Eighth Edition

College Writing Skills

John Langan

McGraw Hill

*Connect
Learn
Succeed*™

Mc
Graw
Hill

Connect
Learn
Succeed™

Published by McGraw-Hill, an imprint of The McGraw-Hill Companies, Inc., 1221 Avenue of the Americas, New York, NY 10020. Copyright © 2011, 2008, 2005, 2001, 1997, 1993, 1989, 1985. All rights reserved. No part of this publication may be reproduced or distributed in any form or by any means, or stored in a database or retrieval system, without the prior written consent of The McGraw-Hill Companies, Inc., including, but not limited to, in any network or other electronic storage or transmission, or broadcast for distance learning.

This book is printed on acid-free paper.

2 3 4 5 6 7 8 9 0 DOC/DOC 0

ISBN: 978-0-07-337165-8
MHID: 0-07-337165-3

Vice President, Editorial: *Michael Ryan*
Sponsoring Editor: *John Kindler*
Editorial Coordinator: *Jesse Hassenger*
Director of Development: *Dawn Groundwater*
Developmental Editor: *Nomi Sofer*
Marketing Manager: *Jaclyn Elkins*
Manager–Project Management Services U.S.: *Lori Hazzard, MPS Limited, A Macmillan Company*
Manuscript Editor: *Sheryl Rose*

Interior Designer: *Maureen McCutcheon*
Cover Designer: *Preston Thomas*
Photo Researcher: *Emily Tietz*
Production Supervisor: *Tandra Jorgensen*
Media Project Manager: *Bethuel Jabez*
Composition: *MPS Limited, A Macmillan Company*
Printing: *45# New Era Thin by R.R. Donnelley & Sons*

Credits: The credits section for this book begins on page C-1 and is considered an extension of the copyright page.

Library of Congress Cataloging-in-Publication Data

Langan, John, 1942-
  College writing skills / John Langan.—8th ed.
      p. cm.
  Includes bibliographical references and index.
  ISBN-13: 978-0-07-337165-8 (alk. paper)
  ISBN-10: 0-07-337165-3 (alk. paper)
  1. English language—Rhetoric. 2. English language—Grammar. 3. Report writing. I. Title.
  PE1471.L34 2010
  808'.042—dc22   2009042359

The Internet addresses listed in the text were accurate at the time of publication. The inclusion of a Web site does not indicate an endorsement by the authors or McGraw-Hill, and McGraw-Hill does not guarantee the accuracy of the information presented at these sites.

www.mhhe.com

Praise for *College Writing Skills* and *College Writing Skills with Readings*

"This is the only text I will use to teach developmental essay writing. The series meets our students' needs!"
—Elaine Herrick, Temple College

"College Writing Skills with Readings has been our developmental textbook of choice for the past ten years for a good reason: His explanations and student examples of the basics of unity (staying focused), coherence (flow and connectedness), and adequate development (support) give our students the tools they need to improve their writing skills."
—Paul Bush, Bowling Green Community College

"College Writing Skills is a student-centered textbook. It asks students to reexamine their attitudes towards writing and then gives them the tools to succeed. Grammar, organization, and development are explained with care and precision. College Writing Skills practices what it preaches by giving clear and accessible explanations for a broad student population."
—Nina Bannett, New York City College of Technology

"All the sections are very manageable and teachers can arrange their courses in a variety of ways while using this text. It breaks down the writing process into clear steps and those steps can be later utilized as tools for revision. The readings are clear and engaging as well as flexible regarding rhetorical style and topic."
—Laurie Sherman, Community College of Rhode Island

"It's a very user friendly text and offers a variety of teaching methods."
—Jessica Carroll, Miami Dade College

"It is sequenced well and places the emphasis on the process of writing from the discovery of a worthy topic to writing and supporting the thesis. The checklists provided in each chapter allow the writer to have a focus for understanding what the instructor is addressing when he or she is evaluating the essay. The readings in the book are both engaging and provocative, which will lead to much discussion in the classroom."
—Alison Reynolds, Midwestern State University

About the Author

John Langan has taught reading and writing at Atlantic Cape Community College near Atlantic City, New Jersey, for more than twenty-five years. The author of a popular series of college textbooks on both writing and reading, John enjoys the challenge of developing materials that teach skills in an especially clear and lively way. Before teaching, he earned advanced degrees in writing at Rutgers University and in reading at Rowan University. He also spent a year writing fiction that, he says, "is now at the back of a drawer waiting to be discovered and acclaimed posthumously." While in school, he supported himself by working as a truck driver, a machinist, a battery assembler, a hospital attendant, and an apple packer. John now lives with his wife, Judith Nadell, near Philadelphia. In addition to his wife and Philly sports teams, his passions include reading and turning on nonreaders to the pleasure and power of books. Through Townsend Press, his educational publishing company, he has developed the nonprofit "Townsend Library"—a collection of more than fifty new and classic stories that appeal to readers of any age.

Contents

To the Instructor   xv

Part 1: Essay Writing   1

1   An Introduction to Writing   2

Point and Support   3
Structure of the Traditional Essay   6
Benefits of Writing the Traditional Essay   11
Writing as a Skill   11
Writing as a Process of Discovery   12
Writing as a Way to Communicate with Others   13
Keeping a Journal   14
Tips on Using a Computer   15
Review Activities   17
Using This Text   20

2   The Writing Process   22

Prewriting   23
Writing a First Draft   31
Revising   33
Editing   35
Review Activities   38

3   The First and Second Steps in Essay Writing   50

Step 1: Begin with a Point, or Thesis   51
Step 2: Support the Thesis with Specific Evidence   60
Practice in Advancing and Supporting a Thesis   67

4   The Third Step in Essay Writing   83
    Step 3: Organize and Connect the Specific Evidence   84
    Introductions, Conclusions, and Titles   94
    Practice in Organizing and Connecting Specific Evidence   102

5   The Fourth Step in Essay Writing   110
    Revising Sentences   111
    Editing Sentences   130
    Practice in Revising Sentences   133

6   Four Bases for Revising Essays   146
    Base 1: Unity   147
    Base 2: Support   150
    Base 3: Coherence   154
    Base 4: Sentence Skills   157
    Practice in Using the Four Bases   161

Part 2: Patterns of Essay Development   175

7   Introduction to Essay Development   176
    Important Considerations in Essay Development   177
    Patterns of Essay Development   182

8   Description   184

    READING: Lou's Place   *Beth Johnson*   194

9   Narration   209

    READING: The Yellow Ribbon   *Pete Hamill*   220

10 Exemplification   230

    READING: Dad   *Andrew H. Malcolm*   241

11   Process   254

READING: **How to Do Well on a Job Interview**
Glenda Davis   263

12   Cause and Effect   276

READING: **Taming the Anger Monster**
Anne Davidson   286

13   Comparison or Contrast   300

READING: **Born to Be Different?**   *Camille Lewis*   311

14   Definition   324

READING: **Television Addiction**   *Marie Winn*   333

15   Division-Classification   343

READING: **Wait Divisions**   *Tom Bodett*   352

16   Argument   363

READING: **Ban the Things. Ban Them All.**   *Molly Ivins*   376

Part 3: Special Skills   385

17   Taking Essay Exams   386

18   Writing a Summary   395

19   Writing a Report   407

20   Writing a Résumé and Cover Letter   412

21   Using the Library and the Internet   419

22   Writing a Research Paper   433

Part 4: Handbook of Sentence Skills   457

SECTION 1: Grammar   458

23 Subjects and Verbs   459
24 Fragments   465
25 Run-Ons   479
26 Regular and Irregular Verbs   492
27 Subject-Verb Agreement   502
28 Additional Information about Verbs   508
29 Pronoun Agreement and Reference   512
30 Pronoun Types   518
31 Adjectives and Adverbs   525
32 Misplaced Modifiers   531
33 Dangling Modifiers   535

SECTION 2: Mechanics   540

34 Manuscript Form   541
35 Capital Letters   544
36 Numbers and Abbreviations   552

SECTION 3: Punctuation   556

37 Apostrophe   557
38 Quotation Marks   565
39 Comma   573
40 Other Punctuation Marks   583

SECTION 4: Word Use   588

41 Spelling Improvement   589
42 Commonly Confused Words   594

43 Effective Word Choice   604

44 Editing Tests   611

45 ESL Pointers   625

    Correction Symbols   639

Credits   C-1

Index   I-1

To the Instructor

College Writing Skills offers students a practical guide to becoming better writers. From mastering the traditional five-paragraph essay and its variations to learning about the finer points of grammar and punctuation, *College Writing Skills* empowers students to take control of their writing and put it to work for them. And now with Connect Writing, a new online writing program, and the soon to come Connect Langan, an online interactive version of *College Writing Skills,* this new edition brings writing closer to where students are and helps take them where you want them to go. Whether online or in class, *College Writing Skills* offers students the tools to succeed.

Key Features of the Book:

- *Four principles are presented as keys to effective writing.* These four principles—unity, support, coherence, and sentence skills—are reinforced throughout the book. **Part 1** focuses on the first three principles. **Parts 2 and 3** show, respectively, how the four principles apply in the different patterns of essay development and other types of writing. **Part 4** serves as a concise handbook of sentence skills.

- *Writing is treated as a process.* The first chapter introduces writing as both a skill and a process of discovery. The second chapter, "The Writing Process," explains and illustrates the sequence of steps in writing an effective essay, focusing on prewriting and revision strategies. More prewriting and revision strategies accompany many of the writing assignments in Part 2.

- *Activities and assignments are numerous and varied.* Part 1 contains more than ninety activities to help students apply and master the four bases, and the entire book has over 250 activities and tests. A variety of writing assignments follows each pattern of essay development in Part 2.

- *Clear thinking is stressed throughout.* In the opening pages of the book, students are introduced to two principles: making a point and providing support to back up that point. These principles, a focus point throughout the book, are the bedrock of clear thinking and clear writing.

- *The traditional essay is emphasized.* Students are asked to write formal essays with an introduction, three supporting paragraphs, and a conclusion.

Writing an essay with an overall thesis statement and in which each of the three supporting paragraphs begins with a topic sentence is more challenging for many students than writing a more free-form essay. The demands are significant, but the rewards are great. As students learn and practice the rules of the five-paragraph essay, professional examples illustrate the variations possible within the essay form.

- *Lively teaching models are provided.* The book includes many high-interest student and professional essays with each chapter in Part 2. After reading papers by other students and professional authors and experiencing the power of writing, students will be encouraged to aim for similar honesty, realism, and detail in their own work.

- *The book is versatile.* Since no two people use an English text in exactly the same way, the material has been organized in a highly accessible manner, so instructors can turn quickly and easily to the skills they want to present.

New to the Eighth Edition

- **Now with Connect Writing:** *College Writing Skills* now comes with innovative Connect Writing software, providing additional guided practice for college writers.
- **Connect Langan (print and online):** The new edition of *College Writing Skills* is available in print and in a soon to be available online format: Connect Langan.
- **Fresh examples and practice exercises.** Exercises have been updated throughout the text, with special emphasis on including current and relevant examples.
- **Part III: Special Skills revised and updated.** Most college students have jobs, and Chapter 20, "Writing a Résumé and Cover Letter," has been updated to include both a functional and a chronological résumé. Information technology changes rapidly, and Chapter 21, "Using the Library and the Internet," has been carefully revised to reflect the current resources available to students in college libraries and online.
- **Three new readings.** Chosen for their appeal and relevance to today's students, these new essays address coming to terms with one's identity, the importance of confronting fears to attain personal growth, and the debate over single-sex education.

Supplements for Instructors

- The *Annotated Instructor's Edition* (ISBN 0-07-734888-5) consists of the student text, complete with answers to all activities and tests, followed by an Instructor's Guide featuring teaching suggestions and a model syllabus.

- The *Online Learning Center* (www.mhhe.com/langan) offers a host of instructional aids and additional resources, including an instructor's manual and test bank, online resources for writing instructors, and more.

Supplements for Students

- The *Online Learning Center* (www.mhhe.com/langan) offers exercises, writing activities, a PowerPoint grammar tutorial, guides to Internet research and avoiding plagiarism, Web links, and more.

You can contact your local McGraw-Hill representative or consult McGraw-Hill's Web site at www.mhhe.com/english for more information on the supplements that accompany *College Writing Skills*.

Acknowledgments

Reviewers who have contributed to this edition through their helpful comments and feedback include:

Nina Bannett, New York City College of Technology
Paul Bush, Bowling Green Community College of Western Kentucky University
Jessica Carroll, Miami Dade College
Neeta Chandra, Cuyahoga Community College
Elaine Herrick, Temple College
L. Adam Mekler, Morgan State University
Stephen Morrow, Oklahoma City Community College
Alison Reynolds, Midwestern State University
Laurie Sherman, Community College of Rhode Island
Mitchell Summerlin, Calhoun Community College

I am also grateful for the talented support of my McGraw-Hill editors, John Kindler and Nomi Sofer. Editorial/marketing team members Jesse Hassenger and Jacklyn Elkins also made valuable contributions to this text. Many thanks to the skilled production and design team—Brett Coker, Preston Thomas, Alexandra Ambrose, Tandra Jorgensen, and permissions editor Marty Moga. Also, I'd like to thank Thomas Brierly for producing the text's media component, and to thank Paul Banks and Andrea Pasquarelli for their work on Connect Writing.

Joyce Stern, Assistant Professor at Nassau Community College, contributed the ESL Tips to the *Annotated Instructor's Edition* of the text. An educator for over thirty years, Professor Stern holds an advanced degree in TESOL from Hunter College. She has been recognized by Nassau Community College's Center for Students with Disabilities for her dedication to student learning.

Donna T. Matsumoto, Assistant Professor of English and the Writing Discipline Coordinator at Leeward Community College in Hawaii, wrote the Teaching Tips for the *Annotated Instructor's Edition*. She has taught writing, women's studies, and American studies for a number of years throughout the University of Hawaii system, at Hawaii Pacific University, and in community schools for adults.

Professor Santi Buscemi made contributions throughout the book; I thank him for his keen editorial eye and tireless work ethic. He is Professor of English and Chair of the Department of English at Middlesex County College in Edison, New Jersey, where he teaches reading and writing.

John Langan

College Writing Skills

Behind every McGraw-Hill education product is research.

Thousands of instructors participate in our course surveys every year, providing McGraw-Hill with longitudinal information on the trends and challenges in your courses. That research, along with reviews, focus groups, and ethnographic studies of both instructor and student workflow, provides the intensive feedback that our authors use to ensure that our revisions continue to provide everything you need to reach your course goals and outcomes.

Some KEY FINDINGS from our Development Writing Course Survey

50% of Developmental English instructors say they have a lab component required each week. **85%** of these respondents say they use the lab to teach grammar and punctuation.

> Connect Writing is built around the five core skill areas instructors say they wanted addressed. Students will see these five areas in all three levels of Connect Writing.

> Students get an individualized learning plan when they take the diagnostic test in Connect Writing. This individualized instruction makes sure that each student gets the practice he or she needs to improve their grammar and punctuation skills.

FOUR BASES Checklist for Cause and Effect

About *Unity*

☑ Have I introduced my essay with a clearly stated thesis and plan of development?

About *Support*

☑ Is each of my main points supported by solid, specific details?

About *Coherence*

☑ Have I used transition words such as *first, another, in addition*, and *also*?

About *Sentence Skills*

☑ Have I used a consistent point of view throughout my essay?

☑ Have I used specific rather than general words?

☑ Have I avoided wordiness and used concise wording?

☑ Are my sentences varied?

☑ Have I checked my writing for spelling and other sentence skills, as listed on the inside back cover of the book?

>The four bases boxes serve to remind students of the core areas they need to address in their writing.

>Students are introduced to writing from the beginning as each assignment chapter starts with a photo and a writing task.

Should cell phones be permitted in class? Look at the photograph above and write an essay in which you argue for or against the use of cell phones in the classroom. Include at least three separate reasons that support your point of view.

College Writing Skills

Essay Writing

Have yourself a merry little Christmas
It may be your last
Next year we may all be living in the past
Have yourself a merry little Christmas
Pop the champagne cork
Next year we may all be living in New York.
No good times like the olden days,
Happy golden days of yore,
Faithful friends who were dear to us
Will be near to us no more.
But at least we all will be together
If the Lord allows.
From now on we'll have to muddle through somehow.
So have yourself a merry little Christmas now.

Have yourself a merry little Christmas,
Let your heart be light
From now on, our troubles will be out of sight
Have yourself a merry little Christmas
Make your yuletide gay
From now on our troubles will be miles away.
Here we are as in olden days,
Happy golden days of yore.
Faithful friends who were dear to us
Gather near to us once more.
Through the years we all will be together
If the fates allow.
Until then, we'll have to muddle through somehow
So have yourself a merry little Christmas now.

Even songwriters often have to write several drafts of lyrics before producing an effective song. Compare this excerpted draft of "Have Yourself a Merry Little Christmas" by Hugh Martin with its final version; what has changed? Choose one revision and explain why and how it makes the lyrics more effective.

PREVIEW

1 An Introduction to Writing

2 The Writing Process

3 The First and Second Steps in Essay Writing

4 The Third Step in Essay Writing

5 The Fourth Step in Essay Writing

6 Four Bases for Revising Essays

1

An Introduction to Writing

This chapter will explain and illustrate

- the importance of supporting a point in writing
- the structure of the traditional essay
- the benefits of writing the traditional essay

This chapter also

- presents writing as both a skill and a process of discovery
- suggests keeping a journal

© Stock Image/SuperStock

What is your ideal job? Write two or more paragraphs about what your ideal job would be and what your daily activities on the job would entail. Be sure to include your reasons for wanting such a job.

The experience I had writing my first college essay helped shape this book. I received a C– for the essay. Scrawled beside the grade was the comment "Not badly written, but ill-conceived." I remember going to the instructor after class, asking about his comment as well as the word *Log* that he had added in the margin at various spots. "What are all these logs you put in my paper?" I asked, trying to make a joke of it. He looked at me a little wonderingly. "Logic, Mr. Langan," he answered, "logic." He went on to explain that I had not thought out my paper clearly. There were actually two ideas rather than one in my thesis, one supporting paragraph had nothing to do with either idea, another paragraph lacked a topic sentence, and so on. I've never forgotten his last words: "If you don't think clearly," he said, "you won't write clearly."

I was speechless, and I felt confused and angry. I didn't like being told that I didn't know how to think. I went back to my room and read over my paper several times. Eventually, I decided that my instructor was right. "No more logs," I said to myself. "I'm going to get these logs out of my papers."

My instructor's advice was invaluable. I learned that clear, disciplined thinking is the key to effective writing. *College Writing Skills* develops this idea by breaking down the writing process into a series of four logical, easily followed steps. These steps, combined with practical advice about prewriting and revision, will help you write strong papers.

Here are the four steps in a nutshell:

1. Discover a clearly stated point, or thesis.
2. Provide logical, detailed support for your thesis.
3. Organize and connect your supporting material.
4. Revise and edit so that your sentences are effective and error-free.

Part 1 of this book explains each of these steps in detail and provides many practice materials to help you master them.

Point and Support

An Important Difference between Writing and Talking

In everyday conversation, you make all kinds of points or assertions. You say, for example, "My boss is a hard person to work for," "It's not safe to walk in our neighborhood after dark," or "Poor study habits keep getting me into trouble." The points that you make concern personal matters as well as, at times, outside issues: "That trade will be a disaster for the team," "Lots of TV commercials are degrading to women," "Students are better off working for a year before attending college."

The people you are talking with do not always challenge you to give reasons for your statements. They may know why you feel as you do, or they may already agree with you, or they simply may not want to put you on the spot; and so they do not always ask why. But the people who read what you write may not know you, agree with you, or feel in any way obliged to you. If you want to communicate effectively with readers, you must provide solid evidence for any point you make. An important difference, then, between writing and talking is this: *In writing, any idea that you advance must be supported with specific reasons or details.*

Think of your readers as reasonable people. They will not take your views on faith, but they are willing to accept what you say as long as you support it. Therefore, remember to support with specific evidence any point that you make.

Point and Support in a Paragraph

In conversation, you might say to a friend who has suggested a movie, "No, thanks. Going to the movies is just too much of a hassle. Parking, people, everything." From shared past experiences, your friend may know what you are talking about so that you will not have to explain your statement. But in writing, your point would have to be backed up with specific reasons and details.

Below is a paragraph, written by a student named Diane Woods, on why moviegoing is a nuisance. A *paragraph* is a short paper of around 150 to 200 words. It usually consists of an opening point, called a *topic sentence,* followed by a series of sentences that support that point.

The Hazards of Moviegoing

Although I love movies, I've found that there are drawbacks to moviegoing. One problem is just the inconvenience of it all. To get to the theater, I have to drive for at least fifteen minutes, or more if traffic is bad. It can take forever to find a parking spot, and then I have to walk across a huge parking lot to the theater. There I encounter long lines, sold-out shows, and ever-increasing prices. And I hate sitting with my feet sticking to the floor because of other people's spilled snacks. Another problem is my lack of self-control at the theater. I often stuff myself with unhealthy calorie-laden snacks. My choices might include a bucket of popcorn, a box of Milk Duds, a giant soda, or all three. The worst problem is some of the other moviegoers. Kids run up and down the aisle. Teenagers laugh and shout at the screen. People of all ages drop soda cups and popcorn tubs, cough and burp, and talk to one another. All in all, I would rather stay home and watch a DVD in the comfort of my own living room.

Notice what the supporting evidence does here. It provides you, the reader, with a basis for understanding *why* the writer makes the point that is made. Through this specific evidence, the writer has explained and successfully communicated the idea that moviegoing can be a nuisance.

The evidence that supports the point in a paper often consists of a series of reasons followed by examples and details that support the reasons. That is true of the paragraph above: three reasons are provided, with examples and details that back up those reasons. Supporting evidence in a paper can also consist of anecdotes, personal experiences, facts, studies, statistics, and the opinions of experts.

The paragraph on moviegoing, like almost any piece of effective writing, has two essential parts: (1) a point is advanced, and (2) that point is then supported. Taking a minute to outline "The Hazards of Moviegoing" will help you understand these basic parts. Write in the following space the point that has been advanced in the paragraph. Then add the words needed to complete the paragraph's outline.

Activity

1

Point Support

_____ ~~The~~ _____

1. _____ inconvenience _____

    a. Fifteen-minute drive to theater

    b. _____ hard find park and ticket _____

    c. Long lines, sold-out shows, and increasing prices

    d. _____

2. Lack of self-control

    a. Often stuff myself with unhealthy snacks

    b. Might have popcorn, candy, soda, or all three

3. _____

    a. _____

    b. _____

    c. People of all ages make noise.

Point and Support in an Essay

An excellent way to learn how to write clearly and logically is to practice the traditional college *essay*—a paper of about five hundred words that typically consists of an introductory paragraph, two to four supporting paragraphs (the norm in this book will be three), and a concluding paragraph. The central idea, or point, developed in any essay is called a *thesis statement* (rather than, as in a paragraph, a topic sentence). The thesis appears in the introductory paragraph, and the specific support for the thesis appears in the paragraphs that follow. The supporting paragraphs allow for a fuller treatment of the evidence that backs up the central point than would be possible in a single-paragraph paper.

Structure of the Traditional Essay
A Model Essay

www.mhhe.com/langan

The following model will help you understand the form of an essay. Diane Woods, the writer of the paragraph on moviegoing, later decided to develop her subject more fully. Here is the essay that resulted.

The Hazards of Moviegoing

<table>
<tr>
<td valign="top" width="22%">

Introductory paragraph

</td>
<td valign="top">

   I am a movie fanatic. My friends count on me to know movie trivia (who was the pigtailed little girl in E.T.: The Extra-Terrestrial? Drew Barrymore) and to remember every big Oscar awarded since I was in grade school (Best Picture, 1994? Forrest Gump). My friends, though, have stopped asking me if I want to go out to the movies. While I love movies as much as ever, the inconvenience of going out, the temptations of the concession stand, and the behavior of some patrons are reasons for me to wait and rent the DVD.

</td>
</tr>
<tr>
<td valign="top">

First supporting paragraph

</td>
<td valign="top">

   To begin with, I just don't enjoy the general hassle of the evening. Since small local movie theaters are a thing of the past, I have to drive for fifteen minutes to get to the nearest multiplex. The parking lot is shared with several restaurants and a supermarket, so it's always jammed. I have to drive around at a snail's pace until I spot another driver backing out. Then it's time to stand in an endless line, with the constant threat that tickets for the show I want will sell out. If we do get tickets, the theater will be so crowded that I won't be able to sit with my friends, or we'll have to sit in a front row gaping up at a giant screen. I have to shell out a ridiculous amount of money—up to $11—for a ticket. That entitles me to sit while my shoes seal themselves to a sticky floor coated with spilled soda, bubble gum, and crushed Raisinets.

</td>
</tr>
<tr>
<td valign="top">

Second supporting paragraph

</td>
<td valign="top">

   Second, the theater offers tempting snacks that I really don't need. Like most of us, I have to battle an expanding waistline. At home I do pretty well by simply not buying stuff that is bad for me. I can make do with snacks like celery and carrot sticks because there is no ice cream in the freezer. Going to the theater, however, is like spending my evening in a 7-Eleven that's been equipped with a movie screen and comfortable seats. As I try to persuade myself to just have a Diet Coke, the smell of fresh popcorn dripping with butter soon

</td>
</tr>
</table>

(continued)

overcomes me. Chocolate bars the size of small automobiles seem to jump into my hands. I risk pulling out my fillings as I chew enormous mouthfuls of Milk Duds. By the time I leave the theater, I feel disgusted with myself.

Many of the other patrons are even more of a problem than the concession stand. Little kids race up and down the aisles, usually in giggling packs. Teenagers try to impress their friends by talking back to the screen, whistling, and making what they consider to be hilarious noises. Adults act as if they were at home in their own living room. They comment loudly on the ages of the stars and reveal plot twists that are supposed to be a secret until the film's end. And people of all ages create distractions. They crinkle candy wrappers, stick gum on their seats, and drop popcorn tubs or cups of crushed ice and soda on the floor. They also cough and burp, squirm endlessly in their seats, file out for repeated trips to the restrooms or concession stands, and elbow me out of the armrest on either side of my seat.

After arriving home from the movies one night, I decided that I was not going to be a moviegoer anymore. I was tired of the problems involved in getting to the theater, resisting unhealthy snacks, and dealing with the patrons. The next day, I arranged to have premium movie channels added to my cable TV service, and I also got a Netflix membership. I may now see movies a bit later than other people, but I'll be more relaxed watching box office hits in the comfort of my own living room.

Third supporting paragraph

Concluding paragraph

Parts of an Essay

"The Hazards of Moviegoing" is a good example of the standard short essay you will write in college English. It is a composition of over five hundred words that consists of a one-paragraph introduction, a three-paragraph body, and a one-paragraph conclusion. The roles of these paragraphs are described and illustrated below.

Introductory Paragraph

The introductory paragraph of an essay should start with several sentences that attract the reader's interest. It should then advance the central idea, or *thesis,* that will be developed in the essay. The thesis often includes a *plan of development*—a preview of the major points that will support the thesis. These supporting points should be listed in the order in which they will appear in the essay. In some cases, the plan of development is presented in a sentence separate from the thesis; in other cases, it is omitted.

1. In "The Hazards of Moviegoing," which sentence or sentences are used to attract the reader's interest?

   a. First sentence

   b. First two sentences

   c. First three sentences

2. In which sentence is the thesis of the essay presented?

   a. Third sentence

   b. Fourth sentence

3. Does the thesis include a plan of development?

   a. Yes

   b. No

4. Write the words in the thesis that announce the three major supporting points in the essay:

   a. _____

   b. _____

   c. _____

Body: Supporting Paragraphs

Most essays have three supporting points, developed at length over three separate paragraphs. (Some essays have two supporting points, others four or more. For the purposes of this book, your goal will be three supporting points unless your instructor indicates otherwise.) Each of the supporting paragraphs should begin with a *topic sentence* that states the point to be detailed in that paragraph. Just as a thesis provides a focus for an entire essay, a topic sentence provides a focus for a supporting paragraph.

1. What is the topic sentence for the first supporting paragraph of the model essay?

   _____

   _____

2. The first topic sentence is then supported by the following details (fill in the missing details):

   a. Have to drive fifteen minutes

   b. _____

   c. Endless ticket line

d. _____

e. _____

f. Sticky floor

3. What is the topic sentence for the second supporting paragraph of the essay?

_____

_____

4. The second topic sentence is then supported by the following details:

a. At home, only snacks are celery and carrot sticks.

b. Theater is like a 7-Eleven with seats.

   (1) Fresh popcorn

   (2) _____

   (3) _____

5. What is the topic sentence for the third supporting paragraph of the essay?

_____

_____

_____

6. The third topic sentence is then supported by the following details:

a. _____

b. _____

c. Adults talk loudly and reveal plot twists.

d. People of all ages create distractions.

Concluding Paragraph

The concluding paragraph often summarizes the essay by briefly restating the thesis and, at times, the main supporting points. In addition, the writer often presents a concluding thought about the subject of the paper.

1. Which two sentences in the concluding paragraph restate the thesis and supporting points of the essay?

a. First and second

b. Second and third

c. Third and fourth

Activity

4

2. Which sentence in the concluding paragraph contains the final thought of the essay?

    a. Second

    b. Third

    c. Fourth

Diagram of an Essay

The following diagram shows you at a glance the different parts of a standard college essay, also known as a *one-three-one-essay*. This diagram will serve as a helpful guide when you are writing or evaluating essays.

TITLE OF THE ESSAY

Introduction

> Opening remarks to catch reader's interest
> Thesis statement
> Plan of development (optional)

Body

> Topic sentence 1 (supporting point 1)
> Specific evidence

> Topic sentence 2 (supporting point 2)
> Specific evidence

> Topic sentence 3 (supporting point 3)
> Specific evidence

Conclusion

> Summary (optional)
> General closing remarks
> (Or both)

You now have an overview of the traditional form of the essay. In Chapter 2, you will learn *how* to go about writing an effective essay. First, though, it will be helpful to consider the following: the benefits of writing traditional essays, the advantage of seeing writing as both a skill and a process of discovery, the value of keeping a journal, and the ways a computer can enhance the writing process.

Benefits of Writing the Traditional Essay

Learning to write a traditional essay offers at least three benefits. First of all, mastering the traditional essay will help make you a better writer. For other courses, you'll often compose papers that will be variations on the essay form—for example, examination essays, reports, and research papers. Becoming comfortable with the basic structure of the traditional essay, with its emphasis on a clear point and well-organized, logical support, will help with almost every kind of writing that you have to do.

Second, the discipline of writing an essay will strengthen your skills as a reader and listener. As a reader, you'll become more critically aware of other writers' ideas and the evidence they provide (or fail to provide) to support those ideas. Essay writing will also help you become a better speaker. You'll be more prepared to develop the three basic parts of an effective speech—an appealing introduction, a solidly developed body, and a well-rounded conclusion—because of your experience writing three-part essays.

Most important, essay writing will make you a stronger thinker. Writing a solidly reasoned traditional essay requires mental discipline and close attention to a set of logical rules. Creating an essay in which there is an overall thesis statement and in which each of three supporting paragraphs begins with a topic sentence is more challenging than writing a free-form or expressive paper. Such an essay obliges you to carefully sort out, think through, and organize your ideas. You'll learn to discover and express just what your ideas are and to develop those ideas in a logical, reasoned way. Traditional essay writing, in short, will train your mind to think clearly, and that ability will prove to be of value in every phase of your life.

Writing as a Skill

A realistic attitude about writing must build on the idea that *writing is a skill,* not a "natural gift." It is a skill like driving, typing, or cooking; and, like any skill, it can be learned. If you have the determination to learn, this book will give you the extensive practice needed to develop your writing skills.

People often fear they are the only ones for whom writing is unbearably difficult. They believe that everyone else finds writing easy or at least tolerable. Such people typically say, "I'm not any good at writing," or "English was not one of my good subjects." They imply that they simply do not have a talent for writing, while others do. Often, the result of this attitude is that people try to avoid writing, and when they do write, they don't try their best. Their attitude becomes a self-fulfilling prophecy: their writing fails chiefly because they have brainwashed themselves into thinking that they don't have the "natural talent" needed to write.

Many people find it difficult to do the intense, active thinking that clear writing demands. It is frightening to sit down before a blank sheet of paper or computer screen and know that an hour later, nothing on it may be worth keeping. It is frustrating to discover how much of a challenge it is to transfer thoughts and feelings from one's head onto the page. It is upsetting to find that an apparently simple subject often turns out to be complicated. But writing is not an automatic process: we will not get something for nothing—and we should not expect to. For almost everyone, competent writing comes from plain hard work—from determination, sweat, and head-on battle. The good news is that the skill of writing can be mastered, and if you are ready to work, you will learn what you need to know.

Writing as a Process of Discovery

In addition to believing that writing is a natural gift, many people falsely believe that writing should flow in a simple, straight line from the writer's head onto the written page. But writing is seldom an easy, one-step journey in which a finished paper comes out in a first draft. The truth is that *writing is a process of discovery* involving a series of steps, and those steps are very often a zigzag journey. Look at the following illustrations of the writing process:

Very often, writers do not discover just what they want to write about until they explore their thoughts in writing. For example, Diane Woods (the author of the paragraph and essay on moviegoing) had been assigned to write about an annoyance in everyday life. She did not know what annoyance she would choose; instead, she just began writing about annoyances in general, in order to discover a topic. One of those annoyances was traffic, which seemed promising, so she began putting down ideas and details that came to her about traffic. One detail was the traffic she had to deal with in going to the movies. That made her think of the traffic in the parking lot at the theater complex. At that point, she realized that moviegoing itself was an annoyance. She switched direction in midstream and began writing down ideas and details about moviegoing.

As Diane wrote, she realized how much other moviegoers annoyed her, and she began thinking that other movie patrons might be her main idea in a paper. But when she was writing about patrons who loudly drop popcorn tubs onto the floor, she realized how much all the snacks at the concession stand tempted her. She changed direction again, thinking now that maybe she could talk about patrons and tempting snacks. She kept writing, just putting down more and more details about her movie experiences, still not having figured out exactly how she would fit both patrons and snacks into the paper. Even though her paper had not quite jelled, she was not worried, because she knew that if she kept writing, it would eventually come together.

The point is that writing is often a process of continuing discovery; as you write, you may suddenly switch direction or double back. You may be working on a topic sentence and realize suddenly that it could be your concluding thought. Or you may be developing a supporting idea and then decide that it should be the main point of your paper. Chapter 2 will treat the writing process more directly. What is important to remember here is that writers frequently do not know their exact destination as they begin to write. Very often they discover the direction and shape of a paper during the process of writing.

Writing as a Way to Communicate with Others

When you talk, chances are you do not treat everyone the same. For example, you are unlikely to speak to your boss in the same way that you chat with a young child. Instead, you adjust what you say to suit the people who are listening to you—your *audience*. Similarly, you probably change your speech each day to suit whatever *purpose* you have in mind when you are speaking. For instance, if you wanted to tell someone how to get to your new apartment, you would speak differently than if you were describing your favorite movie.

To communicate effectively, people must constantly adjust their speech to suit their purpose and audience. This same idea is true for writing. When you write for others, it is crucial to know both your purpose for writing and the audience who will be reading your work. The ability to adjust your writing to suit your purpose and audience will serve you well not only in the classroom but also in the workplace and beyond.

TIP: Purpose and audience, further explained on page 178, are special focuses of each of the nine patterns of essay development in Part 2.

Keeping a Journal

Because writing is a skill, it makes sense that the more you practice writing, the better you will write. One excellent way to get practice in writing, even before you begin composing essays, is to keep a daily or almost daily journal. Writing in a journal will help you develop the habit of thinking on paper and will show you how ideas can be discovered in the process of writing. A journal can make writing a familiar part of your life and can serve as a continuing source of ideas for papers.

At some point during the day—perhaps during a study period after your last class of the day, or right before dinner, or right before going to bed—spend fifteen minutes or so writing in your journal. Keep in mind that you do not have to plan what to write about, or be in the mood to write, or worry about making mistakes as you write; just write down whatever words come out. You should write at least one page in each session.

© Jamie Grill/Corbis

You may want to use a notebook that you can easily carry with you for on-the-spot writing. You can also use the journal provided in Appendix A of this book. Or you may decide to write on loose-leaf paper that can be transferred later to a journal folder on your desk. Many students choose to keep their journals on their home computer or laptop. No matter how you proceed, be sure to date all entries.

Your instructor may ask you to make journal entries a specific number of times a week, for a specific number of weeks. He or she may have you turn in your journal every so often for review and feedback. If you are keeping the journal on your own, try to make entries three to five times a week every week of the semester.

Tips on Using a Computer

www.mhhe.com/langan

- If you are using your school's computer center, allow enough time. You may have to wait for a computer or printer to be free. In addition, you may need several sessions at a computer and printer to complete your paper.

- Every word-processing program allows you to save your writing by pressing one or more keys. Save your work frequently as you write your draft. A saved file is stored safely on the computer or network. A file that is not saved will be lost if the computer crashes or if the power is turned off.

- Keep your work in two places—the hard drive or network you are working on and a backup USB drive. At the end of each session with a computer, copy your work onto the USB drive or e-mail a copy to yourself. Then, if the hard drive or network fails, you'll have the backup copy.

- Print out your work at least at the end of every session. Then you will have not only your most recent draft to work on away from the computer but also a copy in case something should happen to your electronic file.

- Work in single spacing so that you can see as much of your writing on the screen at one time as possible. Just before you print out your work, change to double spacing.

- Before making major changes in a paper, create a copy of your file. For example, if your file is titled "Worst Job," create a file called "Worst Job 2." Then make all your changes in that new file. If the changes don't work out, you can always go back to the original file.

Using a Computer at Each Stage of the Writing Process

Following are some ways to make word processing a part of your writing. Note that this section may be more meaningful *after* you have worked through Chapter 2 of this book.

Prewriting

If you're a fast typist, many kinds of prewriting will work well on a computer. With freewriting in particular, you can get ideas onto the screen almost as quickly as they occur to you. A passing thought that could be productive is not likely to get lost. You may even find it helpful, when freewriting, to dim the monitor screen so that you can't see what you're typing. If you temporarily can't see the screen, you won't have to worry about grammar or spelling or typing errors (all of which do not matter in prewriting); instead, you can concentrate on getting down as many ideas and details as possible about your subject.

After any initial freewriting, questioning, and list-making on a computer, it's often very helpful to print out a hard copy of what you've done. With a clean print-out in front of you, you'll be able to see everything at once and revise and expand your work with handwritten comments in the margins of the paper.

If you have prepared a list of items, you may be able to turn that list into an outline right on the screen. Delete the ideas you feel should not be in your paper (saving them at the end of the file in case you change your mind), and add any new ideas that occur to you. Then use the cut and paste functions to shuffle the supporting ideas around until you find the best order for your paper.

Word processing also makes it easy for you to experiment with the wording of the point of your paper. You can try a number of versions in a short time. After you have decided on the version that works best, you can easily delete the other versions—or simply move them to a temporary "leftover" section at the end of the paper.

Writing Your First Draft

Like many writers, you may want to write out your first draft by hand and then type it into the computer for revision. Even as you type your handwritten draft, you may find yourself making some changes and improvements. And once you have a draft on the screen, or printed out, you will find it much easier to revise than a handwritten one.

If you feel comfortable composing directly on a computer, you can benefit from its special features. For example, if you have written an anecdote in your freewriting that you plan to use in your paper, simply copy the story from your freewriting file and insert it where it fits in your paper. You can refine it then or later. Or if you discover while typing that a sentence is out of place, cut it out from where it is and paste it wherever you wish. And if while writing you realize that an earlier sentence can be expanded, just move your cursor back to that point and type in the additional material.

Revising

It is during revision that the virtues of word processing really shine. All substituting, adding, deleting, and rearranging can be done easily within an existing file. All changes instantly take their proper places within the paper, not scribbled above the line or squeezed into the margin. You can concentrate on each change you want to make, because you never have to type from scratch or work on a messy draft. You can carefully go through your paper to check that all your supporting evidence is relevant and to add new support as needed here and there. Anything you decide to eliminate can be deleted in a keystroke. Anything you add can be inserted precisely where you choose. If you change your mind, all you have to do is delete or cut and paste. Then you can sweep through the paper, focusing on other changes, such as improving word choice, increasing sentence variety, and eliminating wordiness.

> **TIP:** If you are like many students, you might find it convenient to print out a hard copy of your file at various points throughout the revision. You can then revise in longhand—adding, crossing out, and indicating changes—and later quickly make those changes in the document.

Editing and Proofreading

Editing and proofreading also benefit richly from word processing. Instead of crossing out mistakes, using correction fluid, or rewriting an entire paper to correct numerous errors, you can make all necessary changes within the most recent draft. If you find editing or proofreading on the screen hard on your eyes, print out a copy. Mark any corrections on that copy, and then transfer them to the final draft.

If the word-processing program you're using includes spelling and grammar checks, by all means use them. The spell-checker function tells you when a word is not in the program's dictionary. Keep in mind, however, that the spell-checker cannot tell you how to spell a name correctly or when you have mistakenly used, for example, *their* instead of *there*. To a spell-checker, *Thank ewe four the complement* is as correct as *Thank you for the compliment*. Also, use the grammar-checker with caution. Any errors it doesn't uncover are still your responsibility.

A word-processed paper, with its clean appearance and handsome formatting, looks so good that you may feel it is in better shape than it really is. Do not be fooled. Take sufficient time to review your grammar, punctuation, and spelling carefully.

Even after you hand in your paper, save the computer file. Your teacher may ask you to do some revising, and then the file will save you from having to type the paper from scratch.

Review Activities

Activity

5

Answering the following questions will help you evaluate your attitude about writing.

1. How much practice were you given writing compositions in high school?

     _____ Much _____ Some _____ Little

2. How much feedback (positive or negative comments) from teachers were you given on your compositions?

    _____ Much _____ Some _____ Little

3. How did your teachers seem to regard your writing?

    _____ Good _____ Fair _____ Poor

4. Do you feel that some people simply have a gift for writing and others do not?

    _____ Yes _____ Sometimes _____ No

5. When do you start writing a paper?

    _____ Several days before it is due

    _____ About a day before it is due

    _____ At the last possible minute

> **EXPLANATION:** Many people who answer *Little* to questions 1 and 2 often answer *Poor, Yes,* and *At the last possible minute* to questions 3, 4, and 5. On the other hand, people who answer *Much* or *Some* to questions 1 and 2 also tend to have more favorable responses to the other questions. The point is that people with little practice in the skill of writing often have understandably negative feelings about their writing ability. They need not have such feelings, however, because writing is a skill that they can learn with practice.

6. What kinds of writing do you do on a computer? What additional types of writing might you want to undertake on the computer?

    _____

    _____

    _____

7. Have you ever kept a diary or journal like the one explained in this chapter? If so, what kinds of ideas, images, or other information have you put into your journal? If you have never kept a journal, why not? Does this fact have anything to do with how you think of writing?

    _____

    _____

    _____

8. In your own words, explain what it means to say that writing is often a zigzag journey rather than a straight-line journey.

    _____

    _____

    _____

    _____

    _____

Following is an excerpt from one student's journal. As you read, look for a general point and supporting material that could be the basis for an interesting paper.

Activity

6

September 6

    My first sociology class was tonight. The parking lot was jammed when I got there. I thought I was going to be late for class. A guard had us park on a field next to the regular lot. When I got to the room, it had the usual painted-cinder-block construction. Every school I have ever been in since first grade seems to be made of cinder block. The students all sat there without saying anything, waiting for the instructor to arrive. I think they were all a bit nervous like me. I hoped there wasn't going to be a ton of work in the course. I think I was also afraid of looking foolish somehow. This goes back to grade school, when I wasn't a very good student and teachers sometimes embarrassed me in class. I didn't like grade school, and I hated high school. Now here I am six years later—in college, of all places. Who would have thought I would end up here? The instructor appeared—a woman who I think was a bit nervous herself. I think I like her. Her name is Barbara Hanlin. She says we should call her Barbara. We got right into it, but it was interestings tuff. I like the fact that she asks questions but then she lets you volunteer. I always hated it when teachers would call on you whether you wanted to answer or not. I also like the fact that she answers the questions and doesn't just leave you hanging. She takes the time to write important ideas on the board. I also like the way she laughs. This class may be OK.

1. If the writer of the journal entry above was looking for ideas for an essay, he could probably find several in this single entry. For example, he might write a story about the apparently roundabout way he wound up in

college. See if you can find in the entry an idea that might be the basis for an interesting essay, and write your point in the space below.

_____

2.   Take fifteen minutes now to write a journal entry on this day in your life. On a separate sheet of paper, just start writing about anything that you have seen, said, heard, thought, or felt today, and let your thoughts take you where they may.

Using This Text

Here is a suggested sequence for using this book if you are working on your own.

1.   After completing this introduction, read Chapters 2 through 6 in Part 1 and work through as many of the activities as you need to master the ideas in these chapters. By the end of Part 1, you will have covered all the basic theory needed to write effective papers.

2.   Work through some of the chapters in Part 2, which describes a number of traditional patterns for organizing and developing essays. You may want to include "Exemplification," "Process," "Comparison or Contrast," and "Argument." Each chapter opens with a brief introduction to a specific pattern, followed by two student essays and one professional essay written in that pattern. Included are a series of questions so that you can evaluate the essays in terms of the basic principles of writing explained in Part 1. Finally, a number of writing topics are presented, along with hints about prewriting and revising to help you plan and write an effective paper.

3.   Turn to Part 3 as needed for help with types of writing you will do in college: exam essays, summaries, reports, the résumé and cover letter, and the research paper. You will see that these kinds of writing are variations of the essay form you have already learned.

4.   In addition, refer to Part 4 as needed for review and practice in the skills needed to write effective, error-free sentences.

5.   Finally, if you are using the alternate version of this book—*College Writing Skills with Readings*—then read some of the selections in Part 5 and respond to the activities that follow the selections.

For your convenience, the book includes the following:

• On the inside back cover, there is a checklist of the four basic steps in effective writing.

• On pages 639–640, there is a list of commonly used correction symbols.

Get into the habit of regularly referring to these guides; they'll help you produce clearly thought-out, well-written essays.

College Writing Skills will help you learn, practice, and apply the thinking and writing skills you need to communicate effectively. But the starting point must be your own determination to do the work needed to become a strong writer. The ability to express yourself clearly and logically can open doors of opportunity for you, both in school and in your career. If you decide—and only you can decide—that you want such language power, this book will help you reach that goal.

2

The Writing Process

This chapter will explain and illustrate

- the sequence of steps in writing an effective essay
- prewriting
- revising
- editing

© Blend Images/Imagestate

Think about an electronic device you use every day. It could be your cell phone, radio, computer, iPod, Palm Pilot, etc. See if you can write for ten minutes about why you couldn't live without it. Don't worry about spelling and punctuation; just get your thoughts down on paper.

Chapter 1 introduced you to the essay form and to some basics of writing. This chapter explains and illustrates the sequence of steps in writing an effective essay. In particular, the chapter focuses on prewriting and revising—strategies that can help with every essay you write.

For many people, writing is a process that involves the following steps:

1. Discovering a thesis—often through prewriting.

2. Developing solid support for the thesis—often through more prewriting.

3. Organizing the thesis and supporting material and writing it out in a first draft.

4. Revising and then editing carefully to ensure an effective, error-free essay.

Learning this sequence will help give you confidence when the time comes to write. You'll know that you can use prewriting as a way to think on paper and to gradually discover just what ideas you want to develop. You'll understand that there are four clear-cut goals—unity, support, organization, and error-free sentences—to aim for in your writing. You'll realize that you can use revision to rework an essay until it is a strong and effective piece of writing. And you'll be able to edit your writing so that your sentences are clear and error free.

Prewriting

If you are like many people, you may have trouble getting started with writing. A mental block may develop when you sit down before a blank sheet of paper. You may not be able to think of an interesting topic or thesis. Or you may have trouble coming up with relevant details to support a possible thesis. And even after starting an essay, you may hit snags—moments when you wonder, What else can I say? or Where do I go next?

The following pages describe five prewriting techniques that will help you think about and develop a topic and get words on paper: (1) freewriting, (2) questioning, (3) making a list, (4) clustering, and (5) preparing a scratch outline. These techniques help you think about and create material, and they are a central part of the writing process.

Technique 1: Freewriting

Freewriting means jotting down in rough sentences or phrases everything that comes to mind about a possible topic. See if you can write nonstop for ten minutes or more. Do not worry about spelling or punctuating correctly, about erasing mistakes, about organizing material, or about finding exact words. Instead, explore an idea by putting down whatever pops into your head. If you get stuck for words, repeat yourself until more words come. There is no need to feel inhibited, since mistakes *do not count* and you do not have to hand in your freewriting.

www.mhhe.com/langan

Freewriting will limber up your writing muscles and make you familiar with the act of writing. It is a way to break through mental blocks about writing. Since you do not have to worry about mistakes, you can focus on discovering what you want to say about a subject. Your initial ideas and impressions will often become clearer after you have gotten them down on paper, and they may lead to other impressions and ideas. Through continued practice in freewriting, you will develop the habit of thinking as you write. And you will learn a helpful technique for getting started on almost any writing you have to do.

Freewriting: A Student Model

Diane Woods's essay "The Hazards of Moviegoing" on pages 6–7 was developed in response to an assignment to write about some annoyance in everyday life. Diane began by doing some general freewriting and thinking about things that annoy her. Here is her freewriting:

> There are lots of things I get annoyed by. One of them that comes to mind is politishans, in fact I am so annoyed by them that I don't want to say anything about them the last thing I want is to write about them. Another thing that bothers me are people who keep complaining about everything. If you're having trouble, do something about it just don't keep complaining and just talking. I am really annoyed by traffic. There are too many cars in our block and its not surprising. Everyone has a car, the parents have cars and the parents are just too induljent and the kids have cars, and theyre all coming and going all the time and often driving too fast. Speeding up and down the street. We need a speed limit sign but here I am back with politiks again. I am really bothered when I have to drive to the movies all the congestion along the way plus there are just so many cars there at the mall. No space even though the parking lot is huge it just fills up with cars. Movies are a bother anyway because the people can be annoying who are sitting there in the theater with you, talking and dropping popcorn cups and acting like they're at home when they're not.

At this point, Diane read over her notes and, as she later commented, "I realized that I had several potential topics. I said to myself, 'What point can I make that I can cover in an essay? What do I have the most information about?' I decided that maybe I could narrow my topic down to the annoyances involved in going to the movies. I figured I would have more details for that topic." Diane then did more focused freewriting to accumulate details for an essay on problems with moviegoing:

> I really find it annoying to go see movies anymore. Even though I love films. Traffic to Cinema Six is awful. I hate looking for a parking place, the lot isn't big enough for the theaters and other stores. You just keep driving to find a parking space and hoping someone will pull out and no one else will pull in ahead of you. Then you don't want there to be a long line and to wind up in one of the first rows with this huge screen right in front of you. Then I'm in the theater with the smell of popcorn all around. Sitting there smelling it trying to ignore it and just wanting to pour a whole bucket of popcorn with melted butter down my throat. I can't stop thinking about the choclate bars either. I love the stuff but I don't need it. The people who are there sometimes drive me nuts. Talking and laughing, kids running around, packs of teens hollaring, who can listen to the movie? And I might run into my old boyfriend—the last thing I need. Also sitting thru all the previews and commercals. If I arrive late enough to miss that junk the movie may be selled out.

Notice that there are errors in spelling, grammar, and punctuation in Diane's freewriting. Diane is not worried about such matters, nor should she be. At this stage, she just wants to do some thinking on paper and get some material down on the page. She knows that this is a good first step, a good way of getting started, and that she will then be able to go on and shape the material.

You should take the same approach when freewriting: explore your topic without worrying at all about being correct. Figuring out what you want to say and getting raw material down on the page should have all of your attention at this early stage of the writing process.

To get a sense of the freewriting process, take a sheet of paper and freewrite about some of the everyday annoyances in your life. See how much material you can accumulate in ten minutes. And remember not to worry about mistakes; you're just thinking on paper.

Activity

1

Technique 2: Questioning

In *questioning,* you generate ideas and details by asking questions about your subject. Such questions include *why, when, where, who,* and *how.* Ask as many questions as you can think of.

www.mhhe.com/langan

Questioning: A Student Model

Here are some questions that Diane Woods might have asked while developing her essay.

Questions	Answers
Why don't I like to go to a movie?	Just too many problems involved.
When is going to the movies a problem?	Could be any time—when a movie is popular, the theater is too crowded; when traffic is bad, the trip is a drag.
Where are problems with moviegoing?	On the highway, in the parking lot, at the concession stand, in the theater itself.
Who creates the problems?	I do by wanting to eat too much. The patrons do by creating disturbances. The theater owners do by not having enough parking space and showing too many commercials.
How can I deal with the problem?	I can stay home and watch movies on DVD or cable TV.

Asking questions can be an effective way of getting yourself to think about a topic from a number of different angles. The questions can really help you generate details about a topic.

Activity

2

To get a sense of the questioning process, use a sheet of paper to ask yourself a series of questions about a good or bad experience that you have had recently. See how many details you can accumulate in ten minutes. And remember again not to be concerned about mistakes, because you are just thinking on paper.

www.mhhe.com/langan

Technique 3: Making a List

In *making a list,* also known as *brainstorming,* you collect ideas and details that relate to your subject. Pile these items up, one after another, without trying to sort out major details from minor ones or trying to put the details in any special order. Your goal is just to make a list of everything about your subject that occurs to you.

Making a List: A Student Model

After Diane did her freewriting about moviegoing, she made up the following list of details.

Traffic is bad between my house and theater

Noisy patrons

Don't want to run into Jeremy

Hard to be on a diet

Kids running in aisles

I'm crowded into seats between strangers who push me off armrests

Not enough parking

Parking lot needs to be expanded

Too many previews

Can't pause or fast-forward as you can with a DVD

Long lines

High ticket prices

Too many temptatons at snack stand

Commercials for food on the screen

Can prepare healthy snacks for myself at home

Tubs of popcorn with butter

Huge choclate bars

Candy has always been my downfall

Movie may be sold out

People who've seen movie before talk along with actors and give away plot twists

People coughing and sneezing

Icky stuff on floor

Teenagers yelling and showing off

One detail led to another as Diane expanded her list. Slowly but surely, more details emerged, some of which she could use in developing her paper. By the time she was done with her list, she was ready to plan an outline of her paragraph and then to write her first draft.

www.mhhe.com/langan

Activity

3

To get a sense of list-making, list on a sheet of paper a series of realistic goals, major or minor, that you would like to accomplish between today and one year from today. Your goals can be personal, academic, or career-related.

Technique 4: Clustering

Clustering, also known as *diagramming* or *mapping,* is another strategy that can be used to generate material for an essay. This method is helpful for people who like to do their thinking in a visual way. In clustering, you use lines, boxes, arrows, and circles to show relationships among the ideas and details that occur to you.

Begin by stating your subject in a few words in the center of a blank sheet of paper. Then, as ideas and details come to you, put them in boxes or circles around the subject and draw lines to connect them to each other and to the subject. Put minor ideas or details in smaller boxes or circles, and use connecting lines to show how they relate as well.

Clustering: A Student Model

Keep in mind that there is no right or wrong way of clustering or diagramming. It is a way to think on paper about how various ideas and details relate to one another. Below is an example of what Diane might have done to develop her ideas.

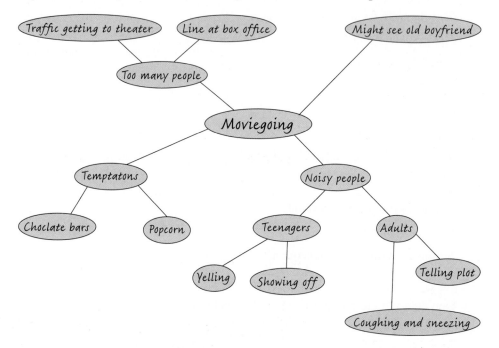

> **TIP:** In addition to helping generate material, clustering can give you an early sense of how ideas and details relate to one another. For example, the cluster for Diane's essay suggests that different kinds of noisy people could be the focus of one paragraph and that different kinds of temptations could be the focus of another paragraph.

Use clustering (diagramming) to organize the list of year-ahead goals that you created for the previous activity (page 28).

Activity

4

www.mhhe.com/langan

Technique 5: Preparing a Scratch Outline

A *scratch outline* is an excellent sequel to the first four prewriting techniques. A scratch outline often follows freewriting, questioning, list-making, or diagramming; or it may gradually emerge in the midst of these strategies. In fact, trying to make a scratch outline is a good way to see if you need to do more prewriting. If you cannot come up with a solid outline, then you know you need to do more prewriting to clarify your main point or its several kinds of support.

In a scratch outline, you think carefully about the point you are making, the supporting items for that point, and the order in which you will arrange those items. The scratch outline is a plan or blueprint to help you achieve a unified, supported, well-organized essay.

When you are planning a traditional essay consisting of an introduction, three supporting paragraphs, and a conclusion, a scratch outline is especially important. It may be only a few words, but it will be the framework on which your whole essay will be built.

Scratch Outline: A Student Model

As Diane was working on her list of details, she suddenly realized what the plan of her essay could be. She could organize many of her details into one of three supporting groups: (1) annoyances in going out, (2) too many tempting snacks, and (3) other people. She then went back to the list, crossed out items that she now saw did not fit, and numbered the items according to the group where they fit. Here is what Diane did with her list:

---

1   *Traffic is bad between my house and the theater*

3   *Noisy patrons*

    ~~Don't want to run into Jeremy~~

(continued)

---

2   Hard to be on a diet

3   Kids running in aisles

3   I'm crowded into seats between strangers who push me off armrests

1   Not enough parking

1   Parking lot needs to be expanded

1   Too many previews

~~Can't pause or fast-forward as you can with a DVD~~

1   Long lines

1   High ticket prices

2   Too many temptatons at snack stand

~~Commercials for food on the screen~~

2   Can prepare healthy snacks for myself at home

2   Tubs of popcorn with butter

~~Candy has always been my downfall~~

2   Huge choclate bars

1   Movie may be sold out

3   People who've seen movie before talk along with actors and give away plot twists

3   People coughing and sneezing

1   Icky stuff on floor

3   Teenagers yelling and showing off

Under the list, Diane was now able to prepare her scratch outline:

Going to the movies offers some real problems.

1. Inconvenience of going out

2. Tempting snacks

3. Other moviegoers

After all her prewriting, Diane was pleased. She knew that she had a promising essay—one with a clear point and solid support. She saw that she could organize the material into a traditional essay consisting of an introduction, several supporting paragraphs, and a conclusion. She was now ready to write the first draft of her essay, using her outline as a guide.

TIP: Chances are that if you do enough prewriting and thinking on paper, you will eventually discover the point and support of your essay.

Create a scratch outline that could serve as a guide if you were to write an essay about your year-ahead goals.

Activity

5

Writing a First Draft

When you write a first draft, be prepared to put in additional thoughts and details that did not emerge during prewriting. And don't worry if you hit a snag. Just leave a blank space or add a comment such as "Do later" and press on to finish the essay. Also, don't worry yet about grammar, punctuation, or spelling. You don't want to take time correcting words or sentences that you may decide to remove later. Instead, make it your goal to state your thesis clearly and develop the content of your essay with plenty of specific details.

Writing a First Draft: A Student Model

Here is Diane's first draft:

Even though I love movies, my friends have stopped asking me to go. There are just too many problems involved in going to the movies.

There are no small theaters anymore, I have to drive fifteen minutes to a big multaplex. Because of a supermarket and restarants, the parking lot is filled. I have to keep driving around to find a space. Then I have to stand in a long line. Hoping that they do not run out of tickets. Finally, I have to pay too much money for a ticket. Putting out that much money, I should not have to deal with a floor that ~~is sticky~~ seems coated with rubber cement. By the end of a movie, my shoes are often sealed to a mix of spilled soda, bubble gum, and other stuff.

(continued)

The theater offers temptatons in the form of snacks I really don't need. Like most of us I have to worry about weight gain. At home I do pretty well by simply watching what I keep in the house and not buying stuff that is bad for me. I can make do with healthy snacks because there is nothing in the house. Going to the theater is like spending my evening in a ~~market~~ 7-Eleven that's been equiped with a movie screen and there are seats which are comfortable. I try to persuade myself to just have a diet soda. The smell of popcorn soon overcomes me. My friends are as bad as I am. Choclate bars seem to jump into your hands, I am eating enormous mouthfuls of milk duds. By the time I leave the theater I feel sick and tired of myself.

Some of the other moviegoers are the worst problem. There are teenagers who try to impress their friends in one way or another. Little kids race up and down the aisles, gigling and laughing. Adults act as if they're watching the movie at home. They talk loudly about the ages of the stars and give away the plot. Other people are droping popcorn tubs or cups of soda crushed ice and soda on the floor. Also coughing a lot and doing other stuff—bms!

I decided one night that I was not going to be a moviegoer anymore. I joined Netflix, and I'll watch movies comfortable in my own living room.

TIP: After Diane finished the first draft, she was able to put it aside until the next day. You will bebefit as well if you can allow some time between finishing a draft and starting to revise.

Activity

6

Team up with someone in your class and see if you can fill in the missing words in the following explanation of Diane's first draft.

1. Diane has a very brief introduction—no more than an opening sentence and a second sentence that states the _____. She knows she can develop the introduction more fully in a later draft.

2. Of Diane's three supporting paragraphs, only the _____ paragraph lacks a topic sentence. She realizes that this is something to work on in the next draft.

3. There are some misspellings—for example, _____. Diane doesn't worry about spelling at this point. She just wants to get down as much of the substance of her paper as possible.

4. There are various punctuation errors, such as the run-on sentences in the

    _____ paragraphs. Again, Diane is focusing on content; she knows she can attend to punctuation and grammar later.

5. At several points in the essay, Diane revises on the spot to make images more

    _____: she changes "is sticky" to "seems coated with rubber cement," "market" to "7-Eleven," and "cups of soda" to "cups of crushed ice and soda."

6. Near the end of her essay, Diane can't think of added details to insert so she

    simply puts the letters "_____" at that point to remind herself to "be more specific" in the next draft. She then goes on to finish her first draft.

7. Her _____ is as brief as her introduction. Diane knows she can

    round off her essay more fully during revision.

Revising

Revising is as much a stage in the writing process as prewriting, outlining, and doing the first draft. *Revising* means rewriting an essay, building on what has already been done, to make it stronger. One writer has said about revision, "It's like cleaning house—getting rid of all the junk and putting things in the right order." But it is not just "straightening up"; instead, you must be ready to roll up your sleeves and do whatever is needed to create an effective essay. Too many students think that the first draft *is* the essay. They start to become writers when they realize that revising a rough draft three or four times is often at the heart of the writing process.

Here are some quick hints that can help make revision easier. First, set your first draft aside for a while. A few hours will do, but a day or two would be better. You can then come back to the draft with a fresh, more objective point of view. Second, work from typed or printed text. You'll be able to see the essay more impartially in this way than if you were just looking at your own familiar handwriting. Next, read your draft aloud. Hearing how your writing sounds will help you pick up problems with meaning as well as with style. Finally, as you do all these things, add your thoughts and changes above the lines or in the margins of your essay. Your written comments can serve as a guide when you work on the next draft.

There are three stages to the revising process:

- revising content

- revising sentences

- editing

Revising Content

To revise the content of your essay, ask these questions:

1. Is my essay **unified**?

   • Do I have a thesis that is clearly stated or implied in the introductory paragraph of my essay?

   • Do all my supporting paragraphs truly support and back up my thesis?

2. Is my essay **supported**?

   • Are there three separate supporting points for the thesis?

   • Do I have specific evidence for each of the three supporting points?

   • Is there plenty of specific evidence for each supporting point?

3. Is my essay **organized**?

   • Do I have an interesting introduction, a solid conclusion, and an accurate title?

   • Do I have a clear method of organizing my essay?

   • Do I use transitions and other connecting words?

Chapters 3 and 4 will give you practice in achieving **unity, support,** and **organization** in your writing.

Revising Sentences

To revise sentences in your essay, ask yourself the following questions:

1. Do I use parallelism to balance my words and ideas?

2. Do I have a consistent point of view?

3. Do I use specific words?

4. Do I use active verbs?

5. Do I use words effectively by avoiding slang, clichés, pretentious language, and wordiness?

6. Do I vary my sentences?

Chapter 5 will give you practice in revising sentences.

Editing

After you have revised your essay for content and style, you are ready to *edit*—check for and correct—errors in grammar, punctuation, and spelling. Students often find it hard to edit their writing carefully. They have put so much, or so little, work into their writing that it's almost painful for them to look at the essay one more time. You may simply have to *will* yourself to perform this important closing step in the writing process. Remember that eliminating sentence-skill mistakes will improve an average essay and help ensure a strong grade on a good essay. Further, as you get into the habit of checking your writing, you will also get into the habit of using the sentence skills consistently. They are an integral part of clear and effective writing.

Chapter 5 and Part 4 of this book will serve as a guide while you are editing your essay for mistakes in **sentence skills.**

An Illustration of the Revising and Editing Processes

Revising with a Second Draft: A Student Model

Since Diane Woods was using a word-processing program on a computer, she was able to print out a double-spaced version of her essay about movies, leaving her plenty of room for revisions. Here is one of her revised paragraphs:

> *Second,*   *tempting*
> The theater offers ~~temptatons in the form of~~ snacks I really don't
>   *battle an expanding waistline.*
> need. Like most of us I have to ~~worry about weight gain.~~ At home I
> do pretty well by simply ~~watching what I keep in the house and~~ not
>   *like celery and carrot sticks*
> buying stuff that is bad for me. I can make do with ~~healthy~~ snacks
>   *no ice cream*   *however*
> because there is ~~nothing~~ in the freezer. Going to the theater is like
> spending my evening in a 7-Eleven that's been equiped with a movie
>   *comfortable*   *As*
> screen and ~~there are~~ seats ~~which are comfortable.~~ I try to persuade
>   *t*   *dripping with butter*
> myself to just have a diet soda. The smell of fresh popcorn soon
> overcomes me. ~~My friends are as bad as I am.~~ Choclate bars seem to
>   *my*   *risk pulling out my fillings as I chew*
> jump into ~~your~~ hands. I ~~am eating~~ enormous mouthfuls of milk duds.
>   *disgusted*
> By the time I leave the theater I feel ~~out of sorts~~ with myself.

Diane made her changes in longhand as she worked on the second draft. As you will see when you complete the activity below, her revision serves to make the paragraph more unified, better supported, and better organized.

Fill in the missing words.

1. To achieve better organization, Diane adds at the beginning of the paragraph the transitional phrase "_____," making it very clear that her second supporting idea is tempting snacks.

2. Diane also adds the transition "_____" to show clearly the difference between being at home and being in the theater.

3. In the interest of (*unity, support, organization*) _____, Diane crosses out the sentence "_____." She realizes this sentence is not a relevant detail but really another topic.

4. To add more (*unity, support, organization*) _____, Diane changes "healthy snacks" to "_____"; she changes "nothing in the freezer" to "_____"; she adds "_____" after "popcorn"; and she changes "am eating" to "_____."

5. In the interest of eliminating wordiness, she removes the words "_____" from the third sentence.

6. In the interest of parallelism, Diane changes "and there are seats which are comfortable" to "_____."

7. For greater sentence variety, Diane combines two short sentences, beginning the first sentence with the subordinating word "_____."

8. To create a consistent point of view, Diane changes "jump into your hands" to "_____."

9. Finally, Diane replaces the vague "out of sorts" with the more precise "_____."

Editing: A Student Model

After typing into her word-processing file all the changes in her second draft, Diane printed out another clean draft of the essay. The paragraph on tempting snacks required almost no more revision, so Diane turned her attention mostly to editing changes, illustrated below with her work on the second supporting paragraph:

> Second, the theater offers tempting snacks I really don't need. Like most of us, I have to battle an expanding waistline. At home I do pretty well by simply not buying stuff that is bad for me. I can make do with snacks like celery and carrot sticks because there is no ice cream in the freezer. Going to the theater, however, is like spending my evening in a 7-Eleven that's been ~~equiped~~ *equipped* with a movie screen and comfortable seats. As I try to persuade myself to just have a Diet ~~soda~~ *Coke*, the smell of fresh popcorn dripping with butter soon overcomes me. ~~Choclate~~ *Chocolate* bars *the size of small automobiles* seem to jump into my hands. I risk pulling out my fillings as I chew enormous mouthfuls of *M*ilk *D*uds. By the time I leave the theater, I feel disgusted with myself.

Once again, Diane makes her changes in longhand right on the printout of her essay. To note these changes, complete the activity below.

Fill in the missing words.

Copyright © 2011 The McGraw-Hill Companies, Inc. All rights reserved.

Activity

8

1. As part of her editing, Diane checked and corrected the _____ of two words, *equipped* and *chocolate*.

2. She added _____ to set off two introductory phrases ("Like most of us" in the second sentence and "By the time I leave the theater" in the final sentence) and also to set off the interrupting word *however* in the fifth sentence.

3. She realized that "milk duds" is a brand name and added _____ to make it "Milk Duds."

4. And since revision can occur at any stage of the writing process, including editing, she made one of her details more vivid by adding the descriptive words "_____."

Review Activities

You now have a good overview of the writing process, from prewriting to first draft to revising to editing. The remaining chapters in Part 1 will deepen your sense of the four goals of effective writing: unity, support, organization or coherence, and sentence skills.

To reinforce the information about the writing process that you have learned in this chapter, you can now work through the following activities:

- taking a writing inventory
- prewriting
- outlining
- revising

Taking a Writing Inventory

Answer the questions below to evaluate your approach to the writing process. This activity is not a test, so try to be as honest as possible. Becoming aware of your writing habits will help you realize changes that may be helpful.

Activity

9

1. When you start work on an essay, do you typically do any prewriting?

   _____ Yes   _____ Sometimes   _____ No

2. If so, which prewriting techniques do you use?

   _____ Freewriting   _____ Diagramming

   _____ Questioning   _____ Scratch outline

   _____ List-making   _____ Other (please describe)

3. Which prewriting technique or techniques work best for you, or which do you think will work best for you?

4. Many students say they find it helpful to handwrite a first draft and then type that draft on a computer. They then print the draft out and revise it by hand. Describe the way you proceed in drafting and revising an essay.

5. After you write the first draft of an essay, do you have time to set it aside for a while so that you can come back to it with a fresh eye?

   _____ Yes   _____ No

---

6. How many drafts do you typically write when working on an essay?_____

7. When you revise, are you aware that you should be working toward an essay that is unified, solidly supported, and clearly organized? Has this chapter given you a better sense that unity, support, and organization are goals to aim for?

8. Do you revise an essay for the effectiveness of its sentences as well as for its content?

   _____ Yes   _____ No

9. Do you typically do any editing of the almost-final draft of an essay, or do you tend to "hope for the best" and hand it in without careful checking?

   _____ Edit   _____ Hope for the best

10. What (if any) information has this chapter given you about *prewriting* that you will try to apply in your writing?

11. What (if any) information has this chapter given you about *revising* that you will try to apply in your writing?

12. What (if any) information has this chapter given you about *editing* that you will try to apply in your writing?

Prewriting

On the following pages are examples of how the five prewriting techniques could be used to develop the topic "Problems of Combining Work and College." Identify each technique by writing F (for freewriting), Q (for questioning), L (for list-making), C (for clustering), or SO (for the scratch outline) in the answer space.

Activity

10

_____ Never enough time

Miss campus parties

Had to study (only two free hours a night)

Give up activities with friends

No time to rewrite papers

Can't stay at school to play video games or talk to friends

Friends don't call me to go out anymore

Sunday no longer relaxed day—have to study

Missing sleep I should be getting

Grades aren't as good as they could be

Can't watch favorite TV shows

Really need the extra money

Tired when I sit down to study at nine o'clock

_____ What are some of the problems of combining work and school?	Schoolwork suffers because I don't have time to study or rewrite papers. I've had to give up things I enjoy, like sleep and touch football. I can't get into the social life at college, because I have to work right after class.
How have these problems changed my life?	My grades aren't as good as they were when I didn't work. Some of my friends have stopped calling me. My relationship with a girl I liked fell apart because I couldn't spend much time with her. I miss TV.
What do I do in a typical day?	I get up at 7 to make an 8 A.M. class. I have classes till 1:30, and then I drive to the supermarket where I work. I work till 7 P.M., and then I drive home and eat dinner. After I take a shower and relax for a half hour, it's about 9. This gives me only a couple of hours to study—read textbooks, do math exercises, write essays. My eyes start to close well before I go to bed at 11.
Why do I keep up this schedule?	I can't afford to go to school without working, and I need a degree to get the accounting job I want. If I invest my time now, I'll have a better future.

_____   Juggling a job and college has created major difficulties in my life.

1. Little time for studying
   a. Not reading textbooks
   b. No rewriting papers
   c. Little studying for tests
2. Little time for enjoying social side of college
   a. During school
   b. After school
3. No time for personal pleasures
   a. Favorite TV shows
   b. Sunday football games
   c. Sleeping late

_____

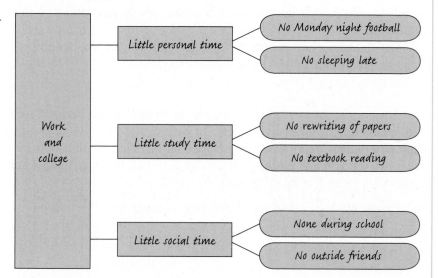

_____   It's hard working and going to school at the same time. I never realized how much I'd have to give up. I won't be quitting my job because I need the money. And the people are friendly at the place where I work. I've had to give up a lot more than I thought. We used to play touch football games every Sunday. They were fun and we'd go out for drinks afterwards. Sundays now are for catch-up work with my courses. I have to catch up because I don't get home every day until 7, I have to eat dinner first before studying. Sometimes I'm so hungry I just eat cookies or chips. Anyway, by the time I take a shower it's 9 P.M. or later and I'm already feeling tired. I've been up since 7 A.M. Sometimes I write an English paper in twenty minutes and don't even read it over. I feel that

I'm missing out on a lot in college. The other day some people I like were sitting in the cafeteria listening to music and talking. I would have given anything to stay and not have to go to work. I almost called in sick. I used to get invited to parties, I don't much anymore. My friends know I'm not going to be able to make it, so they don't bother. I can't sleep late on weekends or watch TV during the week.

Outlining

As already mentioned (see page 29), outlining is central to writing a good essay. An outline lets you see, and work on, the bare bones of an essay, without the distraction of a clutter of words and sentences. It develops your ability to think clearly and logically. Outlining provides a quick check on whether your essay will be *unified*. It also suggests right at the start whether your essay will be adequately *supported*. And it shows you how to plan an essay that is *well organized*.

The following two exercises will help you develop the outlining skills so important to planning and writing a solid essay.

Activity

11

One key to effective outlining is the ability to distinguish between major ideas and details that fit under those ideas. In each of the four lists below, major and supporting items are mixed together. Working in pairs, put the items into logical order by filling in the outline that follows each list. In items 3 and 4, one of the three major ideas is missing and must be added.

1. Thesis: My high school had three problem areas.

Involved with drugs
Leaky ceilings
Students
Unwilling to help after class
Formed cliques
Teachers
Buildings
Ill-equipped gym
Much too strict

a. _____

   (1) _____

   (2) _____

b. _____

   (1) _____

   (2) _____

c. _____

   (1) _____

   (2) _____

2. Thesis: Working as a dishwasher in a restaurant was my worst job.

Ten-hour shifts
Heat in kitchen
Working conditions

a. _____

(1) _____

(2) _____

Minimum wage
Hours changed every week
No bonus for overtime
Hours
Pay
Noisy work area

b. _____

(1) _____

(2) _____

c. _____

(1) _____

(2) _____

3. Thesis: Running is an ideal way to get needed exercise.

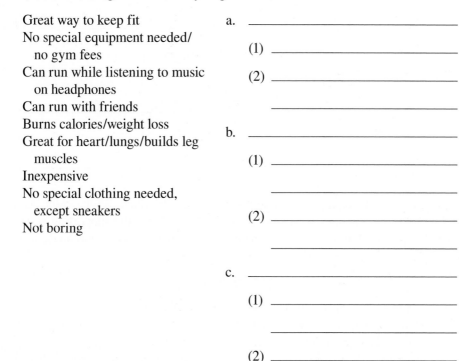

Great way to keep fit
No special equipment needed/
    no gym fees
Can run while listening to music
    on headphones
Can run with friends
Burns calories/weight loss
Great for heart/lungs/builds leg
    muscles
Inexpensive
No special clothing needed,
    except sneakers
Not boring

a. _____

(1) _____

(2) _____

_____

b. _____

(1) _____

_____

(2) _____

_____

c. _____

(1) _____

_____

(2) _____

4. Thesis: The Internet is an invaluable tool for college students.

E-mail instructor/classmates
Research
Take online courses
Access online learning centers/
  extra help
Find information for term papers
Test preparation/
  practice exercises
Schedule more flexible if you can
  study online
Read more about important topics
Save money/time traveling to
  class
Keep up even if you need to be
  absent

a. _____

_____

(1) _____

(2) _____

_____

(3) _____

_____

b. _____

(1) _____

_____

(2) _____

_____

c. _____

(1) _____

_____

(2) _____

_____

Activity

12

Read the following essay and outline it in the spaces provided. Write out the central point and topic sentences, and summarize in a few words the supporting material that fits under each topic sentence. One item is summarized for you as an example.

Losing Touch

Steve, a typical American, stays home on workdays. He logs onto his e-mail. Evenings, he listens to his iPod, watches a DVD, or surfs the Internet. On many days, Steve doesn't talk to any other human beings, and he doesn't see any people except those on television. Steve is imaginary, but his lifestyle is very common. More and more, the inventions of modern technology seem to be cutting us off from contact with our fellow human beings.

Thesis: _____

_____

The world of business is one area in which technology is isolating us. Many people now work alone at home. With access to a large central computer, employees such as secretaries, insurance agents, and accountants do their jobs at display terminals in their own homes. They no longer have to actually see the people they're dealing with. In addition, employees are often paid in an impersonal way. Workers' salaries are automatically credited to their bank accounts, eliminating the need for paychecks. Fewer people stand in line with their coworkers to receive their pay or cash their checks. Finally, personal banking is becoming a detached process. Customers interact with machines rather than people to deposit or withdraw money from their accounts. Even some bank loans are approved or rejected, not in an interview with a loan officer, but by a computer program.

First topic sentence: _____

_____

Support: 1. Many people now work alone at home.

2. _____

_____

3. _____

_____

a. _____

_____

b. _____

_____

Another area that technology is changing is entertainment. Music, for instance, was once a group experience. People listened to music in concert halls or at small social gatherings. For many people now, however, music is a solitary experience. Walking along the street or sitting in their living rooms, they wear headphones to build a wall of music around them. Movie entertainment is changing, too. Movies used to be social events. Now, some people are not going out to see a movie. Some are choosing to wait for a film to appear on cable television or DVD. Instead of being involved with the laughter, applause, or hisses of the audience, viewers watch movies in the isolation of their own living rooms.

Second topic sentence: _____

_____

Support: 1. _____

_____

2. _____

_____

Education is a third important area in which technology is separating us from others. From elementary schools to colleges, students spend more and more time sitting by themselves in front of computers. The computers give them feedback, while teachers spend more time tending the computers and less time interacting with their classes. A similar problem occurs in homes. As more families buy computers, increasing numbers of students practice their math and reading skills with software programs instead of with their friends, brothers and sisters, and parents. Last, alienation is occurring as a result of DVDs. People are buying DVDs on subjects such as cooking, real estate investment, speaking, and speed-reading. They then practice their skills at home rather than by taking group classes in which a rich human interaction can occur.

Third topic sentence: _____

_____

Support: 1. _____

_____

2. _____

_____

3. _____

_____

> Technology, then, seems to be driving human beings apart. Soon, we may
> no longer need to communicate with other human beings to do our work,
> entertain ourselves, or pursue an education. Machines will be the coworkers
> and companions of the future.

Revising

Following is the second supporting paragraph from an essay called "Problems of Combining School and Work." The paragraph is shown in four different stages of development: (1) first draft, (2) revised second draft, (3) edited next-to-final draft, (4) final draft. The four stages appear in scrambled order. Write the number 1 in the answer blank for the first draft, and number the remaining stages in sequence. To help you get started, a few comments about the changes made in draft 2 are included here. Add to these, but also record the changes made in drafts 3 and 4.

Changes in draft 2: _Adds information about sports he/she used to play._____

_Removes sentence beginning "Psychologists say . . ."_____

_____

Changes in draft 3: _____

_____

_____

_____

Activity

13

Changes in draft 4: _____

_____

_____   I have also given up some personal pleasures in my life. On sundays for example I used to play softball or football, now I use the entire day to study. Good old-fashioned sleep is another lost pleasure for me now. I never get as much as I like because their just isn't time. Finally I miss having the chance to just sit in front of the TV, on weeknights. In order to watch the whole lineup of movies and sports that I used to watch regularly. These sound like small pleasures, but you realize how important they are when you have to give them up.

_____   I've had to give up pleasures in my life. I use to spend sundays playing games, now I have to study. Im the sort of person who needs a lot of sleep, but I dont have the time for that either. Sleeping nine or ten hours a night woul'dnt be unusual for me. Psycologists say that each individual need a different amount of sleep, some people need as little as five hours, some need as much as nine or ten. So I'm not unusual in that. But Ive given up that pleasure too. And I can't watch the TV shows I use to enjoy. This is another personal pleasure Ive lost because of doing work and school. These may seem like small things, but you realize how good they are when you give them up.

_____   Besides missing the social side of college life, I've also had to give up some of my special personal pleasures. I used to spend Sunday afternoons, for example, playing lob-pitch softball or touch football depending on the season. Now I use Sunday as a catch-up day for my studies. Another pleasure I've lost is sleeping late on days off and weekends. I once loved mornings when I could check the clock, bury my head in the pillow, and drift off for another hour. These days I'm forced to crawl out of bed the minute the alarm lets out its piercing ring. Finally, I no longer have the chance to just sit watching the movies and sports programs that I enjoy. A leisurely night of Monday Night Football or a network premiere of a Tom Hanks movie is a pleasure of the past for me now.

_____   Besides missing the social side of college life, I've also had to give up some of my special personal pleasures. I used to spend sunday afternoons, for example playing lob-pitch softball or touch football depending on the season. Now I use the day as a catch-up day for my studies. Another pleasure I've lost is sleeping late on days off and weekends. I once loved mornings when I could check the clock, then burying my head in the pillow, and you drift off to sleep for another hour. These days I'm forced to get out of bed the minute the alarm lets out it's ring. Finally I no longer have the chance to just sit watching the movies and also programs with sports that I enjoy. A leisurely night of Monday Night Football or a network premiere of a Tom Hanks movie is a pleasure of the past for me now.

After you have done that, explain why you think that drafts 2, 3, and 4 are each better than the one that preceded them. In other words, explain what improvements that writer has made to each. As you do this, consider the following questions:

1. Is this version of the paragraph better unified, supported, and organized than the previous one? (Review the Revising Content questions on page 34.)

2. Has the student revised sentences? (Review the Revising Sentences questions on page 34.)

3. Has the student edited for mistakes in grammer, punctuation, and spelling? Which ones?

3

The First and Second Steps in Essay Writing

This chapter will show you how to

• start an essay with a point, or thesis

• support that point, or thesis, with specific evidence

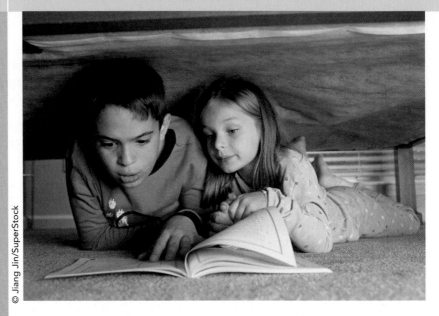

© Jiang Jin/SuperStock

Describe a favorite childhood place that made you feel secure, safe, private, or in a world of your own. Begin with a thesis statement, something like this: "_____was a place that made me feel_____when I was a child." Remember to keep the point of your thesis statement in mind as you describe this place. Include only details that will support the idea that your place was one of security, safety, privacy, or the like.

Chapter 2 emphasized how prewriting and revising can help you become an effective writer. This chapter focuses on the first two steps in writing an effective essay:

1. Begin with a point, or thesis.

2. Support the thesis with specific evidence.

The chapters that follow will focus on the third and fourth steps in writing:

3. Organize and connect the specific evidence (pages 84–109).

4. Write clear, error-free sentences (pages 110–145).

Step 1: Begin with a Point, or Thesis

Your first step in writing is to discover what point you want to make and to write that point out as a single sentence. There are two reasons for doing this. You want to know right from the start if you have a clear and workable thesis. Also, you will be able to use the thesis as a guide while writing your essay. At any stage you can ask yourself, Does this support my thesis? With the thesis as a guide, the danger of drifting away from the point of the essay is greatly reduced.

Understanding Thesis Statements

In Chapter 1, you learned that effective essays center around a thesis, or main point, that a writer wishes to express. This central idea is usually presented as a *thesis statement* in an essay's introductory paragraph.

A good thesis statement does two things. First, it tells readers an essay's *topic.* Second, it presents the writer's *attitude, opinion, idea,* or *point* about that topic. For example, look at the following thesis statement:

Owning a pet has several important benefits.

In this thesis statement, the topic is *owning a pet;* the writer's main point is that owning a pet *has several important benefits.*

For each thesis statement below, single-underline the topic and double-underline the main point that the writer wishes to express about the topic.

Activity 1

EXAMPLES   Our company president should be fired for three main reasons.

The Internet has led to new kinds of frustration in everyday life.

1. Having to care for a child requires hard work, commitment, and patience.
2. Celebrities are often poor role models because of the ways they dress, talk, and behave.
3. My first night as a security guard turned out to be one of the most frightening experiences of my life.
4. SUVs are inferior to cars because they are harder to control, more expensive, and dangerous to the environment.
5. The twentieth century produced three inventions that dramatically changed the lives of all Americans.
6. Stress in the fast-food workplace has led to serious physical, psychological, and emotional problems for employees.

7. Advertisers target young people when marketing cigarettes, alcohol, and adult movies.

8. Christian Bale's varied film roles demonstrate his versatility as an actor.

9. American carmakers need to produce vehicles that are fuel efficient, safe, and less expensive.

10. Being successful at any job requires punctuality, dependability, and ambition.

Writing a Good Thesis I

www.mhhe.com/langan

Now that you know how thesis statements work, you can begin writing your own. To start, you need a topic that is neither too broad nor too narrow. Suppose, for example, that an instructor asks you to write a paper on marriage. Such a subject is too broad to cover in a five-hundred-word essay. You would have to write a book to support adequately any point you might make about the general subject of marriage. What you would need to do, then, is limit your subject. Narrow it down until you have a thesis that you can deal with specifically in about five hundred words. In the box that follows are (1) several general subjects, (2) a limited version of each general subject, and (3) a thesis statement about each limited subject.

General Subject	Limited Subject	Thesis
Marriage	Honeymoon	A honeymoon is perhaps the worst way to begin a marriage.
Family	Older sister	My older sister helped me overcome my shyness.
Television	TV preachers	TV evangelists use sales techniques to promote their messages.
Children	Disciplining of children	My husband and I have several effective ways of disciplining our children.
Sports	Players' salaries	Players' high salaries are bad for the game, for the fans, and for the values our children are developing.

Sometimes a subject must go through several stages of limiting before it is narrow enough to write about. Below are four lists reflecting several stages that writers went through in moving from a general subject to a narrow thesis statement. Number the stages in each list from 1 to 5, with 1 marking the broadest stage and 5 marking the thesis.

List 1

___3___ Major league baseball players

___1___ Athletes

___5___ Major league pitchers' salaries too high

___2___ Professional athletes

___4___ Major league pitchers

List 2

___4___ John Philip Souza

___2___ American composers

___5___ Music 101 taught me to appreciate Souza's band music.

___1___ Music

___3___ Band music

List 3

___2___ Retail companies

___1___ Supermarkets

___4___ Dealing with customers

___3___ Working in a supermarket

___5___ I've learned how to handle unpleasant supermarket customers.

List 4

___2___ Camping

___4___ First camping trip

___3___ Summer vacation

___5___ My first camping trip was a disastrous experience.

___1___ Vacations

Later in this chapter, you will get more practice in narrowing general subjects to thesis statements.

How to Limit and Focus Your Thesis

You have just learned that it is important to *limit* a topic. One way to do this is by clustering, which is also a good way to gather information. (If necessary, turn back to page 28 to review how to cluster.) Let's say your instructor assigns a paper on physical exercise. Obviously, this is far too broad a topic for a short paper. Therefore, you can try to cluster ideas around this topic as a way to limit it to an aspect of the topic that you know most about or that you are most interested in.

Here's an example of how one student began to use this method to limit her topic:

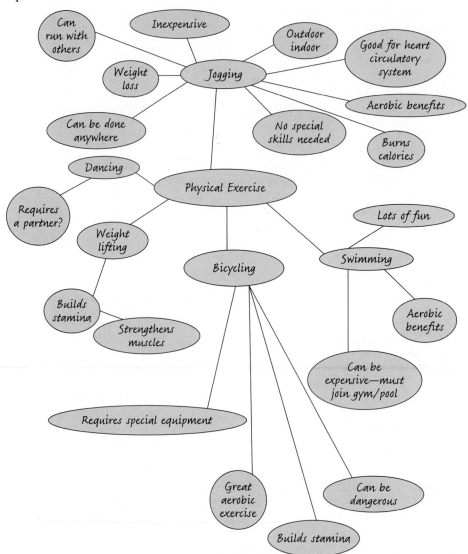

Immediately after completing this exercise, the student realized that the type of physical exercise she knew most about was running. So, she decided to limit her essay to that topic. However, she also knew that she would have to *focus* on a main point about running and that her clustering suggested several different main points. Here are just three:

- Running is an easy way to get needed exercise: it is inexpensive, can be done almost anywhere, and requires few special skills.

- Running benefits the lungs, circulatory system, and the leg muscles.

- Running burns calories and helps maintain a healthy weight.

To determine which of these three main points she could most easily write about, the student used another prewriting technique, making a list. (If necessary, turn back to pages 26–28 to review list making.) In fact, she listed everything she knew about each of her three potential thesis statements:

Easy way to get exercise	Benefits circulatory system, lungs, muscles	Helps maintain a healthy weight
Can be done outside or inside	Strengthens heart muscle	Lost 20 pounds in one year jogging three times a week
No special training needed	Strengthens lungs, improves breathing	
Inexpensive	Slows pulse rate	
No special location needed	Increases blood supply	
No uniform or special clothing required		
Can be done with others		
Can be done while listening to music on headset		

It is obvious from what we see here that the interests of the student favor writing about why running is an easy way to get exercise.

As you can see, limiting or narrowing a topic is extremely important. However, you will also have to *focus* on a main point. Writers should always be committed to the ideas they are discussing. So, if possible, always write about the main point that you know most about, that you are most interested in, or that you are most passionate about.

Below is an list of thesis statements that make or focus on different main points about the same topic. Each can be the foundation of a very different essay.

Topic	Main Point
Some professional athletes	act as negative role models for young people.
Some professional athletes	have to train year round.

Some professional athletes	have caused themselves harm by taking steroids.
Some professional athletes	contribute time and money to worthy causes.
Some professional athletes	forget they are members of a team that needs to work together.
Going to college	demands careful time management.
Going to college	enables people to appreciate different cultures and lifestyles.
Going to college	provides students with analytical skills that can lead to rewarding careers.
Going to college	requires study habits different from those used in high school.
Conserving energy at home	saves residents a great deal of money.
Conserving energy at home	reduces air pollution caused by the burning of fossil fuels.
Conserving energy at home	doesn't require a change in lifestyle.
Conserving energy at home	reduces our dependence on foreign sources of energy.
The Internet	should be regulated to protect children.
The Internet	is an inexpensive way to transmit information.
The Internet	is a valuable academic tool.
The Internet	enables millions of people to speak out on important social and political issues.

As you can see, you can write several different thesis statements about the same topic. In each case, of course, your purpose will help determine your main point and may even help shape the organization of your paper. Below is a list of several different thesis statements written on "heating costs." Each serves a different purpose.

Purpose	**Thesis**
To analyze	A home energy audit revealed that we can reduce home heating costs by $500 a year.
To explain a cause	Our home heating costs were high because of poor insulation, drafty windows, and an inefficient furnace.

To contrast	Homes using passive solar energy have lower heating bills than others.
To explain an effect	Higher heating costs have made architects design more energy-efficient homes.
To explain a process	Lowering home heating costs is easy if one follows three-basic steps.
To offer a solution	People who own older homes should have an energy audit to find ways to reduce heating costs.
To classify	Heating costs can be reduced by using fossil-fuel alternatives: solar, wind, and geothermal.
To explain advantages	Reducing heating costs not only saves money, but it also increases the value of a home and helps the environment.
To explain disadvantages	Installing solar panels will reduce heating costs, but they are unsightly and expensive.

Writing a Good Thesis II

When writing thesis statements, people often make mistakes that undermine their chances of producing an effective essay. One mistake is to simply announce the subject rather than state a true thesis. A second mistake is to write a thesis that is too broad, and a third is to write a thesis that is too narrow. A fourth error is to write a thesis containing more than one idea. Here are tips for avoiding such mistakes and writing good thesis statements.

1 Write Statements, Not Announcements

The subject of this paper will be my parents.

I want to talk about the crime wave in our country.

The baby-boom generation is the concern of this essay.

In this first group, the sentences are not thesis statements but announcements of a topic. For instance, "The subject of this paper will be my parents" does not make a point about the parents but merely tells, in a rather weak and unimaginative way, the writer's general subject. Remember, a thesis statement must make a point about a limited subject. Effective thesis statements based on the above sentences could be as follows:

My parents each struggled with personal demons.

The recent crime wave in our city has several apparent causes.

The baby-boom generation has changed American society in key ways.

2 Avoid Statements That Are Too Broad

Disease has shaped human history.

Insects are fascinating creatures.

Men and women are very different.

In the preceding examples, each statement is too broad to be supported adequately in a student essay. For instance, "Disease has shaped human history" would require far more than a five-hundred-word essay. In fact, there are many lengthy books written on the exact same topic. Remember, your thesis statement should be focused enough that it can be effectively supported in a five-paragraph essay. Revised thesis statements based on the topics in the above sentences could be as follows:

In the mid-1980s, AIDS changed people's attitudes about dating.

Strength, organization, and communication make the ant one of nature's most successful insects.

Men and women are often treated very differently in the workplace.

3 Avoid Statements That Are Too Narrow

Here are three statements that are too narrow:

The speed limit near my home is sixty-five miles per hour.

A hurricane hit southern Florida last summer.

A person must be at least thirty-five years old to be elected president of the United States.

In this third group, there is no room in any of the three statements for support to be given. For instance, "The speed limit near my home is sixty-five miles per hour" is too narrow to be expanded into a paper. It is a simple fact that does not require any support. Such a statement is sometimes called a *dead-end statement:* there is no place to go with it. Remember, a thesis statement must be broad enough to require support in an essay. Successful thesis statements based on the preceding sentences are as follows:

The speed limit near my home should be lowered to fifty-five miles per hour for several reasons.

Federal officials made a number of mistakes in their response to the recent Florida hurricane.

The requirement that a U.S. president must be at least thirty-five years old is unfair and unreasonable.

4 Make Sure Statements Develop Only One Idea

Here are three statements that contain more than one idea:

> One of the most serious problems affecting young people today is bullying, and it is time more kids learned the value of helping others.

> Studying with others has several benefits, but it also has drawbacks and can be difficult to schedule.

> Teachers have played an important role in my life, but they were not as important as my parents.

In this fourth group, each statement contains more than one idea. For instance, "One of the most serious problems affecting young people today is bullying, *and* it is time more kids learned the value of helping others" clearly has two separate ideas ("One of the most serious problems affecting young people today is bullying" *and* "it is time more kids learned the value of helping others"). The reader is asked to focus on two separate points, each of which more logically belongs in an essay of its own. Remember, the point of an essay is to communicate a *single* main idea to readers. To be as clear as possible, then, try to limit your thesis statement to the single key idea you want your readers to know. Revised thesis statements based on each of the examples above are as follows:

> One of the most serious problems affecting young people today is bullying.

> Studying with others has several benefits.

> Teachers have played an important role in my life.

Write TN in the space next to the two statements that are too narrow to be developed in an essay. Write TB beside the two statements that are too broad to be covered in an essay. Then, in the spaces provided, revise one of the too-narrow statements and one of the too-broad statements to make them each an effective thesis.

Activity 3

_____ 1. The way our society treats elderly people is unbelievable.

TN 2. Enrollment at Freestone State College increased by 10 percent.

_____

_____

TB 3. California has much to offer the tourist.

_____

_____

_____ 4. I failed my biology course.

_____

_____

www.mhhe.com/langan

Step 2: Support the Thesis with Specific Evidence

The first essential step in writing a successful essay is to formulate a clearly stated thesis. The second basic step is to support the thesis with specific reasons or details.

To ensure that your essay will have adequate support, you may find an informal outline very helpful. Write down a brief version of your thesis idea, and then work out and jot down the three points that will support the thesis.

Here is the scratch outline that was prepared by the author of the earlier essay on moviegoing:

> *Moviegoing is a problem.*
> 1. *Inconvenience of going out*
> 2. *Tempting snacks*
> 3. *Other moviegoers*

A scratch outline like this one looks simple, but developing it often requires a great deal of careful thinking. The time spent on developing a logical outline is invaluable, though. Once you have planned the steps that logically support your thesis, you will be in an excellent position to go on to write an effective essay.

Activities in this section will give you practice in the crucial skill of planning an essay clearly.

Activity

4

Following are ten informal outlines. Working with a partner, complete any five of them by adding a third logical suppoing point (*c*) that will parallel the two already provided (*a* and *b*).

1. The first day on a new job can be nerve-racking.

    a. Meeting new people

    b. Finding your way around a new place

    c. _____

2. My stepmother has three qualities I admire.

   a. Patience

   b. Thoughtfulness

   c. _Kind_ _____

3. My summer job on a landscaping crew had several advantages.

   a. Learned how to follow directions

   b. Great people to work for

   c. _Earn to some salaury_ _____

4. College students should live at home.

   a. Stay in touch with family

   b. Avoid distractions of dorm or apartment life

   c. _____

5. _____ is the worst job I've ever had.

   a. Difficult boss

   b. Poor pay

   c. _____

6. College is stressful for many people.

   a. Worry about grades

   b. Worry about being accepted

   c. _____

7. My high school algebra teacher was excellent.

   a. Extra help after class

   b. Great practice handouts for tests

   c. _____

8. The college library is the best place to study.

   a. Quiet and well lit

   b. Nothing to tempt me away from my books

   c. _____

9. Buying a used car is better than buying a new one.

    a. Used cars are less likely to be stolen than new cars.

    b. Used cars don't lose their value as quickly as most new cars.

    c. _____

10. Many companies use annoying practices to increase sales.

    a. Junk mail

    b. Spam e-mail

    c. _____

The Importance of *Specific* Details

Just as a thesis must be developed with three supporting points, each supporting point must be developed with specific details. Specific details are valuable in two key ways. First, details excite the reader's interest. They make writing a pleasure to read, for we all enjoy learning particulars about people, places, and things. Second, details serve to explain a writer's points. They give the evidence needed for us to see and understand general ideas.

All too often, the body paragraphs in essays contain only vague generalities, rather than the specific supporting details that are needed to engage and convince a reader. Here is what one of the paragraphs in "The Hazards of Moviegoing" would have looked like if the writer had not detailed her supporting evidence vividly:

> Some of the other patrons are even more of a problem than the theater itself. Many people in the theater often show themselves to be inconsiderate. They make noises and create disturbances at their seats. Included are people in every age group, from the young to the old. Some act as if they were at home in their own living room watching TV. And people are often messy, so that you're constantly aware of all the food they're eating. People are also always moving around near you, creating a disturbance and interrupting your enjoyment of the movie.

The following box contrasts the vague support in the preceding paragraph with the specific support in the essay.

Vague Support	Specific Support
1. Many people in the theater show themselves to be inconsiderate. They make noises and create disturbances at their seats. Included are people in every age group, from the young to the old. Some act as if they were at home in their own living room watching TV.	1. Little kids race up and down the aisles, usually in giggling packs. Teenagers try to impress their friends by talking back to the screen, whistling, and making what they consider to be hilarious noises. Adults act as if they were at home in their own living room and comment loudly on the ages of the stars or why movies aren't as good anymore.
2. And people are often messy, so that you're constantly aware of all the food they're eating.	2. And people of all ages crinkle candy wrappers, stick gum on their seats, and drop popcorn tubs or cups of crushed ice and soda on the floor.
3. People are also always moving around near you, creating a disturbance and interrupting your enjoyment of the movie.	3. They also cough and burp, squirm endlessly in their seats, file out for repeated trips to the restrooms or concession stand, and elbow you out of the armrest on either side of your seat.

The effective paragraph from the essay provides details that make vividly clear the statement that patrons are a problem in the theater. The writer specifies the exact age groups (little kids, teenagers, and adults) and the offenses of each (giggling, talking and whistling, and loud comments). She specifies the various food excesses (crinkled wrappers, gum on seats, dropped popcorn and soda containers). Finally, she provides concrete details that enable us to see and hear other disturbances (coughs and burps, squirming, constant trips to restrooms, jostling for elbow room). The ineffective paragraph asks us to guess about these details; the effective paragraph describes the details in a specific and lively way.

In the strong paragraph, then, sharp details capture our interest and enable us to share the writer's experience. They provide pictures that make us feel we are there. The particulars also enable us to understand clearly the writer's point that patrons are a problem. Aim to make your own writing equally convincing by providing detailed support.

Activity 5

Write S in front of the two selections below that provide specific evidence to support the opening point. Write X in front of the two selections in which the opening point is followed by vague, general, wordy sentences.

_____ 1. The tree house my father and I built was a masterpiece.

It had three floors, each of which was about 75 square feet. There were two windows made of real glass on each floor, allowing sunlight to flood in and making the place pleasant and cheerful. The walls were made of sweet-smelling cedar planks Dad and I salvaged from a landfill. On the bottom floor was a small cast-iron stove, which gave off enough heat to keep us toasty on the coldest winter day. The second floor had an old rocking chair on which I read my favorite comics every summer afternoon. On the top floor, Dad had set up a telescope from which we observed the glories of the night sky.

_____ 2. Our first camping trip in Keystone State Forest was disappointing.

Many of the animals we had hoped to see on our walk just weren't there. Some smaller animals were, but we had seen them before in our backyards. The forest was rather quiet. It was not what we had expected. The weather didn't cooperate either. It was dreadful for most of our stay. Then there were the bugs! We had planned for the trip well, spending a lot of money on provisions and special equipment. But much of it was a waste because we left much earlier than we had intended. We came home frustrated and soured on the whole idea of camping.

_____ 3. Some things are worse when they're "improved."

A good cheesecake, for one thing, is perfect. It doesn't need pineapple, cherries, blueberries, or whipped cream smeared all over it. Plain old American blue jeans, the ones with five pockets and copper rivets, are perfect too. Manufacturers only made them worse when they added flared legs, took away the pockets, tightened the fit, and plastered white logos and designers' names all over them.

_____ 4. Pets can be more trouble than children.

My dog, unlike my children, has never been completely housebroken. When he's excited or nervous, he still has an occasional problem. My dog, unlike my children, has never learned how to take care of himself when we're away, despite the fact that we've given him plenty of time to do so. We don't have to worry about our grown children anymore. However, we still have to hire a dog-sitter.

The Importance of *Adequate* Details

One of the most common and most serious problems in students' writing is inadequate development. You must provide *enough* specific details to fully support the point in a body paragraph of an essay. You could not, for example, include a paragraph about a friend's unreliability and provide only a one- or two-sentence example. You would have to extend the example or add several other examples showing your friend as an unreliable person. Without such additional support, your paragraph would be underdeveloped.

Students may try to disguise unsupported paragraphs through repetition and generalities. Do not fall into this "wordiness trap." Be prepared to do the plain hard work needed to ensure that each paragraph has solid support.

Both of the following body paragraphs were written on the same topic, and each has a clear opening point. Which paragraph is adequately developed? Which one has only several particulars and uses mostly vague, general, wordy sentences to conceal that it is starved for specific details?

Activity

6

Eternal Youth?—No, Thanks

I wouldn't want to be a teenager again, first of all, because I wouldn't want to worry about talking to girls. I still remember how scary it was to call up a girl and ask her out. My heart would race, my pulse would pound, and perspiration would trickle down my face, adding to my acne by the second. I never knew whether my voice would come out deep and masculine, like a television anchorman's, or squeaky, like a little boy's. Then there were the questions: Would she be at home? If she was, would she want to talk to me? And if she did, what would I say? The one time I did get up the nerve to take a girl in my homeroom to a movie, I was so tongue-tied that I stared silently at the box of popcorn in my lap until the feature finally started. Needless to say, I wasn't very interesting company.

Terrors of My Teenage Years

I wouldn't want to be a teenager again, first of all, because I wouldn't want to worry about talking to girls. Calling up a girl to ask her out was something that I completely dreaded. I didn't know what words to express or how to express them. I would have all the symptoms of nervousness when I got on the phone. I worried a great deal about how I would sound, and I had a lot of doubts about the girl's reaction. Once, I managed to call up a girl to go out, but the evening turned out to be a disaster. I was too unsure of myself to act in a confident way. I couldn't think of anything to say and just kept quiet. Now that I look back on it, I really made a fool of myself. Agonizing over my attempts at relationships with the opposite sex made adolescence a very uncomfortable time.

The first paragraph offers a series of well-detailed examples of the author's nerve-racking experiences, as a teenager, with girls. The second paragraph, on the other hand, is underdeveloped. For instance, the second paragraph makes only the general observation "I would have all the symptoms of nervousness when I got on the phone," but the first paragraph states, "My heart would race, my pulse would pound, and perspiration would trickle down my face."

The second paragraph makes the general statement "I worried a great deal about how I would sound," but in the first paragraph the author wonders if his voice will "come out deep and masculine, like a television anchorman's, or squeaky, like a little boy's." And the second paragraph has no specific description of the evening that turned into a disaster. In summary, the second paragraph lacks the full, detailed support needed to develop its opening point convincingly.

Activity

7

Write a paragraph supporting one of the following points:

1.   My room is a mess.
2.   Our cafeteria offers a variety of ethnic foods.
3.   _____ is a dangerous driver.
4.   Shirley is the most helpful neighbor on our street.

Afterward, consider reading your paragraph to a small group of classmates. The best paragraphs are sure to be those with plenty of specific details.

Practice in Advancing and Supporting a Thesis

Identifying the Parts of an Essay

Each cluster below contains one topic, one thesis statement, and two supporting sentences. In the space provided, label each item as follows:

Activity

8

> T—topic
> TH—thesis statement
> S—supporting sentence

Group 1

_____ a. Films based on historical events are sometimes shown in class.

_____ b. Making history more interesting

_____ c. Some history teachers use innovative methods to increase student interest.

_____ d. Instructors ask students to write short plays dramatizing historical events.

Group 2

_____ a. Vegetarian diets

_____ b. Staying away from meat can reduce intake of fat and cholesterol.

_____ c. Eating vegetables helps the environment because raising veggies uses less energy than raising animals.

_____ d. Vegetarianism benefits both the individual and the environment.

Group 3

_____ a. Medicine

_____ b. Antibiotics have enabled doctors to control many diseases that were once fatal.

_____ c. Organ transplants have prolonged the lives of tens of thousands of people.

_____ d. Advances in modern medicine have had great success in helping people.

Group 4

_____ a. Reading

_____ b. Parents can take steps to encourage their children to enjoy reading.

_____ c. The adults' own behavior can influence children to become readers.

_____ d. Parents can make sure the physical environment of the home encourages reading.

Group 5

_____ a. Insects perform many helpful functions for human beings.

_____ b. Insects are essential to the growth of many important crops.

_____ c. Insects

_____ d. Insects protect the environment by removing wastes and controlling disease-causing germs.

Activity

9

This activity will sharpen your sense of the parts of an essay. The essay that follows, "Coping with Old Age," has no indentations starting new paragraphs. Read this essay carefully, and then double-underline the thesis and single-underline the topic sentence for each of the three supporting paragraphs and the first sentence of the conclusion. Write the numbers of those sentences in the spaces provided at the end.

Coping with Old Age

^{1}I recently read about an area of the former Soviet Union where many people live to be well over a hundred years old. ^{2}Being 115 or even 125 isn't considered unusual there, and these old people continue to do productive work right up until they die. ^{3}The United States, however, isn't such a healthy place for older people. ^{4}Since I retired from my job, I've had to cope with the physical, mental, and emotional stresses of being "old." ^{5}For one thing, I've had to adjust to physical changes. ^{6}Now that I'm over sixty, the trusty body that carried me around for years has turned traitor. ^{7}Aside from the deepening wrinkles on my face and neck, and the wiry gray hairs that have replaced my brown hair, I face more frightening changes. ^{8}I don't have the energy I used to. ^{9}My eyes get tired. ^{10}Once in a while, I miss something that's said to me. ^{11}My once faithful feet seem to have lost their comfortable soles, and I sometimes feel I'm walking on marbles. ^{12}In order to fight against

(continued)

this slow decay, I exercise whenever I can. [13]I walk, I stretch, and I climb stairs. [14]I battle constantly to keep as fit as possible. [15]I'm also trying to cope with mental changes. [16]My mind was once as quick and sure as a champion gymnast. [17]I never found it difficult to memorize answers in school or to remember the names of people I met. [18]Now, I occasionally have to search my mind for the name of a close neighbor or favorite television show. [19]Because my mind needs exercise, too, I challenge it as much as I can. [20]Taking a college course like this English class, for example, forces me to concentrate. [21]The mental gymnast may be a little slow and out of shape, but he can still do a backflip or turn a somersault when he has to. [22]Finally, I must deal with the emotional impact of being old. [23]Our society typecasts old people. [24]We're supposed to be unattractive, senile, useless leftovers. [25]We're supposed to be the crazy drivers and the cranky customers. [26]At first, I was angry and frustrated that I was considered old at all. [27]And I knew that people were wrong to stereotype me. [28]Then I got depressed. [29]I even started to think that maybe I was a castoff, one of those old animals that slow down the rest of the herd. [30]But I have now decided to rebel against these negative feelings. [31]I try to have friends of all ages and to keep up with what's going on in the world. [32]I try to remember that I'm still the same person who sat at a first-grade desk, who fell in love, who comforted a child, who got a raise at work. [33]I'm not "just" an old person. [34]Coping with the changes of old age has become my latest full-time job. [35]Even though it's a job I never applied for, and one for which I had no experience, I'm trying to do the best I can.

Thesis statement in "Coping with Old Age": _____

Topic sentence of first supporting paragraph: _____

Topic sentence of second supporting paragraph: _____

Topic sentence of third supporting paragraph: _____

First sentence of the conclusion: _____

Evaluating Thesis Statements

As was explained on pages 57–59, some writers announce a subject instead of stating a true thesis idea. Others write a dead-end thesis statement that is too narrow to need support or development. Contrasting with such a dead-end statement is the statement that is wide open—too broad to be adequately supported in the limited

www.mhhe.com/langan

space of a five-hundred-word essay. Other thesis statements are vague or contain more than one idea. They suggest that the writer has not thought out the main point sufficiently.

Write A beside each sentence that is an announcement rather than a thesis statement. Write OK beside the statement in each pair that is a clear, limited point that could be developed in an essay.

1. _____ a. I want to discuss what it means to be a good citizen.

   _____ b. Being a good citizen means becoming informed about important social, environmental, and political issues.

2. _____ a. I made several mistakes in the process of trying to win the respect and affection of my teenage stepson.

   _____ b. My thesis in this paper is relationships between stepparents and stepchildren.

3. _____ a. Successful teamwork requires focusing on the group's goals, not your own.

   _____ b. This paper explains how to work well in a team.

4. _____ a. This paper will be about sharing housework.

   _____ b. Deciding who will perform certain unpleasant household chores can be the crisis that makes or breaks a marriage.

5. _____ a. I want to show how cardiology has changed in the last 20 years.

   _____ b. The advances in cardiology in the last 20 years have been miraculous.

Write TN beside each statement that is too narrow to be developed in an essay. Write OK beside the statement in each pair that is a clear, limited point.

1. _____ a. I had squash, tomatoes, and corn in my garden last summer.

   _____ b. Vegetable gardening can be a frustrating hobby.

2. _____ a. The main road into our town is lined with billboards.

   _____ b. For several reasons, billboards should be abolished.

3. _____ a. The addition of a fifty-seat computer lab at our college has made it possible to expand the computer-science, mathematics, and English curricula.

   _____ b. Our college just added a fifty-seat computer lab.

4. _____ a. Nathaniel Hawthorne's novel The Scarlet Letter is about the Puritans.

    _____ b. Nathaniel Hawthorne's novel The Scarlet Letter criticizes Puritan morality.

5. _____ a. Americans are living longer than before because of better diets, a cleaner environment, and advanced medical care.

    _____ b. The average American can now expect to live longer than before.

Activity 12

Write TB bside each statement that is too broad to be developed in an essay. Write OK beside the statement in each pair that is a clear, limited point.

1. _____ a. After-school art and athletic clubs provide healthy outlets for young people.

    _____ b. After-school art and athletic clubs at Garfield Junior High School have helped reduce the number of thefts, gang wars, and acts of vandalism once common in our community.

2. _____ a. Modern life makes people suspicious and unfriendly.

    _____ b. A frightening experience in my neighborhood has caused me to be a much more cautious person in several ways.

3. _____ a. The attacks of 9/11 dramatized the heroism we have come to expect from our police and firefighters.

    _____ b. Americans responded well during the attacks of 9/11.

4. _____ a. Learning new skills can be difficult and frustrating.

    _____ b. Learning to write takes work, patience, and a sense of humor.

5. _____ a. I didn't get along with my family, so I did many foolish things.

    _____ b. Running away from home taught me that my parents weren't as terrible as I thought.

Activity 13

For each pair, write 2 beside the statement that contains more than one idea. Write OK beside the statement that is a clear, limited point.

1. _____ a Working with old people changed my stereotypical ideas about the elderly.

    _____ b. My life has moved in new directions since the rewarding job I had working with older people last summer.

2. _____ a. The new architecture on this campus is very unpleasant, although the expansion was desperately needed.

   _____ b. Our new college library building is ugly, intimidating, and inefficient.

3. _____ a. Forest fires are one way nature creates new habitats.

   _____ b. Forest fires destroy lives and property, but they do provide some benefits to the environment.

4. _____ a. My roommate and I are compatible in most ways, but we still have conflicts at times.

   _____ b. My roommate has his own unique systems for studying, writing term papers, and cleaning our room.

5. _____ a. Although the Modern Language Department offers first-rate instruction in several European languages, many professors and students see the need to offer Arabic, Chinese, and Hindi as well.

   _____ b. Many professors and students believe there is a need for courses in Arabic, Chinese, and Hindi.

Completing Thesis Statements

Activity

14

Complete the following thesis statements by adding a third supporting point that will parallel the two already provided. You might want to first check the section on parallelism in Chapter 5 (page 111) to make sure you understand parallel form.

1. A successful camping trip requires familiarity with the terrain, a good tent and sleeping bag, and _____.

2. A good salesperson needs to like people, to be aggressive, and _____

   _____.

3. Rather than blame myself for failing the course, I blamed the instructor, my adviser, and even _____.

4. Anyone who buys an old house planning to fix it up should be prepared to put in a lot of time, hard work, and _____.

5. Our old car guzzles gas, makes funny noises, and _____

   _____.

6. My mother, my boss, and my _____ are three people who are very important in my life right now.

7. Before you begin an exercise program, decide on your exercise goals, pick an activity that can help you achieve those goals, and _____

    _____.

8. Some restaurant patrons seem to leave their honesty, their cleanliness, and their _____ at home.

9. During my first semester at college, I had to learn how to manage my time, my diet, and _____.

10. The three best things I have done for someone else are working with Habitat for Humanity, becoming a Big Sister to a neighborhood child, and

    _____.

Writing a Thesis Statement

Write a thesis for each group of supporting statements. This activity will give you practice in writing an effective essay thesis—one that is neither too broad nor too narrow. It will also help you understand the logical relationship between a thesis and its supporting details.

1. Thesis: _____
   a. My first car was a rebellious-looking one that matched the way I felt and acted as a teenager.
   b. My next car reflected my more mature and practical adult self.
   c. My latest car seems to tell me that I'm aging; it shows my growing concern with comfort and safety.

2. Thesis: _____
   a. All the course credits that are accumulated can be transferred to a four-year school.
   b. Going to a two-year college can save a great deal of money in tuition and other fees.
   c. If the college is nearby, there are also significant savings in everyday living expenses.

3. Thesis: _____

   a. First, I tried simply avoiding the snacks aisle of the supermarket.

   b. Then I started limiting myself to only five units of any given snack.

   c. Finally, in desperation, I began keeping the cellophane bags of snacks in a padlocked cupboard.

4. Thesis: _____

   a. Thomas Jefferson wrote the Declaration of Independence and helped lead the American Revolution.

   b. As third president of the United States, he negotiated the Louisiana Purchase, which doubled the size of the country.

   c. He donated the first books in the Library of Congress.

5. Thesis: _____

   a. Many students who intend to go to law school major in English.

   b. Studying writing and literature is excellent preparation for a career in teaching.

   c. After earning undergraduate degrees in English, some students pursue a master's degree in business administration.

Limiting a Topic and Writing a Thesis Statement

The following two activities will give you practice in distinguishing general from limited subjects and in writing a thesis.

Activity

16

Look carefully at the ten general subjects and ten limited subjects below. Then write a thesis statement for any five of them.

> **HINT:** To create a thesis statement for a limited subject, ask yourself, What point do I want to make about _____ (*my limited subject*)?

General Subject

  1. Apartment

  2. Self-improvement

Limited Subject

  1. Sharing an apartment with a roommate

  2. Behavior toward others

3. Family	3. My mother
4. Eating	4. Fast-food restaurants
5. Automobiles	5. Bad driving habits
6. Health	6. Regular exercise
7. Owning a house	7. Do-it-yourself home repairs
8. Baseball	8. Free-agent system
9. Parenthood	9. Being a single parent
10. Pollution	10. Noise pollution

Thesis statements for five of the limited subjects:

_____

_____

_____

_____

_____

_____

_____

_____

_____

_____

_____

_____

_____

Here is a list of ten general subjects. Limit five of the subjects. Then write a thesis statement about each of the five limited subjects.

Activity

17

General Subject	Limited Subject
1. Pets	_____
2. Teenagers	_____

3. Television   _____

4. Work   _____

5. College   _____

6. Doctors   _____

7. Diets   _____

8. Home heating   _____

9. Money   _____

10. Music   _____

Thesis statements for five of the limited subjects:

_____

_____

_____

_____

_____

_____

_____

_____

_____

_____

_____

_____

_____

_____

_____

Providing Specific Evidence

Provide three details that logically support each of the following points. Your details can be drawn from your own experience, or they can be invented. In each case, the details should show *specifically* what the point expresses only generally. State your details briefly in several words rather than in complete sentences.

EXAMPLE

We quickly spruced up the apartment before our guest arrived.

1. *Hid toys and newspapers in spare closet*
2. *Vacuumed pet hairs off sofa*
3. *Sprayed air freshener around living room*

1. The hike up to the mountain lookout was exciting.

   _____

   _____

   _____

2. My hometown is worth visiting.

   _____

   _____

   _____

3. There are several reasons why I put off studying.

   _____

   _____

   _____

4. Working at the hospital has taught me many valuable skills.

   _____

   _____

   _____

5. I have several ways to earn extra cash.

   _____

   _____

   _____

6. My car needs repairs.

    _____

    _____

    _____

7. Friday evening, I didn't sit still for a minute.

    _____

    _____

    _____

8. My best friends are very different, but I love each of them.

    _____

    _____

    _____

    _____

Identifying Adequate Supporting Evidence

Activity

19

The following body paragraphs were taken from student essays. Two of the paragraphs provide sufficient details to support their topic sentences convincingly. Write AD for *adequate development* beside those paragraphs. Three paragraphs use vague, wordy, general, or irrelevant sentences instead of real supporting details. Write U for *underdeveloped* beside those paragraphs.

_____   1.   Another consideration in adopting a dog is the cost. Initial fees for shots and a license might add up to $50. Annual visits to the vet for heartworm pills, rabies and distemper shots, and general checkups could cost $100 or more. Then there is the cost of food. A twenty-five-pound bag of dry food (the cheapest kind) costs around $15. A large dog can eat that much in a couple of weeks.

_____   2.   People can be cruel to pets simply by being thoughtless. They don't think about a pet's needs, or they simply ignore those needs. It never occurs to them that their pet can be experiencing a great deal of discomfort as a result of their failure to be sensitive. The cruelty is a result of the basic lack of attention and concern—qualities that should be there, but aren't.

_____ 3.   If I were in charge of the nighttime programming on a TV network, I would make changes. I would completely eliminate some shows. In fact, all the shows that proved to be of little interest would be canceled. Commercials would also change so that it would be possible to watch them without wanting to turn off the TV. I would expand the good shows so that people would come away with an even better experience. My ideal network would be a great improvement over the average lineup we see today on any of the major networks.

_____ 4.   A friend's rudeness is much more damaging than a stranger's. When a friend says sharply, "I don't have time to talk to you just now," you feel hurt instead of angry. When a friend shows up late for lunch or a shopping trip, with no good reason, you feel that you're being taken for granted. Worst, though, is when a friend pretends to be listening to you but his or her wandering eyes show a lack of attention. Then you feel betrayed. Friends, after all, are supposed to make up for the thoughtless cruelties of strangers.

_____ 5.   Giving my first shampoo and set to a real person, after weeks of practicing on wigs, was a nerve-racking experience. The customer was a woman who acted very sure about what she came for. She tried to describe what she wanted, and I tried without much success to understand what she had in mind. Every time I did something, she seemed to be indicating in one way or another that it was not what she wanted. I got more and more nervous as I worked on her hair, and the nervousness showed. The worst part of the ordeal happened at the very end, when I added the final touches. Nothing, to this woman, had turned out right.

Adding Details to Complete an Essay

The following essay needs specific details to back up the ideas in the supporting paragraphs. Using the spaces provided, add a sentence or two of clear, convincing details for each supporting idea. This activity will give you practice at supplying specific details and an initial feel for writing an essay.

Life without Television

Introduction

When my family's only television set went to the repair shop the other day, my parents, my sister, and I thought we would have a terrible week. How could we get through the long evenings in such a quiet house? What would it be like without all the shows to keep us company? We soon realized,

(continued)

though, that living without television for a while was a stroke of good fortune. It became easy for each of us to enjoy some activities alone, to complete some postponed chores, and to spend rewarding time with each other and friends.

First supporting paragraph

First of all, with no television to compete for our time, we found plenty of hours for personal interests. We all read more that week than we had read during the six months before. _____

_____

_____

We each also enjoyed some hobbies we had ignored for ages. _____

_____

_____

_____

In addition, my sister and I both stopped procrastinating with our

homework. _____

_____

_____

_____

Second supporting paragraph

Second, we did chores that had been hanging over our heads for too long. There were many jobs around the house that had needed attention for

some time. _____

_____

_____

(continued)

We also had a chance to do some long-postponed shopping. _____

_____

_____

_____

And each of us also caught up with e-mail and did paperwork that was long

overdue. _____

_____

_____

    Finally, and probably most important, we spent time with each other.
Instead of just being in the same room together while we stared at a screen,

we actually talked for many pleasant hours. _____

_____

_____

Moreover, for the first time in years, my family played some games

together. _____

_____

_____

And because we didn't have to worry about missing this or that show,
we had some family friends over on a couple of evenings and spent an

enjoyable time with them. _____

_____

_____

**Third
supporting
paragraph**

Conclusion

Once our television returned, we were not prepared to put it in the attic. But we had a sense of how it can take over our lives if we are not careful. We are now more selective. We turn on the set for our favorite shows, certain sports events, and the news, but we don't leave it running all evening. As a result, we find we can enjoy television and still have time left over for other activities and interests.

© Comstock Select/Corbis

What are some ways besides watching TV that you and your family or friends spend quality time together? Write about one of these activities and why you enjoy it.

The Third Step in Essay Writing

4

© Tim Pannell/Corbis

This chapter will show you how to

- organize and connect specific evidence in the body paragraphs of an essay
- begin and end an essay with effective introductory and concluding paragraphs

In the previous chapter, you helped complete one student's essay about life without television. Without television, the student had time to enjoy a host of other activities he or she otherwise would not have had time to do. Write an essay about what, in your life, keeps you from completing tasks or doing what you enjoy. Also include what you would do with your time if this obstacle was removed.

You know from Chapter 3 that the first two steps in writing an effective essay are advancing a thesis and supporting it with specific evidence. This chapter deals with the third step: organizing and connecting the supporting information in a paper. You'll also learn how to start an essay with a suitable introductory paragraph and how to finish it with a well-rounded concluding paragraph.

Step 3: Organize and Connect the Specific Evidence

As you are generating the specific details needed to support a thesis, you should be thinking about ways to organize and connect those details. All the details in your essay must *cohere*, or stick together, so that your reader will be able to move smoothly from one bit of supporting information to the next. This section shows you how to organize and connect supporting details by using (1) common methods of organization, (2) transitions, and (3) other connecting words.

Common Methods of Organization

Two common methods used to organize the supporting material in an essay are time order and emphatic order. (You will learn more specific methods of development in Part 2 of this book.)

Time order, or *chronological order,* simply means that details are listed as they occur in time. *First* this is done; *next* this; *then* this; *after* that, this; and so on. Here is an outline of an essay in this book that uses time order:

www.mhhe.com/langan

Thesis

> To exercise successfully, you should follow a simple plan consisting of arranging the time, making preparations, and warming up properly.
>
> 1. To begin with, set aside a regular hour for exercise.
>
> 2. Next, prepare for your exercise session.
>
> 3. Finally, do a series of warm-up activities.

Fill in the missing words: The topic sentences in the essay use the words or phrases

_____, _____, and _____ to help show time order.

Here is one supporting paragraph from the essay:

> Next, prepare for your exercise session. You do this, first, by not eating or drinking anything for an hour before the session. Why risk an upset stomach? Then, dress comfortably in something that allows you to move freely. Because you'll be in your own home, there's no need to invest in a high-fashion dance costume. A loose T-shirt and shorts are good. A
>
> *(continued)*

bathing suit is great in summer, and in winter long underwear is warm and comfortable. If your hair tends to flop in your eyes, pin it back or wear a headband or scarf. After dressing, prepare the exercise area. Turn off the phone and lock the door to prevent interruptions. Shove the coffee table out of the way so that you won't bruise yourself on it. Finally, get out the simple materials you'll need to exercise on.

Fill in the missing words: The paragraph uses the following words to help show

time order: _____, _____, _____, _____,

and _____.

    Emphatic order is sometimes described as "saving the best till last." It is a way to put *emphasis* on the most interesting or important detail by placing it in the last part of a paragraph or in the final supporting paragraph of an essay.

www.mhhe.com/langan

> **TIP:** In cases where all the details seem equal in importance, the writer should impose a personal order that seems logical or appropriate.

    The last position in a paper is the most emphatic position because the reader is most likely to remember the last thing read. *Finally, last of all,* and *most important* are typical words or phrases showing emphasis. Here is an outline of an essay in this book that uses emphatic order:

Celebrities lead very stressful lives.   **Thesis**

1. *For one thing, celebrities don't have the privacy an ordinary person does.*

2. *In addition, celebrities are under constant pressure.*

3. *Most important, celebrities must deal with the stress of being in constant danger.*

Fill in the missing words: The topic sentences in the essay use the words or

phrases _____, _____, and _____ to

help show emphatic order.

Here is the third supporting paragraph from the essay:

> Most important, celebrities must deal with the stress of being in constant danger. The friendly grabs, hugs, and kisses of enthusiastic fans can quickly turn into uncontrolled assaults on a celebrity's hair, clothes, and car. Celebrities often get strange letters from people who become obsessed with their idols or from people who threaten to harm them. Worst of all, threats can turn into deeds. The attempt to kill Ronald Reagan and the murder of John Lennon came about because two unbalanced people tried to transfer the celebrity's fame to themselves. Famous people must live with he fact that they are always fair game—and never out of season.

Fill in the missing phrase: The words _____ are used to mark the most emphatic detail in the paragraph.

Some essays use a combination of time order and emphatic order. For example, the essay on moviegoing in Chapter 1 (page 6) includes time order: the writer first describes getting to the theater, then the theater itself, and finally the behavior of audience members during the movie. At the same time, the writer uses emphatic order, ending with the most important reason for her dislike of moviegoing: "Some of the other patrons are even more of a problem than the theater itself."

Activity

1

Part A Read the essays listed below (page numbers are in parentheses) and identify their method of organizing details—time order, emphatic order, or a combination of both.

1. "Adopting a Handicap" (page 210)

   _____

2. "A Vote for McDonald's" (page 303)

   _____

3. "Look on the Bright Side" (page 231)

   _____

Part B Now see if you can complete the explanations that follow.

The essay titled "Adopting a Handicap" uses (*add the missing word*)

_____ order. The author begins with the challenge of learning to sit properly in the wheelchair, then moves on to learning to move in the wheelchair, and ends with several problems that occurred next, during the church service. "A Vote for McDonald's" uses (*add the missing word*) _____ order. The writer presents three advantages of eating at McDonald's and ends with the most important one: reasonable prices. "Look on the Bright Side" uses a

combination of (*add the missing words*) _____ and _____ order. It moves from something that took place one morning, to one that took place at lunchtime, to one that took place one evening. It ends with one of "the worst and best examples of human behavior" that the author witnessed.

Transitions

Transitional Words

Transitions signal the direction of a writer's thoughts. They are like the road signs that guide travelers. In the box that follows are some common transitions, grouped according to the kind of signal they give to readers. Note that certain words provide more than one kind of signal.

www.mhhe.com/langan

Common Transitions

Addition Signals: one, first, second, the third reason, also, next, and, in addition, moreover, further, furthermore, finally, last, similarly, likewise, as well, too, besides.

Time Signals: first, then, next, after, as before, while, meanwhile, soon, now, during, finally, after a while, as soon as, at that time, by then, during, since, suddenly, then, thereafter, by then, in a few hours, by that time.

Space Signals: next to, across, on the opposite side, to the left, to the right, above, below, near, nearby, beside, on top of, under, over, underneath, far from.

Change-of-Direction Signals: but, however, yet, in contrast, although, otherwise, still, on the contrary, on the other hand, nevertheless, instead, nonetheless, otherwise, even though.

Illustration Signals: for example, for instance, specifically, as an illustration, once, such as.

Conclusion Signals: therefore, consequently, thus, then, as a result, in summary, to conclude, last, finally.

Other Transitions: Conjunctive Adverbs and Transitional Phrases

A conjunctive adverb is a word that, when used after a semicolon, connects two independent (main) clauses. A transitional phrase is a group of words that, when used after a semicolon, connects two independent (main) clauses.

Conjunctive adverb: Napoleon successfully invaded Russia in 1812; **however,** he did not occupy it for long.

Transitional phrase: Jean Piaget made major contributions to child psychology; **in fact,** he proved that children and adults reason differently.

Like transitional words, conjunctive adverbs and transitional phrases signal the direction of the writer's thoughts and guide the reader.

Activity

2

1. Underline the three *addition* signals in the following selection:

> To create the time you need to pass difficult courses, find some easy courses. These are the ones that combine the least amount of work with the fewest tests and the most lenient professors. One way to find such courses is to ask friends and classmates about courses in which they received A's after attending only 25 percent of the classes. Also, inquire around to see which instructors lecture with the same notes every year and give the same tests. Photocopies of the class notes are usually cheap and widely available. Another great way of finding simple courses is to pick up a copy of the master schedule and study it carefully. Find the telltale course titles that signal an easy glide through a painless subject. Look for titles like "History of the Animated Cartoon," "Arts and Crafts for Beginners," and "Rock Music of the 1950s."

2. Underline the four *time* signals in the following selection:

> After you've snagged the job of TV sports reporter, you have to begin working on the details of your image. First, invest in two or three truly loud sports jackets. Look for gigantic plaid patterns in odd color combinations

(continued)

like purple and green or orange and blue. These should become familiar enough to viewers so that they will associate that crazy jacket with that dynamic sportscaster. Next, try to cultivate a distinctive voice that will be just annoying enough to be memorable. A nasal whine or a gravelly growl will do it. Be sure to speak only in tough, punchy sentences that seem to be punctuated with imaginary exclamation points. Finally, you must share lots of pompous, obnoxious opinions with your viewers. Your tone of voice must convey the hidden message "I dare anyone to disagree with me." If the home teams lose, call them bums. If players strike, talk sarcastically about the good old days. If a sports franchise leaves town, say, "Good riddance."

3. Underline the three *space* signals in the following selection:

The vegetable bin of my refrigerator contained an assortment of weird-looking items. Next to a shriveled, fuzz-coated lemon were two oranges covered with blue fuzz. To the right of the oranges was a bunch of carrots that had begun to sprout points, spikes, knobs, and tendrils. The carrots drooped into U shapes as I picked them up with the tips of my fingers. Near the carrots was a net bag of onions; each onion had sent curling shoots through the net until the whole thing resembled a mass of green spaghetti. The most horrible item, though, was a head of lettuce that had turned into a pool of brown goo. It had seeped out of its bag and coated the bin with a sticky, evil-smelling liquid.

4. Underline the two *change-of-direction* signals in the following selection:

Taking small children on vacation, for instance, sounds like a wonderful experience for the entire family. But vacations can be scary or emotionally overwhelming times for children. When children are taken away from their usual routine and brought to an unfamiliar place, they can become very frightened. That strange bed in the motel room or the unusual noises in

(continued)

Grandma's spare bedroom may cause nightmares. On vacations, too, children usually clamor to do as many things in one day as they can and to stay up past their usual bedtime. And since it is vacation time, parents may decide to give in to the children's demands. A parental attitude like this, however, can lead to problems. After a sixteen-hour day of touring the amusement park, eating in a restaurant, and seeing a movie, children can experience sensory and emotional overload. They become cranky, unhappy, or even rebellious and angry.

5. Underline the two *illustration* signals in the following selection:

Supermarkets also use psychology to encourage you to buy. For example, in most supermarkets, the milk and the bread are either at opposite ends of the store or located far away from the first aisle. Even if you've stopped at the market only for staples like these, you must pass hundreds of items to reach them. The odds are that, instead of leaving with just a quart of milk, you'll leave with additional purchases as well. Special displays, such as a pyramid of canned green beans in an aisle and a large end display of cartons of paper towels, also increase sales. Because you assume that these items are a good buy, you may pick them up. However, they may not even be on sale! Store managers know that the customer is automatically attracted to a display like this, and they will use it to move an overstocked product.

6. Underline the two *conclusion* signals in the following selection:

Finally, my grandmother was extremely thrifty. She was one of those people who hoard pieces of used aluminum foil after carefully scrubbing off the cake icing or beef gravy. She had a drawer full of old eyeglasses that dated back at least thirty years. The lens prescriptions were no longer accurate, but Gran couldn't bear to throw away "a good pair of glasses." She kept them "just in case," but we could never figure out what situation would involve a desperate need for a dozen pairs of old eyeglasses. We never realized the true extent of Gran's thriftiness, though, until after she died. Her house was to be sold, and therefore we cleaned out its dusty attic. In one corner was a cardboard box filled with two- and three-inch pieces of string. The box was labeled, in Gran's spidery hand, "String too short to be saved."

Transitional Sentences

Transitional sentences, or *linking sentences,* are used between paragraphs to help tie together the supporting paragraphs in an essay. They enable the reader to move smoothly from the idea in one paragraph to the idea in the next paragraph.

Here is the linking sentence used in the essay on moviegoing:

Many of the other patrons are even more of a problem than the concession stand.

The words *concession stand* remind us of the point of the first supporting paragraph, while *Many of the other patrons* presents the point to be developed in the second supporting paragraph.

Following is a brief sentence outline of an essay. The second and third topic sentences serve as transitional, or linking, sentences. Each reminds us of the point in the preceding paragraph and announces the point to be developed in the current paragraph. In the spaces provided, add the words needed to complete the second and third topic sentences.

Activity

3

Thesis

The most memorable sites I visited in Washington, D.C., were the Capitol Building, the Lincoln Memorial, and the Vietnam Memorial.

Our first stop was Capitol Hill, the very symbol of our democratic system. . . .

First supporting paragraph

After leaving the _____, we walked along the Mall to the

_____

_____ . . . .

Second supporting paragraph

A short distance to the right of the _____ is the

_____

_____ . . . .

Other Connecting Words

In addition to transitions, there are three other kinds of connecting words that help tie together the specific evidence in a paper: *repeated words, pronouns,* and *synonyms.*

www.mhhe.com/langan

Repeated Words

Many of us have been taught—correctly—not to repeat ourselves in writing. However, repeating *key* words helps tie together the flow of thought in a paper. Below, repeated words remind readers of the selection's central idea.

> One reason for studying psychology is to help you deal with your children. Perhaps your young daughter refuses to go to bed when you want her to and bursts into tears at the least mention of "lights out." A little knowledge of psychology comes in handy. Offer her a choice of staying up until 7:30 with you or going upstairs and playing until 8:00. Since she gets to make the choice, she does not feel so powerless and will not resist. Psychology is also useful in rewarding a child for a job well done. Instead of telling your ten-year-old son what a good boy he is when he makes his own bed, tell him how neat it looks, how happy you are to see it, and how proud of him you are for doing it by himself. The psychology books will tell you that being a good boy is much harder to live up to than doing one job well.

Pronouns

Pronouns (*he, she, it, you, they, this, that,* and others) are another way to connect ideas. Also, using pronouns in place of other words can help you avoid needless repetition. (Note, however, that pronouns should be used with care to avoid the problems described on pages 513–515.) Here is a selection that makes good use of pronouns:

> Another way for people to economize at an amusement park is to bring their own food. If they pack a nourishing, well-balanced lunch of cold chicken, carrot sticks, and fruit, they will avoid having to pay high prices for hamburgers and hot dogs. They will also save on calories. Also, instead of filling up on soft drinks, they should bring a thermos of iced tea. Iced tea is more refreshing than soda, and it is a great deal cheaper. Every dollar that is not spent at a refreshment stand is one that can be spent on another ride.

Synonyms

Synonyms are words alike in meaning. Using synonyms can also help move the reader easily from one thought to the next. In addition, the use of synonyms increases variety and interest by avoiding needless repetition.

Note the synonyms for *method* in the following selection:

> Several methods of fund-raising work well with small organizations. One technique is to hold an auction, with everyone either contributing an item from home or obtaining a donation from a sympathetic local merchant. Because all the merchandise and the services of the auctioneer have been donated, the entire proceeds can be placed in the organization's treasury. A second fund-raising procedure is a car wash. Club members and their children get together on a Saturday and wash all the cars in the neighborhood for a few dollars apiece. A third, time-tested way to raise money is to hold a bake sale, with each family contributing homemade cookies, brownies, layer cakes, or cupcakes. Sold by the piece or by the box, these baked goods will satisfyingly fill both the stomach and the pocketbook.

Read the selection below and then answer the questions about it that follow.

Activity

4

> [1]When I think about my childhood in the 1930s, life today seems like the greatest of luxuries. [2]In our house, we had only a wood-burning cookstove in the kitchen to keep us warm. [3]In the morning, my father would get up in the icy cold, go downstairs, and light a fire in the black iron range. [4]When he called us, I would put off leaving my warm bed until the last possible minute and then quickly grab my school clothes. [5]The water pitcher and washing basin in my room would be layered with ice, and my breath would come out as white puffs as I ran downstairs. [6]My sisters and I would all dress—as quickly as possible—in the chilly but bearable air of the kitchen. [7]Our schoolroom, once we had arrived, didn't provide much relief from the cold. [8]Students wore woolen mitts that left their fingers free but covered their palms and wrists. [9]Even with these, we occasionally suffered chilblains. [10]The throbbing swellings on our hands made writing a painful process. [11]When we returned home in the afternoon, we spent all our indoor hours in the warm kitchen. [12]We hated to leave it at bedtime to make the return trip to those cold bedrooms and frigid sheets. [13]My mother made up hot-water bottles and gave us hot bricks to tuck under the covers, but nothing could eliminate the agony of that penetrating cold when we first slid under the bedclothes.

1. How many times is the key word *cold* used? _____

2. Write here the pronoun that is used for *father* (sentence 4): _____

3. Write here the words in sentence 3 that are used as a synonym for *cookstove:*

_____ ; write in the words in sentence 10 that are used as a

synonym for *chilblains:* _____; write in the word in

sentence 12 that is used as a synonym for *cold:* _____.

Introductions, Conclusions, and Titles

So far, this chapter has discussed ways to organize and connect the supporting paragraphs of an essay. A well-organized essay, however, also needs a strong introductory paragraph, an effective concluding paragraph, and a good title.

Introductory Paragraph

www.mhhe.com/langan

Functions of the Introduction

A well-written introductory paragraph performs four important roles:

1. It attracts the reader's interest, encouraging him or her to continue reading the essay.

2. It supplies any background information that the reader may need to understand the essay.

3. It presents a thesis statement. This clear, direct statement of the main idea of the paper usually appears near the end of the introductory paragraph.

4. It indicates a plan of development. In this preview, the major supporting points for the thesis are listed in the order in which they will be presented. In some cases, the thesis and plan of development appear in the same sentence. However, writers sometimes choose not to describe the plan of development.

Common Methods of Introduction

Here are some common methods of introduction. Use any one method, or a combination of methods, to introduce your subject to the reader in an interesting way.

- **Begin with a broad, general statement of your topic and narrow it down to your thesis statement.** Broad, general statements ease the reader into your thesis statement by first introducing the topic. In the example below, the writer talks generally about diets and then narrows down to comments on a specific diet.

Bookstore shelves today are crammed with dozens of different diet books. The American public seems willing to try any sort of diet, especially the ones that promise instant, miraculous results. And authors are more than willing to invent new fad diets to cash in on this craze. Unfortunately, some of these fad diets are ineffective or even unsafe. One of the worst fad diets is the Palm Beach plan. It is impractical, doesn't achieve the results it claims, and is a sure route to poor nutrition.

- **Start with an idea or a situation that is the opposite of the one you will develop.** This approach works because your readers will be surprised, and then intrigued, by the contrast between the opening idea and the thesis that follows it.

When I decided to return to school at age thirty-five, I wasn't at all worried about my ability to do the work. After all, I was a grown woman who had raised a family, not a confused teenager fresh out of high school. But when I started classes, I realized that those "confused teenagers" sitting around me were in much better shape for college than I was. They still had all their classroom skills in bright, shiny condition, while mine had grown rusty from disuse. I had to learn how to locate information in a library, how to write a report, and even how to speak up in class discussions.

- **Explain the importance of your topic to the reader.** If you can convince your readers that the subject in some way applies to them, or is something they should know more about, they will want to keep reading.

Diseases like scarlet fever and whooping cough used to kill more young children than any other cause. Today, however, child mortality due to disease has been almost completely eliminated by medical science. Instead, car accidents are the number-one killer of our children. And most of the children fatally injured in car accidents were not protected by car seats, belts, or restraints of any kind. Several steps must be taken to reduce the serious dangers car accidents pose to children.

- **Use an incident or a brief story.** Stories are naturally interesting. They appeal to a reader's curiosity. In your introduction, an anecdote will grab the reader's attention right away. The story should be brief and should be related to your main idea. The incident in the story can be something that happened to you, something you have heard about, or something you have read about in a newspaper or magazine.

Early Sunday morning, the young mother dressed her little girl warmly and gave her a candy bar, a picture book, and a well-worn stuffed rabbit. Together, they drove downtown to a Methodist church. There the mother told the little girl to wait on the stone steps until children began arriving for Sunday school. Then the young mother drove off, abandoning her five-year-old because she couldn't cope with being a parent anymore. This incident is one of thousands of cases of child neglect and abuse that occur annually. Perhaps the automatic right to become a parent should no longer exist. Would-be parents should be forced to apply for parental licenses for which they would have to meet three important conditions.

- **Ask one or more questions.** You may simply want the reader to think about possible answers, or you may plan to answer the questions yourself later in the paper.

What is love? How do we know that we are really in love? When we meet that special person, how can we tell that our feelings are genuine and not merely infatuation? And, if they are genuine, will these feelings last? Love, as we all know, is difficult to define. But most people agree that true and lasting love involves far more than mere physical attraction. Love involves mutual respect, the desire to give rather than take, and the feeling of being wholly at ease.

- **Use a quotation.** A quotation can be something you have read in a book or an article. It can also be something that you have heard: a popular saying or proverb ("Never give advice to a friend"), a current or recent advertising slogan ("Can you hear me now?"), or a favorite expression used by friends or family ("My father always says . . ."). Using a quotation in your introductory paragraph lets you add someone else's voice to your own.

> "Fish and visitors," wrote Benjamin Franklin, "begin to smell after three days." Last summer, when my sister and her family came to spend their two-week vacation with us, I became convinced that Franklin was right. After only three days of my family's visit, I was thoroughly sick of my brother-in-law's lame jokes, my sister's endless complaints about her boss, and their children's constant invasions of our privacy.

The box that follows summarizes the six kinds of introductions. Read the introductions that come after it and, in the space provided, write the letter of the kind of introduction used in each case.

A. General to narrow	D. Incident or story
B. Starting with an opposite	E. Questions
C. Stating importance of topic	F. Quotation

_____ 1. The ad, in full color on a glossy magazine page, shows a beautiful kitchen with gleaming counters. In the foreground, on one of the counters, stands a shiny new food processor. Usually, a feminine hand is touching it lovingly. Around the main picture are other, smaller shots. They show mounds of perfectly sliced onion rings, thin rounds of juicy tomatoes, heaps of matchstick-sized potatoes, and piles of golden, evenly grated cheese. The ad copy tells you how wonderful, how easy, food preparation will be with a processor. Don't believe it. My processor turned out to be expensive, difficult to operate, and very limited in its use.

_____ 2. My father stubbornly says, "You can often tell a book by its cover," and when it comes to certain paperbacks, he's right. When you're browsing in the drugstore or supermarket and you see a paperback featuring an attractive young woman in a low-cut dress fleeing from a handsome dark figure in a shadowy castle, you know exactly what you're getting. Every romance novel has the same elements: an innocent heroine, an exotic setting, and a cruel but fascinating hero.

_____ 3. We Americans are incredibly lazy. Instead of cooking a simple, nourishing meal, we pop a frozen dinner into the oven. Instead of studying a daily newspaper, we are contented with the capsule summaries on the network news. Worst of all, instead of walking even a few blocks to the local convenience store, we jump into our cars. This dependence on the automobile, even for short trips, has robbed us of a valuable experience—walking. If we drove less and walked more, we would save money, become healthier, and discover fascinating things about our surroundings.

www.mhhe.com/langan

Concluding Paragraph

A concluding paragraph is your chance to remind the reader of your thesis idea and bring the paper to a natural and graceful end.

Common Methods of Conclusion

You may use any one of the methods below, or a combination of methods, to round off your paper.

- **End with a summary and final thought.** When army instructors train new recruits, each of their lessons follows a three-step formula:

  1. Tell them what you're going to tell them.
  2. Tell them.
  3. Tell them what you've told them.

An essay that ends with a summary is not very different. After you have stated your thesis ("Tell them what you're going to tell them") and supported it ("Tell them"), you restate the thesis and supporting points ("Tell them what you've told them"). However, don't use the exact wording you used before. Here is a summary conclusion:

> Online shopping at home, then, has several advantages. Such shopping is convenient, saves you money, and saves you time. It is not surprising that growing numbers of people are doing the majority of their shopping on the Internet, for everything from turnip seeds to televisions.

Note that the summary is accompanied by a final comment that rounds off the paper and brings the discussion to a close. This combination of a summary and a final thought is the most common method of concluding an essay.

- **Include a thought-provoking question or short series of questions.** A question grabs the reader's attention. It is a direct appeal to your reader to think further about what you have written. A question should follow logically from the points you have already made in the paper. A question must deal with one of these areas:

1. Why the subject of your paper is important
2. What might happen in the future
3. What should be done about this subject
4. Which choice should be made

In your conclusion, you may provide an answer to your question. Be sure, though, that the question is closely related to your thesis. Here is an example:

> What, then, will happen when most of the population will be over sixty years old? Retirement policies could change dramatically, with the age-sixty-five testimonial dinner and gold watch postponed for five or ten years. Even television would change as the Red Bull generation replaces the Pepsi generation. Glamorous gray-haired models would sell everything from toilet paper to televisions. New soap operas and situation comedies would reveal the secrets of the "sunset years." It will be a different world indeed when the young find themselves outnumbered.

- **End with a prediction or recommendation.** Like questions, predictions and recommendations also involve your readers. A prediction states what may happen in the future:

> If people stopped to think before acquiring pets, there would be fewer instances of cruelty to animals. Many times, it is the people who adopt pets without considering the expense and responsibility involved who mistreat and neglect their animals. Pets are living creatures. They do not deserve to be treated as carelessly as one would treat a stuffed toy.

A recommendation suggests what should be done about a situation or problem:

> Stereotypes such as the ditzy blonde, harried executive, and annoying in-law are insulting enough to begin with. In magazine ads or television commercials, they become even more insulting. Now these unfortunate characters are not just being laughed at; they are being turned into hucksters to sell products to an unsuspecting public. Consumers should boycott companies whose advertising continues to use such stereotypes.

In the space provided, note how each concluding paragraph ends: with a summary and final thought (write S in the space), with a prediction or recommendation (write P/R), or with a question (write Q).

_____ 1. Disappointments are unwelcome, but regular, visitors in everyone's life. We can feel depressed about them, or we can try to escape from them. The best thing, though, is to accept a disappointment and then try to use it somehow: step over the unwelcome visitor and then get on with life.

_____ 2. Saving the environment is up to each of us. Levels of harmful emissions would drop dramatically if we chose to carpool or take public transportation more often. Conserving fuel and electricity at home by sealing up leaky windows and using energy-saving light bulbs would help too. What will you do to conserve?

_____ 3. Some people dream of starring roles, their names in lights, and their pictures on the cover of People magazine. I'm not one of them, though. A famous person gives up private life, feels pressured all the time, and is never completely safe. So let someone else have that cover story. I'd rather lead an ordinary, but calm, life than a stress-filled one.

Titles

A title is usually a very brief summary of what your paper is about. It is often no more than several words. You may find it easier to write the title *after* you have completed your paper.

Following are the introductory paragraphs for two of the essays in this text, along with the titles of the essays.

Introductory paragraph

I'm not just a consumer—I'm a victim. If I order a product, it is sure to arrive in the wrong color, size, or quantity. If I hire people to do repairs, they never arrive on the day scheduled. If I owe a bill, the computer is bound to overcharge me. Therefore, in self-defense, I have developed the following consumer's guide to complaining effectively.

Title: How to Complain

Introductory paragraph

Schools divide people into categories. From first grade on up, students are labeled "advanced" or "deprived" or "remedial" or "antisocial." Students pigeonhole their fellow students, too. We've all known the "brain," the "jock," the "dummy," and the "teacher's pet." In most cases, these narrow labels are misleading and inaccurate. But there is one label for a certain type of college student that says it all: "zombie."

Title: Student Zombies

Note that you should not underline the title. Nor should you put quotation marks around it. On the other hand, you should capitalize all but small connecting words in the title. Also, you should skip a space between the title and the first line of the text. (See "Manuscript Form," page 541.)

Write an appropriate title for each of the introductory paragraphs that follow.

1. Returning to my hometown of Mercyville after five years, I discovered several newcomers on the same street as the pharmacy, hardware store, and restaurants I had patronized. A store selling African art had opened next to my favorite pizzeria. A few doors down was a Thai take-out restaurant, and across the street a Hindu grocer had set up shop. In the storefront where Charlie's Hamburgers was once located, I found a fancy Hungarian bistro featuring an elegant New Year's Eve dinner for $65.

    Title: _____

2. When my parents bought a new home in a small town outside Chicago, they decided to fence in our yard so that our two Labrador retrievers wouldn't wander off. The contractor they hired informed them that they would have to apply for a building permit, which would cost $150. After the shock wore off, my father went to town hall with the check, but the clerk informed him that he would have to submit a written request for the permit as well as a plot plan of our property. When he returned two hours later, the office was closed, and he had to return on Monday. After submitting everything, he learned that the town planning committee would not meet to consider our application for two months. When they did meet, they refused to grant our permit because the proposed fence crossed a "designated wetlands" area, and they refused to refund our $150.

    Title: _____

3. Having the ideal job doesn't depend only on the amount of money it pays, the working conditions, or the opportunities for advancement. It also has to do with one's fellow employees and, of course, the boss. While most people realize that bosses need to exercise careful supervision over the workplace and the employees, they prefer bosses who socialize with workers, make few demands, and look the other way when they don't perform well. Unfortunately, such supervisors too often turn out to be inefficient, disorganized, and unpredictable. A better alternative is someone who enforces rules predictably and demands that workers meet reasonable expectations.

    Title: _____

© Getty

For further practice in writing titles, write an appropriate title for the image pictured here.

Practice in Organizing and Connecting Specific Evidence

You now know the third step in effective writing: organizing the specific evidence used to support the thesis of a paper. This closing section will expand and strengthen your understanding of the third step in writing. You will work through the following series of activities:

- organizing through time or emphatic order

- providing transitions

- identifying transitions and other connecting words
- completing transitional sentences
- identifying introductions and conclusions

Organizing through Time or Emphatic Order

Use time order to organize the scrambled lists of supporting ideas below. Write *1* beside the supporting idea that should come first in time, *2* beside the idea that logically follows, and *3* beside the idea that comes last in time.

Activity

8

1. Thesis: When I was a child, Disney movies frightened me more than any other kind.

    _____   As a five-year-old, I was terrified by the movie *Pinocchio,* about a puppet transformed into a boy.

    _____   Although I saw *Bambi* when I was old enough to begin poking fun at "baby movies," the scene during which Bambi's mother is killed has stayed with me to this day.

    _____   About a year after *Pinocchio,* I gripped my seat in fear as the witches and goblins of *Fantasia* flew across the screen.

2. Thesis: Observing three important rules will help you write better research papers.

    _____   Follow the format for including researched material required by your instructor.

    _____   Start the project early, immediately after it is assigned.

    _____   Use note cards, not notebook paper, to record the facts and ideas you research.

3. Thesis: Applying for unemployment benefits was a confusing, frustrating experience.

    _____   It was difficult to find both the office and a place to park.

    _____   When I finally reached the head of the line after four hours of waiting, the clerk had problems processing my claim.

    _____   There was no one to direct or help me when I entered the large office, which was packed with people.

Activity

9

Use emphatic order (order of importance) to arrange the following scrambled lists of supporting ideas. For each thesis, write 1 in the blank beside the point that is perhaps less important or interesting than the other two, 2 beside the point that appears more important or interesting, and 3 beside the point that should be most emphasized.

1. Thesis: My part-time job has been an invaluable part of my life this year.

    _____   Better yet, it has taught me how to get along with many kinds of people.

    _____   Since it's in the morning, it usually keeps me from staying up too late.

    _____   Without it, I would have had to drop out of school.

2. Thesis: Our soccer team was awarded three special honors for winning the state championship.

    _____   Three of our team members won college athletic scholarships

    _____   Our victory was written up in major newspapers.

    _____   Each team member received a gold medal.

3. Thesis: Donna is my most loyal friend.

    _____   She has taken time to do special favors for me.

    _____   She's always there in real emergencies or emotional crises.

    _____   She once lent me her favorite necklace to wear on a date.

Providing Transitions

Activity

10

In the spaces provided, add appropriate transitions to tie together the sentences and ideas in the following essay. Draw from the words given in the boxes above the paragraphs. Use each word only once.

Annoying People

President Richard Nixon used to keep an enemies list of all the people he didn't especially like. I'm ashamed to confess it, but I, too, have an enemies list—a mental one. On this list are all the people I would gladly live without, the ones who cause my blood pressure to rise to the boiling point. The top three places on the list go to people with annoying nervous habits, people who talk in movie theaters, and people who talk on cell phones while driving.

Greenfield Community College

One College Drive
Greenfield, MA 01301
(413) 775-1190
http://www.gcc.mass.edu/offices/bookstore/

The last day to return Fall 2011 textbooks is September 13, 2011 with your receipt only. Returns from September 14th - 20th require your sales receipt and proof of add/drop. No returns honored after September 20, 2011 for Fall term.

Cust. None

08-Sep-11 1:44p	Clerk: Admin
Trans. #: 10171479	Reg: 2

9780073371658	*College Writing Skil*	
1 @ $100.50	$100.50	*

	Sub-total:	$100.50
	Total:	**$100.50**

* *Non-Tax Items*
  Items: 1   *Units: 1*

Payment Via:

VISA/MC $100.50

VISA ************2747
Approval: 164049
TroutD: 34006

Purchases made by check require a ten business day waiting period for a cash refund.

The College Store
Greenfield Community College
One College Drive
Greenfield, MA 01301
(413) 775-1190
http://www.gcc.mass.edu/offices/bookstore/

Textbook Refund Policy

Fall & Spring semester textbooks are returnable for one week from the first day of classes, with a sales receipt and in the same condition as sold. The cover and pages of new textbook(s) must be free from any marks or other signs of wear and any shrink wrap still intact.

Proof of add/drop, valid ID and your sales receipt are required for all textbook returns during the second week of Fall or Spring classes. The textbook(s) returned must match the required or optional book(s) for the dropped class(es) and must be in the same condition as sold, with no marks or signs of wear on the cover or pages of new texts. Shrink wrap must be intact.

January and Summer Session books are returnable for one week from the beginning of classes, with a sales receipt and in the same condition as sold. One week course books may be returned with a receipt, within 24 hours or purchase. The cover and pages of new textbooks must be free from any marks or other signs of wear and any shrink wrap still intact.

Defective books (missing pages, pages out of order, blurred print, etc.) should be returned to the College Store, with the sales receipt, as soon as the defect is discovered within the same semester purchased.

General Merchandise Return

If you need to return non textbook items purchased at the College Store, the original register receipt must accompany the merchandise and the product must be in original condition. Computer software is not returnable once opened. Electronics are only returnable if in the original unopened package. Defective merchandise can be exchanged or returned with a sales receipt if returnable to our vendor. We reserve the right to refuse a refund or exchange at any time.

Buyback Information

The College Store offers daily buybacks throughout the year during our regular store hours. The College Store also offers end of semester buybacks in December and May and beginning buybacks in September and January.
For exact dates and other up to date information please visit the College Store website at http://www.gcc.mass.edu/offices/bookstore/ or inquire in person.

The College Store
Greenfield Community College
One College Drive
Greenfield, MA 01301
(413) 775-1190
http://www.gcc.mass.edu/offices/bookstore/

Textbook Refund Policy

Fall & Spring semester textbooks are returnable for one week

For example	First of all	Another	However

_____, there are the people with annoying nervous habits.

_____, there are the ones who make faces. When in deep thought, they twitch, squint, and frown, and they can be a real distraction when

I'm trying to concentrate during an exam. _____ type of nervous character makes useless designs. These people bend paper clips into abstract sculptures or string the clips into necklaces as they talk.

_____, neither of these groups is as bad as the people who make noises. These individuals, when they are feeling uncomfortable, bite their fingernails or crack their knuckles. If they have a pencil in their hands, they tap it rhythmically against whatever surface is handy—a desk, a book, a head. Lacking a pencil to play with, they jingle the loose change or keys in their pockets. These people make me wish I were hard of hearing.

On the contrary	Then	As a result	After	Second

A _____ category of people I would gladly do away with is the ones who talk in movie theaters. These people are not content to sit back,

relax, and enjoy the film they have paid to see. _____, they feel compelled to comment loudly on everything from the hero's hairstyle to

the appropriateness of the background music. _____, no one hears a

word of any dialogue except theirs. _____ these people have been in the

theater for a while, their interest in the movie may fade. _____ they will start discussing other things, and the people around them will be treated to an instant replay of the latest family scandal or soap-opera episode. These stories may be entertaining, but they don't belong in a movie theater.

In addition	But	Last of all

(continued)

_____, there are the people who talk on the phone while they're driving. One of the things that irritates me about them is the way they seem to be showing off. They're saying, "Look at me! I'm so important

I have to make phone calls in my car." _____, such behavior is just plain dangerous. Instead of concentrating on adjusting carefully to everchanging traffic conditions, they're weaving all over the road or getting much too close to the car in front of them as they gossip with a friend, make an appointment with a doctor, or order a pizza.

So long as murder remains illegal, the nervous twitchers, movie talkers,

and cell-phone users of the world are safe from me. _____ if ever I am granted the power of life or death, these people had better think twice about annoying me. They might not have long to live.

Identifying Transitions and Other Connecting Words

Activity

11

The following sentences use connecting words to help tie ideas together. The connecting words you are to identify are set off in italics. In the space, write T for *transition,* RW for *repeated word,* S for *synonym,* or P for *pronoun.*

_____   1. The Statue of Liberty stands watch in New York Harbor. In *her* right hand she holds the torch of freedom.

_____   2. Plants like poinsettias and mistletoe are pretty. *They* are also poisonous.

_____   3. A strip of strong cloth can be used as an emergency fan-belt replacement. *In addition,* a roll of duct tape can be used to patch a leaky hose temporarily.

_____   4. The battleship *Arizona* was sunk during the attack on Pearl Harbor in 1941. Entombed in the *vessel* are the bodies of sailors who made the ultimate sacrifice for their country.

_____   5. The molded plastic chairs in the classrooms are hard and uncomfortable. When I sit in one of these *chairs,* I feel as if I were sitting in a bucket.

_____   6. One way to tell if your skin is aging is to pinch a fold of skin on the back of your hand. If *it* doesn't smooth out quickly, your skin is losing its youthful tone.

_____   7. I never eat sloppy joes. *They* look as if they've already been eaten.

———— 8. Clothing intended just for children seems to have vanished. *Instead,* children wear scaled-down versions of everything adults wear.

———— 9. Naturalism was the literary movement that described the individual's struggle in a hostile world. Among those writers who embraced *naturalism* were Theodore Dreiser and Upton Sinclair.

———— 10. The giant cockroaches in Florida are the subject of local legends. A visitor, according to one tale, saw one of the *insects*, thought it was a Volkswagen, and tried to drive it away.

———— 11. Some thieves scour garbage cans for credit-card receipts. *Then* they use the owner's name and card number to order merchandise by phone.

———— 12. Switzerland did not take sides in World War I or II. *It* remained neutral in both.

———— 13. There are many phobias other than the ones described in psychology textbooks. I have *phobias,* for instance, about toasters and lawn mowers.

———— 14. My back problems seem to be getting better because I am trying the exercises the team trainer taught me. *As a result,* I might not have to have surgery.

Completing Transitional Sentences

Following are brief sentence outlines from two essays. In each outline, the second and third topic sentences serve as transitional, or linking, sentences. Each reminds us of the point in the preceding paragraph and announces the point to be developed in the current paragraph. In the spaces provided, add the words needed to complete the second and third topic sentences.

Activity

12

Thesis 1

To prepare for a long automobile trip, you should check tire pressure and condition, replace worn belts and hoses, and make sure the engine oil and other fluids are at proper levels.

First supporting paragraph

To ensure your safety, start by checking the pressure and condition of your tires. . . .

Second supporting paragraph

After making sure that _____

_____, you should _____

_____. . . .

Third supporting paragraph	Once you are certain that _____ _____ . . . .

Thesis 2

Cheaper cost, greater comfort, and superior electronic technology make watching football at home more enjoyable than attending a game at the stadium.

First supporting paragraph	For one thing, watching the game on TV eliminates the cost of attending the game. . . .

Second supporting paragraph	In addition to saving me money, watching the game at home is more _____ than sitting in a stadium. . . .

Third supporting paragraph	Even more important than _____ and _____, though, is the _____ that makes a televised game better than the "real thing." . . .

Identifying Introductions and Conclusions

Activity

13

The following box lists six common kinds of introductions and three common kinds of conclusions. Read the three pairs of introductory and concluding paragraphs that follow. Then, in the space provided, write the letter of the kind of introduction and conclusion used in each paragraph.

Introductions	Conclusions
A. General to narrow	G. Summary and final thought
B. Starting with an opposite	H. Question(s)
C. Stating importance of topic	I. Prediction or recommendation
D. Incident or story	
E. Question(s)	
F. Quotation	

_____   Shortly before Easter, our local elementary school sponsored a fund-raising event at which classroom pets and their babies—hamsters, guinea pigs, and chicks—were available for adoption. Afterward, as I was driving home, I saw a hand drop a baby hamster out of the car ahead of me. I couldn't avoid running over the tiny creature. One of the parents had taken the pet, regretted the decision, and decided to get rid of it. Such people have never stopped to consider the several real obligations involved in owning a pet.

Pair 1

_____   A pet cannot be thrown onto a trash heap when it is no longer wanted or tossed into a closet if it begins to bore its owner. A pet, like us, is a living thing that needs attention and care. Would-be owners, therefore, should think seriously about their responsibilities before they acquire a pet.

_____   What would life be like if we could read each other's minds? Would communications be instantaneous and perfectly clear? These questions will never be answered unless mental telepathy becomes a fact of life. Until then, we will have to make do with less perfect means of communication. Letters, telephone calls, and e-mail messages do have serious drawbacks.

Pair 2

_____   Neither letters, phone calls, nor e-mails guarantee perfect communication. With all our sophisticated skills, we human beings often communicate less effectively than howling wolves or chattering monkeys. We always seem to find some way to foul up the message.

_____   "Few things are harder to put up with," said Mark Twain, "than the annoyance of a good example." Twain obviously knew the problems faced by siblings cursed with older brothers or sisters who are models of perfection. All our lives, my older sister Shelley and I have been compared. Unfortunately, in competition with my sister's virtues, my looks, talents, and accomplishments always ended up on the losing side.

Pair 3

_____   Although I always lost in the sibling contests of looks, talents, and accomplishments, Shelley and I have somehow managed not to turn into deadly enemies. Feeling like the dud of the family, in fact, helped me to develop a drive to succeed and a sense of humor. In our sibling rivalry, we both managed to win.

5

The Fourth Step in Essay Writing

This chapter will show you how to

- revise so that your sentences flow smoothly and clearly
- edit so that your sentences are error free

© Image Source/Corbis

What differences do you notice about the two students in the photograph above? Most likely, you can identify with both of them. Thinking about your own experiences in the classroom, write an essay about one or more teachers or instructors who have conducted classes that made you glad to learn or, alternatively, left you daydreaming in class. Once you have written your first draft, read it aloud to make sure all your sentences flow smoothly and clearly.

Up to now, this book has emphasized the first three goals in effective writing: unity, support, and coherence. This chapter focuses on the fourth goal of writing effectively: sentence skills. You'll learn how to revise an essay so that your sentences flow smoothly and clearly. Then you'll review how to edit a paper for mistakes in grammar, punctuation, and spelling.

Revising Sentences

These strategies will help you to revise your sentences effectively:

- Use parallelism.
- Use a consistent point of view.
- Use specific words.
- Use active verbs.
- Use concise words.
- Vary your sentences.

Use Parallelism

Words in a pair or a series should have parallel structure. By balancing the items in a pair or a series so that they have the same kind of structure, you will make the sentence clearer and easier to read. Notice how the parallel sentences that follow read more smoothly than the nonparallel ones.

www.mhhe.com/langan

Nonparallel (Not Balanced)

My job includes checking the inventory, initialing the orders, and *to call* the suppliers.

The game-show contestant was told to be cheerful, charming, and *with enthusiasm.*

Grandmother likes to read mystery novels, to do needlepoint, and *surfing* the Internet.

We painted the trim in the living room; *the wallpaper was put up by a professional.*

Parallel (Balanced)

My job includes checking the inventory, initialing the orders, and calling the suppliers.
(A balanced series of *-ing* words: *checking, initialing, calling*)

The game-show contestant was told to be cheerful, charming, and enthusiastic.
(A balanced series of descriptive words: *cheerful, charming, enthusiastic*)

Grandmother likes to read mystery novels, to do needlepoint, and to surf the Internet.
(A balanced series of *to* verbs: *to read, to do, to surf*)

We painted the trim in the living room; a professional put up the wallpaper.
(Balanced verbs and word order: *We painted . . . ; a professional put up . . .*)

Balanced sentences are not a skill you need worry about when writing first drafts. But when you rewrite, you should try to put matching words and ideas into matching structures. Such parallelism will improve your writing style.

Cross out and revise the unbalanced part of each of the following sentences.

EXAMPLE   Chocolate makes me gain weight, lose my appetite, and ~~breaking~~ *break* out in hives.

1. Florida is famous for its wonderful weather, theme parks that are family oriented, and great fishing.

2. Many people share the same three intense fears: being in high places, working with numbers, and speeches.

3. The garden boasted a line of fruit trees that were mature, several rows of vegetables, and a large stand of rose bushes.

4. The History Channel offers many programs that are timely, well researched, and that people find interesting.

5. To become a dancer, Lola is taking lessons, working in amateur shows, and auditioned for professional companies.

6. Juan's last job offered security; a better chance for advancement is offered by his new job.

7. Cell phones allow us to communicate, store important information, and they can even be used to take photographs.

8. Because the dying woman was dignified and with courage, she won everyone's respect.

9. The candidate for governor promised that she would cut taxes, reform public education, and do something to rebuild roads and bridges.

10. If we're not careful, we'll leave the next generation polluted air, contaminated water, and forests that are dying.

Use a Consistent Point of View

Consistency with Verbs

www.mhhe.com/langan

Do not shift verb tenses unnecessarily. If you begin writing a paper in the present tense, do not shift suddenly to the past. If you begin in the past, do not shift without reason to the present. Notice the inconsistent verb tenses in the following example:

Incorrect: The gardener breaks up the hard earth with a shovel, added peat moss and other compost, then blends the soil evenly.

Correct: The gardener breaks up the hard earth with a shovel, adds peat moss and other compost, then blends the soil evenly.

Correct: The gardener broke up the hard earth with a shovel, added peat moss and other compost, then blended the soil evenly.

Make the verbs in each sentence consistent with the *first* verb used. Cross out the incorrect verb and write the correct form in the space at the left.

Activity

2

EXAMPLE

_____*ran*_____ Aunt Flo tried to kiss her little nephew, but he ~~runs~~ out of the room.

_____ 1. An aggressive news photographer knocked a reporter to the ground as the movie stars arrive for the Academy Awards.

_____ 2. The winning wheelchair racer in the marathon slumped back in exhaustion and asks for some ice to soothe his blistered hands.

_____ 3. George Washington won his first battle when he defeats the Hessians in Trenton, New Jersey.

_____ 4. Charles Conrad and Alan Bean landed on the moon in 1969 and gathered rock samples, which they bring back to Earth for examination.

_____ 5. John Steinbeck wrote his masterpiece The Grapes of Wrath in 1939, but he does not win the Nobel Prize until 1962.

_____ 6. Galileo (1564–1642) did not invent the telescope, but he improves upon it in order to observe the heavens better.

_____ 7. Ralph ripped open the bag of cheese puffs with his teeth, grabs handfuls of the salty orange squiggles, and stuffed them into his mouth.

_____ 8. From his perch high up on the rocky cliff, the eagle spots a whitetailed rabbit and swooped down toward his victim.

_____ 9. An American physicist was the first to measure the speed of light accurately when he calculates it at just over 186,000 miles per second.

_____ 10. When the great earthquake struck San Francisco in 1906, the entire city burns to the ground in less than twenty-four hours.

Consistency with Pronouns

When writing a paper, you should not shift your point of view unnecessarily. Be consistent in your use of first-, second-, or third-person pronouns.

Point of View		
	Singular	Plural
First-person pronouns	I (my, mine, me)	we (our, us)
Second-person pronouns	you (your)	you (your)
Third-person pronouns	he (his, him)	they (their, them)
	she (her)	
	it (its)	

TIP: Any person, place, or thing, as well as any indefinite pronoun such as *one, anyone, someone,* and so on (page 514), is a third-person word.

For instance, if you start writing in the first person, *I,* do not jump suddenly to the second person, *you.* Or if you are writing in the third person, *they,* do not shift unexpectedly to *you.* Look at the following examples.

Inconsistent

One of the fringe benefits of my job is that *you* can use a company credit card for gasoline.

(The most common mistake people make is to let *you* slip into their writing after they start with another pronoun.)

Though *we* like most of *our* neighbors, there are a few *you* can't get along with.

(The writer begins with the first-person pronouns *we* and *our* but then shifts to the second-person *you*.)

Consistent

One of the fringe benefits of my job is that *I* can use a company credit card for gasoline.

Though *we* like most of *our* neighbors, there are a few *we* can't get along with.

Cross out inconsistent pronouns in the following sentences, and revise with the correct form of the pronoun above each crossed-out word.

Activity

3

EXAMPLE   When I examined the used car, ~~you~~ *I* could see that one of the front fenders had been replaced.

1. Many people are ignorant of side effects that diets can have on your health.

2. I am always nervous when the dentist examines my teeth because you never know what she will find.

3. It is expensive for us to take public transportation to work every day, but what choice do you have if you can't afford a car?

4. During the border crisis, each country refused to change their aggressive stance.

5. If you go to Chicago, one should visit the Art Institute.

6. We don't have enough money to travel to Egypt, but you can learn about the pyramids on the Discovery Channel.

7. Maria loves algebra problems because solving them gives you a sense of accomplishment.

8. It's hard for us to pay for health insurance, but you don't dare go without it.

9. People often take a first-aid course so that we can learn how to help choking and heart attack victims.

10. There are several ways you can impress your new boss. For example, one should dress well, arrive at work on time, and complete tasks efficiently.

www.mhhe.com/langan

Use Specific Words

To be an effective writer, you must use specific words rather than general words. Specific words create pictures in the reader's mind. They help capture interest and make your meaning clear. Compare the following sentences:

General	Specific
The plane landed at the airport.	The United Airlines 747 landed at Reagan National Airport.
Animals came into the place.	Hungry lions padded silently into the sawdust-covered arena.
The man signed the paper.	The biology teacher hastily scribbled his name on the course withdrawal slip.

The specific sentences create clear pictures in our minds. The details *show* us exactly what has happened.

Here are four ways to make your sentences specific.

1. Use exact names.

    Luke fixed the muffler on his car.

    Luke fixed the muffler on his *2007 Chevrolet Impala*.

2. Use lively verbs.

    The flag *moved* in the breeze.

    The flag *fluttered* in the breeze.

3. Use descriptive words (modifiers) before nouns.

    A man strained to lift the crate.

    A *heavyset, perspiring* man strained to lift the *heavy wooden* crate.

4. Use words that relate to the senses—sight, hearing, taste, smell, touch.

    The tourists enjoyed a picnic lunch of cheese, bread, and olives.

    The tourists enjoyed a picnic lunch of *sharp* cheese, *crusty* bread, and *spicy* olives. (*taste*)

    The campers built a fire of pine and cedar.

    The campers built a fire of *aromatic* pine and cedar. (*smell*)

    A noise told the crowd that there were two minutes left to play.

A *piercing whistle* told the *cheering* crowd that there were two minutes left to play. (*hearing*)

When he returned, all he found in the refrigerator was bread and milk.

When he returned, all he found in the refrigerator was *stale* bread and *sour* milk. (*taste*)

Neil stroked the kitten's fur until he felt its tiny claws on his hand.

Neil stroked the kitten's *velvety* fur until he felt its tiny, *needle-sharp* claws on his hand. (*touch*)

Fran placed a sachet in her bureau drawer.

Fran placed a *lilac-scented* sachet in her bureau drawer. (*smell*)

Revise the following sentences, replacing vague, indefinite words with sharp, specific ones.

EXAMPLE   *Several of our appliances* broke down at the same time.

Our washer, refrigerator, and television broke . . .

1. The new home came with *energy-saving appliances*.

   _____

   _____

   _____

2. I swept aside the *things* on my desk to spread out the road map.

   _____

   _____

   _____

3. Large *trees* shaded the valley.

   _____

   _____

   _____

4. *Several sections* of the newspaper were missing.

   _____

   _____

   _____

Activity

4

5. The doctor examined *various parts of my body* before diagnosing my illness as bronchitis.

_____

_____

_____

Again, you will practice changing vague, indefinite writing into lively, image-filled writing that helps capture the reader's interest and makes your meaning clear. With the help of the methods described on pages 116–117, add specific details to the five sentences that follow. Note the two examples.

EXAMPLES   The person got off the bus.

The teenage boy bounded down the steps of the shiny yellow

school bus.

She worked hard all summer.

All summer, Eva sorted peaches and blueberries in the hot,

noisy canning factory.

1. The car would not start.

_____

_____

_____

2. The desk was cluttered.

_____

_____

_____

3. The woman was overjoyed at finding her lost son.

_____

_____

_____

4. My room needs cleaning.

_____

_____

_____

5. A vehicle blocked traffic.

_____

_____

_____

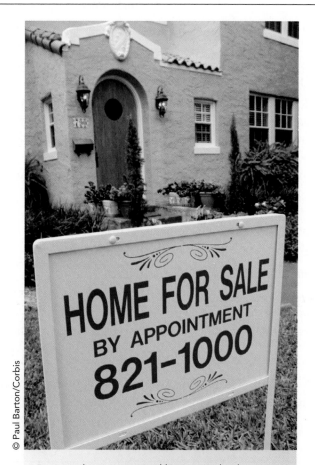

© Paul Barton/Corbis

Rewrite the sign pictured here using lively, image-filled writing that will grab people's attention.

Use Active Verbs

When the subject of a sentence performs the action of the verb, the verb is in the *active voice*. When the subject of a sentence receives the action of a verb, the verb is in the *passive voice*.

Passive voice uses a form of the verb *to be* (*am, is, are, was, were*) and the past participle of the main verb (usually the same as its past-tense form). Look at the following active and passive forms.

Passive	Active
The computer *was turned on* by Hakim.	Hakim *turned on* the computer.
The car's air conditioner *was fixed* by the mechanic.	The mechanic *fixed* the car's air conditioner.
The stream *was diverted* by the engineers.	The engineers *diverted* the stream.
The novel A Country Doctor *was written* by Sarah Orne Jewett.	Sarah Orne Jewett *wrote* the novel A Country Doctor.
In World War II, France, Holland, Norway, Hungary, Poland, Russia, and other countries *were invaded* by Germany.	In World War II, Germany *invaded* France, Holland, Norway, Hungary, Poland, Russia and other countries.

In general, active verbs are more effective than passive verbs. Active verbs give your writing a simpler and more vigorous style.

Activity

6

Revise the following sentences, changing verbs from the passive to the active voice and making any other word changes necessary.

EXAMPLE   Fruits and vegetables are painted often by artists.

Artists often paint fruits and vegetables.

1. Many unhealthy foods are included in the typical American diet.

    _____

2. The North Atlantic Treaty Organization (NATO) was established by the United States, Great Britain, and nine other countries in 1949.

    _____

    _____

3. The soldier's wounds were attacked by gangrene-producing bacteria.

    _____

4. A second Nobel Prize was won by Marie Curie in 1911.

_____

5. Final grades will be determined by the instructor on the basis of class performance.

_____

Use Concise Words

Wordiness—using more words than necessary to express a meaning—is often a sign of lazy or careless writing. Your readers may resent the extra time and energy they must spend when you have not done the work needed to make your writing direct and concise.

www.mhhe.com/langan

Here are two examples of wordy sentences:

> In this paper, I am planning to describe the hobby that I enjoy of collecting old comic books.   **Wordy**

> In Ben's opinion, he thinks that cable television will change and alter our lives in the future.

Omitting needless words improves these sentences:

> I enjoy collecting old comic books.   **Clear**

> Ben thinks that cable television will change our lives.

Following is a list of some wordy expressions that could be reduced to single words.

Wordy Form	Short Form
at the present time	now
in the event that	if
in the near future	soon
due to the fact that	because
for the reason that	because
is able to	can
in every instance	always
in this day and age	today
during the time that	while

(continued)

a large number of	many
big in size	big
red in color	red
five in number	five
return back	return
good benefit	benefit
commute back and forth	commute
postponed until later	postponed

Activity 7

Revise the following sentences, omitting needless words.

1. The bird was purple, red, orange, and yellow in color, and its body was extremely large in size.

   _____

   _____

2. Controlling the quality and level of the television shows that children watch is a continuing challenge to parents that they must meet on a daily basis.

   _____

   _____

3. A large number of people are now seeking out various electronic devices as presents to give to others on their birthdays.

   _____

   _____

4. In 1962, Linus Pauling, who was an American, was awarded the Nobel Prize, which was given to him for his attempts to limit the making of nuclear arms and to curtail the spread of nuclear testing.

   _____

   _____

5. I found out recently that Benito Mussolini (1883–1945), the dictator of the fascist nation of Italy for a period lasting nearly twenty-one years, was named after the Mexican political leader who went by the name of Benito Juarez (1806–1872).

_____

_____

_____

6. In today's uncertain economic climate, it is clear that people, namely, average middle-class working people, have great difficulty saving much money or putting anything aside for emergencies.

_____

_____

7. We thought the television program that was on last night was enjoyable, whereas our parents reacted with dislike to the content of the show.

_____

_____

8. Because of the bad weather, the school district felt it would be safer to cancel classes and let everyone stay home than to risk people having accidents on the way to school.

_____

_____

9. Out of all the regrets in my life so far, one of my greatest ones to the present time is that I did not take additional art classes when I was still in high school and had a chance to do so.

_____

_____

10. It seems obvious to me, and it should be to everyone else, too, that people can be harmed as much by emotional abuse as by physical abuse, even if you don't lay a hand on them.

_____

_____

Vary Your Sentences

One part of effective writing is to vary the kinds of sentences you write. If every sentence follows the same pattern, writing may become monotonous to read. This section explains four ways you can create variety and interest in your writing style. It also describes coordination and subordination—two important techniques for achieving different kinds of emphasis in writing.

The following are four methods you can use to revise simple sentences, making them more complex and sophisticated:

- Add a second complete thought (coordination).
- Add a dependent thought (subordination).
- Begin with a special opening word or phrase.
- Place adjectives or verbs in a series.

Revise by Adding a Second Complete Thought

When you add a second complete thought to a simple sentence, the result is a *compound* (or double) sentence. The two complete statements in a compound sentence are usually connected by a comma and a joining or coordinating word (*and, but, for, or, nor, so, yet*).

A compound sentence is used to give equal weight to two closely related ideas. The technique of showing that ideas have equal importance is called *coordination*. Following are some compound sentences. In each case, the sentence contains two ideas that the writer considers equal in importance.

Greg worked on the engine for three hours, but the car still wouldn't start.

Bananas were on sale this week, so I bought a bunch for the children's lunches.

We laced up our roller blades, and then we moved cautiously onto the rink.

Activity

8

Combine the following pairs of simple sentences into compound sentences. Use a comma and a logical joining word (*and, but, for, so*) to connect each pair of statements.

> **HINT:** If you are not sure what *and, but, for,* and *so* mean, review pages 482–483.

EXAMPLE   The weather was cold and windy.
Al brought a thick blanket to the football game.

The weather was cold and windy, so Al brought a thick blanket to the football game.

1. My son can't eat peanut butter snacks or sandwiches.
   He is allergic to peanuts.

   _____

   _____

2. I tried to sleep.
   The thought of tomorrow's math exam kept me awake.

   _____

   _____

3. The poet Ezra Pound left America in 1908.
   He was dissatisfied with the artistic climate of his native country.

   _____

   _____

4. My philosophy professor believes that every student can learn.
   He spends much of his extra time tutoring his students.

   _____

   _____

5. I didn't have enough money to buy my parents an anniversary present.
   I offered to mow their lawn for the whole summer.

   _____

   _____

Revise by Adding a Dependent Thought

When you add a dependent thought to a simple sentence, the result is a *complex* sentence.* A dependent thought begins with one of the following subordinating words:

www.mhhe.com/langan

---

*The two parts of a complex sentence are sometimes called an *independent clause* and a *dependent clause*. A *clause* is simply a word group that contains a subject and a verb. An independent clause expresses a complete thought and can stand alone. A dependent clause does not express a complete thought in itself and depends on the independent clause to complete its meaning. Dependent clauses always begin with a dependent or subordinating word.

Subordinating Words

after	if, even if	when, whenever
although, though	in order that	where, wherever
as	since	whether
because	that, so that	which, whichever
before	unless	while
even though	until	who
how	what, whatever	whose

A complex sentence is used to emphasize one idea over another. Look at the following complex sentence:

Although the exam room was very quiet, I still couldn't concentrate.

The idea that the writer wishes to emphasize here—*I still couldn't concentrate*—is expressed as a complete thought. The less important idea—*Although the exam room was very quiet*—is subordinated to the complete thought. The technique of giving one idea less emphasis than another is called *subordination*.

Following are other examples of complex sentences. In each case, the part starting with the dependent word is the less emphasized part of the sentence.

Even though I was tired, I stayed up to watch the horror movie.

Before I take a bath, I check for spiders in the tub.

When Ivy feels nervous, she pulls on her earlobe.

Activity

9

Use logical subordinating words to combine the following pairs of simple sentences into sentences that contain a dependent thought. Place a comma after a dependent statement when it starts the sentence.

EXAMPLE   Rita bit into the hard taffy.
She broke a filling.

When Rita bit into the hard taffy, she broke a filling.

_____

1. Many Americans blamed President Herbert Hoover for the Great Depression, which began in 1929.
   They elected Franklin Roosevelt president in 1932.

_____

_____

2. The bear turned over the rotten log.
   Fat white grubs crawled in every direction.

   _____

   _____

3. Europe had suffered a great deal of damage during World War II.
   The United States helped rebuild its infrastructure and economy.

   _____

   _____

4. Some people are allergic to wool.
   They buy sweaters made only from synthetic fibers.

   _____

   _____

5. An older woman in my typing class can type almost one hundred words a minute.
   She is having trouble landing a secretarial job.

   _____

   _____

Revise by Beginning with a Special Opening Word or Phrase

Among the special openers that can be used to start sentences are *-ed* words, *-ing* words, *-ly* words, *to* word groups, and prepositional phrases. Here are examples of all five kinds of openers:

-ed word

   Concerned about his son's fever, Paul called a doctor.

-ing word

   Humming softly, the woman browsed through the rack of dresses.

-ly word

   Hesitantly, Sue approached the instructor's desk.

to word group

To protect her hair, Eva uses the lowest setting on her blow dryer.

Prepositional phrase

During the exam, drops of water fell from the ceiling.

Activity 10

Combine each of the following pairs of simple sentences into one sentence by using the opener shown at the left and omitting repeated words. Use a comma to set off the opener from the rest of the sentence.

EXAMPLE   *-ing* word   The pelican scooped small fish into its baggy bill. It dipped into the waves.

Dipping into the waves, the pelican scooped small fish into its baggy bill.

1. Frederico ran into the burning building.
   He did not hesitate.

Preposi-
tional
phrase

_____

_____

to word
group

2. Eva and Olaf wanted to find the shortest route over the mountain.
   They bought a map of the local hiking trails.

_____

_____

Preposi-
tional
phrase

3. The accused murderer grinned at the witnesses.
   He did this during the trial.

_____

_____

-ed word

4. The vet's office was noisy and confusing.
   It was crowded with nervous pets.

_____

_____

Prepositio-
nal phrase

5. Thomas Alva Edison finally discovered the right filament for his light bulb.
   He had tested thousands of materials.

_____

_____

Revise by Placing Adjectives or Verbs in a Series

Various parts of a sentence may be placed in a series. Among these parts are adjectives (descriptive words) and verbs. Here are examples of both in a series:

Adjectives

I gently applied a *sticky new* Band-Aid to the *deep, ragged* cut on my finger.

Verbs

The truck *bounced* off a guardrail, *sideswiped* a tree, and *plunged* down the embankment.

Combine the simple sentences into one sentence by using adjectives or verbs in a series and by omitting repeated words. Use a comma when necessary between adjectives or verbs in a series.

Activity

11

EXAMPLE Jesse spun the basketball on one finger.
He rolled it along his arms.
He dribbled it between his legs.

Jesse spun the basketball on one finger, rolled it along his arms,

and dribbled it between his legs.

1. The bobcat sat high on a rock.
It stared down at the unsuspecting rodent.
It leaped upon its prey.

_____

_____

2. Some Native Americans lived in the desert.
They built permanent homes.
These homes were usually made of adobe.
Adobe resembles stucco.

_____

_____

3. By 6 A.M., I had read the textbook chapter.
   I had taken notes on it.
   I had studied the notes.
   I had drunk eight cups of coffee.

   _____

   _____

4. The exterminator approached the wasps' nests hanging under the eaves.
   The nests were large.
   The nests were papery.
   The eaves were old.
   The eaves were wooden.

   _____

   _____

5. Reeds bordered the pond.
   The reeds were slim.
   The reeds were brown.
   The pond was green.
   The pond was stagnant.

   _____

   _____

Editing Sentences

After revising sentences in a paper so that they flow smoothly and clearly, you need to edit the paper for mistakes in grammar, punctuation, mechanics, usage, and spelling. Even if a paper is otherwise well written, it will make an unfavorable impression on readers if it contains such mistakes. To edit a paper, check it against the agreed-upon rules, or conventions, of written English—simply called *sentence skills* in this book. Here are the most common of these conventions:

> ✓   Write complete sentences rather than fragments.
> ✓   Do not write run-on sentences.
> ✓   Use verb forms correctly.
> ✓   Make sure that subject, verbs, and pronouns agree.

(continued)

✓   Eliminate faulty modifiers.

✓   Use pronoun forms correctly.

✓   Use capital letters when needed.

✓   Use the following marks of punctuation correctly: apostrophe,
     quotation marks, comma, semicolon, colon, hyphen, dash, parentheses.

✓   Use correct manuscript form.

✓   Eliminate slang, clichés, and pretentious words.

✓   Check for possible spelling errors.

✓   Eliminate careless errors.

These sentence skills are treated in detail in Part 4 of this book, and they can be referred to easily as needed. Both the list of sentence skills on the inside back cover of this book and the correction symbols on pages 639–640 include page references so that you can turn quickly to any skill you want to check.

Hints about Editing

These hints can help you edit the next-to-final draft of a paper for sentence-skill mistakes:

1. Have at hand two essential tools: a good dictionary and a grammar handbook (you can use the one in this book beginning on page 457).

2. Use a sheet of paper to cover your essay so that you will expose only one sentence at a time. Look for errors in grammar, spelling, and typing. It may help to read each sentence out loud. If a sentence does not read clearly and smoothly, chances are something is wrong.

3. Pay special attention to the kinds of errors you tend to make. For example, if you tend to write run-ons or fragments, be especially on the lookout for those errors.

4. Try to work on a typewritten or word-processed draft, where you'll be able to see your writing more objectively than you can on a handwritten page; use a pen with colored ink so that your corrections will stand out.

TIP: A series of editing tests appears on pages 611–624. You will probably find it most helpful to take these tests after reviewing the sentence skills in Part 4.

Proofreading

Proofreading means closely checking the final, edited draft of your paper for typos and other careless errors. A helpful strategy is to read your paper backward, from the last sentence to the first. This helps keep you from getting caught up in the flow of the paper and missing small mistakes. Here are six helpful proofing symbols:

Proofing Symbol	Meaning	Example
∧	insert missing letter or word	ach*i*eve
ℓ	omit	draw two two conclusions
⌒⌒	reverse order of words or letters	lived happily after ever
#	add space	all#right
‿	close up space	base ball
cap, lc	Add a capital (or a lowercase) letter	*cap* My english *lc* Class

After you mark corrections on the page, enter them into your word processer file, then reprint the page.

In the spaces below this paragraph, write the numbers of the ten word groups that contain fragments or run-ons. Then, in the spaces between the lines, edit by making the necessary corrections. One is done for you as an example.

A unique object in my family's living room is an ashtray. *lc* Which I made in second grade. I can still remember the pride I felt. When I presented it to my mother. Now, I'm amazed that my parents didn't hide it away at the back of a shelf it is a remarkably ugly object. The ashtray is made out of brown clay that I had tried to mold into a perfect circle, unfortunately my class was only forty-five minutes long. The best I could do was to shape it into a lopsided oval. Its most distinctive feature, though, is the grooves carved into its rim. I had theorized that each groove could hold a cigarette or cigar, I made at least fifty of them.   I somehow failed to consider that the only person who smoked in my family was my father.   Who smoked about five cigars a year.   Further, although our living room is decorated in sedate tans and blues, my ashtray is bright purple.   My favorite color at the time.   For variety, it has stripes around its rim they are colored neon green.   My parents have proudly displayed my little masterpiece on their coffee table for the past ten years.   If I ever wonder if my parents love me.   I look at that ugly ashtray, the answer is plain to see.

1. _____   3. _____   5. _____   7. _____   9. _____

2. _____   4. _____   6. _____   8. _____   10. _____

Practice in Revising Sentences

You now know the fourth step in effective writing: revising and editing sentences. You also know that practice in *editing* sentences is best undertaken after you have worked through the sentence skills in Part 4. The focus in this section, then, will be on *revising* sentences—using a variety of methods to ensure that your sentences flow smoothly and are clear and interesting. You will work through Review Tests on the following:

- using parallelism
- using a consistent point of view
- using specific words
- using active verbs
- using concise words
- varying your sentences

Using Parallelism

Review Test   1

Cross out the unbalanced part of each sentence. In the space provided, revise the unbalanced part so that it matches the other item or items in the sentence.

EXAMPLE   Cigarette smoking is expensive, disgusting, and ~~a health risk~~. *unhealthy*

1. Langston Hughes (1902–1967) wrote plays, poetry, and he was an essayist.

   _____

2. The president likes reading mystery novels, to listen to bluegrass, and playing golf.

   _____

3. Many mothers who have gone back to school have to budget their time between their studies, their jobs, and taking care of their families.

   _____

4. The keys to improving grades are to take effective notes in class, to plan study time, and preparing carefully for exams.

   _____

5. Qualities that I look for in friends are a sense of humor, being kind, and dependability.

   _____

6. Janine is very talented: she is a gourmet cook, a published poet, and she takes great photographs.

   _____

7. Housekeeping shortcuts will help you speed up doing laundry, cleaning rooms, and food on the table.

   _____

8. Studying a little every day is more effective than to cram.

   _____

9. The chickens travel on a conveyor belt, where they are plucked, washed, rinsed, and bags are put on them.

   _____

10. The speaker impressed the audience because of his clear, reasonable presentation with friendliness as well.

   _____

Review Test 2

Cross out the unbalanced part of each sentence. In the space provided, revise the unbalanced part so that it matches the other item or items in the sentence.

1. Paying college tuition and not studying is as sensible as to buy tickets to a movie and not watching it. _____

2. The best programming on television includes news coverage, show on science, and children's series. _____

3. Curling overgrown vines, porch furniture that was rotted, and sagging steps were my first impressions of the neglected house. _____

4. Alex Haley's career included writing several short stories and essays, authoring <u>Roots</u>, the novel that made him famous, and he also edited <u>The Autobiography of Malcolm X</u>. _____

5. The college provides three ways to earn extra money while attending school: serve as a lab assistant, tutoring fellow students in the learning lab, and working in one of the many federally sponsored work-study programs.

   _____

6. While waiting for the exam to start, small groups of nervous students glanced over their notes, drank coffee, and were whispering to each other.

   _____

7. In many ways, starting college at forty is harder than to start at eighteen.

   _____

8. Well-written poetry impresses me as much as any skyscraper that is found in the city. _____

9. The homeless woman shuffled along the street, bent over to pick something up, and was putting it in her shopping bag. _____

10. A teamsters' strike now would mean interruptions in food deliveries, a slow-down in the economy, and losing wages for workers. _____

Using a Consistent Point of View

Review Test   3

Change verbs as needed in the following selection so that they are consistently in the past tense. Cross out each incorrect verb and write the correct form above it, as shown in the example. You will need to make ten additional corrections.

My uncle's shopping trip last Thursday was discouraging to him. First of
all, he had to drive around for fifteen minutes until he ~~finds~~ *found* a parking space.
There was a half-price special on paper products in the supermarket, and
every spot is taken. Then, when he finally got inside, many of the items on
his list were not where he expected. For example, the pickles he wanted
are not on the same shelf as all the other pickles. Instead, they were in a
refrigerated case next to the bacon. And the granola was not on the cereal
shelves but in the health-food section. Shopping thus proceeds slowly.
About halfway through his list, he knew there would not be time to cook
dinner and decides to pick up a barbecued chicken. The chicken, he learned,
was available at the end of the store he had already passed. So he parks his
shopping cart in an aisle, get the chicken, and came back. After adding half
a dozen more items to his cart, he suddenly realizes it contained someone
else's food. So he retraced his steps, found his own cart, transfers the
groceries, and continued to shop. Later, when he began loading items onto
the checkout counter, he notices that the barbecued chicken was missing.
He must have left it in the other cart, certainly gone by now. Feeling totally
defeated, he returned to the deli counter and says to the clerk, "Give me
another chicken. I lost the first one." My uncle told me that when he saw the
look on the clerk's face, he felt as if he'd flunked Food Shopping.

Review Test   4

Cross out inconsistent pronouns in the following sentences, and revise with the correct form of the pronoun above each crossed-out word.

EXAMPLE   Dog owners should put tags on their dogs in case ~~you~~ *they* lose their pets.

1. Students who get a good night's sleep before a major exam find that you do a lot better than if thay spent the whole night studying.

2. All you could hear was the maddening rattle of the heating register, even though I buried my face in the pillow.

3. When we answer the telephone at work, you are supposed to say the company's name.

4. Every time Alex attends a rock concert, he reminds himself that listening to loud music can damage your hearing.

5. When people go to Disney land, you sometimes have to wait to get into the most popular attractions.

6. Last year, we went to an aquatic park where you were allowed to swim with dolphins.

7. When I first began to work as a waitress, I was surprised at how rude some customers were to you.

8. When you drive on the highway, I get disgusted at the amount of trash I see.

9. Students may not leave the exam room unless you have turned in the exam.

10. Nina wanted to just browse through the store, but in every department a salesperson came up and asked to help you.

Using Specific Words

Review Test   5

Revise the following sentences, changing vague, indefinite words to sharp, specific ones.

1. *We were exhausted* after shoveling snow all day.

_____

_____

_____

2. The *food choices* in the cafeteria were unappetizing.

_____

_____

_____

3. *Bugs* invaded our kitchen and pantry this summer.

_____

_____

_____

4. All last week, *the weather was terrible.*

_____

_____

_____

5. My mathematics teacher *is excellent.*

_____

_____

_____

Review Test 6

With the help of the methods described on pages 116–117, add specific details to the sentences that follow.

1. The salesperson was obnoxious.

_____

_____

_____

2. The kitchen was cheery.

_____

_____

_____

3. My city is a cultural paradise.

   _____

   _____

   _____

4. The lounge area was busy.

   _____

   _____

   _____

5. A passenger on the bus was acting strangely.

   _____

   _____

   _____

Using Active Verbs

Review Test | **7**

Revise the following sentences, changing verbs from the passive to the active voice and making any other necessary word changes.

EXAMPLE   Soccer is played by children all over the world.

   Children all over the world play soccer.

1. The pizza restaurant was closed by the health inspector.

   _____

2. Huge stacks of donated books were sorted by the workers in the library.

   _____

3. A poem about Chicago entitled "City of Big Shoulders" was written by Carl Sandburg.

   _____

4. In 1928, the antibiotic penicillin was discovered by Sir Alexander Fleming.

   _____

5. Nearly a million tons of tobacco are grown by American farmers each year.

   _____

6. An additional charge was placed on our phone bill by the telephone company.

   _____

7. The building of a new community library was made possible by a grant from a large corporation.

   _____

   _____

8. Stress is relieved by physical activity, meditation, and relaxation.

   _____

9. Taxes will be raised by the federal government to pay for highway improvements.

   _____

10. Studies show that violent behavior among young children is increased by watching violent TV programs.

    _____

    _____

Using Concise Words

Review Test   8

Revise the following sentences, omitting needless words.

1. I finally made up my mind and decided to look for a new job.

   _____

   _____

2. Scientists who study botany classify or think of the tomato as a type of fruit, but most other people today think of it as a vegetable.

   _____

   _____

3. Tamika realized suddenly that her date had stood her up and was not going to show up.

_____

_____

4. At this point in time, we are not exactly sure what the causes of Alzheimer's disease are, but we are aware of the fact that it rarely attacks younger people who are below the age of sixty.

_____

_____

5. The salesperson advised us not to buy the laptop at this time because it was going to have a drop in price in the very near future.

_____

_____

Review Test   9

Revise the following sentences, omitting needless words.

1. The policy at our company at the present time is that there are two coffee breaks, with each of them being fifteen minutes long.

_____

_____

2. I am of the opinion that the police are more likely to stop cars painted the color red than cars that are painted in another color.

_____

_____

3. I have a strong preference for candy over fruit, which, in my opinion, doesn't taste as good as candy does.

_____

_____

4. Majoring in liberal arts during your first year in college can help you explore varoius types of academic majors, and doing so will help you decide what discipline you want to study.

_____

_____

5. Many people are of the opinion that children should be required by law to attend school until they reach the age of sixteen years old.

_____

_____

Varying Your Sentences

Review Test 10

Combine each of the following groups of simple sentences into one longer sentence. Omit repeated words. Various combinations are often possible, so try to find the combination in each group that flows most smoothly and clearly.

1. Buddhism is a major world religion.
   The religion was founded in Asia about 2,500 years ago.
   It was founded by a Hindu philosopher
   This philosopher came to be called Buddha.

_____

_____

2. The physical therapist watched.
   Julie tried to stand on her weakened legs.
   They crumpled under her.

_____

_____

3. There were parking spaces on the street.
   Richard pulled into an expensive garage.
   He did not want to risk damage to his new car.

_____

_____

4. The sun set over a valley.
The valley was lush with vegetation
The vegetation was green.
The vegetation provided food for many different animals.
The vegetation also provided habitats for them.

_____

_____

5. The rainstorm flooded our basement.
The rainstorm was sudden.
The rainstorm was terrible.
It knocked slates off the roof.
It uprooted a young tree.

_____

_____

Review Test 11

Combine each of the following groups of simple sentences into two longer sentences. Omit repeated words. Various combinations are often possible, so try to find combinations in each group that flow most smoothly and clearly.

1. Skateboarding is a popular sport.
It takes a lot of practice.
The rider stands on a narrow plank
The board is mounted on a set of wheels
The rider maneuvers the board by shifting his or her weight.

_____

_____

_____

2. Vern works as a model.
He has to look his best.
He gained ten pounds recently.

He had to take off the extra weight.
He would have lost his job.

_____

_____

_____

3. Digital cameras do not use film.
   They can display a photograph only a few seconds after it is taken.
   These photographs can also be viewed on a computer screen.
   They can be seen on a television as well.

_____

_____

_____

4. The lion was hungry.
   It watched the herd of gazelle closely.
   A young or sick animal wandered away from the group.
   The lion would move in for the kill.

_____

_____

_____

5. My aunt decided to find a helpful form of exercise.
   She was suffering from arthritis.
   She learned that swimming is very healthful.
   It works every muscle group in the body without straining the muscles.

_____

_____

_____

Review Test   12

Combine the sentences in the following paragraph into four sentences. Omit repeated words. Try to find combinations in each case that flow as smoothly and clearly as possible.

Lena and Miles wanted a vacation. They wanted a vacation that was nice. They wanted one that was quiet. They wanted one that was relaxing. They rented a small lakeside cabin. Their first day there was very peaceful. The situation quickly changed. A large family moved into a nearby cabin. They played music at top volume. They raced around in a speedboat with a loud whining engine. Lena and Miles were no longer very relaxed. They packed up their things. They drove off. They returned to their quiet apartment.

_____

_____

_____

_____

_____

_____

_____

_____

_____

_____

_____

Four Bases for Revising Essays

This chapter will
show you how to
evaluate an essay for

- unity
- support
- coherence
- sentence skills

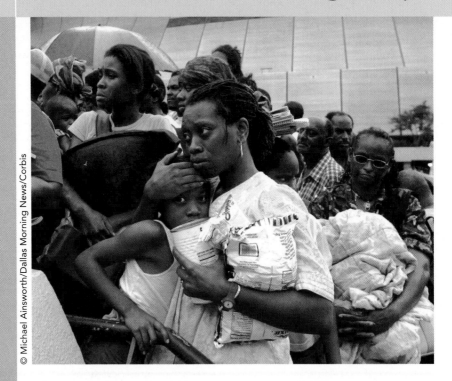

© Michael Ainsworth/Dallas Morning News/Corbis

*What emotions come to mind as you look at this photograph
taken in the aftermath of Hurricane Katrina? Write an essay
about a tragedy you have experienced in your own life. What
was the experience like and how did it change you—for better
or worse? After writing the first draft of your essay, check that
you have covered the four bases of writing: unity, support,
coherence, and sentence skills.*

In the preceding chapters, you learned four essential steps in writing an
effective paper. The box below shows how the steps lead to four standards, or bases, you can use in revising an essay.

Four Steps $\longrightarrow$	Four Bases
1 If you advance a single point and stick to that point,	your paper will have *unity*.
2 If you support the point with specific evidence,	your paper will have *support*.
3 If you organize and connect the specific evidence,	your paper will have *coherence*.
4 If you write clear, error-free sentences,	your paper will demonstrate effective *sentence skills*.

This chapter discusses these four bases—unity, support, coherence, and sentence skills—and shows how the four bases can be used to evaluate and revise a paper.

Base 1: Unity

Understanding Unity

The following student essays are on the topic "Problems or Pleasures of My Teenage Years." Which one makes its point more clearly and effectively, and why?

Teenage Pranks   Essay 1

1   Looking back at some of the things I did as a teenager makes me break out in a sweat. The purpose of each adventure was fun, but occasionally things got out of hand. In my search for good times, I was involved in three notable pranks, ranging from fairly harmless to fairly serious.

2   The first prank proved that good, clean fun does not have to be dull. As a high school student, I was credited with making the world's largest dessert. With several friends, I spent an entire year collecting boxes of Jell-O. Entering our school's indoor pool one night, we turned the water temperature up as high as it would go and poured in box after box of the strawberry powder. The next morning, school officials arrived to find the pool filled with thirteen thousand gallons of the quivering, rubbery stuff. No one was hurt by the prank, but we did suffer through three days of a massive cleanup.

3   Not all my pranks were harmless, and one involved risking my life. As soon as I got my driver's license, I wanted to join the Fliers' Club.

(continued)

Membership in this club was limited to those who could make their cars fly a distance of at least ten feet. The qualifying site was an old quarry field where friends and I had built a ramp made of dirt. I drove my battered Ford Pinto up this ramp as fast as it would go. The Pinto flew ten feet, but one of the tires exploded when I landed. The car rolled on its side, and I luckily escaped with only a bruised arm.

Risking my own life was bad enough, but there was another prank in which   4
other people could have been hurt, too. On this occasion, I accidentally set a valley on fire. Two of my friends and I were sitting on a hill sharing a few beers. It was a warm summer night, and there was absolutely nothing to do. The idea came like a thunderclap. We collected a supply of large plastic trash bags, emergency highway flares, and a half tank of helium left over from a science-fair experiment. Then we began to construct a fleet of UFOs. Filling the bags with helium, we tied them closed with wire and suspended several burning flares below each bag. Our UFOs leaped into the air like an army of invading Martians. Rising and darting in the blackness, they convinced even us. Our fun turned into horror, though, as we watched the balloons begin to drop onto the wooded valley of expensive homes below. Soon, a brushfire started and, quickly sobered, we hurried off to call the fire department anonymously.

Every so often, I think back on the things that I did as a teenager. I   5
chuckle at the innocent pranks and feel lucky that I didn't harm myself or others with the not-so-innocent ones. Those years were filled with wild times. Today I'm older, wiser—and maybe just a little more boring.

Essay 2

Problems of My Adolescence

In the unreal world of television situation comedies, teenagers are   1
carefree, smart, funny, wisecracking, secure kids. In fact, most of them are more "together" than the adults on the shows. This, however, isn't how I recall my teenage years at all. As a teen, I suffered. Every day, I battled the terrible physical, family, and social troubles of adolescence.

For one thing, I had to deal with a demoralizing physical problem—acne.   2
Some days, I would wake up in the morning with a red bump the size of a taillight on my nose. Since I worried constantly about my appearance anyway, acne outbreaks could turn me into a crying, screaming maniac. Plastering on a layer of (at the time) orange-colored Clearasil, which didn't

(continued)

fool anybody, I would slink into school, hoping that the boy I had a crush on would be absent that day. Within the last few years, however, treatments for acne have improved. Now, skin doctors prescribe special drugs that clear up pimples almost immediately. An acne attack could shatter whatever small amount of self-esteem I had managed to build up.

In addition to fighting acne, I felt compelled to fight my family. As a teenager, I needed to be independent. At that time, the most important thing in life was to be close to my friends and to try out new, more adult experiences. Unfortunately, my family seemed to get in the way. My little brother, for instance, turned into my enemy. We are close now, though. In fact, Eddie recently painted my new apartment for me. Eddie used to barge into my room, make calls on my cell phone, and read my e-mail. I would threaten to tie him up and leave him in a garbage dumpster. He would scream, my mother would yell, and all hell would break loose. My parents, too, were enemies. They wouldn't let me stay out late, wear the clothes I wanted to wear, or hang around with the friends I liked. So I tried to get revenge on them by being miserable, sulky, and sarcastic at home.

Worst of all, I had to face the social traumas of being a teenager. Things that were supposed to be fun, like dates and dances, were actually horrible. On the few occasions when I had a real date, I agonized over everything—my hair, my weight, my pimples. After a date, I would come home, raid the kitchen, and drown my insecurities in a sea of junk food. Dances were also stressful events. My friends and I would sneak a couple of beers just to get up the nerve to walk into the school gym. Now I realize that teenage drinking is dangerous. I read recently that the number-one killer of teenagers is drunk driving. At dances, I never relaxed. It was too important to look exactly right, to act really cool, and to pretend I was having fun.

I'm glad I'm not a teenager anymore. I wouldn't ever want to feel so unattractive, so confused, and so insecure again. I'll gladly accept the crow's-feet and stomach bulge of adulthood in exchange for a little peace of mind.

Fill in the blanks.

Essay _____ makes its point more clearly and effectively because _____

_____

_____

Activity 1

> EXPLANATION: Essay 1 is more effective because it is unified. All the details in this essay are on target; they support and develop each of its three topic sentences ("The first prank proved that good, clean fun does not have to be dull"; "Not all my pranks were harmless, and one involved risking my life"; and "Risking my own life was bad enough, but there was another prank where other people could have been hurt, too").
>
>   On the other hand, essay 2 contains some details irrelevant to its topic sentences. In the first supporting paragraph (paragraph 2), for example, the sentences "Within the last few years, however, treatments for acne have improved. Now, skin doctors prescribe special drugs that clear up pimples almost immediately" do not support the writer's topic statement that she had to deal with the physical problem of acne. Such details should be left out in the interest of unity.

www.mhhe.com/langan

The difference between these first two essays leads us to the first base, or standard, of effective writing: *unity*. To achieve unity is to have all the details in your paper related to your thesis and to your three supporting topic sentences. Each time you think of something to put into your paper, ask yourself whether it relates to your thesis and your supporting points. If it does not, leave it out. For example, if you were writing a paper about the problems of being unemployed and then spent a couple of sentences talking about the pleasures of having a lot of free time, you would be missing the first and most essential base of good writing.

Revising for Unity

Activity

2

Go back to essay 2 and cross out the two sentences in the second supporting paragraph (paragraph 3) and the two sentences in the third supporting paragraph (paragraph 4) that are off target and do not support their topic sentences.

Base 2: Support

Understanding Support

The following essays were written on "Dealing with Disappointment." Both are unified, but one communicates more clearly and effectively. Which one, and why?

Dealing with Disappointment

Essay 1

One way to look at life is as a series of disappointments. Life can certainly appear that way because disappointment crops up in the life of everyone more often, it seems, than satisfaction. How disappointments are handled can have a great bearing on how life is viewed. People can react negatively by sulking or by blaming others, or they can try to understand the reasons behind the disappointment.

Sulking is one way to deal with disappointment. This attitude—Why does everything always happen to me?—is common because it is easy to adopt, but it is not very productive. Everyone has had the experience of meeting people who specialize in feeling sorry for themselves. A sulky manner will often discourage others from wanting to lend support, and it prevents the sulker from making positive moves toward self-help. It becomes easier just to sit back and sulk. Unfortunately, feeling sorry for oneself does nothing to lessen the pain of disappointment. It may, in fact, increase the pain. It certainly does not make future disappointments easier to bear.

Blaming others is another negative and unproductive way to cope with disappointment. This all-too-common response of pointing the finger at someone else doesn't help one's situation. This posture will lead only to anger, resentment, and, therefore, further unhappiness. Disappointment in another's performance does not necessarily indicate that the performer is at fault. Perhaps expectations were too high, or there could have been a misunderstanding as to what the performer actually intended to accomplish.

A positive way to handle disappointment is to try to understand the reasons behind the disappointment. An analysis of the causes of disappointment can have an excellent chance of producing desirable results. Often understanding alone can help alleviate the pain of disappointment and can help prevent future disappointments. Also, it is wise to try to remember that what would be ideal is not necessarily what is reasonable to expect in any given situation. The ability to look disappointment squarely in the face and then go on from there is the first step on the road back.

Continuous handling of disappointment in a negative manner can lead to a negative view of life itself. Chances for personal happiness in such a state of being are understandably slim. Learning not to expect perfection in an imperfect world and keeping in mind those times when expectations were actually surpassed are positive steps toward allowing the joys of life to prevail.

Essay 2

Reactions to Disappointment

Ben Franklin said that the only sure things in life are death and taxes.   1
He left something out, however: disappointment. No one gets through
life without experiencing many disappointments. Strangely, though, most
people seem unprepared for disappointment and react to it in negative
ways. They feel depressed or try to escape their troubles instead of using
disappointment as an opportunity for growth.

One negative reaction to disappointment is depression. For example,   2
Helen, a woman trying to win a promotion, works hard for over a year in her
department. Helen is so sure she will get the promotion, in fact, that she
has already picked out the car she will buy when her salary increase comes
through. However, the boss names one of Helen's coworkers to the spot. The
fact that all the other department employees tell Helen that she is the one
who really deserved the promotion doesn't help her deal with the crushing
disappointment. Deeply depressed, Helen decides that all her goals are
doomed to defeat. She loses her enthusiasm for her job and can barely force
herself to show up every day. Helen tells herself that she is a failure and that
doing a good job just isn't worth the work.

Another negative reaction to disappointment, and one that often   3
follows depression, is the desire to escape. Jamal fails to get into the college
his brother is attending, the college that was the focus of all his dreams,
and decides to escape his disappointment. Why worry about college at
all? Instead, he covers up his real feelings by giving up on his schoolwork
and getting completely involved with friends, parties, and "good times." Or
Carla doesn't make the varsity basketball team—something she wanted very
badly—and so refuses to play sports at all. She decides to hang around with
a new set of friends who get high every day; then she won't have to confront
her disappointment and learn to live with it.

The positive way to react to disappointment is to use it as a chance   4
for growth. This isn't easy, but it's the only useful way to deal with an
inevitable part of life. Helen, the woman who wasn't promoted, could have
handled her disappointment by looking at other options. If her boss doesn't
recognize her talent and hard work, perhaps she could transfer to another
department. Or she could ask the boss how to improve her performance
so that she would be a shoo-in for the next promotion. Jamal, the boy who
didn't get into the college of his choice, should look into other schools.
Going to another college may encourage him to be his own person, step out
of his brother's shadow, and realize that being turned down by one college
isn't a final judgment on his abilities or potential. Rather than escape into

(continued)

drugs, Carla could improve her basketball skills for a year or pick up another sport—like swimming or tennis—that would probably turn out to be more useful to her as an adult.

Disappointments are unwelcome but regular visitors to everyone's life.   5
We can feel depressed about them, or we can try to escape from them.
The best thing, though, is to accept a disappointment and then try to use it somehow: step over the unwelcome visitor on the doorstep and get on with life.

Fill in the blanks.

Essay _____ makes its point more clearly and effectively because _____

_____

_____

Activity

3

EXPLANATION: Here, essay 2 is more effective, for it offers specific examples of the ways people deal with disappointment. We see for ourselves the kinds of reactions people have to disappointment.

Essay 1, on the other hand, gives us no specific evidence. The writer tells us repeatedly that sulking, blaming others, and trying to understand the reasons behind a disappointment are the reactions people have to a letdown. However, the writer never *shows* us any of these responses in action. Exactly what kinds of disappointments is the writer talking about? And how, for instance, does someone analyze the causes of disappointment? Would a person write a list of causes on a piece of paper, or review the causes with a concerned friend, or speak to a professional therapist? In an essay like this, we would want to see *examples* of how sulking and blaming others are negative ways of dealing with disappointment.

Consideration of these two essays leads us to the second base of effective writing: *support*. After realizing the importance of specific supporting details, one student writer revised a paper she had done on being lost in the woods as the worst experience of her childhood. In the revised paper, instead of talking about "the terror of being separated from my parents," she referred to such specifics as "tears streamed down my cheeks as I pictured the faces I would never see again"

www.mhhe.com/langan

and "I clutched the locket my parents had given me as if it were a lucky charm that could help me find my way back to the campsite." All your papers should include such vivid details.

Revising for Support

Activity

4

On a separate sheet of paper, revise one of the three supporting paragraphs in "Dealing with Disappointment" by providing specific supporting examples.

Base 3: Coherence

Understanding Coherence

The following two essays were written on the topic "Positive or Negative Effects of Television." Both are unified, and both are supported. However, one communicates more clearly and effectively. Which one, and why?

Essay 1

Harmful Effects of Watching Television

In a recent cartoon, one character said to another, "When you think of the awesome power of television to educate, aren't you glad it doesn't?" It's true that television has the power to educate and to entertain, but unfortunately, these benefits are outweighed by the harm it does to dedicated viewers. Television is harmful because it creates passivity, discourages communication, and presents a false picture of reality.   **1**

Television makes viewers passive. Children who have an electronic babysitter spend most of their waking hours in a semiconscious state. Older viewers watch tennis matches and basketball games with none of the excitement of being in the stands. Even if children are watching <u>Sesame Street</u> or <u>Barney & Friends</u>, they are being educated passively. The child actors are going on nature walks, building crafts projects, playing with animals, and participating in games, but the little viewers are simply watching. Older viewers watch guests discuss issues with Oprah Winfrey, but no one will turn to the home viewers to ask their opinion.   **2**

Worst of all, TV presents a false picture of reality that leaves viewers frustrated because they don't have the beauty or wealth of the characters on television. Viewers absorb the idea that everyone else in the United States owns a lavish apartment, a suburban house, a sleek car, and an   **3**

(continued)

---

expensive wardrobe. Every detective, police officer, oil baron, and lawyer, male or female, is suitable for a pinup poster. The material possessions on TV shows and commercials contribute to the false image of reality. News anchors and reporters, with their perfect hair and makeup, must fit television's standard of beauty. From their modest homes or cramped apartments, many viewers tune in daily to the upper-middle-class world that TV glorifies.

Television discourages communication. Families watching television do   4
very little talking except for brief exchanges during commercials. If Uncle Bernie or the next-door neighbors drop in for a visit, the most comfortable activity for everyone may be not conversation but watching ESPN. The family may not even be watching the same set; instead, in some households, all the family members head for their own rooms to watch their own sets. At dinner, plates are plopped on the coffee table in front of the set, and the meal is wolfed down during NBC Nightly News. During commercials, the only communication a family has all night may consist of questions like "Do we have any popcorn?" and "Where's TV Guide?"

Television, like cigarettes or saccharin, is harmful to our health. We   5
are becoming isolated, passive, and frustrated. And, most frightening, the average viewer now spends more time watching television than ever before.

The Benefits of Television

We hear a lot about the negative effects of television on the viewer.   1
Obviously, television can be harmful if it is watched constantly to the exclusion of other activities. It would be just as harmful to listen to CDs all the time or to eat constantly. However, when television is watched in moderation, it is extremely valuable, as it provides relaxation, entertainment, and education.

First of all, watching TV has the value of sheer relaxation. Watching   2
television can be soothing and restful after an eight-hour day of pressure, challenges, or concentration. After working hard all day, people look forward to a new episode of a favorite show or yet another showing of Casablanca or Anchorman. This period of relaxation leaves viewers refreshed and ready to take on the world again. Watching TV also seems to reduce stress in some people. This benefit of television is just beginning to be recognized. One doctor, for example, advises his patients with high blood pressure to relax in the evening with a few hours of television.

Essay 2

(continued)

In addition to being relaxing, television is entertaining. Along with the standard comedies, dramas, and game shows that provide enjoyment to viewers, television offers a variety of movies and sports events. Moreover, viewers can pay a monthly fee and receive special cable programming or Direct TV. Viewers can watch first-run movies, rock and classical music concerts, and specialized sports events, like international soccer and Grand Prix racing. Viewers can also buy or rent movies and TV shows on DVD. Still another growing area of TV entertainment is video games. PlayStation, Xbox, and Nintendo consoles allow the owner to have a video-game arcade in the living room.   3

Most important, television is educational. Preschoolers learn colors, numbers, and letters from public television programs, like Sesame Street, that use animation and puppets to make learning fun. On the Discovery Channel, science shows for older children go on location to analyze everything from volcanoes to rocket launches. Adults, too, can get an education (college credits included) from courses given on television. Also, television widens our knowledge by covering important events and current news. Viewers can see and hear presidents' speeches, state funerals, natural disasters, and election results as they are happening.   4

Perhaps because television is such a powerful force, we like to criticize it and search for its flaws. However, the benefits of television should not be ignored. We can use television to relax, to have fun, and to make ourselves smarter. This electronic wonder, then, is a servant, not a master.   5

Activity 5

Fill in the blanks.

Essay _____ makes its point more clearly and effectively because _____

_____

_____

EXPLANATION: In this case, essay 2 is more effective because the material is organized clearly and logically. Using emphatic order, the writer develops three positive uses of television, ending with the most important use: television as an educational tool. The writer includes transitional words that act as signposts, making movement from one idea to the next easy to follow. The major transitions include *First of all, In addition,* and *Most important;*

(continued)

transitions within paragraphs include such words as *Moreover, Still another, too,* and *Also.* And this writer also uses a linking sentence ("In addition to being relaxing, television is entertaining") to tie the first and second supporting paragraphs together clearly.

Although essay 1 is unified and supported, the writer does not have any clear and consistent way of organizing the material. The most important idea (signaled by the phrase *Worst of all*) is discussed in the second supporting paragraph instead of being saved for last. None of the supporting paragraphs organizes its details in a logical fashion. The first supporting paragraph, for example, discusses older viewers, then goes to younger viewers, then jumps back to older people again. The third supporting paragraph, like the first, leaps from an opening idea (families talking only during commercials) to several intervening ideas and then back to the original idea (talking during commercials). In addition, essay 1 uses practically no transitional devices to guide the reader.

These two essays lead us to the third base of effective writing: *coherence.* All the supporting ideas and sentences in a paper must be organized so that they cohere, or "stick together." As has been discussed in Chapter 4, key techniques for tying together the material in a paper include a clear method of organization (such as time order or emphatic order), transitions, and other connecting words.

www.mhhe.com/langan

Revising for Coherence

On a separate sheet of paper, revise one of the three supporting paragraphs in "Harmful Effects of Watching Television" by providing a clear method of organizing the material and transitional words.

Activity

6

Base 4: Sentence Skills

Understanding Sentence Skills

Following are the opening paragraphs from two essays. Both are unified, supported, and organized, but one version communicates more clearly and effectively. Which one, and why?

> **"revenge"**
>
> ¹Revenge is one of those things that everyone enjoy. ²People don't like   1
> to talk about it, though. ³Just the same, there is nothing more tempting,
> more satisfying, or with the reward of a bit of revenge. ⁴The purpose is
> not to harm your victims. ⁵But to let them know that you are upset about
> something they are doing. ⁶Careful plotting can provide you with relief from
> bothersom coworkers, gossiping friends, or nagging family members.
>
> ⁷Coworkers who make comments about the fact that you are always   2
> fifteen minutes late for work can be taken care of very simply. ⁸The first
> thing that you should do is to get up extra early one day. ⁹Before the sun
> comes up, drive to each coworker's house, reach under the hood of his car,
> and disconnected the center wire that leads to the distrib. cap. ¹⁰The car will
> be unharmed, but it will not start, and your friends at work will all be late for
> work on the same day. ¹¹If your lucky, your boss might notice that you are the
> only one there and will give you a raise. ¹²Later if you feel guilty about your
> actions you can call each person anonymously and tell them how to get the
> car running. . . .

> **A Bit of Revenge**
>
> Revenge is one of those things that everyone enjoys. People don't like   1
> to talk about it, though. Just the same, there is nothing more tempting, more
> satisfying, or more rewarding than a bit of revenge. The purpose is not to
> harm your victims but to let them know that you are upset about something
> they are doing to you. Careful plotting can provide you with relief from
> bothersome coworkers, gossiping friends, or nagging family members.
>
> Coworkers who make comments about the fact that you are always   2
> fifteen minutes late for work can be taken care of very simply. The first thing
> that you should do is to get up extra early one day. Before the sun comes up,
> drive to each coworker's house. Reach under the hood of your coworker's car
> and disconnect the center wire that leads to the distributor cap. The car will
> be unharmed, but it will not start, and your friends at work will all be late
> for work on the same day. If you're lucky, your boss might notice that you
> are the only one there and will give you a raise. Later, if you feel guilty about
> your actions, you can call your coworkers anonymously and tell them how
> to get their cars running again. . . .

Fill in the blanks.

Essay _____ makes its point more clearly and effectively because _____

_____

_____

EXPLANATION: Essay 2 is more effective because it uses *sentence skills*, the fourth base of competent writing. Here are the sentence-skills mistakes in essay 1:

- The title should not be set off in quotation marks.
- The first letter of the title should be capitalized.
- The singular subject *everyone* in sentence 1 should have a singular verb: *enjoy* should be *enjoys.*
- There is a lack of parallelism in sentence 3: *with the reward* of should be *more rewarding.*
- Word group 5 is a fragment; it can be corrected by attaching it to the previous sentence.
- The word *bothersom* in sentence 6 is misspelled; it should be *bothersome.*
- The word *disconnected* in sentence 9 should be *disconnect* to be consistent in tense with *reach*, the other verb in the sentence.
- The word *distrib.* in sentence 9 should be spelled out in full: *distributor.*
- The first *your* in sentence 11 stands for *you are;* an apostrophe and an *e* must be added: *you're.*
- Commas must be added in sentence 12 to set off the interrupting words.
- The words *each person* and *the car* in sentence 12 need to be changed to plural forms to agree with *them.*

Revising for Sentence Skills

Here are the final three paragraphs from the two essays. Edit the sentences in the first essay to make the corrections needed. Note that comparing essays 1 and 2 will help you locate the mistakes. This activity will also help you identify some of the sentence skills you may want to review in Part 4.

**Essay 1,
Last Part**

. . . [13]Gossiping friends at school are also perfect targets for a simple act   3
of revenge. [14]A way to trap either male or female friends are to leave phony
messages on their lockers. [15]If the friend that you want to get is male, leave
a message that a certain girl would like him to stop by her house later that
day. [16]With any luck, her boyfriend will be there. [17]The girl won't know what's
going on, and the victim will be so embarrassed that he probably won't leave
his home for a month. [18]The plan works just as well for female friends, too.

[19]When Mom and Dad and your sisters and brothers really begin to   4
annoy you, harmless revenge may be just the way to make them quite
down for a while. [20]The dinner table, where most of the nagging probably
happens, is a likely place. [21]Just before the meal begins, throw a handful of
raisins into the food. [22]Wait about 5 minutes and, after everyone has began
to eat, clamp your hand over your mouth and begin to make odd noises.
[23]When they ask you what the matter is, point to a raisin and yell, "Bugs!"
[24]Dumping the food in the disposal, the car, will head quickly for mcdonald's
[25]That night, you'll have your first quiet, peaceful meal in a long time.

[26]Well-planned revenge does not have to hurt anyone. [27]The object   5
is simply to let other people know that they are beginning to bother you.
[28]You should remember, though, to stay on your guard after completing your
revenge. [29]The reason for this is simple,. coworkers, friends, and family can
also plan revenge on you.

**Essay 2,
Last Part**

. . . Gossiping friends at school are also perfect targets for a simple act   3
of revenge. A way to trap either male or female friends is to leave phony
messages on their lockers. If the friend that you want to get is male, leave a
message that a certain girl would like him to stop by her house later that day.
With any luck, her boyfriend will be there. The girl won't know what's going
on, and the victim will be so embarrassed that he probably won't leave his
home for a month. The plan works just as well for female friends, too.

(continued)

When Mom and Dad and your sisters and brothers really begin to annoy   4
you, harmless revenge may be just the way to make them quiet down for a
while. The dinner table, where most of the nagging probably happens, is a
likely place. Just before the meal begins, throw a handful of raisins into the
food. Wait about five minutes and, after everyone has begun to eat, clamp
your hand over your mouth and begin to make odd noises. When they ask
you what the matter is, point to a raisin and yell, "Bugs!" They'll all dump their
food in the disposal, jump into the car, and head quickly for McDonald's. That
night, you'll have your first quiet, peaceful meal in a long time.

Well-planned revenge does not have to hurt anyone. The object is   5
simply to let other people know that they are beginning to bother you.
You should remember, though, to stay on your guard after completing your
revenge. The reason for this is simple. Coworkers, friends, and family can also
plan revenge on you.

Practice in Using the Four Bases

You are now familiar with four standards, or bases, of effective writing: *unity,
support, coherence,* and *sentence skills.* In this section you will expand and
strengthen your understanding of the four bases as you evaluate and revise essays
for each of them.

www.mhhe.com/langan

Revising Essays for Unity

Both of the following essays contain irrelevant sentences that do not relate to the
thesis of the essay or support the topic sentence of the paragraph in which they
appear. Cross out the irrelevant sentences and write the numbers of those sentences
in the spaces provided.

Activity

9

Playing on the Browns

Essay 1

[1]For the past three summers, I have played first base on a softball team   1
known as the Browns. [2]We play a long schedule, including playoffs, and
everybody takes the games pretty seriously. [3]In that respect, we're no different
from any other of the thousand or so teams in our city. [4]But in one respect,
we <u>are</u> different. [5]In an all-male league, we have a woman on the team—me.
[6]Thus I've had a chance to observe something about human nature by seeing

(continued)

how the men have treated me. [7]Some have been disbelieving; some have been patronizing; and, fortunately, some have simply accepted me.

[8]One new team in the league was particularly flabbergasted to see me start the game at first base. [9]Nobody on the Comets had commented one way or the other when he saw me warming up, but playing in the actual game was another story. [10]The Comets' first-base coach leaned over to me with a disbelieving grin and said, "You mean, you're starting, and those three guys are on the bench?" [11]I nodded and he shrugged, still amazed. [12]He probably thought I was the manager's wife. [13]When I came up to bat, the Comet pitcher smiled and called to his outfielders to move way in on me. [14]Now, I don't have a lot of power, but I'm not exactly feeble. [15]I used to work out on the exercise machines at a local health club until it closed, and now I lift weights at home a couple of times a week. [16]I wiped the smirks off their faces with a line drive double over the left fielder's head.

2

The number of the irrelevant sentence: _____

[17]The next game, we played another new team, the Argyles, and their attitude was patronizing. [18]The Argyles had seen me take batting practice, so they didn't do anything so rash as to draw their outfield way in. [19]They had respect for my ability as a player. [20]However, they tried to annoy me with phony concern. [21]For example, a redheaded Argyle got on base in the first inning and said to me, "You'd better be careful, hon. [22]When you have your foot on the bag, somebody might step on it. [23]You can get hurt in this game." [24]I was mad, but I have worked ou several mental techniques to control my anger because it interferes with my playing ability. [25]Well, this delicate little girl survived the season without injury, which is more than I can say for some of the he-men on the Argyles.

3

The number of the irrelevant sentence: _____

[26]Happily, most of the teams in the league have accepted me, just as the Browns did. [27]The men on the Browns coached and criticized me (and occasionally cursed me) just like anyone else. [28]Because I'm a religious person, I don't approve of cursing, but I don't say anything about it to my

4

(continued)

teammates. [29] They are not amazed when I get a hit or stretch for a wide throw. [30] My average this year was higher than the averages of several of my teammates, yet none of them acted resentful or threatened. [31] On several occasions I was taken out late in a game for a pinch runner, but other slow players on the team were also lifted at times for pinch runners. [32] Every woman should have a team like the Browns!

The number of the irrelevant sentence: _____

[33] Because I really had problems only with the new teams, I've concluded that it's when people are faced with an unfamiliar situation that they react defensively. [34] Once a rival team has gotten used to seeing me on the field, I'm no big deal. [35] Still, I suspect that the Browns secretly feel we're a little special. [36] After all, we won the championship with a woman on the team.

5

How to Con an Instructor

Essay 2

[1] Enter college, and you'll soon be reminded of the old saying "The pen is mightier than the sword." [2] That person behind the instructor's desk holds your future in his or her ink-stained hands. [3] So your first important assignment in college has nothing to do with required readings, examinations, or even the hazards of registration. [4] It is, instead, how to con an instructor.

1

[5] The first step in conning an instructor is to use body language. [6] You may be able to convince your instructor that you are special without even saying a word. [7] When you enter the classroom, be sure to sit in the front row. [8] That way, the instructor can't possibly miss you. [9] Then, as the instructor lectures, take notes frantically. [10] The instructor will be flattered that you think so much of his or her words that you want to write them all down. [11] A felt-tip pen is superior to a pen or pencil; it will help you write faster and prevent aching wrists. [12] While you are writing, be sure to smile at the instructor's jokes and nod violently in agreement with every major point. [13] Most important, as class continues, sit with your body pitched forward and your eyes wide open, fixed firmly, as if hypnotized, on your instructor's face. [14] Make your whole body suggest that you are watching a star.

2

The number of the irrelevant sentence: _____

¹⁵Once you have mastered body language, it is time to move on to the second phase of conning the instructor: class participation. ¹⁶Everyone knows that the student who is most eager to learn is the one who responds to the questions that are asked and even comes up with a few more. ¹⁷Therefore, be sure to be responsive. ¹⁸Questions such as "How does this affect the future of the United States?" or "Don't you think that someday all this will be done by computer?" can be used in any class without prior knowledge of the subject matter. ¹⁹Many students, especially in large classes, get lost in the crowd and never do anything to make themselves stand out: ²⁰Another good participation technique is to wait until the instructor has said something that sounds profound and then ask him or her to repeat it slowly so you can get it down word for word in your notes. ²¹No instructor can resist this kind of flattery.

3

The number of the irrelevant sentence: _____

²²However, the most advanced form of conning an instructor happens after class. ²³Don't be like the others who slap their notebooks closed, snatch up their books, and rush out the door before the echoes of the final bell have died away. ²⁴Did you ever notice how students begin to get restless about five minutes before class ends, even if there's no clock on the wall? ²⁵Instead, be reluctant to leave. ²⁶Approach the instructor's desk hesitantly, almost reverently. ²⁷Say that you want to find out more about the topic. ²⁸Is there any extra reading you can do? ²⁹Even better, ask if the instructor has written anything on the topic—and whether you could borrow it. ³⁰Finally, compliment your instructor by saying that this is the most interesting course you've ever taken. ³¹Nothing beats the personal approach for making an instructor think you care.

4

The number of the irrelevant sentence: _____

³²Body language, questions, after-class discussions—these are the secrets of conning an instructor that every college student should know. ³³These kinds of things go on in high school, too, and they're just as effective on that level. ³⁴Once you master these methods, you won't have to worry about a thing—until the final exam.

5

The number of the irrelevant sentence: _____

Revising Essays for Support

Both of the essays below lack supporting details at certain key points. In each essay, identify the spots where details are needed.

Activity

10

Essay 1

Formula for Happiness

1
¹Everyone has his or her own formula for happiness. ²As we go through life, we discover the activities that make us feel best. ³I've already discovered three keys to happiness. ⁴I depend on karate, music, and self-hypnosis.

2
⁵Karate helps me feel good physically. ⁶Before taking karate lessons, I was tired most of the time, my muscles felt like foam rubber, and I was twenty pounds overweight. ⁷After three months of these lessons, I saw an improvement in my physical condition. ⁸Also, my endurance has increased. ⁹At the end of my workday, I used to drag myself home to eat and watch television all night. ¹⁰Now, I have enough energy to play with my children, shop, or see a movie. ¹¹Karate has made me feel healthy, strong, and happy.

The spot where supporting details are needed occurs after sentence _____.

3
¹²Singing with a chorus has helped me achieve emotional well-being by expressing my feelings. ¹³In situations where other people would reveal their feelings, I would remain quiet. ¹⁴Since joining the chorus, however, I have an outlet for joy, anger, or sadness. ¹⁵When I sing, I pour my emotions into the music and don't have to feel shy. ¹⁶For this reason, I most enjoy singing certain kinds of music, since they demand real depth of feeling.

The first spot where supporting details are needed occurs after sentence _____.

The second spot occurs after sentence _____.

4
¹⁷Self-hypnosis gives me peace of mind. ¹⁸This is a total relaxation technique, which I learned several years ago. ¹⁹Essentially I breathe deeply and concentrate on relaxing all my muscles. ²⁰I then repeat a key suggestion to myself. ²¹Through self-hypnosis, I have gained control over several bad habits that have long been haunting me. ²²I have also learned to reduce the stress that goes along with my secretarial job. ²³Now I can handle the boss's demands or unexpected work without feeling tense.

The first spot where supporting details are needed occurs after sentence _____.

The second spot occurs after sentence _____.

---

²⁴In short, my physical, emotional, and mental well-being have been greatly increased through karate, music, and self-hypnosis. ²⁵These activities have become important elements in my formula for happiness.   5

Essay 2

Problems of a Foreign Student

¹About ten months ago I decided to leave my native country and come to the United States to study. ²When I got here, I suddenly turned into someone labeled "foreign student." ³A foreign student, I discovered, has problems. ⁴Whether from Japan, like me, or from some other country, a foreign student has to work twice as hard as Americans do to succeed in college.   1

⁵First of all, there is the language problem. ⁶American students have the advantage of comprehending English without working at it. ⁷But even they complain that some professors talk too fast, mumble, or use big words. ⁸As a result, they can't take notes fast enough to keep up, or they misunderstand what was said. ⁹Now consider my situation. ¹⁰I'm trying to cope with a language that is probably one of the hardest in the world to learn. ¹¹Dozens of English slang phrases—"mess around," "hassle," "get into"—were totally new to me. ¹²Other language problems gave me trouble, too.   2

The spot where supporting details are needed occurs after sentence _____.

---

¹³Another problem I face has to do with being a stranger to American culture. ¹⁴For instance, the academic world is much different in Japan. ¹⁵In the United States, instructors seem to treat students as equals. ¹⁶Many classes are informal, and the relationship between instructor and student is friendly; in fact, students call some instructors by their first names. ¹⁷In Japan, however, the instructor-student relationship is different. ¹⁸Lectures, too, are more formal, and students show respect by listening quietly and paying attention at all times. ¹⁹This more casual atmosphere occasionally makes me feel uncomfortable in class.   3

The spot where supporting details are needed occurs after sentence _____.

> [20]Perhaps the most difficult problem I face is social. [21]American students may have some trouble making new friends or may feel lonely at times. [22]However, they usually manage to find other people with the same background, interests, or goals. [23]It is twice as hard to make friends, though, if a person has trouble making the small talk that can lead to a relationship. [24]I find it difficult to become friends with other students because I don't understand some aspects of American life. [25]Students would rather talk to someone who is familiar with these things.   4

The spot where supporting details are needed occurs after sentence _____.

> [26]Despite all the challenges that I, as a foreign student, have to overcome, I wouldn't give up this chance to go to school in the United States. [27]Each day, the problems seem a little bit less overwhelming. [28]Like a little child who is finally learning to read, write, and make sense of things, I am starting to enjoy my experience of discovering a brand-new world.   5

Revising Essays for Coherence

Both of the essays that follow could be revised to improve their coherence. Answer the questions about coherence that come after each essay.

Activity

11

Essay 1

> **Noise Pollution**
>
> [1]Natural sounds—waves, wind, birdsong—are so soothing that companies   1
> sell recordings of them to anxious people seeking a relaxing atmosphere at home or in the car. [2]One reason why "environmental sounds" are big business is that ordinary citizens, especially city dwellers, are bombarded by noise pollution. [3]On the way to work, on the job, and on the way home, the typical urban resident must cope with a continuing barrage of unpleasant sounds.
>   [4]The noise level in an office can be unbearable. [5]From nine to   2
> five o'clock, phones and fax machines ring, computer keyboards chatter, intercoms buzz, and copy machines thump back and forth. [6]Every time the receptionists can't find people, they resort to a nerve-shattering public

(continued)

address system. [7] And because the managers worry about the employees' morale, they graciously provide the endless droning of canned music. [8] This effectively eliminates any possibility of a moment of blessed silence.

[9] Traveling home from work provides no relief from the noisiness of the office. [10] The ordinary sounds of blaring taxi horns and rumbling buses are occasionally punctuated by the ear-piercing screech of car brakes. [11] Taking a shortcut through the park will bring the weary worker face to face with chanting religious cults, freelance musicians, screaming children, and barking dogs. [12] None of these sounds can compare with the large radios many park visitors carry. [13] Each radio blasts out something different, from heavy-metal rock to baseball, at decibel levels so strong that they make eardrums throb in pain. [14] If there are birds singing or wind in the trees, the harried commuter will never hear them.   3

[15] Even a trip to work at 6 or 7 a.m. isn't quiet. [16] No matter which route a worker takes, there is bound to be a noisy construction site somewhere along the way. [17] Hard hats will shout from third-story windows to warn their coworkers below before heaving debris out and sending it crashing to earth. [18] Huge front-end loaders will crunch into these piles of rubble and back up, their warning signals letting out loud, jarring beeps. [19] Air hammers begin an earsplitting chorus of rat-a-tat-tat sounds guaranteed to shatter sanity as well as concrete. [20] Before reaching the office, the worker is already completely frazzled.   4

[21] Noise pollution is as dangerous as any other kind of pollution. [22] The endless pressure of noise probably triggers countless nervous breakdowns, vicious arguments, and bouts of depression. [23] And imagine the world problems we could solve, if only the noise stopped long enough to let us think.   5

---

1. In "Noise Pollution," what is the number of the sentence to which the transition word *Also* could be added in paragraph 2? _____

2. In the last sentence of paragraph 2, to what does the pronoun *This* refer?

    _____

3. .What is the number of the sentence to which the transition word *But* could be added in paragraph 3? _____

4. What is the number of the sentence to which the transition word *Then* could be added in paragraph 4? _____

5. What is the number of the sentence to which the transition word *Meanwhile* could be added in paragraph 4? _____

6. What word is used as a synonym for *debris* in paragraph 4? _____

7. How many times is the key word *sounds* used in the essay? _____

8. The time order of the three supporting paragraphs is confused. What is the number of the supporting paragraph that should come first? _____ Second? _____ Third? _____

Weight Loss   Essay 2

[1] The big fraternity party turned out to be the low point of my first year at college. [2] I was in heaven until I discovered that my date with handsome Greg, the fraternity vice president, was a hoax: he had used me to win the "ugliest date" contest. [3] I ran sobbing back to the dorm, wanting to resign from the human race. [4] Then I realized that it was time to stop kidding myself about my weight. [5] Within the next two years, I lost forty-two pounds and turned my life around. [6] Losing weight gave me self-confidence socially, emotionally, and professionally.   **1**

[7] I am more outgoing socially. [8] Just being able to abandon dark colors, baggy sweaters, and tent dresses in favor of bright colors, T-shirts, and designer jeans made me feel better in social situations. [9] I am able to do more things. [10] I once turned down an invitation for a great camping trip with my best friend's family, making up excuses about sun poisoning and allergies. [11] Really, I was too embarrassed to tell them that I couldn't fit into the bathroom in their Winnebago! [12] I made up for it last summer when I was one of the organizers of a college backpacking trip through the Rockies.   **2**

[13] Most important, losing weight helped me seek new professional goals. [14] When I was obese, I organized my whole life around my weight, as if it were a defect I could do nothing about. [15] With my good grades, I could have chosen almost any major the college offered, but I had limited my goal to teaching kindergarten because I felt that little children wouldn't judge how I looked. [16] Once I was no longer fat, I realized that I love working with all sorts of people. [17] I became a campus guide and even had small parts in college theater productions. [18] As a result, last year I changed my major to public relations. [19] The area fascinates me, and I now have good job prospects there.   **3**

(continued)

^{20}I have also become more emotionally honest. ^{21}Rose, at the college   **4**
counseling center, helped me see that my "fat and jolly" personality had
been false. ^{22}I was afraid others would reject me if I didn't always go along
with their suggestions. ^{23}I eventually put Rose's advice to the test. ^{24}My
roommates were planning an evening at a Greek restaurant. ^{25}I loved the
restaurant's atmosphere, but there wasn't much I liked on the menu. ^{26}Finally,
in a shaky voice I said, "Actually, I'm not crazy about lamb. ^{27}How about
Chinese food?" ^{28}They scolded me for not mentioning it before, and we
had dinner at a Chinese restaurant. ^{29}We all agreed it was one of our best
evenings out.

^{30}Fortunately, the low point of my first year turned out to be the turning   **5**
point, leading to what promises to be an exciting senior year. ^{31}Greg's cruel
joke became a strange sort of favor, and I've gone from wanting to resign
from the human race to welcoming each day as a source of fresh adventure
and self-discovery.

1. In "Weight Loss," what is the number of the sentence to which the transition

   words *For one thing* could be added in paragraph 2? _____

2. What is the number of the sentence to which the transition word *Also* could be

   added in paragraph 2? _____

3. What is the number of the sentence to which the transition word *But* could be

   added in paragraph 2? _____

4. In sentence 11, to what does the pronoun *them* refer? _____

   _____

5. What is the number of the sentence to which the transition word *However*

   could be added in paragraph 3? _____

6. What word is used as a synonym for *obese* in paragraph 3? _____

7. How many times is the keyword *weight* used in the essay? _____

8. What is the number of the supporting paragraph that should be placed in the

   emphatic final position? _____

Revising Essays for All Four Bases: Unity, Support, Coherence, and Sentence Skills

In this activity, you will evaluate and revise two essays in terms of all four bases: unity, support, coherence, and sentence skills. Comments follow each supporting paragraph. Circle the letter of the statement that applies in each case.

Activity

12

Chiggers

Essay 1

I had lived my whole life not knowing what chiggers are. I thought they 1 were probably a type of insect Humphrey Bogart encountered in The African Queen. I never had any real reason to care, until one day last summer. Within twenty-four hours, I had vividly experienced what chigger bites are, learned how to treat them, and learned how to prevent them.

First of all, I learned that chiggers are the larvae of tiny mites found in the 2 woods and that their bites are always multiple and cause intense itching. A beautiful summer day seemed perfect for a walk in the woods. I am definitely not a city person, for I couldn't stand to be surrounded by people, noise, and concrete. As I walked through the ferns and pines, I noticed what appeared to be a dusting of reddish seeds or pollen on my slacks. Looking more closely, I realized that each speck was a tiny insect. I casually brushed off a few and gave them no further thought. I woke up the next morning feeling like a victim staked to an anthill by an enemy wise in the ways of torture. Most of my body was speckled with measlelike bumps that at the slightest touch burned and itched like a mosquito bite raised to the twentieth power. When antiseptics and calamine lotion failed to help, I raced to my doctor for emergency aid.

a. Paragraph 2 contains an irrelevant sentence.

b. Paragraph 2 lacks supporting details at one key spot.

c. Time order in paragraph 2 is confused.

d. Paragraph 2 contains two run-ons.

Healing the bites of chiggers, as the doctor diagnosed them to be, is not 3 done overnight. It seems that there is really no wonder drug or commercial product to help. The victim must rely on a primitive home remedy and mostly wait out the course of the painful bites. First, the doctor explained, the skin must be bathed carefully with warm soapy water. An antihistamine spray applied several hours later will not cure the bites but will soothe the intense itching and help prevent infection. A few days after the treatment,

(continued)

the bites finally healed. Although I was in pain, and desperate for relief, I followed the doctor's instructions.

a.   Paragraph 3 contains an irrelevant sentence.

b.   Paragraph 3 lacks supporting details at one key spot.

c.   Time order in paragraph 3 is confused.

d.   Paragraph 3 contains one fragment.

Most important of all, I learned what to do to prevent getting chigger **4**
bites in the future. Mainly, of course, stay out of the woods in the summertime. But if the temptation is too great on an especially beautiful day, I'll be sure to wear the right type of clothing, like a long-sleeved shirt, long pants, knee socks, and closed shoes. In addition, I'll cover myself with clouds of superstrength insect repellent. I will then shower thoroughly as soon as I get home, I also will probably burn all my clothes if I notice even one suspicious red speck.

a.   Paragraph 4 contains an irrelevant sentence.

b.   Paragraph 4 lacks supporting details at one key spot.

c.   Paragraph 4 lacks transitional words.

d.   Paragraph 4 contains a run-on and a fragment.

I will never forget my lessons on the cause, cure, and prevention of **5**
chigger bites. I'd gladly accept the challenge of rattlesnakes and scorpions in the wilds of the West but will never again confront a siege of chiggers in the pinewoods.

Essay 2

The Hazards of Being an Only Child

Many people who have grown up in multichild families think that being **1**
an only child is the best of all possible worlds. They point to such benefits as the only child's annual new wardrobe and the lack of competition for parental love. But single-child status isn't as good as people say it is. Instead of having everything they want, only children are sometimes denied certain basic human needs.

Only children lack companionship. An only child can have trouble **2**
making friends, since he or she isn't used to being around other children.

(continued)

Often, the only child comes home to an empty house; both parents are working, and there are no brothers or sisters to play with or to talk to about the day. At dinner, the single child can't tell jokes, giggle, or throw food while the adults discuss boring adult subjects. An only child always has his or her own room but never has anyone to whisper to half the night when sleep doesn't come. Some only children thrive on this isolation and channel their energies into creative activities like writing or drawing. Owing to this lack of companionship, an only child sometimes lacks the social ease and self-confidence that come from being part of a close-knit group of contemporaries.

a.   Paragraph 2 contains an irrelevant sentence.

b.   Paragraph 2 lacks supporting details at one key spot.

c.   Paragraph 2 lacks transitional words.

d.   Paragraph 2 contains one fragment and one run-on.

Second, only children lack privacy. An only child is automatically the center of parental concern. There's never any doubt about which child tried to sneak in after midnight on a weekday. And who will get the lecture the next morning. Also, whenever an only child gives in to a bad mood, runs into his or her room, and slams the door, the door will open thirty seconds later, revealing an anxious parent. Parents of only children sometimes don't even understand the child's need for privacy. For example, they may not understand why a teenager wants a lock on the door or a personal telephone. After all, the parents think, there are only the three of us, there's no need for secrets.   3

a.   Paragraph 3 contains an irrelevant sentence.

b.   Paragraph 3 lacks supporting details at one key spot.

c.   Paragraph 3 lacks transitional words.

d.   Paragraph 3 contains one fragment and one run-on.

Most important, only children lack power. They get all the love; but if something goes wrong, they also get all the punishment. When a bottle of perfume is knocked to the floor or the television is left on all night, there's no little sister or brother to blame it on. Moreover, an only child has no recourse when asking for a privilege of some kind, such as permission to stay out late or to take an overnight trip with friends. There are no other siblings to point to and say, "You let them do it. Why won't you let me?" With no   4

(continued)

allies their own age, only children are always outnumbered, two to one. An only child hasn't a chance of influencing any major family decisions, either.

a. Paragraph 4 contains an irrelevant sentence.

b. Paragraph 4 lacks supporting details at one key spot.

c. Paragraph 4 lacks transitional words.

d. Paragraph 4 contains one fragment and one run-on.

Being an only child isn't as special as some people think. It's no fun being 5 without friends, without privacy, and without power in one's own home. But the child who can triumph over these hardships grows up self-reliant and strong. Perhaps for this reason alone, the hazards are worth it.

Patterns of Essay Development

PART 2

© Lawrence Manning/Corbis

© Eddie Gerald/Alamy

Yahoo! Used with permission.

PREVIEW

7 Introduction to Essay Development

8 Description

9 Narration

10 Exemplification

11 Process

12 Cause and Effect

13 Comparison or Contrast

14 Definition

15 Division-Classification

16 Argument

What do all of the images shown here have in common? They can all be classified as news sources. Think about the many different formats available for getting the news today. Then select three formats and write an essay in which you discuss the unique qualities of each.

7 Introduction to Essay Development

This chapter will

- introduce you to nine patterns of essay development
- explain the importance of understanding the nature and length of an assignment
- explain the importance of knowing your subject, your purpose, and your audience
- explain the three different points of view used in writing
- show you how to conduct a peer review and personal review

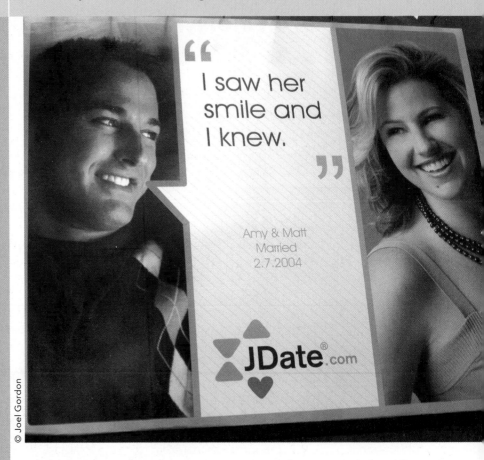

Who is the intended audience of this advertisement? Write a description of the intended audience.

Important Considerations in Essay Development

When you begin work on particular types of essays, keep in mind several general considerations about writing; they are discussed in the following pages.

Understanding the Nature and Length of an Assignment

In all likelihood, your college writing assignments will have a good deal of variety. Sometimes you will be able to write on a topic of your own choosing or on a point you discover within a given topic; at other times you may be given a very specific assignment. In any case, do not start writing a paper until you know exactly what is expected.

First of all, be clear about *what kind of paper* the instructor has in mind. Should it be primarily a research paper summarizing other people's ideas? Should it consist entirely of your own ideas? Should it consist of a comparison of your ideas with those of a given author? Should it be something else? If you are not sure about the nature of an assignment, other students may be confused as well. Do not hesitate, then, to ask an instructor about an assignment. Most instructors are more than willing to provide an explanation. They would rather spend a few minutes of class time explaining an assignment than spend hours reading student essays that miss the mark.

Second, find out right at the start *how long* a paper is expected to be. Many instructors will indicate the approximate length of the papers they assign. Knowing the expected length of a paper will help you decide exactly how detailed your treatment of a subject should be.

Knowing Your Subject

Whenever possible, try to write on a subject that interests you. You will then find it easier to put more time into your work. Even more important, try to write on a subject that you already know something about. If you do not have direct experience with the subject, you should at least have indirect experience—knowledge gained through thinking, reading, or talking about the subject as well as from prewriting.

If you are asked to write on a topic about which you have no experience or knowledge, do whatever research is required to gain the background information you may need. Chapter 21, "Using the Library and the Internet," will show you how to look up relevant information. Without direct or indirect experience, or the information you gain through research, you may not be able to provide the specific evidence needed to develop an essay.

Knowing Your Purpose and Audience

The three most common purposes of writing are *to inform, to persuade*, and *to entertain*. As noted previously, much of the writing you do in this book will involve some form of argumentation or persuasion. You will advance a point or thesis and then support it in a variety of ways. To some extent, also, you will write papers to inform—to provide readers with information about a particular subject. And since, in practice, writing often combines purposes, you might also find yourself at times providing vivid or humorous details to entertain your readers.

Your audience will be primarily your instructor and sometimes other students. Your instructor is really a symbol of the larger audience you should see yourself writing for—educated adult readers who expect you to present your ideas in a clear, direct, organized way. If you can learn to write to persuade or inform such a general audience, you will have accomplished a great deal.

It will also be helpful for you to write some papers for a more specific audience. By doing so, you will develop an ability to choose words and adopt a tone and point of view that are just right for a given audience. This part of the book includes assignments asking you to write with very specific purposes in mind and for very specific audiences.

www.mhhe.com/langan

Determining Your Point of View

When you write, you can take any of three approaches, or points of view: first person, second person, or third person.

First-Person Approach

In the first-person approach—a strongly individualized point of view—you draw on your own experience and speak to your audience in your own voice, using pronouns like *I, me, mine, we, our*, and *us*.

The first-person approach is most common in narrative essays based on personal experience. It also suits other essays where most of the evidence presented consists of personal observation.

Here is a first-person supporting paragraph from an essay on camping:

> First of all, I like comfort when I'm camping. My motor home, with its completely equipped kitchen, shower stall, toilet, double bed, and flatscreen television, resembles a mobile motel room. I can sleep on a real mattress, clean sheets, and fluffy pillows. Next to my bed are devices that make me feel at home: a Bose radio, an alarm clock, and a remote control. Unlike the poor campers huddled in tents, I don't have to worry about cold, rain, heat,
>
> *(continued)*

or annoying insects. After a hot shower, I can slide into my best nightgown, sit comfortably on my down-filled quilt, and read the latest best seller while a thunderstorm booms outside.

Second-Person Approach

In the second-person approach, the writer speaks directly to the reader, using the pronoun *you*. The second-person approach is considered appropriate for giving direct instructions and explanations to the reader. That is why *you* is used throughout this book.

   You should plan to use the second-person approach only when writing a process essay. Otherwise, as a general rule, never use the word *you* in writing.

> **TIP:** If using *you* has been a common mistake in your writing, you should review the rule about pronoun point of view on pages 114–115.

Third-Person Approach

The third-person approach is by far the most common point of view in academic writing. In the third person, the writer includes no direct references to the reader (*you*) or the self (*I, me*). Third person gets its name from the stance it suggests—that of an outsider or "third person" observing and reporting on matters of public rather than private importance. In this approach, you draw on information achieved through observation, thinking, or reading.

   Here is a similar paragraph on camping, recast in the third person. Note the third-person pronouns *their, them,* and *they,* which all refer to *campers* in the first sentence.

First of all, modern campers bring complete bedrooms with them. Winnebagos, Airstream motor homes, and Fleetwood recreational vehicles lumber into America's campgrounds every summer like mobile motel rooms. All the comforts of home are provided inside. Campers sleep on real mattresses with clean sheets and fluffy pillows. Next to their beds are the same gadgets that litter their night tables at home—Bose radios, alarm clocks, and remote controls. It's not necessary for them to worry about

(continued)

annoyances like cold, heat, rain, or buzzing insects, either. They can sit comfortably in bed and read the latest best sellers while a thunderstorm booms outside.

Using Peer Review

In addition to having your instructor as an audience for your writing, you will benefit from having other students in your class as an audience. On the day a paper is due, or on a day when you are writing papers in class, your instructor may ask you to pair up with another student (or students). That student will read your paper, and you will read his or her paper.

Ideally, read the other paper aloud while your peer listens. If that is not practical, read it in a whisper while your peer looks on. As you read, both you and your peer should look and listen for spots where the paper does not read smoothly and clearly. Check or circle the trouble spots where your reading snags.

Your peer should then read your paper, marking possible trouble spots. Then each of you should do three things.

1 Identification

At the top of a separate sheet of paper, write the title and author of the paper you have read. Under it, write your name as the reader of the paper.

2 Scratch Outline

"X-ray" the paper for its inner logic by making up a scratch outline. The scratch outline need be no more than twenty words or so, but it should show clearly the logical foundation on which the essay is built. It should identify and summarize the overall point of the paper and the three areas of support for the point.

Your outline can look like this:

Point: _____

Support:

(1) _____

(2) _____

(3) _____

For example, here is a scratch outline of the essay on moviegoing on page 4:

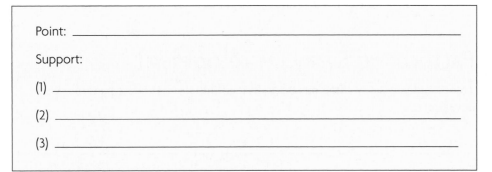

Point: _____

Support:

(1) _____

(2) _____

(3) _____

3 Comments

Under the outline, write a heading: "Comments." Here is what you should comment on:

- Look at the spots where your reading of the paper snagged. Are words missing or misspelled? Is there a lack of parallel structure? Are there mistakes with punctuation? Is the meaning of a sentence confused? Try to figure out what the problems are and suggest ways to fix them.

- Are there spots in the paper where you see problems with *unity, support,* or *organization*? (You'll find it helpful to refer to the Four Bases checklist on the inside back cover of this book.) If so, offer comments. For example, you might say, "More details are needed in the first supporting paragraph," or, "Some of the details in the last supporting paragraph don't really back up your point."

- Finally, note something you really liked about the paper, such as good use of transitions or an especially realistic or vivid specific detail.

After you have completed your evaluation of the paper, give it to your peer. Your instructor may give you the option of rewriting a paper in light of the feedback you get. Whether or not you rewrite, be sure to hand in the peer-evaluation form with your paper.

Doing a Personal Review

1. While you're writing and revising an essay, you should be constantly evaluating it in terms of *unity, support*, and *coherence*. Use as a guide the detailed checklist on the inside back cover of the book.

2. After you've finished the next-to-final draft of an essay, check it for the *sentence skills* listed on the inside back cover. It may also help to read the paper out loud. If a given sentence does not sound right—that is, if it does

not read clearly and smoothly—chances are something is wrong. Then revise or edit as needed until your paper is error-free.

Patterns of Essay Development

Traditionally, essay writing has been divided into the following patterns of development:

- Description
- Narration
- Exposition

Exemplification	Comparison or contrast
Process	Definition
Cause and effect	Division-classification

- Argument

A *description* is a verbal picture of a person, place, or thing. In *narration,* a writer tells the story of something that happened.

In *exposition,* the writer provides information about and explains a particular subject. Patterns of development within exposition include giving examples (*exemplification*), detailing a *process* of doing or making something, analyzing *causes and effects, comparing or contrasting, defining* a term or concept, and *dividing* something into parts or *classifying* it into categories.

Finally, in *argument,* a writer attempts to support a controversial point or to defend a position on which there is a difference of opinion.

The pages ahead present individual chapters on each pattern. You will have a chance, then, to learn nine different patterns or methods for organizing material in your papers. Each pattern has its own internal logic and provides its own special strategies for imposing order on your ideas. As you practice each pattern, keep these two points in mind:

- **While each essay that you write will involve one predominant pattern, very often one or more additional patterns may be involved**. For example, consider the two student essays in Chapter 10, "Exemplification." The first essay there, "Look on the Bright Side" (pages 231–233), is developed through a series of *examples*. But there is also an element of *narration,* because the writer presents examples that occur as he proceeds through his day. In the second essay, "Altered States" (pages 233–234), *exemplification* is again the predominant pattern, but in a lesser way the author is also explaining the *causes* of altered states of mind.

- **No matter which pattern or patterns you use, each essay will probably involve some form of argumentation**. You will advance a point and then go on to support that point. In "Look on the Bright Side," for instance, the author uses *exemplification* to support his point that people inflict little cruelties on each other. In "The Diner at Midnight," a writer supports the point that a particular diner is depressing by providing a number of *descriptive details* (see pages 186–187). In "A Night of Violence," another writer claims that a certain experience in his life was frightening and then uses a *narrative* to persuade us of the truth of this statement (see pages 211–212). Yet another author states that a fast-food restaurant can be preferable to a fancy one and then supplies *comparative information* about both to support his statement (see page 303, "A Vote for McDonald's"). Much of your writing, in short, will have the purpose of persuading your reader that the idea you have advanced is valid.

The Progression in Each Chapter

In Chapters 8 through 16, after each type of essay development is explained, student essays and a professional essay illustrating that pattern are presented, followed by questions about the essays. The questions relate to unity, support, and coherence—principles of effective writing explained earlier in this book and outlined on the inside back cover. You are then asked to write your own essay. In most cases, the first assignment is fairly structured and provides a good deal of guidance for the writing process. The other assignments offer a wide choice of writing topics. In each case, one assignment involves writing an essay with a specific purpose and for a specific audience. And in three instances (exemplification, cause and effect, and comparison or contrast), the final assignments require outside reading of literary works; a student model is provided for each of these assignments.

8

Description

This chapter will explain and illustrate how to

- develop a descriptive essay
- write a descriptive essay
- revise a descriptive essay

In addition, you will read and consider

- two student descriptive essays
- one professional descriptive essay

© Photographers Choice RF/SuperStock

Think about your college graduation day and write an essay about what you imagine it will be like. How will you feel? What sights and sounds will surround you? Will your family and friends be there to congratulate you? Describe the day and bring it to life in your essay.

When you describe someone or something, you give your readers a picture in words. To make the word picture as vivid and real as possible, you must observe and record specific details that appeal to your readers' senses (sight, hearing, taste, smell, and touch). More than any other type of essay, a descriptive paper needs sharp, colorful details.

Here is a sentence in which there is almost no appeal to the senses: "In the window was a fan." In contrast, here is a description rich in sense impressions: "The blades of the rusty window fan clattered and whirled as they blew out a stream of warm, soggy air." Sense impressions in this second example include sight (*rusty window fan, whirled*), hearing (*clattered*), and touch (*warm, soggy air*). The vividness and sharpness provided by the sensory details give us a clear picture of the fan and enable us to share the writer's experience.

In this chapter, you will be asked to describe a person, place, or thing sharply, by using words rich in sensory details. To prepare for this assignment, read the student essays and the professional essay that follow and work through the questions that accompany each piece of writing.

Student Essays to Consider

Family Portrait

My great-grandmother, who is ninety-five years old, recently sent me a **1** photograph of herself that I had never seen before. While cleaning out the attic of her Florida home, she came across a studio portrait she had had taken about a year before she married my great-grandfather. This picture of my great-grandmother as a twenty-year-old girl and the story behind it have fascinated me from the moment I began to consider it.

The young woman in the picture has a face that resembles my own **2** in many ways. Her face is a bit more oval than mine, but the softly waving brown hair around it is identical. The small, straight nose is the same model I was born with. My great-grandmother's mouth is closed, yet there is just the slightest hint of a smile on her full lips. I know that if she had smiled, she would have shown the same wide grin and down-curving "smile lines" that appear in my own snapshots. The most haunting feature in the photo, however, is my great-grandmother's eyes. They are an exact duplicate of my own large, dark brown ones. Her brows are plucked into thin lines, which are like two pencil strokes added to highlight those fine, luminous eyes.

I've also carefully studied the clothing and jewelry in the photograph. **3** Although the photo was taken seventy-five years ago, my great-grandmother is wearing a blouse and skirt that could easily be worn today. The blouse is

(continued)

---

made of heavy eggshell-colored satin and reflects the light in its folds and hollows. It has a turned-down cowl collar and smocking on the shoulders and below the collar. The smocking (tiny rows of gathered material) looks hand-done. The skirt, which covers my great-grandmother's calves, is straight and made of light wool or flannel. My great-grandmother is wearing silver drop earrings. They are about two inches long and roughly shield-shaped. On her left wrist is a matching bracelet. My great-grandmother can't find this bracelet now, despite our having spent hours searching through the attic for it. On the third finger of her left hand is a ring with a large, square-cut stone.

The story behind the picture is as interesting to me as the young woman   4
it captures. Great-Grandmother, who was earning twenty-five dollars a week as a file clerk, decided to give her boyfriend (my great-grandfather) a picture of herself. She spent almost two weeks' salary on the skirt and blouse, which she bought at a fancy department store downtown. She borrowed the earrings and bracelet from her older sister, Dorothy. The ring she wore was a present from another young man she was dating at the time. Great-Grandmother spent another chunk of her salary to pay the portrait photographer for the hand-tinted print in old-fashioned tones of brown and tan. Just before giving the picture to my great-grandfather, she scrawled at the lower left, "Sincerely, Beatrice."

When I study this picture, I react in many ways. I think about the trouble   5
that my great-grandmother went to in order to impress the young man who was to be my great-grandfather. I laugh when I look at the ring, which was probably worn to make him jealous. I smile at the serious, formal inscription my great-grandmother used at this stage of the budding relationship. Sometimes, I am filled with a mixture of pleasure and sadness when I look at this frozen long-ago moment. It is a moment of beauty, of love, and—in a way—of my own past.

The Diner at Midnight

I've been in lots of diners, and they've always seemed to be warm, busy,   1
friendly, happy places. That's why, on a recent Monday night, I stopped in a diner for a cup of coffee. I was returning home after an all-day car trip and needed something to help me get through the last forty-five miles. I'd been visiting my cousins, whom I try to get together with at least twice a year. A diner at midnight, however, was not the place I had expected—it was different, and lonely.

(continued)

Even the outside of the diner was uninviting. My Focus pulled to a halt in   2
front of the dreary gray aluminum building, which looked like an old railroad car.
A half-lit neon sign, sputtering the message "Fresh baked goods daily," reflected
on the surface of the rain-slick parking lot. Only half a dozen cars and a battered
pickup were scattered around the lot. An empty paper coffee cup made a
hollow scraping sound as it rolled in small circles on one cement step close to
the entrance. I pulled hard at the balky glass door, and it banged shut behind me.

The diner was quiet when I entered. As there was no hostess on duty,   3
only the faint odor of stale grease and the dull hum of an empty refrigerated
pastry case greeted me. The outside walls were lined with vacant booths that
squatted back to back in their black vinyl upholstery. On each black-and-white
checkerboard-patterned table were the usual accessories—glass salt and
pepper shakers, ketchup bottle, sugar packets—silently waiting for the next
morning's breakfast crowd. I glanced through the round windows on the two
swinging metal doors leading to the kitchen. I could see only part of the
large, apparently deserted cooking area, with a shiny stainless-steel range
and blackened pans of various sizes and shapes hanging along a ledge.

I slid onto one of the cracked vinyl seats at the Formica counter. Two men   4
in rumpled work shirts also sat at the counter, on stools several feet apart,
smoking cigarettes and staring wearily into cups of coffee. Their faces sprouted
what looked like a day-old stubble of beard. I figured they were probably shift
workers who, for some reason, didn't want to go home. Three stools down from
the workers, I spotted a thin young man with a mop of curly black hair. He was
dressed in new-looking jeans and a black polo shirt, unbuttoned at the neck. He
wore a blank expression as he picked at a plate of limp french fries. I wondered
if he had just returned from a disappointing date. At the one occupied booth
sat a middle-aged couple. They hadn't gotten any food yet. He was staring off
into space, idly tapping his spoon against the table, while she drew aimless
parallel lines on her paper napkin with a bent dinner fork. Neither said a word
to the other. The people in the diner seemed as lonely as the place itself.

Finally, a tired-looking waitress approached me with her thick order pad.   5
I ordered the coffee, but I wanted to drink it fast and get out of there. My
car, and the solitary miles ahead of me, would be lonely. But they wouldn't
be as lonely as that diner at midnight.

About Unity

1. In which supporting paragraph of "The Diner at Midnight" does the topic
   sentence appear at the paragraph's end, rather than the beginning?
   a. paragraph 2
   b. paragraph 3
   c. paragraph 4

Questions

1

2. Which sentence in paragraph 1 of "The Diner at Midnight" should be eliminated and why should it be eliminated? (*Write your answer here.*)

_____

_____

3. Which sentence in paragraph 3 of "Family Portrait" should be eliminated and why? (*Write your answer here.*)

_____

_____

About Support

4. In paragraph 3 of "Family Portrait," the writer goes beyond the mere mention of clothing and jewelry. Focus on ane item and summarize the details she includes to make the object clearer to the reader. (*Write your answer here.*)

_____

_____

_____

5. Label as sight, touch, hearing, or smell all the sensory details in the following sentences taken from the two essays. The first one is done for you as an example.

                sight   *smell*

   a. "As there was no hostess on duty, only the faint odor of stale grease and
        hearing   *sight*
     the dull hum of an empty refrigerated pastry case greeted me."

   b. "He was staring off into space, idly tapping his spoon against the table, while she drew aimless parallel lines on her paper napkin with a bent dinner fork."

   c. "The blouse is made of heavy eggshell-colored satin and reflects the light in its folds and hollows."

   d. Her brows are plucked into thin lines, which are like two pencil strokes added to highlight those fine, luminous eyes.

6. Could the author have added more details to her description of her great-grandmother? Provide two or three you would add. (*Write your answer here.*)

_____

About Coherence

7. Which method of organization does paragraph 2 of "Family Portrait" use?

   a. Time order

   b. Emphatic order

8. What sentence in paragraph 2 of "Family Portrait" serves as a transition?
   (*Write the first words.*)

   _____

9. Find at least four transitions and connecting words in paragraph 4 of "The
   Diner at Midnight." Remember that repeated words, pronouns, and synonyms
   can act as connectors.

   _____

   _____

About the Introduction and Conclusion

10. What method discussed in Chapter 4 is used in the introduction to "The
    Diner at Midnight?"

    _____

Developing a Descriptive Essay

Considering Purpose and Audience

The main purpose of a descriptive essay is to make readers see—or hear, taste, smell,
or feel—what you are writing about. Vivid details are the key to descriptive essays,
enabling your audience to picture and, in a way, experience what you describe.

As you start to think about your own descriptive essay, choose a topic that appeals
strongly to at least one of your senses. It's possible to write a descriptive essay, maybe
even a good one, about a boiled potato. But it would be easier (not to mention more
fun) to describe a bowl of potato salad, with its contrasting textures of soft potato,
crisp celery, and spongy hard-boiled egg: the crunch of the diced onion, the biting
taste of the bits of pickle, the salad's creamy dressing and its tangy seasonings. The
more senses you involve, the more likely your audience is to enjoy your paper.

Also, when selecting your topic, consider how much your audience already
knows about it. If your topic is a familiar one—for instance, potato salad—you can
assume your audience already understands the general idea. However, if you are
presenting something new or unfamiliar to your readers—perhaps a description of
one of your relatives or a place where you've lived—you must provide background
information.

Once you have selected your topic, focus on the goal or purpose of your essay. What message do you hope to convey to your audience? For instance, if you chose as your topic a playground you used to visit as a child, decide what dominant impression you want to communicate. Is your goal to make readers see the park as a pleasant play area, or do you want them to see it as a dangerous place? If you choose the second option, focus on conveying that sense of danger to your audience. Then jot down any details that support that idea. You might describe broken beer bottles on the asphalt, graffiti sprayed on the metal jungle gym, or a pack of loud teenagers gathered on a nearby street corner. In this case, the details support your overall purpose, creating a threatening picture that your audience can see and understand.

Visualizing the Subject

Physical description relies solely on sense impressions. Of course, all five senses can be used when describing. However, perhaps the most important sense is sight, and many of us can be classified as visual learners. Therefore, one advantage that description has over other methods of development is that it allows the writer to visualize his or her subject before describing it in words.

If you like to draw or paint, make an image of your subject before you start writing about him, her, or it. If possible, use different colors to reveal the complexity of your subject, apply perspective to give your picture depth and contrast, or add small details like a tiny mole, a button on a shirt, or a stain on a tie.

When you are done, use the picture as inspiration as you gather information during prewriting.

Including People and Events in the Description of a Place

Discussing the type of people who are in a place can sometimes give clues to its character and help describe it. The same can be said for what happens there. For example, a bar where middle-aged men quietly drink beer and watch a hockey game on TV is one thing; a bar where young people dance to loud music is quite another. The author of "The Diner at Midnight" describes the restaurant's patrons in paragraph 3 in order to reinforce the lonely atmosphere of the place. We learn about two men sitting at the counter several feet apart as if "they didn't want to go home." A little further down, we spot a young man with "a blank expression." Finally, at a booth sit a middle-aged couple, neither of whom is speaking to the other.

You might even describe animals and their actions to enliven your description of a place. Say you're writing about a zoo. It might be worth discussing the antics of chimpanzees or the majestic pacing of a tiger as it struts within its habitat.

Finally, consider including dialogue. You will learn more about creating dialogue in Chapter 9, "Narration." For now just remember that dialogue can sometimes reveal a great deal about a person or a place. For example, our first clue that the owner of the café in "Lou's Place" (an essay appearing later in this chapter) is rather feisty is his response to a woman who wants to know if he's open: "I'm here, aren't I?" Later, when another customer asks for breakfast, Lou says, "I'm reading the paper. . . . Eggs are in the refrigerator."

Development through Prewriting

When Cindy, the author of "Family Portrait," sat down to think about a topic for her essay, she looked around her apartment for inspiration. First she thought about describing her own bedroom. But she had moved into the apartment only recently and hadn't done much in the way of decorating, so the room struck her as too bare and sterile. Then she looked out her window, thinking of describing the view. That seemed much more promising: she noticed the sights and sounds of children playing on the sidewalks and a group of older men playing cards, as well as smells— neighbors' cooking and exhaust from passing traffic. She was jotting down some details for such an essay when she glanced up at the framed portrait of her great-grandmother on her desk. "I stopped and stared at it, as I often do, wondering again about this twenty-year-old girl who became my great-grandmother," she said. "While I sat there studying it, I realized that the best topic of all was right under my nose."

As she looked at the photograph, Cindy began to freewrite. This is what she wrote:

> Great-Grandma is twenty in the picture. She's wearing a beautiful skirt and blouse and jewelry she borrowed from Dorothy. Looks a lot like me— nose, eyes, mouth. She's shorter than I am but you really can't tell in picture. Looks a lot like old photos I've seen of Grandma too—all the Diaz women resemble each other. Earrings and bracelet are of silver and they match. Ring might be amber or topaz? We've laughed about the "other man" who gave it to her. Her brown hair is down loose on her shoulders. She's smiling a little. That doesn't really look like her—her usual smile is bigger and opens her mouth. Looking at the photo makes me a little sad even though I really like it. Makes me realize how much older she's getting and I wonder how long she'll be with us. It's funny to see a picture of your great-grandmother at a younger age than you are now—stirs up all kinds of weird feelings. Picture was taken at a studio in Houston to give to Great-Grandpa. Signed "Sincerely, Beatrice." So serious! Hard to imagine them being so formal with each other.

Cindy looked over her notes and thought about how she might organize her essay. First she thought only of describing how the photograph *looked*. With that in mind, she thought her main points might be (1) what her great-grandmother's face looked like and (2) what her great-grandmother was wearing. But she was stuck for a third main point.

Studying her notes again, Cindy noticed two other possible main points. One was her own emotional reaction to the photo—how it made her feel. The other was the story of the photo—how and why it was taken. Not sure which of those two she would use as her third main point, she began to write. Her first draft follows.

First Draft

Family Portrait

I have a photograph of my great-grandmother that was taken seventy-five years ago, when she was only twenty. She sent it to me only recently, and I find it very interesting.

In the photo, I see a girl who looks a good deal like I do now at twenty-two. Like most of the women in her family, including me, the girl in the picture has the Diaz family nose, waving brown hair, and large brown eyes. Her mouth is closed and she is smiling slightly. That isn't my great-grandmother's usual big grin that shows her teeth and her "smile lines."

In the photo, Great-Grandmother is wearing a very pretty skirt and blouse. They look like something that would be fashionable today. The blouse is made of heavy satin. The satin falls in lines and hollows that reflect the light. It has a turned-down cowl collar and smocking on the shoulders and under the collar. Her skirt is below her knees and looks like it is made of light wool. She is wearing jewelry. Her silver earrings and bracelet match. She had borrowed them from her sister. Dorothy eventually gave them both to her, but the bracelet has disappeared. On her left hand is a ring with a big yellow stone.

When I look at this photo, I feel conflicting emotions. It gives me pleasure to see my great-grandmother as a pretty young woman. It makes me sad, too, to think how quickly time passes and realize how old she is getting. It amuses me to read the inscription to my great-grandfather, her boyfriend at the time. She wrote, "Sincerely, Beatrice." It's hard for me to imagine them ever being so formal with each other.

My great-grandmother had the photograph taken at a studio near where she worked in Houston. She spent nearly two weeks' salary on the outfit she wore for it. She must have really wanted to impress my great-grandfather to go to all that trouble and expense.

Development through Revising

Cindy showed this first draft to her classmate Elena, who read it and returned it with these notes jotted in the margin:

Reader's Comments

Was this the first time you'd seen it? Where's it been? And "very interesting" doesn't really say anything. Be more specific about why it interests you.

The "Diaz family nose" isn't helpful for someone who doesn't know the Diaz family—describe it!

Nice beginning, but I still can't quite picture her. Can you add more specific detail? Does anything about her face really stand out?

Color?
This is nice—I can picture the material.

What is smocking?

How—what are they like?

Family Portrait

I have a photograph of my great-grandmother that was taken seventy-five years ago, when she was only twenty. She sent it to me only recently, and I find it very interesting.

In the photo, I see a girl who looks a good deal like I do now at twenty-two. Like most of the women in her family, including me, the girl in the picture has the Diaz family nose, waving brown hair, and large brown eyes. Her mouth is closed and she is smiling slightly. That isn't my great-grandmother's usual big grin that shows her teeth and her "smile lines."

In the photo, Great-Grandmother is wearing a very pretty skirt and blouse. They took like something that would be fashionable today. The blouse is made of heavy satin. The satin falls in lines and hollows that reflect the light. It has a turned-down cowl collar and smocking on the shoulders and under the collar. Her skirt is below her knees and looks like it is made of light wool. She is wearing jewelry. Her silver earrings and bracelet match. She had borrowed them from her sister. Dorothy eventually gave them both to her, but the bracelet has disappeared. On her left hand is a ring with a big yellow stone.

(continued)

It'd make more sense for the main points of the essay to be about your great-grandma and the photo. How about making this—your reaction—the conclusion of the essay?

This is interesting stuff—she really did go to a lot of trouble to have the photo taken. I think the story of the photograph deserves to be a main point.

When I look at this photo, I feel conflicting emotions. It gives me pleasure to see my great-grandmother as a pretty young woman. It makes me sad, too, to think how quickly time passes and realize how old she is now. It amuses me to read the inscription to my great-grandfather, her boyfriend at the time. She wrote, "Sincerely, Beatrice." It's hard for me to imagine them ever being so formal with each other.

My great-grandmother had the photograph taken at a studio near where she worked in Houston. She spent nearly two weeks' salary on the outfit she wore for it. She must have really wanted to impress my great-grandfather to go to all that trouble and expense.

Making use of Elena's comments and her own reactions upon rereading her essay, Cindy wrote the final draft that appears on pages 185–186.

A Professional Essay to Consider

Read the following professional essay. Then answer the questions and read the comments that follow.

Lou's Place

by Beth Johnson

Imagine a restaurant where your every whim is catered to, your every want satisfied, your every request granted without hesitation. The people on the staff live to please you. They hover anxiously as you sample your selection, waiting for your judgment. Your pleasure is their delight, your dissatisfaction their dismay.   1

Lou's isn't that kind of place.   2

At Lou's Kosy Korner Koffee Shop, the mock abuse flows like a cup of spilled 3 Folgers. Customers are yelled at, lectured, blamed, mocked, teased, and ignored. They pay for the privilege of pouring their own coffee and scrambling their own eggs. As in a fond but dysfunctional family, Lou displays his affection through criticism and insults, and his customers respond in kind. If Lou's had a slogan, it might be, "If I'm polite to you, ask yourself what's wrong."

Lou's is one of three breakfast joints located in the business district of a small 4 mid-Atlantic town. The county courthouse is nearby, supplying a steady stream of lawyers, jurors, and office workers looking for a bite to eat. A local trucking firm also provides Lou with customers as its drivers come and go in town. Lou's is on the corner. Beside it is a jewelry shop ("In Business Since 1946—Watch Repairs Our Speciality") and an upscale home accessories store that features bonsai trees and hand-painted birdhouses in its window. There's a bus stop in front of Lou's. Lou himself has been known to storm out onto the sidewalk to shoo away people who've dismounted from the bus and lingered too long on the corner.

The sign on Lou's front door says "Open 7 A.M.–3 P.M." But by 6:40 on a brisk 5 spring morning, the restaurant's lights are on, the door is unlocked, and Lou is settled in the booth nearest the door, with the *Philadelphia Inquirer* spread over the table. Lou is sunk deep into the booth's brown vinyl seat, its rips neatly mended with silver duct tape. He is studying the box scores from the night before as a would-be customer pauses on the sidewalk, unsure whether to believe the sign or her own eyes. She opens the door enough to stick her head in.

"Are you open?" she asks.   6

Without lifting his eyes from the paper, Lou answers. "I'm here, aren't I?"   7

Unsure how to interpret this remark, the woman enters and sits at a booth. Lou 8 keeps studying the paper. He begins to hum under his breath. The woman starts tracing a pattern on the glass-topped table with her fingernail. She pulls out her checkbook and pretends to balance it. After a few long minutes, Lou apparently reaches a stopping point in his reading. He rises, his eyes still on the folded newspaper he carries with him. His humming breaks into low-volume song as he trudges behind the counter. "Maaaaaaaake someone happy . . . Make-make-maaaaaake someone happy," he croons as he lifts the steaming pot that has infused the room with the rich aroma of freshly brewed coffee. He carries it to the woman's table, fills her cup, and drops two single-serving containers of half-and-half nearby. He then peers over the tops of his reading glasses at his customer. "You want anything else, dear?" he asks, his bushy gray eyebrows rising with the question.

She shakes her head. "I'm meeting someone. I'll order when he gets here."   9

Lou nods absently, his eyes back on his paper. As he shuffles back to his seat, 10 he mutters over his shoulder, "Hope he shows up before three. I close then."

Lou reads his paper; the woman drinks her coffee and gazes around the room. 11 It's a small restaurant: just an eight-seat counter and seven padded booths. A grill, coffeepots, and a huge stainless-steel refrigerator line the wall behind the counter.

Under the glass top of the tables is the breakfast menu: it offers eggs, pancakes, home fries, bacon, and sausage. A wall rack holds Kellogg's Jumbo Packs of single-serving cereals: smiling toucans and cheerful tigers offer Froot Loops and Frosted Flakes.

Two poster-size photographs hang side by side at the far wall. One is of Lou and 12 his wife on their wedding day. They appear to be in their midtwenties. He is slim, dark-haired, beaming; his arm circles the shoulders of his fair-haired bride. The other photo shows the same couple in an identical pose—only in this one, Lou looks much as he is today. His short white hair is parted at the side; a cropped white beard emphasizes his prominent red mouth. His formerly slim figure now expands to take up much of the photograph. But the smile is the same as he embraces his silver-haired wife.

The bell at the door tinkles; two sleepy-eyed men in flannel shirts, work boots, 13 and oil-company caps walk in. Lou glances up and grunts at them; they nod. One picks up an *Inquirer* from the display stand and leaves two quarters on the cash register. They drop onto seats at the counter, simultaneously swivel to look at the woman in the booth behind them, and then turn back. For a few minutes, they flip through the sports section. Lou doesn't move. One man rises from his seat and wanders behind the counter to find cups and the coffeepot. He fills the cups, returns to his seat, and immerses himself in the paper. There is no noise but the occasional slurping of men sipping hot coffee.

Minutes pass. Finally one of the men speaks. "Lou," he says. "Can I maybe get 14 some breakfast?"

"I'm reading the paper," says Lou. "Eggs are in the refrigerator."   15

The man sighs and lumbers behind the counter again. "In some restaurants, 16 they actually cook for ya," he says, selecting eggs from the carton.

Lou doesn't raise his eyes. "In some restaurants, they wouldn't let a guy with a 17 face like yours in."

The room falls silent again, except for the splatter of grease on the grill and 18 the scrape of the spatula as the customer scrambles his eggs. He heaps them onto his plate, prepares some toast, and returns to his seat. The bell at the door begins tinkling as the breakfast rush begins—men, mostly, about half in work clothes and the rest in suits. They pour in on a wave of talk and laughter. Lou reluctantly rises and goes to work behind the counter, volleying comments with the regulars:

"Three eggs, Lou," says one.   19

"Three eggs. One heart attack wasn't enough for you? You want some bacon 20 grease on top of that?"

A large red-haired man in blue jeans and a faded denim shirt walks in with 21 a newspaper, which he reads as he waits for his cup of takeout coffee. "Anything good in the paper, Dan?" Lou asks.

"Not a thing," drawls Dan. "Not a *damn* thing. The only good thing is that the 22 machine down the street got my fifty cents instead of you."

Lou flips pancakes as the restaurant fills to capacity. The hum of voices fills the 23 room as the aromas of coffee, bacon, eggs, and toasting bread mingle in the air. A group of suits* from the nearby courthouse slide into the final empty booth. After a moment one rises, goes behind the counter, and rummages in a drawer.

"Whatcha need, Ben?" Lou asks, pouring more batter.   24

"Rag," Ben answers. He finds one, returns to the booth, and wipes crumbs off 25 the tabletop. A minute later he is back to drop a slice of ham on the hot grill. He and Lou stand side by side attending to their cooking, as comfortable in their silence as an old married couple. When the ham is sizzling and its rich fragrance reaches the far corners of the room, Ben slides it onto a plate and returns to his booth.

Filled plate in hand, Lou approaches a woman sitting at the counter. Her golden 26 hair contrasts with her sunken cheeks and her wrinkled lips sucking an unfiltered Camel. "You wanna I put this food in your ashtray, or are you gonna move it?" Lou growls. The woman moves the ashtray aside.

"Sorry, Lou," she says.   27

"I'm not really yelling at you, dear," he answers.   28

"I know," says the woman. "I'm glad *you're* here this morning." She lowers her 29 voice. "That girl you've got working here sometimes, Lou—she doesn't *like* me." Lou rolls his eyes, apparently at the poor taste of the waitress, and moves down to the cash register. As he rings up a bill, a teenage girl enters and walks by silently. Lou glares after her. "Start the day with a 'Good morning,' please," he instructs.

"Good morning, Lou," she replies obediently.   30

"*Very* nice," he mutters, still punching the cash-register buttons. "Thank you 31 *so* much for your concern. I get up at the crack of dawn to make your breakfast, but don't bother saying 'good morning' to *me*."

The day's earliest arrival, the woman in the booth, has been joined by a com- 32 panion. They order eggs and hash browns. As Lou slides the filled plates before them, he reverts briefly to the conventional manners he saves for first-timers. "Enjoy your meal," he says.

"Thank you," says the woman. "May I have some hot sauce?"   33

Lou's reserve of politeness is instantly exhausted. "Hot sauce. Jeez. She wants *hot* 34 *sauce*!" he announces to the room at large. "Anything else? Some caviar on the side, maybe?" He disappears behind the counter, reemerging with an enormous red bottle. "Here you are. It's a new bottle. Don't use it all, please. I'd like to save a little for other customers. Hey, on second thought, use it all if you want. Then I'll know you'll like my chili." Laughing loudly at his own joke, he refills the woman's coffee cup without being asked. Golden-brown coffee splashes into her saucer. Lou ignores it.

Lou's waitress, Stacy, has arrived, and begins taking orders and delivering 35 meals. Lou alternates between working the grill and clearing tables. Mid-stride, he halts before the golden-haired woman at the counter, who has pushed her plate aside and is lighting another cigarette. "What? What is this?" he demands.

"Looouuu . . ." she begins soothingly, a stream of smoke jetting from her mouth 36 with the word.

---

suits: business executives or professionals (people wearing business suits).

"Don't 'Lou' me," he retorts. "You don't eat your toast, you don't eat your po- 37
tatoes, you barely touch your eggs. Whatcha gonna live on? Camels?"

"Awww, Lou," she says, but she pulls her plate back and eats a few more bites. 38

As the rush of customers slows to a trickle, Lou returns to the register, mak- 39
ing change and conversation, talking Phillies and the weather. One of the flannel-
shirted men rises from his counter seat and heads for the door, dropping his money
on the counter. " 'Bye, Stacy," he says to the waitress. "Have a nice day."

" 'Bye, Mel," she replies. "You too."   40

"What about me?" Lou calls after Mel.   41

Mel doesn't pause. "Who cares what kind of a day *you* have?"   42

Mel disappears into the morning sunshine; the Camel lady pulls a crossword 43
puzzle out of her purse and taps an unlit cigarette rapidly against the counter.
Stacy wipes the tables and empties a wastebasket of its load of dark, wet coffee
grounds. Lou butters a piece of toast and returns to his favorite booth. He spreads
out his newspaper again, then glances up to catch the eye of the hot-sauce woman.
"Where's your friend?" he asks.

"He left," she replies.   44

"He left you, eh?" Lou asks.   45

"No, he didn't *leave* me. He just had to go to work . . ."   46

"Dump him," Lou responds automatically. "And now, if you don't mind *very* 47
much, I would like to finish my newspaper."

Questions
2

About Unity

1. What is the thesis of Johnson's essay? If it is stated directly, locate the relevant
   sentence or sentences. If it is implied, state the thesis in your own words.

   _____

2. Which statement would best serve as a topic sentence for paragraph 13?

   a. Many of Lou's customers are, like him, interested in the Philadelphia
      sports teams.

   b. Lou doesn't mind if customers serve themselves coffee.

   c. Lou apparently disliked the two men in oil-company caps who came into
      the restaurant.

   d. Regular customers at Lou's are used to taking care of themselves while
      Lou reads his paper.

About Support

3. In paragraph 3, Johnson claims that Lou and his customers are fond of one
   another. How does she support that claim in the case of the golden-haired
   woman who is first mentioned in paragraph 26?

   _____

   _____

4. We are told that customers enjoy the unusual atmosphere of Lou's coffee shop. What detail in paragraph 25 supports this idea?

_____

_____

5. Find a paragraph that appeals to three senses and identify those senses.

_____

About Coherence

6. Which sentence in paragraph 31 contains a change-of-direction signal?

_____

_____

7. Which sentence in paragraph 23 begins with a time signal? (*Write the opening words of that sentence.*)

_____

8. The sentence that makes up paragraph 38 includes which of the following types of transition?
   a. time
   b. addition
   c. change of direction
   d. conclusion

About the Introduction and Conclusion

9. Johnson begins with a situation that is the opposite of the one that will be developed. Rewrite paragraph 1 using another method for introducing essays explained in Chapter 4: a broad statement that gets narrowed, a question, or a brief story.

_____

_____

10. "Lou's Place" ends with a comment by Lou that characterizes the mood of his shop. Rewrite this conclusion by using another method for concluding essays as explained in Chapter 4, summarizing the description of the shop or predicting something about the future of the shop or its owner.

_____

_____

Writing Assignment | Writing a Descriptive Essay

1   Write an essay about a particular place that you can observe carefully or already know well. Choose one of the following or another place you think of.

Pet shop

Playroom in a day-care center

Laundromat

Bar or nightclub on Saturday night (or Sunday morning)

Video arcade

Electronics store

Athletic locker room after a major loss or win

© James Leynse/Corbis

Waiting room in a train or bus station or airport

Classroom you have revisited in your old high school

House of horrors or similar attraction at an amusement park

Library study area

Your bedroom or the bedoom of someone you know

Antique shop or some other small shop

Prewriting

a.   Like all essays, a descriptive essay must have a thesis. It should state your dominant impression about your subject. Write a short sentence that names the place you are describing and your dominant impression of it. Don't worry if your thesis doesn't feel just right—you can always revise a later. For now, just express a workable topic. Here are some examples.

The pet shop was noisy.

The restaurant was crowded.

The bus terminal was frightening.

The locker room was in an uproar.

The day-care's playroom was a joyous mess.

The beach was lonely.

b. Once you have written your sentence, make a list of as many details as you can to support that general impression. For example, this is the list made by the writer of "The Diner at Midnight":

Tired workers at counter

Rainy parking lot

Vacant booths

Quiet

Few cars in lot

Dreary gray building

Lonely young man

Silent middle-aged couple

Out-of-order neon sign

No hostess

Couldn't see anyone in kitchen

Tired-looking waitress

c. Organize your paper according to one or a combination of the following:

Physical order—move from left to right or from far to near, or follow some other consistent order.

Size—Begin with large features or objects and work down to smaller ones.

A special order—Use an order that is appropriate to your subject.

For example, the writer of "The Diner at Midnight" builds his essay around the dominant impression of loneliness. The paper is organized in terms of physical order (from the parking lot to the entrance to the interior); a secondary method of organization is size (large parking lot to smaller diner to still smaller people).

d. Use as many senses as possible in describing a scene. Chiefly you will use sight, but to some extent you may be able to use touch, hearing, smell, and perhaps even taste. Remember that it is through the richness of your sense impressions that the reader will gain a picture of the scene.

e. Proceed to write the first draft of your essay.

Revising

After you have completed the first draft of the paper, set it aside for a while—if possible, until the next day. When you review the draft, try to do so as critically as you would if it were not your own work. Ask yourself these questions:

FOUR BASES Checklist for Description

About *Unity*

☑ Does my essay have a clearly stated thesis, including a dominant impression?

☑ Is there any irrelevant material that should be eliminated or rewritten?

About *Support*

☑ Have I provided rich, specific details that appeal to a variety of senses (sight, hearing, smell, taste, touch)?

About *Coherence*

☑ Have I organized my essay in some consistent manner—physical order, size, time progression, or another way that is appropriate to my subject?

☑ Have I used transition words to help readers follow my train of thought?

☑ Do I have a concluding paragraph that provides a summary, a final thought, or both?

About *Sentence Skills*

☑ Have I used a consistent point of view throughout my essay?

☑ Have I used specific rather than general words?

☑ Have I avoided wordiness and used concise wording?

☑ Are my sentences varied?

☑ Have I proofread my essay for spelling and other sentence skills, as listed on the inside back cover of the book?

As you revise your essay through one or more additional drafts, continue to refer to this checklist until you can answer yes to each question.

Writing | Assignment

2

Write an essay about a family portrait. (The picture may be of an individual or a group.)

Prewriting

a. Decide how you will organize your essay. Your decision will depend on what seems appropriate for the photograph. Two possibilities are these:

As in "Family Portrait," you might use the first supporting paragraph to describe the subjects' faces, the second to describe their clothing and jewelry, and the third to describe the story behind the picture.

Another possible order might be, first, the people in the photograph (and how they look); second, the relationships among the people (and what they are doing in the photo); and third, the story behind the picture (time, place, occasion, other circumstances).

b. Make a scratch outline for your essay, based on the organization you have chosen.

c. Using your scratch outline as a guide, make a list of details that support each of your main points. As practice in doing this, complete the following list of details based on "Family Portrait":

A. Great-Grandmother's face

   Small, straight nose

   Slight smile on her full lips

   Large, dark eyes

   _____

   _____

   _____

B. Great-Grandmother's clothing and jewelry

   Blouse of heavy satin

   Blouse is eggshell-colored

   Cowl collar

(continued)

> *Smocking on blouse*
> *Light wool skirt*
>
> _____
>
> _____
>
> _____
>
> C. *Story behind the photo*
> *Great-Grandmother spent two weeks' salary on clothing*
> *Borrowed jewelry from sister*
>
> _____
>
> _____

d. Use your scratch outline and list of details to write your first draft.

Revising

> **HINT:** Refer to the FOUR BASES Checklist for Description provided on page 202 with Writing Assignment 1.

Writing Assignment

3   Write an essay that explains your dominant impression of a large building or of an outdoor setting you visit often. Do you like going there, or do you have to go there because of family obligations, your job, or some other responsibility? What is it about the place that draws you or that makes you dread having to go there? Here are examples of such places. Choose one of these or select your own topic.

Crowded city neighborhood

Skyscraper

Warehouse

Park or playground

Shopping mall during the holidays

Forest in the fall or winter

Site of an outdoor wedding

Baseball, football, or soccer stadium

Outdoor amusement park

Campground

Harbour

Beach, lakefront, or other natural setting during a particular season

Writing Assignment

4

Writing for a Specific Purpose and Audience

Option A

In this descriptive essay, you will write with a specific purpose and for a specific audience. Imagine that you have subscribed to an online dating service. Clients of the service are asked to create a detailed profile and submit photographs. Write a paper in which you describe yourself. Your goal is to give interested members of the dating service a good sense of what you are like.

Prewriting

a. Decide how you will organize your profile. What aspects of yourself will you describe? Remember, your profile will include photos, so viewers of the site will see for themselves what you look like. Therefore, it won't be necessary to describe your appearance.

You might organize your profile in terms of describing your attitudes and beliefs, your interests, and your personal habits. Other ideas you might use as main points could be your hopes for the future, how you spend a typical day, or your imaginary perfect date.

b. Focus on each of the main points you've decided to write on, and ask yourself questions to generate details to support each one. For example, if you were going to write about your perfect date, you would ask questions like these:

Where would I go?

What would I do?

What time of day would the date occur?

Why would I enjoy this date so much?

How would I travel to my destination?

Continue questioning until you have a number of rich, specific, sensory details to support each of your main points.

c. Plan a brief introductory paragraph that will indicate how you'll organize your profile. For instance, one student might write, "I'm Terry Jefferson. I'm going to tell you something about what I believe, what I enjoy doing, and what I hope to accomplish in the future."

d. Write the first draft of your profile.

Revising

Once you have the first draft of your paper completed, read it to a partner who will give you honest feedback. You and your partner should consider these questions:

FOUR BASES Checklist for Description

About *Unity*

✔ Does my introduction indicate a clear plan of development?

About *Support*

✔ Have I filled each of my supporting paragraphs with rich, descriptive details that help potential dates vividly imagine me?

About *Coherence*

✔ Is my profile clearly organized according to three main points?

✔ Have I rounded off my profile with an appropriate concluding paragraph?

About *Sentence Skills*

✔ Have I used a consistent point of view throughout?

✔ Have I used specific rather than general words?

✔ Have I avoided wordiness and used concise wording?

✔ Are my sentences varied?

✔ Have I proofread my profile, referring to the list of sentence skills on the inside back cover?

Option B

Imagine that you are working for a travel agency and have been asked to write a letter to prospective clients advertising a wonderful vacation destination you have already visited yourself. It might be a large city, a seaside town, an archeological site, a theme park that caters to families, a resort for honeymooners, a dude ranch, a lake, or a mountain hideaway. Then again, you might want to advertise a cruise or even a vacation that involves public service, like the kinds sponsored by Habitat for Humanity. Your purpose is, of course, to get your clients to sign up for the vacation you are advertising. Focus on a particular type of audience: college students, young professionals, families, singles, or senior citizens, for example.

Prewriting

a. First, gather details about the physical appearance, sounds, smells, and even tastes of the setting your clients will visit. Talk about how it feels to swim in a crystal-clear lagoon or describe the taste of a crab sandwich you bought at a straw-covered beach shack. Describe the natural setting, as well the kind of weather your clients can expect.

Discuss what the living and dining accommodations are like as well. By the way, if you are advertising a public-service vacation, you might have to tell them about the tents they'll be sleeping in or the outdoor toilets they'll use. In any case, use as many senses as possible.

b. Keeping the type of audience you have chosen in mind, tell your readers about the kinds of people they are likely to meet, both the tourists and permanent residents.

Are the tourists mostly single, young married couples, families?

Are most of the people young, middle-aged, older? Or is there a mix of ages?

Are these people friendly, helpful, interesting?

Where do they come from?

What do they talk about?

Are they fun-loving and active or more private and sedate?

What about the people who work or live at the place? Are they friendly, helpful, etc.?

c. Finally, provide details about the activities your clients might pursue during the vacation. Does the place offer hang gliding, scuba diving, tours of famous landmarks? Again, if this is a public-service vacation, will your readers be digging wells, framing houses, or constructing schoolhouses?

d. After reading the notes you have gathered, write a rough outline that might look like this:

A. The place

    1. Location

    2. Accommodations

    3. Food

B. The people

    1. Other tourists

    2. Staff

    3. Locals

C. Activities

    1. Water sports

    2. Guided tours

    3. Tennis/golf

e. Now, plan your introductory and concluding sections. In your introduction, state a thesis that is intended to persuade your readers. In addition, prepare them for the points you are going to cover and the order in which you will cover them. For example, you might write:

The setting and accommodations, the people, and the activities make a week at Crystal Bay Resort the ideal family beach vacation.

Your conclusion might summarize or remind your readers of the best reasons to book the vacation. Naturally, you will have to mention the cost of accommodations and travel as well.

Drafting

Write your rough draft by following your outline closely, but don't be a slave to it. If new ideas or details pop into your mind, put them down. You can fix any inconsistencies or repetitions when it comes time to revise. Just be as detailed as you can at this point.

Revising

Read your first draft to a classmate who is willing to listen carefully and work hard at providing valuable feedback. Turn back to the FOUR BASES Checklist for Description on page 202 for questions to consider while revising.

Narration

© James Leynse/Corbis

This chapter will explain and illustrate how to

- develop a narrative essay
- write a narrative essay
- revise a narrative essay

In addition, you will read and consider

- two student narrative essays
- one professional narrative essay

Imagine that you are the owner of your own very successful company, which you have built from the ground up. You have been asked to share your experience with a group of young entrepreneurs who have hopes of owning their own businesses someday. Write a narrative of your success story, including the type of business you own, how you came up with the idea, and how you managed to make it a success.

Children beg to hear a beloved story read again and again. Over dinner, tired adults tell each other about their day. A restless class is hushed when a teacher says, "Let me tell you something strange that happened to me once." Whatever our age, we never outgrow our hunger for stories. Just as our ancestors entertained and instructed each other with tales of great hunts and battles, of angry gods and foolish humans, we still love to share our lives and learn about others through storytelling.

Narration is storytelling, whether we are relating a single story or several related ones. Through narration, we make a statement clear by relating in detail something that has happened to us. In the story we tell, we present the details in the order in which they happened. A person might say, for example, "I was really embarrassed the day I took my driver's test," and then go on to develop that statement with an account of the experience. If the story is sharply detailed, we will be able to see and understand just why the speaker felt that way.

In this chapter, you'll be asked to tell a story that illustrates a specific point. To prepare for this assignment, first read the student essays and the professional essay that follow and work through the questions that accompany each piece of writing. All three essays use narratives to develop their points.

Student Essays to Consider

Adopting a Handicap

My church recently staged a "Sensitivity Sunday" to make our congregation more aware of the problems faced by people with physical disabilities. We were asked to "adopt a disability" for several hours one Sunday morning. Some members, like me, chose to use wheelchairs. Others wore sound-blocking earplugs, hobbled around on crutches, or wore blindfolds.   1

Just sitting in the wheelchair was instructive. I had never considered before how awkward it would be to use one. As soon as I sat down, my weight made the chair begin to roll. Its wheels were not locked, and I fumbled clumsily to correct that. Another awkward moment occurred when I realized I had no place to put my feet. I fumbled some more to turn the metal footrest into place. I felt psychologically awkward as well, as I took my first uneasy look at what was to be my only means of transportation for several hours. I realized that for many people, "adopting a wheelchair" is not a temporary experiment. That was a sobering thought as I sank back into my seat.   2

Once I sat down, I had to learn how to cope with the wheelchair. I shifted around, trying to find a comfortable position. I thought it might be restful, even kind of nice, to be pushed around for a while. I glanced around to see who would be pushing me and then realized I would have to navigate the contraption by myself! My palms reddened and my wrist and forearm muscles started to ache as I tugged at the heavy metal wheels. I realized, as I veered this way and that, that steering and turning were not going to be easy tasks. Trying to make a right-angle turn from one aisle to another, I steered straight into a pew. I felt as though everyone was staring at me and commenting on my clumsiness.   3

(continued)

When the service started, other problems cropped up to frustrate me 4
further. Every time the congregation stood up, my view was blocked. I could
not see the minister, the choir, or the altar. Also, as the church's aisles were
narrow, I seemed to be in the way no matter where I parked myself. For
instance, the ushers had to squeeze by me to pass the collection plate. This
made me feel like a nuisance. Thanks to a new building program, however,
our church will soon have the wide aisles and well-spaced pews that will
make life easier for the disabled. After the service ended, when people
stopped to talk to me, I had to strain my neck and look up at them. This
made me feel like a little child being talked down to and added to my sense
of powerlessness. *omit*

My wheelchair experiment was soon over. It's true that it made an 5
impression on me. I no longer resent large tax expenditures for ramp-
equipped buses, and I wouldn't dream of parking my car in a space marked
"Handicapped Only." But I also realize how little I know about the daily life
of a truly disabled person. A few hours of voluntary "disability" gave me
only a hint of the challenges, both physical and emotional, that people with
handicaps must overcome.

A Night of Violence

According to my history instructor, Adolf Hitler once said that he wanted to 1
sign up "brutal youths" to help him achieve his goals. If Hitler were still alive,
he wouldn't have any trouble recruiting the brutal youths he wanted; he
could get them right here in the United States. I know, because I was one of
them. As a teenager, I ran with a gang. And it took a frightening incident for
me to see how violent I had become.

The incident was planned one Thursday night when I was out with 2
my friends. I was still going to school once in a while, but most of my
friends weren't. We spent our days on the streets, talking, showing off,
sometimes shoplifting a little or shaking people down for a few dollars.
My friends and I were close, maybe because life hadn't been very good
to any of us. On this night, we were drinking wine and vodka on the
corner. For some reason, we all felt tense and restless. One of us came up
with the idea of robbing one of the old people who lived in the high-rise
close by. We would just knock him or her over, grab the money, and party
with it.

(continued)

The robbery did not go as planned. After about an hour, and after more wine and vodka, we spotted an old man. He came out of the glass door of the building and started up the street. Pine Street had a lot of antique stores as well as apartment buildings. Stuffing our bottles in our jacket pockets, we closed in behind him. Suddenly, the old man whipped out a homemade wooden club from under his jacket and began swinging. The club thudded loudly against Victor's shoulder, making him yelp with pain. When we heard that, we went crazy. We smashed our bottles over the old man's head. Not content with that, Victor kicked him savagely, knocking him to the ground. As we ran, I kept seeing him sprawled on the ground, blood from our beating trickling into his eyes. Victor, the biggest of us, had said, "We want your money, old man. Hand it over."   3

Later, at home, I had a strong reaction to the incident. My head would not stop pounding, and I threw up. I wasn't afraid of getting caught; in fact, we never did get caught. I just knew I had gone over some kind of line. I didn't know if I could step back, now that I had gone so far. But I knew I had to. I had seen plenty of people in my neighborhood turn into the kind of people who hated their lives, people who didn't care about anything, people who wound up penned in jail or ruled by drugs. I didn't want to become one of them.   4

That night, I realize now, I decided not to become one of Hitler's "brutal youths." I'm proud of myself for that, even though life didn't get any easier and no one came along to pin a medal on me. I just decided, quietly, to step off the path I was on. I hope my parents and I will get along better now, too. Maybe the old man's pain, in some terrible way, had a purpose.   5

Questions

1

About Unity

1. Which essay lacks an opening thesis statement? *Write a thesis statement that might work for that essay.*

   I Thruc it is very unclear about a night at violence

2. Which sentence in paragraph 4 of "Adopting a Handicap" should be omitted in the interest of paragraph unity? (*Write the opening words.*)

   my veiw was blocked.

3. What sentence in paragraph 3 of "A Night of Violence" should be omitted in the interest of paragraph unity? (*Write the opening words.*)

   "not content with that"

4. Reread the conclusions to both essays. Which one contains a sentence introducing a new topic and should be eliminated? (*Write the opening words of that sentence.*)

   it is very good in both conclusions.

About Support

5. a. Find a sentence in "Adopting a Handicap" that contains words appealing to both sight and touch. (*Write the opening words.*)

   hand and bland

   b. Find a sentence in "A Night of Violence" that contains words appealing to hearing. (*Write the opening words.*)

   got to loud from guy screwed

6. In a narrative, the main method of organization is time order. Which sentence in paragraph 3 of "A Night of Violence" is placed out of order? (*Write the opening words.*)

   "When"

7. Reread paragraph 4 of "Adopting a Handicap." Then, record three details that support that paragraph's topic sentence.

   No park

   not fit

   stop to talk

About Coherence

8. The first stage of the writer's experience in "Adopting a Handicap" might be called *sitting down in the wheelchair*. What are the other two stages of the experience?

9. List four transitions in paragraph 3 of "A Night of Violence." What type of transitions are they?

after   _after_   _as well as_   _when_

_as_

About the Introduction and Conclusion

10. What method of writing introductions explained in Chapter 4 is used in the first paragraph of "A Night of Violence?

"according to

Developing a Narrative Essay

Considering Purpose and Audience

The main purpose of a narrative essay is to make a point by telling your audience a story. Colorful details and interesting events that build up to a point of some kind make narrative essays enjoyable for readers and writers alike.

At one time or another, you have probably listened to someone tell a rambling story that didn't seem to go anywhere. You might have impatiently wondered, "Where is this story going?" or "Is there a point here?" Keep such questions in mind as you think about your own narrative essay. To satisfy your audience, your story must have some overall purpose and point.

Also keep in mind that your story should deal with an event or a topic that will appeal to your audience. A group of young children, for example, would probably be bored by a narrative essay about your first job interview. They might, however, be very interested if you wrote about a time you were chased by a pack of mean dogs or when you stood up to a bully in your school. In general, narrative essays that involve human conflict—internal or external—are entertaining to readers of all ages.

Using Dialogue

In Chapter 8, you learned that including people in an essay about a place is important to communicating something about its character or atmosphere. Of course, people are essential to narration as are what they do and what they say. You can convey much about a person through the dialogue he or she has with others or even through the interior conversations he or she has while thinking silently. But dialogue can also be used to move the plot or action of the story along, to tell what happened before the story began, and to reveal other important facts that will make the story clearer, more suspenseful, or more meaningful.

For example, in "A Night of Violence" Victor's brutal tendencies become clear when he says, "We want your money, old man. Hand it over." You will see a great deal more dialogue in Pete Hamill's essay "The Yellow Ribbon" (pages 220–221). Here, dialogue reveals much about the plot: that Vingo had been sentenced to four years in prison, that he had given his wife the option to "forget" him, and that he asked her to tie a yellow handkerchief on a large oak near their home if she intended to welcome him home. It also reveals a lot about Vingo's character. Fair minded and reasonable, he admits that he deserved to have been in prison: "I did it and I went to jail. If you can't do the time, don't do the crime."

Some Rules for Using Dialogue

Use dialogue especially in the narrative essays you write, but remember to observe a few simple rules:

1. Place quotation marks around the words, and start a new paragraph when a new character begins speaking. For this reason, it is easy to tell that there are two different speakers in the following exchange between Vingo and a young girl he has met on the bus. The girl asks:

   > "Are you married?"
   > "I don't know."
   > "You don't know?" she said.
   > "Well, when I was in the can I wrote to my wife," he said. "I told her, I said, Martha, I understand if you can't stay married to me. I told her that I was gonna be away for a long time, and if she couldn't stand it, if the kids kept askin' questions, if it hurt her too much, well, she could just forget about me. Get a new guy—she's a wonderful woman, really something—and forget about me. I told her she didn't have to write me or nothing. And she didn't. Not for three and a half years."
   > "And you're going home now, not knowing?"
   > "Yeah," he said shyly.

2. Record people's words exactly as they speak them, complete with slang and errors in grammar and pronunciation. Notice that, in the dialogue quoted above, Vingo says "gonna" rather than "going to" and "askin'" rather than "asking." He also uses a double negative when he says "I told her she didn't have to write me or nothing." This is not the kind of writing expected in a college essay, but it is completely appropriate when you are recording dialogue. Remember that you are trying to capture the words— the very sounds—that the character uttered just as he or she said them.

3. Make sure your reader knows who is speaking at any given time. In "The Yellow Ribbon" passage quoted above, Hamill uses tag lines like "she said" to explain that the girl is the speaker. Later, when we read "he said

shyly," we know it's Vingo who is talking. One way to make sure that readers can identify the speaker is to use tag lines like "she said," "Johann replied," or "the man shouted."

4. Set off tag lines from quotations with commas, as in *"Yeah," he said shyly*. However, if a tag line is used in the middle of a quotation, place commas before and after it, as in paragraph 20 of "The Yellow Ribbon": *"Wow," the girl said, "Wow."*

As you can see from the previous example, commas and periods appear within quotation marks, but colons and semicolons appear outside of them. Finally, if the quotation is a question, end it with a question mark without the comma, as in *"You don't know?" she said*.

Development through Prewriting

Freewriting is a particularly helpful prewriting technique as you're planning your narrative essay. As you think about the story you want to relate, many ideas will crowd into your mind. Simply writing them down in free-form style will jog loose details you may have forgotten and also help you determine what the central point of your story really is.

> **TIP:** For more about freewriting, see pages 23–25.

Lisa, the writer of "Adopting a Handicap," spent a half hour freewriting before she wrote the first draft of her essay. Here is what she came up with:

Our church was planning a building renovation to make the church more accessible to handicapped people. Some people thought it was a waste of money and that the disabled could get along all right in the church the way it was. Not many disabled people come to our church anyway. Pastor Henry gave a sermon about disabilities. He suggested that we spend one Sunday pretending to be disabled ourselves. We got to choose our disability. Some people pretended to be blind or deaf or in need of crutches. I chose to use a wheelchair. I thought it might be fun to have someone push me around. It was a lot scarier and more

(continued)

disturbing than I expected. We borrowed wheelchairs and crutches from the local nursing home. I didn't like sitting down in the wheelchair. I didn't know how to work it right. It rolled when I didn't want it to. I felt clumsy trying to make it move. I even ran into a pew. I felt silly pretending to be disabled and also sort of disrespectful because for most people sitting in a wheelchair isn't a choice. It also bothered me to think what it'd be like if I couldn't get up again. It turned out that nobody was going to push me around. I thought Paula would, but instead she put on a blindfold and pretended to be blind. She knocked over a cup of coffee before the morning was over. She told me later she felt really panicky when that happened. Sitting down so low in the wheelchair was weird. I couldn't see much of anything. People ignored me or talked to me like I was a little kid. I was glad when the morning was over. Making the wheels turn hurt my hands and arms.

As Lisa read over her freewriting passage, she decided that the central point of her story was her new realization of how challenging it would be to be truly disabled. To support that central point, she realized, she would need to concentrate on details that demonstrated the frustrations she felt. She created a scratch outline for the first draft of her essay:

Thesis statement: A church experiment led to my spending the morning in a wheelchair.

1. Sitting in the wheelchair
   a. Awkward because it rolled
   b. Awkward because footrest was out of place
   c. Psychologically awkward
2. Moving the wheelchair
   a. I thought someone would push me.

(continued)

    b. It was hard to make the chair move and it hurt my hands.

    c. It was difficult to steer.

  3. Ways the wheelchair affected me

    a. I couldn't see.

    b. I felt in the way.

    c. I felt funny talking to people as they bent down over me.

Development through Revising

Lisa based her first draft on her scratch outline. Here is the draft:

First Draft

Adopting a Handicap

The pastor at our church suggested that we each "adopt a disability" for a few hours on Sunday morning. Some members, like me, chose to use wheelchairs. Others wore earplugs, used crutches, or wore blindfolds.

It surprised me that I felt nervous about sitting down in my wheelchair. I'm not sure why I felt scared about it. I guess I realized that most people who use wheelchairs don't do it by choice—they have to.

When I sat down, I thought my friend Paula would push me around. We had talked about her doing that earlier. But she decided instead to "adopt" her own disability and she pretended to be blind. I saw her with a blindfold on, trying to fix herself a cup of coffee and knocking it off the table as she stirred it. So I had to figure out how to make the chair move by myself. It wasn't so easy. Pushing the wheels made my hands and arms sore. I also kept bumping into things. I felt really awkward. I even had trouble locking the wheels and finding the footrest.

I couldn't see well as I sat down low in my chair. When the rest of the congregation stood up, I could forget about seeing entirely. People would nod or chuckle at something that had happened up at the front of the church and I could only guess what was going on. Instead of sitting in the pew with everyone else, I was parked out in the aisle, which was really too narrow for the chair. The new building program our church is planning will make that problem better by widening the aisles and making the pews farther apart. It's going to be expensive, but it's a worthwhile thing. Another thing I disliked was how I felt when people talked to me. They had to lean down as though I was a kid, and I had to stare up at them as though I was too. One person I talked to who seemed to understand what I was experiencing was Don Henderson, who mentioned that his brother-in-law uses a wheelchair.

Lisa read over her first draft. Then she showed it to her roommate. After hearing her roommate's comments, Lisa read the essay again. This time she made a list of comments about how she thought it could be improved:

- The introduction should explain why the pastor wanted us to adopt disabilities.
- The second paragraph is sort of weak. Instead of saying, "I'm not sure why I felt scared," I should try to put into specific words what was scary about the experience.
- The stuff about Paula doesn't really add to my main point. The story is about me, not Paula.
- Maybe I shouldn't talk so much about the new building program. It's related to people with disabilities, but it doesn't really support the idea that my morning in a wheelchair was frustrating.
- Eliminate the part about Don Henderson. It doesn't contribute to my feeling frustrated.
- The essay ends too abruptly. I need to wrap it up with some sort of conclusion.

With that list of comments in hand, Lisa returned to her essay. She then wrote the version that appears on pages 210–211.

A Professional Essay to Consider

Read the following professional essay. Then answer the questions and read the comments that follow.

The Yellow Ribbon

by Pete Hamill

They were going to Fort Lauderdale, the girl remembered later. There were six of 1
them, three boys and three girls, and they picked up the bus at the old terminal
on 34th Street, carrying sandwiches and wine in paper bags, dreaming of golden
beaches and the tides of the sea as the gray cold spring of New York vanished behind them. Vingo was on board from the beginning.

As the bus passed through Jersey and into Philly, they began to notice that 2
Vingo never moved. He sat in front of the young people, his dusty face masking
his age, dressed in a plain brown ill-fitting suit. His fingers were stained from cigarettes and he chewed the inside of his lip a lot, frozen into some personal cocoon of
silence.

Somewhere outside of Washington, deep into the night, the bus pulled into a 3
Howard Johnson's, and everybody got off except Vingo. He sat rooted in his seat,
and the young people began to wonder about him, trying to imagine his life: Perhaps he was a sea captain, maybe he had run away from his wife, he could be an
old soldier going home. When they went back to the bus, the girl sat beside him and
introduced herself.

"We're going to Florida," the girl said brightly. "You going that far?"   4
"I don't know," Vingo said.   5
"I've never been there," she said. "I hear it's beautiful."   6
"It is," he said quietly, as if remembering something he had tried to forget.   7
"You live there?"   8
"I did some time there in the Navy. Jacksonville."   9
"Want some wine?" she said. He smiled and took the bottle of Chianti and took 10
a swig. He thanked her and retreated again into silence. After a while, she went
back to the others, as Vingo nodded into sleep.

In the morning they awoke outside another Howard Johnson's, and this time 11
Vingo went in. The girl insisted that he join them. He seemed very shy and ordered
black coffee and smoked nervously, as the young people chattered about sleeping
on the beaches. When they went back on the bus, the girl sat with Vingo again, and
after a while, slowly and painfully and with great hesitation, he began to tell his
story. He had been in jail in New York for the last four years, and now he was going
home.

"Four years!" the girl said. "What did you do?"   12
"It doesn't matter," he said with quiet bluntness. "I did it and I went to jail. If 13
you can't do the time, don't do the crime. That's what they say and they're right."
"Are you married?"   14
"I don't know."   15
"You don't know?" she said.   16

"Well, when I was in the can I wrote to my wife," he said. "I told her, I said, 17
Martha, I understand if you can't stay married to me. I told her that. I said I was
gonna be away a long time, and that if she couldn't stand it, if the kids kept askin'
questions, if it hurt her too much, well, she could just forget me. Get a new guy—
she's a wonderful woman, really something—and forget about me. I told her she
didn't have to write me or nothing. And she didn't. Not for three and a half years."

"And you're going home now, not knowing?" 18

"Yeah," he said shyly. "Well, last week, when I was sure the parole was com- 19
ing through I wrote her. I told her that if she had a new guy, I understood. But if
she didn't, if she would take me back she should let me know. We used to live in
this town, Brunswick, just before Jacksonville, and there's a great big oak tree just
as you come into town, a very famous tree, huge. I told her if she would take me
back, she should put a yellow handkerchief on the tree, and I would get off and
come home. If she didn't want me, forget it, no handkerchief, and I'd keep going on
through."

"Wow," the girl said. "Wow." 20

She told the others, and soon all of them were in it, caught up in the approach 21
of Brunswick, looking at the pictures Vingo showed them of his wife and three
children, the woman handsome in a plain way, the children still unformed in a
cracked, much-handled snapshot. Now they were twenty miles from Brunswick
and the young people took over window seats on the right side, waiting for the approach of the great oak tree. Vingo stopped looking, tightening his face into the
ex-con's mask, as if fortifying himself against still another disappointment. Then
it was ten miles, and then five and the bus acquired a dark hushed mood, full of
silence, of absence, of lost years, of the woman's plain face, of the sudden letter on
the breakfast table, of the wonder of children, of the iron bars of solitude.

Then suddenly all of the young people were up out of their seats, screaming 22
and shouting and crying, doing small dances, shaking clenched fists in triumph and
exaltation. All except Vingo.

Vingo sat there stunned, looking at the oak tree. It was covered with yellow 23
handkerchiefs, twenty of them, thirty of them, maybe hundreds, a tree that stood
like a banner of welcome blowing and billowing in the wind, turned into a gor-
geous yellow blur by the passing bus. As the young people shouted, the old con
slowly rose from his seat, holding himself tightly, and made his way to the front of
the bus to go home.

About Unity

1. The thesis of Hamill's essay is implied rather than stated directly. See if you
   can state the thesis in your own words.

   he being kinda of weird.

Questions

2

2. The main point in paragraph 2 is not stated; it is implied. Write a topic sentence for that paragraph.

_____ he vour move _____

3. What is the topic sentence of paragraph 11? (*Write the opening words.*)

_____

About Support

4. "His fingers were stained from cigarettes and he chewed the inside of his lip a lot, frozen in some personal cocoon of silence." This line from paragraph 2 supports the idea that

   a. Vingo had been drinking.

   b. Vingo was nervous.

   c. Vingo was a hostile person.

   d. Vingo knew the young peope were watching him.

5. Hamill writes in paragraph 11 that Vingo seemed very shy. Find at least two pieces of evidence in the essay to support the idea that Vingo was shy.

   _____ ordered to black colfer he vy _____

   _____ seen shy _____

   _____

6. Hamill implies that despite his crime, Vingo was an honorable man. Find evidence that supports that point.

   _____

   _____

About Coherence

7. Because this is the story of a trip, it is appropriate that Hamill uses place names to signal the passing of time. But he also uses other types of transitions like those appearing on pages 87–90. List four place names and four other transitions used in this essay.

Place Names	**Other Transitions**
Time Signal	as
save	bos Pebre
Same	suddeny

8. What sentence in paragraph 19 begins with a transition word that indicates contrast? (*Write the opening words.*)

    _____ *When* _____ " *Time Signal* " _____

About the Introduction and Conclusion

9. Reread the introduction. How do you think Hamill learned about this story?

    _____ *I Think it is very good!* _____

10. The author does not use one of the methods for writing conclusions discussed on pages 98–100. How does he end this essay? What kind of welcome might we expect Vingo to receive when he walks into his home? Why didn't Hamill tell us about this?

    _____ *he will be happy when he* _____
    _____ *got home. he did learn about* _____
    _____ *the trip* _____
    _____

Writing a Narrative Essay

Write an essay narrating an experience in which a certain emotion was predominant. The emotion might be disappointment, happiness, frustration, embarrassment, or any of the following:

Fear	Shock	Nervousness	Loss
Courage	Love	Hate	Respect
Jealousy	Anger	Surprise	Confidence
Sadness	Nostalgia	Shyness	Shame
Satisfaction	Relief	Humility	Envy
Guilt	Greed	Pity	Loneliness

The experience should be limited in time. Note that each of the three essays presented in this chapter describes an experience that occurred within a relatively short period. One writer described her frustration in acting like a disabled person at a morning church service; another detailed the terror of a minute's mugging that had lifelong consequences; Pete Hamill described an overnight bus trip and its thrilling conclusion.

© Rachel Epstein/PhotoEdit

© Simon Marcus/Corbis

© BananaStock/Alamy

Prewriting

a. Think of an experience or event in your life in which you felt a certain emotion. Then spend at least ten minutes freewriting about that experience. Do not worry at this point about such matters as spelling or grammar or putting things in the right order; instead, just try to get down as many details as you can think of that seem related to the experience.

b. This preliminary writing will help you decide whether your topic is promising enough to continue working on. If it is not, choose another emotion. If it is, do three things:

First, write out the thesis in a single sentence, underlining the emotion you will focus on. Here are three sample sentences like the one you might write:

"My first day in high school was one of the <u>scariest</u> of my life."

"Playing on the freshman soccer team gave me the <u>confidence</u> to try out for the versity."

"What I recently learned about the men and women serving in the military has increased my <u>respect</u> for them enormously.

Second, think about the source of the emotion. What made your first day one of the "scariest," or what was it about playing on the freshman team that gave you "confidence"? What details can you add to explain this emotion so as to "hook" your readers and keep them interested?

c. Using your list as a guide, prepare a rough draft of your paper.

Revising

Once you have a first draft of your essay completed, consider the following checklist as you work on a second draft:

FOUR BASES Checklist for Narration

About *Unity*

☑ Do I state the thesis of my narrative in the introductory paragraph?

☑ If not in the introductory paragraph, is the thesis cleary implied somewhere in the essay?

☑ Are there any portions of the essay that do not support the thesis and should therefore be eliminated or rewritten?

About *Support*

☑ Do I have enough details, including dialogue?

☑ Have I included enough vivid, exact details that will help my readers experience the event as it actually happened?

About *Coherence*

☑ Have I included time signals such as *first, then, next, after, while, during,* and *finally* to help connect details as the reader moves from the beginning to the middle to the end of the narrative?

About *Sentence Skills*

☑ Have I used a consistent point of view throughout my essay?

☑ Have I used specific rather than general words?

☑ Have I avoided wordiness and used concise wording?

☑ Are my sentences varied?

☑ Have I checked for spelling and other sentence skills, as listed on the inside back cover of the book?

Writing Assignment

2

Think of an experience in your life that supports one of the statements below:

If you never have a dream, you'll never have a dream come true.—popular saying

For fools rush in where angels fear to tread.—Alexander Pope

Before I got married I had six theories about bringing up children; now I have six children and no theories.—John Wilmot, Earl of Rochester

There are some things you learn best in calm, and some in storm.—Willa Cather

Success is 99 percent perspiration and 1 percent inspiration.—Thomas Edison

Lying is an indispensable part of making life tolerable.—Bergen Evans

What a tangled web we weave / When first we practice to deceive.—Walter Scott

There's a sucker born every minute.—P. T. Barnum

We lie loudest when we lie to ourselves.—Eric Hoffer

All marriages are happy. It's the living together afterward that causes all the trouble.—Raymond Hul

Hoping and praying are easier but do not produce as good results as hard work.—Andy Rooney

A little learning is a dangerous thing.—Alexander Pope

Nothing is as good as it seems beforehand.—George Eliot

You don't like weak women / You get bored too quick / And you don't like strong women / 'Cause they're hip to your tricks.—Joni Mitchell

Give a pig a finger, and he'll take the whole hand.—folk saying

Life shrinks or expands in proportion to one's courage.—Anaïs Nin

When I got to the end of my long journey in life / I realized I was the architect of my own destiny.—Amado Nervo

A fool and his money are soon parted.—popular saying

From what we get, we can make a living; what we give, however, makes a life.—Arthur Ashe

No matter how lovesick a woman is, she shouldn't take the first pill that comes along.—Dr. Joyce Brothers

Fear not those who argue but those who dodge.—Marie von Ebner-Eschenback

Trust in Allah, but tie your camel.—old Muslim proverb

Think of an experience you have had that demonstrates the truth of one of the above statements or another noteworthy saying—perhaps one that has been a guidepost for your life. Then, using one of these statements as your thesis, write a narrative essay about that experience. As you develop your essay, refer to the suggestions in the following prewriting strategies and rewriting strategies.

Prewriting

The key to the success of your essay will be your choice of an incident from your life that illustrates the truth of the statement you have chosen. Here are some guidelines to consider as you choose such an incident:

- The incident should include a *conflict,* or a source of tension. That conflict does not need to be dramatic, such as a fistfight between two characters.

Equally effective is a quieter conflict, such as a conflict between a person's conscience and desires, or a decision that must be made, or a difficult situation that has no clear resolution.

- The incident should be limited in time. It would be difficult to do justice in such a brief essay to an experience that continued over several weeks or months.

- The incident should evoke a definite emotional response in you so that it might draw a similar response from your reader.

- The incident must *fully support* the statement you have chosen, not merely be linked by some of the same ideas. Do not, for example, take the statement "We lie loudest when we lie to ourselves" and then write about an incident in which someone just told a lie. The essay should demonstrate the cost of being untruthful to oneself.

Here is how one student tested whether her plan for her narrative essay was a good one:

- What statement have I chosen as my thesis?
  The chains of habit are too weak to be felt until they are too strong to be broken.—Samuel Johnson

- Does the incident I have chosen include some kind of tension?

  Yes. I am going to write about the day I tried to purchase an expensive new shirt but was told that I had maxed out my credit card. When I tried a second card and then a third, I was told that they too had reached their balance limits. What an embarrassment. That day I realized something about myself—I get the urge to buy things whenever I am lonely, depressed, or just bored. I also learned that in order to battle that urge, I would have to change my values, my outlook on life. I would have to learn that happiness does not result simply from having nice things.

- Is the incident limited in time?

  Yes. I am going to write about events that happened in one day.

- Does the incident evoke an emotional response in me?

  Yes. I was embarrassed and ashamed of myself.

- Does the incident support the statement I have chosen?

  Yes. I was a "shopaholic," but I did not realize that I was caught in the "chains" of this habit until I was embarrassed into making major changes in my outlook on life.

Revising

After you have put your essay away for a day, read it to a friend or classmate who will give you honest feedback. You and your reader should consider these questions:

FOUR BASES Checklist for Narration

About *Unity*

☑ Have I included the essay's thesis (my chosen statement) in my introductory paragraph, or is it clearly implied?

☑ Does each paragraph, and each sentence within that paragraph, help either to keep the action moving or to reveal important things about the characters?

☑ Are there portions of the essay that do not support my thesis and therefore should be eliminated or rewritten?

About *Support*

☑ Do I have enough details, including dialogue?

☑ Have I included enough vivid, exact details that will help my readers experience the event as it actually happened?

About *Coherence*

☑ Do transitional words and phrases, and linking sentences between paragraphs, help make the sequence of events clear?

☑ Should I break up the essay by using bits of interesting dialogue instead of narration?

About *Sentence Skills*

☑ Have I used a consistent point of view throughout my essay?

☑ Have I used specific rather than general words?

☑ Have I avoided wordiness and used concise wording?

☑ Are my sentences varied?

☑ Have I checked for spelling and other sentence skills, as listed on the inside back cover of the book?

Continue revising your work until you and your reader can answer "yes" to each question.

Writing Assignment

3

Writing for a Specific Purpose and Audience

In this narrative essay, you will write with a specific purpose and for a specific audience.

Option 1 Imagine that you are in a town fifty miles from home, that your car has broken down several miles from a gas station, and that you are carrying no money. You're afraid you are going to have a terrible time, but the friendly people who help you turn your experience into a positive one. It is such a good day, in fact, that you don't want to forget what happened.

Write a narrative of the day's events in your journal so that you can read it ten years from now and remember exactly what happened. Begin with the moment you realize your car has broken down and continue until you're safely back home. Include a thesis at either the beginning or the end of your narration.

Option 2 Imagine that a friend or sister or brother has to make a difficult decision of some kind. Perhaps he or she must decide how to deal with a troubled love affair, or a problem with living at home, or a conflict with a boss or coworker. Write a narrative from your own experience that will teach him or her something about the decision that must be made.

Option 3 Pete Hamill writes about an incident that helps affirm our faith in people's fidelity and courage. Write the story of an incident in your life or in the life of someone you know that has strengthened your belief in the goodness, fairness, honesty, faithfulness, charity, or other positive qualities in people.

www.mhhe.com/langan

10

Exemplification

This chapter will explain and illustrate how to

• develop an exemplification essay

• write an exemplification essay

• revise an exemplification essay

In addition, you will read and consider

• two student exemplification essays

• one professional exemplification essay

© AP Photo/James Nachtwey/VII

Did the events of 9/11 bring people in the United States together or are we a more divided nation? Use examples found in the media, in this photograph, or in your own daily observations to support your point.

In our daily conversations, we often provide examples—details, particulars, and specific instances—to explain statements that we make. Here are several statements and supporting examples:

Statement	Examples
The first day of school was frustrating.	My sociology course was canceled. Then, I couldn't find the biology lab. And the lines at the bookstore were so long that I went home without buying my textbooks.
That washing machine is unreliable.	The water temperature can't be predicted; it stops in midcycle; and it sometimes shreds my clothing.
My grandfather is a thrifty person.	He washes and reuses aluminum foil. He wraps gifts in newspaper. And he's worn the same Sunday suit for twenty years.

In each case, exemplification helps us see for ourselves the truth of the statement that has been made. In essays, too, explanatory examples help your audience fully understand your point. Lively, specific examples also add interest to your paper.

In this chapter, you will be asked to use exemplification to support your thesis. First read the student essays and the professional essay that follow and work through the questions that accompany the essays. All three essays use exemplification to develop their points.

www.mhhe.com/langan

Student Essays to Consider

Look on the Bright Side

Some people have a tendency to look for and remember the worst in life. Don't get me wrong; I do not wear rose-colored glasses. Yes, there's plenty of filth, evil, and corruption in the world to make anyone depressed. However, if you focus on the negative, you will never win the battle to achieve happiness. In fact, for every corrupt politician there is one who is an honest and dedicated public servant; for every doctor who is in it for the money, there is one who truly cares about patients, and for every stock-market cheat, there is a business executive who works hard, makes money

1

(continued)

honestly, and has a conscience. But you don't have to work on Wall Street or in Washington to see that there are pulses and minuses to being human. You can see both good and evil in the people anywhere.

Every day I walk from the bus stop to the office where I work. On my way   2
is a tiny patch of ground that was once strewn with rubbish and broken glass. The city is trying to make a "pocket park" out of it by planting trees and flowers. Every day this spring, I watched the skinny saplings put out tiny leaves. When I walked past I always noted how big the tulips were getting and made bets with myself on when they should bloom. To pass time as I walk, I often make silly little bets with myself such as predicting that the next man I see will be wearing a blue tie. But last Wednesday, I noticed that someone had uprooted the trees and trampled the budding tulips. I felt sick that some people can destroy such beauty for no apparent reason. However, the following Saturday, when I was downtown shopping, I saw a group of Boy Scouts cleaning up another empty lot. There were twelve of them accompanied by two adults, and everyone seemed to be having a great time picking up glass, throwing old mattresses into a dumpster, and repainting a wall that was covered with graffiti.

At lunchtime last Friday, I witnessed another example of meanness   3
and stupidity, but this too was tempered by good will and kindness. I was waiting in a long line at McDonald's. Also in the line was a young mother with two tired, impatient children clinging to her legs. She was trying to calm them down, but it was obvious that their whining was about to give way to full-fledged tantrums. The lines barely moved, and the lunchtime tension increased. Then, one of the children began to cry and scream. As people stared angrily at the helpless mother, the little boy's screams echoed through the restaurant. Finally, a man shouted in the mother's face: "Lady, don't bring your kids to a public place if you can't control them!" A young woman chimed in with another piece of cruel criticism. Out of nowhere, however, came an elderly gentleman who stopped, knelt down next to the child, and started making funny faces. I learned later that he was an experienced grandfather who knew how to entertain the little ones. Within seconds tears and screams turned into smiles and giggles, and even the lines seemed to be moving faster. Meanwhile, the elderly man's companion waited for him near the exit.

Among the worst and best examples of human behaviour came one   4
evening as I was heading home after a double shift at work. It was about 11 P.M. when I passed an old woman huddled in a doorway. Wrapped in a dirty blanket and clucthing a cheap vinyl bag packed with her belongings, she was one of the "street people" our society leaves to fend for themselves. Approaching the woman from the opposite direction were three teenagers. Talking and laughing loudly, they began to shout crude remarks at her. Then they did even

(continued)

more cruel things to torment her. The woman stared helplessly at them, like a wounded animal surrounded by hunters. In a few seconds, however, two police officers in a patrol car arrived and quickly scared the scoundrels away. While one of the men went into a nearby Starbucks to get her some coffee, the other asked her if she wanted to be taken to a shelter. Then helping here ro her feet, he wrapped her in clean blanket he had taken from the trunk of the car and sat her carefully in the back seat. In a few moments, the second officer came out with the coffee as well as a bountiful sandwich he had purchased with his own money. It was probably the first meal she had in days.

That night, I went home and began to think about what I had just   5
witnessed. The world may be filled with mean-spirited creeps, but it doesn't take much work to find good-hearted, cheerful people who love their fellow human beings and are willing to help whenever they can. That idea, and the belief that with a little effort I too might be able to make a difference, made me sleep a lot better that night.

Altered States

Most Americans are not alcoholics. Most do not cruise seedy city   1
streets looking to score crack cocaine or heroin. Relatively few try to con their doctors into prescribing unneeded mood-altering medications. And yet, many Americans are traveling through life with their minds slightly out of kilter. In its attempt to cope with modern life, the human mind seems to have evolved some defense strategies. Confronted with inventions like television, the shopping center, and the Internet, the mind will slip—all by itself—into an altered state.

Never in the history of humanity have people been expected to sit   2
passively for hours, staring at moving pictures emanating from an electronic box. Since too much exposure to flickering images of police officers, detectives, and talk-show hosts can be dangerous to human sanity, the mind automatically goes into a state of TV hypnosis. The eyes see the sitcom or the dog-food commercial, but the mind goes into a holding pattern. None of the televised images or sounds actually enter the brain. This is why, when questioned, people cannot remember commercials they have seen five seconds before or why the TV cops are chasing a certain suspect. In this hypnotic, trancelike state, the mind resembles an armored armadillo. It rolls up in self-defense, letting the stream of televised information pass by harmlessly.

(continued)

If the TV watcher arises from the couch and goes to a shopping mall,   3
he or she will again cope by slipping into an altered state. In the mall,
the mind is bombarded with the sights, smells, and sounds of dozens of
stores, restaurants, and movie theaters competing for its attention. There
are hundreds of questions to be answered. Should I start with the upper
or lower mall level? Which stores should I look in? Should I bother with
the sweater sale at J. Crew? Should I eat fried chicken or try the healthier
sounding Pita Wrap? Where is my car parked? To combat this mental
overload, the mind goes into a state resembling the whiteout experienced
by mountain climbers trapped in a blinding snowstorm. Suddenly, everything
looks the same. The shopper is unsure where to go next and cannot
remember what he or she came for in the first place. The mind enters this
state deliberately so that the shopper has no choice but to leave. Some kids
can be in a shopping mall for hours, but they are exceptions to the rule.

But no part of everyday life so quickly triggers the mind's protective   4
shutdown mode as that favorite pastime of the new millennium: cruising the
Internet. A computer user sits down with the intention of briefly checking
his or her e-mail or looking up a fact for a research paper. But once tapped
into the immense storehouse of information, entertainment, and seemingly
intimate personal connections that the Internet offers, the user loses all
sense of time and priorities. Prospects flood the mind: Should I explore
the rise of Nazi Germany? Play a trivia game? Hear the life story of a lonely
stranger in Duluth? With a mind dazed with information overload, the
user numbly hits one key after another, leaping from topic to topic, from
distraction to distraction. Hours fly by as he or she sits hunched over the
keyboard, unable to account for the time that has passed.

Therefore, the next time you see TV viewers, shoppers, or Internet   5
surfers with eyes as glazed and empty as polished doorknobs, you'll know
these people are in a protective altered state. Be gentle with them. They are
merely trying to cope with the mind-numbing inventions of modern life.

Questions

1

About Unity

1. Which sentence in paragraph 3 of "Altered States" should be omitted in the
   interest of paragraph unity? (*Write the opening words.*)

   _____ Some kids can be in a shopping mall

2. Which supporting paragraph in one of the essays lacks a topic sentence?

   _____

3. Find a sentence in one of the paragraphs of "Look on the Bright Side" that does not belong in the eassy. Write the opening words below, and explain why it doesn't belong.

_____

_____

About Support
4. Which idea paragraph 4 "Look on the Bright Side" is not supported with details? Write the opening words below and explain how would you fix this problem.

_____

_____

5. The last sentence in paragraph 3 of "Look on the Bright Side" seems out of place. Rewrite it so that it actually helps support that paragraphs topic sentence. (Hint: You might want to combine it with a sentence that appears earlier in the paragraph.)

_____

_____

_____

6. What three pieces of evidence does the writer of "Altered States" offer to support the statement that the Internet is an "immense storehouse of information, entertainment, and seemingly intimate personal connections"?

_____

_____

_____

About Coherence
7. In paragraph 3 of "Look on the Bright Side," which four *time* signals does the author begin sentences with? (*Write the four signals here.*)

_____   _____   _____   _____

8. What sentence in "Altered States" indicates that the author has used emphatic order, saving his most important point for last? (*Write the opening words.*)

_____

About the Introduction and Conclusion

9. Which of the two essays provides a clue to its development? Write the title of the essay and a brief outline of that plan below.

_____

_____

_____

_____

10. a.   What method discussed in Chapter 4 is used in the conclusion of "Altered States"?

_____

b.   What method discussed in Chapter 4 is used in the inroduction of "Look on the Bright Side"?

_____

Developing an Exemplification Essay
Considering Purpose and Audience

Using Various Types of Examples All examples act as concrete representations of the abstract idea you are trying to communicate, but there are several kinds you can choose from depending on your purpose and audience. Varying the types of examples will help make your writing interesting. Readers would certainly become bored if you simply listed the different kinds of sports or other extra-curricular activities your college offers in an attempt to prove that there are many good ways to spend your time. So, you might also include a couple of anecdotes (brief stories) about the interesting club trips you have been on in the past year or the fascinating people you met while planning a language-club fundraiser last semester.

Mention People, Places, Actions, and Things Some effective examples refer to people, places, actions, and things that readers recognize or can relate to. If you wanted to prove that your town is making a strong effort to improve the environment, you might mention actions like the building of the new sewer treatment plan, the reduction in bus fares to encourage the use of public trans-portation, the funding of an empty-lot cleanup project. If you were trying to prove that Virginia contributed a great deal to the founding of our country, you might mention figures such as George Washington, Thomas Jefferson, and Patrick Henry.

Mention Facts and Events You could use facts if you wanted to explain that ancient Athens was not a democracy in the modern sense because poor people could not participate in government, women had no voice in the affairs of the city, and Athenians owned slaves. You might discuss World War I, World War II, the Korean War, the Vietnam War, and the Persian Gulf War to prove that, in the twentieth century, Americans fought in many global conflicts.

Include Anecdotes Anecdotes are brief, informative stories that can serve as examples. Although they are brief, they go beyond the mere mention of something and actually tell a complete story that serves to make an abstract idea more understandable. There are several such stories in "Look on the Bright Side," an essay that appeared earlier in this chapter.

Using Only Relevant Examples Examples should always relate directly to the idea that they are being used to support. Let's say you are trying to prove that taking public transportation can sometimes be inconvenient. Telling your readers that you often read on the bus while traveling to work won't help you. In fact, being able to read while commuting is an advantage. Neither will it help to say that bus fares have risen lately. Remember that you are trying to explain the term "inconvenient," not "expensive." A better example would be the fact that three days this week the bus was so crowded you had to stand up for the entire half-hour trip.

Development through Prewriting

When Cedric, the student author of "Altered States," was considering a topic for his exemplification essay, he looked around his dorm for inspiration. He first considered writing about examples of some different types of people: jocks, dorks, goths. Then he thought about examples of housekeeping in dorm rooms: the Slob Kingdom, the Neat Freak Room, and the Packrat's Place.

"But that evening I was noticing how my roommate acted as he was cruising the Internet," Cedric said. "He sat down to write his brother a brief e-mail, and three hours later he was still there, cruising from Web site to Web site. His eyes were glassy and he seemed out of touch with reality. It reminded me of how spaced out I get when I go to a busy shopping mall. I began to think about how our minds have to adjust to challenges that our grandparents didn't grow up with. I added 'watching television' as the third category, and I had a pretty good idea what my essay would be about."

Cedric had his three categories, but he needed to do some more work to generate supporting details for each. He used the technique of clustering, or diagramming, to help inspire his thinking. Here is what his diagram looked like:

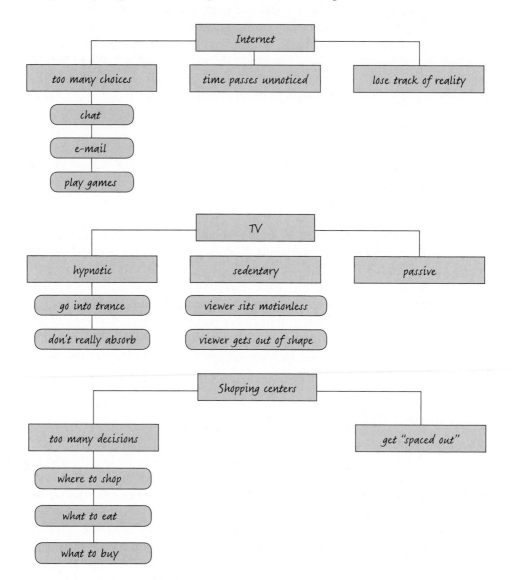

Looking at his diagram, Cedric saw that he would have no trouble supporting the thesis that people's minds go into an "altered state" when they watch TV, go to shopping centers, or use the Internet. As he quickly jotted down details in cluster form, he had easily come up with enough ideas for his essay. He started writing and produced this first draft.

Altered States   First Draft

Modern life makes demands on the human mind that no other period of history has made. As society becomes more and more complex, the mind has developed some defense mechanisms. Confronted with inventions like the Internet, television, and the shopping center, the mind will slip—all by itself—into an altered state.

Cruising the Internet can quickly make the mind slip into a strange state. A computer user sits down to check his e-mail or look up something. But once tapped into the Internet, the user loses all sense of time. He can chat with strangers, research any topic, play a game, or shop for any product. Some people begin to think of the online world and online friends as more real than the people in their own homes. While my roommate is absorbed in the Internet, he can even have brief conversations with people who come into our room, yet not be able to remember the conversations later. He sits there in a daze from information overload. He seems numb as he hits key after key, going from Web site to Web site.

Then there's TV. Growing up, our grandparents could not have imagined the idea of sitting passively for hours, staring at moving pictures emanating from a box. It's not a normal state of affairs, so the mind goes into something like a hypnotic trance. You see the sitcom or the dog-food commercial, but your mind goes into a holding pattern. You don't really absorb the pictures or sounds. Five minutes after I watch a show I can't remember commercials I've seen or why the TV cops are chasing a certain suspect.

If the TV watcher arises from the couch and journeys into the real world, he often goes to the shopping center. Here, the mind is bombarded with the sights, smells, and sounds of dozens of stores, restaurants, and movie theaters competing for its attention. Dazed shoppers begin to feel like mountain climbers trapped in a blinding snowstorm. Suddenly, everything looks the same. My father is the worst of all when it comes to shopping in an altered state. He comes back from the mall looking like he'd been through a war. After about fifteen minutes of shopping, he can't concentrate enough to know what he's looking for.

Internet surfers, TV viewers, and shoppers all have one thing in common. They're just trying to cope with the mind-numbing inventions of modern life. I hope that someday we'll turn away from such inventions and return to a simpler and more healthy way of life.

Development through Revising

Cedric showed his first-draft essay to a classmate for her critique. She returned his essay with these comments:

Altered States

Modern life makes demands on the human mind that no other period of history has made. As society becomes more and more complex, the mind has developed some defense mechanisms. Confronted with inventions like the Internet, television, and the shopping center, the mind will slip—all by itself—into an altered state.

Cruising the Internet can quickly make the mind slip into a strange state. A computer user sits down to check his e-mail or look up something. But once tapped into the Internet, the user loses all sense of time. He can chat with strangers, research any topic, play a game, or shop for any product. Some people begin to think of the online world and online friends as more real than the people in their own homes. While my roommate is absorbed in the Internet, he can even have brief conversations with people who come into our room, yet not be able to remember the conversations later. He sits there in a daze from information overload. He seems numb as he hits key after key, going from Web site to Web site.

Then there's TV. Growing up, our grandparents could not have imagined the idea of sitting passively for hours, staring at moving pictures emanating from a box. It's not a normal state of affairs, so the mind goes into something like a hypnotic trance. You see the sitcom or the dog-food commercial, but your mind goes into a holding pattern. You don't really absorb the pictures or sounds. Five minutes after I watch a show I can't remember commercials I've seen or why the TV cops are chasing a certain suspect.

If the TV watcher arises from the couch and journeys into the real world, he often goes to the shopping center. Here, the mind is bombarded with

(continued)

Reader's Comments

This seems to me like a separate topic—people's relationships with people they meet on the Internet.

Sometimes you write about "a user," other times about "you," and then about "my roommate." It's confusing. Also, is the paragraph about your roommate on the Internet or what people in general are like?

These last two sentences are good. I'd like to read more about this "altered state" you think people go into.

The idea of the "hypnotic trance" is interesting, but you need more details to back it up.

The point of view is a problem again. You skip from "you" to "I."

the sights, smells, and sounds of dozens of stores, restaurants, and movie theaters competing for its attention. Dazed shoppers begin to feel like mountain climbers trapped in a blinding snowstorm. Suddenly, everything looks the same. My father is the worst of all when it comes to shopping in an altered state. He comes back from the mall looking like he'd been through a war. After about fifteen minutes of shopping, he can't concentrate enough to know what he's looking for.

Internet surfers, TV viewers, and shoppers all have one thing in common. They're just trying to cope with the mind-numbing inventions of modern life. I hope that someday we'll turn away from such inventions and return to a simpler and more healthy way of life.

Good image!

I don't think this works. The essay isn't about your father. It should be about modern shoppers, not just one man.

This final sentence seems to introduce a new topic—that we shouldn't get caught up in TV and the Internet, etc.

Cedric read his classmate's comments and reviewed the essay himself. He agreed with her criticisms about point of view and the need for stronger supporting details. He also decided that the Internet was his strongest supporting point and should be saved for the last paragraph. He then wrote the final version of his essay, the version that appears on pages 233–234.

A Professional Essay to Consider

Read the following professional essay. Then answer the questions and read the comments that follow.

Dad
by Andrew H. Malcolm

www.mhhe.com/langan

The first memory I have of him—of anything, really—is his strength. It was 1 in the late afternoon in a house under construction near ours. The unfinished wood floors had large, terrifying holes whose yawning darkness I knew led to nowhere good. His powerful hands, then age thirty-three, wrapped all the way around my tiny arms, then age four, and easily swung me up to his shoulders to command all I surveyed.

The relationship between a son and his father changes over time. It may   2
grow and flourish in mutual maturity. It may sour in resented dependence or
independence. With many children living in single-parent homes today, it may
not even exist.

But to a little boy right after World War II, a father seemed a god with strange   3
strengths and uncanny powers enabling him to do and know things that no mortal
could do or know. Amazing things, like putting a bicycle chain back on, just like
that. Or building a hamster cage. Or guiding a jigsaw so it formed the letter F;
I learned the alphabet that way in those pretelevision days, one letter or number
every other evening plus a review of the collection. (The vowels we painted red
because they were special somehow.)

He seemed to know what I thought before I did. "You look like you could use   4
a cheeseburger and a chocolate shake," he would say on hot Sunday afternoons.
When, at the age of five, I broke a neighbor's garage window with a wild curveball
and waited in fear for ten days to make the announcement, he seemed to know
about it already and to have been waiting for something.

There were, of course, rules to learn. First came the handshake. None of those   5
fishy little finger grips, but a good firm squeeze accompanied by an equally strong
gaze into the other's eyes. "The first thing anyone knows about you is your handshake," he would say. And we'd practice it each night on his return from work, the
serious toddler in the battered Cleveland Indians cap running up to the giant father
to shake hands again and again until it was firm enough.

When my cat killed a bird, he defused the anger of a nine-year-old with a   6
little chat about something called "instinked." The next year, when my dog got run
over and the weight of sorrow was just too immense to stand, he was there, too,
with his big arms and his own tears and some thoughts on the natural order of life
and death, although what was natural about a speeding car that didn't stop always
escaped me.

As time passed, there were other rules to learn. "Always do your best." "Do   7
it now." "NEVER LIE!" And, most important, "You can do whatever you have to
do." By my teens, he wasn't telling me what to do anymore, which was scary and
heady at the same time. He provided perspective, not telling me what was around
the great corner of life but letting me know there was a lot more than just today and
the next, which I hadn't thought of.

When the most important girl in the world—I forget her name now—turned   8
down a movie date, he just happened to walk by the kitchen phone. "This may
be hard to believe right now," he said, "but someday you won't even remember
her name."

One day, I realize now, there was a change. I wasn't trying to please him so   9
much as I was trying to impress him. I never asked him to come to my football
games. He had a high-pressure career, and it meant driving through most of Friday
night. But for all the big games, when I looked over at the sideline, there was

that familiar fedora. And, by God, did the opposing team captain ever get a firm handshake and a gaze he would remember.

Then, a school fact contradicted something he said. Impossible that he could **10** be wrong, but there it was in the book. These accumulated over time, along with personal experiences, to buttress[1] my own developing sense of values. And I could tell we had each taken our own, perfectly normal paths.

I began to see, too, his blind spots, his prejudices, and his weaknesses. I never **11** threw these up at him. He hadn't to me, and, anyway, he seemed to need protection. I stopped asking his advice; the experiences he drew from no longer seemed relevant to the decisions I had to make. On the phone, he would go on about politics at times, why he would vote the way he did or why some incumbent was a jerk. And I would roll my eyes to the ceiling and smile a little, though I hid it in my voice.

He volunteered advice for a while. But then, in more recent years, politics and **12** issues gave way to talk of empty errands and, always, to ailments—his friends', my mother's, and his own, which were serious and included heart disease. He had a bedside oxygen tank, and he would ostentatiously[2] retire there during my visits, asking my help in easing his body onto the mattress. "You have very strong arms," he once noted.

From his bed, he showed me the many sores and scars on his misshapen body **13** and all the bottles of medicine. He talked of the pain and craved much sympathy. He got some. But the scene was not attractive. He told me, as the doctor had, that his condition would only deteriorate. "Sometimes," he confided, "I would just like to lie down and go to sleep and not wake up."

After much thought and practice ("You can do whatever you have to do"), one **14** night last winter, I sat down by his bed and remembered for an instant those terrifying dark holes in another house thirty-five years before. I told my father how much I loved him. I described all the things people were doing for him. But, I said, he kept eating poorly, hiding in his room, and violating other doctors' orders. No amount of love could make someone else care about life, I said: it was a two-way street. He wasn't doing his best. The decision was his.

He said he knew how hard my words had been to say and how proud he was **15** of me. "I had the best teacher," I said. "You can do whatever you have to do." He smiled a little, and we shook hands, firmly, for the last time.

Several days later, at about 4 A.M., my mother heard Dad shuffling about their **16** dark room. "I have some things I have to do," he said. He paid a bundle of bills. He composed for my mother a long list of legal and financial what-to-do's "in case of emergency." And he wrote me a note.

Then he walked back to his bed and laid himself down. He went to sleep, **17** naturally. And he did not wake up.

---

[1]*buttress:* strengthen and support.
[2]*ostentatiously:* dramatically.

About Unity

1. What is the thesis of Malcolm's essay "dad"? (Write the first words.)

   _____

2. Which statement would best serve as a topic sentence for paragraph 6?
   a. My dad loved my dog as much as I did.
   b. Pets were a subject that drew my dad and me together.
   c. My dad helped me make sense of life's tragedies.
   d. I was angry at my cat for killing a bird.

3. Write a sentence that might serve as the topic sentence of paragraph 10.

   _____

About Support

4. List the details Malcolm uses in paragraph 3 to support the idea that his father "seemed a god with strange strengths and uncanny powers."

   _____

   _____

   _____

5. With which sentence does Malcolm support his statement in paragraph 14 that his father "wasn't doing his best"? (*Write the opening words.*)

   _____

6. What point or idea does the anecdote in paragraph 8 suppoprt?

   _____

About Coherence

7. What event makes Malcolm begin to see his father in more realistic, less idealized terms?

   _____

8. In paragraph 6, find each of the following:
   a. two time transition signals

      _____   _____

   b. one addition transition signal

      _____

    c. one change-of-direction transition signal

_____

9. Which method of organization does Malcolm use in his essay?
    a. Time
    b. Emphatic

About the Conclusion
10. The conclusion of "Dad" is made up of
    a. a summary of the narrative and a final thought.
    b. a question about fatherhood.
    c. the last event of the story about Malcolm and his father.
    d. a prediction of what kind of father Malcolm hopes to be himself.

Writing an Exemplification Essay

Writing Assignment 1

For this assignment, you will complete an unfinished essay by adding appropriate supporting examples. Here is the incomplete essay:

Problems with My Apartment

When I was younger, I fantasized about how wonderful life would be when I moved into my own apartment. Now I'm a bit older and wiser, and my dreams have turned into nightmares. My apartment has given me nothing but headaches. From the day I signed the lease, I've had to deal with an uncooperative landlord, an incompetent janitor, and inconsiderate neighbors.

First of all, my landlord has been uncooperative. . . .

I've had a problem not only with my landlord but also with an incompetent janitor. . . .

> Perhaps the worst problem has been with the inconsiderate neighbors who live in the apartment above me. . . .

> Sometimes, my apartment seems like a small, friendly oasis surrounded by hostile enemies. I never know what side trouble is going to come from next: the landlord, the janitor, or the neighbors. Home may be where the heart is, but my sanity is thinking about moving out.

© Journal-Courier/Steve Warmowski/ The Image Works

If you do not have experience with living in an apartment, write instead about problems of living in a dormitory or problems of living at home. Revise the introduction and conclusion so that they fit your topic. Problems of living in a dorm might include these:

Restrictive dorm regulations

Inconsiderate students on your floor

A difficult roommate

Problems of living at home might be these:

Lack of space

Inconsiderate brothers and sisters

Conflict with your parent or parents

Prewriting

a. Generate details for your paper by using questioning as a prewriting technique. Write answers to the following questions. *(Use separate paper.)*

How has the landlord been uncooperative?

In what ways have you been inconvenienced?

Has he (or she) been uncooperative more than once?

How have you reacted to the landlord's lack of cooperation?

What has been the landlord's reaction?

What kinds of things have you said to each other?

What is the most uncooperative thing the landlord has done?

Who is the janitor?

What has he (or she) tried to fix in the apartment?

In what ways has the janitor been incompetent?

How has the janitor inconvenienced you?

Has the janitor's incompetence cost you money?

What is the worst example of the janitor's incompetence?

Who are the neighbors?

How long have they lived upstairs?

What kind of problems have you had with them?

Have these problems occurred more than once?

If you have spoken to the neighbors about the problems, how did they respond?

What is the worst problem with these neighbors?

b. Use the details generated by your questioning to flesh out the three paragraphs with details and examples. Remember that you may use one extended example in each paragraph (as in "Look on the Bright Side") or several brief examples (as in "Altered States").

c. As you write your first draft, keep asking yourself these questions:

Do my examples truly show my landlord as *uncooperative?*

Do my examples truly show the janitor as *incompetent?*

Do my examples truly show my neighbors as *inconsiderate?*

d. Write the first draft of your essay.

© Anton Vengo/SuperStock

Revising

After you have completed the first draft of the paper, set it aside for a while if you can. When you review it, try to do so as critically as you would if it were not your own work. Better yet, read it aloud to a friend or classmate whose judgment you trust. Read the essay with these questions in mind:

FOUR BASES Checklist for Exemplification

About *Unity*

☑ Do I have a clearly stated (or implied) thesis?

About *Support*

☑ Have I provided *relevant* specific details for the landlord's uncooperativeness, the janitor's incompetence, and the neighbors' inconsiderateness?

☑ Have I provided *enough* specific details to support each of the three qualities?

About *Coherence*

☑ Have I used transitions, including transitions between paragraphs, to help readers follow my train of thought?

☑ Do I have a concluding paragraph that provides a summary or final thought or both?

About *Sentence Skills*

☑ Have I used a consistent point of view throughout my essay?

☑ Have I used specific rather than general words?

☑ Have I avoided wordiness and used concise wording?

☑ Are my sentences varied?

☑ Have I proofread my essay for sentence skills, as listed on the inside back cover of the book?

As you revise your essay through one or more additional drafts, continue to refer to this checklist until you can answer yes to each question.

Writing | Assignment

2

Write an exemplification essay on the outstanding qualities (good or bad) of a person you know well. This person might be a member of your family, a friend, a roommate, a boss, a neighbor, an instructor, or someone else.

You may approach this assignment in one of two ways. You may choose to write about three related qualities of one person. For example, "My brother is stubborn, bad-tempered, and suspicious." Or you may write about one quality that is apparent in three different aspects of a person's life. For example, "My sister's patience is apparent in her relationships with her students, her husband, and her teenage son."

Just to jog your thinking, here are some descriptive words that can be applied to people. You are *not* restricted to writing about these qualities. Write about whatever qualities the person you choose possesses.

Honest	Persistent	Flirtatious	Spineless
Bad-tempered	Shy	Irresponsible	Good-humored
Ambitious	Sloppy	Stingy	Cooperative
Prejudiced	Hardworking	Aggressive	Disciplined
Considerate	Outgoing	Trustworthy	Sentimental
Argumentative	Supportive	Courageous	Defensive
Softhearted	Suspicious	Compulsive	Dishonest
Energetic	Lazy	Jealous	Insensitive
Patient	Cynical	Modest	Neat
Reliable	Independent	Sarcastic	
Generous	Stubborn	Self-centered	

Prewriting

a. Ask yourself questions to come up with supporting details for your thesis. For instance, if you are writing about your sentimental father, you would ask questions like these:

> Why do I think of Dad as being sentimental?
>
> When have I seen him be sentimental?
>
> What sort of occasions make him sentimental?
>
> Where are some places he's become sentimental about?
>
> Whom does Dad become sentimental about?
>
> What are some memorable examples of Dad's acting sentimental?

b. Look over the material generated by your questioning and decide what your three main points will be.

c. Decide on the order of your supporting paragraphs. If one of your main points seems stronger than the others, consider making it the final point in the body of the essay.

d. Decide whether to use one extended example or two or three brief examples to support each main point.

e. Prepare a scratch outline for your essay. To find your main points and supporting examples, draw on details generated by your questioning.

f. Write the first draft of your essay.

Revising
Refer to the guidelines for revising provided on page 248.

Writing Assignment

3 Write an exemplification essay based upon an outside reading. It might be a selection recommended by your instructor, or it might be a piece by one of the following authors, all of whom have written books of essays that should be available in your college library.

Annie Dillard	David Sedaris
Malcolm Gladwell	Amy Tan
Ellen Goodman	Deborah Tannen
Molly Ivins	Henry David Thoreau
Maxine Hong Kingston	Calvin Trillin
George Orwell	Alice Walker
Anna Quindlen	E. B. White
Richard Rodriguez	Marie Winn
Andy Rooney	

Base your essay on some idea in the selection you have chosen, and provide a series of examples to back up your idea. Of course, you may want to draw information from the reading selection by quoting from it or making other types of references. However, you might also want to use examples from other sources, perhaps something else you have read, a movie you have seen, or a personal experience.

The following student essay on capital punishment was inspired by and takes information from George Orwell's essay "A Hanging," which you can find online (the essay appears on page 675 of *College Writing Skills with Readings*).

However, the paper also uses examples from *The Green Mile*, a 1999 movie about the recollections of Paul Edgecomb during one year when he was a corrections officer in charge of inmates on death row.

Paying Attention to a Death

In "A Hanging" (1931), George Orwell narrates the execution of a Burmese man in such a way that no reader can avoid realizing the enormity of taking a human life. The Green Mile (1999), a movie based on a Stephen King novel, makes the same statement. The essay focuses on the last few moments in the life of a man we hardly get to know. The film covers the events of an entire year and allows us to see into the hearts of both prisoners and guards. But the messages are identical: no one, not even a legally constituted government, has the right to violate the sanctity of human life.   **1**

The moments leading to the hanging in Orwell's essay are filled with tension. Six tall guards, two of them armed with rifles, lead the prisoner, "a puny wisp of a man," who is both chained to their belts and handcuffed. Suddenly, the procession to the gallows is interrupted by a friendly dog that licks the prisoner's face and wags its "whole body wild with glee at finding so many human beings together." The scene is heavy with irony. This friendly animal, full of life and energy, contrasts markedly with the officials leading the prisoner to his death. "What is the point of all of this?" the presence of the dog suggests. In The Green Mile, a death-row prisoner called Del adopts a pet mouse that he names "Mr. Jingles." Del is a small, soft-spoken, endearing little man, who is able to train the mouse as if it were a very smart dog. He bonds with the tiny creature so poignantly that the silliness and brutality of his impending execution become clear. Here is a man who, literally, couldn't hurt a mouse—why not just keep him imprisoned for life?   **2**

Both essay and film defend the sanctity and dignity of human life. In "A Hanging," Orwell mentions that the prisoner moves to avoid a puddle on his way to the gallows. Why does he do this if not from some innate human need to keep his dignity intact, even to the last? Seconds before he is killed, he begins "crying out to his god." The repeated "Ram! Ram! Ram!" is his own death knell. The guards grow gray, finally realizing that the hooded, faceless little man on the platform is, after all, a human being. In The Green Mile, Del is finally electrocuted, but the manner in which he dies provides us a painful reminder of the sacredness that capital punishment violates. Guard Percy Wetmore, a sadistic coward, is given the job of preparing Del for the chair. This involves placing a wet sponge on his head so that electricity will flow more efficiently through his body and result in less pain. Demonically,   **3**

(continued)

Wetmore decides to leave the sponge dry. When the switch is thrown, Del writhes in agony, his suffering beyond belief. Then, the chair bursts into flame in a scene from which viewers will want to turn away.

Interestingly, the author of "A Hanging" never tells about the crime for which the prisoner was executed. He leaves this information out intentionally. For Orwell, capital punishment is wrong, no matter the crime. A similar statement is made in The Green Mile. John Coffee, an African American, sits on death row, having been wrongly convicted of killing two white girls. Coffee is a giant—seven feet tall and muscular—but he is as gentle as Del and his mouse. Moreover, he has magical healing powers that he uses to cure Paul Edgecomb, the death-row superintendent, of a severe urinary infection, to bring Mr. Jingles back to life, and even to save the warden's wife from a deadly cancer. Near the end of the movie, we discover that the girls' real killer is another death-row inmate, and we hope for John Coffee's release. But it is not to be; the real killer dies without confessing. Yes, Edgecomb gives Coffee the option to escape, but the gentle giant declines, explaining that the world is just too evil and that he is just "dog tired."   4

Only a few moments after the execution of the Burmese prisoner, Orwell's prison officials attempt to forget that they have just killed a man. They make silly jokes, smoke cigarettes, and take a drink, even though it is still early morning. The Green Mile ends with Paul Edgecomb, now 108 years old, recalling Coffee's execution and explaining that living to see all of his friends and relatives die is his punishment for letting Coffee go to the chair. "We each owe a death," he says. "There are no exceptions. But, Oh God, sometimes the Green Mile seems so long." Standing only a few yards away from the body, Orwell's warders pretend to ignore the horror they have committed. They are trying to hide the moon with a sheet, as my grandmother would say. At least Paul Edgecomb accepts the enormous significance of Coffee's wrongful death. And for that reason, we too can feel his pain and regret as if they were our own.   5

Writing | Assignment

4 Writing for a Specific Purpose and Audience
In this exemplification essay, you will write with a specific purpose and for a specific audience. Imagine that you have completed a year of college and have agreed to take part in your college's summer orientation program for incoming

students. You will be meeting with a small group of new students to help them get ready for college life.

Prepare a presentation to the new students in which you make the point that college is more demanding than high school. Make vividly clear—using several hypothetical students as examples—just what the consequences of being unprepared for those demands can be. Focus on three areas of college and the demands of each. Some areas you might consider are these: instructors, class attendance, time management, class note-taking, choosing courses, studying a textbook, work habits, balancing work and social life, and getting help when it is needed. Each of the areas you choose should be developed in a separate paragraph. Each paragraph should have its own detailed examples.

www.mhhe.com/langan

11

Process

This chapter will explain and illustrate how to

- develop a process essay
- write a process essay
- revise a process essay

In addition, you will read and consider

- two student process essays
- one professional process essay

© Mike Watson Images/Corbis

Write an essay that informs a reader how to perform a particular hobby or activity you enjoy. Depending on the hobby or activity you are writing about, you may prefer to use a humorous approach.

Every day we perform many activities that are *processes,* that is, series of steps carried out in a definite order. Many of these processes are familiar and automatic: for example, loading film into a camera, diapering a baby, or making an omelet. We are thus seldom aware of the sequence of steps making up each activity. In other cases—for example, when someone asks us for directions to a particular place, or when we try to read and follow directions for a new table game that someone has given us—we may be painfully conscious of the whole series of steps involved in the process.

In this chapter, you will be asked to write a process essay—one that explains clearly how to do or make something. To prepare for this assignment, you should first read the student process papers and the professional essay and then answer the questions that follow them.

Student Essays to Consider

Successful Exercise

Regular exercise is something like the weather—we all talk about it, 1
but we tend not to do anything about it. Exercise classes on television and
exercise programs on DVDs—as well as instructions in books, magazines, and
pamphlets—now make it easy to have a low-cost personal exercise program
without leaving home. However, for success in exercise, you should follow
a simple plan consisting of arranging time, making preparations, and starting
off at a sensible pace.

Everyone has an excuse for not exercising: a heavy schedule at work 2
or school; being rushed in the morning and exhausted at night; too many
other responsibilities. However, one solution is simply to get up half an hour
earlier in the morning. Look at it this way: if you're already getting up too
early, what's an extra half hour? Of course, that time could be cut to fifteen
minutes earlier if you could lay out your clothes, set the breakfast table,
fill the coffeemaker, and gather your books and materials for the next day
before you go to bed.

Next, prepare for your exercise session. To begin with, get yourself 3
ready by not eating or drinking anything before exercising. Why risk an upset
stomach? Then, dress comfortably in something that allows you to move
freely. Since you'll be in your own home, there's no need to invest in a high-
fashion dance costume. A loose T-shirt and shorts are good. A bathing suit
is great in summer, and in winter long underwear is warm and comfortable.
If your hair tends to flop in your eyes, pin it back or wear a headband or
scarf. Prepare the exercise area, too. Turn off the phone and lock the door to
prevent interruptions. Shove the coffee table out of the way so you won't
bruise yourself on it or other furniture. Then get out the simple materials
you'll need to exercise with.

Finally, use common sense in getting started. Common sense isn't so 4
common, as anyone who reads the newspapers and watches the world can
tell you. If this is your first attempt at exercising, begin slowly. You do not
need to do each movement the full number of times at first, but you should
try each one. After five or six sessions, you should be able to do each one the
full number of times. Try to move in a smooth, rhythmic way; this will help
prevent injuries and pulled muscles. Pretend you're a dancer and make each
move graceful, even if it's just getting up off the floor. After the last exercise,
give yourself five minutes to relax and cool off—you have earned it. Finally,
put those sore muscles under a hot shower and get ready for a great day.

(continued)

Establishing an exercise program isn't difficult, but it can't be achieved by   5
reading about it, talking about it, or watching models exercise on television.
It happens only when you get off that couch and do something about it. As
my doctor likes to say, "If you don't use it, you'll lose it."

How to Complain

I'm not just a consumer—I'm a victim. If I order a product, it is sure to   1
arrive in the wrong color, size, or quantity. If I hire people to do repairs, they
never arrive on the day scheduled. If I owe a bill, the computer program is
bound to overcharge me. Therefore, in self-defense, I have developed the
following consumer's guide to complaining effectively.

The first step is getting organized. I save all sales slips and original boxes.   2
Also, I keep a special file for warranty cards and appliance guarantees. This
file does not prevent a product from falling apart the day after the guarantee
runs out. One of the problems in our country is the shoddy workmanship
that goes into many products. However, these facts give me the ammunition
I need to make a complaint. I know the date of the purchase, the correct
price (or service charge), where the item was purchased, and an exact
description of the product, including model and serial numbers. When I
compose my letter of complaint, I find it is not necessary to exaggerate. I
just stick to the facts.

The next step is to send the complaint to the person who will get   3
results quickly. My experience has shown that the president of the company
is the best person to contact. I call the company to find out the president's
name and make sure I note the proper spelling. Then I write directly to
that person, and I usually get prompt action. For example, the head of AMF
arranged to replace my son's ten-speed "lemon" when it fell apart piece
by piece in less than a year. Another time, the president of a Philadelphia
department store finally had a twenty-dollar overcharge on my bill
corrected after I had spent three months arguing uselessly with a computer
program.

If I get no response to a written complaint within ten days, I follow   4
through with a personal telephone call. When I had a new bathtub installed
a few years ago, the plumber left a gritty black substance on the bottom of
the tub. No amount of scrubbing could remove it. I tried every cleanser on
the supermarket shelf, but I still had a dirty tub. The plumber shrugged off

(continued)

my complaints and said to try Comet. The manufacturer never answered my letter or e-mail. Finally, I made a personal phone call to the president of the firm. Within days a well-dressed executive showed up at my door. In a business suit, white shirt, striped tie, and rubber gloves, he cleaned the tub. Before he left, he scolded me in an angry voice, "You didn't have to call the president." The point is, I did have to call the president. No one else cared enough to solve the problem.

Therefore, my advice to consumers is to keep accurate records, and   5
when you have to complain, go right to the top. It has always worked for me.

About Unity

Questions

1

1. The (*fill in the correct answer:* first, second, third) _____ supporting paragraph of "Successful Exercise" lacks a topic sentence. Write a topic sentence that expresses its main point:

   _____

   _____

2. Which sentence from paragraph 4 of "Successful Exercise" should be omitted in the interest of paragraph unity? (*Write the first words.*)

   _____

3. Which sentence in paragraph 2 of "How to Complain" should be omitted in the interest of paragraph unity? (*Write the opening words.*)

   _____

About Support

4. Which sentence in paragraph 3 of "Successful Exercise" needs to be followed by more supporting details? (*Write the opening words.*)

   _____

5. Which supporting paragraph in "How to Complain" uses one extended example? Write the number of that paragraph and tell (in just a few words) what the example was about.

   _____

   _____

6. Which supporting paragraph in "How to Complain" depends on two short examples? Write the number of that paragraph and tell (in just a few words) what each example was about.

_____

_____

About Coherence

7. Paragraph 3 of "Successful Exercise" uses four transitions. What type of transitions are they? List them here.

_____   _____   _____

_____   _____

8. In "How to Complain," what transitions are used to maintain coherence

between paragraphs 1 and 2? _____

Between 2 and 3? _____

About the Introduction and Conclusion

9. Which method for writing introductions discussed in Chapter 4 is used in "Successful Exercise?"

_____

10. Which method for writing conclusions discussed in Chapter 4 is used in "Successful Exercise?"

_____

Developing a Process Essay

Considering Purpose and Audience

On any newsstand, you will see magazine cover stories with titles such as "How to Impress Your Boss" or "How to Seduce Anyone." Promising readers directions or information, these articles are popular versions of process essays.

In general, the purpose of a process essay is to explain the steps involved in an action, process, or event. Some process essays give readers instructions; others provide information. The type of essay you write depends on your purpose and topic.

Begin by asking yourself what you want your readers to know. If, for example, you want your audience to know how to make the ultimate chocolate chip cookie, your process essay would include directions telling them what to do and how to do it. On the other hand, if you want your readers to know how a cookie is digested, you would detail the events in the body as it turns food into energy.

No matter what your main point, keep your audience in mind as you work. As with any essay, select a topic that will interest readers. College students, for example, might be interested in an essay on how to get financial aid but be bored by one on how to prepare for retirement.

Finally, evaluate how much your readers already know about your topic. An audience unfamiliar with it might require you to explain technical terms. If you are explaining how to protect your computer from viruses, for example, you might have to define "firewall." If you are explaining how to check a car's tire pressure, you might have to describe a pressure gauge.

Deciding on Structure, Content, and Style

- As with other types of papers, include a thesis. In a process paper, your thesis might explain your purpose—why it is important to learn how to change the oil in your car or why learning to prepare a room for painting is worth knowing. On the other hand, it might explain something definitive about the process. For example, you might begin a paper on the digestive process by stating that, "the human body is a truly marvelous machine." Then, of course, you would have to show just how marvelous it is as you explain how it digests food.

- Use language that is easy to follow and not unnecessarily complex. If you are explaining how to do something, your readers may be executing your instructions as they read them for the first time. So be as clear as you can to avoid unintentionally misleading the reader.

- In most cases, list each step in chronological or time order. (See page 87 for words that signal time.)

- Explain each step in a separate paragraph. If two steps are done or occur simultaneously, connect separate paragraphs with phrases such as "At the same time."

- When giving information about a process, use the right verb tense. If you are explaining something that happened only once, use the past tense: "After Mount Vesuvius erupted, it covered the city of Pompeii with pumice and ash." However, if you are discussing something that recurs, use the present tense: "During the next phase of digestion, food passes down the esophagus to the stomach."

- If you are writing directions (something this book does), you will probably want to write in the second person, directly addressing your audience as "you." However, if you are presenting information, as in the examples about Pompeii and digestion above, you should write in the more formal third person.

> **TIP:** For more information about third- and second-person points of view, see pages 178–179.

Development through Prewriting

A process essay requires the writer to think through the steps involved in an activity. As Marian, the author of "How to Complain," thought about possible topics for her essay, she asked herself, What are some things I do methodically, step by step? A number of possibilities occurred to her, including getting herself and her children ready for school in the morning, shopping for groceries (from preparing a shopping list to organizing her coupons), and the one she finally settled on: effective complaining. "People tell me I'm 'so organized' when it comes to getting satisfaction on things I buy," Marian said. "I realized that I do usually get results when I complain because I go about complaining in an organized way. To write my essay, I just needed to put those steps into words."

Marian began by making a list of the steps she follows when she makes a complaint. This is what she wrote:

Save sales slips and original boxes

Engrave items with ID number in case of burglary

Write or e-mail letter of complaint

Save or make photocopy of letter

Create file of warranties and guarantees

Send complaint letter directly to president

Call company for president's name

Follow through with telephone call if no response

Make thank-you call after action is taken

Next, she numbered those steps in the order in which she performs them. She struck out some items she realized weren't really necessary to the process of complaining:

1   Save sales slips and original boxes
    ~~Engrave items with ID number in case of burglary~~
4   Write or e-mail letter of complaint
    ~~Save or make photocopy of letter~~
2   Create file of warranties and guarantees
5   Send complaint letter directly to president
3   Call company for president's name
6   Follow through with telephone call if no response
    ~~Make thank-you call after action is taken~~

Next, she decided to group her items into three steps: (1) getting organized, (2) sending the complaint to the president, and (3) following up with further action.

With that preparation done, Marian wrote her first draft.

How to Complain

First Draft

Because I find that a consumer has to watch out for herself and be ready to speak up if a product or service isn't satisfactory, I have developed the following consumer's guide to complaining effectively.

The first step is getting organized. I save all sales slips, original boxes, warranty cards, and appliance guarantees. This file does not prevent a product from falling apart the day after the guarantee runs out. One of the problems in our country is the shoddy workmanship that goes into many products. That way I know the date of the purchase, the correct price, where the item was purchased, and an exact description of the product.

The next step is to send the complaint to the person who will get results quickly. I call the company to find out the president's name and then I write directly to that person. For example, the head of AMF arranged to replace my son's bike. Another time, the president of a Philadelphia

(continued)

department store finally had a twenty-dollar overcharge on my bill corrected.

If I get no response to a written complaint within ten days, I follow through with a personal telephone call. When I had a new bathtub installed a few years ago, the plumber left a gritty black substance on the bottom of the tub. I tried everything to get it off. Finally, I made a personal phone call to the president of the firm. Within days a well-dressed executive showed up at my door. In a business suit, white shirt, striped tie, and rubber gloves, he cleaned the tub. Before he left, he said, "You didn't have to call the president."

Therefore, my advice to consumers is to keep accurate records, and when you have to complain, go right to the top. It has always worked for me.

Development through Revising

After she had written the first draft, Marian set it aside for several days. When she reread it, she was able to look at it more critically. These are her comments:

I think this first draft is OK as the "bare bones" of an essay, but it needs to be fleshed out everywhere. For instance, in paragraph 2, I need to explain why it's important to know the date of purchase etc. And in paragraph 3, I need to explain more about what happened with the bike and the department store overcharge. In paragraph 4, especially, I need to explain how I tried to solve the problem with the bathtub before I called the president. I want to make it clear that I don't immediately go to the top as soon as I have a problem—I give the people at a lower level a chance to fix it first. All in all, my first draft looks as if I just rushed to get the basic ideas down on paper. Now I need to take the time to back up my main points with better support.

With that self-critique in mind, Marian wrote the version of "How to Complain" that appears on pages 256–257.

A Professional Essay to Consider

Read the following professional essay. Then answer the questions and read the comments that follow.

How to Do Well on a Job Interview
by Glenda Davis

www.mhhe.com/langan

Ask a random selection of people for a listing of their least favorite activities, **1** and right up there with "getting my teeth drilled" is likely to be "going to a job interview." The job interview is often regarded as a confusing, humiliating, and nerve-racking experience. First of all, you have to wait for your appointment in an outer room, often trapped there with other people applying for the same job. You sit nervously, trying not to think about the fact that only one of you may be hired. Then you are called into the interviewer's office. Faced with a complete stranger, you have to try to act both cool and friendly as you are asked all sorts of questions. Some questions are personal: "What is your greatest weakness?" Others are confusing: "Why should we hire you?" The interview probably takes about twenty minutes but seems like two hours. Finally, you go home and wait for days and even weeks. If you get the job, great. But if you don't, you're rarely given any reason why.

The job-interview "game" may not be much fun, but it is a game you *can* win **2** if you play it right. The name of the game is standing out of the crowd—in a positive way. If you go to the interview in a Bozo the Clown suit, you'll stand out of the crowd, all right, but not in a way that is likely to get you hired.

Here are guidelines to help you play the interview game to win: **3**

Present yourself as a winner. Instantly, the way you dress, speak, and move **4** gives the interviewer more information about you than you would think possible. You doubt that this is true? Consider this: a professional job recruiter, meeting a series of job applicants, was asked to signal the moment he decided *not* to hire each applicant. The thumbs-down decision was often made *in less than forty-five seconds—even before the applicant thought the interview had begun.*

How can you keep from becoming a victim of an instant "no" decision?   **5**

- *Dress appropriately.* This means business clothing: usually a suit and tie or a conservative dress or skirt suit. Don't wear casual student clothing. On the other hand, don't overdress: you're going to a job interview, not a party. If you're not sure what's considered appropriate business attire, do some spying before the interview. Walk past your prospective place of employment at lunch or quitting time and check out how the employees are dressed. Your goal is to look as though you would fit in with that group of people.

- *Pay attention to your grooming.* Untidy hair, body odor, dandruff, unshined shoes, a hanging hem, stains on your tie, excessive makeup or cologne, a sloppy job of shaving—if the interviewer notices any of these, your prospect of being hired takes a probably fatal hit.

- *Look alert, poised, and friendly.* When that interviewer looks into the waiting room and calls your name, he or she is getting a first impression of your behavior. If you're slouched in your chair, dozing or lost in the pages of a magazine; if you look up with an annoyed "Huh?"; if you get up slowly and wander over with your hands in your pockets, he or she will not be favorably impressed. What *will* earn you points is rising promptly and walking briskly toward the interviewer. Smiling and looking directly at that person, extend your hand to shake his or hers, saying, "I'm Lesley Brown. Thank you for seeing me today."

- *Expect to make a little small talk.* This is not a waste of time; it is the interviewer's way of checking your ability to be politely sociable, and it is your opportunity to cement the good impression you've already made. The key is to follow the interviewer's lead. If he or she wants to chat about the weather for a few minutes, do so. But don't drag it out; as soon as you get a signal that it's time to talk about the job, be ready to get down to business.

Be ready for the interviewer's questions. The same questions come up again 6 and again in many job interviews. *You should plan ahead for all these questions!* Think carefully about each question, outline your answer, and memorize each outline. Then practice reciting the answers to yourself. Only in this way are you going to be prepared. Here are common questions, what they really mean, and how to answer them:

- *"Tell me about yourself."* This question is raised to see how organized you are. The *wrong* way to answer it is to launch into a wandering, disjointed response or—worse yet—to demand defensively, "What do you want to know?" or "What do you mean?" When this question comes up, you should be prepared to give a brief summary of your life and work experience—where you grew up, where your family lives now, where you went to school, what jobs you've had, and how you happen to be here now looking for the challenge of a new job.

- *"What are your strengths and weaknesses?"* In talking about your strong points, mention traits that will serve you well in this particular job. If you are well organized, a creative problem-solver, a good team member, or a quick learner, be ready to describe specific ways those strengths have served you in the past. Don't make the mistake of saying, "I don't have any real weaknesses." You'll come across as more believable if you admit a flaw—but make it one that an employer might actually like. For instance, admit that you are a workaholic or a perfectionist.

- *"Why should we hire you?"* Remember that it is up to *you* to convince the interviewer that you're the man or woman for this job. If you just sit there and hope that the interviewer will magically discern your good qualities, you are likely to be disappointed. Don't be afraid to sell yourself. Tell the recruiter that from your research you have learned that the interviewer's company is one you would like to work for, and that you believe the company's needs and your skills are a great match.

- *"Why did you leave your last job?"* This may seem like a great opportunity to cry on the interviewer's shoulder about what a jerk your last boss was or how unappreciated you were. It is not. The experts agree: never bad-mouth *anyone* when you are asked this question. Say that you left in order to seek greater responsibilities or challenges. Be positive, not negative. No matter how justified you may feel about hating your last job or boss, if you give voice to those feelings in an interview, you're going to make the interviewer suspect that you're a whiner and hard to work with.

- *"Do you have any questions?"* This is the time to stress one last time how interested you are in this particular job. Ask a question or two about specific aspects of the job, pointing out again how well your talents and the company's needs are matched. Even if you're dying to know how much the job pays and how much vacation you get, don't ask. There will be time enough to cover those questions after you've been offered the job. Today, your task is to demonstrate what a good employee you would be.

Send a thank-you note. Once you've gotten past the interview, there is one 7 more chance for you to make a fine impression. As soon as you can—certainly no more than one or two days after the interview—write a note of thanks to your interviewer. In it, briefly remind him or her of when you came in and what job you applied for. As well as thanking the interviewer for seeing you, reaffirm your interest in the job and mention again why you think you are the best candidate for it. Make the note courteous, businesslike, and brief—just a paragraph or two. If the interviewer is wavering between several equally qualified candidates, such a note could tip the scales in your favor.

No amount of preparation is going to make interviewing for a job your favorite 8 activity. But if you go in well-prepared and with a positive attitude, your potential employer can't help thinking highly of you. And the day will come when you are the one who wins the job.

About Unity

1. Either of two sentences in "How to Do Well on a Job Interview" might serve as the thesis. Write the opening words of either of these sentences:

_____

_____

_____

2. Which statement would make the best topic sentence for paragraph 4?
   a. Beauty is only skin-deep.
   b. Interviewers care only about how applicants dress.
   c. Professional job recruiters meet many applicants for a single job.
   d. You should present yourself as a winner because first impressions count a lot.

3. Write an appropriate topic sentence for the list item that talks about strengths and weaknesses in paragraph 6.

_____

_____

About Support

4. What does the author mean by "dress appropriately" in paragraph 5?

_____

5. According to Davis, what is the best reason for sending a thank-you note?

_____

_____

About Coherence

6. In paragraph 1, what three transitional words or phrases are used to begin sentences as the author describes the process of interviewing?

_____   _____   _____

7. The main method of organization of paragraph 1 is
   a. time order.
   b. emphatic order.

8. Find three change-of-direction signals in the first list item of paragraph 5. (*Write them here.*)

_____ _____ _____

About the Introduction and Conclusion

9. Which statement best describes the introductory paragraph of "How to Do Well on a Job Interview"?

   a. It begins with a broad, general statement about job interviews and narrows it down to the thesis statement.

   b. It describes a typical job interview and its aftermath.

   c. It explains the importance of doing well on a job interview.

   d. It asks a series of questions that encourage readers to think about how they prepare for a job interview.

10. What method for writing conclusions explained in Chapter 4 does Davis use?

_____

Writing a Process Essay

Writing Assignment

1

Choose a topic from the list below to use as the basis for a process essay.

- How to shop for groceries in a minimum amount of time
- How to choose a car, rent an apartment, or buy a house
- How to do household cleaning efficiently
- How to gain or lose weight
- How to get over a broken heart
- How to plan an event (party, wedding, garage sale, etc.)
- How to choose a pet
- How to quit smoking (or another bad habit)

© WoodyStock/Alamy

Prewriting

a. Freewrite for ten minutes on the topic you have tentatively chosen. Don't worry about spelling, grammar, organization, or anything other than getting your thoughts down on the page. If ideas are still flowing at the end of ten minutes, keep on writing. This freewriting will give you a base of raw material that you can draw on in the next phase of your work. Judging from your freewriting, do you think you have enough material to support a process essay? If so, keep following the steps below. If not, choose another topic and freewrite about *it* for ten minutes.

b. Develop a single clear sentence that will serve as your thesis. Your thesis can either (1) say it is important that your readers know about this process ("Knowing how to choose a pet wisely can ensure that the two of you have a happy relationship") or (2) state your opinion of this process ("Quitting smoking is the most important single thing you can do for your health").

c. Make a list of the steps you are describing. Here, for example, is the list prepared by the author of "Successful Exercise."

Wear comfortable, loose clothing

Clear an area for exercise

Lock the door and turn off the phone

Tie hair back

Move smoothly and gracefully

Start slowly

Take hot shower afterward

Make time—get up early, give up a TV show

Get out weights or other equipment

Turn on music

Cool down

d. Number your items in time order. Strike out items that do not fit in the list; add others as they occur to you. Thus:

> 2 Wear comfortable, loose clothing
>
> 4 Clear an area for exercise
>
> 6 Lock the door and turn off the phone
>
> 3 Tie hair back
>
> 8 Move smoothly and gracefully
>
> 7 Start slowly
>
> 10 Take hot shower afterward
>
> 1 Make time—get up early, give up a TV show
>
> 5 Get out weights or other equipment
>
> ~~Turn on music~~
>
> 9 Cool down

e. After making the list, decide how the items can be grouped into a minimum of three steps. For example, with "Successful Exercise," you might divide the process into (1) setting a regular time, (2) preparing for exercise, and (3) doing the exercise. With a topic like "How to Quit Smoking," you might divide the process into (1) keeping a journal of your smoking, (2) preparing mentally and physically, and (3) getting through the first days.

f. Use your list as a guide to write the first rough draft of your paper. Do not expect to finish your paper in one draft. You should be ready to write a series of drafts as you work toward the goals of unity, support, and coherence.

Revising

After you have completed the first draft of the paper, set it aside for a while if you can. Then read the paper out loud to a friend or classmate whose judgment you respect. Keep these points in mind as you hear your own words, and ask your friend to respond to them as well:

FOUR BASES Checklist for Process

About *Unity*

   ✔   Does my essay describe the steps in a clear, logical way?

About *Support*

   ✔   Does the essay describe the necessary steps so that a reader could perform the task described, or is essential information missing?

About *Coherence*

   ✔   Have I used transitions such as *first, next, also, then, after, now, during,* and *finally* to make the essay move smoothly and clearly from one step to another?

   ✔   Do I have a concluding paragraph that provides a summary or final thought or both?

About *Sentence Skills*

   ✔   Have I used a consistent point of view throughout my essay?

   ✔   Have I used specific rather than general words?

   ✔   Have I avoided wordiness and used concise wording?

   ✔   Are my sentences varied?

   ✔   Have I proofread my essay for spelling and other sentence skills, as listed on the inside back cover of the book?

As you revise your essay through one or more additional drafts, continue to refer to this list until you can answer yes to each question.

Writing Assignment

2   Write an essay in which you explain how something is done or happens rather than how to do something. Focus on a limited subject. For example, instead of trying to discuss the workings of the U.S. government, explain the process by which a bill presented in Congress eventually becomes law. Instead of explaining how students are treated at your college, discuss a particular process they must go through, like orientation or registration. Instead of discussing ways in which families manage to stay together through rough times, explain how your family dealt with your grandmother's serious illness or how you compensated for the loss of income when one of your parents was out of work. Then again, you might explain what you are doing right now to meet your tuition payments and other bills on a limited salary while you attend college.

Here are other topics you might choose:

A coming-of-age ceremony like a confirmation or bar/bat mitzvah

A religious ceremony or service with which you are familiar

How a particular disease is or was treated

How people in your culture or another culture meet and get married

How a certain product is made (perhaps something the company you work for makes)

How a fast-food restaurant prepares for a lunch-time crowd

How professional athletic teams draft players

How a choral or theater group or an athletic team prepares for a major performance or game

How you broke bad news to your parents or other loved ones

How you told your parents or other loved ones something you were sure they would refuse to accept

How to break a bad habit or achieve a major goal

Prewriting

a. Write about a topic you know a lot about. However, if necessary, gather more detail by reading about your topic in the library or on the Internet. Don't put this information directly into your essay as you would into a research paper. Instead, just add it to what you already know—your store of knowledge about the topic. Then, use freewriting, listing, or some other information-gathering technique to put down information.

b. Look over your notes and make a list of steps involved in the process.

c. Considering your list, decide how you can divide the items listed into three steps. For instance, look at the following list of items compiled by a student for the process of registering for college courses. Fill in the blanks in the scratch outline that follows.

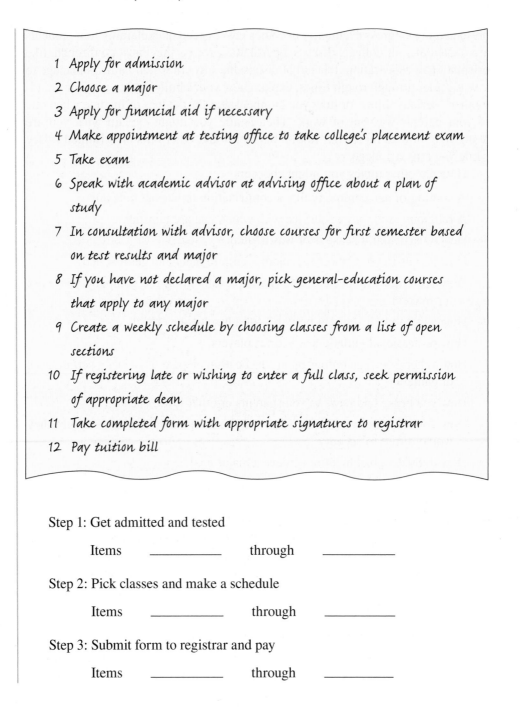

1 Apply for admission
2 Choose a major
3 Apply for financial aid if necessary
4 Make appointment at testing office to take college's placement exam
5 Take exam
6 Speak with academic advisor at advising office about a plan of study
7 In consultation with advisor, choose courses for first semester based on test results and major
8 If you have not declared a major, pick general-education courses that apply to any major
9 Create a weekly schedule by choosing classes from a list of open sections
10 If registering late or wishing to enter a full class, seek permission of appropriate dean
11 Take completed form with appropriate signatures to registrar
12 Pay tuition bill

Step 1: Get admitted and tested

     Items   _____ through   _____

Step 2: Pick classes and make a schedule

     Items   _____ through   _____

Step 3: Submit form to registrar and pay

     Items   _____ through   _____

d. You have just prepared the beginnings of a scratch outline. Finish the outline by filling in information under each main point. Then use this outline as a guide as you write the first draft of your paper.

Revising

As you read through your first draft and subsequent drafts, ask yourself these questions:

FOUR BASES Checklist for Process

About *Unity*

☑ Have I introduced my essay with either a statement of the importance of the process or my opinion of the process?

About *Support*

☑ Have I provided a clear step-by-step description of the process?

About *Coherence*

☑ Have I divided the items in the process into at least three logical steps (main points of the essay)?

☑ Have I used transitions such as *first, next, also, then, during,* and *finally* to help readers follow my train of thought?

About *Sentence Skills*

☑ Have I used a consistent point of view throughout my essay?

☑ Have I used specific rather than general words?

☑ Have I avoided wordiness and used concise wording?

☑ Are my sentences varied?

☑ Have I checked for spelling and other sentence skills, as listed on the inside back cover of the book?

As you revise your essay through one or more additional drafts, continue to refer to this checklist until you can answer yes to each question.

Writing | Assignment

3 Most process analysis papers provide straightforward instructions or explanations. However, sometimes you can take an ironic approach. That is, you can explain how to do something by recommending the very opposite. Doing so can make for interesting—even humorous—writing. For example, let's say you want to provide advice about classroom etiquette, a guide to impressing your instructor. You could take an ironic stance by discussing "How Not to Impress Your English Professor." Here is a paragraph that might appear in such an essay.

> While seated in class, never remove your hat, even though the instructor has indicated that wearing a hat in class is rude. Don't bother turning off your cell phone or putting it on "vibrate," either. If someone calls during class, make sure to answer the phone and talk in a normal voice, at least until the professor and your classmates stare you down. Another annoying cell phone trick involves "texting" someone, especially during a test. This will surely arouse the instructor's suspicion that you are cheating. Finally, never come to class without your iPod turned on and the earphones plugged snugly into your ears. Turning up the volume to create a bit of distracting background noise adds a nice touch.

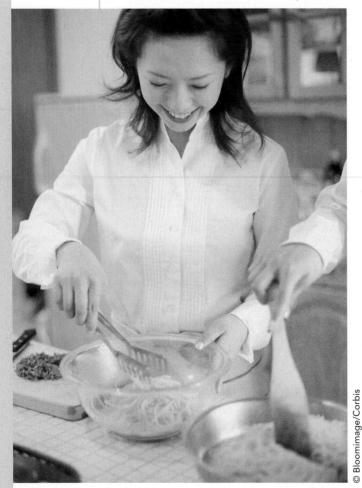

© Bloomimage/Corbis

Here are some topics you might want to write about. In any case, pick a topic that will yield a paper both you and your readers will enjoy. How to

- Flunk out of college
- Lose friends and annoy people
- Anger the police officer who has just asked you to pull your car to the side of the road
- Make certain a first date is not followed by a second
- Put on 10 pounds in a week

- Choose clothes that don't flatter you
- Waste money on a particular activity you do often
- Waste energy at home
- Waste valuable time when you're supposed to be studying
- Procrastinate—put off doing something important

Writing Assignment

4

Writing for a Specific Purpose and Audience

In this process essay, you will write with a specific purpose and for a specific audience. Imagine that you have a younger brother or sister who has asked you to be a guest editor of his or her high school paper. Prepare an informal essay in which you summarize, in your own words, the steps involved in successfully managing your time in college or in preparing for and taking an essay exam.

www.mhhe.com/langan

12

Cause and Effect

This chapter will explain and illustrate how to

- develop a cause-and-effect essay

- write a cause-and-effect essay

- revise a cause-and-effect essay

In addition, you will read and consider

- two student cause-and-effect essays

- one professional cause-and-effect essay

Craig Sjodin/© ABC/Courtesy Everett Collection

Write an essay in which you discuss the causes or effects of our society's fascination with reality TV. An essay on the causes would discuss why Americans are so intrigued with reality television shows. An essay on the effects would show how this fascination with reality TV has affected American society.

Why did Gail decide to move out of her parents' house? What made you quit a well-paying job? Why are horror movies so popular? Why has Ben acted so depressed lately? Why did our team fail to make the league play-offs?

Every day we ask questions like these and look for answers. We realize that many actions do not occur without causes, and we realize also that a given action can have a series of effects—good or bad. By examining the causes or effects of an action, we seek to understand and explain things that happen in our lives.

You will be asked in this chapter to do some detective work by examining the cause of something or the effects of something. First read the student essays and the professional essay that follow and work through the questions that accompany the essays. All three essays support their thesis statements by explaining a series of causes or a series of effects.

Student Essays to Consider

The Joys of an Old Car

Some of my friends can't believe that my car still runs. Others laugh when they see it parked outside the house and ask if it's an antique. But they aren't being fair to my twenty-year-old Toyota Corolla. In fact, my "antique" has opened my eyes to the rewards of owning an old car. 1

One obvious reward of owning my old Toyota is economy. Twenty years ago, when my husband and I were newly married and nearly broke, we bought the car—a shiny red year-old leftover—for a mere $4,200. Today it would cost four times as much. We save money on insurance, since it's no longer worthwhile for us to have collision coverage. Old age has even been kind to the Toyota's engine, which has required only three major repairs in the last several years. And it still delivers twenty-eight miles per gallon in the city and forty-one on the highway—not bad for a senior citizen. 2

I've heard that when a Toyota passes the twenty-thousand-mile mark with no problems, it will probably go on forever. I wouldn't disagree. Our Toyota breezed past that mark many years ago. Since then, I've been able to count on it to sputter to life and make its way down the driveway on the coldest, snowiest mornings. When my boss got stuck with his brand-new BMW in the worst snowstorm of the year, I sauntered into work on time. The single time my Toyota didn't start, unfortunately, was the day I had a final exam. The Toyota may have the body of an old car, but beneath its elderly hood hums the engine of a teenager. 3

Last of all, having the same car for many years offers the advantage of familiarity. When I open the door and slide into the driver's seat, the soft vinyl surrounds me like a well-worn glove. I know to the millimeter exactly how much room I have when I turn a corner or back into a curbside parking space. When my gas gauge points to "empty," I know that 1.3 gallons are still in reserve, and I can plan accordingly. The front wheels invariably begin to shake when I go more than fifty-five miles an hour, reminding me that I am exceeding the speed limit. With the Toyota, the only surprises I face come from other drivers. 4

I prize my twenty-year-old Toyota's economy and dependability, and most of all, its familiarity. It is faded, predictable, and comfortable, like a well-worn pair of jeans. And, like a well-worn pair of jeans, it will be difficult to throw away. 5

We Have Nothing to Fear

During the Great Depression, President Roosevelt claimed that, "We have   1
nothing to fear but fear itself." He wanted to inspire people as a way to
spur the economy. In his Nobel Prize acceptance speech of 1949, William
Faulkner, the great American novelist, said that, "the basest of all things is
to be afraid." Uttered more than a half century ago, both these ideas still
have relevance. Some young people make important life decisions based on
deep-seated anxieties. They fear that they won't be accepted by others, that
they won't find a mate, or that they just aren't living life to the fullest. As
a result, they pervert their identities, becoming people they don't want to
become and living lives they never intended.

Why is it that so many of us spend money—often money we don't   2
have—on costly toys we don't need? Deep in the pits of our stomachs is the
gnawing fear that, without such toys, our friends will abandon us and that we
will have to sit home weekends watching sitcom reruns. We are frightened
we won't fit in, so frightened, in fact, that we have become blind to the
true meaning of friendship. We have forgotten that, to people of character,
possessions and image are far less important than integrity, honesty, and
compassion. Such people are worth knowing, and they are everywhere. To
find them, all we need to do is to show a little character ourselves.

Some of my friends—both men and women—fear they will never be   3
able to attract and keep a lifelong partner. Therefore, they make gargantuan
efforts to re-create themselves in the Hollywood image. They follow
ludicrous diets, exercise for hours each week, and drink expensive commercial
concoctions to curb their appetites and lose weight. One of my friends even
turned herself into an anorexic. Looking forward to their more mature years,
they plan to get collagen injections, hair plugs, and even breast implants.
How much easier might their lives be if they simply trusted in the goodness
of someone who might love them for whom they are and not for the
smoothness of their skins or the fullness of their hair?

However, the fear that causes the greatest damage to the human spirit   4
is the one that makes people question the value and fullness of their own
lives. Too many of us—young and old alike, if the truth be told—are afraid
that we might miss out on "the good life," which, the media tells us, is part
of a life fulfilled. Influenced by the glitz of Hollywood and Madison Avenue,
we equate happiness with owning the best of everything. So, we take a
second and even a third job to afford the sexiest car, the biggest house, or
the largest television set. This is the worst perversion of all, for it turns us
into slaves. We don't own the car, the house, the television set; they own

(continued)

us. What else can we call it but slavery? The irony is, of course, that, in seeking the good life, we have lost it. Instead of rushing off to an evening of more work, how many of us have the luxury to come home after work and talk—really talk—to each other over dinner, to go for long walks, or simply to sit in the yard with neighbors and watch the sun set?

Who needs this cowering to silly fears, this getting and spending, this changing ourselves to fit into some ridiculous image created by a plastic society? Our moral vision has been blurred, and we need to realize, once more, that the true source of happiness, the measure of a life fulfilled, is the ability to see eternal beauty in the night sky, to become inspired by gently falling snow, and to recognize the image of God in the face of a child. 5

About Unity

1. Which supporting paragraph in "The Joys of an Old Car" lacks a topic sentence?

   a. 2

   b. 3

   c. 4

2. Which sentence in paragraph 3 of "The Joys of an Old Car" should be omitted in the interest of paragraph unity? (*Write the opening words.*)

   _____

3. Rewrite the thesis statement of "The Joys of an Old Car" to include a plan of development.

   _____

   _____

   _____

About Support

4. In paragraph 3 of "We Have Nothing to Fear," how does the author support the idea that some of her friends are afraid they won't be able to attract and keep lifelong partners?

   _____

   _____

   _____

5. After which sentence in paragraph 2 of "We Have Nothing to Fear" is more detail needed? (*Write the first words here.*)

_____

6. In "The Joys of an Old Car," what examples support the topic sentence in paragraph 2?

_____

_____

_____

_____

About Coherence

7. Which sentence in "We Have Nothing to Fear" serves as a linking sentence between paragraphs? (*Write the first words.*)

_____

8. Paragraph 3 of "We Have Nothing to Fear" contains two transitional words or phrases. List those words or phrases.

_____   _____

9. What are the two transition words or phrases in "The Joys of an Old Car" that signal two major points of support for the thesis?

_____   _____

About the Introduction and Conclusion

10. Which method for concluding essays explained in Chapter 4 does "The Joys of an Old Car" use?

   a. Summary and final thought

   b. Thought-provoking question

   c. Recommendation

Developing a Cause-and-Effect Essay

Considering Purpose and Audience

The purpose of cause-and-effect essays is to explain to your audience (1) the causes of an event or situation; (2) the effects of an event or situation; or more rarely (3) both causes and effects.

The type of essay you write depends on your topic and main point. If you want to tell readers the impact a person had on your life, your essay would focus on *effects*. If you want to explain why you moved out of your family home, it would focus on *causes*.

Cause-and-effect essays are like process essays. However, while process papers explain *how* something happens, cause-and-effect papers discuss the *reasons for or results* of an event or situation. Exams in science, history, economics, and other courses include questions that demand the explanation of causes, effects, or both. For example, you might be asked to explain the economic causes of the Russian Revolution or the atmospheric effects of cutting down trees in the rain forest.

At first, the process can seem simple. However, analyzing causes and effects is often complicated. For example, in the essay "We Have Nothing to Fear," the writer claims that many young people desire to possess the same type of clothing or electronic gadgets that their friends have. This stems from an *ultimate* or primary cause: the fear of being alone. A more *proximate* cause (one that is closer to the effect) is the desire to be popular, part of a group. In short, the writer has not simply discussed a cause but has explained a causal chain: (1) fear of being alone (ultimate cause); (2) desire to be popular (proximate cause); (3) need to have what others have (effect). Of course, the author could have extended the chain to explain the cause behind the fear of being alone: low self-esteem, difficult family life, or peer pressure, for example.

Analyzing effects can also be tricky because one cause may lead to multiple effects. In addition, one cause may yield a long-term effect as well as an immediate effect. Take the case of a young construction worker who decided to go back to college to study architecture five years after having graduated from high school. The immediate effects of his decision include (1) having to budget his money more carefully because he had to quit his job; (2) having less time to socialize with friends; and (3) getting a lot less physical exercise. However, there are several long-term effects as well: (1) securing a high-paying, white-collar position after graduation; (2) making new friends at college and at his new job; and (3) developing new tastes in music and film as a result of having to take college humanities courses.

Depending on your topic and purpose, you can decide whether to focus on causes or effects. If you want to balance your paper, you can discuss both. Consider each of the following scenarios and decide whether it requires discussing causes, effects, or both.

1. A young couple decides to buy a two-family house and rent out the top floor to tenants.

2. A new television reality show becomes an instant sensation, and the "actors" achieve instant fame.

3. Some patients of a local doctor demand she write them prescriptions for drugs when they know they can cure themselves by changing their diets and lifestyles.

Students writing on the first item might focus on effects; those writing on the second might discuss causes. The third item might be approached by writing about both.

Whichever approach you choose, remember that you can't discuss effects without at least mentioning causes, and vice versa. While discussing the problems that the young couple had with their tenants (effects of their decision to rent out the second floor), you might also explain their reason for becoming landlords in the first place: to earn rent money that would help them meet their mortgage payments.

As with all essays, pick a topic that appeals to your readers. An essay on the negative effects of steroids on professional athletes may interest sports fans; it might not appeal to people who dislike sports. In addition, make your main point clear so that your audience can follow the cause-and-effect relationship. You might even announce specific causes or effects by signaling them to readers: "One effect steroid use has on athletes is to . . ."

Development through Prewriting

The best essays are often those written about a topic that the author genuinely cares about. When Janine, the author of "The Joys of an Old Car," was assigned a cause-and-effect essay, she welcomed the assignment. She explains, "My husband and I believe in enjoying what we have and living simply, rather than 'keeping up with the Joneses.' Our beat-up old car is an example of that way of life. People often say to me, 'Surely you could buy a nicer car!' I enjoy explaining to them why we keep our old 'clunker.' So when I heard 'cause-and-effect essay,' I immediately thought of the car as a topic. Writing this essay was just an extension of a conversation I've had many times."

Although Janine had often praised the virtues of her old car to friends, she wasn't sure how to divide what she had to say into three main points. To get started, she made a list of all the good things about her car. Here is what she wrote:

> *Starts reliably*
>
> *Has needed few major repairs*
>
> *Reminder of Bill's and my first days of marriage*
>
> *Gets good gas mileage*
>
> *Don't need to worry about scratches and scrapes*

(continued)

I know exactly how much room I need to turn and park

Saves money on insurance

I'm very comfortable in it

No car payments

Cold weather doesn't seem to bother it

Don't worry about its being stolen

Uses regular gas

Can haul anything in it—dog, plants—and not worry about dirt

Know all its little tics and shimmies and don't worry about them

When Janine reviewed her list, she saw that the items fell into three major categories. There was (1) the car's economy, (2) its familiarity, and (3) its dependability. She went back and noted which category each of the items best fit. Then she crossed out those items that didn't seem to belong in any of the categories.

3 *Starts reliably*

1 *Has needed few major repairs*

~~*Reminder of Bill's and my first days of marriage*~~

1 *Gets good gas mileage*

~~*Don't need to worry about scratches and scrapes*~~

2 *I know exactly how much room I need to turn and park*

1 *Saves money on insurance*

2 *I'm very comfortable in it*

1 *No car payments*

3 *Cold weather doesn't seem to bother it*

~~*Don't worry about its being stolen*~~

(continued)

1   Uses regular gas
~~Can haul anything in it—dog, plants—and not worry about dirt~~
2   Know all its little tics and shimmies and don't worry about them

Now Janine had three main points and several items to support each point. She produced this as a first draft:

First Draft

The Joys of an Old Car

When people see my beat-up old car, they sometimes laugh at it. But I tell them that owning a twenty-year-old Toyota has its good points.

One obvious reward is economy. My husband and I bought the car when we were newly married. We paid $4,200 for it. That seemed like a lot of money then, but today we'd spend four times that much for a similar car. We also save money on insurance. In the twenty years we've had it, the Toyota has needed only a few major repairs. It even gets good gas mileage.

I like the familiar feel of the car. I'm so used to it that driving anything else feels very strange. When I visited my sister recently, I drove her new Prius to the grocery store. Everything was so unfamiliar! I couldn't even figure out how to turn on the radio. I was relieved to get back to my own car.

Finally, my car is very dependable. No matter how cold and snowy it is, I know the Toyota will start quickly and get me where I need to go. Unfortunately, one day it didn't start, and naturally that day I had a final exam. But otherwise it just keeps on going and going.

My Toyota reminds me of a favorite piece of clothing that you wear forever and can't bear to throw away.

Development through Revising

Janine traded first drafts with a classmate, Sharon, and each critiqued the other's work before it was revised. Here is Janine's first draft again, with Sharon's comments in the margins.

The Joys of an Old Car

When people see my beat-up old car, they sometimes laugh at it. But I tell them that owning a twenty-year-old Toyota has its good points.

One obvious reward is economy. My husband and I bought the car when we were newly married. We paid $4,200 for it. That seemed like a lot of money then, but today we'd spend four times that much for a similar car. We also save money on insurance. In the twenty years we've had it, the Toyota has needed only a few major repairs. It even gets good gas mileage.

I like the familiar feel of the car. I'm so used to it that driving anything else feels very strange. When I visited my sister recently, I drove her new Prius to the grocery store. Everything was so unfamiliar! I couldn't even figure out how to turn on the radio. I was relieved to get back to my own car.

Finally, my car is very dependable. No matter how cold and snowy it is, I know the Toyota will start quickly and get me where I need to go. Unfortunately, one day it didn't start, and naturally that day I had a final exam. But otherwise it just keeps on going and going.

My Toyota reminds me of a favorite piece of clothing that you wear forever and can't bear to throw away.

Reader's Comments

How? Is the insurance less expensive just because the car is old?

Here would be a good place for a specific detail—how good is the mileage?

This topic sentence doesn't tie in with the others—shouldn't it say "Second," or "Another reason I like the car . . . ."?

This is too much about your sister's car and not enough about yours.

This is a good comparison. But draw it out more—how is the car like comfortable old clothes?

Making use of Sharon's comments, Janine wrote the final version of "The Joys of an Old Car" that appears on page 277.

A Professional Essay to Consider

Read the following professional essay. Then answer the questions and read the comments that follow.

Taming the Anger Monster
by Anne Davidson

Laura Houser remembers the day with embarrassment.   1

"My mother was visiting from Illinois," she says. "We'd gone out to lunch and   2
done some shopping. On our way home, we stopped at an intersection. When the
light changed, the guy ahead of us was looking at a map or something and didn't
move right away. I leaned on my horn and automatically yelled—well, what I
generally yell at people who make me wait. I didn't even think about what I was
doing. One moment I was talking and laughing with my mother, and the next I
was shouting curses at a stranger. Mom's jaw just dropped. She said, 'Well, I guess
you've been living in the city too long.' That's when I realized that my anger was
out of control."

Laura has plenty of company. Here are a few examples plucked from the head-   3
lines of recent newspapers:

- Amtrak's Washington–New York train: When a woman begins to use her
  cell phone in a designated "quiet car," her seatmate grabs the phone and
  smashes it against the wall.

- Reading, Mass.: Arguing over rough play at their ten-year-old sons' hockey
  practice, two fathers begin throwing punches. One of the dads beats the
  other to death.

- Westport, Conn.: Two supermarket shoppers get into a fistfight over who
  should be first in a just-opened checkout line.

Reading these stories and countless others like them which happen daily, it's hard
to escape the conclusion that we are one angry society. An entire vocabulary has
grown up to describe situations of out-of-control fury: road rage, sideline rage,
computer rage, biker rage, air rage. Bookstore shelves are filled with authors'
advice on how to deal with our anger. Court-ordered anger management classes
have become commonplace, and anger-management workshops are advertised in
local newspapers.

Human beings have always experienced anger, of course. But in earlier, more   4
civil decades, public displays of anger were unusual to the point of being aberrant.
Today, however, whether in petty or deadly forms, episodes of unrepressed rage
have become part of our daily landscape.

What has happened to us? Are we that much angrier than we used to be? Have   5
we lost all inhibitions about expressing our anger? Are we, as a society, literally
losing our ability to control our tempers?

Why Are We So Angry?

According to Sybil Evans, a conflict-resolution expert in New York City, there are 6 three components to blame for our societal bad behavior: time, technology and tension.

What's eating up our time? To begin with, Americans work longer hours and 7 are rewarded with less vacation time than people in any other industrial society. Over an average year, for example, most British employees work 250 hours less than most Americans; most Germans work a full 500 hours less. And most Europeans are given four to six weeks vacation every year, compared to the average American's two weeks. To make matters worse, many Americans face long stressful commutes at the beginning and end of each long workday.

Once we Americans finally get home from work, our busy day is rarely done. 8 We are involved in community activities; our children participate in sports, school programs, and extracurricular activities; and our houses, yards and cars cry out for maintenance. To make matters worse, we are reluctant to use the little bit of leisure time we do have to catch up on our sleep. Compared with Americans of the nineteenth and early twentieth centuries, most of us are chronically sleep deprived. While our ancestors typically slept nine-and-a-half hours a night, many of us feel lucky to get seven. We're critical of "lazy" people who sleep longer, and we associate naps with toddlerhood. (In doing so, we ignore the example of successful people including Winston Churchill, Albert Einstein, and Napoleon, all of whom were devoted to their afternoon naps.)

The bottom line: we are time-challenged and just plain tired—and tired people 9 are cranky people. We're ready to blow—to snap at the slow-moving cashier, to tap the bumper of the slowpoke ahead of us, or to do something far worse.

Technology is also to blame for the bad behavior so widespread in culture. 10 Amazing gadgets were supposed to make our lives easier—but have they? Sure, technology has its positive aspects. It is a blessing, for instance, to have a cell phone on hand when your car breaks down far from home or to be able to "instant message" a friend on the other side of the globe. But the downsides are many. Cell phones, pagers, fax machines, handheld computers and the like have robbed many of us of what was once valuable downtime. Now we're *always* available to take that urgent call or act on that last-minute demand. Then there is the endless pressure of feeling we need to keep up with our gadgets' latest technological developments. For example, it's not sufficient to use your cell phone for phone calls. Now you must learn to use the phone for text-messaging and downloading games. It's not enough to take still photos with your digital camera. You should know how to shoot ultra high-speed fast-action clips. It's not enough to have an enviable CD collection. You should be downloading new songs in MP3 format. The computers in your house should be connected by a wireless router, and online via high-speed DSL service.

In other words, if it's been more than ten minutes since you've updated your technology, you're probably behind.

In fact, you're not only behind; you're a stupid loser. At least, that's how most 11 of us end up feeling as we're confronted with more and more unexpected technologies: the do-it-yourself checkout at the supermarket, the telephone "help center" that offers a recorded series of messages, but no human help. And feeling like losers makes us frustrated and, you guessed it, angry. "It's not any one thing but lots of little things that make people feel like they don't have control of their lives," says Jane Middleton-Moz, an author and therapist. "A sense of helplessness is what triggers rage. It's why people end up kicking ATM machines."

Her example is not far-fetched. According to a survey of computer users in 12 Great Britain, a quarter of those under age 25 admitted to having kicked or punched their computers on at least one occasion. Others confessed to yanking out cables in a rage, forcing the computer to crash. On this side of the Atlantic, a Wisconsin man, after repeated attempts to get his daughter's malfunctioning computer repaired, took it to the store where he had bought it, placed it in the foyer, and attacked it with a sledgehammer. Arrested and awaiting a court appearance, he told local reporters, "It feels good, in a way." He had put into action a fantasy many of us have had—that of taking out our feelings of rage on the machines that so frustrate us.

Tension, the third major culprit behind our epidemic of anger, is intimately 13 connected with our lack of time and the pressures of technology. Merely our chronic exhaustion and our frustration in the face of a bewildering array of technologies would be enough to cause our stress levels to skyrocket, but we are dealing with much more. Our tension is often fueled by a reserve of anger that might be the result of a critical boss, marital discord, or (something that many of today's men and women experience, if few will admit it) a general sense of being stupid and inadequate in the face of the demands of modern life. And along with the challenges of everyday life, we now live with a widespread fear of such horrors as terrorist acts, global warming, and antibiotic-resistant diseases. Our sense of dread may be out of proportion to actual threats because of technology's ability to so constantly bombard us with worrisome information. Twenty-four hours a day news stations bring a stream of horror into our living rooms. As we work on our computers, headlines and graphic images are never more than a mouseclick away.

The Result of Our Anger

Add it all together—our feeling of never having enough time; the chronic aggravation 14 caused by technology; and our endless, diffuse sense of stress—and we become time bombs waiting to explode. Our angry outbursts may be briefly satisfying, but afterwards we are left feeling—well, like jerks. Worse, flying off the handle is a self-perpetuating behavior. Brad Bushman, a psychology professor at Iowa State University, says, "Catharsis is worse than useless." Bushman's research has shown that when people vent their anger, they actually become more, not less, aggressive. "Many people think of anger as the psychological equivalent of the steam in a pressure cooker. It has to be released, or it will explode. That's not true. The people who react by hitting, kicking, screaming, and swearing just feel more angry."

Furthermore, the unharnessed venting of anger may actually do us physical [15] harm. The vigorous expression of anger pumps adrenaline into our system and raises our blood pressure, setting the stage for heart attack and strokes. Frequently angry people have even been shown to have higher cholesterol levels than even-tempered individuals.

How to Deal with Our Anger

Unfortunately, the culprits behind much of our anger—lack of time, frustrating [16] technology, and mega-levels of stress—are not likely to resolve themselves anytime soon. So what are we to do with the anger that arises as a result?

According to Carol Tavris, author of *Anger: The Misunderstood Emotion,* [17] the keys to dealing with anger are common sense and patience. She points out that almost no situation is improved by an angry outburst. A traffic jam, a frozen computer, or a misplaced set of car keys are annoying. To act upon the angry feelings those situations provoke, however, is an exercise in futility. Shouting, fuming, or leaning on the car horn won't make traffic begin to flow, the screen unlock, or keys materialize.

Patience, on the other hand, is a highly practical virtue. People who take the [18] time to cool down before responding to an anger-producing situation are far less likely to say or do something they will regret later. "It is as true of the body as of arrows," Tavris says, "that what goes up must come down. Any emotional arousal will simmer down if you just wait long enough." When you are stuck in traffic, in other words, turn on some soothing music, breathe deeply, and count to ten—or thirty or forty, if need be.

Anger-management therapist Doris Wild Helmering agrees. "Like any feeling, [19] anger lasts only about three seconds," she says. "What keeps it going is your own negative thinking." As long as you focus on the idiot who cut you off on the expressway, you'll stay angry. But if you let the incident go, your anger will go with it. "Once you come to understand that you're driving your own anger with your thoughts," adds Helmering, "you can stop it."

Experts who have studied anger also encourage people to cultivate activities that [20] effectively vent their anger. For some people, it's reading the newspaper or watching TV, while others need more active outlets, such as using a treadmill, taking a walk, hitting golf balls, or working out with a punching bag. People who succeed in calming their anger can also enjoy the satisfaction of having dealt positively with their frustrations.

For Laura Houser, the episode in the car with her mother was a wake-up call. "I [21] saw myself through her eyes," she said, "and I realized I had become a chronically angry, impatient jerk. My response to stressful situations had become habitual—I automatically flew off the handle. Once I saw what I was doing, it really wasn't that hard to develop different habits. I simply decided I was going to treat other people the way I would want to be treated." The changes in Laura's life haven't benefited only her former victims. "I'm a calmer, happier person now," she reports. "I don't lie in bed at night fuming over stupid things other people have done and my own enraged responses." Laura has discovered the satisfaction of having a sense of control over her own behavior—which ultimately is all any of us can control.

Questions 2

About Unity

1. Which of the following statements best represents the implied thesis of "Taming the Anger Monster"?

   a. People today have lost their ability to control their anger and to behave in a civil fashion.

   b. Anger would last only a few seconds if we didn't keep it going with negative thinking.

   c. While technology has its positive aspects, it has made us constantly available to others and frustrates us with the need to master its endless new developments.

   d. Our out-of-control anger has understandable causes, but common sense and patience are more satisfying than outbursts of rage.

2. Write a topic sentence that covers what is discussed in paragraphs 3 and 4.

   _____

3. What sentence in paragraph 17 serves as the topic sentence for paragraphs 16 through 18? (*Write the first words.*)

   _____

   _____

About Support

4. The essay is about one main effect and three possible causes. What is the one main effect? What are the three causes?

   Effect: _____

   Three causes: _____

5. Trace the line of causation in paragraph 11. What is the ultimate cause, the proximate cause, and the effect?

   Ultimate cause: _____

Proximate cause: _____

Effect: _____

About Coherence

6. What is the best description of the organization of this essay?

    a. Introduction, Thesis, Three Supporting Parts, Conclusion

    b. Introduction, Thesis, Four Supporting Parts, Conclusion

    c. Introduction, Thesis, Five Supporting Parts

    d. Thesis, Six Supporting Parts, Conclusion

7. As shown by the outline below, "Taming the Anger Monster" bears a general resemblance to the traditional one-three-one essay model. Fill in the missing paragraph numbers.

    Introduction: Paragraphs: _____

    Supporting Point 1:   Paragraph(s)   _____

    Supporting Point 2:   Paragraph(s)   _____

    Supporting Point 3:   Paragraph(s)   _____

    Supporting Point 4:   Paragraphs   _____

    Supporting Point 5:   Paragraphs   _____

    Conclusion: Paragraph: _____

8. What are the three addition signals used to introduce the three causes of anger?

    _____   _____   _____

About the Introduction and Conclusion

9. What method best describes the introduction to "Taming the Anger Monster"?

    a. Quotation

    b. Broad, general statement narrowing to thesis

    c. Idea that is the opposite of the one to be developed

    d. Anecdote and questions

10. What is the relationship between the essay's first paragraph and its concluding paragraph?

    _____

    _____

Writing a Cause-and-Effect Essay

Writing | Assignment

1   In scratch-outline form, on a separate piece of paper, provide brief causes *or* effects for at least *four* of the ten statements below. The first is done for you as an example. Make sure that you have three *separate* and *distinct* items for each statement—don't provide two rewordings that say essentially the same thing. Also, indicate whether the items you have listed are causes or effects.

When you have finished your four scratch outlines, decide which of them would provide the best basis for a cause-and-effect essay that you will write.

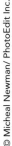
© Micheal Newman/ PhotoEdit Inc.

1. Many youngsters are terrified of school.
   Causes:

   a. _____

   b. _____

   c. _____

2. Having more mothers in the workforce has changed the way many kids grow up.

3. Americans tend to get married later in life than they used to.

4. Society would benefit if nonviolent criminals were punished in ways other than jail time.

© Greg Hinsdale/Corbis

5. Among winners of prestigious academic awards, a high percentage are children of immigrant families who recently arrived in this country.

6. My relationship with (*name a relative or friend*) _____ has changed over time.

7. Growing up in my family has influenced my life in significant ways.

8. A bad (or good) teacher can have long-lasting impact on a student.

9. The average workweek should be no more than thirty hours.

10. It is easy to fall into an unhealthy diet in our society.

Prewriting

a. Look at the outline you produced in the previous step. You will now use it as the basis for a cause-and-effect essay. The statement will serve as your thesis,

© Bubbles Photolibrary/Alamy

and the three causes or effects will function as your main points. Make sure that each of your main points is a *separate* and *distinct* point, not a restatement of one of the other points.

b. Decide whether you will support each of your main points with several short examples or with one extended example. You may want to freewrite about each of these examples for a few minutes, or you may want to make up a list of as many details as you think of that would go with each of the examples.

c. Write a first draft of an introduction that attracts the reader's interest, states your thesis, and presents a plan of development.

Revising

After you have completed the first draft of the paper, set it aside for a while (if possible). Then read it aloud to a friend or classmate. As you listen to your words, you should both keep these questions in mind:

FOUR BASES Checklist for Cause and Effect

About *Unity*

✓ Does the essay have a clearly stated thesis?

✓ Is there any irrelevant material that should be eliminated or rewritten?

About *Support*

✓ Have I backed up each main point with one extended example or several shorter examples?

✓ Do I have enough detailed support?

About *Coherence*

✓ Have I used transition words to help readers follow my train of thought?

✓ Have I provided a concluding paragraph to wrap up the essay?

About *Sentence Skills*

✓ Have I used a consistent point of view throughout my essay?

✓ Have I used specific rather than general words?

✓ Have I avoided wordiness and used concise wording?

✓ Are my sentences varied?

✓ Have I checked for spelling and other sentence skills, as listed on the inside back cover of the book?

As you revise your essay through one or more additional drafts, continue to refer to this list until you can answer yes to each question.

Writing Assignment

2   If friendly aliens from a highly developed civilization decided to visit our planet, they would encounter a contradictory race of beings—us. We humans would have reasons to feel both proud and ashamed of the kind of society the aliens would encounter. Write an essay explaining whether you would be proud or ashamed of the state of the human race today. Give reasons for your feelings.

Prewriting

a. You will probably have an instant gut reaction to the question, Am I more proud of or ashamed of the human race? Go with that reaction; you will find it easier to come up with supporting points for the thesis that occurred to you immediately.

b. Generate supporting details for your thesis by making a list. Title it "Reasons I am proud of the human race" or "Reasons I am ashamed of the human race." Then list as many items as you can think of. Don't worry about whether the reasons are important or silly, significant or trivial. Just write down as many as possible.

c. Review your list and ask yourself if some of the items could be grouped into one category. For instance, a list of reasons to be proud of humanity might include items such as "We've come up with cures for major diseases," "We've developed the computer," and "We've invented wonderful communication devices like the cellular telephone, the Internet, movies, and TV." All of these could be grouped into a category called "Important inventions." That category, in turn, could serve as a main supporting point in your essay.

d. As described in step *c*, decide on three supporting points. Write a scratch outline that includes those points and the examples (one extended example or several shorter ones). The point described in step c would be outlined like this:

Point: The human race has come up with wonderful inventions that benefit all society.

  1. Cures for diseases
  2. Computers
  3. Communication devices, including cell phones, the Internet, and TV

e. Using your scratch outline, write a first draft of the paper. Include an introduction that states your thesis and plan of development, and a conclusion that reminds readers of your thesis and leaves them with a final point to consider.

Revising

As you work through subsequent drafts, ask yourself these questions:

FOUR BASES Checklist for Cause and Effect

About *Unity*

☑ Have I introduced my essay with a clearly stated thesis and plan of development?

About *Support*

☑ Is each of my main points supported by solid, specific details?

About *Coherence*

☑ Have I used transition words such as *first, another, in addition*, and *also*?

About *Sentence Skills*

☑ Have I used a consistent point of view throughout my essay?

☑ Have I used specific rather than general words?

☑ Have I avoided wordiness and used concise wording?

☑ Are my sentences varied?

☑ Have I checked my writing for spelling and other sentence skills, as listed on the inside back cover of the book?

Writing Assignment

3

Write a cause-and-effect essay in which you advance an idea about a poem, story, play, film, literary essay, or novel. The work you choose may be assigned by your instructor or may require your instructor's approval. To develop your idea, use a series of two or more reasons and specific supporting evidence for each reason. A student model follows.

Paul's Suicide

Paul, the main character in Willa Cather's short story "Paul's Case," is a young man on a collision course with death. As Cather reveals Paul's story, we learn about elements of Paul's personality that inevitably come together   1

(continued)

and cause his suicide. Paul takes his own life as a result of his inability to conform to his society, his passive nature, and his emotional isolation.

First of all, Paul cannot conform to the standards of his own society.   **2**
At school, Paul advertises his desire to be part of another, more glamorous world by wearing fancy clothes that set him apart from the other students. At home on Cordelia Street, Paul despises everything about his middle-class neighborhood. He hates the houses "permeated by kitchen odors," the "ugliness and commonness of his own home," and the respectable neighbors sitting on their front stoops every Sunday, "their stomachs comfortably protruding." Paul's father hopes that Paul will settle down and become like the young man next door, a nearsighted clerk who works for a corporate steel magnate. Paul, however, is repelled by the young man and all he represents. It seems inevitable, then, that Paul will not be able to cope with the office job his father obtains for him at the firm of Denny & Carson; and this inability to conform will, in turn, lead to Paul's theft of $1,000.

Paul's suicide is also due, in part, to his passive nature. Throughout his   **3**
life, Paul has been an observer and an onlooker. Paul's only escape from the prison of his daily life comes from his job as an usher at Pittsburgh's Carnegie Hall; he lives for the moments when he can watch the actors, singers, and musicians. However, Paul has no desire to <u>be</u> an actor or musician. As Cather says, "What he wanted was to see, to be in the atmosphere, float on the wave of it, to be carried out . . . away from everything." Although Paul steals the money and flees to New York, these uncharacteristic actions underscore the desperation he feels. Once at the Waldorf in New York, Paul is again content to observe the glamorous world he has craved for so long: "He had no especial desire to meet or to know any of these people; all he demanded was the right to look on and conjecture, to watch the pageant." During his brief stay in the city, Paul enjoys simply sitting in his luxurious rooms, glimpsing the show of city life through a magical curtain of snow. At the end, when the forces of ordinary life begin to close in again, Paul kills himself. But it is typical that he does not use the gun he has bought. Rather, more in keeping with his passive nature, Paul lets himself fall under the wheels of a train.

Finally, Paul ends his life because he is emotionally isolated. Throughout   **4**
the story, not one person makes any real contact with Paul. His teachers do not understand him and merely resent the attitude of false bravado that he uses as a defense. Paul's mother is dead; he cannot even remember her. Paul is completely alienated from his father, who obviously cares for him but who cannot feel close to this withdrawn, unhappy son. To Paul, his father is only the man waiting at the top of the stairs, "his hairy legs sticking out

(continued)

of his nightshirt," who will greet him with "inquiries and reproaches." When Paul meets a college boy in New York, they share a night on the town. But the "champagne friendship" ends with a "singularly cool" parting. Paul is not the kind of person who can let himself go or confide in one of his peers. For the most part, Paul's isolation is self-imposed. He has drifted so far into his fantasy life that people in the "real" world are treated like invaders. As he allows no one to enter his dream, there is no one Paul can turn to for understanding.

The combination of these personality factors—inability to conform,   5
passivity, and emotional isolation—makes Paul's tragic suicide inevitable. Before he jumps in front of the train, Paul scoops a hole in the snow and buries the carnation that he has been wearing in his buttonhole. Like a hothouse flower in the winter, Paul has a fragile nature that cannot survive in its hostile environment.

Writing | Assignment
4

Writing for a Specific Purpose and Audience

Imagine that several friends say they are having a hard time learning anything in Professor X's class. You volunteer to attend the class to see for yourself. You also get information from your friends about the course requirements and the assignments Professor X makes.

After attending class, you write a letter addressed to both Professor X and your friends politely calling attention to causes of the learning problems students are having in the class. To organize your essay, try developing each cause in a separate supporting paragraph. In the second part of each supporting paragraph, suggest changes that could be made to deal with each problem.

Remember, however, that teaching and learning involve both instructors and students. So don't put the blame on the professor alone. Mention at least one deficiency in your friends' approach to the class and suggest ways in which they might correct it.

www.mhhe.com/langan

13

Comparison or Contrast

This chapter will explain and illustrate how to

- develop an essay of comparison or contrast
- write an essay of comparison or contrast
- revise an essay of comparison or contrast

In addition, you will read and consider

- two student essays of comparison or contrast
- one professional essay of contrast

© vario images GmbH & Co.KG/Alamy

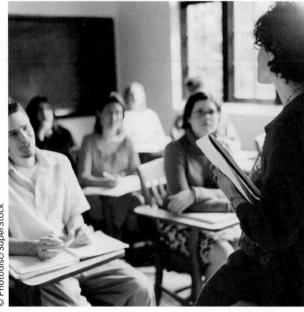

© Photodisc/SuperStock

Looking at the two photographs above, write an essay in which you compare or contrast lecture classes with smaller classes.

Comparison and contrast are two thought processes we go through constantly in everyday life. When we *compare* two things, we show how they are similar; when we *contrast* two things, we show how they are different. We may compare or contrast two brand-name products (for example, Pepsi and Coca-Cola), two television shows, two cars, two teachers, two jobs, two friends, or two possible solutions to a problem we are facing. The purpose of comparing or contrasting is to understand each of the two things more clearly and, at times, to make judgments about them.

You will be asked in this chapter to write an essay of comparison or contrast. To prepare for this assignment, first read about the two methods of development you can use in writing your essay. Then read the student essays and the professional essay that follow and work through the questions that accompany the essays.

Methods of Development

A comparison or contrast essay calls for one of two types of development. Details can be presented *one side at a time* or *point by point*. Each format is illustrated below.

One Side at a Time

Look at the following supporting paragraph from "A Vote for McDonald's," one of the model essays that will follow.

> For one thing, going to the Chalet is more difficult than going to McDonald's. The Chalet has a jacket-and-tie rule, which means I have to dig a sport coat and tie out of the back of my closet, make sure they're semiclean, and try to steam out the wrinkles somehow. The Chalet also requires reservations. Since it is downtown, I have to leave an hour early to give myself time to find a parking space within six blocks of the restaurant. The Chalet cancels reservations if a party is more than ten minutes late. Going to McDonald's, on the other hand, is easy. I can feel comfortable wearing my jeans or warm-up suit. I don't have to do any advance planning. I can leave my house whenever I'm ready and pull into a doorside parking space within fifteen minutes.

The first half of this paragraph fully explains one side of the contrast (the difficulty of going to the Chalet). The second half of the paragraph deals entirely with the other side (the ease of going to McDonald's). When you use this method, be sure to follow the same order of points of contrast (or comparison) for each side. An outline of the paragraph shows how the points for each side are developed in a consistent sequence.

Outline   **One Side at a Time**

> Thesis: Going to the Chalet is more difficult than going to McDonald's.
> 1. Chalet
>   a. Dress code
>   b. Advance reservations
>   c. Leave an hour early
>   d. Find parking space
> 2. McDonald's
>   a. Casual dress
>   b. No reservations
>   c. Leave only fifteen minutes ahead of time
>   d. Plenty of free parking

Point by Point

Now look at the supporting paragraph below, which is taken from another essay you will read, "Studying: Then and Now":

> Ordinary studying during the term is another area where I've made changes. In high school, I let reading assignments go. I told myself that I'd have no trouble catching up on two hundred pages during a fifteen-minute ride to school. College courses have taught me to keep pace with the work. Otherwise, I feel as though I'm sinking into a quicksand of unread material. When I finally read the high school assignment, my eyes would run over the words but my brain would be plotting how to get the car for Saturday night. Now, I use several techniques that force me to really concentrate on my reading.

The paragraph contrasts two styles of studying point by point. The following outline illustrates the point-by-point method.

Point by Point Outline

Thesis: Studying is something I do differently in college than in high school.

1. Keeping up with reading assignments
   a. High school
   b. College
2. Concentration while reading
   a. High school
   b. College

When you begin writing a comparison or contrast paper, you should decide right away which format you will use: one side at a time or point by point. Use that format as you create the outline for your paper. Remember that an outline is an essential step in planning and writing a clearly organized paper.

Student Essays to Consider

A Vote for McDonald's

For my birthday this month, my wife has offered to treat me to dinner at the restaurant of my choice. I think she expects me to ask for a meal at the Chalet, the classiest, most expensive restaurant in town. However, I'm going to eat my birthday dinner at McDonald's. When I compare the two restaurants, the advantages of eating at McDonald's are clear. 1

For one thing, going to the Chalet is more difficult than going to McDonald's. The Chalet has a jacket-and-tie rule, which means I have to dig a sport coat and tie out of the back of my closet, make sure they're semiclean, and try to steam out the wrinkles somehow. The Chalet also requires reservations. Since it is downtown, I have to leave an hour early to give 2

(continued)

myself time to find a parking space within six blocks of the restaurant. The Chalet cancels reservations if a party is more than ten minutes late. Going to McDonald's, on the other hand, is easy. I can feel comfortable wearing my jeans or warm-up suit. I don't have to do any advance planning. I can leave my house whenever I'm ready and pull into a doorside parking space within fifteen minutes.

The Chalet is a dimly lit, formal place. While I'm struggling to see   3
what's on my plate, I worry that I'll knock one of the fragile glasses off the table. The waiters at the Chalet can be uncomfortably formal, too. As I awkwardly pronounce the French words on the menu, I get the feeling that I don't quite live up to their standards. Even the other diners can make me feel uncomfortable. And though the food at the Chalet is gourmet, I prefer simpler meals. I don't like unfamiliar food swimming in a pasty white sauce. Eating at the Chalet is, to me, less enjoyable than eating at McDonald's. McDonald's is a pleasant place where I feel at ease. It is well lit, and the bright-colored decor is informal. The employees serve with a smile, and the food is easy to pronounce and identify. I know what I'm going to get when I order a certain type of sandwich.

The most important difference between the Chalet and McDonald's,   4
though, is price. Dinner for two at the Chalet, even without appetizers or desserts, would easily cost $100. And the $100 doesn't include the cost of parking the car and tipping the waiter, which can come to an additional $20. Once, I forgot to bring enough money. At McDonald's, a filling meal for two will cost around $10. With the extra $110, my wife and I can eat at McDonald's eleven more times, or go to the movies five times, or buy tickets to a football game.

So, for my birthday dinner, or any other time, I prefer to eat at   5
McDonald's. It is convenient, friendly, and cheap. And with the money my wife saves by taking me to McDonald's, she can buy me what I really want for my birthday—a new Sears power saw.

Studying: Then and Now

One June day, I staggered into a high school classroom to take my final   1
exam in United States History IV. I had made my usual desperate effort to cram the night before, with the usual dismal results—I had gotten only to page 75 of a four-hundred-page textbook. My study habits in high school,

(continued)

obviously, were a mess. But in college, I've made an attempt to reform my note-taking, studying, and test-taking skills.

As I took notes in high school classes, I often lost interest and began doodling, drawing Martians, or seeing what my signature would look like if I married the cute guy in the second row. Now, however, I try not to let my mind wander, and I pull my thoughts back into focus when they begin to go fuzzy. In high school, my notes often looked like something written in another language. In college, I've learned to use a semiprint writing style that makes my notes understandable. When I would look over my high school notes, I couldn't understand them. There would be a word like "Reconstruction," then a big blank, then the word "important." Weeks later, I had no idea what Reconstruction was or why it was important. I've since learned to write down connecting ideas, even if I have to take the time to do it after class. Taking notes is one thing I've really learned to do better since high school days.

Ordinary studying during the term is another area where I've made changes. In high school, I let reading assignments go. I told myself that I'd have no trouble catching up on two hundred pages during a fifteen-minute ride to school. College courses have taught me to keep pace with the work. Otherwise, I feel as though I'm sinking into a quicksand of unread material. When I finally read the high school assignment, my eyes would run over the words but my brain would be plotting how to get the car for Saturday night. Now, I use several techniques that force me to really concentrate on my reading.

In addition to learning how to cope with daily work, I've also learned to handle study sessions for big tests. My all-night study sessions in high school were experiments in self-torture. Around 2:00 A.M., my mind, like a soaked sponge, simply stopped absorbing things. Now, I space out exam study sessions over several days. That way, the night before can be devoted to an overall review rather than raw memorizing. Most important, though, I've changed my attitude toward tests. In high school, I thought tests were mysterious things with completely unpredictable questions. Now, I ask instructors about the kinds of questions that will be on the exam, and I try to "psych out" which areas or facts instructors are likely to ask about. These practices really work, and for me they've taken much of the fear and mystery out of tests.

Since I've reformed, note-taking and studying are not as tough as they once were. And I am beginning to reap the benefits. As time goes on, my college test sheets are going to look much different from the red-marked tests of my high school days.

2

3

4

5

About Unity

1. Which supporting paragraph in "A Vote for McDonald's" has its topic sentence within the paragraph, rather than at the beginning? (*Write the paragraph number and the opening words of the topic sentence.*)

_____

2. Which sentence in paragraph 4 of "A Vote for McDonald's" should be omitted in the interest of paragraph unity? (*Write the opening words.*)

I forget

3. In which supporting paragraph in "Studying: Then and Now" is the topic sentence at the end rather than at the beginning, where it generally belongs in

student essays? _____

About Support

4. In paragraph 3 of "A Vote for McDonald's," what three points does the writer make to support his statement that, for him, dining at McDonald's is a more pleasant experience than dining at the Chalet?

_____

_____

_____

5. In paragraph 3 of "A Vote for McDonald's," what sentence should be followed up by supporting details? (*Write the opening words of that sentence.*)

The waiter at the chat let can be uncomfortable

6. Which sentence in paragraph 3 of "Studying: Then and Now" needs to be followed by more supporting details? (*Write the opening words.*)

The No technology have No explain

About Coherence

7. In paragraph 2 of "A Vote for McDonald's," what "change of direction" signal does the author use to indicate that he has finished discussing the Chalet and is

now going to discuss McDonald's? _____

8. Write the words in paragraph 4 of "A Vote for McDonald's" that indicate the writer has used emphatic order in organizing his supporting points.

Price

About the Introduction and Conclusion

9. Which sentence best describes the opening paragraph of "Studying: Then and Now"?

   a. It begins with a broad statement that narrows down to the thesis.

   b. It explains the importance of the topic to the reader.

   c. It uses an incident or a brief story.

   d. It asks a question.

10. The conclusion of "Studying: Then and Now" falls into which category?

    a. Some observations and a prediction

    b. Summary and final thought

    c. Question or series of questions

Developing a Comparison or Contrast Essay

Considering Purpose and Audience

The purpose of a comparison or contrast essay is to make a point by showing readers that two distinct items are either similar or different. Whether you choose to compare or contrast two items depends on the specific point you want to convey to readers. Suppose, for instance, the main point of your essay is that home-cooked hamburgers are superior to fast-food burgers. To convince your audience of your claim, you might contrast the two items, pointing out those differences—price, taste, and nutrition—that make the homemade dish better. If, however, your main point is that tap water is just as good as store-bought bottled water, you could compare the two, pointing out the similarities that support your main point. Tap water and bottled water, for example, might be equally clean, fresh, and mineral-rich. In both examples above, comparing or contrasting is used to convince readers of a larger main point.

As you think about your own essay, ask yourself what two things you wish to discuss. Then determine whether you want to focus on the differences between the two items or their similarities. You may even decide that you want to do both. If, say, you choose as your topic Macintoshes and PCs, you may write paragraphs on the similarities and differences between the two computer systems. But remember, no matter what topic you select, be sure that your comparison or contrast is connected to a main point that readers can see and understand.

Be sure to keep your audience in mind when planning your essay. If you were writing about Macs and PCs for computer majors, for example, you could assume your readers were familiar with the two systems. On the other hand, if your audience were made up of liberal arts majors, you could not make such an assumption, and it would be up to you to provide background information. Thinking about your audience will help you determine the tone of your essay as well. Once again, if you are writing for an audience of programmers, it is appropriate to write in an objective, technical tone. But if you are writing for a more general audience, you should assume a friendly, informal tone.

Development through Prewriting

When Jesse, one of the student writers featured earlier, had to choose two things to compare or contrast, the Chalet and McDonald's quickly came to mind: "My wife and I had been talking that morning about where I wanted to go for my birthday," he said. "I'd been thinking how I would explain to her that I'd really prefer McDonald's. So the comparisons and contrasts between the two restaurants were fresh in my mind."

To generate ideas for his paper, Jesse turned to the technique of freewriting. Without concerning himself with organization, finding the perfect word, or even spelling, he simply wrote whatever came into his mind as he asked himself, Why would I rather eat at McDonald's than at the Chalet? Here is what Jesse came up with:

> The Chalet is a beautiful restaurant and it's sweet of Lilly to want to take me there. But I honestly like McDonald's better. To me, food is food, and a meal at the Chalet is not eleven times better than a meal at McDonald's but that's what it costs. I like a plain cheeseburger better than something I can't pronounce or identify. The waiters at the Chalet are snooty and make me feel awkward—how can you enjoy eating when you're tensed up like that? Have to wear jacket and tie to the Chalet and I've gained weight; not sure jacket will even fit. Sweats or jeans are great at McDonald's. Desserts at Chalet are great, better than McCookies or whatever they're called. Parking is a hassle at the Chalet and easy at McD's. No tipping at McD's, either. I don't know why they keep it so dark at the Chalet—guess it's supposed to be relaxing, but seems creepy to me. McD's is bright and cheerful.

As Jesse looked over his freewriting, he saw that most of what he had written fell into three categories that he could use as the three supporting points of his essay. Using these three points, he prepared this first scratch outline for the essay:

I'd rather eat my special dinner at McDonald's than at the Chalet.
1. *Can wear anything I want to McD's.*
2. *Waiters, lighting, menu at Chalet make me feel awkward.*
3. *Chalet is <u>much</u> more expensive than McD's.*

Next, Jesse went back and inserted some supporting details that fit in with his three main points.

I'd rather eat my special dinner at McDonald's than at the Chalet.
1. *Going to the Chalet is a hassle.*
    a. *Have to wear jacket, tie to Chalet*
    b. *Have to make reservations*
    c. *Long drive; trouble parking*
2. *Waiters, lighting, menu at Chalet make me feel awkward.*
    a. *Waiters are snooty*
    b. *Lighting is dim*
    c. *French names on menu don't mean anything to me*
3. *Chalet is <u>much</u> more expensive than McD's.*
    a. *Meal costs eleven times as much*
    b. *Parking, tips on top of that*
    c. *Rather spend that money on other things*

Working from this scratch outline, Jesse wrote the following first draft of his essay.

A Vote for McDonald's

First Draft

Lilly has offered to take me anywhere I want for my birthday dinner. She thinks I'll choose the Chalet, but instead I want to eat at McDonald's.

The Chalet has a jacket-and-tie rule, and I hate wearing a jacket and tie, and the jacket's probably too tight for me anyway. I have to dig them out of

(continued)

the closet and get them cleaned. I can wear any old thing to McDonald's. We'd also have to leave the house early, since the Chalet requires reservations. Since it is downtown, I have to leave an hour early so I'm sure to have time to park. The Chalet cancels reservations if a party is more than ten minutes late. Going to McDonald's, on the other hand, is easy. I don't have to do any advance planning. I can leave my house whenever I'm ready.

McDonald's is a pleasant place where I feel at ease. It is bright and well lit. The employees serve with a smile, and the food is easy to pronounce and identify. I know what I'm going to get when I order a certain type of sandwich. I like simple meals more than gourmet ones. The Chalet is dimly lit. While I'm struggling to see what's on my plate, I worry that I'll knock one of the glasses off the table. The waiters at the Chalet can be uncomfortably formal, too. I get the feeling that I don't quite live up to their standards. Even the other diners can make me feel uncomfortable.

There's a big price difference between the Chalet and McDonald's. Dinner for two at the Chalet can easily cost $100, even without any "extras" like appetizers and dessert. And the $100 doesn't include the cost of parking the car and tipping the waiter. Once, I forgot to bring enough money. At McDonald's, a meal for two will cost around $10.

So, for my birthday dinner, or any other time, I prefer to eat at McDonald's. It is convenient, friendly, and cheap.

Development through Revising

Jesse put the first draft of his essay aside and took it to his writing class the next day. His instructor asked Jesse and the other students to work in small groups reading their drafts aloud and making suggestions for revision to one another. Here are the notes Jesse made on his group's comments:

- *I need to explain that Lilly is my wife.*
- *I'm not consistent in developing my paragraphs. I forgot to do a "one side at a time" or "point by point" comparison. I think I'll try "one side at a time." I'll describe in each paragraph what the Chalet is like, then what McDonald's is like.*

(continued)

> - *I could use more support for some of my points, like when I say that the waiters at the Chalet make me uncomfortable. I should give some examples of what I mean by that.*
> - *I want to say something about what I'd rather do with the money we save by going to McDonald's. For me that's important—we can "eat" that money at the Chalet, or do other things with it that we both enjoy.*

After making these observations about his first draft, Jesse proceeded to write the version of his essay that appears on page 303.

A Professional Essay to Consider

Read the following professional essay. Then answer the questions and read the comments that follow.

Born to Be Different?

by Camille Lewis

Some years ago, when my children were very young, I cut a cartoon out of 1 a magazine and taped it to my refrigerator. It showed a young couple welcoming friends over for Christmas. The hosts rather proudly announce that instead of dolls, they have given their little daughter her own set of tools. And sure enough, the second panel shows their little girl playing in her room, a wrench in one hand and a hammer in the other. But she's making the wrench say, "Would you like to go to the prom, Barbie?" and the hammer answer, "Oh, Ken! I'd love to!"

Oh my, did that cartoon strike a chord. I grew up with *Ms.* magazine and the 2 National Organization of Women and a firm belief that gender differences were *learned,* not inborn. Other parents may have believed that pink and baby dolls and kindergarten teaching were for girls, and blue and trucks and engineering were for boys, but by golly, *my* kids were going to be different. They were going to be raised free of all that harmful gender indoctrination. They were just going to be *people.*

I don't remember exactly when I began to suspect I was wrong. Maybe it was 3 when my three-year-old son, raised in a "no weapons" household, bit his toast into a gun shape and tried to shoot the cat. Maybe it was when his younger brother nearly levitated out of his car seat, joyously crowing "backhoe!" upon spotting his first piece of earth-moving equipment. Maybe it was when my little daughter first lined up her stuffed animals and began teaching them their ABC's and bandaging their boo-boos.

It wasn't that my sons couldn't be sweet and sensitive, or that my daughter 4
wasn't sometimes rowdy and boisterous. But I had to rethink my earlier assump-
tions. Despite my best efforts not to impose gender-specific expectations on them,
my boys and my girl were, well, different. *Really* different.

Slowly and hesitantly, medical and psychological researchers have begun con- 5
firming my observations. The notion that the differences between the sexes (beyond
the obvious anatomical ones) are biologically based is fraught[1] with controversy. Such
beliefs can easily be misinterpreted and used as the basis for harmful, oppressive
stereotypes. They can be overstated and exaggerated into blanket statements about
what men and women "can" and "can't" do; about what the genders are "good" and
"bad" at. And yet, the unavoidable fact is that studies are making it ever clearer
that, as groups, men and women differ in almost every measurable aspect. Learning
about those differences helps us understand why men and women are simultaneously so attracted and fascinated, and yet so frequently stymied and frustrated, by
the opposite sex. To dig into what it really means to be masculine and feminine helps
to depersonalize our responses to one another's behavior—to avoid the "*My* perceptions and behaviors are normal; *yours* don't make sense" trap. Our differences are
deep-rooted, hard-wired, and present from the moment of conception.

To begin with, let's look at something as basic as the anatomy of the brain. Typi- 6
cally, men have larger skulls and brains than women. But the sexes score equally well
on intelligence tests. This apparent contradiction is explained by the fact that our brains
are apportioned differently. Women have about 15 percent more "gray matter" than
men. Gray matter, made up of nerve cells and the branches that connect them, allows
the quick transference of thought from one part of the brain to another. This high concentration of gray matter helps explain women's ability to look at many sides of an argument at once, and to do several tasks (or hold several conversations) simultaneously.

Men's brains, on the other hand, have a more generous portion of "white matter." 7
White matter, which is made up of neurons, actually inhibits the spread of information.
It allows men to concentrate very narrowly on a specific task, without being distracted
by thoughts that might conflict with the job at hand. In addition, men's larger skulls
contain more cerebrospinal fluid, which cushions the brain. Scientists theorize that
this reflects men's history of engaging in warfare and rough sports, activities which
bring with them a high likelihood of having one's head banged about.

Our brains' very different makeup leads to our very different methods of 8
interacting with the world around us. Simon Baron-Cohen, author of *The Essential Difference: Men, Women and the Extreme Male Brain,* has labeled the classic
female mental process as "empathizing." He defines empathizing as "the drive to
identify another person's emotions and thoughts, and to respond to these with an
appropriate emotion." Empathizers are constantly measuring and responding to the
surrounding emotional temperature. They are concerned about showing sensitivity

---

[1] *fraught:* filled.

to the people around them. This empathetic quality can be observed in virtually all aspects of women's lives: from the choice of typically female-dominated careers (nursing, elementary school teaching, social work) to reading matter popular mainly with women (romantic fiction, articles about relationships, advice columns about how people can get along better) to women's interaction with one another (which typically involves intimate discussion of relationships with friends and family, and sympathy for each others' concerns). So powerful is the empathizing mindset that it even affects how the typical female memory works. Ask a woman when a particular event happened, and she often pinpoints it in terms of an occurrence that had emotional content: "That was the summer my sister broke her leg," or "That was around the time Gene and Mary got into such an awful argument." Likewise, she is likely to bring her empathetic mind to bear on geography. She'll remember a particular address not as 11th and Market Streets but being "near the restaurant where we went on our anniversary," or "around the corner from Liz's old apartment."

In contrast, Baron-Cohen calls the typical male mindset "systemizing," which he 9 defines as "the drive to analyze and explore a system, to extract underlying rules that govern the behavior of a system." A systemizer is less interested in how people feel than in how things work. Again, the systematic brain influences virtually all aspects of the typical man's life. Male-dominated professions (such as engineering, computer programming, auto repair, and mathematics) rely heavily on systems, formulas, and patterns, and very little on the ability to intuit another person's thoughts or emotions. Reading material most popular with men includes science fiction and history, as well as factual "how-to" magazines on such topics as computers, photography, home repair, and woodworking. When they get together with male friends, men are far less likely to engage in intimate conversation than they are to share an activity: watching or playing sports, working on a car, bowling, golfing, or fishing. Men's conversation is peppered with dates and addresses, illustrating their comfort with systems: "Back in 1996 when I was living in Boston . . ." or "The best way to the new stadium is to go all the way out Walnut Street to 33rd and then get on the bypass. . . ."

One final way that men and women differ is in their typical responses to problem- 10 solving. Ironically, it may be this very activity—intended on both sides to eliminate problems—that creates the most conflict between partners of the opposite sex. To a woman, the *process* of solving a problem is all-important. Talking about a problem is a means of deepening the intimacy between her and her partner. The very anatomy of her brain, as well as her accompanying empathetic mindset, makes her want to consider all sides of a question and to explore various possible solutions. To have a partner who is willing to explore a problem with her is deeply satisfying. She interprets that willingness as an expression of the other's love and concern.

But men have an almost completely opposite approach when it comes to deal- 11 ing with a problem. Everything in their mental makeup tells them to focus narrowly on the issue, solve it, and get it out of the way. The ability to fix a problem quickly and efficiently is, to them, a demonstration of their power and competence. When a man hears his female partner begin to describe a problem, his strongest impulse is to listen briefly and then tell her what to do about it. From his perspective, he has made a helpful and loving gesture; from hers, he's short-circuited a conversation that could have deepened and strengthened their relationship.

The challenge that confronts men and women is to put aside ideas of "better" and   12
"worse" when it comes to their many differences. Our diverse brain development, our ways of interacting with the world, and our modes of dealing with problems all have their strong points. In some circumstances, a typically feminine approach may be more effective; in others, a classically masculine mode may have the advantage. Our differences aren't going to disappear: my daughter, now a middle-schooler, regularly tells me she loves me, while her teenage brothers express their affection by grabbing me in a headlock. Learning to understand and appreciate one another's gender-specific qualities is the key to more rich and rewarding lives together.

Questions

2

About Unity

1. Which of the following statements best represents the implied thesis of "Born to Be Different"?

    a. Although the author believed that gender differences were learned rather than inborn, experience with her own children convinced her otherwise.

    b. Researchers have classified the typical female mental process as "empathizing" and the typical male process as "systemizing."

    c. Many of the differences in the ways men and women think and behave may be due to their biological makeup.

    d. In order to live together happily, men and women need to appreciate and understand their gender-based differences.

2. Which statement would best serve as a topic sentence for paragraphs 6 and 7?

    a. Because of their different construction, men's and women's brains function differently.

    b. Women are skilled at doing several tasks or holding several conversations simultaneously.

    c. Although men's brains are larger than women's, men and women score equally on tests of intelligence.

    d. Men's brains have a larger allocation of white matter, which contributes to the ability to focus narrowly on a particular task.

3. What statement below would best serve as the topic sentence of paragraph 11?

    a. Men solve problems quickly to demonstrate power and competence.

    b. Men's approach to solving problems usually involves giving instructions.

    c. Men's gestures of love are often unhelpful to women.

    d. Men's approach to problem solving is the opposite of women's.

About Support

4. Paragraph 8 states that the "empathizing" mindset "can be observed in virtually all aspects of women's lives." What evidence does Lewis provide to support that claim?

_____

_____

_____

5. According to the author, what are the three major differences between men and women?

_____

_____

_____

About Coherence

6. Has the author presented her evidence one side at a time or point by point? Explain your answer.

_____

_____

_____

7. As shown by the outline below, the organization of "Born to Be Different?" resembles the traditional one-three-one essay model. Fill in the missing paragraph numbers.

Introduction:	Paragraphs	_____
Supporting Point 1:	Paragraph(s)	_____
Supporting Point 2:	Paragraph(s)	_____
Supporting Point 3:	Paragraph(s)	_____
Conclusion:	Paragraph	_____

8. What are the three contrast signals used to introduce the main supporting paragraphs in the essay? Where do they occur? (*Write the paragraph number after the signal.*)

_____   _____   _____

About the Introduction and Conclusion

9. What method best describes the introductory paragraph to the essay?

    a. Broad, general statement narrowing to a thesis

    b. Questions

    c. Idea that is the opposite of the one to be developed

    d. Anecdote

10. With which common method of conclusion does the essay end?

    a. A summary and final thought

    b. Questions that prompt the reader to think further about what's been written

    c. A prediction

Writing a Comparison or Contrast Essay

Writing Assignment

1   Write an essay of comparison or contrast on one of these topics:

Two teachers you've had

Two jobs you'd held

Two bosses you've worked for

Two restaurants you've eaten in

Two parenting styles you've observed

Two friends you've had

Two pets you've had or seen

Two sports you're acquainted with

Two singers or bands you've heard

Two dates you've been on

Two places you've lived

Prewriting

a.   As you select your topic, keep in mind that you won't be merely *describing* the two things you're writing about—you will be emphasizing the ways they are alike or different.

b.   Make two columns on a sheet of paper, one for each of the two things you'll write about. In the left-hand column, jot down words or phrases that describe the first of the two. Write anything that comes into your head about that half of your topic. Then go back and write a corresponding word or phrase about the item in the right-hand column. For example, here is one student's list of characteristics about two games. He began brainstorming for words and phrases to describe Scrabble.

Scrabble   Volleyball

quiet

involves words

played sitting down

involves small group of people

can let mind wander when it's not your turn

mental concentration, not physical

part chance—don't know what letters you'll get

part strategy and skill

some see as boring, nerdy game

Then he wrote a corresponding list of characteristics for volleyball, which helped him modify and add to his first list:

Scrabble	Volleyball
quiet	noisy, talking and yelling
involves words	involves ball and a net
played sitting down	played standing up, jumping
involves as few as two players	involves twelve players
can let mind wander when it's not your turn	have to stay alert every minute
mental concentration, not physical	mental and physical concentration required
part chance (what letters you get), part strategy and skill	mostly skill, strategy; little chance
some see as boring, nerdy game	seen as glamorous—stars get advertising contracts
players' sizes don't matter	being tall helps

c.   Your list of characteristics will help you decide if the two things you are writing about are more alike (in which case you'll write an essay *comparing* them) or different (in which case you'll emphasize how they *contrast*).

d.   As you look over your lists, think how the characteristics you've written down (and others that occur to you) could fit into three categories that can serve as your supporting points. Prepare a scratch outline for your essay based on these three supporting points.

For instance, the student writing about Scrabble and volleyball came up with these three groupings of characteristics. Fill in the blanks in his outline to indicate the supporting points.

Thesis: Although they are two of my favorite activities, Scrabble and volleyball could hardly be more different.

Point   _____

Scrabble requires a board and letter tiles.

Volleyball needs a ball and net.

Scrabble can be played by two people.

Twelve people are needed for a volleyball game.

Scrabble can be played anywhere there's room for two people to sit down.

Volleyball needs a large room and high ceilings or an outdoor playing area.

Point   _____

You have to concentrate mentally to play Scrabble.

You need mental and physical concentration to play volleyball.

It doesn't matter what size you are to play Scrabble.

It helps to be tall to play volleyball.

There's some chance involved in playing Scrabble.

Chance is not a big part of volleyball.

Point   _____

Scrabble players are seen as nerdy by the general public.

Star volleyball players are seen as glamorous by the public.

Volleyball players get contracts to endorse athletic shoes.

Scrabble players don't endorse anything, even dictionaries.

Volleyball players are admired for the power of their spike.

Scrabble players are admired for the number of unusual two-letter words they know.

e. Decide which method of development you will use to design your essay: one side at a time or point by point. Be consistent in your use of one method or the other in each of your paragraphs.

f. Write the first draft of your essay.

Revising

Reread your essay and then show it to a friend or classmate who will give you honest feedback. You should both review it with these questions in mind:

FOUR BASES Checklist for Comparison or Contrast

About *Unity*

☑ Have I made it clear in my opening paragraph what two things I am writing about, and whether I will compare or contrast them?

About *Support*

☑ Do my supporting points offer three areas in which I will compare or contrast my two subjects?

About *Coherence*

☑ Have I consistently used a single method of development—one side at a time or point by point—in each supporting paragraph?

☑ Have I used transition words to help readers follow my train of thought?

☑ If one area of comparison or contrast is stronger than the others, am I using emphatic order and saving that area for my final supporting paragraph?

☑ Have I rounded off my essay with an appropriate concluding paragraph?

About *Sentence Skills*

☑ Have I avoided wordiness and used concise wording?

☑ Are my sentences varied?

☑ Have I checked my writing for spelling and other sentence skills, as listed on the inside back cover of the book?

As you revise your essay through one or more additional drafts, continue to refer to this list until you and your reader can answer yes to each question.

Writing | Assignment

2 Write an essay in which you contrast two attitudes on a controversial subject. You may want to contrast your views with those of someone else, or contrast the way you felt about the subject in the past with the way you feel now. You might consider writing about one of these subjects:

Legalization of narcotics

Abortion

Men and women serving together in military units

Prayer in public schools

Nuclear power plants

Homosexual couples adopting children

Fertility methods that allow older women to have children

Welfare reform

The death penalty

Euthanasia

Prostitution

The public's right to know about elected officials' private lives

The Iraq war

© Bob Daemmrich/PhotoEdit

Prewriting

a. To gather information for the point of view that contrasts with your own, you will need to do some research. You'll find useful material if you go to the library and search through article indexes for recent newsmagazines. (If you need help, ask your instructor or the research librarian.) Or interview friends and acquaintances whose attitude on the subject is different from yours.

b. To generate ideas for your essay, try the following two-part exercise.

- Part 1: Pretend that a visitor from Mars who has never heard of the topic of your paper has asked you to explain it, as well as why you take the attitude you do toward it.

© Peter M. Fisher/Corbis

Using the technique of freewriting—not worrying about sentence structure, organization, spelling, repetition, etc.—write an answer for the Martian. Throw in every reason you can think of for your attitude.

- Part 2: Now the Martian asks you to do the same, taking the opposing point of view. Remember that it's up to you to make this interplanetary visitor understand both sides of the issue, so really try to put yourself in the other person's shoes as you represent the contrasting attitude.

c. As you look over the writing on both sides of the issue you've done for the Martian, note the strongest points on both sides. From them, select your three main supporting points. Are there other thoughts in your writing that can be used as supporting details for those points?

d. Write your three supporting paragraphs. Decide whether it is more effective to contrast your attitude and the opposing attitude point by point within each paragraph, or by devoting the first half of each paragraph to one side's attitude and then contrasting it with the other's.

e. In your concluding paragraph, summarize the contrast between your attitude and the other point of view. Consider closing with a final comment that makes it clear why you stand where you do.

Revising

Refer to the guidelines for rewriting provided on page 319.

Writing Assignment

3

Write an essay that contrasts two characters or two points of view in one or more poems, stories, plays, or novels. The work you choose may be assigned by your instructor, or it may require your instructor's approval. For this assignment, your essay may have two supporting paragraphs, with each paragraph representing one side of the contrast. A student model follows.

Warren and Mary

1

In "Death of the Hired Man," Robert Frost uses a brief incident—the return of Silas, an aging farmhand—to dramatize the differences between a husband and wife. As Warren and Mary talk about Silas and reveal his story, the reader learns their story, too. By the end of the poem, Warren and Mary emerge as contrasting personalities; one is wary and reserved, while the other is open and giving.

(continued)

Warren is a kindly man, but his basic decency is tempered by practicality   2
and emotional reserve. Warren is upset with Mary for sheltering Silas, who is
barely useful and sometimes unreliable: "What use he is there's no depending
on." Warren feels that he has already done his duty toward Silas by hiring him
the previous summer and is under no obligation to care for him now. "Home,"
says Warren, "is the place where, when you have to go there/They have to
take you in." Warren's home is not Silas's home, so Warren does not have a
legal or moral duty to keep the shiftless old man. Warren's temperament,
in turn, influences his attitude toward Silas's arrival. Warren hints to Mary—
through a condescending smile—that Silas is somehow playing on her
emotions or faking his illness. Warren considers Silas's supposed purpose in
coming to the farm—to ditch the meadow—nothing but a flimsy excuse for
a free meal. The best that Warren can find to say about Silas is that he does
have one practical skill: the ability to build a good load of hay.

Mary, in contrast, is distinguished by her giving nature and her   3
concentration on the workings of human emotion. In caring for Silas, Mary
sees not his lack of ability or his laziness but the fact that he is "worn out"
and needs help. To Mary, home represents not obligation ("They have to
take you in") but unconditional love: "I should have called it/Something
you somehow haven't to deserve." Mary is observant, not only of outer
appearances but also of the inner person; this is why she thinks not that Silas
is trying to trick them but that he is a desperate man trying to salvage a little
self-respect. She realizes, too, that he will never ditch the meadow, and she
knows that Silas's insecurity prompted his arguments with the college boy
who helped with the haying. Mary is also perceptive enough to see that Silas
could never humble himself before his estranged brother. Mary's attitude is
more sympathetic than Warren's; whereas Warren wonders why Silas and his
brother don't get along, Mary thinks about how Silas "hurt my heart the way
he lay/And rolled his old head on that sharp-edged chairback."

In describing Silas, Warren and Mary describe themselves. We see a   4
basically good man whose spirit has been toughened by a hard life. Warren,
we learn, would have liked to pay Silas a fixed wage but simply couldn't
afford to. Life has taught Warren to be practical and to rein in his emotions.
In contrast, we see a nurturing woman, alert to human feelings, who could
never refuse to care for a lonely, dying man. Warren and Mary are both
decent people. This is the reason why, as Mary instinctively feels, Silas
chooses their home for his final refuge.

Writing Assignment

Writing for a Specific Purpose and Audience

In this comparison or contrast essay, you will write with a specific purpose and for a specific audience.

Option 1 Your niece or nephew is finishing high school soon and is thinking about getting a job instead of going to college. You would prefer to see him or her give college a try. Write him or her a letter in which you compare and contrast the advantages and disadvantages of each course of action. Use the one-side-at-a-time method in making your analysis.

Option 2 Write a letter to your boss in which you compare your abilities with those of the ideal candidate for a position to which you'd like to be promoted. Use the point-by-point method, discussing each desired qualification and then describing how well you measure up to it. Use the requirements of a job you are familiar with, ideally a job you would really like to apply for someday.

www.mhhe.com/langan

14

Definition

This chapter will explain and illustrate how to

- develop a definition essay
- write a definition essay
- revise a definition essay

In addition, you will read and consider

- two student definition essays
- one professional definition essay

© Digital Vision/Getty Images

What does it mean to be a successful student? What qualities and attributes does a successful student possess? Looking at the photograph above and thinking about these questions, write an essay in which you define what it means to be a successful student.

In talking with other people, we sometimes offer informal definitions to explain just what we mean by a particular term. Suppose, for example, we say to a friend, "Larry is really an inconsiderate person." We might then explain what we mean by "inconsiderate" by saying, "He borrowed my accounting book 'overnight' but didn't return it for a week. And when I got it back, it was covered with coffee stains." In a written definition, we make clear in a more complete and formal way our own personal understanding of a term. Such a definition typically starts with one meaning of a term. The meaning is then illustrated with a series of details.

In this chapter, you will be asked to write an essay in which you define and illustrate a term. To prepare for this assignment, first read the student essays and the professional essay that follow and work through the questions that accompany the essays.

Student Essays to Consider

Definition of a Football Fan

What is a football fan? The word "fan" is an abbreviation of "fanatic," meaning "an insane or crazy person." In the case of football fans, the term is appropriate. They behave insanely, they are insane about the past, and they are insanely loyal. **1**

Football fans wear their official team T-shirts and warm-up jackets to the mall, the supermarket, the classroom, and even—if they can get away with it—to work. If the team offers a giveaway item, the fans rush to the stadium to claim the hat or sports bag or water bottle that is being handed out that day. Baseball fans go similarly nuts when their favorite teams give away some attractive freebie. Football fans just plain behave insanely. Even the fact that fans spend the coldest months of the year huddling on icy metal benches in places like Chicago proves it. In addition, football fans decorate their houses with football-related items of every kind. To them, team bumper stickers belong not only on car bumpers, but also on fireplace mantels and front doors. When they go to a game, which they do as often as possible, they also decorate their bodies. True football fans not only put on their team jackets and grab their pennants but also paint their heads to look like helmets or wear glow-in-the-dark cheeseheads. At the game, these fans devote enormous energy to trying to get a "wave" going. **2**

Football fans are insanely fascinated by the past. They talk about William "Refrigerator" Perry's 1985 Super Bowl touchdown as though it had happened last week. They describe the "Fog Bowl" as if dense fog had blanketed yesterday's game, not 1988's playoff match between the Philadelphia Eagles and the Chicago Bears. They excitedly discuss John Elway's final game before **3**

(continued)

retiring—when he won the 1999 Super Bowl and received MVP honors—as if it were current news. And if you can't manage to get excited about such ancient history, they look at you as though you were the insane one.

Last of all, football fans are insanely loyal to the team of their choice, often dangerously so. Should their beloved team lose three in a row, fans may begin to react negatively as a way to hide their broken hearts. They still obsessively watch each game and spend the entire day afterward reading and listening to the postgame commentary in newspapers, on TV sports segments, and on sports radio. Further, this intense loyalty makes fans dangerous. To anyone who dares to say to a loyal fan that another team has better players or coaches or, God forbid, to anyone wandering near the home cheering section wearing the jacket of the opposing team, physical damage is a real possibility. Bloody noses, black eyes, and broken bones are just some of the injuries inflicted on people cheering the wrong team when fans are around. In 1997, one man suffered a concussion at a game in Philadelphia when Eagles fans beat him up for wearing a jacket with another team's insignia.

From February through August, football fans act like any other human beings. They pay their taxes, take out the garbage, and complain about the high cost of living. But when September rolls around, the colors and radios go on, the record books come off the shelves, and the devotion returns. For the true football fan, another season of insanity has begun.

Student Zombies

Schools divide people into categories. From first grade on up, students are labeled "advanced" or "deprived" or "remedial" or "antisocial." Students pigeonhole their fellow students, too. We've all known the "brain," the "jock," the "dummy," and the "teacher's pet." In most cases, these narrow labels are misleading and inaccurate. But there is one label for a certain type of college student that says it all: "zombie."

Zombies are the living dead. Most of us haven't known a lot of real zombies personally, but we do know how they act. We have horror movies to guide us. The special effects in horror movies are much better these days. Over the years, we've learned from the movies that zombies stalk around graveyards, their eyes glued open by Hollywood makeup artists, bumping like cheap toy robots into living people. Zombie students in college do just about the same thing. They stalk around campus, eyes glazed, staring

(continued)

off into space. When they do manage to wander into a classroom, they sit down mechanically and contemplate the ceiling. Zombie students rarely eat, dance, talk, laugh, or toss Frisbees on campus lawns. Instead, they vanish when class is dismissed and return only when some mysterious zombie signal summons them back into a classroom. The signal may not occur for weeks.

Zombies are controlled by some mysterious force. According to   3
legend, real zombies are corpses that have been brought back to life to do the bidding of a voodoo master. Student zombies, too, seem directed by a strange power. They continue to attend school although they have no apparent desire to do so. They show no interest in college-related activities like tests, grades, papers, and projects. And yet some inner force compels them to wander through the halls of higher education.

An awful fate awaits all zombies unless something happens to break the   4
spell they're under. In the movies, zombies are often shot, stabbed, drowned, electrocuted, and run over by large vehicles, all to no avail. Finally the hero or heroine realizes that a counterspell is needed. Once that spell is cast, with the appropriate props of chicken feet, human hair, and bats' eyeballs, the zombie-corpse can return peacefully to its coffin. The only hope for a student zombie to change is for him or her to undergo a similarly traumatic experience. Sometimes the evil spell can be broken by a grade transcript decorated with large red "F's." At other times a professor will succeed through a private, intensive exorcism session. But in other cases zombies blunder around for years until they are gently persuaded by the college administration to head for another institution. Then they enroll in a new college or get a job in the family business.

Every college student knows that it's not necessary to see Night of the   5
Living Dead or The Dead Don't Die to see zombies in action—or nonaction. Forget the campus film series or the late-late show. Just sit in a classroom and wait. You know what you're looking for—the students who walk in without books or papers and sit in the very last row of seats. The ones with personal stereos plugged into their ears don't count as zombies—that's a whole different category of "student." Day of the Living Dead is showing every day at a college near you.

About Unity

1. Which supporting paragraph in "Definition of a Football Fan" has a topic sentence buried within the paragraph, rather than at the paragraph's beginning? *(Write the paragraph number and the opening words of the topic sentence.)*

Questions

1

2. What sentence in paragraph 2 of "Definition of a Football Fan" should be omitted in the interest of paragraph unity? *(Write the opening words.)*

3. Which sentence in paragraph 2 of "Student Zombies" should be omitted in the interest of paragraph unity? *(Write the opening words.)*

4. What sentence in the final paragraph of "Student Zombies" introduces a new topic and so should be eliminated? *(Write the opening words.)*

About Support

5. Which essay develops its definitions through a series of comparisons?

6. After which sentence in paragraph 4 of "Definition of a Football Fan" is more support needed? *(Write the opening words.)*

7. In the second paragraph of "Definition of a Football Fan," how many examples are given of fans' "insane" behavior? *(Circle the letter of the answer.)*
    a. two   b. four   c. six

About Coherence

8. Which paragraph in "Definition of a Football Fan" begins with a transitional phrase? _____

9. Which sentence in paragraph 2 of "Student Zombies" begins with a change-of-direction transitional word? *(Write the opening words.)*

About the Introduction and Conclusion

10. Which method of introduction is used in the opening paragraph of "Student Zombies"? *(Circle the letter of the answer.)*
    a. Anecdote
    b. Idea that is the opposite of the one to be developed
    c. Quotation
    d. Broad, general statement narrowing to a thesis
    e. Questions

Developing a Definition Essay

Considering Purpose and Audience

When you write a definition essay, your main purpose is to explain to readers your understanding of a key term or concept, while your secondary purpose is to persuade them that your definition is a legitimate one. Keep in mind that a definition essay does not simply repeat a word's dictionary meaning. Instead, it conveys what a particular term means *to you*. For example, if you were to write about the term *patriotism*, you might begin by presenting your definition of the word. You might say patriotism means turning out for Fourth of July parades, displaying the flag, or supporting the government. Or perhaps you think patriotism is about becoming politically active and questioning government policy. Whatever definition you choose, be sure to provide specific instances so that readers can fully understand your meaning of the term. For example, in writing an essay on patriotism, you might describe three people whom you see as truly patriotic. Writing about each person will help ensure that readers see and understand the term as you do.

As with other essay forms, keep your audience in mind. If, for instance, you were proposing a new definition of patriotism, an audience of war veterans might require different examples than would an audience of college students.

Development through Prewriting

Brian, the author of "Definition of a Football Fan," spent a few minutes jotting down a number of possible essay topics, keeping in mind the question, "What do I know a good deal about, or at least have an interest in exploring?" Here is his list of topic ideas. Notice how they reflect Brian's interest in outdoor activities, sports, and history:

Definition of . . .

A person who fishes

A soccer goalie

A reenactor of Civil War battles

People who vacation at Gettysburg

A bodybuilder

A Green Bay Packers fan

A history buff

A Little League coach

After looking over his list, Brian selected "A Green Bay Packers fan" as the topic that interested him most. He thought it would lend itself well to a lighthearted essay that defined the sometimes nutty fans of the Wisconsin football team. After giving it further thought, however, Brian decided to broaden his topic to include all football fans. "I realized I just didn't know enough specifically about Green Bay fans to support an entire essay," he said.

A person who likes to think in visual terms, Brian decided to develop ideas and details about his topic by clustering his thoughts.

Football fans

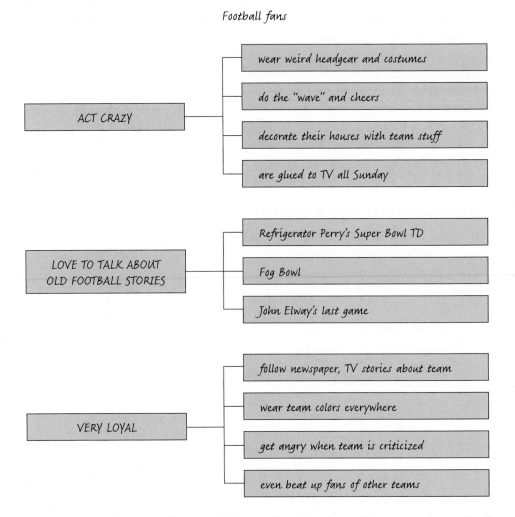

When he looked over his diagram, Brian realized that he could characterize each of his three main topics as a kind of "insanity." He decided on a thesis (he would define football fans as insane) that would indicate his essay's plan of development ("they behave insanely, they are insane about the past, and they are insanely loyal").

With that thesis and plan of development in mind, Brian wrote the first draft of his essay.

Definition of a Football Fan

First Draft

Football fans are by definition crazy. They behave insanely, they are insane about the past, and they are insanely loyal.

If their team gives away something free, the fans rush to the stadium to get the hat or whatever. Football fans just plain behave insanely. Baseball fans go similarly nuts when their favorite teams give away some attractive freebie. But football fans are even worse. Football fans freeze themselves in order to watch their favorite game. In addition, football fans decorate their houses with football-related items of every kind. When they go to a game, which they do as often as possible, the true football fans make themselves look ridiculous by decorating themselves in weird team-related ways. At the game, these fans do the "wave" more than they watch the game.

Football fans love to talk about the past. They talk about William "Refrigerator" Perry's 1985 Super Bowl touchdown as though it had happened last week. They still get all excited about 1988's "Fog Bowl." They talk about John Elway's final game as though it's today's news, though it happened in 1999. They think everyone should be as excited as they are about such old stories.

Last of all, football fans are insanely loyal to the team of their choice. Football fans wear their team T-shirts and warm-up jackets everywhere, even to work. Of course, if they have to dress up in business clothes, they can't do that. Should their beloved team lose three in a row, their fans may begin to criticize their team. But these reactions only hide their broken hearts. They still obsessively watch each game and read all the newspaper stories about it. This intense loyalty makes fans dangerous. To anyone who dares to say to a loyal fan that another team is better or, God forbid, to anyone wandering near the home cheering section wearing the jacket of the opposing team, physical damage is a real possibility. Incidents of violence in football stadiums have increased in recent years and are a matter of growing concern.

Football fans really act as if they're crazy. They behave insanely, they are crazy about the past, and they're too loyal.

Development through Revising

The next day, Brian showed his first draft to a study partner from his composition class. She returned it with comments noted in the margins.

Definition of a Football Fan

Football fans are by definition crazy. They behave insanely, they are insane about the past, and they are insanely loyal.

If their team gives away something free, the fans rush to the stadium to get the hat or whatever. Football fans just plain behave insanely. Baseball fans go similarly nuts when their favorite teams give away some attractive freebie. But football fans are even worse. Football fans freeze themselves in order to watch their favorite game. In addition, football fans decorate their houses with football-related items of every kind. When they go to a game, which they do as often as possible, the true football fans make themselves look ridiculous by decorating themselves in weird team-related ways. At the game, these fans do the "wave" more than they watch the game.

Football fans love to talk about the past. They talk about William "Refrigerator" Perry's 1985 Super Bowl touchdown as though it had happened last week. They still get all excited about 1988's "Fog Bowl." They talk about John Elway's final game as though it's today's news, though it happened in 1999. They think everyone should be as excited as they are about such old stories.

Last of all, football fans are insanely loyal to the team of their choice. Football fans wear their team T-shirts and warm-up jackets everywhere, even to work. Of course, if they have to dress up in business clothes, they can't do that. Should their beloved team lose three in a row, their fans may begin to criticize their team. But these reactions only hide their broken hearts. They still obsessively watch each game and read all the newspaper stories about it. This intense loyalty makes fans dangerous. To anyone who dares to say to a loyal fan that another team is better or, God forbid, to anyone wandering near the home cheering section wearing the jacket of the opposing

(continued)

Reader's Comments

Huh? I guess this is about the weather—make it clearer.

Like what? Details here.

Details needed. How do they decorate themselves?

I'm not a football fan, so I don't understand these references. Can you briefly explain them?

Shouldn't this be in the second paragraph? It seems to belong to "they behave insanely," not "loyalty."

This doesn't support your topic statement, so take it out.

team, physical damage is a real possibility. Incidents of violence in football stadiums have increased in recent years and are a matter of growing concern.

Football fans really act as if they're crazy. They behave insanely, they are crazy about the past, and they're too loyal.

Kind of a boring way to end it. You're just repeating your thesis.

After reading his classmate's comments, Brian went to work on his next draft. As he worked, he read his essay aloud several times and noticed places where his wording sounded awkward or too informal. (Example: "If their team gives away a freebie, the fans rush to the stadium to get the hat or whatever.") A few drafts later, he produced the version of "Definition of a Football Fan" that appears on page 325–326.

A Professional Essay to Consider

Read the following professional essay. Then answer the questions and read the comments that follow.

Television Addiction
by Marie Winn

The word "addiction" is often used loosely and wryly in conversation. People 1 will refer to themselves as "mystery book addicts" or "cookie addicts." E. B. White writes of his annual surge of interest in gardening, "We are hooked and are making an attempt to kick the habit." Yet nobody really believes that reading mysteries or ordering seeds by catalogue is serious enough to be compared to an addiction to heroin or alcohol. The word "addiction" is here used jokingly to denote a tendency to overindulge in some pleasurable activity.

People often refer to being "hooked on TV." Does this, too, fall into the light-2 hearted category of eating cookies and other pleasures that people pursue with unusual intensity, or is there a kind of television viewing that falls into the more serious category of destructive addiction?

When we think about addiction to drugs or alcohol, we frequently focus on 3 negative aspects, ignoring the pleasures that accompany drinking or taking drugs. And yet the essence of any serious addiction is a pursuit of pleasure, a search for a "high" that normal life does not supply. It is only the inability to function without the addictive substance that is dismaying, the dependence of the organism upon a certain experience and an increasing inability to function without it. Thus a person will take two or three drinks at the end of the day not merely for the pleasure drinking provides, but also because he "doesn't feel normal" without them.

An addict does not merely pursue a pleasurable experience and need to experi-   4
ence it in order to function normally. He needs to repeat it again and again. Something about that particular experience makes life without it less than complete. Other potentially pleasurable experiences are no longer possible, for under the spell of the addictive experience, his life is peculiarly distorted. The addict craves an experience, and yet he is never really satisfied. The organism may be temporarily sated, but soon it begins to crave again.

Finally, a serious addiction is distinguished from a harmless pursuit of pleasure   5
by its distinctly destructive elements. A heroin addict, for instance, leads a damaged life: his increasing need for heroin in increasing doses prevents him from working, from maintaining relationships, from developing in human ways. Similarly, an alcoholic's life is narrowed and dehumanized by his dependence on alcohol.

Let us consider television viewing in the light of the conditions that define seri-   6
ous addictions.

Not unlike drugs and alcohol, the television experience allows the participant   7
to blot out the real world and enter into a pleasurable and passive mental state. The worries and anxieties of reality are as effectively deferred by becoming absorbed in a television program as by going on a "trip" induced by drugs or alcohol. And just as alcoholics are only vaguely aware of their addiction, feeling that they control their drinking more than they really do ("I can cut it out any time I want—I just like to have three or four drinks before dinner"), people similarly overestimate their control over watching television. Even as they put off other activities to spend hour after hour watching television, they feel they could easily resume living in a different, less passive style. But somehow or other while the television set is present in their homes, the click doesn't sound. With television pleasures available, those other experiences seem less attractive, more difficult somehow.

A heavy viewer (a college English instructor) observes: "I find television al-   8
most irresistible. When the set is on, I cannot ignore it. I can't turn it off. I feel sapped, will-less, enervated. As I reach out to turn off the set, the strength goes out of my arms. I sit there for hours and hours."

The self-confessed television addict often feels he "ought" to do other things—   9
but the fact that he doesn't read and doesn't plant his garden or sew or crochet or play games or have conversations means that those activities are no longer as desirable as television. In a way the heavy viewer's life is as imbalanced by his television "habit" as a drug addict's or an alcoholic's. He is living in a holding pattern, as it were, passing up the activities that lead to growth or development or a sense of accomplishment. This is one reason people talk about their television viewing so ruefully, so apologetically. They are aware that it is an unproductive experience, that almost any other endeavor is more worthwhile by any human measure.

Finally, it is the adverse effect of television viewing on the lives of so many **10** people that defines it as a serious addiction. The television habit distorts the sense of time. It renders other experiences vague and curiously unreal while taking on a greater reality for itself. It weakens relationships by reducing and sometimes eliminating normal opportunities for talking, for communicating.

And yet television does not satisfy, else why would the viewer continue to **11** watch hour after hour, day after day? "The measure of health," writes Lawrence Kubie, "is flexibility . . . and especially the freedom to cease when sated." But the television viewer can never be sated with his television experiences—they do not provide the true nourishment that satiation requires—and thus he finds that he cannot stop watching.

About Unity

1. Winn's thesis is not presented directly in the essay. See whether you can state it in your own words.

_____

_____

2. Which statement would best serve as a topic sentence for paragraph 4?
   a. Addicts enjoy pleasurable experiences more than nonaddicts.
   b. Addicts feel that their lives are not really complete.
   c. Addicts would give up their addiction if other pleasurable experiences were available.
   d. Addicts need to endlessly repeat the experience on which they are dependent.

3. Which statement would best serve as a topic sentence for paragraph 7?
   a. People become television addicts because they have more troubled lives than most other people.
   b. Television addicts develop a distorted perception of reality and lose self-control.
   c. Few experiences in life are as pleasurable as watching television.
   d. Alcoholics often believe they have more control over their drinking than they really do.

About Support

4. The author defines TV as an addiction by first defining
   a. being hooked on TV.
   b. serious addiction.
   c. a heavy viewer.
   d. the real world.

5. The topic sentence of paragraph 5 states, "Finally, a serious addiction is distinguished from a harmless pursuit of pleasure by its distinctly destructive elements." What details does the author use to support this point?

_____

_____

6. Paragraph 8
   a. supports the idea in paragraph 7 that TV addicts overestimate their control over TV watching.
   b. raises a point not dealt with elsewhere.
   c. supports the idea in paragraph 9 that TV addicts are stuck in a living holding pattern.

About Coherence

7. Which paragraph fully signals the author's switch from discussing addiction in general terms to talking specifically about addiction to television? _____

8. What key transitional word is used twice in the essay? _____

About the Introduction and Conclusion

9. Which statement best describes the introductory paragraph of Winn's essay?
   a. It explains the importance of the topic of television addiction.
   b. It tells an anecdote that illustrates the nature of television addiction.
   c. It presents a type of "addiction" very different from the one discussed in the essay.

10. Which statement best describes the conclusion of "Television Addiction"?
   a. Winn recommends that the television addict try to "kick the habit."
   b. Winn summarizes the points made in the body of the essay.
   c. Winn comments on the damage television does to society at large.

Writing a Definition Essay

Writing Assignment

1 Below are an introduction, a thesis, and supporting points for an essay that defines the word *maturity*. Using a separate sheet of paper, plan out and write the supporting paragraphs and a conclusion for the essay.

The Meaning of Maturity

Being a mature student does not mean being an old-timer. Maturity is not measured by the number of years a person has lived. Instead, the yard-stick of maturity is marked by the qualities of self-denial, determination, and dependability.

Self-denial is an important quality in the mature student. . . .

Determination is another characteristic of a mature student. . . .

Although self-denial and determination are both vital, probably the most important measure of maturity is dependability. . . .

In conclusion, . . .

Prewriting

a. Prepare examples for the three qualities of maturity. For each quality, you should have either one extended example that takes up an entire paragraph or two or three shorter examples that together form enough material for a paragraph.

b. To generate these details, ask yourself questions like these, based on the topic sentence of the first supporting paragraph:

What could I do, or what have I done, that would be an example of self-denial?

What has someone I know ever done that could be described as self-denial?

What kind of behavior on the part of a student could be considered self-denial?

Write down quickly whatever answers occur to you. As when you freewrite, don't worry about grammar, punctuation, or spelling. Instead, concentrate on getting down as many details relating to self-denial as you can think of. Then repeat the questioning and writing process, substituting "determination" and "dependability" for "self-denial."

c. Now go through the material you have compiled. If you think of other details as you read, jot them down. Next, decide just what information you will use in each supporting paragraph. List the details in the order in which you will present them.

d. Now write the first draft of your essay.

Revising

After you have completed the first draft of the essay, set it aside for a while (if possible). When you reread what you have written, prepare for rewriting by asking yourself these questions:

FOUR BASES Checklist for Definition

About *Unity*

☑ Have I eliminated or rewritten any irrelevant material?

About *Support*

☑ Have I provided enough details to support each of the three characteristics of maturity?

About *Coherence*

☑ Have I used transition words to help readers follow my train of thought?

☑ Does my concluding paragraph provide a summary or a final thought or both?

About *Sentence Skills*

☑ Have I used a consistent point of view throughout my essay?

☑ Have I used specific rather than general words?

☑ Have I avoided wordiness and used concise wording?

☑ Are my sentences varied?

☑ Have I checked my writing for spelling and other sentence skills, as listed on the inside back cover of the book?

As you revise your essay through one or more additional drafts, continue to refer to this list until you can answer yes to each question.

Writing Assignment

Choose one of the terms below as the subject of a definition essay. Each term refers to a certain kind of person.

Slob
Cheapskate
Loser
Good neighbor
Busybody
Whiner
Con artist
Optimist
Pessimist
Team player
Bully
Scapegoat
Religious person
Hypocrite
Snob
Tease
Practical joker
Procrastinator
Loner
Pig
Type A

© BananaStock/SuperStock

© Joel Gordon

Prewriting

a. As you devise your opening paragraph, you may want to refer to the dictionary definition of the term. If so, be sure to use only one meaning of the term. (Dictionaries often provide several different meanings for a term.) *Don't* begin your paper with the overused phrase "According to Webster. . . ."

b. Remember that the thesis of a definition essay is a version of "What _____ means to me." The thesis presents what *your* experience has made *you* think the term actually means.

c. As you plan your supporting paragraphs, think of different parts or qualities of your term. Here, for example, are the three-part divisions of the student essays considered in this chapter:

> Football fans are crazy in terms of their behavior, their fascination with the past, and their loyalty.

> Student zombies are the "living dead," are controlled by a "mysterious force," and are likely to suffer an "awful fate."

d. Support each part of your division with either a series of examples or a single extended example.

e. You may find outlining to be the most helpful prewriting strategy for your definition essay. As a guide, write your thesis and three supporting points in the spaces below.   .

Thesis: _____

Support: 1. _____

2. _____

3. _____

Revising

Once you have the first draft of your essay completed, read it aloud to a friend or classmate. The two of you should review it with these questions in mind:

FOUR BASES Checklist for Definition

About *Unity*

✔ Does my thesis statement indicate how I define the term, and does it indicate my plan of development for the essay?

✔ Does each of my supporting paragraphs have a clear topic sentence?

About *Support*

✔ Have I supported each of my three topic sentences with one extended example or a series of examples?

About *Coherence*

✔ Have I rounded off my essay with an appropriate concluding paragraph?

About *Sentence Skills*

✔ Have I used a consistent point of view throughout my essay?

✔ Have I used specific rather than general words?

✔ Have I avoided wordiness and used concise wording?

✔ Are my sentences varied?

✔ Have I proofread my essay for spelling and other sentence skills, as listed on the inside back cover of the book?

Writing | Assignment

3   Write an essay that defines one of these terms:

Persistence	Responsibility	Fear
Rebellion	Insecurity	Arrogance
Sense of humor	Assertiveness	Conscience
Escape	Jealousy	Class
Laziness	Practicality	Innocence
Danger	Nostalgia	Freedom
Curiosity	Gentleness	Violence
Common sense	Depression	Shyness
Soul	Obsession	Idealism
Family	Christianity	Spirituality

Writing | Assignment

4   Writing for a Specific Purpose and Audience
In this definition essay, you will write with a specific purpose and for a specific audience.

You work in a doctor's office and have been asked to write a brochure that will be placed in the waiting room. The brochure is intended to tell patients what a healthy lifestyle is. Write a definition of *healthy lifestyle* for your readers, using examples wherever appropriate. Your definition might focus on both mental and physical health and might include eating, sleeping, exercise, and recreational habits.

Alternatively, you might decide to take a playful point of view and write a brochure defining an *unhealthy lifestyle*.

www.mhhe.com/langan

Division-Classification

This chapter will explain and illustrate how to

- develop a division-classification essay
- write a division-classification essay
- revise a division-classification essay

In addition, you will read and consider

- two student division-classification essays
- one professional division-classification essay

Visit an online bookstore like Powell's at http://www.powells .com.psection/psection.html and browse through the categories of books. Or visit Amazon at http://www.amazon.com and browse through the categories of music. Then design your own site selling something similar (you can be as creative as you like). Provide at least five different categories for your "product" and explain what distinguishes each one.

When you return home from your weekly trip to the supermarket with five bags packed with your purchases, how do you sort them out? You might separate food items from nonfood items (like toothpaste, paper towels, and detergent). Or you might divide and classify the items into groups intended for the freezer compartment, the refrigerator, and the kitchen cupboards. You might even put the items into groups like "to be used tonight," "to be used soon," and "to be used last." Sorting supermarket items in such ways is just one simple example of how we spend a great deal of our time organizing our environment in one manner or another.

In this chapter, you will be asked to write an essay in which you divide or classify a subject according to a single principle. To prepare for this assignment, first read the student essays and the professional essay that follow and work through the questions that accompany the essays.

Student Essays to Consider

Mall People

© BananaStock/SuperStock

Just what goes into "having fun"? For many people, "fun" involves getting out of the house, seeing other people, having something interesting to look at, and enjoying a choice of activities, all at a reasonable price. Going out to dinner or to the movies may satisfy some of those desires, but often not all. But an attractive alternative does exist in the form of the free-admission shopping mall. Teenagers, couples on dates, and the nuclear family can all be observed having a good time at the mall. 1

Teenagers are drawn to the mall to pass time with pals and to see and be seen by other teens. The guys saunter by in sneakers, T-shirts, and blue jeans, complete with a package of cigarettes sticking out of a pocket. The girls stumble along in midriff-baring tank tops, with a cell phone tucked snugly in the rear pocket of their low-waisted jeans. Traveling in a gang that resembles a wolf pack, the teenagers make the shopping mall their hunting ground. Mall managers have obviously made a decision to attract all this teenage activity. The kids' raised voices, loud laughter, and occasional shouted obscenities can be 2

(continued)

heard from as far as half a mall away. They come to "pick up girls," to "meet guys," and just to "hang out."

Couples find fun of another sort at shopping malls. The young lovers are 3 easy to spot because they walk hand in hand, stopping to sneak a quick kiss after every few steps. They first pause at a jewelry store window so that they can gaze at diamond engagement rings and platinum wedding bands. Then, they wander into furniture departments in the large mall stores. Finally, they drift away, their arms wrapped around each other's waist.

Mom, Dad, little Jenny, and Fred Jr., visit the mall on Friday and Saturday 4 evenings for inexpensive recreation. Hearing the music of the antique carousel housed there, Jenny begs to ride her favorite pony with its shining golden mane. Shouting, "I'm starving!" Fred Jr., drags the family toward the food court, where he detects the seductive odor of pizza. Mom walks through a fabric store, running her hand over the soft velvets and slippery silks. Meanwhile, Dad has wandered into an electronics store and is admiring the sound system he'd love to buy someday. The mall provides something special for every member of the family.

Sure, some people visit the mall in a brief, businesslike way, just to pick 5 up a specific purchase or two. But many more are shopping for inexpensive recreation. The teenagers, the dating couples, and the nuclear families all find cheap entertainment at the mall.

Genuine Draft

The other night, my six-year-old son turned to me and asked for a light 1 beer. My husband and I sat there for a moment, stunned, and then explained to him that beer was only for grown-ups. I suddenly realized how many beer ads appear on television and how often they appear. To my little boy, it must seem that every American drinks beer after work, or after playing softball, or while watching a football game. Brewers have pounded audiences with all kinds of campaigns to sell beer. There seems to be an ad to appeal to the self-image of every beer drinker.

One type of ad attracts people who think of themselves as 2 grown-up kids. Budweiser's animated frogs, squatting on lily pads and croaking, "Bud," "Weis," "Er," are a perfect example of this type. The frogs are an example of the wonders of computer animation, which is being increasingly mixed in with real-life action in advertisements. The

(continued)

campaign was an immediate hit with the underage set as well as with adult beer-drinkers. Within weeks, the frogs were as recognizable to children as Tony the Tiger or Big Bird. They became so popular that the new Bud ads were a feverishly anticipated part of the Super Bowl—as much a part of the entertainment as the game itself or the halftime show. These humorous ads suggest that beer is part of a lighthearted approach to life.

A second kind of ad is aimed not at wanna-be kids but at macho men, guys who think of themselves as "men's men," doing "guy things" together. One campaign features men who see themselves as victims of their nagging wives. Ads in this series show men howling with laughter about how they've fooled their wives into thinking they're home doing chores (by leaving dummy-stuffed pants lying under leaky sinks or broken furnaces) while they're really out drinking. Beer is a man's drink, the ads seem to say, and women are a nuisance to be gotten around.   3

European and European-sounding beers such as Löwenbräu and Heineken like to show handsome, wealthy-looking adults enjoying their money and leisure time. A typical scene shows such people enjoying an expensive hobby in a luxurious location. Beer, these ads tell us, is an essential part of the "good life." This type of ad appeals to people who want to see themselves as successful and upper class.   4

To a little boy, it may well seem that beer is necessary to every adult's life. After all, we need it to make us laugh, to bond with our friends, and to celebrate our financial success. At least, that's what advertisers tell him—and us.   5

Questions

1

About Unity

1. In which supporting paragraph in "Genuine Draft" is the topic sentence at the end rather than, as is more appropriate for student essays, at the beginning?

   _____

2. Which sentence in paragraph 2 of "Mall People" should be omitted in the interest of paragraph unity? (*Write the opening words.*)

   _____

3. What sentence in paragraph 2 of "Genuine Draft" should be omitted in the interest of paragraph unity? (*Write the opening words.*)

   _____

About Support

4. After which sentence in paragraph 3 of "Mall People" are more supporting details needed? (*Write the opening words.*)

_____

5. Which paragraph in "Genuine Draft" lacks sufficient specific details? _____

6. Label as *sight, touch, hearing,* or *smell* all the sensory details in the following sentences taken from "Mall People."

   a. "Hearing the music of the antique carousel housed there, Jenny begs to ride her favorite pony with its shining golden mane."

   b. "Shouting, 'I'm starving!' Fred Jr., drags the family toward the food court, where he detects the seductive odor of pizza."

   c. "Mom walks through a fabric store, running her hand over the soft velvets and slippery silks."

About Coherence

7. What are the time transition words used in paragraph 3 of "Mall People"?

_____ _____ _____

8. Which topic sentence in "Genuine Draft" functions as a linking sentence between paragraphs? (*Write the opening words.*)

_____

About the Introduction and Conclusion

9. What kind of introduction is used in "Genuine Draft"? (*Circle the appropriate letter.*)

   a. Broad, general statement narrowing to a thesis
   b. Idea that is the opposite of the one to be developed
   c. Quotation
   d. Anecdote
   e. Questions

10. What conclusion technique is used in "Mall People"? (*Circle the appropriate letter.*)

   a. Summary
   b. Prediction or recommendation
   c. Question

Developing a Division-Classification Essay
Considering Purpose and Audience

When writing a division-classification essay, your purpose is to present your audience with your own unique way of dividing and classifying a particular topic. To write a successful essay, you will need to first choose a topic that interests readers and lends itself to being divided and classified. Once you pick your topic, you will then have to come up with your own unique sorting system—one that readers will be able to understand.

For example, if you choose clothing, there are a number of ways to sort this topic into categories. You could divide clothing by the function it serves: shirts and jackets (to cover the upper body), pants and skirts (for the lower body), and shoes and socks (for the feet). Or you could divide clothes according to the materials they are made from: animal products, plant products, and synthetic materials. A more interesting, and potentially humorous, way to divide clothes is by fashion: clothes that are stylish, clothes that are going out of style, and clothes that are so unattractive that they never were in style. Notice that in all three of these cases, the broad topic of clothing has been divided into categories according to a particular principle (function, materials, and fashion). When you divide your topic for your essay, be sure to come up with your own division principle and make it clear to your readers.

Once you've selected your topic and figured out how to divide it, you will need to provide specific details so that readers fully understand the categories you made. For the example about fashion above, you might classify plaid bell-bottom pants as part of the "going out of style" category, while blue jeans might belong in the "clothes that are stylish" group and a mustard-yellow velour jacket might fit in the "never stylish" group. Whatever divisions you make, be sure to include enough details to make your division-classification method—your main point—clear to your readers. Equally important, keep your audience in mind. An audience of fashion-conscious young people, for instance, would probably have very different opinions about what is and isn't stylish than an audience of middle-aged bankers. Or an audience made up of the parents of middle-school students who are clamoring for "cool" clothes would have much more interest in clothing styles than the parents of students about to enter college.

Development through Prewriting

Julia, the writer of "Mall People," believed from her observations that "people at malls" would make a good topic for a division-classification essay. But she did not immediately know how she wanted to group those people or what she wanted to say about them. She decided to begin her prewriting by making a list of observations about mall shoppers. Here is what she came up with:

Families with kids

Lots of snacking

Crowds around special displays—automobiles, kiddie rides

Older people walking in mall for exercise

Groups of teenagers

Women getting made over at makeup counter

Dating couples

Blind woman with Seeing Eye dog

Lots of people talking and laughing rather than shopping

Interviewers stopping shoppers to fill out questionnaires

Kids hanging out, meeting each other

As Julia reviewed her list, she concluded that the three largest groups of "mall people" were families with children, groups of teens, and dating couples. She decided to organize her essay around those three groups. To further flesh out her idea, she created a scratch outline that her essay would follow. Here is the scratch outline Julia prepared:

Thesis statement: Mall offers inexpensive fun for several groups.

1. Teens

    a. Roam in packs

    b. Dress alike

    c. Meet new people

(continued)

2. *Dating couples*
    a. *Act romantic*
    b. *Window-shop for future home*
    c. *Have lovers' quarrels*
3. *Families*
    a. *Kids' activities*
    b. *Cheap food*
    c. *Adults shop*

Julia's list and outline prepared her to write the first draft of her essay.

First Draft

Mall People

Malls aren't only places to go shopping. They also offer free or at least cheap fun and activities for lots of people. Teenagers, dating couples, and families all like to visit the mall.

Teenagers love to roam the mall in packs, like wolves. They often dress alike, depending on the latest fashion. They're noisy and sometimes rude, and mall security officers sometimes kick them out of the building. Then they find somewhere else to go, maybe one of the warehouse-sized amusement and video-game arcades that are springing up everywhere. Those places are fun, but they tend to be more expensive than just "hanging out" at the mall. Teens are usually not as interested in shopping at the mall as they are in picking up members of the opposite sex and seeing their friends.

Dating couples also enjoy wandering around the mall. They are easy to spot because they walk along holding hands and sometimes kissing. They stare at diamond rings and wedding bands and shop for furniture together. Sometimes they have spats and one of them stomps off to sulk on a bench for a while.

Little kids and their parents make up a big group of mall-goers. There is something for every member of the family there. There are usually some special displays that interest the kids, and Mom and Dad can always find

(continued)

things they like to window-shop for. Another plus for the family is that there is inexpensive food, like burgers and pizza, available at the mall's food court.

Development through Revising

After Julia completed her first draft, she put it aside. She knew from previous experience that she was a better critic of her own writing after she took a break from it. The following morning, when Julia read over her first draft, she noticed several places where it could be improved. Here are the observations she put in her writing journal:

- My first paragraph does present a thesis (malls offer inexpensive entertainment), and it tells how I'm going to develop that thesis (by discussing three groups of people). But it isn't very interesting. I think I could do a better job of drawing readers in by describing what is fun about malls.
- Some of the details in the essay aren't necessary; they don't support my main idea. For instance, the stuff about teens being kicked out of the mall and about dating couples having fights doesn't have anything to do with the entertainment malls provide. I'll eliminate this.
- Some of my statements that do support the main idea need more support. For example, when I say there are "special displays that interest the kids" in paragraph 4, I should give an example of such a display. I should also back up the idea that many teens dress alike.

With these observations in mind, Julia returned to her essay and revised it, producing the version that appears on page 344.

A Professional Essay to Consider

Now read the following professional essay. Then answer the questions and read the comments that follow.

Wait Divisions
by Tom Bodett

I read somewhere that we spend a full third of our lives waiting. I've also **1** read that we spend a third of our lives sleeping, a third working, and a third at our leisure. Now either somebody's lying, or we're spending all our leisure time waiting to go to work or sleep. That can't be true or league softball and Winnebagos never would have caught on.

So where are we doing all of this waiting, and what does it mean to an impatient **2** society like ours? Could this unseen waiting be the source of all our problems? A shrinking economy? The staggering deficit? Declining mental health and moral apathy? Probably not, but let's take a look at some of the more classic "waits" anyway.

The very purest form of waiting is what we'll call the *Watched-Pot Wait*. This **3** type of wait is without a doubt the most annoying of all. Take filling up the kitchen sink. There is absolutely nothing you can do while this is going on but keep both eyes glued to the sink until it's full. If you try to cram in some extracurricular activity, you're asking for it. So you stand there, your hands on the faucets, and wait. A temporary suspension of duties. During these waits it's common for your eyes to lapse out of focus. The brain disengages from the body and wanders around the imagination in search of distraction. It finds none and springs back into action only when the water runs over the edge of the counter and onto your socks.

The phrase "a watched pot never boils" comes of this experience. Pots don't **4** care whether they are watched or not; the problem is that nobody has ever seen a pot actually come to a boil. While people are waiting, their brains turn off.

Other forms of the Watched-Pot Wait would include waiting for your dryer to **5** quit at the Laundromat, waiting for your toast to pop out of the toaster, or waiting for a decent idea to come to mind at a typewriter. What they all have in common is that they render the waiter helpless and mindless.

A cousin to the Watched-Pot Wait is the *Forced Wait*. Not for the weak of will, **6** this one requires a bit of discipline. The classic Forced Wait is starting your car in the winter and letting it slowly idle up to temperature before engaging the clutch. This is every bit as uninteresting as watching a pot, but with one big difference. You have a choice. There is nothing keeping you from racing to work behind a stone-cold engine save[1] the thought of the early demise of several thousand dollars' worth of equipment you haven't paid for yet. Thoughts like that will help you get through a Forced Wait.

Properly preparing packaged soup mixes also requires a Forced Wait. Direc- **7** tions are very specific on these mixes. "Bring three cups of water to boil, add mix,

---

[1]*save:* except.

simmer three minutes, remove from heat, let stand five minutes." I have my doubts that anyone has actually done this. I'm fairly spineless when it comes to instant soups and usually just boil the bejeezus out of them until the noodles sink. Some things just aren't worth a Forced Wait.

8   All in all Forced Waiting requires a lot of a thing called patience, which is a virtue. Once we get into virtues I'm out of my element and can't expound on the virtues of virtue, or even lie about them. So let's move on to some of the more farreaching varieties of waiting.

9   The *Payday Wait* is certainly a leader in the long-term anticipation field. The problem with waits that last more than a few minutes is that you have to actually do other things in the meantime. Like go to work. By far the most aggravating feature

What, in your opinion, is worth waiting for? Think about this question and create a scratch outline for a division-classification essay on things you feel are worth waiting for.

of the Payday Wait is that even though you must keep functioning in the interludes,[2] there is less and less you are able to do as the big day draws near. For some of us the last few days are best spent alone in a dark room for fear we'll accidentally do something that costs money. With the Payday Wait comes a certain amount of hope that we'll make it, and faith that everything will be all right once we do.

With the introduction of faith and hope, I've ushered in the most potent wait **10** class of all, the *Lucky-Break Wait*, or the *Wait for One's Ship to Come In*. This type of wait is unusual in that it is for the most part voluntary. Unlike the Forced Wait, which is also voluntary, waiting for your lucky break does not necessarily mean that it will happen.

Turning one's life into a waiting game of these proportions requires gobs of the **11** aforementioned faith and hope, and is strictly for the optimists among us. For these people life is the thing that happens to them while they're waiting for something to happen to them. On the surface it seems as ridiculous as following the directions on soup mixes, but the Lucky-Break Wait performs an outstanding service to those

---

[2]*interludes:* times in between.

who take it upon themselves to do it. As long as one doesn't come to rely on it, wishing for a few good things to happen never hurt anybody.

In the end it is obvious that we certainly do spend a good deal of our time 12 waiting. The person who said we do it a third of the time may have been going easy on us. It makes a guy wonder how anything at all gets done around here. But things do get done, people grow old, and time boils on whether you watch it or not.

The next time you're standing at the sink waiting for it to fill while cooking 13 soup mix that you'll have to eat until payday or until a large bag of cash falls out of the sky, don't despair. You're probably just as busy as the next guy.

Questions

2

About Unity

1. The thesis of Bodett's essay is not presented directly. See if you can state it in your own words.

   _____

2. In paragraph 2, Bodett introduces several possible effects of waiting, then dismisses them with a "probably not." Is it a sign of careless writing that Bodett mentions irrelevant topics and then dismisses them? Or does he intend a particular effect by introducing unnecessary topics? If he does intend an effect, how would you describe it?

   _____

   _____

About Support

3. Bodett writes of four "classic waits": the Watched-Pot Wait, the Forced Wait, the Payday Wait, and the Lucky-Break Wait. For which two "waits" does he provide several examples?

   _____   _____

4. Bodett refers to the first two waits as cousins. How does he differentiate between them?

   _____

   _____

5. How does Bodett support his claim that the Forced Wait "requires a bit of discipline"?

   _____

   _____

About Coherence

6. Bodett's essay does not follow the strict one-three-one model (introduction, three supporting paragraphs, conclusion) often used in student essays. Instead, its form is a looser one that includes an introduction, four topics for development (the four "waits"), and a conclusion. Indicate in the following outline how the paragraphs of Bodett's essay are broken up:

Introduction: Paragraph(s)   _____

Topic 1:   Paragraph(s)   _____

Topic 2:   Paragraph(s)   _____

Topic 3:   Paragraph(s)   _____

Topic 4:   Paragraph(s)   _____

Conclusion: Paragraph(s)   _____

7. Which words in the first sentence of paragraph 6 link that sentence to the preceding three paragraphs?

_____

8. Bodett organizes the waits
   a. from the most harmful to the least harmful.
   b. from the shortest waits to the longest.
   c. from the most difficult wait to the easiest one.
   d. in no particular order.

About the Introduction and Conclusion

9. Which method best describes the introduction to "Wait Divisions"?
   a. Quotation
   b. Idea that is the opposite of the one to be developed
   c. Anecdote
   d. Broad, general statement narrowing to thesis

10. In what way does the first sentence in paragraph 13 serve as a summary of Bodett's main points?

_____

_____

Writing a Division-Classification Essay

Writing | Assignment

1 Shown below are an introduction, a thesis, and supporting details for a classification essay on stress in college. Using separate paper, plan out and write the supporting paragraphs and a conclusion for the essay.

College Stress

Jack's heart pounds as he casts panicky looks around the classroom. He doesn't recognize the professor, he doesn't know any of the students, and he can't even figure out what the subject is. In front of him is a test. At the last minute his roommate awakens him. It's only another anxiety dream. The very fact that dreams like Jack's are common suggests that college is a stressful situation for young people. The causes of this stress can be academic, financial, and personal.

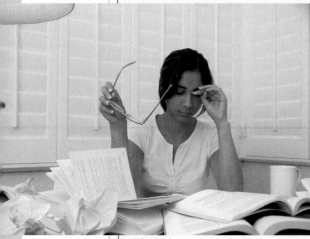
© Myrleen Ferguson Cate/PhotoEdit

Academic stress is common. . . .

In addition to academic stress, the student often feels financial pressure. . . .

Along with academic and financial worries, the student faces personal pressures. . . .

In conclusion . . .

Prewriting

a. To develop some ideas for the division-classification essay in Writing Assignment 1, freewrite for five minutes apiece on (1) *academic,* (2) *financial,* and (3) *personal* problems of college students.

b. Then add to the material you have written by asking yourself these questions:

> What are some examples of academic problems that are stressful for students?
>
> What are some examples of financial problems that students must contend with?
>
> What are some examples of personal problems that create stress in students?

Write down quickly whatever answers occur to you. As with freewriting, do not worry at this stage about writing correct sentences. Instead, concentrate on getting down as much information as you can think of that supports each of the three points.

c. Now go through all the material you have accumulated. Perhaps some of the details you have written down may help you think of even better details that would fit. If so, write down these additional details. Then make decisions about the exact information that you will use in each supporting paragraph. List the details in the order in which you will present them (1, 2, 3, and so on).

d. Now write the first draft of your essay.

Revising

After you have completed the first draft of the essay (and ideally have set it aside for a while), you should prepare yourself to rewrite by asking the following questions:

FOUR BASES Checklist for Division-Classification

About *Unity*

- ✔ Have I introduced my essay with a clearly stated thesis?
- ✔ Have I eliminated or rewritten any irrelevant material?

About *Support*

- ✔ Have I provided relevant examples for each of the three kinds of stress?
- ✔ Have I provided enough details to support each of the three kinds of stress?

About *Coherence*

- ✔ Have I used transition words to help readers follow my train of thought?
- ✔ Have I added a concluding paragraph that rounds out and completes the essay?

About *Sentence Skills*

- ✔ Have I used a consistent point of view throughout my essay?
- ✔ Have I used specific rather than general words?
- ✔ Have I avoided wordiness and used concise wording?
- ✔ Are my sentences varied?
- ✔ Have I checked my essay carefully for spelling and other sentence skills, as listed on the inside back cover of the book?

As you revise your essay, continue to refer to this list until you can answer yes to each question.

Writing | Assignment

2

Choose one of the following subjects as the basis for a division-classification essay:

Music	Pet owners
Videos	Junk food
TV shows	College courses
Fiction	Dating couples
Comic strips	Shoppers
Vacations	Bosses
Answering-machine messages	Parties
Breakfast foods	Advertisements
Pets	Catalogs
Attitudes toward exercise	Technology

Prewriting

a. For a division-classification essay, the prewriting strategy that may be especially helpful is outlining. The success of your essay will depend on your division of your topic into three well-balanced parts. To create those three parts, you must use the same rule, or principle, of division for each. Most topics can be divided in several ways according to several principles. For example, the topic "Hit movies" could be divided in the following ways:

> By *film categories:* Action, comedy, romance
>
> By *intended audience:* Families, dating couples, teens

The topic "My favorite books" could be divided like this:

> By *book categories:* Novels, how-to books, biographies
>
> By *purpose they serve for me:* Escape, self-improvement, amusement

The topic "Places to eat" could be divided in these ways:

> By *cost:* Cheap, moderate, expensive
>
> By *type of food:* American, Italian, Chinese

If you look back at the essays that appear earlier in this chapter, you'll see that the topics are divided according to the following principles:

> "Mall People" is divided by *groups of shoppers:* Teens, dating couples, families

"Genuine Draft" is divided by *beer-drinkers' self-images:* Grown-up kids, men's men, upper class

"Wait Divisions" is divided by *types of waits:* Watched-Pot Wait, Forced Wait, Payday Wait, Lucky-Break Wait

The important point to remember is to divide your topic consistently, according to a single principle. It would be illogical, for example, to divide the topic "Places to eat" into "American" (type of food served), "Italian" (type of food served), and "Expensive" (cost). For the essay to be balanced and consistent, choose one principle of division and stick to it.

b.   As you consider a topic for your own paper, think of principles of division you might use. Test them by filling out this outline and answering the question.

Topic: _____

Principle of division: _____

Three-part division of topic: _____

   1.   _____

   2.   _____

   3.   _____

Have I used the same principle of division for each of the three parts?

When you are confident that you have chosen a topic of interest to you that you can divide into three parts according to one principle, you are ready to begin writing.

c.   Before writing your first draft, you may want to freewrite on each of the three parts, make lists, or ask and answer questions to generate the supporting details you will need to develop your ideas.

Revising

Once you have completed a first draft of your essay, share it with a friend or classmate. You should both review it with these questions in mind:

FOUR BASES Checklist for Division-Classification

About *Unity*

✔ Have I included the essay's thesis in my introductory paragraph?

✔ Does my thesis state my topic and the principle of division I have chosen?

✔ Have I eliminated irrelevant material that does not support my thesis?

About *Support*

✔ Have I backed up statements in my essay with relevant examples or illustrations?

✔ Have I provided enough details to support each of the three kinds of stress?

About *Coherence*

✔ Is each of the paragraphs in the body of my essay based on one division of my topic?

✔ Have I used transition words to help readers follow my train of thought?

✔ Have I included a concluding paragraph that provides a sense of completion to the essay?

✔ Have I used linking sentences between paragraphs to help tie those paragraphs together?

About *Sentence Skills*

✔ Have I used a consistent point of view throughout my essay?

✔ Have I used specific rather than general words?

✔ Have I avoided wordiness and used concise wording?

✔ Are my sentences varied?

✔ Have I proofread my essay for spelling and other sentence skills, as listed on the inside back cover of the book?

As you revise your essay, continue to refer to this list until you and your reader can answer yes to each question.

Writing | Assignment

3 Writing for a Specific Purpose and Audience

In this division-classification essay, you will write with a specific purpose and for a specific audience.

Option 1 Your younger sister or brother has moved to another city and is about to choose a roommate. Write her or him a letter about what to expect from different types of roommates. Label each type of roommate ("The Messy Type," "The Neatnik," "The Loud-Music Lover," etc.), and explain what it would be like to live with each.

Option 2 Unsure about your career direction, you have gone to a vocational counseling service. To help you select the type of work you are best suited for, a counselor has asked you to write a detailed description of your ideal job. You will present this description to three other people who are also seeking to choose a career.

To describe your ideal job, divide work life into three or more elements, such as

Activities done on the job

Skills used on the job

Physical environment

People you work with and under

How the job affects society

In your essay, explain your ideals for each element. Use specific examples where possible to illustrate your points.

Argument

This chapter will explain and illustrate how to

- develop an argument essay
- write an argument essay
- revise an argument essay

In addition, you will read and consider

- two student argument essays
- one professional argument essay

Should cell phones be permitted in class? Look at the photograph above and write an essay in which you argue for or against the use of cell phones in the classroom. Include at least three separate reasons that support your point of view.

Do you know someone who enjoys a good argument? Such a person likes to challenge any sweeping statement we might make. For example, when we say something like "Ms. Lucci doesn't grade fairly," he or she comes back with "Why do you say that? What are your reasons?"

Our questioner then listens carefully as we state our case, judging if we really do have solid evidence to support our point of view. We realize that saying, "Ms. Lucci just doesn't, that's all," sounds weak and unconvincing, so we try to come up with stronger evidence to back up our statement. Such a questioner may make us feel uncomfortable, but we may also feel grateful to him or her for helping us clarify our opinions.

The ability to put forth sound and compelling arguments is an important skill in everyday life. You can use argument to make a point in a class discussion, persuade a friend to lend you money, or talk an employer into giving you a day off. Becoming skilled in clear, logical reasoning can also help you see through faulty arguments that others may make. You'll become a better critic of advertisements, newspaper articles, political speeches, and the other persuasive appeals you see and hear every day.

In this chapter, you will be asked to write an essay in which you defend a position with a series of solid reasons. In a general way, you have done the same thing—making a point and then supporting it—with all the essays in this book. The difference here is that argument advances a *controversial* point, a point that at least some of your readers will not be inclined to accept. To prepare for this assignment, first read about five strategies you can use in advancing an argument. Then read the student essays and the professional essay that follow and work through the questions that accompany the essays.

Strategies for Argument

Because argument assumes controversy, you have to work especially hard to convince readers of the validity of your position. Here are five strategies you can use to help win over readers whose viewpoint may differ from yours.

1 Use Tactful, Courteous Language

In an argument essay, you are attempting to persuade readers to accept your viewpoint. It is important, therefore, not to anger them by referring to them or their opinions in rude or belittling terms. Stay away from sweeping statements like "Everybody knows that . . ." or "People with any intelligence agree that. . . ." Also, keep the focus on the issue you are discussing, not on the people involved in the debate. Don't write, "*My opponents* say that orphanages cost less than foster care." Instead, write, "*Supporters of orphanages* say that orphanages cost less than foster care." Terms like *my opponents* imply that the argument is between you and anyone who disagrees with you. By contrast, a term such as *supporters of orphanages* suggests that those who don't agree with you are nevertheless reasonable people who are willing to consider differing opinions.

2 Point Out Common Ground

Another way to persuade readers to consider your opinion is to point out common ground—opinions that you share. Find points on which people on all sides of the argument can agree. Perhaps you are arguing that there should be an 11 P.M. curfew for juveniles in your town. Before going into detail about your proposal, remind readers who oppose such a curfew that you and they share certain goals: a safer city, a lower crime rate, and fewer gang-related tragedies. Readers will be more receptive to your idea once they have considered how you and they think alike.

3   Acknowledge Differing Viewpoints

It is a mistake to simply ignore points of view that conflict with yours. Acknowledging other viewpoints strengthens your position in several ways. First, it helps you spot flaws in the opposing position—as well as in your own argument. Second, and equally important, it gives the impression that you are a reasonable person, willing to look at an issue from all sides. Readers will be more likely to consider your point of view if you indicate a willingness to consider theirs.

At what point in your essay should you acknowledge opposing arguments? The earlier the better—ideally, in the introduction. By quickly establishing that you recognize the other side's position, you get your readers on board with you, ready to hear what else you have to say.

One effective technique is to *cite the opposing viewpoint in your thesis statement.* You do this by dividing your thesis into two parts. In the first part, you acknowledge the other side's point of view; in the second, you state your opinion, suggesting that yours is the stronger viewpoint. In the following example, the opposing viewpoint is underlined once; the writer's own position is underlined twice:

> Although some students believe that studying a foreign language is a waste of time, two years of foreign-language study should be required of all college graduates.

For another example of a thesis that acknowledges an opposing viewpoint, look at this thesis statement, taken from the essay titled "Once Over Lightly: Local TV News" (page 368):

> While local TV newscasts can provide a valuable community resource, too often such programs provide mere entertainment at the expense of solid news.

Another effective technique is to use one or two sentences (separate from the thesis) in the introduction to acknowledge the alternative position. Such sentences briefly state the "other side's" argument. To see this technique at work, look at the introduction to the essay "Teenagers and Jobs" (page 367), noting the sentence "Many people argue that working can be a valuable experience for the young."

A third technique is to *use a paragraph within the body of your essay to summarize opposing opinions in greater detail.* To do this successfully, you must spend some time researching those opposing arguments. A fair, evenhanded summary of the other side's ideas will help convince readers that you have looked at the issue from all angles before deciding where you stand. Imagine, for instance, that you are

Arguments can be made through visual images as well. What visual argument is suggested by this photograph? Is it effective? Why or why not?

© Mary Kate Denny/PhotoEdit

writing an essay arguing that the manufacture and sale of handguns should be outlawed. You would begin by doing some library research to find information on both sides of the issue, making sure to pay attention to material that argues against your viewpoint. You might also talk with local representatives of the National Rifle Association or other organizations that support gun ownership. Having done your research, you would be in a good position to write a paragraph summarizing the opposing viewpoints. In this paragraph, you might mention that many citizens believe that gun ownership is a right guaranteed by the Constitution and that gun owners fear that outlawing handguns would deprive law-abiding people of protection against gun-toting criminals. Once you had demonstrated that you understood opposing views, you would be in a stronger position to present your own point of view.

4   When Appropriate, Grant the Merits of Differing Viewpoints

Sometimes an opposing argument contains a point whose validity you cannot deny. What should you do then? The strongest strategy is to admit that the point is a good one. You will lose credibility if you argue against something that clearly makes sense. Admit the merit of one aspect of the other argument while making it clear that you still believe your argument to be stronger overall. Suppose that you were arguing against the use of computers in writing classrooms. You might say, "Granted, students who are already accustomed to computers can use them to write papers more quickly and efficiently"—admitting that the other side has a valid point. But you could quickly follow this admission with a statement making your own viewpoint clear: "But for students like me who write and think in longhand, a computer in the classroom is more a hindrance than a help; it would require too long a learning curve to be of any value to me."

5 Rebut Differing Viewpoints

Sometimes it may not be enough simply to acknowledge other points of view and present your own argument. When you are dealing with an issue that your readers feel strongly about, you may need to *rebut* the opposing arguments. To *rebut* means to point out problems with an opposing view, to show where an opponent's argument breaks down.

Imagine that you are writing an essay arguing that your college should use money intended to build a campus health and fitness center to upgrade the library instead. From reading the school paper, you know that supporters of the center say it will help attract new students to the college. You rebut that point by citing a study conducted by the admissions office that shows that most students choose a college because they can afford it and because they like its academic programs and facilities. You also emphasize that many students, already financially strapped, would have trouble paying the proposed fee for using the center.

A rebuttal can take two forms: (1) You can first mention all the points raised by the other side and then present your counterargument to each of those points. (2) You can present the first point raised by the opposition and rebut that point, then move on to the second opposing point and rebut that, and so on.

Student Essays to Consider

Teenagers and Jobs

"The pressure for teenagers to work is great, and not just because of 1 the economic plight in the world today. Much of it is peer pressure to have a little bit of freedom and independence, and to have their own spending money. The concern we have is when the part-time work becomes the primary focus." These are the words of Roxanne Bradshaw, educator and officer of the National Education Association. Many people argue that working can be a valuable experience for the young. However, working more than about fifteen hours a week is harmful to adolescents because it reduces their involvement with school, encourages a materialistic and expensive lifestyle, and increases the chance of having problems with drugs and alcohol.

Schoolwork and the benefits of extracurricular activities tend to go by 2 the wayside when adolescents work long hours. As more and more teens have filled the numerous part-time jobs offered by fast-food restaurants and malls, teachers have faced increasing difficulties. They must both keep the attention of tired pupils and give homework to students who simply don't have time to do it. In addition, educators have noticed less involvement

(continued)

---

in the extracurricular activities that many consider a healthy influence on young people. School bands and athletic teams are losing players to work, and sports events are poorly attended by working students. Those teens who try to do it all—homework, extracurricular activities, and work—may find themselves exhausted and prone to illness. A recent newspaper story, for example, described a girl in Pennsylvania who came down with mononucleosis as a result of aiming for good grades, playing on two school athletic teams, and working thirty hours a week.

Another drawback of too much work is that it may promote materialism   3
and an unrealistic lifestyle. Some parents claim that working helps teach adolescents the value of a dollar. Undoubtedly that can be true. It's also true that some teens work to help out with the family budget or to save for college. However, surveys have shown that the majority of working teens use their earnings to buy luxuries—computers, video-game systems, clothing, even cars. These young people, some of whom earn $500 or more a month, don't worry about spending wisely—they can just about have it all. In many cases, experts point out, they are becoming accustomed to a lifestyle they won't be able to afford several years down the road, when they no longer have parents paying for car insurance, food, lodging, and so on. At that point, they'll be hard-pressed to pay for necessities as well as luxuries.

Finally, teenagers who work a lot are more likely than others to get   4
involved with alcohol and drugs. Teens who put in long hours may seek a quick release from stress, just like the adults who need to drink a couple of martinis after a hard day at work. Stress is probably greater in our society today than it has been at any time in the past. Also, teens who have money are more likely to get involved with drugs.

Teenagers can enjoy the benefits of work while avoiding its drawbacks,   5
simply by limiting their work hours during the school year. As is often the case, a moderate approach will be the most healthy and rewarding.

Once Over Lightly: Local TV News

Are local television newscasts a reliable source of news? Do they   1
provide in-depth coverage and analysis of important local issues? Unfortunately, all too often they do not. While local TV newscasts can provide a valuable community resource, too often such programs provide mere entertainment at the expense of solid news. In their battle for high ratings, local programs emphasize news personalities at the expense of

(continued)

stories. Visual appeal has a higher priority than actual news. And stories and reports are too brief and shallow.

Local TV newscasters are as much the subject of the news as are the stories they present. Nowhere is this more obvious than in weather reports. Weatherpersons spend valuable news time joking, drawing cartoons, chatting about weather fronts as "good guys" and "bad guys," and dispensing weather trivia such as statistics about relative humidity and record highs and lows for the date. Reporters, too, draw attention to themselves. Rather than just getting the story, the reporters are shown jumping into or getting out of helicopters to get the story. When reporters interview crime victims or the residents of poor neighborhoods, the camera angle typically includes them and their reaction as well as their subjects. When they report on a storm, they stand outside in the storm, their styled hair blowing, so we can admire how they "brave the elements." Then there are the anchorpersons, who are chosen as much for their looks as their skills. They, too, dilute the news by putting their personalities at center stage.

Often the selection of stories and the way they are presented are based on visual impact rather than news value. If a story is not accompanied by an interesting film clip, it is not likely to be shown on the local news. The result is an overemphasis on fires and car crashes and little attention to such important issues as the economy. A tractor-trailer spill on the highway slightly injures one person and inconveniences motorists for only an hour. But because it provides dramatic pictures—the big truck on its side, its load spilled, emergency personnel running around, lots of flashing lights—it is given greater emphasis in the local newscast than a rise in local taxes, which has far more lasting effect on the viewer. "If it bleeds, it leads" is the unofficial motto of many local news programs. A story that includes pictures of death and destruction, no matter how meaningless, is preferable on the local news to a solid, important story without flashy visuals. The mania for visuals is so strong that local news programs will even slap irrelevant visuals onto an otherwise strong story. A recent story on falling oil prices, for example, was accompanied by footage of a working oil well that drew attention away from the important economic information in the report.

On the average, about half a minute is devoted to a story. Clearly, stories that take less than half a minute are superficial. Even the longest stories, which can take up to several minutes, are not accompanied by meaningful analysis. Instead, the camera jumps from one location to another, and the newscaster simplifies and trivializes the issues. For instance, one recent "in-depth" story about the homeless consisted of a glamorous reporter talking

2

3

4

(continued)

to a homeless person and asking him what should be done about the problem. The poor man was in no condition to respond thoughtfully. The story then cut to an interview with a city bureaucrat who mechanically rambled on about the need for more government funding. Is raising taxes the answer to every social problem? There were also shots of homeless people sleeping in doorways and on top of heating vents, and there were interviews with people in the street, all of whom said that something should be done about the terrible problem of homelessness. There was, in all of this, no real exploration of the issue and no proposed solution. It was also apparent that the homeless were just the issue of the week. After the week's coverage was over, the topic was not mentioned again.

Because of the emphasis on newscasters' personalities and on the visual   5 impact of stories and the short time span for stories, local news shows provide little more than diversion. What viewers need instead is news that has real significance. Rather than being amused and entertained, we need to deal with complex issues and learn uncomfortable truths that will help us become more responsible consumers and citizens.

About Unity

Questions

1

1. Which paragraph in "Once Over Lightly" lacks a topic sentence? _____
   Write a topic sentence for the paragraph:

   _____

2. What sentence in paragraph 4 of "Once Over Lightly" should be omitted in the interest of paragraph unity? *(Write the opening words.)*

   _____

3. Which sentence in paragraph 4 of "Teenagers and Jobs" should be omitted in the interest of paragraph unity? *(Write the opening words.)*

   _____

About Support

4. Which sentence in paragraph 4 of "Teenagers and Jobs" needs to be followed by more supporting details? Which sentence in paragraph 2 of "Once Over Lightly" needs to be followed by supporting details? *(Write the opening words of each sentence.)*

   _____

   _____

5. In "Teenagers and Jobs," which supporting paragraph raises an opposing idea and then argues against that idea? _____ What transition word is used to signal the author's change of direction? _____

6. In paragraph 2 of "Once Over Lightly," the topic sentence is supported by details about three types of newscasters. What are those three types?

_____   _____   _____

About Coherence

7. Which two paragraphs of "Teenagers and Jobs" begin with an addition transition, and what are those words?

_____   _____

8. Write the change-of-direction transition and the illustration transition in paragraph 3 of "Once Over Lightly."

   Change of direction: _____   *Illustration:* _____

About the Introduction and Conclusion

9. Two methods of introduction are used in "Teenagers and Jobs." Circle the letters of these two methods.

   a. Broad, general statement narrowing to thesis

   b. Idea that is the opposite of the one to be developed

   c. Quotation

   d. Anecdote

   e. Questions

10. Both essays end with the same type of conclusion. What method do they use?

   a. Summary only

   b. Summary and recommendation

   c. Prediction

Developing an Argument Essay

Considering Purpose and Audience

When you write an argument essay, your main purpose is to convince readers that your particular view or opinion on a *controversial* issue is correct. In addition, at times, you may have a second purpose for your argument essay: to persuade your audience to take some sort of action.

To convince readers in an argument essay, it is important to provide them with a clear main point and plenty of logical evidence to back it up. Say, for example, you want to argue that public schools should require students to wear uniforms. In this case, you might do research to gather as much evidence as possible to support your point. You may check to see, for instance, if uniforms are cheaper than the alternative. Perhaps you could find out if schools with uniforms have a lower rate of violence than those without them. You may even look for studies to see if students' academic performance improves when school uniforms are adopted. As you search for evidence, be sure that it clearly links to your topic and supports the main point you are trying to get across to your audience,

While consideration of your audience is important for all essay forms, it is absolutely critical to the success of your argument essay. Depending on the main point you choose, your audience may be firmly opposed to your view or somewhat supportive of it. As you begin planning your own argument essay, then, consider what your audience already knows, and how it feels, about the main point of your argument. Using the example above, for instance, ask yourself what opinion your audience holds about school uniforms. What are likely to be their objections to your argument? Why would people *not* support your main point? What, if anything, are the merits of the opposing point of view? To "get inside the head" of your opposition, you might even want to interview a few people you're sure will disagree with you: say, for instance, a student with a very funky personal style who you know would dislike wearing a uniform. By becoming aware of the points of view your audience might have, you will know how to proceed in researching your rebuttal to their arguments.

TIP: For more information on how to deal with opposing views in your essay, see pages 265–367. By directly addressing your opposition, you add credibility to your argument and increase the chances that others will be convinced that your main point is valid.

Development through Prewriting

Before choosing a topic for her essay, Anna, the writer of "Teenagers and Jobs," asked herself what controversial subject she was particularly well qualified to argue. She wanted to select something she cared about, something she could sink her teeth into. As a person who had been an active member of her high school community—she had worked on the newspaper, played basketball, and sung in a chorus—Anna first thought of writing about student apathy. It had always bothered her to see few students taking advantage of the opportunities available to them in school. But as she thought more about individual students she knew and their reasons for not getting more involved in school and extracurricular activities, she changed her opinion. "I realized that 'apathy' was not really the problem," she explained. "Many of them worked so much that they literally didn't have time for school life."

After narrowing her thesis to the idea of "teenagers and work," Anna made a list of what she perceived as the bad points of students' working too much:

No time for real involvement in school and school activities

Students leave right after school—can't stay for clubs, practices

Don't have time to attend games, other school functions

Students sleep in class and skip homework

Stress, extra money contribute to drug and alcohol use

Teachers frustrated trying to teach tired students

Having extra money makes teens materialistic

Some get so greedy they drop out of school to work full-time

Students miss the fun of being young, developing talents and social abilities

Students burn out, even get sick

Hanging around older coworkers can contribute to drug, alcohol use

Buying luxuries gives teens unrealistic idea of standard of living

As she reviewed and revised her list of points, Anna identified three main points to develop in her essay. Those she identified as points 1, 2, and 3. She realized that some of the other items she had jotted down were related ideas that might be used to support her main topics. She marked those with the number of the main idea they supported, in parentheses, like this: (1). She also crossed out points that did not fit.

1 No time for real involvement in school and school activities

(1) Students leave right after school—can't stay for clubs, practices

(1) Don't have time to attend games, other school functions

Students sleep in class and skip homework

(continued)

2 *Stress, extra money contribute to drug and alcohol use*

(1) *Teachers frustrated trying to teach tired students*

3 *Having extra money makes teens materialistic*

(3) *Some get so greedy for money they drop out of school to work full-time*

~~*Students miss the fun of being young, developing talents and social abilities*~~

~~*Students burn out, even get sick*~~

(2) *Hanging around older coworkers can contribute to drug, alcohol use*

(3) *Buying luxuries gives teens unrealistic idea of standard of living*

Referring to this list, Anna wrote the following first draft of her essay.

First Draft

Teenagers and Jobs

Many people think that working is a valuable experience for young people. But when teenagers have jobs, they are too likely to neglect their schoolwork, become overly materialistic, and get into trouble with drugs and alcohol.

Schoolwork and the benefits of extracurricular activities tend to go by the wayside when adolescents work long hours. As more and more teens have taken jobs, teachers have faced increasing difficulties. They must both keep the attention of tired pupils and give homework to students who simply don't have time to do it. In addition, educators have noticed less involvement in extracurricular activities. School bands and athletic teams are losing players to work, and sports events are poorly attended by working students. Those teens who try to do it all—homework, extracurricular activities, and work—may find themselves exhausted and burned out.

Another drawback of too much work is that it may promote materialism and an unrealistic lifestyle. Most working teens use their earnings to buy luxuries. These young people don't worry about spending wisely—they can just about have it all. They are becoming accustomed to a lifestyle they won't be able to afford several years down the road, when they have to support themselves.

(continued)

Finally, teenagers who work are more likely than others to get involved with alcohol and drugs. Teens who put in long hours may seek a quick release from stress, just like the adults who need to drink a couple of martinis after a hard day at work. Also, teens who have money are more likely to get involved with drugs.

In short, teens and work just don't mix.

Development through Revising

Anna's instructor had offered to look over students' first drafts and suggest improvements for revision. Here is the note she wrote at the end of Anna's work:

Anna—Good beginning. While I think your thesis is overstated, it and each of your main topics are on the right track. Here are some points to consider as you write your next draft:

- Many teenagers find working a limited number of hours a week to be a good experience. I think it's a mistake to state flatly that it's always a negative thing for teenagers to have jobs. Think about acknowledging that there can be good points to students' working part-time.

- You do a pretty good job of supporting your first main point ("Schoolwork and the benefits of extracurricular activities tend to go by the wayside when adolescents work long hours") by noting the effect of too much work on scholastic achievement and extracurricular activities. You less effectively support points 2 and 3 ("Another drawback of too much work is that it may promote materialism and an unrealistic lifestyle" and "Finally, teenagers who work are more likely than others to get involved with alcohol and drugs"). Show how teens become too materialistic; don't just state that they do. And what evidence do you have that working teens use drugs and alcohol more than others?

- Throughout the essay, can you come up with evidence beyond your own observations to support the idea that too much working is detrimental to teens? Look in the magazine indexes in the library and on the Internet for studies or stories that might support your thesis.

I'll look forward to seeing your final draft.

After considering her instructor's comments, Anna wrote the version of "Teenagers and Jobs" that appears on page 367.

A Professional Essay to Consider

Read the following professional essay. Then answer the questions and read the comments that follow.

Ban the Things. Ban Them All.
by Molly Ivins

www.mhhe.com/langan

Guns. Everywhere guns.   1

Let me start this discussion by pointing out that I am not anti-gun. I'm pro-knife.   2
Consider the merits of the knife.

In the first place, you have to catch up with someone to stab him. A general   3
substitution of knives for guns would promote physical fitness. We'd turn into a
whole nation of great runners. Plus, knives don't ricochet. And people are seldom
killed while cleaning their knives.

As a civil libertarian,[1] I of course support the Second Amendment. And I be-   4
lieve it means exactly what it says: "A well-regulated militia being necessary to the
security of a free state, the right of the people to keep and bear arms shall not be
infringed."[2] Fourteen-year-old boys are not part of a well-regulated militia. Members of wacky religious cults are not part of a well-regulated militia. Permitting
unregulated citizens to have guns is destroying the security of this free state.

I am intrigued by the arguments of those who claim to follow the judicial   5
doctrine of original intent. How do they know it was the dearest wish of Thomas
Jefferson's heart that teenage drug dealers should cruise the cities of this nation
perforating their fellow citizens with assault rifles? Channeling?[3]

There is more hooey spread about the Second Amendment. It says quite clearly   6
that guns are for those who form part of a well-regulated militia, i.e., the armed
forces including the National Guard. The reasons for keeping them away from everyone else get clearer by the day.

The comparison most often used is that of the automobile, another lethal ob-   7
ject that is regularly used to wreak great carnage. Obviously, this society is full of
people who haven't got enough common sense to use an automobile properly. But
we haven't outlawed cars yet.

We do, however, license them and their owners, restrict their use to presumably   8
sane and sober adults and keep track of who sells them to whom. At a minimum,
we should do the same with guns.

In truth, there is no rational argument for guns in this society. This is no   9
longer a frontier nation in which people hunt their own food. It is a crowded,

---

[1]*civil libertarian:* someone actively concerned with protecting rights guaranteed to the individual by law.
[2]*infringed:* violated.
[3]*channeling:* serving as a medium in order to communicate with spirits.

overwhelmingly urban country in which letting people have access to guns is a continuing disaster. Those who want guns—whether for target shooting, hunting or potting⁴ rattlesnakes (get a hoe)—should be subjected to the same restrictions placed on gun owners in England, a nation in which liberty has survived nicely without an armed populace.

The argument that "guns don't kill people" is patent nonsense. Anyone who **10** has ever worked in a cop shop knows how many family arguments end in murder because there was a gun in the house. Did the gun kill someone? No. But if there had been no gun, no one would have died. At least not without a good footrace first. Guns do kill. Unlike cars, that is all they do.

Michael Crichton makes an interesting argument about technology in his **11** thriller *Jurassic Park*. He points out that power without discipline is making this society into wreckage. By the time someone who studies the martial arts becomes a master—literally able to kill with bare hands—that person has also undergone years of training and discipline. But any fool can pick up a gun and kill with it.

"A well-regulated militia" surely implies both long training and long discipline. **12** That is the least, the very least, that should be required of those who are permitted to have guns, because a gun is literally the power to kill. For years, I used to enjoy taunting my gun-nut friends about their psychosexual hangups—always in a spirit of good cheer, you understand. But letting the noisy minority in the National Rifle Association force us to allow this carnage to continue is just plain insane.

I do think gun nuts have a power hangup. I don't know what is missing in their **13** psyches that they need to feel they have the power to kill. But no sane society would allow this to continue.

Ban the damn things. Ban them all.   **14**

You want protection? Get a dog.   **15**

About Unity

1. Which of the following statements best represents the implied thesis of the essay?

    a. The author is pro-knife.

    b. The Second Amendment is poorly understood.

    c. Despite arguments to the contrary, people without long training and discipline should not be allowed to have guns.

    d. In his novel *Jurassic Park,* Michael Crichton argues that power without discipline is wrecking society.

2. Which statement would best serve as a topic sentence for paragraphs 5 and 6?

    a. Drug dealers should not be allowed to purchase assault rifles.

    b. Ivins is interested in other people's points of view concerning gun ownership.

Questions

2

---

⁴*potting:* shooting with a potshot (an easy shot).

  c. Thomas Jefferson was opposed to the idea of a "well-regulated militia."

  d. Applying the original intent of the Second Amendment to modern circumstances is not clear-cut and must be done with common sense.

3. Which is the topic sentence of paragraph 9?

  a. "In truth, there is no rational argument for guns in this society."

  b. "This is no longer a frontier nation in which people hunt their own food."

  c. "It is a crowded, overwhelmingly urban country in which letting people have access to guns is a continuing disaster."

  d. "Those who want guns . . . should be subjected to the same restrictions placed on gun owners in England. . . ."

About Support

4. Why does Ivins contrast the use of martial arts with the use of guns?

  a. To support the idea that gun owners should be required to study the martial arts

  b. To support the idea that a martial arts master can kill with his bare hands

  c. To support the idea that power without discipline is dangerous

  d. To support the idea that guns are more practical than the martial arts

5. Which statement best expresses the implied point of paragraph 10?

  a. Guns kill people.

  b. Many family arguments are surprisingly violent.

  c. Many arguments end in death only because a gun was handy.

  d. Guns and cars are similar.

6. In what ways, according to Ivins, is the knife preferable to the gun? Is Ivins really "pro-knife," or is she making some other point in her discussion of knives versus guns?

  _____

  _____

  _____

About Coherence

7. In paragraph 3, Ivins uses three addition signals—one to introduce each of her three reasons for being pro-knife. What are those three signals? (Two are *not* in the list of addition signals on page 376.)

  _____ _____ _____

8. In paragraph 7, Ivins acknowledges an opposing point of view when she mentions that automobiles, like guns, "wreak great carnage." In paragraph 8, what sentence includes a "change of direction" signal indicating that Ivins will present her argument against that point of view? *(Write the first few words of that sentence.)*

_____

About the Introduction and Conclusion

9. Ivins's introduction consists of three very brief paragraphs. Which statement best describes the style of her introduction?

   a. It presents an anecdote that is related to the topic of unregulated gun ownership.

   b. It presents a provocative question that grabs the reader's attention.

   c. It makes a startling point that at first seems unrelated to the topic.

   d. It presents a quotation that puts the topic in some sort of historical context.

10. Which of these best describes the conclusion of "Ban the Things"?

   a. It makes a blunt recommendation.

   b. It asks a thought-provoking question.

   c. It narrates an anecdote about guns.

   d. It predicts what will happen if guns are not banned.

Writing an Argument Essay

Writing | **Assignment**

1

Write an essay in which you argue *for* or *against* any one of the three comments below (options 1–3). Support and defend your argument by drawing on your reasoning ability and general experience.

Option 1 In many ways, television has proved to be one of the worst inventions of modern times. All too often, television is harmful because of the shows it broadcasts and the way it is used in the home.

Option 2 Many of society's worst problems with drugs result from the fact that they are illegal. During Prohibition, Americans discovered that making popular substances unlawful causes more problems than it solves. Like alcohol and tobacco, drugs should be legal in this country.

© Tony Freeman/PhotoEdit

Option 3 Statistics show that newly licensed teenage boys cause a higher number of serious automobile accidents than any other group. It is evident that many young men are too reckless and impulsive to be good drivers. To protect the larger society, the age at which a boy can earn his license should be raised to eighteen.

Prewriting

a. Take a few minutes to think about the three options. Which one in particular are you for or against, and *why?*

b. One a sheet of paper, make a brief outline of support for your position on one of the options. (Remember, you may choose to argue *against* one of the three comments, as well as for it.) Preparing the outline will give you a chance to think further about your position. And the outline will show whether you have enough support for your position. (If you find that you don't, choose another position and prepare another outline.)

c. Next, decide how you will develop each of your three supporting points. Make up brief outlines of three supporting paragraphs. In addition to preparing brief outlines, you may want to use other prewriting techniques. You may want to freewrite or ask questions or make up lists.

d. Decide in which order you want to present your paragraphs. *Emphatic order* (in which you *end* with your most important reason) is often the most effective way to organize an argument. You reader is most likely to remember your final reason.

e. As you write, think of your audience as a jury that will ultimately believe or disbelieve your argument. Have you presented a convincing case? Do you need more details? If *you* were on the jury, would you be favorably impressed with this argument?

f. Proceed to write the first draft of your essay.

Revising

After you have completed the first draft of the essay, set it aside for a while (if possible). When you review it, ask a friend or classmate for feedback. You should both consider the following questions:

FOUR BASES Checklist for Argument

About *Unity*

☑ Does each paragraph in my essay have a clear topic sentence?

☑ Are there portions of the essay that do not support my thesis and therefore should be eliminated or rewritten?

About *Support*

☑ Have I provided persuasive details to support my argument?

☑ Does my final supporting paragraph include a strong argument for my position?

About *Coherence*

☑ Have I acknowledged the opposing point of view, showing that I am a reasonable person willing to consider other arguments?

☑ Have I used transition words to help readers follow my train of thought?

☑ Have I provided a concluding paragraph to summarize my argument or add a final persuasive touch?

About *Sentence Skills*

☑ Is my language tactful and courteous in order to avoid insulting anyone who doesn't agree with me?

☑ Have I used specific rather than general words?

☑ Have I avoided wordiness and used concise wording?

☑ Are my sentences varied?

☑ Have I checked my writing for spelling and other sentence skills, as listed on the inside back cover of the book?

As you revise your essay through added drafts, continue to refer to this list until you and your reader can answer yes to each question.

Writing Assignment

2

Write an essay in which you argue *for* or *against* any one of the three comments below. Support and defend your argument by drawing on your reasoning ability and general experience.

Option 1 Giving students grades does more harm than good. Schools should re-place grades with written evaluations of the student's strengths and weaknesses. These would benefit both students and parents.

Option 2 Jails are overcrowded. Furthermore, jails often function as "schools for crime" in which petty lawbreakers learn to become hardened criminals. Of course, it is necessary to put violent criminals in jail to protect others. But society would benefit if nonviolent criminals received punishments other than jail sentences.

Option 3 Physical punishment "works" in the sense that it may stop a child from misbehaving, but adults who frequently spank and hit are also teaching children that violence is a good method of accomplishing a goal. Nonviolent methods are a more effective way of training children.

Prewriting

a. As you write your opening paragraph, acknowledge the opposing point of view before stating your thesis. If you have trouble figuring out what the "other side" would argue, completing this exercise will give you practice in acknowledging another way of looking at the question.

In each item, you will see a statement and then a question related to that statement. Write *two* answers to each question. Your first will answer yes to the question and briefly explain why. The other will answer no to the question, and also state why. The first item is done for you as an example:

1. Smoking has been proved to be bad for health. Should it therefore be made illegal?

Yes: *Because smoking has been shown to have so many negative effects on health, the sale of tobacco should be made illegal.*

No: *Although smoking has been linked to various health problems, adults should have the right to make their own decision about whether or not to smoke. Smoking should not be made illegal.*

2. Animals feel pain when they are killed for food. Is eating animals therefore immoral?

Yes: _____

No: _____

3. Professional boxing often leads to serious injury. Should it be outlawed?

Yes: _____

_____

No: _____

_____

4. Some high school students are sexually active. Should birth control devices and information be given out by high schools to their students?

Yes: _____

_____

No: _____

_____

b. Make a list of the thoughts that support your argument. Don't worry about repetition, spelling, or grammar at this point. Just write down everything that occurs to you.

c. Once you have written down all the thoughts that occur to you, identify what you see as your strongest points. Select your three main supporting points. Are there other thoughts in your list that you can use as supporting details for those points?

d. Write your three supporting paragraphs. Keep in mind that you are writing for an audience of people who, initially, will not all agree with you. It isn't enough to state your opinion. You must show *why* you feel as you do, persuading your reader that your point of view is valid.

e. Your concluding paragraph is your final chance to persuade your readers to accept your argument. Consider ending with a prediction of what will happen if your point of view does not prevail. Will an existing situation grow worse? Will a new problem arise?

Revising
Follow the suggestions for revising provided on page 381.

Writing Assignment 3

Write an essay in which you argue *for* or *against* any one of the three comments below. Support and defend your argument by drawing on your reasoning ability and general experience.

© BananaStock/Imagestate

Option 1 Junk food is available in school cafeterias and school vending machines, and the cafeteria menus do not encourage the best eating habits. But good education should include good examples as well as classwork. Schools should practice what they preach about a healthy diet and stop providing junk food.

Option 2 By the time many students reach high school, they have learned the basics in most subjects. Some still have much to gain from the education that high schools offer, but others might be better off spending the next four years in other ways. For their benefit, high school attendance should be voluntary.

Option 3 Many of today's young people are mainly concerned with prestigious careers, making money, and owning things. It seems we no longer teach the benefits of spending time and money to help the community, the country, or the world. Our country can strengthen these human values and improve the world by requiring young people to spend a year working in some type of community service.

Writing Assignment

4   Writing for a Specific Purpose and Audience

In this argument essay, you will write with a specific purpose and for a specific audience.

Option 1 You'd like to live in a big city, but your parent or spouse refuses to budge from the suburbs. Write him or her a letter in which you argue the advantages of city life. Since the success of your argument will depend to some degree on how well you overcome the other person's objections to city life, be sure to address those as well. Use specific, colorful examples wherever possible.

Option 2 Find an editorial in your local newspaper that you either strongly agree with or strongly disagree with. Write a letter to the editor responding to that editorial. State why you agree or disagree with the position taken by the paper. Provide several short paragraphs of supporting evidence for your position. Actually send your letter to the newspaper. When you turn in a copy of your letter to your instructor, also turn in the editorial that you are responding to.

www.mhhe.com/langan

PART 3

Special Skills

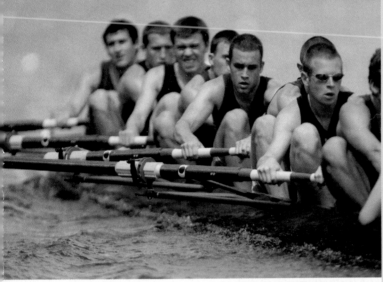

© Steve Boyle/NewSport/Corbis

Write an essay about a skill you have learned outside of the classroom, which has helped you succeed in college. Maybe it is teamwork, persistence, time management, or something else. Be sure to provide specific examples of how this skill has been beneficial to you.

PREVIEW

17 Taking Essay Exams

18 Writing a Summary

19 Writing a Report

20 Writing a Résumé and Cover Letter

21 Using the Library and the Internet

22 Writing a Research Paper

17

Taking Essay Exams

© Comstock/Imagestate

www.mhhe.com/langan

Visit AltaVista at http://www.altavista.com and enter the phrase "taking an essay exam" into the search box. Then visit a handful of the sites that AltaVista finds and choose one to recommend to your classmates. Write a one-paragraph review of the site to hand in to your instructor. Was it helpful? What advice did it offer?

Essay exams are perhaps the most common type of writing you will do in school. They include one or more questions to which you must respond in detail, writing your answers in a clear, well-organized manner. Many students have trouble with essay exams because they do not realize there is a sequence to follow that will help them do well on such tests. This section describes five basic steps needed to prepare adequately for an essay test and to take the test. It is assumed, however, that you are already doing two essential things: first, attending class regularly and taking notes on what happens in class; second, reading your textbook and other assignments and taking notes on them. If you are *not* consistently going to class, reading your text, and taking notes in both cases, you are likely to have trouble with essay exams and other tests as well.

To write an effective exam essay, follow these five steps:

Step 1: Anticipate ten probable questions.

Step 2: Prepare and memorize an informal outline answer for each question.

Step 3: Look at the exam carefully and do several things.

Step 4: Prepare a brief, informal outline before writing your essay answer.

Step 5: Write a clear, well-organized essay.

The following pages explain and illustrate these steps.

Step 1: Anticipate Ten Probable Questions

Because exam time is limited, the instructor can give you only several questions to answer. He or she will focus on questions dealing with the most important areas of the subject. You can probably guess most of them.

Go through your class notes with a colored pen and mark off those areas where your instructor has spent a good deal of time. The more time spent on any one area, the better the chance you will get an essay question on it. If the instructor spent a week talking about present-day changes in the traditional family structure, or the importance of the carbon molecule, or the advantages of capitalism, or key early figures in the development of psychology as a science, you can reasonably expect that you will get a question about the emphasized area.

In both your class notes and your textbooks, pay special attention to definitions and examples and to basic lists of items (enumerations). Enumerations in particular are often a key to essay questions. For instance, if your instructor spoke at length about causes of the Great Depression, effects of water pollution, or advantages of capitalism, you should probably expect a question such as What were the causes of the Great Depression? or What are the effects of water pollution? or What are the advantages of capitalism?

If your instructor has given you a study guide, look there for probable essay questions. (Some instructors choose essay questions from those listed in study guides.) Look for clues to essay questions on any short quizzes that you might have been given. Finally, consider very carefully any review that the instructor provides. Always write down such reviews—your instructor has often made up the test or is making it up at the time of the review and is likely to give you valuable hints about it. Take advantage of them! Note also that if the instructor does not offer to provide a review, do not hesitate to *ask* for one in a friendly way. Essay questions are likely to come from areas the instructor may mention.

An Illustration of Step 1

A psychology class was given one day to prepare for an essay exam on stress—a subject that had been covered in class and by a chapter in the textbook for the course. One student, Mark, read carefully through his class notes and the textbook chapter. On the basis of the headings, major enumerations, and definitions he noted, he decided that there were five likely essay questions:

1. What are the common sources of stress?
2. What are the types of conflict?
3. What are the defense mechanisms that people use to cope with stress?
4. What effects can stress have on people?
5. What are the characteristics of a well-adjusted person?

Step 2: Prepare and Memorize an Informal Outline Answer for Each Question

Write out each question you have made up and, under it, list the main points that need to be discussed. Put important supporting information in parentheses after each main point. You now have an informal outline that you can memorize.

Pick out a *key word* in each part, and then create a *catchphrase* to help you remember the key words.

> **TIP:** If you have spelling problems, make up a list of words you might have to spell in writing your answers. For example, if you are having a psychology test on the principles of learning, you might want to study such terms as *conditioning, reinforcement, Pavlov, reflex, stimulus,* and so on.

An Illustration of Step 2

After identifying the likely questions on the exam, Mark made up an outline answer for each of the questions. For example, here is the outline answer that he made up for the first question:

Common sources of stress:

1. (Pressure)(internal and external)
2. (Anxiety)(sign of internal conflict)
3. (Frustration)(can't reach desired goal)
4. (Conflict)(three types of approach-avoidance)
   P A F C (People are funny creatures.)

See whether you can complete the following explanation of what Mark has done in preparing for the essay question.

     First, Mark wrote down the heading and then numbered the sources of stress under it. Also, in parentheses beside each point he added _____. Then he circled the four key words, and he wrote down the first _____ of each word underneath his outline. Mark then used the first letter in each key word to make up a catchphrase that he could easily remember. Finally, he _____ himself over and over until he could recall all four of the sources of stress that the first letters stood for. He also made sure that he recalled the supporting material that went with each idea.

Part 1
Make a list of the steps that Mark took in preparing for an essay test question on the common causes of stress.

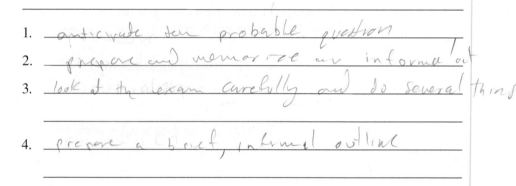

1. anticipate ten probable question
2. prepare and memorize an informat out
3. look at the exam carefully and do several things
4. prepare a brief, informal outline

Part 2
After you have done that, pretend that you have been told that you will be tested on a particular chapter of a textbook in a history, sociology, biology, or other class you are taking. Write a list of five sample essay questions that might be on the test. Then, like Mark, write out an outline answer for each question.

Step 3: Look at the Exam Carefully and Do Several Things

1. Get an overview of the exam by reading *all* the questions on the test.
2. Note *direction words (compare, illustrate, list,* and so on) for each question. Be sure to write the kind of answer that each question requires. For example, if a question says "illustrate," do not "compare." The list on the next page will help clarify the distinctions among various direction words.

3. Budget your time. Write in the margin the number of minutes you should spend for each essay. For example, if you have three essays worth an equal number of points and a one-hour time limit, figure twenty minutes for each essay. Make sure you are not left with only a couple of minutes to do a high-point essay.

4. Start with the easiest question. Getting a good answer down on paper will help build up your confidence and momentum. Number your answers plainly so that your instructor knows what question you are answering first.

An Illustration of Step 3

When Mark received the exam, the question was "Describe the four common sources of stress in our lives." Mark circled the direction word *describe,* which meant he should explain in detail each of the four causes of stress. He also jotted a "30" in the margin when the instructor said that students would have a half hour to write the answer.

Activity

2

Complete the short matching quiz below. It will help you review the meanings of some of the direction words listed in the box below.

1. List ___B___   a. Tell in detail about something.

2. Contrast ___d___   b. Give a series of points and number them 1, 2, 3, etc.

3. Define ___e___   c. Give a condensed account of the main points.

4. Summarize ___C___   d. Show differences between two things.

5. Describe ___A___   e. Give the normal meaning of a term.

www.mhhe.com/langan

Direction Words

Term	Meaning
Compare	Show similarities between things.
Contrast	Show differences between things.
Criticize	Give the positive and negative points of a subject as well as evidence for those positions.
Define	Give the formal meaning of a term.
Describe	Tell in detail about something.
Diagram	Make a drawing and label it.
Discuss	Give details and, if relevant, the positive and negative points of a subject as well as evidence for those positions.

(continued)

Enumerate	List points and number them 1, 2, 3, and so on.
Evaluate	Give the positive and negative points of a subject as well as your judgment about which outweighs the other and why.
Illustrate	Explain by giving examples.
Interpret	Explain the meaning of something.
Justify	Give reasons for something.
List	Give a series of points and number them 1, 2, 3, and so on.
Outline	Give the main points and important secondary points. Put main points at the margin and indent secondary points under the main points. Relationships may also be described with logical symbols, as follows:

1. _____

    a. _____

    b. _____

2. _____

Prove	Show to be true by giving facts or reasons.
Relate	Show connections among things.
State	Give the main points.
Summarize	Give a condensed account of the main points.
Trace	Describe the development or history of a subject.

Step 4: Prepare a Brief, Informal Outline before Writing Your Essay Answer

Use the margin of the exam or a separate piece of scratch paper to jot down quickly, as they occur to you, the main points you want to discuss in each answer. Then decide in what order you want to present these points in your response. Write 1 in front of the first item, 2 beside the second, and so on. You now have an informal outline to guide you as you answer your essay question.

If a question on the exam is similar to the questions you anticipated and outlined at home, quickly write down the catchphrase that calls back the content of the outline. Below the catchphrase, write the key words represented by each letter in the catchphrase. The key words, in turn, will remind you of the concepts they represent. If you have prepared properly, this step will take only a minute or so, and you will have before you the guide you need to write a focused, supported, organized answer.

An Illustration of Step 4

Mark immediately wrote down his catchphrase, "People are funny creatures." He next jotted down the first letters in his catchphrase and then the key words that went with each letter. He then filled in several key details and was ready to write his essay answer. Here is what his brief outline looked like:

> *People are funny creatures.*
>
> P   *Pressure (internal and external)*
>
> A   *Anxiety (internal conflict)*
>
> F   *Frustration (prevented from reaching goal)*
>
> C   *Conflict (approach-avoidance)*

Step 5: Write a Clear, Well-Organized Essay

If you have followed steps 1 through 4, you are ready to write an effective essay, keeping in mind the principles of good writing: unity, support, coherence, and clear, error-free sentences.

Start with a sentence that clearly states what your essay will be about. Then, make sure that everything in your essay relates to that sentence.

Second, although you must take time limitations into account, provide as much support as possible for each of your main points.

Third, use transitions such as *first, next, then, however,* and *finally* to guide your reader.

Last, leave time to proofread for sentence mistakes. Look for omitted, miswritten, or misspelled words (if you are allowed, bring a dictionary). Check for awkward phrasings or incorrect punctuation, or anything else that makes your writing unclear or distracts your reader. Cross out mistakes and make corrections neatly above them. To add or change a point, insert an asterisk at the appropriate spot, put another asterisk at the bottom of the page, and add the corrected material there.

An Illustration of Step 5

Read Mark's answer, reproduced below, and then do the activity that follows.

> *There are four common sources of stress in our lives. The first one is*
>
> *pressure, which can be internal or external. Internal pressure occurs*

when a person tries to live up to his or her own goals and standards. This kind of pressure can help (when a person strives to be a better musician, for instance) or hurt (as when someone tries to reach impossible standards of beauty). External pressure occurs when people must compete, deal with rapid change, or cope with outside demands. Another source of stress is anxiety. People who are ~~anxous~~ anxious often don't know why they feel this way. Some psychologists think anxiety comes from some internal conflict, like feeling angry and trying hard to repress this ~~angry feeling~~ anger. A third source of stress is frustration, which occurs when people are prevented from reaching goals or obtaining certain needs. For example, a woman may do poorly on an important exam because she has a bad cold. She feels angry and frustrated because she could not reach her goal of an A or B grade. The most common source of stress is conflict. Conflict results when a person is faced with two incompatible ~~goals~~ desires. The person may want both goals (a demanding career and motherhood, for instance). This is called approach-approach. Or a person may want to avoid both choices (avoidance-avoidance). Or a person may be both attracted to and repelled by a desire (as a woman who wants to marry a gambler). This is approach-avoidance.

The following sentences comment on Mark's essay. Fill in the missing word or words in each case.

Activity

3

1. Mark begins with a sentence that clearly states what his essay
    _____have_____. Always begin with such a clear statement!

2. Notice the _____who_____ that Mark made when writing and
    proofreading his paper. He neatly crossed out miswritten or unwanted words,
    and he used insertion signs (^) to add omitted words.

3. The four signal words that Mark used to guide his readers, and himself, through
    the main points of his answer are _____The first_____, _____for instance_____,
    _____as when_____, and _____another_____.   Third

        For examp

Activity

4

In Part 2 of Activity 1, you were asked to write five questions (as well as an informal outline for each) that you might use for an essay exam in another course you are taking. Use the outline you made for one of these questions as the basis for an answer you might provide on an essay exam.

Before you begin writing, read this sample essay, which responds to the following question: "Explain the major difference between ancient Athenian democracy and contemporary American democracy." Note that the essay begins with a clear thesis statement.

Ancient Athens had a direct form of democracy; America has a representative form of democracy. In Athens, all men could participate in the Assembly, the body where laws governing every aspect of Athenian life—from taxes to religious observances—were debated and voted upon. Each man, no matter how rich or poor, could speak his mind and cast a vote. In the United States, the people do not, as a rule, make laws directly. Instead, they elect representatives to legislative bodies to do that. In the federal government, for example, these two bodies are the House of Representatives and the Senate. Members of these groups can debate an decide on laws independent of the wishes of those who elected them. Although deliberations of the House and Senate are open, legislators usually hear from their constituents only when controversial laws are being discussed. However, no matter what the majority of people in a congressional district or state think about a particular proposal, a representative or senator may vote as he or she pleases. (Of course, he or she may pay a price for ignoring their opinions in the next election.) The closest thing we have to Athenian democracy is a referendum or plebiscite, which is also known as a ballot question. This is proposed law that every citizen can vote upon. Such questions appear on the ballot every two years when we vote in local, state, and national elections.

Writing a Summary

© Bill Aron/PhotoEdit

This chapter will
explain and illustrate
how to

• summarize an
article

• summarize a book

*Find an article in your school or local newspaper about which
you can write an essay-length summary. Include an introductory
paragraph in which you state the article's thesis.*

At some point in a course, your instructor may ask you to write a summary of a book, an article, a TV show, or the like. In a *summary* (also referred to as a *précis* or an *abstract*), you reduce material in an original work to its main points and key supporting details. Unlike an outline, however, a summary does not use symbols such as I, A, 1, 2, etc., to indicate the relations among parts of the original material.

A summary may consist of a single word, a phrase, several sentences, or one or more paragraphs. The length of any summary you prepare will depend on your instructor's expectations and the length of the original work. Most often, you will be asked to write a summary consisting of one or more paragraphs.

Writing a summary brings together a number of important reading, study, and writing skills. To condense the original assigned material, you must preview, read, evaluate, organize, and perhaps outline it. Summarizing, then, can be a real aid to understanding; you must "get inside" the material and realize fully what is being said before you can reduce its meaning to a few words.

How to Summarize an Article

To write a summary of an article, follow the steps described below. If the assigned material is a TV show or film, adapt the suggestions accordingly.

1. Take a few minutes to preview the work. You can preview an article in a magazine by taking a quick look at the following:

   a. *Title.* A title often summarizes what an article is about. Think about the title for a minute and about how it may condense the meaning of the article.

   b. *Subtitle.* A subtitle, if given, is a short summary appearing under or next to the title. For example, in a *Newsweek* article titled "Growing Old, Feeling Young," the following caption appeared: "Not only are Americans living longer, they are staying active longer—and their worst enemy is not nature, but the myths and prejudices about growing old." In short, the subtitle, the caption, or any other words in large print under or next to the title often provide a quick insight into the meaning of an article.

   c. *First and last several paragraphs.* In the first several paragraphs, the author may introduce you to the subject and state the purpose of the article. In the last several paragraphs, the writer may present conclusions or a summary. The previews or summaries can give you a quick overview of what the entire article is about.

   d. *Other items.* Note any heads or subheads that appear in the article. They often provide clues to the article's main points and give an immediate sense of what each section is about. Look carefully at any pictures, charts, or diagrams that accompany the article. Page space in a magazine or journal is limited, and such visual aids are generally used only to illustrate important points in the article. Note any words or phrases set off in *italic type* or **boldface type;** such words have probably been emphasized because they deal with important points in the article.

2. Read the article for all you can understand the first time through. Do not slow down or turn back. Check or otherwise mark main points and key supporting details. Pay special attention to all the items noted in the preview. Also, look for definitions, examples, and enumerations (lists of items), which often indicate key ideas. You can also identify important points by turning any headings into questions and reading to find the answers to the questions.

3. Go back and reread more carefully the areas you have identified as most important. Also, focus on other key points you may have missed in your first reading.

4. Take notes on the material. Concentrate on getting down the main ideas and the key supporting points.

5. Prepare the first draft of your summary, keeping these points in mind:

www.mhhe.com/langan

   a. Identify at the start of the summary the title and author of the work. Include in parentheses the date of publication. For example, "In 'Leaking with a Vengeance' (*Time,* October 13, 2003), Michael Duffy states. . . ."

   b. Do not write an overly detailed summary. Remember that the purpose of a summary is to reduce the original work to its main points and essential supporting details.

   c. Express the main points and key supporting details in your own words. Do not imitate the style of the original work.

   d. Quote from the material only to illustrate key points. Also, limit your quotations. A one-paragraph summary should not contain more than one or two quoted sentences or phrases.

   e. Preserve the balance and proportion of the original work. If the original devoted 70 percent of its space to one idea and only 30 percent to another, your summary should reflect that emphasis.

   f. Revise your first draft, paying attention to the four bases of effective writing (*unity, support, coherence,* and *sentence skills*) explained in Part One.

   g. Write the final draft of the paper.

A Model Summary of an Article

Here is a model summary of a magazine article:

> In "How to Heal a Hypochondriac" (*Time,* October 6, 2003), Michael Lemonick reports on research into ways of dealing with hypochondria, a thinking disorder that makes healthy people believe that they are suffering from one or more serious diseases. Not only do hypochondriacs genuinely suffer from their disorder but they create a significant burden on the health care system. Research suggests that hypochondriacs fall into three categories: those who have a variant of obsessive-compulsive disorder,
>
> *(continued)*

those who had a stressful life event that triggered the hypochondria, and those who are hypersensitive to any physical symptoms. Cognitive therapy, in which patients are trained to direct their attention away from their symptoms, and antidepressant medication both seem helpful in treating hypochondria. The most difficult part of treatment is suggesting that a patient suffers from hypochondria without angering or embarrassing him or her.

Activity

1

Write an essay-length summary of the following article. Include a short introductory paragraph that states the thesis of the article. Then summarize in your three supporting paragraphs the three important areas in which study skills can be useful. Your conclusion might be a single sentence restating the thesis.

Power Learning

Jill had not done as well in high school as she had hoped. Since college involved even more work, it was no surprise that she didn't do better there.   1

The reason for her so-so performance was not a lack of effort. She   2
attended most of her classes and read her textbooks. And she never missed handing in any assignment, even though it often meant staying up late the night before homework was due. Still, she just got by in her classes. Before long, she came to the conclusion that she simply couldn't do any better.

Then one day, one of her instructors said something to make her think   3
otherwise. "You can probably build some sort of house by banging a few boards together," he said. "But if you want a sturdy home, you'll have to use the right techniques and tools. Building carefully takes work, but it gets better results. The same can be said of your education. There are no shortcuts, but there are some proven study skills that can really help. If you don't use them, you may end up with a pretty flimsy education."

Jill signed up for a study-skills course and found out a crucial fact—that   4
learning how to learn is the key to success in school. Certain dependable skills have made the difference between disappointment and success for generations of students. These techniques won't free you from work, but they will make your work far more productive. They include three important areas: time control, classroom note-taking, and textbook study.

(continued)

Time Control

Success in college depends on time control. *Time control* means that   5
you deliberately organize and plan your time, instead of letting it drift by.
Planning means that you should never be faced with an overdue term paper
or a cram session the night before a test.

Three steps are involved in time control. *First*, you should prepare a   6
large monthly calendar. Buy a calendar with a large white block around
each date, or make one yourself. At the beginning of the college semester,
circle important dates on this calendar. Circle the days on which tests are
scheduled; circle the days when papers are due. This calendar can also be
used to schedule study plans. At the beginning of the week, you can jot
down your plans for each day. An alternative method would be to make
plans for each day the night before. On Tuesday night, for example, you
might write down "Read Chapter 5 in psychology" in the Wednesday block.
Hang this calendar where you will see it every day—your kitchen, bedroom,
even your bathroom!

The *second step* in time control is to have a weekly study schedule for   7
the semester—a chart that covers all the days of the week and all the waking
hours in each day. Below is part of one student's schedule:

Time	Mon.	Tue.	Wed.	Thurs.	Fri.	Sat.
6:00 a.m.						
7:00	Breakfast	Breakfast	Breakfast	Breakfast	Breakfast	
8:00	Math	STUDY	Math	STUDY	Math	Breakfast
9:00	STUDY	Biology	STUDY	Biology	STUDY	Job
10:00	Psychology	↓	Psychology	↓	Psychology	
11:00		English		English		
12:00	Lunch		Lunch		Lunch	↓

On your own schedule, fill in all the fixed hours in each day—hours for
meals, classes, job (if any), and travel time. Next, mark time blocks that you
can *realistically* use for study each day. Depending on the number of courses
you are taking and the demands of these courses, you may want to block
off five, ten, or even twenty or more hours of study time a week. Keep in
mind that you should not block off time that you do not truly intend to use
for study. Otherwise, your schedule will be a meaningless gimmick. Also,
remember that you should allow time for rest and relaxation. You will be
happiest, and able to accomplish the most, when you have time for both
work and play.

(continued)

The *third step* in time control is to make a daily or weekly to-do list.   **8**
This may be the most valuable time-control method you ever use. On this
list, write down the things you need to do for the following day or the
following week. If you choose to write a weekly list, do it on Sunday night.
If you choose to write a daily list, do it the night before. Here is part of one
student's daily list:

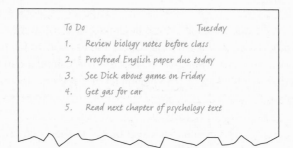

To Do   Tuesday
1.   Review biology notes before class
2.   Proofread English paper due today
3.   See Dick about game on Friday
4.   Get gas for car
5.   Read next chapter of psychology text

You may use a three-by-five-inch notepad or a small spiral-bound
notebook for this list. Carry the list around with you during the day. Always
concentrate on doing the most important items first. To make the best
use of your time, mark high-priority items with an asterisk and give them
precedence over low-priority items. For instance, you may find yourself
wondering what to do after dinner on Thursday evening. Among the items
on your list are "Clean inside of car" and "Review chapter for math quiz."
It is obviously more important for you to review your notes at this point;
you can clean out the car some other time. As you complete items on your
to-do list, cross them out. Do not worry about unfinished items. They can
be rescheduled. You will still be accomplishing a great deal and making more
effective use of your time.

Classroom Note-Taking

One of the most important single things you can do to perform well in   **9**
a college course is to take effective class notes. The following hints should
help you become a better note-taker.

First, attend class faithfully. Your alternatives—reading the text, reading   **10**
someone else's notes, or both—cannot substitute for the class experience
of hearing ideas in person as someone presents them to you. Also, in class
lectures and discussions, your instructor typically presents and develops the
main ideas and facts of the course—the ones you will be expected to know
on exams.

(continued)

Another valuable hint is to make use of abbreviations while taking notes. **11** Using abbreviations saves time when you are trying to get down a great deal of information. Abbreviate terms that recur frequently in a lecture and put a key to your abbreviations at the top of your notes. For example, in sociology class, *eth* could stand for *ethnocentrism;* in a psychology class, *STM* could stand for *short-term memory.* (When a lecture is over, you may want to go back and write out the terms you have abbreviated.) Also, use *e* for *example; def* for *definition; info* for *information;* + for *and;* and so on. If you use the same abbreviations all the time, you will soon develop a kind of personal shorthand that makes taking notes much easier.

A third hint for taking notes is to be on the lookout for signals of **12** importance. Write down whatever your instructor puts on the board. If he or she takes the time to put material on the board, it is probably important, and the chances are good that it will come up later on exams. Always write down definitions and enumerations. Enumerations are lists of items. They are signaled in such ways as "The four steps in the process are . . ."; "There were three reasons for . . ."; "The two effects were . . ."; "Five characteristics of . . ."; and so on. In your notes, always number such enumerations (1, 2, 3, etc.). They will help you understand relationships among ideas and organize the material of the lecture. Watch for emphasis words—words your instructor may use to indicate that something is important. Examples of such words are "This is an important reason . . ."; "A point that will keep coming up later . . ."; "The chief cause was . . ."; "The basic idea here is . . ."; and so on. Always write down the important statements announced by these and other emphasis words. Finally, if your instructor repeats a point, you can assume that it is important. You might put an *R* for *repeated* in the margin so that later you will know that your instructor stressed it.

Next, be sure to write down the instructor's examples and mark them **13** with an *e.* The examples help you understand abstract points. If you do not write them down, you are likely to forget them later, when they are needed to help make sense of an idea.

Also, be sure to write down the connections between ideas. Too many **14** students merely copy terms the instructor puts on the board. They forget that, as time passes, the details that serve as connecting bridges between ideas quickly fade. You should, then, write down the relationships and connections in class. That way you'll have them to help tie together your notes later on.

Review your notes as soon as possible after class. You must make them **15** as clear as possible while they are fresh in your mind. A day later may be too

(continued)

late, because forgetting sets in very quickly. Make sure that punctuation is clear, that all words are readable and correctly spelled, and that unfinished sentences are completed (or at least marked off so that you can check your notes with another student's). Add clarifying or connecting comments wherever necessary. Make sure that important ideas are clearly marked. Improve the organization if necessary so that you can see at a glance main points and relationships among them.

Finally, try in general to get down a written record of each class. You must do this because forgetting begins almost immediately. Studies have shown that within two weeks you are likely to have forgotten 80 percent or more of what you have heard. And in four weeks you are lucky if 5 percent remains! This is so crucial that it bears repeating: To guard against the relentlessness of forgetting, it is absolutely essential that you write down what you hear in class. Later you can concentrate on working to understand fully and to remember the ideas that have been presented in class. And then, the more complete your notes are, the more you are likely to learn.   16

Textbook Study

In many college courses, success means being able to read and study a textbook skillfully. For many students, unfortunately, textbooks are heavy going. After an hour or two of study, the textbook material is as formless and as hard to understand as ever. But there is a way to attack even the most difficult textbook and make sense of it. Use a sequence in which you preview a chapter, mark it, take notes on it, and then study the notes.   17

Previewing

Previewing a selection is an important first step to understanding. Taking the time to preview a section or chapter can give you a bird's-eye view of the way the material is organized. You will have a sense of where you are beginning, what you will cover, and where you will end.   18

There are several steps in previewing a selection. First, study the title. The title is the shortest possible summary of a selection and will often tell you the limits of the material you will cover. For example, the title "FDR and the Supreme Court" tells you to expect a discussion of President Roosevelt's dealings with the Court. You know that you will probably not encounter any material dealing with FDR's foreign policies or personal life. Next, quickly read over the first and last paragraphs of the selection; these may contain important introductions to, and summaries of, the main ideas. Then   19

(continued)

briefly examine the headings and subheadings in the selection. Together, the headings and subheadings are a mini-outline of what you are reading. Headings are often main ideas or important concepts in capsule form; subheadings are breakdowns of ideas within main areas. Finally, read the first sentence of some paragraphs, look for words set off in **boldface** or *italics*, and look at pictures or diagrams. After you have previewed a selection in this way, you should have a good general sense of the material to be read.

Marking

You should mark a textbook selection at the same time that you read   20
it through carefully. Use a felt-tip highlighter to shade material that seems important, or use a ballpoint pen and put symbols in the margin next to the material: stars, checks, or NB (*nota bene*, Latin for "note well"). What to mark is not as mysterious as some students believe. You should try to find ain ideas by looking for clues: definitions and examples, enumerations, and emphasis words.

1. *Definitions and examples:* Definitions are often among the most   21
    important ideas in a selection. They are particularly significant in introductory courses in almost any subject area, where much of your learning involves mastering the specialized vocabulary of that subject. In a sense, you are learning the "language" of psychology or business or whatever the subject might be.

    Most definitions are abstract, and so they usually are followed by   22
    one or more examples to help clarify their meaning. Always mark off definitions and at least one example that makes a definition clear to you. In a psychology text, for example, we are told that "rationalization is an attempt to reduce anxiety by deciding that you have not really been frustrated." Several examples follow, among them: "A young man, frustrated because he was rejected when he asked for a date, convinces himself that the girl is not very attractive or interesting."

2. *Enumerations:* Enumerations are lists of items (causes, reasons,   23
    types, and so on) that are numbered 1, 2, 3, . . . or that could easily be numbered. They are often signaled by addition words. Many of the paragraphs in this book, for instance, use words like *First of all, Another, In addition,* and *Finally* to signal items in a series. Other textbooks also use this very common and effective organizational method.

3. *Emphasis words:* Emphasis words tell you that an idea is important.   24
    Common emphasis words include phrases such as *a major event,*

(continued)

a key feature, the chief factor, important to note, above all, and *most of all.* Here is an example: "The most significant contemporary use of marketing is its application to nonbusiness areas, such as political parties."

Note-Taking

Next, you should take ntes. Go through the chapter a second time, rereading the most important parts. Try to write down the main ideas in a simple outline form. For example, in taking notes on a psychology selection, you might write down the heading "Defense Mechanisms." Below the heading you would define them, number and describe each kind, and give an example of each.

25

Defense Mechanisms

a. *Definition: unconscious attempts to reduce anxiety*

b. *Kinds:*

(1) *Rationalization: An attempt to reduce anxiety by deciding that you have not really been frustrated.*

Example: A man turned down for a date decides that the woman was not worth going out with anyway.

(2) *Projection: Projecting onto other people motives or thoughts of one's own.*

Example: A wife who wants to have an affair accuses her husband of having one.

Studying Notes

To study your notes, use repeated self-testing. For example, look at the heading "Defense Mechanisms" and say to yourself, "What are the kinds of defense mechanisms?" When you can recite them, then say to yourself, "What is rationalization?" "What is an example of rationalization?" Then ask yourself, "What is projection?" "What is an example of projection?" After you learn each section, review it, and then go on to the next section.

26

Do not simply read your notes; keep looking away and seeing if you can recite them to yourself. This self-testing is the key to effective learning.

27

(continued)

Summary: Textbook Study

In summary, remember this sequence for dealing with a textbook: 28
preview, mark, take notes, study the notes. Approaching a textbook in
this methodical way will give you very positive results. You will no longer
feel bogged down in a swamp of words, unable to figure out what you are
supposed to know. Instead, you will understand exactly what you have to do
and how to go about doing it.

Take a minute now to evaluate your own study habits. Do you practice   29
many of the above skills to take effective classroom notes, control your
time, and learn from your textbooks? If not, perhaps you should. The skills
are not magic, but they are too valuable to ignore. Use them carefully and
onsistently, and they will make academic success possible for you. Try them,
and you won't need convincing.

Write an essay-length summary of a broadcast of the CBS television show
60 Minutes. In your first sentence, include the date of the show. For example, "The
September 6, 2007, broadcast of CBS's *60 Minutes* dealt with three subjects most
people would find of interest. The first segment of the show centered on . . . ; the
second segment examined . . . ; the final segment discussed. . . . " Be sure to use
parallel form in describing the three segments of the show. Then summarize each
segment in the three supporting paragraphs that follow.

Activity 2

Write an essay-length summary of a cover story of interest to you in a recent issue
of *Time, Newsweek,* or *U.S. News & World Report.*

Activity 3

How to Summarize a Book

To write a summary of a book, first preview the book by briefly looking at the
following:

www.mhhe.com/langan

1. *Title.* A title is often the shortest possible summary of what a book is
   about. Think about the title and how it may summarize the whole book.

2. *Table of contents.* The contents will tell you the number of chapters in
   the book and the subject of each chapter. Use the contents to get a general
   sense of how the book is organized. You should also note the number of
   pages in each chapter. If thirty pages are devoted to one episode or idea
   and an average of fifteen pages to other episodes or ideas, you should

probably give more space in your summary to the contents of the longer chapter.

3. *Preface.* Here you will probably find out why the author wrote the book. Also, the preface may summarize the main ideas developed in the book and may describe briefly how the book is organized.

4. *First and last chapters.* In these chapters, the author may preview or review important ideas and themes developed in the book.

5. *Other items.* Note how the author has used headings and subheadings to organize information in the book. Check the opening and closing paragraphs of each chapter to see if these paragraphs contain introductions or summaries. Look quickly at charts, diagrams, and pictures in the book, since they are probably there to illustrate key points. Note any special features (index, glossary, appendixes) that may appear at the end of the book.

Next, adapt steps 2 through 5 for summarizing an article on pages 396–397.

Activity

4

Write an essay-length summary of a book you have read.

Writing a Report

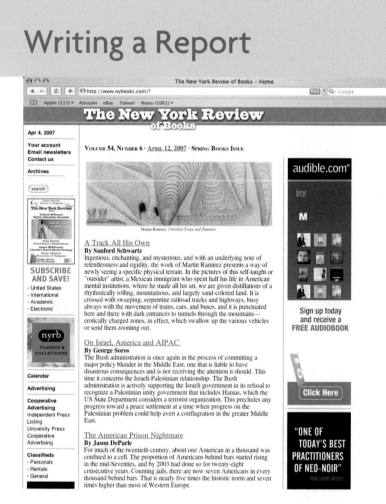

This chapter will explain and illustrate

- the two parts of a report

  PART 1: A summary of the work

  PART 2: Your reaction to the work

This chapter also includes

- points to keep in mind when writing a report
- a model report

To gain a sense of how to review a text, visit the New York Review of Books Web site at http://www.nybooks.com and choose a review to read. Write a short paragraph explaining why you chose that review and what you've learned from it.

Each semester, you will probably be asked by at least one instructor to read a book or an article and write a paper recording your response to the material. In these reports or reaction papers, your instructor will most likely expect you to do two things: *summarize the material* and *detail your reaction to it*. The following pages explain both parts of a report.

Part 1 of a Report: A Summary of the Work

To develop the first part of a report, do the following. (An example follows, on page 409.)

1. Identify the author and title of the work, and include in parentheses the publisher and publication date. With magazines, give the date of publication.

2. Write an informative summary of the material. Condense the content of the work by highlighting its main points and key supporting points. (See pages 396–397 for a complete discussion of summarizing techniques.) Use direct quotations from the work to illustrate important ideas.

Do *not* discuss in great detail any single aspect of the work while neglecting to mention other equally important points. Summarize the material so that the reader gets a general sense of *all* key aspects of the original work. Also, keep the summary objective and factual. Do not include in the first part of the paper your personal reaction to the work; your subjective impression will form the basis of the second part of the paper.

Part 2 of a Report: Your Reaction to the Work

To develop the second part of a report, do the following:

1. Focus on any or all of the questions below. (Check with your instructor to see whether you should emphasize specific points.)

   a. How is the assigned work related to ideas and concerns discussed in the course? For example, what points made in the course textbook, class discussions, or lectures are treated more fully in the work?

   b. How is the work related to problems in our present-day world?

   c. How is the work related to your life, experiences, feelings, and ideas? For instance, what emotions did it arouse in you? Did it increase your understanding of an issue or change your perspective?

2. Evaluate the merit of the work: the importance of its points; its accuracy, completeness, and organization; and so on. You should also indicate here whether you would recommend the work to others, and why.

Points to Keep in Mind When Writing a Report

Here are some important matters to consider as you prepare a report:

1. Apply the four basic standards of effective writing (unity, support, coherence, and clear, error-free sentences).

a. Make sure each major paragraph presents and then develops a single main point. For example, in the model report that follows, a paragraph summarizes the book, and the three paragraphs that follow detail three separate reactions that the student writer had. The student then closes the report with a short concluding paragraph.

b. Support with specific reasons and details any general points or attitudes you express. Statements such as "I agreed with many ideas in this article" and "I found the book very interesting" are meaningless without specific evidence that shows why you feel as you do. Look at the model report to see how the main point or topic sentence of each paragraph is developed by specific supporting evidence.

c. Organize the material in the paper. Follow the basic *plan of organization* already described: an introduction, a summary consisting of one or more paragraphs, a reaction consisting of two or more paragraphs, and a conclusion. Use *transitions* to connect the parts of the paper.

d. Proofread the paper for grammar, mechanics, punctuation, and word use.

2. Document quotations from all works by giving the page number in parentheses after the quoted material (see the model report). You may use quotations in the summary and reaction parts of the paper, but do not rely too much on them. Use them only to emphasize key ideas.

A Model Report

Here is a report written by a student in an introductory sociology course. Look at the paper closely to see how it follows the guidelines for report writing described in this chapter.

A Report on I Know Why the Caged Bird Sings

In I Know Why the Caged Bird Sings (New York: Bantam Books, 1971), **1**   Introductory
Maya Angelou tells the story of her earliest years. Angelou, a dancer, poet,   paragraph
and television producer as well as a writer, has continued her life story in
three more volumes of autobiography. I Know Why the Caged Bird Sings is
the start of Maya Angelou's story; in this book, she writes with crystal clarity
about the pains and joys of being black in America.

(continued)

PART 1:
SUMMARY
Topic
sentence
for
summary
paragraph

I Know Why the Caged Bird Sings covers Maya Angelou's life from
age three to age sixteen. We first meet her as a gawky little girl in a white
woman's cut-down lavender silk dress. She has forgotten the poem she
had memorized for the Easter service, and all she can do is rush out of
the church. At this point, Angelou is living in Stamps, Arkansas, with her
grandmother and uncle. The town is rigidly segregated: "People in Stamps
used to say that the whites in our town were so prejudiced that a Negro
couldn't buy vanilla ice cream" (40). Yet Angelou has some good things in her
life: her adored older brother Bailey, her success in school, and her pride in
her grandmother's quiet strength and importance in the black community.
There is laughter, too, as when a preacher is interrupted in midsermon by an
overly enthusiastic woman shouting, "Preach it, I say preach it!" The woman,
in a frenzied rush of excitement, hits the preacher with her purse; his false
teeth fly out of his mouth and land at Angelou's feet. Shortly after this
incident, Angelou and her brother are taken by her father to live in California
with their mother. Here, at age eight, she is raped by her mother's boyfriend,
who is mysteriously murdered after receiving only a suspended sentence for
his crime. She returns, silent and withdrawn, to Stamps, where the gloom
is broken when a friend of her mother introduces her to the magic of great
books. Later, at age thirteen, Angelou returns to California. She learns how
to dance. She runs away after a violent family fight and lives for a month
in a junkyard. She becomes the first black female to get a job on the San
Francisco streetcars. She graduates from high school eight months pregnant.
And she survives.

2

PART 2:
REACTION
Topic
sentence
for first
reaction
paragraph

I was impressed with the vividness of Maya Angelou's writing style. For
example, she describes the lazy dullness of her life in Stamps: "Weekdays
revolved in a sameness wheel. They turned into themselves so steadily and
inevitably that each seemed to be the original of yesterday's rough draft"
(93). She also knows how to bring a scene to life, as when she describes her
eighth-grade graduation. For months, she has been looking forward to this
event, knowing she will be honored for her academic successes. She is even
happy with her appearance: her hair has become pretty, and her yellow
dress is a miracle of hand-sewing. But the ceremony is spoiled when the
speaker—a white man—implies that the only success available to blacks is in
athletics. Angelou remembers: "The man's dead words fell like bricks around
the auditorium and too many settled in my belly. . . . The proud graduating
class of 1940 had dropped their heads" (152). Later, Angelou uses a crystal-
clear image to describe her father's mistress sewing: "She worked the thread
through the flowered cloth as if she were sewing the torn ends of her life

3

(continued)

together" (208). With such vivid details and figures of speech, Maya Angelou re-creates her life for her readers.

I also reacted strongly to the descriptions of injustices suffered by   4   Topic sentence for second reaction paragraph
blacks two generations ago. I was as horrified as the seven-year-old Maya when some "powhitetrash" girls torment her dignified grandmother, calling her "Annie" and mimicking her mannerisms. In another incident, Mrs. Cullinan, Angelou's white employer, decides that Marguerite (Angelou's given name) is too difficult to pronounce and so renames her Mary. This loss of her name—a "hellish horror" (91)—is another humiliation suffered at white hands, and Angelou leaves Mrs. Cullinan's employ soon afterward. Later, Angelou encounters overt discrimination when a white dentist tells her grandmother, "Annie, my policy is I'd rather stick my hand in a dog's mouth than in a nigger's" (160)—and only slightly less obvious prejudice when the streetcar company refuses to accept her application for a conductor's job. We see Angelou over and over as the victim of a white society.

Although I was saddened to read about the injustices, I rejoiced in   5   Topic sentence for third reaction paragraph
Angelou's triumphs. Angelou is thrilled when she hears the radio broadcast of Joe Louis's victory over Primo Carnera: "A Black boy. Some Black mother's son. He was the strongest man in the world" (114). She weeps with pride when the class valedictorian leads her and her fellow eighth-graders in singing the Negro National Anthem. And there are personal victories, too. One of these comes after her father has gotten drunk in a small Mexican town. Though she has never driven before, she manages to get her father into the car and drives fifty miles through the night as he lies intoxicated in the backseat. Finally, she rejoices in the birth of her son: "He was beautiful and mine. Totally mine. No one had bought him for me" (245). Angelou shows us, through these examples, that she is proud of her race—and of herself.

I Know Why the Caged Bird Sings is a remarkable book. Angelou   6   Concluding paragraph
could have been just another casualty of race prejudice. Yet by using her intelligence, sensitivity, and determination, she succeeds in spite of the odds against her. And by writing with such power, she lets us share her defeats and joys. She also teaches us a vital lesson: With strength and persistence, we can all escape our cages—and sing our songs.

Writing a Résumé and Cover Letter

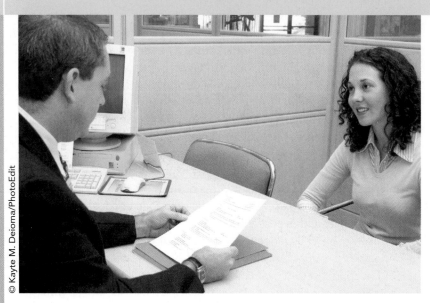

© Kayte M. Deioma/PhotoEdit

Write an essay about your first job interview. What was the job for? Did the interview go well? How did you feel before, during, and after the interview? Is there anything you would have done differently?

When applying for a job through the mail, you should ordinarily send (1) a résumé and (2) a cover letter.

Résumé

A résumé is a summary of your personal background and your qualifications. It helps potential employers see at a glance whether you are suited for a job opening. Two sample job résumés follow: a chronological résumé for someone just out of college; and a functional résumé for a more experienced person.

Chronological Résumé

ERIC KURLAND
27 Hawkins Road
Clarksboro, New Jersey 08020
609-723-2166
Ekurland@email.com

Professional objective	A challenging position in the computer technology field.
Education	2005 to present: Rowan University, Glassboro, New Jersey Degree: B.S. (in June)
Major courses	Introduction to Computer Science I and II Data Structures and Algorithms I and II Programming Languages Programming in Pascal Assembly Language Operating Systems I and II
Related courses	Introduction to Discrete Mathematics I and II Calculus I and II Entrepreneurship and Small Business Management Organizational Behavior
Special school project	Chaired study group that advised local business on advantages of installing computerized payroll system. The group projected comparative cost figures, developed a time-sharing purchase plan, and prepared a budget.
Work experience	2007 to present: Salesperson at Radio Shack Interact with customers, maintain inventory control, repair equipment. Wrote computer program in Visual Basic that demonstrates multimedia aspects of Dell Inspiron Laptop T6400 for use in homes and small businesses. 2003–2006: Word processor, theater usher, and child-care aide.

(continued)

<u>Skills</u>	Mastery of computer languages: C++, Visual Basic, Pascal, and COBOL. Excellent math skills. Detail-oriented, relate easily to coworkers and customers, and show initiative for problem-solving.
<u>References</u>	Available upon request from Rowan University Placement Office, Glassboro, New Jersey 08028.

Functional Résumé

MOLLY CORNELL
9061 Shadow Glen Way
Fort Myers, FL 33966
239-973-0987
Mcornell@email.com

<u>Objective</u> Instructional designer in corporate training and development

<u>Summary of Qualifications</u>

- Write successful proposals that have secured $10 million in training contracts.

- Design and deliver successful training programs tailored to needs of IT professionals and sales personnel in the pharmaceutical and telecommunication industries.

- Able to address complex training issues and diverse client needs.

- Knowledge of all major design software programs including Microsoft Publisher, Lotus Notes, and ACT.

<u>Professional Experience</u>

- Created 13 new distance learning programs, which increased client participation by between 15 and 30 percent.

- Designed a new product line that secured a two-year training contract with Merck, Inc.

(continued)

- Supervised delivery of two training programs for Verizon, Inc., which resulted in renewal of major contract.

- Wrote six proposals for new business that brought in $8 million in increased revenue for 2006–2008.

Employment History	
	2006 to present: Assistant Director of Training, Acme Consultants, Fort Myers, FL
	2005–2006: Proposal Writer, Instructional Design Systems, Alexandria, VA
Education	2005 to present: Completing MS in Instructional Design, Freewald Online University, Minneapolis, MN
	2000: BA in Technical Writing, St. Bonaventure University, St. Bonaventure, NY
	3.75/4.0 GPA
Special Skills	Speak and read Russian.
References	Provided upon request.

Points to Note about the Résumé

1. Your résumé, along with your cover letter, is your introduction to a potential employer. First impressions count, so make the resume neat!

www.mhhe.com/langan

a. Prepare your résumé on a computer. This way you can change it easily if the need arises. Print it on good-quality letter paper (8½ by 11 inches).

b. Proofread very carefully for sentence-skills and spelling mistakes. A potential employer will see such mistakes as signs of carelessness. In addition, get someone else to proofread the résumé for you.

c. Be brief and to the point; limit it to one page if possible.

d. Use a format like that of the model résumés (consider also the variations described below). Balance the résumé on the page so that you have roughly the same margins on all sides.

e. Start with the most recent education/employment experience and work backward in time.

2. Point out strengths, not weaknesses. Don't include "Special Training" if you have had none. Don't refer to your grade-point average if it is less than a B. On the other hand, include a main heading like "Extracurricular Activities" if the activities or awards seem relevant. For example, if Eric Kurland had been vice president of the Computer Club in college he should have mentioned that.

   If you have no work experience related to the job for which you're applying, list the jobs you have had. Any job that shows a period of responsible employment may favorably impress a potential employer.

3. List the names of references on the résumé, but get the permission of people you cite before including their names. You can also give the address of a placement office file that holds references, as shown on Eric Kurland's résumé. Or you can simply say that you will provide references on request, as Molly Cornell did.

Cover Letter

The purpose of the cover letter that goes with your résumé is to introduce yourself briefly and to try to make an employer interested in you. You should include only the high points of the information in your résumé.

Following is the cover letter that Eric Kurland sent with his résumé.

---

27 Hawkins Road
Clarksboro, New Jersey 08020
May 13, 2009

Mr. George C. Arline
Personnel Manager, Indesco Associates
301 Sharptown Road
White Plains, New York 10019

Dear Mr. Arline:

I would like to be considered as a candidate for the assistant computer programmer position advertised in the *Philadelphia Inquirer* on April 28, 2009.

I am currently finishing my degree in Computer Science at Rowan University. I have taken every required computer course offered at Rowan and have a solid background in the following computer languages: C++, Visual Basic, Pascal, and COBOL. In addition to my computer background, I have supplemented my education with business and mathematics courses.

(continued)

My knowledge of computers and the business field goes beyond my formal classroom education. For the past three years I have worked part-time at Radio Shack, where I have gained experience in sales and inventory control. Also, on my own initiative, I designed a demonstration program for the Compaq Presario 5062 and developed promotional fliers about the program.

In short, I believe I have the up-to-date computer background and professional drive needed to contribute to your organization. I have enclosed a copy of my résumé to give you further details about my experience. Sometime next week, I'll give you a call to see whether I can come in for an interview at your convenience. I look forward to speaking with you then.

Sincerely,

Eric Kurland
Eric Kurland

Points to Note about the Cover Letter

www.mhhe.com/langan

1. Your letter should do the following:
   a. In the first paragraph, state that you are an applicant for a job and identify the source through which you learned about the job.

   Here is how Eric Kurland's letter might have opened if his source had been the college placement office: "I learned through the placement office at Rowan University of the assistant computer programmer position at your company. I would like to be considered as a candidate for the job."

   Sometimes an ad will list only a box number (such as Y 172) to reply to. Your inside address should then be:

   Y 172
   Philadelphia Inquirer
   Philadelphia, Pennsylvania 19101

   Dear Sir or Madam:

   b. In the second paragraph, briefly state your qualifications for the job and refer the reader to your résumé.
   c. In the last paragraph, state your willingness to come for an interview. If you can be available for an interview only at certain times, indicate this.

2. As with your résumé, neatness is crucial. Follow the same hints for the letter that you did for the résumé.

   a. Print the letter on good paper.

   b. Proofread *very carefully* for sentence-skills mistakes and spelling mistakes. Use the checklist of sentence skills on the inside back cover.

   c. Be brief and to the point: use no more than one page.

   d. Use a format like the model letter. Keep roughly the same margin on all sides.

   e. Use punctuation and spelling in the model letter as a guide. For example:

      (1) Skip two spaces between the inside address and the salutation ("Dear Mr. Arline").

      (2) Use a colon after the salutation.

      (3) Sign your name at the bottom, in addition to typing it.

Activity

1

Clip a job listing from a newspaper or copy a job description posted in your school placement office. The job should be one that you feel you are qualified for or that you would one day like to have.

Write a résumé and a cover letter for the job. Use the models already considered as guides.

Use the checklist on the inside back cover as a guide in your writing.

This chapter will explain and illustrate how to

- research topics using the library
- research topics using the Internet
- evaluate Internet sources

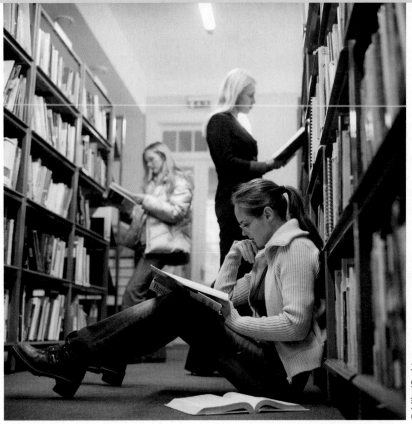

© Mika/Corbis

Write a letter to a new student on campus in which you describe the various uses of the college library.

This chapter provides the basic information you need to use your college library and the Internet with confidence. You will learn that for most research topics there are two basic steps you should take:

1. Find books on your topic.

2. Find articles on your topic.

You will learn, too, that while the library is the traditional place for doing such research, a home computer with Internet access now enables you to thoroughly investigate any topic.

Using the Library

Most students know that libraries provide study space, computer workstations, and copying machines. They are also aware of a library's reading area, which contains recent copies of magazines and newspapers. But the true heart of a library consists of a *main desk, the library's catalog(s) of holdings, book stacks,* and *the periodicals storage area.* Each of these will be discussed in the pages that follow.

Main Desk

The main desk is usually located in a central spot. Check with the main desk to see whether a brochure describes the layout and services of the library. You might also ask whether the library staff provides tours. If not, explore your library to find each of the areas in the activity below.

Activity

1

Make up a floor plan of your college library. Label the main desk, catalogs (in print or computerized), book stacks, and periodicals storage area.

Library Catalog

The library catalog will be your starting point for almost any research project. In most libraries, the catalog can be accessed on computer terminals. Increasingly, local and college library catalogs can be accessed online, so you may be able to check their book holdings via your personal computer.

Finding a Book: Author, Title, and Subject

There are three ways to look up a book: according to *author, title,* or *subject.* Suppose you want to see if the library has the book *A Tribe Apart,* by Patricia Hersch. You could check for the book through:

1. An author search, in which you would look under *Hersch, Patricia*
2. A title search, in which you would look under *Tribe Apart, A.*
3. A subject search. In this case, since the subject of the book is "teenagers," you would look under that term.

Here is the author entry in a computerized card catalog for Hersch's book *A Tribe Apart:*

Author:	Hersch, Patricia
Title:	A tribe apart: a journey into the heart of American adolescence
Publisher:	New York: Ballantine, 1998
LC Subjects:	Teenagers—United States
Call Number:	HQ796.H43
Location:	Gibbsboro
Status:	Available

Note that in addition to giving you the publisher (Ballantine) and year of publication (1998), the entry also tells you the *call number*—where to find the book in the library. If the computerized catalog is part of a network of libraries, you may also learn at what branch or location the book is available. If the book is not at your library, you can probably arrange for an interlibrary loan.

Using Subject Headings to Research a Topic

Generally, if you are looking for a particular book, it is easier to search by *author* or *title*. On the other hand, if you are researching a topic, then you should search by *subject*.

The subject section performs three valuable functions:

- It will give you a list of books on a given topic.

- It will often provide related topics that might have information on your subject.

- It will suggest more-limited topics, helping you narrow your general topic.

Chances are you will be asked to do a research paper of about five to fifteen pages. You do not want to choose a topic so broad that it could be covered only by an entire book or more. Instead, you want to come up with a limited topic that can be adequately supported in a relatively short paper. As you search the subject section, take advantage of ideas that it might offer on how you can narrow your topic.

Part A Team up with a partner in class and answer the following questions about your library's catalog.

1. Is your library's catalog an actual file of cards in drawers, or is it computerized?

   _____

2. Which type of catalog search will help you research and limit a topic?

   _____

Activity

2

Part B Use your library's catalog to answer the following questions.

1. What is the title of one book by Anna Quindlen? _____

   _____

2. What is the title of one book by Bill Geist?

   _____

3. Who is the author of *A Tree Grows in Brooklyn?* (Remember to look up the title under *Tree,* not *A.*)

   _____

4. Who is the author of *Seven Habits of Highly Effective People?*

   _____

5. List two books and their authors dealing with the subject of adoption.

   a. _____

   b. _____

6. Look up a book titled *When Bad Things Happen to Good People* or *Silent Spring* and give the following information:

   a. Author _____

   b. Publisher _____

   c. Date of publication _____

   d. Call number _____

   e. One subject heading _____

7. Look up a book written by Deborah Tannen or Garrison Keillor and give the following information:

   a. Title _____

   b. Publisher _____

   c. Date of publication _____

   d. Call number _____

   e. One subject heading _____

Book Stacks

The book stacks are the library shelves where books are arranged according to their call numbers. The call number, as distinctive as a Social Security number, always appears on the catalog entry for any book. It is also printed on the spine of every book in the library.

If your library has open stacks (ones that you are permitted to enter), here is how to find a book. Suppose you are looking for *A Tribe Apart,* which has the call number HQ796.H43 in the Library of Congress system. (Libraries using the Dewey decimal system have call letters made up entirely of numbers rather than letters and numbers. However, you use the same basic method to locate a book.) First, you go to the section of the stacks that holds the *H*'s. When you locate the *H*'s, you look for the *HQ*'s. After that, you look for *HQ796*. Finally, you look for *HQ796.H43,* and you have the book.

If your library has closed stacks (ones you are not permitted to enter), you will have to write down the title, author, and call number on a request form. (Such forms will be available near the card catalog or computer terminals.) You'll then give the form to a library staff person, who will locate the book and bring it to you.

Use the book stacks to answer one of the following sets of questions. Choose the questions that relate to the system of classifying books used by your library.

Activity

3

Option 1: Library of Congress system (letters and numbers)

1. Books in the E184.6–E185.9 area deal with
   a. Benjamin Franklin.
   c. American presidents.
   b. American Indians.
   d. African Americans.

2. Books in the HM–HN65 area deal with
   a. sociology.
   c. economics.
   b. history.
   d. psychology.

3. Books in the M1–M220 area deal with
   a. painting.
   c. music.
   b. sculpture.
   d. architecture.

Option 2: Dewey decimal system (numbers)

1. Books in the 200–299 area deal with
   a. language.
   c. religion.
   b. philosophy.
   d. sports.

2. Books in the 370–372 area deal with
   a. education.
   c. the military.
   b. death.
   d. waste disposal.

3. Books in the 613 area deal with

    a. wildflowers.   c. drugs.

    b. health.   d. the solar system.

Periodicals

The second step in researching a topic is to locate relevant periodicals: *magazines, journals, and newspapers.* They contain recent or very specialized information about a subject, which may not be available in a book.

The library keeps a catalogue of the periodicals to which it subscribes. However, to find a particular article in periodical you will need to consult a periodical index.

Following are some widely used indexes.

Readers' Guide to Periodical Literature

One way to research is to use the volumes of the *Readers' Guide,* found in almost every libary. They list articles published in more than one hundred popular magazines, such as *Newsweek, Health, Ebony,* and *Popular Science.* Articles appear alphabetically under both subject and author. For example, if you wanted to learn the titles of articles published on the subject of child abouse within a certain time span, you would look under the heading "Child abuse." Following is a typical entry from the *Guide.*

Subject heading   *Title of article*   *Author of article*   *"Illustrated"*

Parenting

The Case for Staying Home C. Wallis il

    Time p51–9 Mr 22 '04

Name of magazine   *Page numbers*   *Date*

Note the sequence in which information is given about the article:

1. Subject heading.
2. Title of the article. In some cases, bracketed words ([ ]) after the title help make clear just what the article is about.
3. Author (if it is a signed article). The author's first name is always abbreviated.
4. Whether the article has a bibliography (*bibl*) or is illustrated with pictures (*il*). Other abbreviations sometimes used are shown in the front of the *Readers' Guide.*

5. Name of the magazine. Before 1988, the *Readers' Guide* used abbreviations for most of the magazines indexed. For example, the magazine *Popular Science* is abbreviated *Pop Sci*. If necessary, refer to the list of magazines in the front of the index to identify abbreviations.

6. Page numbers on which the article appears.

8. Date when the article appeared. Dates are abbreviated: for example, *Mr* stands for March, *Ag* for August, *O* for October. Other abbreviations are shown in the front of the *Guide.*

The *Readers' Guide* is published in monthly supplements. At the end of a year, a volume is published covering the entire year. You will see in your library large green volumes titled, for instance, *Readers' Guide 2000* or *Readers' Guide 2007.* You will also see the small monthly supplements for the current year.

The drawback of the *Readers' Guide* is that it gives you only a list of articles; you must then go to your library's catalog to see if the library actually has copies of the magazines that contain those articles. If you're lucky and it does, you must take the time to locate the relevant issue and then to read and take notes on the articles or to make copies of them.

The *Readers' Guide* may also be available at your library online. If so, you can quickly search for articles on a given subject simply by typing in a key word or key phrase.

Online Databases

Most college and public libraries now provide online computer-search services known as online databases or library subscription services. Using any of these services, you will be able to type in key words and quickly search many periodicals for articles on your subject. Some databases, such as General Science Index, are discipline specific, but others, such as Academic Search Premier, are more general.

Often, articles you find will be shown as "full text." That means that you can print out the entire article from your computer. In other cases, only an abstract (summary) of the article will be available. However, abstracts are valuable too, for they allow you to determine whether the article is relevant to your research and if you should continue searching for the full text.

Finally, database articles appear in *html* or *pdf* format or in both. Articles in .html (hypertext markup language) have been reformatted for publication on the Internet. Those in .pdf (portable document format) are exact reproductions of a print document. Note that some databases are among many compiled by the same provider. EBSCOhost, Infotrac, and ProQuest are such providers.

Here are a few online databases that have proven useful for new student researchers.

Academic Search Premier covers a variety of disciplines and includes full-text articles and abstracts of articles from over 4,400 periodicals.

Cumulative Index to Nursing and Allied Health Literature (CINAHL) provides access to articles found in over 1,800 professional journals in the health professions.

ERIC (Education Resources Information Center) makes available articles from professional journals, reports, and speeches having to do with education.

General Science Index lists articles on biology, chemistry, physics, and the other physical sciences.

Wilson Humanities Index covers over 500 English-language periodicals in disciplines such as archaeology, the classics, art, history, theater, music, literature, philosophy, and religion.

JSTOR (Journal Storage) provides full-text articles found in back issues of journals in the humanities, social sciences, and natural sciences.

CGP (Catalog of U.S. Government Publications) contains documents published by the U.S. government.

New York Times **Index** lists articles published in this newspaper since 1913.

PsychInfo is published by the American Psychological Association. It includes abstracts of books, articles, and doctoral dissertations in psychology. It also provides access to full-text articles through PsycARTICLES.

Activity 4

At this point in the chapter, you now know the two basic steps in researching a topic in the library. What are the steps?

1. _____

2. _____

Activity 5

1. Look up a recent article on nursing home costs using one of your library's periodicals indexes or online databases, and fill in the following information:

   a. Name of the index you used _____

   b. Article title _____

   c. Author (if given) _____

   d. Name of magazine _____

   e. Pages _____ f. Date _____

2. Look up a recent article on organ donation using one of your library's periodicals indexes or online databases, and fill in the following information:

   a. Name of the index you used _____

b. Article title _____

c. Author (if given) _____

d. Name of magazine _____

e. Pages _____ f. Date _____

Using the Internet

Before you begin searching the Internet, find out what databases your local and school libraries subscribe to. You may be able to do enough research using these online resources and print sources available in your library. If not, you can search for material on the Internet.

Finding Additional Books on Your Topic

To find current books on your topic, go online and search for one of the large commercial online booksellers such as Amazon or Barnes & Noble. They will list helpful books that you might want to buy. Many of these are used and are, therefore, discounted. However, if you don't want to buy the book, just jot down the author's name, the title, the publisher, and the date of publication. Take this information to your college library and see if the book is on the shelves. If not, request an interlibrary loan. Tour librarian will forward your request to the nearest library that has the book. Be aware, however, that it may take a week or longer to get the book.

A Note on the Library of Congress

You can also find additional books on your topic by visiting the Library of Congress Web site (www.loc.gov). Located in Washington, D.C., the Library of Congress, has copies of all books published in the United States. Its online catalog contains about twelve million entries. You can browse this catalog by subject or search by key words. The search form permits you to check just those books that interest you. After you find a given book, click on the "Full Record" option to view publication information and call number. You can then try to obtain the book from your college library or through an interlibrary loan.

Other Points to Note

After you have found the books you think might relate to your topic, print out a list of them. This way you can go to the library prepared to find just those you want to borrow. In fact, since many libraries are now accessible online, you might want to search your library's electronic catalogs on your home computer even when the library is closed. You can then go to the library as soon as it opens and start checking out the books you need right away.

Finding Articles on Your Topic

Online Magazines and Newspaper Articles

As already mentioned, your library probably subscribes to online databases such as Academic Search Premiere or JSTOR, which you can use to find relevant articles on your subject. Another online research service, one that you can subscribe to individually on a home computer, is eLibrary. You may be able to get a free seven-day trial subscription or pay for a monthly subscription at a limited cost. The service provides millions of newspaper and magazine articles as well as many thousands of book chapters and television and radio transcripts. After typing in one or more key words on the eLibrary Web site, you'll get long lists of articles that may relate to your subject.

www.mhhe.com/langan

Search Engines

An Internet search engine will help you go through a vast amount of information on the Web to find articles about almost any topic. As with other resources, choosing the appropriate key words is important to beginning a search. For example, if you are thinking of doing a paper on road rage, type "road rage." Within a second or so, you will get a list of over three million articles and sites on the Web about road rage!

You should then narrow your topic by adding other key words. For instance, if you typed "preventing road rage," you would get a list of over one million articles and sites. If you narrowed your potential topic further by typing "educational programs for preventing road rage," you would get a list of almost a half million items. Some search engines, such as Google, do good job of returning hits that are genuinely relevant to your search, so just scanning the early part of a list may be enough to provide you with the information you need.

As discussed above, sometimes you get too much information. So, try making your key words more specific, or use different combinations of key words. You might also try another search engine. Finally, many search engines have an Advanced Search feature for tips on successful searching.

www.mhhe.com/langan

Evaluating Internet Sources

Keep in mind that the quality and reliability of information you find on the Internet may vary widely. Anyone with a bit of computer know-how can create a Web site and post information there. That person may be a Nobel Prize winner, a leading authority in a specialized field, a high school student, or a crackpot. Be careful, then, to look closely at the source in the following ways:

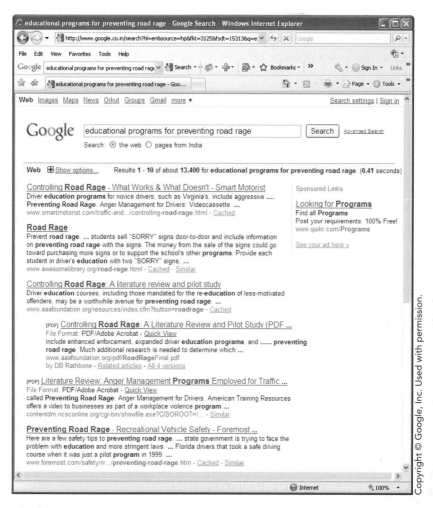

Results from a key word search on Google using "educational programs for preventing road rage" in the search box.

1. **Internet address**   In a Web address, the three letters following the "dot" are the domain. The most common domains are .com, .edu, .gov, .net, and .org. A common misconception is that a Web site's reliability can be determined by its domain. This is not the case, as almost anyone can get a Web address ending in .com, .edu, .org, or any of the other domains. Therefore, it is important that you examine every Web site carefully, considering the three points that follow.

2. **Author**   What credentials does the author have (if any)? Has the author published other material on the topic?

3. **Internal evidence** Does the author seem to proceed objectively—presenting all sides of a topic fairly before arguing his or her own views? Does the author produce solid, adequate support for his or her views?

4. **Date** Is the information up-to-date? Check at the top or bottom of the document for copyright, publication, or revision dates. Knowing such dates will help you decide whether the material is current enough for your purposes.

Activity

6

Part A Go to www.google.com and search for "education." Then complete the items below.

1. How many items did your search yield? _____

2. In the early listings, you will probably find each of the following domains: edu, gov, org, and com. Pick one site with each domain and write its full address.

   a. Address of one .com site you found: _____

   b. Address of one .gov site: _____

   c. Address of one .org site: _____

   d. Address of one .edu site: _____

Part B Circle *one* of the sites you identified above and use it to complete the following evaluation. Answers will vary.

3. Name of site's author or authoring institution: _____

4. Is site's information current (within two years)? _____

5. Does the site serve obvious business purposes (with advertising or attempts to sell products)? _____

6. Does the site have an obvious connection to a governmental, commercial, business, or religious organization? If so, which one?

   _____

7. Does the site's information seem fair and objective?

   _____

   _____

8. Based on the information above, would you say the site appears reliable?

   _____

Practice in Using the Library and the Internet

Use your library or the Internet to research a subject that interests you. Select one of the following areas or (with your instructor's permission) an area of your own choice:

Activity

7

Assisted suicide
Interracial adoption
Ritalin and children
Sexual harassment
Gay marriage
Greenhouse effect
Nursing home costs
Pro-choice movement today
Pro-life movement today
Health insurance reform
Pollution of drinking water
Problems of retirement
Cremation
Capital punishment
Prenatal care
Acid rain
New aid for people with disabilities
New remedies for allergies
Censorship on the Internet
Prison reform
Drug treatment programs
Sudden infant death syndrome
New treatments for insomnia
Organ donation
Child abuse
Voucher system in schools
Food poisoning (salmonella)
Alzheimer's disease
Holistic healing
Best job prospects today
Heroes for today

Computer use and carpal tunnel
  syndrome
Noise control
Animals nearing extinction
Animal rights movement
Antigay violence
Drug treatment programs for
  adolescents
Fertility drugs
Witchcraft today
New treatments for AIDS
Mind-body medicine
Origins of Kwanzaa
Hazardous substances in the home
Airbags
Gambling and youth
Nongraded schools
Forecasting earthquakes
Ethical aspects of hunting
Ethics of cloning
Recent consumer frauds
Stress reduction in the workplace
Sex on television
Everyday addictions
Toxic waste disposal
Self-help groups
Telephone crimes
Date rape
Steroids
Surrogate mothers
Vegetarianism

Research the topic first through a subject search in your library's catalog or that of an online bookstore. Then research the topic through a periodicals index (print or online). On a separate sheet of paper, provide the following information:

1. Topic

2. Three books that either cover the topic directly or at least touch on the topic in some way. Include the following:

   Author

   Title

   Place of publication

   Publisher

   Date of publication

3. Three articles on the topic published in 2006 or later. Include the following:

   Title of article

   Author (if given)

   Title of magazine

   Date

   Pages (if given)

4. Finally, write a paragraph describing just how you went about researching your topic. In addition, include a photocopy or printout of one of the three articles.

Writing a Research Paper

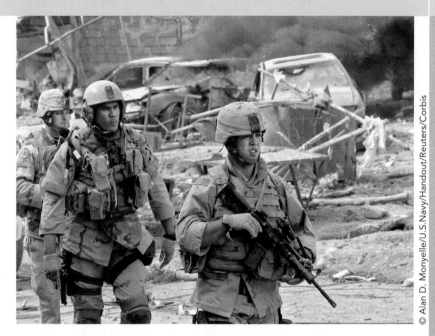

22

© Alan D. Monyelle/U.S.Navy/Handout/Reuters/Corbis

If you were to write a research paper on war, what would you focus on? War itself is too broad a topic to cover in one research paper. You would need to select a more limited topic to write about, for example, the effect of war on the economy. Looking at the above photograph of American soldiers in Iraq, can you think of some other limited topics of war you might cover in a research paper?

Step 1: Select a Topic That You Can Readily Research

Researching at a Local Library

First of all, do a subject search of your library's catalog and see whether there are several books on your general topic. For example, if you initially choose the broad topic "parenting," try to find at least three books on being a parent. Make sure that the books are actually available on the library shelves.

This chapter will explain and illustrate

- the six steps in writing a research paper:

  STEP 1: Select a topic that you can readily research.

  STEP 2: Limit your topic and make the purpose of your paper clear.

  STEP 3: Gather information on your limited topic.

  STEP 4: Plan your paper and take notes on your limited topic.

  STEP 5: Write the paper.

  STEP 6: Use an acceptable format and method of documentation.

This chapter also provides

- a model research paper

Next, go to a periodicals index in your library to see if there are a fair number of magazine, newspaper, or journal articles on your subject. You can use the *Readers' Guide to Periodical Literature* (found in just about every library) to find articles that appear in the back issues of periodicals that your library may keep. But you may find that your library subscribes to a provider of electronic databases such as EBSCOhost, which will allow you access to articles published in a far greater range of publications. For instance, when Sonya Philips, author of the model research paper "Successful Families," visited her local library, she connected to EBSCOhost and typed "parenting" in the search box. In seconds, EBSCOhost came back with hundreds of hits—titles, publication information, and the complete text of articles about parenting.

Researching on the Internet

The first step is to go to the subjects section of a library's electronic catalog or large online bookseller to find relevant books (don't worry—you don't have to buy any books; you're just browsing for information). Two of the largest online booksellers are Barnes & Noble and Amazon.

As Sonya Philips explains, "Barnes & Noble has a category called 'Parenting and Family.' When I clicked on that, I got a bunch of subcategories, including one for 'Teenagers.' I clicked on 'Teenagers,' and that brought up a list of hundreds of books! I went through the list, and when I got to a book that sounded promising, I just clicked on that title and up like magic came reviews of the book—and sometimes a table of contents and a summary as well! This information helped me decide on the dozen or so books I eventually picked out that seemed relevant to my paper. I then went to my local library and found five of those titles on the shelves. Another title was a recent paperback, so I asked the research librarian to help me get the book through interlibrary loan."

Next, determine whether magazine or newspaper articles on your topic are available online. The simplest way is to use an Internet search engine, such as Google. Here's what Sonya did.

"First I typed in the word 'parenting' in the key word box." I got more than eight million hits! So I tried more specific search terms. I tried 'parenting and teenagers' first, but that was still too general. So I narrowed the topic even more: 'parenting and teenagers and television' and 'parenting and teenagers and homeschooling.' This reduced the number of hits a lot. I was still getting thousands, but I could see that some of the first ones looked promising. In fact, I found some useful sites, like 'The Television Project,' which is an online resource that doesn't exist anywhere else.

"To look just for magazine and newspaper articles, I went directly to the site of some popular publications, such as *Time* and *Newsweek*.

I was able to search for recent articles, but I saw that I would have to pay a fee of about two dollars to read each article online. So, I noted the date and page number of the articles, and I looked up the ones that were available in the library's reading room. Between doing that and using EBSCOhost, I found plenty of recent material related to my subject."

So, the first step in doing a research paper is to find out if both books and articles are available on your chosen topic. If so, pursue your topic. Otherwise, choose another one. You can't write a paper on a topic for which research materials are not available.

Step 2: Limit Your Topic and Make the Purpose of Your Paper Clear

A research paper should *thoroughly* develop a *limited* topic. The paper should be narrow and deep rather than broad and shallow. Therefore, as you read through books and articles, look for ways to limit your general topic.

For instance, as Sonya read materials on the general topic "parenting," she chose to limit her topic to the particular problems of parents raising children in today's culture. She then decided to limit it even more by focusing on what successful parents do to deal with those challenges. To take other examples, the general topic "drug abuse" might be narrowed to "successful drug treatment programs for adolescents." After reading about the worldwide problem of overpopulation, you might decide to limit your paper to the birth control policies enforced by the Chinese government.

The subject headings in your library's catalog and periodicals indexes will give you helpful ideas about how to limit your subject. For example, under the subject heading "parenting" in the book file were several related headings, such as "moral and ethical considerations of parenting" and "stepparenting." In addition, there was a list of seventy books, including several titles that suggested limited directions for research: parents and discipline, parenting and adolescent girls, how parents can protect their kids from violence. Under the subject heading "Parenting" in the library's periodicals index were subheadings and titles of many articles that suggested additional limited topics: how parents can limit the impact of TV on kids, keeping the lines of communication open between parents and teenagers, and secrets to raising a successful teen.

Do not expect to limit your topic and make your purpose clear all at once. You may have to do quite a bit of reading as you work out the limited focus of your paper. Note that many research papers have one of two general purposes: (1) to defend a point (for example, to provide evidence that elected officials should be limited to a single term) or (2) to present information (for example, to discuss the effects of diet on heart disease).

Step 3: Gather Information on Your Limited Topic

After limiting your topic, begin gathering relevant information. A helpful way to proceed is to sign out the books that you need from your library and photocopy relevant articles from magazines, newspapers, or journals. You should also print out articles directly from your library's databases or the Internet.

Then sit and work on these materials in a quiet, unhurried place.

Step 4: Plan Your Paper and Take Notes on Your Limited Topic

Preparing a Scratch Outline

As you carefully read through the material you have gathered, think about the content and organization of your paper. Begin deciding what information you will present and how you will arrange it. Prepare a scratch outline that shows both the paper's thesis and the areas that support the thesis. Try to include at least three areas of support.

Thesis: _____

Support: (1) _____

                (2) _____

                (3) _____

Following is the outline that Sonya Philips made for her paper on successful parenting.

Thesis: Parents can do things to overcome the negative influences hurting their families.

Support: (1) Create quality time with families

                (2) Increase families' sense of community

                (3) Minimize the impact of media and technology

---

Note-Taking

With this tentative outline in mind, you can begin taking notes on the information that you expect to include in your paper. Write your notes on four-by-six-inch or five-by-eight-inch cards, or in a computer file. Don't use loose-leaf or notebook paper; doing so makes it harder to organize your notes as you prepare to draft your paper. Notes should be in the form of *direct quotations and summaries in your own words*. At times, you may also *paraphrase*—use your own words in place of someone else's. Since most research involves condensing, you will probably summarize much more often than you will paraphrase. (For more information on summarizing, see pages 396–397.)

A *direct quotation* must be written *exactly* as it appears in the original work. But, you may omit words that are not relevant to your point as long as you don't change the meaning. To show such an omission, use three spaced periods (known as *ellipsis points*) in place of the deleted words:

www.mhhe.com/langan

        We cannot guarantee that bad things will happen, but we can argue that good things are not happening. It is the contention of this report that increasing numbers of young people are left to their own devices at a critical time in their development.

Original passage

Direct quotation with an ellipsis

> "We cannot guarantee that bad things will happen, but we can argue that good things are not happening. . . . [I]ncreasing numbers of young people are left to their own devices at a critical time in their development."

(Note the four dots in the above example; the first dot is the period at the end of the sentence. The capital letter in brackets shows that the word was capitalized by the student and not by the author of the quotation.)

In a *summary,* you condense the original material and use your own words. Below is one of Sonya Philips's summary note cards.

> *Movie content*
>
> *Study conducted in 2006 showed that of PG-13 movies, 91 percent had crude language, 89 percent had obscene language, 45 percent had actual or suggested sex. Worrisome because most parents assume PG-13 movies are OK for their kids.*
>
> *Medved and Medved, 62*

Remember that, in a *paraphrase,* you report the information in your own words and style without condensing it.

Keep the following in mind as you research:

- Write on only one side of each card.

- Write only one kind of information, from one source, on any one card. For example, the sample card on the previous page has information on only one idea (movie content) from one source (Medved and Medved).

- At the top of each card, write a heading that summarizes its content. This will help you organize different kinds of information.

- Identify the source and page number at the bottom.

Always record the exact source and page from which you take each piece of information. In a research paper, you must document all information that is not common knowledge or not a matter of historical record. For example, the birth and death dates of Dr. Martin Luther King Jr. are established facts and do not need documenting. On the other hand, the average number of hours worked in the United States this year compared with the average number worked in 1980 is a specialized fact and should be documented. In addition, as you read several sources on a subject, you will develop a sense of what authors regard as generally shared, or common, information and what is more specialized information that requires documentation.

Read the following paragraphs from books that a student might use to gather material for a research paper. Then, using note cards, create three separate note cards for each:

1. In the first note card, use a direct quotation in which you indicate the omission of certain words or phrases by using ellipses.

2. In the second note card, write a paraphrase of the paragraph.

3. In the third note card, write a summary of the paragraph.

Provide a heading for each card and identify the author and the page number. You will end up with six complete note cards.

Paragraph A: Taken from page 1 of *The Sea Around Us,* by Rachel Carson.
   Beginnings are apt to be shadowy, and so it is with the beginnings of the great mother of life, the sea. Many people have debated how and when the earth got its oceans, and it is not surprising that their explanations do not always agree. For the plain and inescapable truth is that no one was there to see, and in the absence of eyewitness accounts there is bound to be a certain amount of disagreement.

Paragraph B: Taken from Robert Ramirez's "The Woolen Sarape," which appeared on page 53 of an essay anthology.
   Many lower-income families of the barrio manage to maintain a comfortable standard of living through the communal action of family members who contribute their wages to the head of the family. Economic need creates interdependence and closeness.

A Caution about Plagiarism

If you fail to document information that is not your own, you will be stealing. The formal term is *plagiarizing*—using someone else's work as your own, whether you borrow a single idea, a sentence, or an entire essay.

   One example of plagiarism is turning in a friend's paper as if it is your own. Another example is copying an article found in a magazine, newspaper, journal, or on the Internet and turning it in as your own. By copying someone else's work, you

www.mhhe.com/langan

risk being failed or even expelled. Equally, plagiarism deprives you of what can be a most helpful learning and organization experience—researching and writing about a selected topic in detail.

Keep in mind, too, that while the Internet has made it easier for students to plagiarize, it has also made it riskier. Teachers can easily discover that a student has taken material from an Internet source by typing a sentence or two from the student's paper into a powerful search engine like Google; that source is then often quickly identified.

With the possibility of plagiarism in mind, then, be sure to take careful, documented notes during your research. Remember that if you use another person's material, *you must acknowledge your source*. When you cite a source properly, you give credit where it is due, you provide your readers with a way to locate the original material on their own, and you demonstrate that your work has been carefully researched.

Activity 2

Here are three sets of passages. Each set begins with an original passage followed by notes on the passage. Both notes include a parenthetical citation, "(24)," crediting the original source. But while one note is an acceptable paraphrase or summary, the other is an unacceptable paraphrase or summary in which the sentences and ideas too closely follow the original, using some of the same structure and the same words as the original. Identify the acceptable note with an A and the unacceptable note with a U.

Set 1: Original Passage

The self-confessed television addict often feels he "ought" to do other things— but the fact that he doesn't read and doesn't plant his garden or sew or crochet or play games or have conversations means that those activities are no longer as desirable as television. In a way the heavy viewer's life is as imbalanced by his television "habit" as a drug addict's or an alcoholic's. He is living in a holding pattern, as it were, passing up the activities that lead to growth or development or a sense of accomplishment. This is one reason people talk about their television viewing so ruefully, so apologetically. They are aware that it is an unproductive experience, that almost any other endeavor is more worthwhile by any human measure.

—Marie Winn, from "Television Addiction,"
in *The Plug-In Drug* (Viking Penguin, 2002)

_____ a. Television addicts may feel they should do other things like play games or have conversations. But they pass up activities that might lead to a sense of accomplishment. Their lives are as imbalanced by their television watching as a drug addict's or alcoholic's. Aware of how unproductive television viewing is, they talk about it apologetically (24).

_____ b. TV addicts feel that they ought to spend their time doing more worthwhile activities. But like alcohol or drugs, TV has taken over their lives. The addicts' apologetic tone when they talk about their TV watching indicates that they know they're wasting time on a completely unproductive activity (24).

Set 2: Original Passage

Now, however, there is growing evidence that restorative naps are making a comeback. Recognizing that most of their employees are chronically sleep-deprived, some companies have set up nap rooms with reclining chairs, blankets and alarm clocks. If unions are truly interested in worker welfare, they should make such accommodations a standard item in contract negotiations. Workers who take advantage of the opportunity to sleep for twenty minutes or so during the workday report that they can go back to work with renewed enthusiasm and energy. My college roommate, Dr. Linda Himot, a psychiatrist in Pittsburgh, who has a talent for ten-minute catnaps between patients, says these respites help her focus better on each patient's problems, which are not always scintillating. And companies that encourage napping report that it reduces accidents and errors and increases productivity, even if it shortens the workday a bit. Studies have shown that sleepy workers make more mistakes and cause more accidents, and are more susceptible to heart attacks and gastrointestinal disorders.

—Jane Brody, from "New Respect for the Nap"
(New York Times, 2001)

_____ a. As employers realize that many workers are short on sleep, they are becoming more open to the idea of napping on the job. Some even provide places for workers to stretch out and nap briefly. Companies that allow napping find their employees are more alert and productive, and even suffer fewer physical ailments (24).

_____ b. Naps are becoming more acceptable. Some companies have done such things as set up nap rooms with reclining chairs and blankets. Naps provide workers with renewed enthusiasm and energy. Although naps shorten the workday a bit, they reduce accidents and increase productivity. Sleep-deprived workers are prone to heart attacks and gastrointestinal disorders (24).

Set 3: Original Passage

Chances are, you are going to go to work after you complete college. How would you like to earn an extra $950,000 on your job? If this sounds appealing, read on. I'm going to reveal how you can make an extra $2,000 a month between the ages of 25 and 65. Is this hard to do? Actually, it is simple for some, but impossible for others. All you have to do is be born a male and graduate from college. If we compare full-time workers, this is how much more the average male college graduate earns over the course of his career. Hardly any single factor pinpoints gender discrimination better than this total. The pay gap, which shows up at all levels of education, is so great that women who work full-time average only two-thirds (67 percent) of what men are paid. This gap does not occur only in the United States. All industrialized nations have it, although only in Japan is the gap larger than in the United States.

> —James Henslin, from *Essentials of Sociology,*
> fourth edition (Allyn & Bacon, 2002)

_____ a. To make an extra $2,000 a month between the ages of 25 and 65, you need to be born male and graduate from college. This adds up to an additional $950,000. The pay gap between genders shows up at all levels of education. It is so great that women who work full time make only two-thirds what men make. The gender gap occurs in all industrialized nations, although only in Japan is it greater than in the U.S. (24).

_____ b. The effect of gender on salary is significant. At all levels of education, a woman who works full time earns about two-thirds as much as a man who works full time. For college graduates, this adds up to a difference of $950,000 over the course of a 40-year working life. The gender gap exists in all industrialized nations, but it is greatest in Japan and the U.S. (24).

Step 5: Write the Paper

www.mhhe.com/langan

Many instructors require an outline. So, start by making a *final outline* which you can use as a guide to write the first draft. You can prepare either a *topic outline* (thesis plus supporting words and phrases); or a *sentence outline* (complete sentences).

In the model paper shown (pages 447–456), a topic outline appears on pages 448–449. Note that roman numerals are used for first-level headings, capital letters for second-level headings, and arabic numbers for third-level headings.

In an *introduction,* include a thesis statement expressing your purpose and indicate the plan of development you will follow. (Pages 94–98) contain information about writing introductions for both essays and research papers. The model research paper uses a two-paragraph introduction (page 449).

Always maintain unity and coherence and provide enough support to develop your thesis. Use the checklist on the inside back cover of this book to make sure that your paper follows all four bases of effective writing.

Step 6: Use an Acceptable Format and Method of Documentation

Format

The model paper in this chapter (pages 455–456) shows acceptable formats for a research paper using the style recommended by the Modern Language Association (MLA). Most English professors require this style. However, if you are writing in another class, such as psychology, sociology, or one of the physical sciences, your instructor may require a different style. So, always check with your professor first.

Documentation of Sources

You must reveal the sources (books, articles, and so on) of borrowed information in your paper. Whether you quote directly, or summarize ideas in your own words, you must acknowledge your sources. In the past, you may have used footnotes. However, the MLA now requires a simpler form of documentation.

www.mhhe.com/langan

Citations within a Paper

When citing a source, you must mention the author's name and the relevant page number. The author's name may appear either in the sentence you are writing or in parentheses following the sentence:

> In The Way We Really Are, Stephanie Coontz writes, "Right up through the 1940s, ties of work, friendship, neighborhood, ethnicity, extended kin, and voluntary organizations were as important a source of identity for most Americans . . ." (37).
>
> "Some . . . are looking for a way to reclaim family closeness in an increasingly fast-paced society. . . . Still others worry about unsavory influences in school—drugs, alcohol, sex, violence" (Kantrowitz and Wingert 66).

There are several points to note about citations within the paper:

- When the author's name is provided in parentheses, only the last name is given.

- There is no punctuation between the author's name and the page number.

- The parenthetical citation is placed after the borrowed material but before the period at the end of the sentence.

- If you are using more than one work by the same author, include a shortened version of the title in the citation. For example, your citation for the quotation above would be (Coontz, *Really Are* 39). Note that a comma appears between the author's name and the title.

- The abbreviation *qtd. in* is used when citing a quotation from another source. For example, a quotation from Edward Wolff on page 2 of the paper was found in a book not by Wolff but by Sylvia Ann Hewlett and Cornel West. The citation is as follows:

The economist Edward Wolff explains the loss of time:

> Over a thirty-year time span, parental time has declined 13 percent. The time parents have available for their children has been squeezed by the rapid shift of mothers into the paid labor force, by escalating divorce rates and the subsequent abandonment of children by their fathers, and by an increase in the number of hours required on the job. The average worker is now at work 163 hours a year more than in 1969, which adds up to an extra month of work annually (qtd. in Hewlett and West 48).

Citations at the End of a Paper

End your paper with a list of works cited that includes all the sources actually used in the paper. (Don't list other sources, no matter how many you have read.) Look at the "Works Cited" page in the model research paper (pages 455–456) and note the following:

- The works-cited list begins on a new page, not on the last page of the paper's text.

- Entries are organized alphabetically according to the authors' last names. Entries are not numbered.

- Entries are double-spaced, with no extra spaces between entries.

- After the first line of an entry, a half-inch indentation separates each additional line in that entry. This arrangement is called a "hanging indent" in the formatting menus for most word processors.

- *Italicize* (do not underline) titles of books, periodicals, and other independently published works.

- Do not include URLs in Web entries.

- Include the publication medium, such as Print, Web, DVD or TV.

- If no publisher's name appears in a Web source, write *n.p.* When no date appears in a Web site, write *n.d.*

Model Entries for a List of Works Cited

Use the following entries as a guide when you prepare your list.

> Bryson, Bill. *The Life and Times of the Thunderbolt Kid: A Memoir.* New York:
> Broadway Books, 2006. Print.

Book by One Author

Note that the author's last name is written first.

> ___. *A Short History of Nearly Everything.* New York: Broadway Books, 2003. Print.

Two or More Entries by the Same Author

If you cite two or more entries by the same author (in the example above, a second book by Bill Bryson is cited), do not repeat the author's name. Instead, begin the line with three hyphens followed by a period. Then give the remaining information as usual. Arrange works by the same author alphabetically by title. The words *A, An,* and *The* are ignored in alphabetizing by title.

> Mortenson, Greg, and Greg Oliver Relin, *Three Cups of Tea.* New York:
> Penguin Books, 2007. Print.

Book by Two or More Authors

For a book with two or more authors, give all the authors' names but reverse only the first author's name.

> Tumulty, Karen. "Maxed-Out Moms." *Time.* 29 Sept. 2008: 42–44. Print.

Magazine Article

> Wilson, Craig. "The Key to Saving Money: Just Don't Spend It." *USA Today.*
> 6 Aug. 2008: D1. Print.

Newspaper Article

The final letter and number refer to page 1 of section D. If the article is not printed on consecutive pages, simply list the first page followed by a plus sign ("+"). In that case, the above example would read "D1+").

> "Equality's Winding Path." Editorial. *New York Times.* 6 Nov. 2008: A28. Print.

Editorial

List an editorial as you would any signed or unsigned article, but indicate the nature of the piece by adding *Editorial* after the article's title.

> Andrews, Elmer. "The Gift and the Craft: An Approach to the Poetry of
> Seamus Heaney." *Twentieth Century Literature* 31.4 (1985): 368–369. Print.

Article in a Professional Journal

> Dunne, Dominick. "Nightmare on Elm Drir Schecter Ed. New York: Library of
> America, 2008. 737. Print.

Selection in an Edited Collection

> Schaefer, Richard. *Sociology: A Brief Introduction.* 7th ed. New York: McGraw
> Hill College, 2008. Print.

Revised or Later Edition

The abbreviations *Rev. ed., 2nd ed., 3rd ed.,* and so on, are placed right after the title.

Chapter or Section in a Book by One Author

> Clinton, Bill. "Model Gifts." *Giving.* New York: Alfred A. Knopf, 2007. 116–136.

Pamphlet	*Funding Your Education, 2007–2008.* Washington: Dept. of Education Office of Federal Student Aid, 2007. Print.
Television Program	"Following the Trail of Toxic E-Waste." *60 Minutes.* Report. Scott Pelle. CBS. 9 Nov. 2008. Television.
Film	*High School Musical 3: Senior Year.* Dir. Kenny Orts. Walt Disney Pictures, 2008. Film.
Sound Recording	Janet Jackson. "Feedback." *Discipline.* Island Def Jam Music Group, 2008. LP.
DVD	"UFOs—Seeing is Believing." *Primetime* Narr. David Mu, ABC, WABC, New York. 16 September 2008. DVD. ABC/2008. DVD.
Personal Interview	Firbank, Matthew. Personal interview. 14 July 2009.
Article in an Online Magazine	Stone, Daniel. "Six Worst Kid Health Habits." *Newsweek.com.* 3 April 2008. 12 Oct. 2008.

The first date (3 April 2008) refers to the issue of the publication in which the article appeared; the second date (12 Oct. 2008) refers to the day when the student researcher accessed the source.

Article in an Online Web Site	"Sunbathing Spiders." *Urban Legends and Superstitions.* 2008. 17 Sept. 2008

The first date (2008) refers to when the material was electronically published, updated, or posted; the second date (17 Sept. 2008) refers to when the student researcher accessed the source.

Article in a Reference Database	Costa, Stefano. "Music in Dreams and the Emergence of the Self." *Journal of American Psychology* 54.1 (2009): 81–83. *Academic Search Premier.* Web. 3 Mar. 2009.

The first date (2009) refers to when the material was electronically published, updated, or posted; the second date (3 Mar. 2009) refers to when the student researcher accessed the source.

Electronic Mail (E-mail) Posting	Graham, Vanessa. "Re: Teenager Problems." Message to Sonya Philips. 12 Apr. 2004. E-mail

Activity 3

On a separate sheet of paper, convert the information in each of the following into the correct form for a list of "Works Cited." Use the appropriate model above as a guide.

1. A book by David Carr called *The Longest Trip Home* and published in New York by HarperCollins in 2008.

2. An article by Julie Appleby titled "Drug Costs for Seniors Growing" on page 1A of the November 12, 2008 issue of *USA Today*.

3. A book by Michael W. Passer and Ronald E. Smith titled *Psychology: The Science of Mind and Behavior* and published in a second edition by McGraw-Hill in New York in 2007.

4. An article by Mark Miller titled "Parting with a Pet" found on May 16, 2007, in the October 8, 2007, issue of *Newsweek Online*.

5. An article titled "Depression in Teenagers" found on April 24, 2007, on the Web site titled *Troubled Teens* which is sponsored by the Aspen Education Group.

Model Paper

While the *MLA Handbook* does not require a title page or an outline for a paper, your instructor may ask you to include one or both. Here is a model title page.

Model Title Page

Successful Families:

Fighting for Their Kids

by

Sonya Philips

English 101

Professor Lessing

5 May 2009

The title should begin about one-third of the way down the page. Center the title. Double-space the lines of the title and your name. Also center and double-space the instructor's name and the date.

Papers written in MLA style use the simple format shown below. There is no title page or outline.

Model First Page of MLA-Style Paper

1/2 inch

Philips 1

1 inch

Sonya Philips
Professor Lessing
English 101
5 May 2007

Successful Families: Fighting for Their Kids

Double-space lines. Leave a one-inch margin on all sides.

It's a terrible time to be a teenager, or even a teenager's parent. That message is everywhere. Television, magazines, and newspapers are all full of frightening stories about teenagers and families. They say that America's families are falling apart, that kids don't care about anything, and that parents have trouble doing anything. . . .

Use this format if your instructor asks you to submit an outline of your paper.

Model Outline Page

Philips i

After the title page, number all pages in the upper-right corner, a half inch from the top. Place your name before the page number. Use small roman numerals on outline pages. Use arabic numerals on pages following the outline.

Outline

Thesis: Although these are difficult times to be raising teenagers, successful families are finding ways to cope with the challenges.

I.   Meeting the challenge of spending quality time together

   A. Barriers to spending quality time

      1.   Increased working hours

      2.   Rising divorce rates

      3.   Women in workforce

   B. Danger of lack of quality time

   C. Ways found to spend time together

      1.   Working less and scaling back lifestyle

      2.   Homeschooling

II. Meeting the challenge of creating sense of community

   A. Lack of traditional community ties

   B. Ways found to create sense of community

     1. Intentional communities

     2. Religious ties

III. Meeting the challenge of limiting the negative impact of media and technology

   A. Negative impact of media and technology

     1. Creation of environment without protection

     2. Flood of uncontrolled, inappropriate information

   B. Ways of controlling media and technology

     1. Banning TV

     2. Using technology in beneficial ways

The word *Outline* (without underlining or quotation marks) is centered one inch from the top. Double-space lines. Leave a one-inch margin on all sides.

Here is a full model paper. It assumes the writer has included a title page.

Philips 1

Successful Families: Fighting for Their Kids

It's a terrible time to be a teenager, or even a teenager's parent. That message is everywhere. Television, magazines, and newspapers are all full of frightening stories about teenagers and families. They say that America's families are falling apart, that kids don't care about anything, and that parents have trouble doing anything about it. Bookstores are full of disturbing titles like these: <u>Parenting Your Out-of-Control Teenager</u>, <u>Teenage Wasteland</u>, <u>Unhappy Teenagers</u>, and <u>Teen Torment</u>. These books describe teenage problems that include apathy, violence, suicide, sexual abuse, depression, loss of values, poor mental health, crime, gang involvement, and drug and alcohol addiction.

Double-space lines of the text. Leave a one-inch margin all the way around the page. Your name and the page number should be typed one-half inch from the top of the page.

Common knowledge is not documented.

This typical citation shows the source by giving the author's last name or (as here, if no author is provided) the title of the article (and if relevant, a page number). "Works Cited" then provides full information about the source.

Naturally, caring parents are worried by all this. Their worry showed in a 2005 national poll in which 76% of parents said that raising children was "a lot harder" than it was when they were growing up ("A Lot Easier Said"). But just as most popular TV shows don't give a realistic view of American teens, these frightening books and statistics do not provide a complete picture of what's going on in families today. The fact is that not all teens and families are lost and without values. While they struggle with problems in our culture like everyone else, successful families are doing what they've always done: finding ways to protect and nurture their children. They are fighting the battle for their families in three ways: by fighting against the loss of quality family time, by fighting against the loss of community, and by fighting against the influence of the media.

Thesis, followed by plan of development.

It's true that these days parents face more challenges than ever before when it comes to finding quality time to spend with their children. The economist Edward Wolff explains the loss of time:

Source is identified by name and area of expertise.

Direct quotations of five typed lines or more are indented ten spaces (or one inch) from the left margin. Quotation marks are not used.

Over a thirty-year time span, parental time has declined 13%. The time parents have available for their children has been squeezed by the rapid shift of mothers into the paid labor force, by escalating divorce rates and the subsequent abandonment of children by their fathers, and by an increase in the number of hours required on the job. The average worker is now at work 163 hours a year more than in 1969, which adds up to an extra month of work annually (qtd. in Hewlett and West 48).

As a result, more children are at home alone than ever before. And this situation does leave children vulnerable to getting into trouble. Richardson and others, in their study of five thousand eighth graders in California, found that children who were home alone after school were twice as likely to experiment with drugs and alcohol as children who had a parent (or another adult) home in the after-school hours.

The abbreviation *qtd.* means *quoted.* No comma is used between the author name and the page number.

But creative parents still come up with ways to be there for their kids. For some, it's been a matter of cutting back on working hours and living more simply. For example, in her book The Shelter of Each Other, Mary Pipher tells the story of a couple with three-year-old twin boys. Eduardo worked sixty-hour weeks at a factory. Sabrina supervised checkers at a Kmart, cared for the boys, and tried to watch over her mother, who had cancer. Money was tight, especially, since day care was expensive and the parents felt they had to keep the twins stylishly dressed and supplied with new toys. The parents were stressed over money problems, their lack of time together, and especially, having so little time with their boys. It bothered them that the twins had begun to cry when their parents picked them up at day care, as if they'd rather stay with the day care workers. Finally, Sabrina and Eduardo made a difficult decision. Sabrina quit her job, and the couple invited her mother (whose illness was in remission) to live with them. With three adults pooling their resources, Sabrina and Eduardo found that they could manage without Sabrina's salary. The family no longer ate out, and they gave up their cable TV. Their sons loved having their grandmother in the house. Sabrina was able to begin doing relaxed, fun projects with the boys. They planted a garden and built a sandbox together. Sabrina observed, "I learned I could get off the merry-go-round" (195). Other parents have gotten off the merry-go-round by working at home, even if it means earning less money than they had previously.

Some parents even homeschool their children as a way to be sure they have plenty of time together. Homeschooling used to be thought of as a choice made only by very religious people or back-to-nature radicals. Now, teaching children at home is much less unusual. It's estimated that as many as two million American children are being homeschooled. Harvard even has an admissions officer whose job it is to review applications from homeschooled kids. Parents who homeschool have different reasons, but

When citing a work in general, not part of a work, it is best to include the author's name in the text instead of using a parenthetical citation. No page number is needed, as the citation refers to the overall findings of the study.

Only the page number is needed, as the author has already been named in the text.

according to a cover story in Newsweek, "some . . . are looking for a way to reclaim family closeness in an increasingly fast-paced society. . . . Still others worry about unsavory influences in school—drugs, alcohol, sex, violence" (Kantrowitz and Wingert 66). Homeschooling is no guarantee that a child will resist those temptations, but some families do believe it's a great way to promote family closeness. One fifteen-year-old, homeschooled since kindergarten, explained why he liked the way he'd been raised and educated. He ended by saying, "Another way I'm different is that I love my family. One guy asked me if I'd been brainwashed. I think it's spooky that liking my family is considered crazy" (Pipher 103).

Many parents can't quit their jobs or teach their children at home. But some parents find a second way to nurture their children, through building community ties. They help their children develop a healthy sense of belonging by creating links with positive, constructive people and activities. In the past, community wasn't so hard to find. In The Way We Really Are, Stephanie Coontz writes, "Right up through the 1940s, ties of work, friendship, neighborhood, ethnicity, extended kin, and voluntary organizations were as important a source of identity for most Americans, and sometimes a more important source of obligation, than marriage and the nuclear family" (37). Even when today's parents were teenagers, neighborhoods were places where kids felt a sense of belonging and responsibility. But today "parents . . . mourn the disappearance of neighborhoods where a web of relatives and friends kept a close eye on everyone's kids. And they worry their own children grow up isolated, knowing more about the cast of Friends than the people in surrounding homes" (Donahue D1).

One way that some families are trying to build old-fashioned community is through "intentional community," or "cohousing." Begun in Denmark in 1972, the cohousing movement is modeled after the traditional village. It brings together a number of families who live in separate houses but share some common space. For instance, families

Ellipsis points show where the student has omitted material from the original source.

The quoted material is not capitalized because the student has blended it into a sentence with an introductory phrase.

might share central meeting rooms, dining areas, gardens, day care, workshops, or office space. They might own tools and lawn mowers together, rather than each household having its own. The point is that they treat their neighbors as extended family, not as strangers. As described by the online site Cohousing.org, cohousing is "a type of collaborative housing that attempts to overcome the alienation of modern subdivisions in which no one knows their neighbors, and there is no sense of community." In its 2007 database, the Intentional Communities Web site estimates that over one thousand such communities exist in North America.

Other families turn to religion as a source of community. Michael Medved and Diane Medved, authors of Saving Childhood, are raising their family in a religious Jewish home. Their children attend Jewish schools, go to synagogue, and follow religious customs. They frequently visit, eat, play with, and are cared for by neighboring Jewish families. The Medveds believe their family is stronger because of their belief "in planting roots—in your home, in your family, in your community. That involves making a commitment, making an investment both physically and emotionally, in your surroundings" (200). Other religious traditions offer families a similar sense of community, purpose, and belonging. Marcus and Tracy Glover are members of the Nation of Islam. They credit the Nation with making their marriage and family strong and breaking a three-generation cycle of single motherhood (Hewlett and West 201–02).

A third way that families are fighting to protect their children is by controlling the impact of the media and technology. Hewlett and West and Pipher use similar words to describe this impact. As they describe growing up today, Hewlett and West write about children living "without a skin" (xiii), and Pipher writes about "houses without walls" (12). These authors mean that today—unlike in the old days, when children were protected from the outside world while they were in their homes—the home offers

Cited material extends from one page to another, so both page numbers are given.

little protection. Even in their own living rooms, all children have to do is to turn on a TV, radio, or computer to be hit with a flood of violence, sick humor, and often weird sexuality. Children are growing up watching shows like The Osbournes, a program that celebrated two spoiled, foul-mouthed children and their father—a burned-out rock star slowed by years of carefree drug abuse. A recent article in Science magazine offered the most damning link yet between TV watching and antisocial behavior. Reporting on the results of its seventeen-year study that followed viewers from youth to adulthood, Science found that the more television a teen watched, the higher the chances he or she would commit violent acts later in life. Of kids who watched an hour or less of TV a day, fewer than 6% of teens went on to commit assaults, robberies, or other violent acts as adults. But nearly 28% of teens who watched TV three or more hours a day did commit crimes of violence (Anderson and Bushman 2377–79). Sadly, many parents seem to have given up even trying to protect their growing kids against the flood of televised garbage. They are like the mother quoted in USA Today as saying, "How can I fight five hundred channels on TV?" (Donahue D1).

Fortunately, some parents are still insisting on control over the information and entertainment that comes into their homes. Some subscribe to "The Television Project," an online educational organization that helps parents "understand how television affects their families and community and proposes alternatives that foster positive emotional, cognitive and spiritual development within families and communities." Others ban TV entirely from their homes. More try to find a way to use TV and other electronics as helpful tools but not allow them to dominate their homes. One family in Nebraska, the Millers, who homeschool their children, described to Mary Pipher their attitude toward TV. They hadn't owned a TV for years, but they bought one so that they could watch the Olympics. The set is now stored in a closet unless a program is on that the family agrees is worthwhile. Some programs the Millers have enjoyed together include the World Cup soccer games, the TV drama Sarah Plain and Tall, and an educational TV course in sign language. Pipher was impressed by the Miller children, and she thought their limited exposure to TV was one reason why. In her words,

> Calm, happy children and relaxed, confident parents are so rare today. Probably most notable were the long attention spans of the children and their willingness to sit and listen to the grown-ups talk. The family had a manageable amount of information to deal with. They weren't stressed by more information than they could assimilate. The kids weren't overstimulated and edgy. Nor were they sexualized in the way most kids now are. (107)

Pipher's words describe children raised by parents who won't give in to the idea that their children are lost. Such parents structure ways to be present in the home, build family ties to a community, and control the impact of the media in their homes. Through their efforts, they succeed in raising nurtured, grounded, successful children. Such parents acknowledge the challenges of raising kids in today's America, but they are up to the job.

The conclusion provides a summary and restates the thesis.

Works Cited

Works cited should be double-spaced. Titles of books, magazines, and the like should be underlined.

"A Lot Easier Said Than Done: Parents Talk about Raising Children in Today's America." *Public Agenda*. Oct 2005. 4 Oct. 2007.

Anderson, Craig A., and Brad J. Bushman. "The Effects of Media Violence on Society." *Science* 29 Mar. 2002: 2377–79. Print.

Coontz, Stephanie. *The Way We Really Are*. New York: Basic Books, 1997. Print.

Donahue, Deirdre. "Struggling to Raise Good Kids in Toxic Times." *USA Today* 1 Oct. 1998: D1+.Print.

Hewlett, Sylvia Ann, and Cornel West. *The War Against Parents*. Boston: Houghton Mifflin, 1998. Print.

Include the date you accessed a Web source—in the first case, 4 October 2007.

Several of these sources—*Public Agenda, Intentional Communities,* and the *Television Project*—are online. By going online and typing the letters after "www." in each citation, you can access any of the sources.

The Intentional Communities Home Page. Fellowship of Intentional Communities. 2 Sept. 2007.

Kantrowitz, Barbara, and Pat Wingert. "Learning at Home: Does It Pass the Test?" *Newsweek* 5 Oct. 1998: 64–70. Print.

Medved, Michael, and Diane Medved. *Saving Childhood.* New York: Putnam, 1996. Print.

Pipher, Mary. *The Shelter of Each Other.* New York: Putnam, 1996. Print.

The Television Project Home Page. The Television Project. *n. d.* Web. 2 Feb. 2007.

"What Is Cohousing?" *Cohousing.* The Cohousing Association of the United States. 10 Sept. 2006. Web. 2 Feb. 2007.

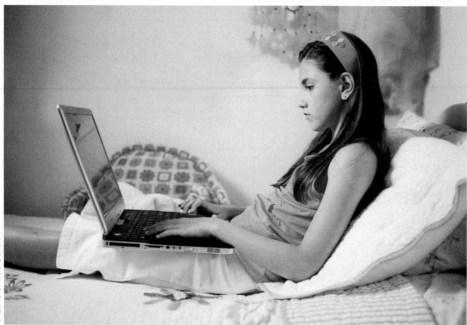

© Zave Smith/Corbis

Although the student writer of the research paper emphasized the impact of TV on children, she referred to the computer as another source of "violence, sick humor, and often weird sexuality." In your opinion, which do you feel is more dangerous for children when unsupervised, the computer or the TV? Why?

Handbook of Sentence Skills

PART 4

LOVER'S LEAP

1827 ———•——— 1973

The poetic lines inscribed on the boulder below is a replica of those carved in 1827 by Thomas W. Farrar.
Thomas W. Farrar was the Founder and first Grand Master of the Masonic Lodge in Alabama 1821-22-24. This historical site donated to the public by Jonas W. Schwab in 1935. The work was done and fence provided by Thomas W. Martin and George B. Ward.

ERECTED BY SHADES CREST GARDEN CLUB, JEFFERSON COUNTY, BIRMINGHAM, ALABAMA
APRIL 18, 1973

© Natalie Hummel

How could you change this sign's wording to make it grammatically correct? What specific errors have been made?

PREVIEW

1 Grammar

2 Mechanics

3 Punctuation

4 Word Use

PREVIEW

CHAPTER 23
Subjects and Verbs

CHAPTER 24
Fragments

CHAPTER 25
Run-Ons

CHAPTER 26
Regular and
Irregular Verbs

CHAPTER 27
Subject-Verb
Agreement

CHAPTER 28
Additional Information
about Verbs

CHAPTER 29
Pronoun Agreement
and Reference

CHAPTER 30
Pronoun Types

CHAPTER 31
Adjectives and
Adverbs

CHAPTER 32
Misplaced Modifiers

CHAPTER 33
Dangling Modifiers

© Bill Aron/PhotoEdit

Can you find any sentence-skills errors in the sign pictured above? What are they?

23

Subjects and Verbs

This chapter will explain two of the basic building blocks of English sentences: subjects and verbs.

KEY TERMS

auxiliary verbs: verbs that work with the main verb to make up the complete verb in a sentence; also called helping verbs. Example: *The woman is working.* (Auxiliary verb: working)

linking verbs: verbs that help describe a subject by connecting it to another word. Example: *The man is handsome.* (Linking verb: is)

preposition: one of a group of words that precede a noun or pronoun and indicate direction, position, placement, duration, or another kind of connection to the other words in the sentence. Examples: *about, above, through, under, with.*

subject: who or what a sentence speaks about; usually a noun or pronoun that acts, is acted upon, or is described. Example: *The boy cries.* (Subject: boy)

verb: what the sentence says about the subject; a word that shows what a subject does or that helps describe the subject by linking it to an adjective. Example: *The boy cries.* (Verb: cries)

Every sentence has a subject and a verb. Who or what the sentence speaks about is called the *subject;* what the sentence says about the subject is the *verb.* In the following sentences, the subject is underlined once; the verb is underlined twice.

The boy cried.
That fish stinks.
Many people applied for the job.
The show is a documentary.

www.mhhe.com/lan

A Simple Way to Find a Subject

If you ask *who* or *what* the sentence is about, your answer will be the subject.

> *Who* is the first sentence about? The <u>boy</u>
>
> *What* is the second sentence about? That <u>fish</u>
>
> *Who* is the third sentence about? Many <u>people</u>
>
> *What* is the fourth sentence about? The <u>show</u>

A Simple Way to Find a Verb

If you ask what the sentence *says about* the subject, your answer will be the verb.

> What does the first sentence *say about* the boy? He <u>cried</u>.
>
> What does the second sentence *say about* the fish? It <u>stinks</u>.
>
> What does the third sentence *say about* the people? They <u>applied</u>.
>
> What does the fourth sentence *say about* the show? It <u>is</u> a documentary.

A second way to find the verb is to put *I, you, we, he, she, it,* or *they* in front of the word you think is a verb. If the result makes sense, you have a verb. For example, you could put *he* in front of *cried* in the first sentence, with the result, *he cried,* making sense. Thus, you know that *cried* is a verb.

Also remember that most verbs show action. In the sentences above, there are three action verbs: *cried, smells,* and *applied.* Other verbs, known as *linking verbs,* do not show action; they give information about the subject. In "The show is a documentary," the linking verb *is* joins the subject (*show*) with a word that identifies or describes it (*documentary*). Other common linking verbs include *am, are, was, were, feel, appear,* and *become.*

Activity

1

In each of the following sentences, draw one line under the subject and two lines under the verb.

1. The ripening <u>tomatoes</u> glistened on the sunny windowsill.

2. <u>Acupuncture</u> <u>reduces</u> the pain of my headaches.

3. <u>Elena</u> <u>twisted</u> a strand of hair around her fingers.

4. My <u>brother</u> <u>built</u> his bookshelves from cinder blocks and wood planks.

5. A <u>jackrabbit</u> <u>bounds</u> up to fifteen feet in one leap.

6. The singer's diamond <u>earrings</u> <u>sparkled</u> in the spotlight.

7. Walt <u>Disney</u> <u>created</u> the cartoon character Mickey Mouse.

8. The Federal Bureau of Investigation (FBI) pursues violators of federal laws.

9. Ferdinand and Isabella of Spain sponsored Columbus's voyages.

10. On April 9, 1865, General Robert E. Lee surrendered to General Ulysses S. Grant.

More about Subjects and Verbs

www.mhhe.com/langan

1. A sentence may have more than one verb, more than one subject, or several subjects and verbs.

   The engine coughed and sputtered.
   Broken glass and empty cans littered the parking lot.
   Marta, Nilsa, and Robert met after class and headed downtown.

2. The subject of the sentence never appears within a prepositional phrase. A *prepositional phrase* is simply a group of words that begins with a preposition. Following is a list of common prepositions.

Prepositions

about	before	by	inside	over
above	behind	during	into	through
across	below	except	like	to
among	beneath	for	of	toward
around	beside	from	off	under
at	between	in	on, onto	with

Crossing out prepositional phrases will help you find the sentence's subject or subjects.

A stream of cold air seeps in through the space below the door.
Specks of dust dance gently in a ray of sunlight.
The amber lights on its sides outlined the tractor-trailer in the hazy dusk.
Members of the club are entitled to use the exercise room.
The golden rays of the May sun reflect on the crystal-clear waters of the icy lake.

3. Many verbs consist of *helping, or auxiliary,* verbs, as seen here in several forms of the verb *work*.

Forms of *work*

work	worked	should work
works	were working	will be working
does work	have worked	can work
is working	had been working	could be working

---

4. Words like *not, just, never, only,* and *always* are not part of the verb, although they may appear within the verb.

   Ruby has never liked cold weather.

   Our boss will not be singing with the choir this year.

   The intersection has not always been this dangerous.

5. A verb preceded by *to* is never the verb of a sentence.

   At night, my son likes to read under the covers.

   Evelyn decided to separate from her husband.

6. An *-ing* word by itself is never the verb of a sentence. (It may be part of the verb, but it must have a helping verb in front of it.) The following is *not* a sentence, because the verb is not complete:

   They going on a trip this weekend.

   This *is* a sentence:

   They are going on a trip this weekend.

Activity

2

Draw a single line under subjects and a double line under verbs. Cross out prepositional phrases as necessary to find the subjects.

1. A large segment of the population supports the new legislation.

2. Two of the films we chose to write about were first released in the 1970s.

3. After more than 2,000 years, some Roman aqueducts are still supplying water to large European cities.

4. Every plant in the dim room bent toward the small window.

5. A glaring headline about the conviction of a local congressman attracted my attention.

6. The novels of John Steinbeck portray the lives of the poor and powerless.

7. The battery tester's tiny red lights suddenly started to flicker.

8. A neighbor of mine does all her work at home and e-mails it to her office.

9. The jar of peppercorns tumbled from the spice shelf and shattered on the floor.

10. A memorial of beautifully sculpted granite stands as tribute to Abraham Lincoln, our 16th president.

Review Test   1

Draw a single line under subjects and a double line under verbs. Cross out prepositional phrases as necessary to find the subjects.

1. Besides winning a Nobel Prize for physics (1903), Marie Curie won a second Noble Prize in chemistry (1911).

2. Like human mothers, sheep and goat mothers develop close bonds with their babies.

3. Before class, Antonietta and Jorge rushed to the coffee machine in the hall.

4. Michelangelo, who spent four years painting the ceiling of the Vatican's Sistine Chapel, was also a great sculptor.

5. In 1954, the United States Supreme Court, in a landmark decision, disallowed segregation of the races in public schools.

6. Ancient Egyptians were branding cattle more than four thousand years ago.

7. Dogs and cats crowded the veterinarian's office on Monday morning.

8. The driver abruptly halted her Jeep and backed up toward a narrow parking place.

9. During the American Revolution, some brides rejected white wedding gowns and wore red as a symbol of rebellion.

10. To spur economic growth, President, John F. Kennedy lowered federal income taxes.

Review Test   2

Write five complete sentences that contain prepositional phrases that come between the subject and the verb. Remember that prepositional phrases begin with words such as *with, to, in, into, about,* and *for.* Then, draw a single line under the subject and a double line under the verb. Finally, draw a line through the prepositional phrase.

24

Fragments

This chapter will explain how to avoid the most common types of fragments. A fragment is a word group that lacks a subject or a verb and/or one that does not express a complete thought.

FRAGMENT:

Whenever I go to school.

"Whenever," a dependent word, cannot introduce a complete thought, so it cannot stand alone.

CORRECT SENTENCE:

Whenever I go to school, I take the bus.

The fragment introduces a complete thought.

Every sentence must have a subject and a verb and must express a complete thought. A word group that lacks a subject or a verb and fails to express a complete thought is a *fragment*. Here are the most common types of fragments:

1. Dependent-word fragments
2. *-ing* fragments
3. Added-detail fragments
4. Missing-subject fragments

Dependent-Word Fragments

Some word groups that begin with *dependent words* are fragments. When you start a sentence with a dependent word, be careful not to create a fragment.

www.mhhe.com/langan

Dependent Words		
after	if, even if	when, whenever
although	in order that	where, wherever
as	since	whether
		(continued)

because	that, so that	which, whichever
before	unless	while
even though	until	who, whom, whose
how	what, whatever	

Below, the word group beginning with *after* is a fragment:

After I cashed my paycheck. I treated myself to dinner.

A dependent statement—which begins with a dependent word like *after*—cannot stand alone; it is a "fragment". It depends on another statement to complete the thought. *After I cashed my paycheck* leaves us hanging. We want to know what happened *after* the writer cashed the check.

To correct the fragment, simply complete the thought:

After I cashed my paycheck, I treated myself to dinner.

As you can see, *dependent statements by themselves are fragments*. They must be attached to a statement that makes sense standing alone.

I won't leave the house. Until I hear from you.

Rick finally picked up the socks. That he had thrown on the floor days ago.

Until I hear from you is a fragment; it does not make sense standing by itself. We want to know *what cannot happen* until I hear from you. Likewise, *That he had thrown on the floor . . .* is not a complete thought. What does *that* refer to?

How to Correct a Dependent-Word Fragment

Often, you correct a dependent-word fragment by attaching it to the sentence that comes after it or to the one that comes before it.

After I cashed my paycheck, I treated myself to dinner.

(The fragment has been attached to the sentence that comes after it.)

Rick finally picked up the socks that he had thrown on the floor days ago.

(The fragment has been attached to the sentence that comes before it.)

You can also connect a dependent-word fragment by removing the dependent word and rewriting the sentence:

I cashed my paycheck and then treated myself to dinner.

I will wait to hear from you.

He had thrown them on the floor days ago.

TIPS

a. Use a comma if a dependent-word group comes at the beginning of a sentence, but not generally if it comes at the *end* of a sentence.

   Comma: After I cashed my paycheck, I treated myself to dinner.

   No comma: I won't leave the house until I hear from you.

b. Sometimes *who, that, which,* or *where* appear not at the very start but near the start of a word group. A fragment can result:

   I drove slowly past the old brick house. The place where I grew up.

   The place where I grew up is not a complete thought. We want to know in the same statement *where was the place?* To correct the fragment attach it to the sentence that came before:

   I drove slowly past the old brick house, the place where I grew up.

Turn each of the following dependent-word groups into a sentence by adding a complete thought. Use a comma after the dependent-word group if a dependent word starts the sentence. Note the examples.

Activity

1

EXAMPLES

Although I felt miserable

Although I felt miserable, I tried to smile for the photographer.

The man who found my wallet

The man who found my wallet returned it the next day.

1. If I don't get a raise soon

   If I don't get a raise soon then
   I will late in class.

2. After visiting the museum

   after visiting the museum, then going to
   Thailand restaurant in the D.C

3. Because I had just gotten paid

   Because I had just gotten paid,

   _____

4. Until the new mall opened

until the new mall opend, I will send a box latter to India.

5. The restaurant that we tried

The restaurant that we tried to order but I waiting for a service who ont show up

Activity

2

Underline the dependent-word fragment in each item. Then rewrite the items, correcting each fragment by attaching it to the sentence that comes before or the sentence that comes after it—whichever sounds more natural. Use a comma after the dependent-word group if it starts the sentence.

1. Whenever I spray deodorant. My cat arches her back. She thinks she is hearing a hissing enemy.

   Whenever I spray deodorant, my cat arches her back. She thinks she is hearing a hissing enemy

2. Philadelphia was originally a Quaker colony. That was founded by William Penn in 1681. By 1777, it had become the capital of the new United States.

   _____

   _____

3. If Kim takes too long saying good-bye to her boyfriend, Her father will start flicking the porch light. Then he will come out with a flashlight.

   _____

   _____

4. Scientists are studying mummified remains, That are thousands of years old, Most of the people were killed by parasites.

   _____

   _____

5. Roman law was first recorded in 450 B.C. in what was known as the "twelve tablets." It lasted for many centuries, Until the fall of the eastern Roman Empire nearly 2,000 years later.

   _____

   _____

-ing and to Fragments

When an *-ing* word appears at or near the start of a word group, a fragment may result. Such fragments often lack a subject and part of the verb. In the items on the following page, underline the word groups that contain *-ing* words. Each is a fragment.

1. Ellen walked all over the neighborhood yesterday. Trying to find her dog Bo. Several people claimed they had seen him only hours before.

2. We sat back to watch the movie. Not expecting anything special. To our surprise, we clapped, cheered, and cried for the next two hours.

3. I telephoned the balloon store. It being the day before our wedding anniversary. I knew my wife would be surprised to receive a dozen heart-shaped balloons.

People sometimes write *-ing* fragments because they think that the subject of one sentence will work for the next word group as well. Thus, in item 1 the writer thinks that the subject *Ellen* in the opening sentence will also serve as the subject for *Trying to find her dog Bo.* But the subject must be in the same sentence.

How to Correct -ing Fragments

1. Attach the fragment to the sentence that comes before it or the sentence that comes after it, whichever makes sense. Item 1 could read "Ellen walked all over the neighborhood yesterday trying to find her dog Bo."

2. Add a subject and change the *-ing* verb part to the correct form of the verb. Item 2 could read "We didn't expect anything special."

3. Change *being* to the correct form of the verb be *(am, are, is, was, were)*. Item 3 could read "It was the day before our wedding anniversary."

How to Correct to Fragments

When *to* appears at or near the start of a word group, a fragment sometimes results:

At the Chinese restaurant, Tim used chopsticks. To impress his date. He spent one hour eating a small bowl of rice.

The second word group is a fragment and can be corrected by adding it to the preceding sentence:

At the Chinese restaurant, Tim used chopsticks to impress his date.

www.mhhe.com/langan

Activity **3**	Underline the *-ing* fragment in each of the following items. Then correct the item by using the method described in parentheses.

EXAMPLE

<u>Including the Arctic Ocean and parts of Canada, the United States, and other countries.</u> The Arctic Circle is the area that surrounds the Earth's North Pole. (Add the fragment to the sentence that comes after it.)

<u>Including the Arctic Ocean and parts of Canada, the United States, and other</u>

<u>countries, the Arctic Circle is the area that surrounds the Earth's North Pole.</u>

1. Ramses II ruled over Egypt from 1279 to 1212 B.C. Making his country stronger than ever before, He was both ambitious and intelligent.
   (Add the fragment to the preceding sentence.)

   _____

   _____

2. A noisy fire truck suddenly raced down the street, Coming to a stop at my house. My home security system had sent a false alarm.
   (Correct the fragment by adding the subject *it* and changing *coming* to the proper form of the verb, *came*.)

   _____

   _____

3. I couldn't find any books on Egyptian history in the library. They had all been checked out. The reason for this being that a research paper had just been assigned to students in an ancient history class.
   (Correct the fragment by changing *being* to the proper form of the verb, *was*.)

   _____

   _____

Activity **4**	Underline the *-ing* or *to* fragment in each item. Then rewrite each item, correcting the fragment by using one of the three methods described above.

1. Looking at the worm on the table. Shelby groaned. She knew she wouldn't like what the biology teacher said next.

   _____

   _____

2. I put a box of baking soda in the freezer. To get rid of the musty smell. However, my ice cubes still taste like old socks.

_____

_____

3. Searching for the right filament for his incandescent light bulb. Thomas Edison (1847–1931) found that a strip of carbonized bamboo could glow for 1,200 hours.

_____

_____

4. Jerome sat quietly at his desk. Fantasizing about the upcoming weekend. He might meet the girl of his dreams at Saturday night's party.

_____

_____

5. To get his company to grow rapidly. Harvey Firestone launched a vigorous marketing compaign. In 1906, he sold 2,000 sets of tires to the Ford Motor Company.

_____

_____

Added-Detail Fragments

Added-detail fragments lack a subject and a verb. They often begin with one of the following words:

also	especially	except	for example
like	including	such as	

Underline the one added-detail fragment in each of the following items:

1. Before a race, I eat starchy foods. Such as bread and spaghetti. The carbohydrates provide quick energy.
2. Bob is taking a night course in auto mechanics. Also, one in plumbing. He wants to save money on household repairs.
3. My son keeps several pets in his room. Including hamsters and mice.

People often write added-detail fragments for much the same reason they write -*ing* fragments. They think the subject and verb in one sentence will serve for the next word group. But the subject and verb must be in *each* word group.

www.mhhe.com/langan

How to Correct Added-Detail Fragments

1. Attach the fragment to the complete thought that precedes it. Item 1 could read "Before a race, I eat starchy foods such as bread and spaghetti."

2. Add a subject and a verb to the fragment to make it a complete sentence. Item 2 could read "Bob is taking a night course in auto mechanics. Also, he is taking one in plumbing."

3. Insert the fragment within the preceding sentence. Item 3 could read "My son keeps several pets, including hamsters and mice, in his room."

Activity

5

Underline the fragment in each of the following items. Then make it a sentence by rewriting it, using the method described in parentheses.

EXAMPLE

My mother likes watching daytime television shows. Especially old movies and soap operas. She says that daytime television is less violent. (Add the fragment to the preceding sentence.)

My mother likes watching daytime television shows, especially old movies and

soap operas.

1. Luis works evenings in a video store. He enjoys the fringe benefits. For example, seeing the new movies first.

    (Correct the fragment by adding the subject and verb *he sees*.)

    _____

    _____

2. Henry Ford (1863–1947) is credited with the invention of the assembly line, not the automobile. Several nineteenth-century inventors had designed self-propelled vehicles. Like the one that ran on high-pressure steam.

    (Attach the fragment to the preceding sentence.)

    _____

    _____

3. Electronic devices keep getting smaller. Such as video cameras and cell phones. Some are so tiny they look like toys.

    (Correct the fragment by inserting it in the preceding sentence.)

    _____

    _____

Underline the added-detail fragment in each item. Then rewrite to correct the fragment. Use one of the three methods described on the previous page.

1. Left-handed students face problems. For example, right-handed desks. Spiral notebooks can also be uncomfortable to use.

   _____

   _____

2. Some European countries remained neutral during World War II. Such as Switzerland and Portugal. Most South American countries refused to take sides as well.

   _____

   _____

3. Hundreds of moths were swarming around the stadium lights. Like large flecks of snow. However, I knew they couldn't be snow—it was eighty degrees outside.

   _____

   _____

4. Trevor buys and sells paper collectors' items. For instance, comic books and movie posters. He sets up a display at local flea markets and carnivals.

   _____

   _____

5. I know why I had to learn certain subjects in high school. Such as American history. Becoming a responsible citizen requires a knowledge of our country's past and of its system of government.

   _____

   _____

Missing-Subject Fragments

In each item below, underline the word group in which the subject is missing:

1. Alicia loved getting wedding presents. But hated writing thank-you notes.
2. Mickey has orange soda and potato chips for breakfast. Then eats more junk food, like root beer and cookies, for lunch.

www.mhhe.com/langan

How to Correct Missing-Subject Fragments

1. Attach the fragment to the preceding sentence. Item 1 could read "Alicia loved getting wedding presents but hated writing thank-you notes."

2. Add a subject (which can often be a pronoun standing for the subject in the preceding sentence). Item 2 could read "Then he eats more junk food, like root beer and cookies, for lunch."

Underline the missing-subject fragment in each item. Then rewrite that part of the item needed to correct the fragment. Use one of the two methods of correction described above.

1. Every other day, Kara runs two miles. Then does fifty sit-ups. She hasn't lost weight, but she looks trimmer and more muscular.

   _____

   _____

2. I like all kinds of fresh pizza. But refuse to eat frozen pizza. The sauce is always dried out, and the crust tastes like leather.

   _____

   _____

3. Many people are allergic to seafood. They break out in hives when they eat it. And can even have trouble breathing.

   _____

   _____

4. When we arrived in Chicago, we took a train from the airport to the center of the city. Then walked a few blocks to our hotel. The trip was easy.

   _____

   _____

5. Next fall, I plan to take a course in calculus. And to join the mathematics club. By the time the year is over, I will have decided whether to become a mathematics teacher.

   _____

   _____

A Review: How to Check for Sentence Fragments

1. Read your paper aloud from the *last* sentence to the *first*. You will be better able to see and hear whether each word group you read is a complete thought.

2. If you think a word group may be a fragment, ask yourself, Does this contain a subject and a verb and express a complete thought?

3. More specifically, be on the lookout for the most common fragments:

    *   Dependent-word fragments (starting with words like *after, because, since, when,* and *before*)

    *   *-ing* and *to* fragments (*-ing* and *to* at or near the start of a word group)

    *   Added-detail fragments (starting with words like *for example, such as, also,* and *especially*)

    *   Missing-subject fragments (a verb is present but not the subject)

Review Test   1

Each word group in the following student paragraph is numbered. In the space provided, write C if a word group is a complete sentence; write F if it is a fragment. You will find eight fragments in the paragraph.

_____   1. ¹I'm starting to think that there is no safe place left. ²To ride

_____   2. a bicycle. ³When I try to ride on the highway, to

_____   3. go school. ⁴I feel like a rabbit being pursued by predators.

_____   4. ⁵Drivers whip past me at high speeds. ⁶And try to see how

_____   5. close they can get to my bike without actually killing me.

_____   6. ⁷When they pull onto the shoulder of the road or make a

_____   7. right turn. ⁸Drivers completely ignore my vehicle. ⁹On city

_____   8. streets, I feel more like a cockroach than a rabbit. ¹⁰Drivers

_____   9. in the city despise bicycles. ¹¹Regardless of an approaching

_____   10. bike rider. ¹²Street-side car doors will unexpectedly open.

_____   11. ¹³Frustrated drivers who are stuck in traffic will make nasty

_____   12. comments. ¹⁴Or shout out obscene propositions. ¹⁵Even

_____ 13. pedestrians in the city show their disregard for me. ¹⁶While

_____ 14. jaywalking across the street. ¹⁷The pedestrian will treat

_____ 15. me, a law-abiding bicyclist, to a withering look of disdain.

_____ 16. ¹⁸Pedestrians may even cross my path deliberately. ¹⁹As if to

_____ 17. prove their higher position in the pecking order of the city

_____ 18. streets. ²⁰Today, bicycling can be hazardous to the rider's

_____ 19. health.

_____ 20.

Now (on separate paper) correct the fragments you have found. Attach the fragments to sentences that come before or after them or make whatever other change is needed to turn each fragment into a sentence.

Review Test   2

Underline the two fragments in each item below. Then make whatever changes are needed to turn the fragments into sentences.

EXAMPLE

Sharon was going to charge her new suit_x *b* But then decided to pay cash instead. She remembered her New Year's resolution_x *t* To cut down on her use of credit cards.

1. We both began to tire. As we passed the halfway mark in the race. But whenever I'd hear Reggie's footsteps behind me. I would pump my legs faster.

2. The American Southwest is home to several Native American nations. Such as the Navajo, the Apache, and the Pueblo. The East is the land of the Huron and Iroquois. Along with the Delaware and the Mohegan.

3. Punching all the buttons on his radio in sequence. Phil kept looking for a good song. He was in the mood to cruise down the highway. And sing at the top of his voice.

4. My children joke that we celebrate "Hanumas." With our Jewish neighbors. We share Hanukkah and Christmas activities. Including making potato pancakes at their house and decorating our tree.

5. Pop artists gained fame in the 1950s. Reacting to the more established art forms like expressionism, which preceded them. They portrayed common images from everyday life. Such as Coke bottles and soup cans.

6. Our landlord often invites her tenants to dinner. And allows them to use her washer and dryer. By doing such things. She has become known as the kindest person in our neighborhood.

7. The alley behind our house was flat. Except for a wide groove in the center. We used to sail paper boats down the groove. Whenever it rained hard enough to create a "river" there.

8. Don passed the computer school's aptitude test. Which qualifies him for nine months of training. Don kidded that anyone could be accepted. If he or she had $4,000.

Review Test   3

Turn each of the following word groups into a complete sentence.

EXAMPLES

With trembling hands

With trembling hands, I headed for the front of the classroom.

As the race wore on

Some runners dropped out as the race wore on.

1. After the storm passed

_____

2. Such as fresh fruits and vegetables

_____

3. During the mystery movie

_____

4. Because we have prepared so well for the exam

_____

5. Enrique, who works at his uncle's restaurant

   _____

6. Swimming across the lake

   _____

7. To enter the rare-book room

   _____

8. Hurrying to get dressed

   _____

9. Up in the attic

   _____

10. E-mailing his parents

    _____

25

Run-Ons

Run-ons are two complete thoughts that are run together with no adequate sign given to mark the break between them. In this text, the term "run-on" refers to both comma splices and fused sentences.

KEY TERMS

clause: a group of words having a subject and a verb.

comma splice: a comma incorrectly used to connect ("splice" together) two complete thoughts. Example:

Comma splice: *I go to school, my brother stays home.*

Correct sentences: *I go to school. My brother stays home.*

dependent clause: a group of words having a subject and a verb that does not express a complete thought and is not able to stand alone; also called a subordinate clause.

fused sentence: a run-on with no punctuation to mark the break between thoughts. Example:

Fused sentence: *I go to school my brother stays home.*

Correct sentences: *I go to school. My brother stays home.*

independent clause: a group of words having a subject and a verb that expresses a complete thought and is able to stand alone.

What Are Run-Ons?

A ***run-on*** consists of two complete thoughts run together without adequate punctuation to signal the break between them.* There are two types of run-ons: fused sentences and comma splices.

www.mhhe.com/langan

---

* Some instructors regard all run-ons as fused sentences. But for many other instructors, and for our purposes in this book, the term *run-on* applies equally to fused sentences and comma splices. The bottom line is that you do not want either fused sentences or comma splices in your writing.

    Some instructors refer to each complete thought in a run-on as an *independent clause.* A *clause* is simply a group of words having a subject and a verb. A clause may be *independent* (expressing a complete thought and able to stand alone) or *dependent* (not expressing a complete thought and not able to stand alone). Using this terminology, we'd say that a run-on is two independent clauses run together with no adequate sign given to mark the break between them.

Fused sentences have no punctuation to mark the break between the two thoughts.

> The bus stopped suddenly I found myself in an old man's lap.

> We heard a noise in the garage two birds had flown in through the open window.

www.mhhe.com/langan

Comma splices are the most common kind of run-on. Students sense that some kind of connection is needed between two thoughts, so they often put a comma at the dividing point. But the comma alone is *not sufficient*. A stronger, clearer mark is needed between the two complete thoughts.

> The bus stopped suddenly. I found myself in an old man's lap.

> We heard a noise in the garage; two birds had flown in through the open window.

A Warning—Words That Can Lead to Run-Ons People often write run-ons when the second complete thought begins with one of the following words:

I	we	there	now
you	they	this	then
he, she, it	that	next	

Be on the alert for run-ons whenever you use one of these words.

Three Ways to Correct Run-Ons

Here are three common methods of correcting a run-on:

1. Use a period and a capital letter to separate sentences:

   The bus stopped suddenly. I found myself in an old man's lap.

   We heard a noise in the garage. Two birds had flown in through the open window.

2. Use a comma and a joining word (*and, but, for, or, nor, so, yet*):

   The bus stopped suddenly, and I found myself in an old man's lap.

   We heard a noise in the garage, for two birds had flown in through the open window.

3. Use a semicolon to connect the two complete thoughts:

The bus stopped suddenly; I found myself in an old man's lap.

We heard a noise in the garage; two birds had flown in through the open window.

A fourth way to correct a run-on is to use *subordination*, which is discussed on page 488.

Method 1: Period and a Capital Letter

Use a period and a capital letter between two complete thoughts if the thoughts are not closely related or if another method would make the sentence too long.

In the following run-ons, locate the point at which one complete thought ends and another begins. Each is a fused sentence: two sentences joined with no punctuation. Reading a sentence aloud helps you hear where the break is. At this point, your voice may drop and pause. Correct each run-on by putting a period at the end of the first thought and a capital letter at the start of the next.

Activity

1

EXAMPLE

Bev's clock radio doesn't work anymore she spilled a glass of soda on it.

1. The men at the door claimed to have paving material left over from another job they wanted to pave our driveway for a "bargain price."

2. Linh, a paralegal who speaks Vietnamese, helps other people from her country write wills she assists others by going with them when they have to appear in court.

3. Vicky has a unique style of dressing she wore a man's tuxedo with a red bow tie to her cousin's wedding.

4. The flower is the most important part of a plant it contains the seeds that enable the plant to reproduce.

5. Humans have managed to adapt to any environment they can survive in Arctic wastes, tropical jungles, and barren deserts.

6. Galileo discovered that two solid objects of different weights fall at the same velocities he also made the first practical telescope for observing the heavens.

7. On our trip to Africa, we traveled to Mozambique and Zimbabwe then we went north to Zambia.

8. Squirrels like to jump from trees onto our roof their footsteps sound like ghosts running around our attic.

9. Today I didn't make good time driving to work every traffic light along the way was red.

10. Since I started using the Internet, I've sent hundreds of e-mails to my friends, I never write letters by hand anymore.

Method 2: Comma and a Joining Word

Another way of correcting a run-on is to use a comma and a joining word to connect the two complete thoughts. Joining words (also called *conjunctions*) include *and, but, for, or, nor, so,* and *yet.* Here are what the four most common joining words mean:

and   in addition

Teresa works full time for an accounting firm, and she takes evening classes.

(*And* means *in addition:* Teresa works full time for an accounting firm; *in addition,* she takes evening classes.)

but   however, on the other hand

I turned to the want ads, but I knew my dream job wouldn't be listed.

(*But* means *however:* I turned to the want ads; *however,* I knew my dream job wouldn't be listed.)

for   because

Lizards become sluggish at night, for they need the sun's warmth to maintain an active body temperature.

(*For* means *because:* Lizards become sluggish at night *because* they need the sun's warmth to maintain an active body temperature.)

so   as a result, therefore

The canoe touched bottom, so Dave pushed it toward deeper water.

(*So* means *as a result:* The canoe touched bottom; *as a result,* Dave pushed it toward deeper water.)

yet but, however, on the other hand

The defenders of the Alamo were vastly outnumbered, yet they refused to surrender.

(*Yet* means *however:* The defenders of the Alamo were vastly outnumbered; *however*, they refused to surrender.)

Insert the joining word *(and, but, for, so)* that logically connects the two thoughts in each sentence.

1. Napoleon may have been a brave general, ___but___ he was afraid of cats.

2. King MacBeth of Scotland (1040–1057) defeated King Duncan in battle, ___and___ he later became the title character in one of Shakespeare's tragedies.

3. The library had just closed, ___so___ I couldn't get any of the reserved books.

4. Maria Montessori is known as a pioneer of modern education, ___for___ she created a system that included "learning games" designed especially for children.

5. The tomato is very popular today, ___but___ it was once thought to be poisonous.

6. Elephants have no thumbs, ___and___ baby elephants suck their trunks.

7. Lonnie heard a noise and looked out the window, ___for___ the only thing there was his reflection.

8. Although I like most creatures, I am not fond of snakes, ___and___ I like spiders even less.

9. My sister wants to exercise more and use her car less, ___and___ she walks to the grocery store.

10. Barry spends hours every day on his computer, ___and___ he often has the television on at the same time.

Activity

2

Activity 3

Add a complete and closely related thought to go with each of the following statements. Use a comma and the indicated joining word when you write the second thought.

EXAMPLE

for I decided to leave school an hour early, _____

for I had a pounding headache. _____

but 1. The corner store is convenient _but it is into_ _____

_____

for 2. Leo attended night class _for test exam,_ _____

_____

and 3. Aisha studied for an hour before dinner _and wash hands_ _____

_____

so 4. Marcia was unable to take Prof. Samuelson's economics class _____

marcia was unable to take prof. so samoulson economic class

but 5. I had enough money to buy dinner _but I can't cook at home._

home.

Activity 4

Correct each run-on with either (1) a period and a capital letter or (2) a comma and a logical joining word. Do not use the same method of correction for every sentence.

Some of the run-ons are fused sentences (there is no punctuation between the two complete thoughts), and some are comma splices (there is only a comma between the two complete thoughts). One sentence is correct.

EXAMPLE

There was a strange odor in the house, ˢᵒBurt called the gas company immediately.

1. Oxygen is an odorless gas discovered independently by Joseph Priestly, and Karl Scheele, it is the third most abundant element in the universe.

2. Cockroaches adapt to any environment, they have even been found living inside nuclear reactors.

3. My dog was panting from the heat, I decided to wet him down with the garden hose.

4. Our science class is working on a weather project with students from Russia. We communicate by computer almost every day.

5. My grandfather is 85 years old, and he goes to work every day.

6. The bristles of the paintbrushes were very stiff, but soaking them in turpentine made them soft again.

7. Chen borrows cassettes from the library to listen to on the way to work, and some are music, and some are recordings of best-selling books.

8. Thomas Paine, who supported the American Revolution, was accused of treason in England. He escaped to France in 1793.

9. Today, there are only eight major planets in our solar system, for astronomers have downgraded Pluto to a dwarf planet.

10. I volunteered to run the Meals on Wheels service in our city. We deliver hot meals to sick or housebound people.

Method 3: Semicolon

A third way to correct a run-ons is to use a semicolon to mark the break between thoughts. When used to correct run-ons, a semicolon can be used alone or with a transitional word.

Semicolon Alone Unlike the comma alone, a semicolon can be used to connect the two complete thoughts:

> Lonnie heard a noise and looked out the window; the only thing he saw was his reflection.

> Lizards become sluggish at night; they need the sun's warmth to maintain an active body temperature.

> We knew a power failure had occurred; all the clocks were forty-seven minutes slow.

Using semicolons can add to sentence variety. For some people, however, the semicolon is a confusing punctuation mark. Keep in mind that if you are not comfortable using it, you can and should use one of the the first two methods of correcting run-ons.

Activity

5

Insert a semicolon where the break occurs between the two complete thoughts in each of the following sentences.

EXAMPLE

The plumber gave me an estimate of $260; I decided to repair the faucet myself.

1. The children stared at the artichokes on their plates they didn't know how to eat the strange vegetable.
2. Ecuador is in South America it is bordered by Colombia and Peru.
3. The Great Wall of China is immense it's the only human construction visible from the moon.
4. Elaine woke up at 3 A.M. to the smell of sizzling bacon her husband was having another insomnia attack.
5. Maya curled up under the covers she tried to get warm by grasping her icy feet with her chilly hands.
6. Honshu is the largest island in Japan it is also the most densely populated.
7. Ice had formed on the inside edge of our window Joey scratched a *J* in it with his finger.
8. Charles peered into the microscope he saw only his own eyelashes.
9. A man in a bear suit walked slowly down the street the children stopped their play to stare at him.
10. Ceylon was declared independent in 1948 later it became known as Sri Lanka.

Semicolon with a Transitional Word A semicolon can be used with a transitional word and a comma to join two complete thoughts.

I tried to cash my paycheck; however, I had forgotten to bring my identification.

Athletic shoes must fit perfectly; otherwise, wearers may injure their feet.

People use seventeen muscles when they smile; on the other hand, they use forty-three muscles when they frown.

Here is a list of transitional words, also known as *adverbial conjunctions*.

Transitional Word	Meaning
however	but
nevertheless	however
on the other hand	however

(continued)

instead	as a substitute
meanwhile	in the intervening time
otherwise	under other conditions
indeed	in fact
in addition	also, and
also	in addition
moreover	in addition
furthermore	in addition
as a result	thus, therefore
thus	as a result
consequently	as a result
therefore	as a result

For each sentence, choose a logical transitional word from the box above, and write it in the space provided. Use a semicolon *before* the connector and a comma *after* it.

Activity

6

EXAMPLE

I dread going to parties; __*however*__, my husband loves meeting new people.

1. Jackie suffers from migraine headaches ___*and*___ her doctor has advised her to avoid caffeine and alcohol.

2. Kryptonite is a fictitious substance that is supposed to be harmful to Superman ___*in fact*___ krypton is a real element, which was discovered in 1989.

3. I try to attend all my math classes ___*also*___ I'll get too far behind to pass the weekly quizzes.

4. We were asleep in our tent ___*meanwhile*___ two bears crept into our campsite and began searching for food.

5. The reporter was tough and experienced ___*while*___ even he was stunned by the tragic events.

A Note on Subordination

A fourth method of joining related thoughts is to use subordination. *Subordination* is a way of showing that one thought in a sentence is not as important as another thought. (Subordination is explained in full on pages 125–126.) Below are three earlier sentences, recast so that one idea is subordinated to (made less important than) the other idea. In each case, the subordinate (or less important) thought is underlined. Note that each subordinate clause begins with a dependent word.

<u>Because the library had just closed</u>, I couldn't get any of the reserved books.

<u>When the canoe touched bottom</u>, Dave pushed the craft toward deeper water.

I didn't make good time driving to work today <u>because every traffic light along the way was red.</u>

www.mhhe.com/langan

A Review: How to Check for Run-Ons

1. To see if a sentence is a run-on, read it aloud and listen for a break marking two complete thoughts. Your voice will probably drop and pause at the break.

2. To check an entire paper, read it aloud from the *last* sentence to the *first*. Doing so will help you hear and see each complete thought.

3. Be on the lookout for words that can lead to run-on sentences:

I	he, she, it	they	this	then	now
you	we	there	that	next	

4. Correct run-ons by using one of the following methods:

   Period and a capital letter

   Comma and a joining word *(and, but, for, or, nor, so, yet)*

   Semicolon, alone or with a transitional word

   Subordination

Review Test 1

Correct each run-on with either (1) a period and a capital letter or (2) a comma (if needed) and the joining word *and, but, for,* or *so.* Do not use the same method of correction for every sentence.

Some of the run-ons are fused sentences (there is no punctuation between the two complete thoughts), and some are comma splices (there is only a comma between the two complete thoughts). One sentence is correct.

1. Slovakia, a country in eastern Europe, was once ruled by the Austro-Hungarian Empire, It is now an independent country.

2. The children in the next car were making faces at other drivers. when I made a face back, they giggled and sank out of sight.

3. Chuck finished reading Mark Twain's *The Adventures of Huckleberry Finn*, then he began to take notes for his report.

4. The branches of the tree were bare, they made a dark feathery pattern against the orange-pink sunset.

5. Ernest hemingway drove an ambulance in World War I, he based the novel *A Farewell to Arms* on that experience.

6. Our class wanted to do something for the earthquake victims, we sent a donation to the Red Cross.

7. My ex-husband hit me just once in our marriage. five minutes later I was packed and walking out the door.

8. Charles Lindbergh took off from Roosevelt Field in New York on May 20, 1927 thirty-three-and-a-half hours later, he landed in Paris, France, completing the first nonstop transatlantic flight.

9. The average American teenager spends thirty-eight hours a week on schoolwork. the average Japanese teenager spends about sixty.

10. We stocked our backpacks with high-calorie candy bars, and we also brought bags of dried apricots and peaches.

Review Test 2

Correct each run-on by using (1) a period and a capital letter, (2) a comma and a joining word, or (3) a semicolon. Do not use one method exclusively.

1. The nervous system works by transmitting signals from all parts of the body to the brain. Then it sends return signals to various organs and muscles.

2. With a groan, Margo pried off her high heels, then she plunged her swollen feet into a bucket of baking soda and hot water.

3. At 2 A.M. the last customer left the diner, a busboy began stacking chairs on the tables for the night.

4. Hypnosis has nothing to do with the occult. It is merely a state of deep relaxation.

5. Many young adults today live at home with their parents this allows them to save money.

6. Many politicians wanted America to remain neutral during world War II the attack on Pearl Harbor in 1941 made that impossible.

7. Early in life, Thomas Edison suffered with deafness, he taught his wife-to-be Morse code while he was courting her.

8. Originally, horses were too small to carry riders very far larger horses had to be bred for use in warfare.

9. The words *month, silver, purple,* and *orange* have something in common, no other English words rhyme with them.

10. I had heard that the Taj Mahal was one of the wonders of the world I planned a special excursion to visit this magnificent tomb.

Review Test 3

Locate and correct the five run-ons in the passage that follows.

My worst experience of the week was going home for lunch, rather than eating at work. My children didn't know I was coming, they had used most of the bread. All I had to make a sandwich with were two thin, crumpled pieces of crust. I sat there eating my tattered sandwich and trying to relax, then the telephone rang. It was for my daughter, who was in the bathroom, she called down to me that I should get the person's name and number. As soon as I sat down again, someone knocked on the door. It was a neatly dressed couple with bright eyes who wanted to talk with me about a higher power in life. I politely got rid of them and went back to finish lunch. I thought I would relax over my coffee. I had to break up a fight between my two young sons about which television channel to watch. As a last bit of frustration, my daughter came downstairs and asked me to drive her over to a friend's house before I went back to work.

Review Test 4

On separate paper, write quickly for five minutes about what you did this past weekend. Don't worry about spelling, punctuation, finding exact words, or organizing your thoughts. Just focus on writing as many words as you can without stopping.

After you have finished, go back and correct any run-ons in your writing.

26

Regular and Irregular Verbs

This chapter will review the principal characteristics of regular and irregular verbs.

KEY TERMS

irregular verb: a verb that has an irregular form in the past tense and past participle. For example, *choose* becomes *chose* or *chosen*.

past participle: one of the principal parts of every verb; formed by adding *-d* or *-ed* to the present; used with the helping verbs *have*, *has*, or *had*, or with a form of *be* (with passive verbs).

present participle: one of the principal parts of every verb; formed by adding *-ing* to the present.

principal parts of verbs: the four parts of every verb: present, past, past participle, and present participle.

verb tense: the times shown by verbs: present, past, and future.

Regular Verbs

A Brief Review of Regular Verbs

Every verb has four principal parts: *present, past, past participle,* and *present participle.* These parts can be used to build all the verb *tenses*—the times shown by verbs.

Most verbs in English are regular. The past and past participle of a regular verb are formed by adding *-d* or *-ed* to the present. The *past participle* is the form of the verb used with the helping verbs *have*, *has*, or *had* (or some form of *be* with passive verbs). The *present participle* is formed by adding *-ing* to the present.

Here are the principal parts of some regular verbs:

Present	Past	Past Participle	Present Participle
shout	shouted	shouted	shouting
prepare	prepared	prepared	preparing
surprise	surprised	surprised	surprising
tease	teased	teased	teasing
frighten	frightened	frightened	frightening

Nonstandard Forms of Regular Verbs

Many people have grown up in communities where nonstandard forms of regular verbs are used in everyday speech. Instead of saying, for example, "That girl *looks* tired," a person using a community dialect might say, "That girl *look* tired." Instead of saying, "Yesterday I *fixed* the car," a person using a community dialect might say, "Yesterday I *fix* the car." Community dialects have richness and power but are a drawback in college and in the world of work, where regular English verb forms must be used.

The following chart compares the nonstandard and the regular verb forms of the verb *work*.

Nonstandard Verb Form		Regular Verb Form	
(Do *not* use in your writing)		(Use for clear communication)	
Present tense			
I works	we works	I work	we work
you works	you works	you work	you work
he, she, it works	they works	he, she, it works	they work
Past tense			
I work	we work	I worked	we worked
you work	you work	you worked	you worked
he, she, it work	they work	he, she, it worked	they worked

To avoid nonstandard usage, memorize the forms shown above for the regular verb *work*. Then use the activities that follow to help make the inclusion of verb endings a writing habit.

Present Tense Endings The verb ending *-s* or *-es* is needed with a regular verb in the present tense when the subject is *he, she, it,* or any *one person or thing*.

He reads every night.

She watches television every night.

It appears they have little in common.

Activity

1

Some verbs in the sentences that follow need *-s* or *-es* endings. Cross out each nonstandard verb form and write the standard form in the space provided.

_____ 1. My radio wake me up every morning with soft music.

_____ 2. Sonya always rave about the beaches in Costa Rica.

_____ 3. My wife watch our baby in the morning, and I take over afternoons.

_____ 4. Alexander live on puget Sound in Tacoma, Washington.

_____ 5. My brain work much better at night than it does in early morning.

Past Tense Endings The verb ending *-d* or *-ed* is needed with a regular verb in the past tense.

This morning I completed my research paper.

The recovering hospital patient walked slowly down the corridor.

Some students hissed when the new assignment was given out.

Activity

2

Some verbs in the sentences that follow need *-d* or *-ed* endings. Cross out each nonstandard verb form and write the standard form in the space provided.

_____ 1. In 1609, an Italian astronomer named Galileo use the telescope to view the moons of Jupiter.

_____ 2. At one time, the F. W. Woolworth Company own more than 1,000 five-and-dime stores across the United States.

_____ 3. We realize a package was missing when we got back from shopping.

_____ 4. Bill was incorrect when he said that Henry Ford invent the automobile.

_____ 5. The driver edge her car into the intersection while the light was still red.

Irregular Verbs

Irregular verbs have irregular forms in past tense and past participle. For example, the past tense of the irregular verb _choose_ is _chose;_ its past participle is _chosen._

Almost everyone has some degree of trouble with irregular verbs. When you are unsure about the form of a verb, you can check the following list of irregular verbs. (The present participle is not shown on this list because it is formed simply by adding _-ing_ to the base form of the verb.) Or you can check a dictionary, which gives the principal parts of irregular verbs.

A List of Irregular Verbs

Present	Past	Past Participle
arise	arose	arisen
awake	awoke _or_ awaked	awoken _or_ awaked
be (am, are, is)	was (were)	been
become	became	become
begin	began	begun
bend	bent	bent
bite	bit	bitten
blow	blew	blown
break	broke	broken
bring	brought	brought
build	built	built
burst	burst	burst
buy	bought	bought
catch	caught	caught
choose	chose	chosen
come	came	come
cost	cost	cost

Present	Past	Past Participle
cut	cut	cut
do (does)	did	done
draw	drew	drawn
drink	drank	drunk
drive	drove	driven
eat	ate	eaten
fall	fell	fallen
feed	fed	fed
feel	felt	felt
fight	fought	fought
find	found	found
fly	flew	flown
freeze	froze	frozen
get	got	got *or* gotten
give	gave	given
go (goes)	went	gone
grow	grew	grown
have (has)	had	had
hear	heard	heard
hide	hid	hidden
hold	held	held
hurt	hurt	hurt
keep	kept	kept
know	knew	known
lay	laid	laid
lead	led	led
leave	left	left
lend	lent	lent
let	let	let
lie	lay	lain
light	lit	lit
lose	lost	lost

Present	Past	Past Participle
make	made	made
meet	met	met
pay	paid	paid
ride	rode	ridden
ring	rang	rung
run	ran	run
say	said	said
see	saw	seen
sell	sold	sold
send	sent	sent
shake	shook	shaken
shrink	shrank	shrunk
shut	shut	shut
sing	sang	sung
sit	sat	sat
sleep	slept	slept
speak	spoke	spoken
spend	spent	spent
stand	stood	stood
steal	stole	stolen
stick	stuck	stuck
sting	stung	stung
swear	swore	sworn
swim	swam	swum
take	took	taken
teach	taught	taught
tear	tore	torn
tell	told	told
think	thought	thought
wake	woke *or* waked	woke *or* waked
wear	wore	worn
win	won	won
write	wrote	written

Activity	Cross out the incorrect verb form in each of the following sentences. Then write the correct form of the verb in the space provided.
3	**EXAMPLE**

flown   After it had flew into the picture window, the dazed bird huddled on the ground.

_____ 1. Before they bought their first house, my parents had chose to live with my grandparents in order to save money.

_____ 2. Before we could find seats, the theater darkened and the opening credits begun to roll.

_____ 3. To be polite, I drunk the slightly sour wine that my grandfather poured from his carefully hoarded supply.

_____ 4. In 1803, the United States payed France $15 million for the Louisiana Territory.

_____ 5. After crossing over land, the power of the hurricane shrinked significantly.

_____ 6. After a day on the noisy construction site, Sam's ears rung for hours with a steady hum.

_____ 7. Because Sylvia had been stinged by wasps, she was taken to the hospital.

_____ 8. If I had went to work ten minutes earlier, I would have avoided being caught in the gigantic traffic snarl.

_____ 9. After the bicycle hit a patch of soft sand, the rider was throwed into the thorny bushes along the roadside.

_____ 10. Anne Sullivan teached Helen Keller to speak and read.

Nonstandard Forms of Three Common Irregular Verbs

People who use nonstandard forms of regular verbs also tend to use nonstandard forms of three common irregular verbs: *be, have,* and *do.* Instead of saying, for example, "My neighbors *are* nice people," a person using a nonstandard form might say, "My neighbors *be* nice people." Instead of saying, "She doesn't agree," they might say, "She *don't* agree." Instead of saying, "We have tickets," they might say, "We *has* tickets."

The following charts compare the nonstandard and the standard forms of *be, have,* and *do.*

Be

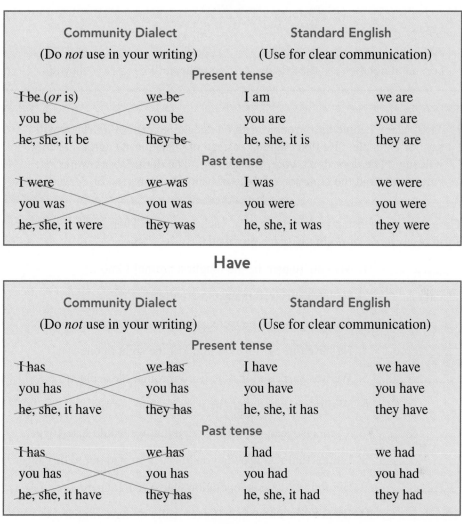

Community Dialect (Do *not* use in your writing)		Standard English (Use for clear communication)	
Present tense			
I be (*or* is)	we be	I am	we are
you be	you be	you are	you are
he, she, it be	they be	he, she, it is	they are
Past tense			
I were	we was	I was	we were
you was	you was	you were	you were
he, she, it were	they was	he, she, it was	they were

Have

Community Dialect (Do *not* use in your writing)		Standard English (Use for clear communication)	
Present tense			
I has	we has	I have	we have
you has	you has	you have	you have
he, she, it have	they has	he, she, it has	they have
Past tense			
I has	we has	I had	we had
you has	you has	you had	you had
he, she, it have	they has	he, she, it had	they had

Do

Community Dialect (Do *not* use in your writing)		Standard English (Use for clear communication)	
Present tense			
I does	we do	I do	we do
you does	you does	you do	you do
he, she, it do	they does	he, she, it does	they do

(continued)

		Past tense		
I done	we done	I did	we did
you done	you done	you did	you did
he, she, it done	they done	he, she, it did	they did

TIP: Many people have trouble with one negative form of *do*. They will say, for example, "He don't agree," instead of, "He doesn't agree," or they will say, "The door don't work," instead of, "The door doesn't work." Be careful to avoid the common mistake of using *don't* instead of *doesn't*.

Activity 4

Cross out the nonstandard verb form in each sentence. Then write the standard form of *be, have,* or *do* in the space provided.

_____ 1. My cat, Tugger, be the toughest animal I know.

_____ 2. He have survived many close calls.

_____ 3. Three years ago, he were caught inside a car's engine.

_____ 4. He have one ear torn off and lost the sight in one eye.

_____ 5. We was surprised that he lived through the accident.

_____ 6. Within weeks, though, he were back to normal.

_____ 7. Then, last year, we was worried that we would lose Tugger.

_____ 8. Lumps that was growing on his back turned out to be cancer.

_____ 9. But the vet done an operation that saved Tugger's life.

_____ 10. By now, we know that Tugger really do have nine lives.

Review Test   1

Cross out the incorrect verb form in each sentence. Then write the correct form or forms in the space provided.

_____ 1. The company I work for has growed to be one of the largest supplies of sports equipment in America.

_____ 2. The thieves would have stole my stereo, but I had had it engraved with a special identification number.

_____ 3. At the Chinese restaurant, Hollis choose his food by the number.

_____ 4. The child lied quietly as his mother signed a lullaby.

_____ 5. The lifeguard swimmed to the young woman who had becomed too tired to get to shore.

_____ 6. Baked potatoes doesn't have as many calories as I thought.

_____ 7. The grizzly bear, with the dart dangling from its side, begun to feel the effects of the powerful tranquilizer.

_____ 8. They knowed for days that molly had winned a scholarship.

_____ 9. Many childhood diseases has almost vanished in the United States.

_____ 10. Nancy sticked notes on the refrigerator with fruit-shaped magnets.

Review Test   2

Write short sentences that use the form requested for the following verbs.

EXAMPLE

Past of *grow* _I grew my own tomatoes last year._

1. Past of *know* _____

2. Present of *take* _____

3. Past participle of *give* _____

4. Past participle of *write* _____

5. Past of *do* _____

6. Past of *talk* _____

7. Present of *begin* _____

8. Past of *go* _____

9. Past participle of *see* _____

10. Present of *drive* _____

27 Subject-Verb Agreement

Subject-verb agreement is the correspondence in number between the subject and the verb of a sentence; plural subjects take plural verbs, and singular subjects take singular verbs. This chapter will review the necessity for subject-verb agreement.

INCORRECT:

The crinkly lines around Joan's mouth gives her a friendly look.

The subject of "crinkly lines" is a plural, so the verb should be "give," not "gives."

CORRECT:

The crinkly lines around Joan's mouth give her a friendly look.

The verb "give" agrees with the plural "crinkly lines."

KEY TERMS

compound subject: two subjects separated by a joining word such as *and*. Compound subjects generally take a plural verb.

indefinite pronoun: a word that refers to people and things that are not named or are not specific. Many indefinite pronouns (such as *one, nobody, nothing,* and *each*) take a singular verb; others, such as *both* or *few*, take plural verbs.

A verb must agree with its subject in number. A *singular subject* (one person or thing) takes a singular verb. A *plural subject* (more than one person or thing) takes a plural verb. Mistakes in subject-verb agreement are sometimes made in the following situations:

1. When words come between the subject and the verb
2. When a verb comes before the subject
3. With compound subjects
4. With indefinite pronouns

Each of these situations is explained in this chapter.

Words between Subject and Verb

Words that come between the subject and the verb do not change subject-verb agreement. In the sentence

The sharp <u>fangs</u> in the dog's mouth <u><u>look</u></u> scary.

the subject *(fangs)* is plural, and so the verb *(look)* is plural. The words that come between the subject and the verb are a prepositional phrase: *in the dog's mouth.* They do not affect subject-verb agreement. (A list of prepositions can be found on page 461.)

To help find the subject of certain sentences, you should cross out prepositional phrases.

The lumpy <u>salt</u> ~~in the shakers~~ <u><u>needs</u></u> to be changed.

An old <u>chair</u> ~~with broken legs~~ <u><u>has</u></u> sat in our basement for years.

Underline the subject and lightly cross out any words that come between the subject and the verb. Then double-underline the verb in parentheses that you believe is correct.

1. Some members of Abraham Lincoln's cabinet (was, were) his political rivals.

2. Chung's trench coat, with its big lapels and shoulder flaps, (make, makes) him feel like a tough private eye.

3. Misconceptions about apes like the gorilla (has, have) turned a relatively peaceful animal into a terrifying monster.

4. The Prado, one of the world's greatest art museums, (is, are) located in Madrid, Spain.

5. In my opinion, a few slices of pepperoni pizza (make, makes) a great evening.

Verb before Subject

A verb agrees with its subject even when the verb comes *before* the subject. Words that may precede the subject include *there, here,* and, in questions, *who, which, what,* and *where.*

Here are some examples of sentences in which the verb appears before the subject:

There <u><u>are</u></u> wild <u>dogs</u> in our neighborhood.

In the distance <u><u>was</u></u> a <u>billow</u> of black smoke.

Here is the newspaper.

Where are the children's coats?

If you are unsure about the subject, ask *who* or *what* of the verb. With the first example above, you might ask, "*What* are in our neighborhood?" The answer, *wild dogs*, is the subject.

Activity 2

Write the correct form of each verb in the space provided.

(is, are)   1. There _____ several reasons that the Americans won the Revolution.

(is, are)   2. Here _____ the notes from yesterday's anthropology lecture.

(do, does)   3. When _____ we take our break?

(was, were)   4. There _____ scraps of yellowing paper stuck between the pages of the cookbook.

(was, were)   5. Near the top of the hill _____ two gigantic pines covered with snow.

Compound Subjects

A *compound subject* is two subjects separated by a joining word, such as *and*. Subjects joined by *and* generally take a plural verb.

A patchwork quilt and a sleeping bag cover my bed in the winter.

Clark and Lois are a contented couple.

When subjects are joined by *either . . . or, neither . . . nor, not only . . . but also,* the verb agrees with the subject closer to the verb.

Neither the negotiator nor the union leaders want the strike to continue.

The nearer subject, *leaders,* is plural, and so the verb is plural.

Neither the union leaders nor the negotiator wants the strike to continue.

In this version, the nearer subject, *negotiator,* is singular, so the verb is singular.

Activity 3

Write the correct form of the verb in the space provided.

1. A watchtower and several cabins _____ over the valley. (look, looks)

2. Spidery cracks and a layer of dust _____ the ivory keys on the old piano.   (cover, covers)

3. Not only France and Great Britain but also Italy _____ to NATO.
    (belong, belongs)

4. In eighteenth-century France, makeup and high heels _____ worn by men.
    (was, were)

5. Neither the director nor the writers of this film _____ ever received an Academy Award.
    (has, have)

Indefinite Pronouns

The following words, known as *indefinite pronouns*, always take singular verbs:

(-*one* words)	(-*body* words)	(-*thing* words)	
one	nobody	nothing	each
anyone	anybody	anything	either
everyone	everybody	everything	neither
someone	somebody	something	

TIP: *Both* always takes a plural verb.

www.mhhe.com/langan

Write the correct form of the verb in the space provided.

Activity 4

1. Neither of the essays _____ plagiarized.
    (was, were)

2. Somebody without much sensitivity always _____ my birthmark.
    (mention, mentions)

3. Both countries _____ great coffee.
    (produce, produces)

4. Everyone _____ the college kite-flying contest in the spring.
    (enter, enters)

5. One of the students in my history class _____ Polish.
    (speak, speaks)

Review Test   1

In the space provided, write the correct form of the verb shown in the margin.

(are, is)

1. Yellowstone National Park, located in Wyoming, Idaho, and Montana, _____ home to Old Faithful, the world's most famous geyser.

(was, were)

2. Each of their children _____ given a name picked at random from a page of the Bible.

(were, was)

3. Near the top of the company's organizational chart _____ the vice president for sales and the director of personnel.

(is, are)

4. Envelopes, file folders, and a telephone book _____ jammed into Lupe's kitchen drawers.

(contains, contain)

5. Neither of the main dishes at tonight's dinner _____ any meat.

(decrease, decreases)

6. A drop in the price of gasoline and other fuels _____ the chances that bus fares will go up soon.

(appear, appears)

7. Many people in my neighborhood _____ to be recycling paper, cans, glass, and plastic.

(make, makes)

8. A good grounding in mathematics _____ it easier to learn physics.

(cleans, clean)

9. In exchange for reduced rent, Karla and James _____ the dentist's office beneath their second-floor apartment.

(is, are)

10. One of the hospital's delivery rooms _____ furnished with bright carpets and curtains to resemble a room at home.

Review Test   2

Cross out the incorrect verb form in each sentence. In addition, underline the subject or subjects that go with the verb. Then write the correct form of the verb in the space provided.

_____ 1. Why has the president and the Senate supported a law banning trade with Iran?

_____ 2. Neither of the cars come equipped with satellite radio.

_____ 3. Three goats, a potbellied pig, and a duck was among the entrants in the pet parade.

_____ 4. The little balls all over my pink sweater looks like woolen goose bumps.

_____ 5. Here is the low-calorie cola and the double-chocolate cake you ordered.

_____ 6. The odor of those perfumed ads interfere with my enjoyment of a magazine.

_____ 7. One of the children in my mother's day-care center have an extraordinary talent for drawing.

_____ 8. A bumper crop of wheat and a decrease in fuel prices makes it possible to for farmers to increase their profits.

_____ 9. A person in his or her forties often begin to think about making a contribution to the world and not just about himself or herself.

_____ 10. Each of the child's thirty-four stuffed animals have a name and an entire life history.

Review Test 3

Complete each of the following sentences using *is, are, was, were, have,* or *has.* Then underline the subject.

EXAMPLE

For me, popcorn at the movies *is like coffee at breakfast.* _____

1. The three women speaking tonight _____

2. The car with the purple fenders _____

3. My boss and her secretary _____

4. Neither of the football players _____

5. Here _____

Additional Information about Verbs

This chapter will provide additional information about verbs, specifically:

- verb tense
- helping verbs
- verbals

KEY TERMS

gerund: a verbal; the *-ing* form of the verb used as a noun. Example: I love *dancing*.

infinitive: a verbal; *to* plus the base form of the verb. Example: I love *to dance*.

participle: a verbal; the *-ing* or *-ed* form of the verb used as an adjective. Example: I love *dancing* bears.

verbals: words formed from verbs that often express action; these include gerunds, infinitives, and participles.

www.mhhe.com/langan

Verb Tense

The time that a verb shows is usually called *tense*. The most common tenses are the simple present, past, and future. In addition, nine other tenses enable us to express more specific ideas about time than the simple tenses do.

Tenses	Examples
Present	I *work*. Tony *works*.
Past	Ellen *worked* on her car.
Future	You *will work* on a new project next week.

(continued)

Tenses	Examples
Present perfect	He *has worked* on his term paper for a month. They *have worked* out a compromise. *Note:* The present perfect tense is used for an action that began in the past and continues in the present.
Past perfect	The nurse *had worked* two straight shifts. *Note:* The past perfect tense is used for a past action that came *before* another past action.
Future perfect	Next Monday, I *will have worked* here exactly two years.
Present progressive	I *am working* on my speech for the debate. You *are working* too hard. The tape recorder *is* not *working* properly.
Past progressive	He *was working* in the basement. The contestants *were working* on their talent routines.
Future progressive	My son *will be working* in our store this summer.
Present perfect progressive	Sarah *has been working* late this week.
Past perfect progressive	Until recently, I *had been working* nights.
Future perfect progressive	My mother *will have been working* as a nurse for forty-five years by the time she retires.

On a separate sheet of paper, write twelve sentences using the twelve verb tenses.

Activity

1

Helping Verbs

These common verbs can either stand alone or "help" other verbs.

be (am, are, is, was, were, being, been)
have (has, having, had)
do (does, did)

Here are examples of the helping verbs:

Used Alone	Used as Helping Verbs
I *was* angry.	I *was growing* angry.
Sue *has* the key.	Sue *has forgotten* the key.
He *did* well in the test.	He *did fail* the previous test.

Nine helping verbs (traditionally known as *modals,* or *modal auxiliaries*) are always used in combination with other verbs. Here are the nine verbs and a sentence example of each:

can	I *can see* the rainbow.
could	I *could* not *find* a seat.
may	The game *may be postponed.*
might	Cindy *might resent* your advice.
shall	I *shall see* you tomorrow.
should	He *should get* his car serviced.
will	Tony *will want* to see you.
would	They *would* not *understand.*
must	You *must* visit us again.

Note from the examples that these verbs have only one form. They do not, for instance, add an *-s* when used with *he, she, it,* or any one person or thing.

Activity

2

On a separate sheet of paper, write nine sentences using the nine helping verbs.

Verbals

Verbals are words formed from verbs. Verbals, like verbs, often express action. They can add variety to your sentences and vigor to your writing style. The three kinds of verbals are *infinitives, participles,* and *gerunds.*

Infinitive

An infinitive is *to* and the base form of the verb.

I love *to dance.*

Lina hopes *to write* for a newspaper.

I asked the children *to clean* the kitchen.

Participle

A participle is a verb form used as an adjective (a descriptive word). The present participle ends in *-ing*. The past participle ends in *-ed* or has an irregular ending.

> *Peering* into the cracked mirror, the *crying* woman wiped her eyes.
>
> The *astounded* man stared at his *winning* lottery ticket.
>
> *Swinging* a sharp ax, Omar split the *rotted* beam.

Gerund

A gerund is the *-ing* form of a verb used as a noun.

> *Swimming* is the perfect exercise.
>
> *Eating* junk food is my diet downfall.
>
> Through *doodling,* people express their inner feelings.

www.mhhe.com/langan

Part A

On a separate sheet of paper, write three sentences using infinitives, three sentences using participles, and three sentences using gerunds.

Activity

3

Part B

Identify the infinitives, participles, and gerunds in the following sentences. Write *I* for infinitive, *P* for participle, and *G* for gerund above each of them.

_____ 1. To teach mathematics is her overwhelming ambition.

_____ 2. Leaping toward his students, the fencing coach demonstrated the art of lunging.

_____ 3. Sleeping is one of my favorite activities, but I don't get to indulge in it very often.

_____ 4. Receiving an award for her work with the homeless was the last thing Marge expected.

_____ 5. Entering the hotdog–eating contest, Steven hoped to break last year's record, but his stomach had other ideas.

29 Pronoun Agreement and Reference

This chapter will provide information on pronoun agreement and reference.

INCORRECT:

Miriam was annoyed when they failed her car for a faulty turn signal.

In this case, "they" should be replaced by a specific noun, such as "the inspectors," so the reader knows who the word "they" refers to.

CORRECT:

Miriam was annoyed when the inspectors failed her car for a faulty turn signal.

Now it is made clear that it was the inspectors who failed the car.

KEY TERMS

indefinite pronouns: a word that refers to people and things that are not named or are not specific. Many indefinite pronouns (such as *one, nobody, nothing,* and *each*) take a singular verb; others, such as *both* or *few*, take plural verbs.

nouns: words that name persons, places, or things.

pronoun: words that take the place of nouns. Pronouns are short-cuts that keep you from unnecessarily repeating words in writing.

pronoun agreement: correspondence in number between the pronoun and the noun it replaces. Example: *Students enrolled in the art class must prove that they can paint.*

pronoun reference: the relationship between the pronoun and the noun in the sentence to which it refers. A sentence may be confusing if a pronoun appears to refer to more than one noun or does not appear to refer to any specific noun.

Nouns name persons, places, or things. *Pronouns* are words that take the place of nouns. In fact, the word *pronoun* means "for a noun." Pronouns are shortcuts that keep you from unnecessarily repeating words in writing. Here are some examples of pronouns:

> Eddie left *his* camera on the bus.
> (*His* is a pronoun that takes the place of *Eddie's*.)
>
> Elena drank the coffee even though *it* was cold.
> (*It* replaces *coffee*.)
>
> As I turned the newspaper's damp pages, *they* disintegrated in my hands.
> (*They* is a pronoun that takes the place of *pages*.)

This chapter presents rules that will help you avoid two common mistakes people make with pronouns. The rules are the following:

1. A pronoun must agree in number with the word or words it replaces.
2. A pronoun must refer clearly to the word it replaces.

Pronoun Agreement

A pronoun must agree in number with the word or words it replaces. If the word a pronoun refers to is singular, the pronoun must be singular; if that word is plural, the pronoun must be plural. (Note that the word a pronoun refers to is known as the *antecedent*.)

> Marie showed me her antique wedding band.
>
> Students enrolled in the art class must provide their own supplies.

In the first example, the pronoun *her* refers to the singular word *Marie;* in the second example, the pronoun *their* refers to the plural word *Students*.

Write the appropriate pronoun *(their, they, them, it)* in the blank space in each of the following sentences.

Activity

1

EXAMPLE

> I opened the wet umbrella and put _____*it*_____ in the bathtub to dry.

1. Kate and Omar left for the movies earlier than usual, because _____ knew the theater would be packed.

2. The clothes were still damp, but I decided to fold _____ anyway.

3. Many people immigrate to America to make a better life for _____ families.

4. Paul's grandparents renewed _____ marriage vows at a huge fiftieth wedding anniversary celebration.

5. The area around San Jose, California, produces fine wines, but _____ is also the home of many high-technology companies.

Indefinite Pronouns

The following words, known as *indefinite pronouns,* are always singular.

(-*one* words)	(-*body* words)	
one	nobody	each
anyone	anybody	either
everyone	everybody	neither
someone	somebody	

If a pronoun in a sentence refers to one of these singular words, the pronoun should be singular.

Somebody left her shoulder bag on the back of a chair.

One of the busboys just called and said he would be an hour late.

Everyone in the club must pay his dues next week.

Each circled pronoun is singular because it refers to an indefinite pronoun.
  There are two important points to remember about indefinite pronouns:

1. In the last example, if everyone in the club was a woman, the pronoun would be *her.* If the club had women and men, the pronoun would be *his or her:*

   Everyone in the club must pay his or her dues next week.

   Some writers follow the traditional practice of using *his* to refer to both women and men. Some now use *his or her* to avoid an implied sexual bias. To avoid using *his* or the somewhat awkward *his or her,* a sentence can often be rewritten in the plural:

   Club members must pay their dues next week.

2. In informal spoken English, *plural* pronouns are often used with the indefinite pronouns. Many people would probably not say,

   Everybody has his or her own opinion about the election.

Instead, they would be likely to say,

> Everybody has their own opinion about the election.

Here are other examples:

> Everyone in the choir must buy their robes.
> Everybody in the line has their ticket ready.
> No one in the class remembered to bring their books.

In such cases, the indefinite pronouns are clearly plural in meaning, and using them helps people avoid the awkward *his or her*. In time, the plural pronoun may be accepted in formal speech or writing. Until then, however, you should use the grammatically correct singular form in your writing.

Underline the correct pronoun.

1. Neither of the potential buyers had really made up (her, their) mind.
2. Not one of the new cashiers knows what (he, they) should be doing.
3. Each of the three sisters was willing to donate (her, their) inheritance to charity.
4. Anyone trying to reduce (his or her, their) salt intake should avoid canned and processed foods.
5. Everybody should bring (his or her, their) own camera to class next week.

Activity

2

Pronoun Reference

A sentence may be confusing and unclear if a pronoun appears to refer to more than one word or does not refer to any specific word. Look at this sentence:

> Miriam was annoyed when they failed her car for a faulty turn signal.

Who failed her car? There is no specific word that *they* refers to. Be clear:

> Miriam was annoyed when the inspectors failed her car for a faulty turn signal.

Here are sentences with other faulty pronoun references. Read the explanations of why they are faulty and look carefully at how they are corrected.

www.mhhe.com/langan

Faulty	Clear
Peter told Alan that his wife was unhappy. (Whose wife is unhappy: Peter's or Alan's? Be clear.)	Peter told Alan, "My wife is unhappy."

Faulty

Kia is really a shy person, but she keeps it hidden.
(There is no specific word that *it* refers to. It would not make sense to say, "Kia keeps shy hidden.")

Marsha attributed her success to her husband's support, which was generous.
(Does *which* mean that Marsha's action was generous or that her husband's support was generous?)

Clear

Kia is really a shy person, but she keeps her shyness hidden.

Generously, Marsha attributed her success to her husband's support.
Or: Marsha attributed her success to her husband's generous support.

Activity

3

Working with a fellow classmate, rewrite each of the following sentences to make clear the vague pronoun reference. Add, change, or omit words as necessary.

EXAMPLE

Susan's mother wondered if she was tall enough to be a model.

Susan's mother wondered if Susan was tall enough to be a model.

1. Jim is a talkative person; sometimes he just can't control it.

   _____

2. At that fast-food restaurant, they give you free glasses with your soft drinks.

   _____

3. Sallie told Anna that she had just been promoted to assistant manager.

   _____

4. Dipping her spoon into the pot of simmering spaghetti sauce, Helen felt it slip out of her hand.

   _____

5. Pete visited the tutoring center because they can help him with his economics course.

   _____

Review Test   1

Underline the correct word in parentheses.

1. Each congressional district sends (its, their) own representative to Washington.

2. I asked at the body shop how quickly (they, the shop employees) could fix my car.

3. The coaches told each member of the football team that (his, their) position was the most important in the game.

4. Pete's sneezing and coughing had gotten better, but he still wasn't over (it, his cold).

5. When someone has a cold, (they, he or she) should take extra vitamin C and drink a lot of fluids.

Review Test 2

Cross out the pronoun error in each of the following sentences, and write the correction in the space provided at the left. Then circle the letter that correctly describes the type of error that was made.

EXAMPLES

his (or her)   Anyone without a ticket will lose ~~their~~ place in the line.

Mistake in   a. pronoun reference (b.) pronoun agreement

Ellen (or Kim)   When Ellen takes her daughter Kim to the park, ~~she~~ enjoys herself.

Mistake in   (a.) pronoun reference b. pronoun agreement

_____ 1. Could someone volunteer their services to clean up after the party?

Mistake in   a. pronoun reference b. pronoun agreement

_____ 2. The referee watched the basketball game closely to make sure they didn't commit any fouls.

Mistake in   a. pronoun reference b. pronoun agreement

_____ 3. If job-hunters want to make a good impression at an interview, he should be sure to arrive on time.

Mistake in   a. pronoun reference b. pronoun agreement

_____ 4. One poll predicts that Robinson will win the gubernatorial election next November, but they have been wrong before.

Mistake in   a. pronoun reference b. pronoun agreement

_____ 5. They disagree about the success of President Roosevelt's attempts to fight the Great Depression.

Mistake in   a. pronoun reference b. pronoun agreement

30

Pronoun Types

This chapter will describe some common types of pronouns:

- subject pronouns

- object pronouns

- possessive pronouns

- demonstrative pronouns

KEY TERMS

demonstrative pronouns: pronouns that point to or single out a person or thing. The four demonstrative pronouns are *this, that, these,* and *those.*

object pronouns: pronouns that function as the objects of verbs or prepositions. Example: *Tony helped me.*

possessive pronouns: pronouns that show ownership or possession. Example: *The keys are mine.*

subject pronouns: pronouns that function as the subjects of verbs. Example: *He is wearing an artificial arm.*

www.mhhe.com/langan

Subject and Object Pronouns

Most pronouns change their form depending on what place they occupy in a sentence. In the box that follows is a list of subject and object pronouns.

Subject Pronouns	Object Pronouns
I	me
you	you (no change)
he	him
she	her
it	it (no change)
we	us
they	them

Subject Pronouns

Subject pronouns are subjects of verbs.

> *He* served as a soldier during the war in Iraq. (*He* is the subject of the verb *served*.)
>
> *They* are moving into our old apartment. (*They* is the subject of the verb *are moving*.)
>
> *We* students should have a say in the decision. (*We* is the subject of the verb *should have*.)

Following are several rules for using subject pronouns—and several kinds of mistakes people sometimes make with subject pronouns.

Rule 1

Use a subject pronoun when you have a compound subject (more than one subject).

Incorrect	Correct
My brother and *me* are Bruce Springsteen fanatics.	My brother and *I* are Bruce Springsteen fanatics.
Him and *me* know the lyrics to all of Bruce's songs.	*He* and *I* know the lyrics to all of Bruce's songs.

> **TIP:** *Rule 1*
> If you are not sure what pronoun to use, try each pronoun by itself in the sentence. The correct pronoun will be the one that sounds right. For example, "Him knows the lyrics to all of Bruce's songs" does not sound right; "He knows the lyrics to all of Bruce's songs" does.

Rule 2

Use a subject pronoun after forms of the verb *be*. Forms of *be* include *am, are, is, was, were, has been, have been,* and others.

> It was *I* who left the light on.
>
> It may be *they* in that car.
>
> It is *he.*

The sentences above may sound strange and stilted to you because they are seldom used in conversation. When we speak with one another, forms such as "It was me,"

"It may be them," and "It is him" are widely accepted. In formal writing, however, the grammatically correct forms are still preferred.

TIP: *Rule 2*
You can avoid having to use a subject pronoun after *be* by simply rewording a sentence. Here is how the preceding examples could be reworded:

> I was the one who left the light on.
>
> They may be in that car.
>
> He is here.

Rule 3

Use subject pronouns after *than* or *as*. The subject pronoun is used because a verb is understood after the pronoun.

> You play better than I (play). (The verb *play* is understood after *I*.)
>
> Jenny is as bored as I (am). (The verb *am* is understood after *I*.)
>
> We don't need the money as much as they (do). (The verb *do* is understood after *they*.)

TIP: *Rule 3*
Avoid mistakes by mentally adding the "missing" verb at the end of the sentence.

Object Pronouns

Object pronouns (me, him, her, us, them) are the objects of verbs or prepositions. (*Prepositions* are connecting words like *for, at, about, to, before, by, with,* and *of*. See also page 461.)

> Tony helped me. (*Me* is the object of the verb *helped*.)
>
> We took *them* to the college. (*Them* is the object of the verb *took*.)
>
> Leave the children with *us*. (*Us* is the object of the preposition *with*.)
>
> I got in line behind *him*. (*Him* is the object of the preposition *behind*.)

People are sometimes uncertain about what pronoun to use when two objects follow a verb.

Incorrect	Correct
I gave a gift to Ray and *she*.	I gave a gift to Ray and *her*.
She came to the movie with Bobbie and *I*.	She came to the movie with Bobbie and *me*.

> **TIP:** If you are not sure what pronoun to use, try each pronoun by itself in the sentence. The correct pronoun will be the one that sounds right. For example, "I gave a gift to she" does not sound right; "I gave a gift to her" does.

Underline the correct subject or object pronoun in each of the following sentences. Then show whether your answer is a subject or object pronoun by circling the S or O in the margin. The first one is done for you as an example.

Activity 1

S   O   1. The sweaters Mom knitted for Victor and (I, me) are too small.

S   O   2. Andrew and (she, her) visited the Tower of London during their trip to England.

S   O   3. The senator praised her opponent by saying that no one had ever run a cleaner compaign than (he, him).

S   O   4. Your grades prove that you worked harder than (they, them).

S   O   5. (We, Us) runners train indoors when the weather turns cold.

S   O   6. (She, Her) and Betty never put the cap back on the toothpaste.

S   O   7. Chris and (he, him) are the most energetic kids in the first grade.

S   O   8. Reading about the ancient Greeks became an obsession for Molly and (him, he).

S   O   9. The rest of (they, them) will be arriving in about ten minutes.

S   O   10. The head of the ticket committee asked Melba and (I, me) to help with sales.

Possessive Pronouns

Here is a list of possessive pronouns:

my, mine	our, ours
your, yours	your, yours
his	their, theirs
her, hers	
its	

Possessive pronouns show ownership or possession.

> Adam revved up *his* motorcycle and blasted off.
>
> The keys are *mine*.

www.mhhe.com/langan

> **TIP:** A possessive pronoun *never* uses an apostrophe. (See also page 561.)

Incorrect	Correct
That coat is *hers'*.	That coat is *hers*.
The card table is *theirs'*.	The card table is *theirs*.

Activity

2

Cross out the incorrect pronoun form in each of the sentences below. Write the correct form in the space at the left.

EXAMPLE

_____hers_____   Those gloves are hers'.

_____   1. I discovered that my car had somehow lost its' rear license plate.

_____   2. Are those seats theirs'?

_____   3. The mayor said that the task of cutting the budget was not hers' alone.

_____   4. The prize-winning entry in the science fair was our's.

_____   5. These books are yours' if you want them.

Demonstrative Pronouns

Demonstrative pronouns point to or single out a person or thing. There are four demonstrative pronouns:

this	these
that	those

Generally speaking, *this* and *these* refer to things close at hand; *that* and *those* refer to things farther away. The four demonstrative pronouns are also commonly used as demonstrative adjectives.

> Is anyone using *this* spoon?
>
> I am going to throw away *these* magazines.
>
> I just bought *that* black pickup truck at the curb.
>
> Pick up *those* toys in the corner.

TIP: Do not use *them, this here, that there, these here,* or *those there* to point out. Use only *this, that, these,* or *those.*

Cross out the incorrect form of the demonstrative pronoun, and write the correct form in the space provided.

Activity

3

EXAMPLE

_____*Those*_____   Them tires look worn.

_____ 1. This here map is out of date.

_____ 2. Leave them keys out on the coffee table.

_____ 3. Them two movies are about life in early New England.

_____ 4. Jack entered that there dog in an obedience contest.

_____ 5. Where are them concert tickets I left here?

Review Test 1

Underline the correct word in the parentheses.

1. If the contract negotiations are left up to (they, them), we'll have to accept the results.

2. (Them, Those) student crafts projects have won several awards.

3. Our history professor asked Philip and (I, me) to prepare a short presentation on the Battle of Princeton.

4. The soldiers believe that victory was (theirs, theirs') so they kept moving forward.

5. I gave the money to (she, her) and asked her to put it in the bank's night deposit slot.

6. The black-masked raccoon stared at Rudy and (I, me) for an instant and then ran away.

7. After spending some time in Florence, Italy, Andrea and (I, me) traveled to Rome.

8. (This here, This) is my cousin Manuel.

9. This coat can't be (hers, her's); it's too small.

10. Because we weren't wearing shoes, Tara and (I, me) had a hard time walking on the sharp gravel.

31

Adjectives and Adverbs

This chapter will describe the principal characteristics of adjectives and adverbs.

KEY TERMS

adjectives: words that describe nouns or pronouns. Example: Yoko is a *wise* woman.

adverbs: words that describe verbs, adjectives, or other adverbs. Example: I walked *quickly* to the store.

Adjectives

What Are Adjectives?

Adjectives describe nouns (names of persons, places, or things) or pronouns.

Yoko is a *wise* woman. (The adjective *wise* describes the noun *woman*.)

She is also *funny*. (The adjective *funny* describes the pronoun *she*.)

I'll carry the *heavy* bag of groceries. (The adjective *heavy* describes the noun *bag*.)

It is *torn*. (The adjective *torn* describes the pronoun *it*.)

Adjectives usually come before the word they describe (as in *wise* woman and *heavy* bag). But they also come after forms of the verb *be* (*is, are, was, were,* and so on). They also follow verbs such as *look, appear, seem, become, sound, taste,* and *smell*.

That road is *slippery*. (The adjective *slippery* describes the road.)

The dogs are *noisy*. (The adjective *noisy* describes the dogs.)

Those customers were *impatient*. (The adjective *impatient* describes the customers.)

Your room looks *neat*. (The adjective *neat* describes the room.)

Using Adjectives to Compare

For all one-syllable adjectives and some two-syllable adjectives, add *-er* when comparing two things and *-est* when comparing three or more things.

> Phil's beard is *longer* than mine, but Lee's is the *longest*.

> Meg may be the *quieter* of the two sisters; but that's not saying much, since they're the *loudest* girls in school.

For some two-syllable adjectives and all longer adjectives, use *more* when comparing two things and *most* when comparing three or more things.

> Liza Minnelli is *more famous* than her sister; but their mother, Judy Garland, is still the *most famous* member of the family.

> The red letters on the sign are *more noticeable* than the black ones, but the Day-Glo letters are the *most noticeable*.

You can usually tell when to use *more* and *most* by the sound of a word. For example, you can probably tell by its sound that "carefuller" would be too awkward to say and that *more careful* is thus correct. But there are many words for which both *-er* or *-est* and *more* or *most* are equally correct. For instance, either "a more fair rule" or "a fairer rule" is correct.

To form negative comparisons, use *less* and *least*.

> During my first dance class, I felt *less graceful* than an injured elephant.

> When the teacher came to our house to complain to my parents, I offered her the *least* comfortable chair in the room.

Points to Remember about Comparing

Point 1

Use only one form of comparison at a time. That is, do not use both an *-er* ending and *more* or both an *-est* ending and *most:*

Incorrect	Correct
My mother's suitcase is always *more heavier* than my father's.	My mother's suitcase is always *heavier* than my father's.
Psycho is still the *most frighteningest* movie I've ever seen.	*Psycho* is still the *most frightening* movie I've ever seen.

Point 2

Learn the irregular forms of the words shown below.

	Comparative (for comparing two things)	Superlative (for comparing three or more things)
bad	worse	worst
good, well	better	best
little (in amount)	less	least
much, many	more	most

Do not use both *more* and an irregular comparative or *most* and an irregular superlative.

Incorrect	Correct
It is *more better* to give than to receive.	It is *better* to give than to receive.
Last night I got the *most worst* snack attack I ever had.	Last night I got the *worst* snack attack I have ever had.

Add to each sentence the correct form of the word in the margin.

EXAMPLES

The _____*worst*_____ job I ever had was babysitting for spoiled four-year-old twins.

The ___*most wonderful*___ day of my life was when my child was born.

1. The _____ chocolate cake I have ever eaten had bananas in it.

2. Aunt Sonja is the _____ of the three sisters.

3. The solutions that Mary offered were _____ than mine.

4. That's the _____ home I've ever seen—it's shaped like a teapot.

5. The Rockies are the world's _____ mountains.

Activity

1

bad

wonderful

good

young

best

unusual

beautiful

Adverbs

What Are Adverbs?

Adverbs describe verbs, adjectives, or other adverbs. They usually end in *-ly*.

The father *gently* hugged the sick child. (The adverb *gently* describes the verb *hugged*.)

www.mhhe.com/langan

Newborns are *totally* innocent. (The adverb *totally* describes the adjective *innocent*.)

The lecturer spoke so *terribly* fast that I had trouble taking notes. (The adverb *terribly* describes the adverb *fast*.)

A Common Mistake with Adverbs and Adjectives

People often mistakenly use an adjective instead of an adverb after a verb.

Incorrect	Correct
Sam needs a haircut *bad*.	Sam needs a haircut *badly*.
She gets along *easy* with others.	She gets along *easily* with others.
You might have lost the race if you hadn't run so *quick* at the beginning.	You might have lost the race if you hadn't run so *quickly* at the beginning.

Activity

2

Underline the adjective or adverb needed.

> **HINT:** Remember that adjectives describe nouns, and adverbs describe verbs and other adverbs.

1. As Mac danced, his earring bounced (rapid, rapidly).

2. We back up all of our files in case there is a (sudden, suddenly) power surge that could damage our computers.

3. I hiccuped (continuous, continuously) for fifteen minutes.

4. The detective opened the door (careful, carefully).

5. The Salvation Army is (heavy, heavily) dependent upon donations from the public.

Well and *Good*

Two words that are often confused are *well* and *good*. *Good* is an adjective; it describes nouns. *Well* is usually an adverb; it describes verbs. But *well* (rather than *good*) is used as an adjective when referring to health.

Team up with a fellow classmate and write *well* or *good* in each of the sentences that follow.

Activity

3

1. Miami fared _____ during the last hurricane because the people took adequate precautions.

2. If I organize the office records too _____, my bosses may not need me anymore.

3. The governor commended the literacy volunteers for the _____ work they had accomplished.

4. When Ernie got AIDS, he discovered who his _____ friends really were.

5. In high school, Jessica always did _____ in history.

Review Test 1

Underline the correct word in parentheses.

1. The waitress poured (littler, less) coffee into my cup than yours.
2. We could not have asked for a (more good, better) teacher in math.
3. The movie is so interesting that the three hours pass (quick, quickly).
4. The talented boy sang as (confident, confidently) as a seasoned performer.
5. Our band played so (good, well) that a local firm hired us for its annual dinner.
6. Tamika is always (truthful, truthfully), even when it might be better to tell a white lie.
7. The Beatles seemed to burst onto the scene very (quick, quickly) but they had been singing for years before they became popular.
8. Shirt and pants in the same color make you look (more thin, thinner) than ones in contrasting colors.
9. John Roebling's prediction that he could build a bridge across New York's East River turned out (good, well); today that structure is known as the Brooklyn Bridge.
10. Our cat likes to sit in the (warmest, most warm) spot in any room—by a fireplace, on a windowsill in the sunshine, or on my lap.

Review Test 2

Write a sentence that uses each of the following adjectives and adverbs correctly.

1. careless _____

2. angrily _____

3. well _____

4. most relaxing _____

5. best _____

6. rapid _____

7. cautious _____

8. brilliantly _____

9. quietly _____

10. fairly _____

32

Misplaced Modifiers

This chapter will describe misplaced modifiers, which are words that, because of awkward placement, do not describe what the author intended them to describe.

INCORRECT:

George couldn't drive to work in his sports car with a broken leg.

The sentence makes it sound as if the car has the broken leg, not George.

CORRECT:

With his broken leg, George couldn't drive to work in his sports car.

The phrase "with a broken leg" has been moved so that it is closer to "George"; now it is more clear whose leg is broken.

Misplaced modifiers are words that, because of awkward placement, do not describe what the writer intended them to describe. A misplaced modifier can make a sentence confusing or unintentionally funny. To avoid this, place words as close as possible to what they describe.

www.mhhe.com/langan

Misplaced Words	Correctly Placed Words
George couldn't drive to work in his small sports car *with a broken leg*. (The sports car had a broken leg?)	With a broken leg, George couldn't drive to work in his small sports car. (The words describing George are now placed next to *George*.)
The toaster was sold to us by a charming salesman *with a money-back guarantee*. (The salesman had a money-back guarantee?)	The toaster with a money-back guarantee was sold to us by a charming salesman. (The words describing the toaster are now placed next to it.)

<table>
<tr><td>

Misplaced Words

He *nearly* brushed his teeth for twenty minutes every night. (He came close to brushing his teeth but in fact did not brush them at all?)

</td><td>

Correctly Placed Words

He brushed his teeth for nearly twenty minutes every night. (The meaning—that he brushed his teeth for a long time—is now clear.)

</td></tr>
</table>

Activity

1

Underline the misplaced word or words in each sentence. Then rewrite the sentence, placing related words together and thereby making the meaning clear.

EXAMPLES

Frozen shrimp lay in the steel pans <u>that were thawing rapidly</u>.

Frozen shrimp that were thawing rapidly lay in the steel pans.

The speaker discussed the problem of crowded prisons <u>at the college</u>.

At the college, the speaker discussed the problem of crowded prisons.

1. The patient talked about his childhood on the psychiatrist's couch.

_____

2. The crowd watched the tennis players with swiveling heads.

_____

3. Vonnie put four hamburger patties on the counter which she was cooking for dinner.

_____

4. Steve carefully hung the new suit that he would wear to his first job interview in the bedroom closet.

_____

5. The novel was about a pioneer family that Annie had borrowed from her cousin.

_____

6. The latest Denzel Washington movie has almost opened in 2,200 theaters across the country.

_____

7. To be cooked properly, the chef advised us to place the casserole in a pre-heated oven.

_____

8. The tenants left town in a dilapidated old car owing two months' rent.

_____

9. The plan was to construct a church on an acre of land made of brick and stone.

_____

10. I discovered an unusual plant in the greenhouse that oozed a milky juice.

_____

Review Test   1

Write MM for *misplaced modifier* or C for *correct* in the space provided for each sentence.

_____ 1. I nearly napped for twenty minutes during the biology lecture.

_____ 2. I napped for nearly twenty minutes during the biology lecture.

_____ 3. The spacecraft traveled nearly 142 million miles to reach Mars.

_____ 4. The spacecraft nearly traveled 142 million miles to reach Mars.

_____ 5. My grandfather prepared breakfast for his family wearing his bathrobe.

_____ 6. Wearing his bathrobe, my grandfather prepared breakfast for his family.

_____ 7. We couldn't read the advertisement on the water tower written in tiny letters.

_____ 8. We couldn't read the advertisement written in tiny letters on the water tower.

_____ 9. I ordered a new telephone from the mail-order catalog shaped like a cartoon character.

_____ 10. I ordered from the mail-order catalog a new telephone shaped like a cartoon character.

Review Test 2

Make the changes needed to correct the misplaced modifier in each sentence.

1. Henry Wadsworth Longfellow wrote that rainbows are flowers that have died and gone to heaven in a poem.

   _____

   _____

2. Because of the storm, I almost arrived two hours late for my first day on the job.

   _____

   _____

3. The youngsters ran through the rooms of their brand new house with smiling faces.

   _____

   _____

4. The photographer pointed the camera at the shy deer equipped with a special night-vision scope.

   _____

   _____

5. Treated with a new drug, the doctor was confident that his patients would recover.

   _____

   _____

33

Dangling Modifiers

This chapter will describe dangling modifiers—descriptive words that open a sentence but do not describe what the author intended them to describe.

> INCORPORATE:
>
> *While reading the newspaper, my dog sat with me on the steps.*
>
> The sentence misleadingly states that the dog was reading the newspaper.
>
> CORRECT:
>
> *While I was reading the newspaper, my dog sat with me on the steps.*
>
> The sentence makes it clear that the subject "I" was reading the newspaper.

A modifier that opens a sentence must be followed immediately by the word it is meant to describe. Otherwise, the modifier is said to be dangling, and the sentence takes on an unintended meaning. For example, in the sentence

> While reading the newspaper, my dog sat with me on the front steps.

the unintended meaning is that the *dog* was reading the newspaper. The writer should have said,

> While reading the newspaper, *I* sat with my dog on the front steps.

The dangling modifier could also be corrected by placing the subject within the opening word group:

> While *I* was reading the newspaper, my dog sat with me on the front steps.

Dangling	Correct
Shaving in front of the steamy mirror, the razor nicked Ed's chin. (*Who* was shaving? The subject *Ed* must be added.)	Shaving in front of the steamy mirror, *Ed* nicked his chin with the razor. *Or* When *Ed* was shaving in front of the steamy mirror, he nicked his chin with a razor.
While turning over the bacon, hot grease splashed my arm. (Who was turning over the bacon? *I* was, not the *hot grease*. The subject *I* must be added.)	While *I* was turning over the bacon, hot grease splashed my arm. *Or* While turning over the bacon, *I* was splashed with hot grease.
To impress the interviewer, punctuality is essential. (Who is to impress the interviewer? You are, not *punctuality*.)	To impress the interviewer, *you* must be punctual. *Or* For *you* to impress the interviewer, punctuality is essential.

The examples above show two ways to correct a dangling modifier.

1. Place the subject *within* the opening word group:

    When *Ed* was shaving in front of the steamy mirror, he nicked his chin.

TIP: In some cases, a subordinating word such as *when* must be added and the verb may have to be changed.

---

2. Place the subject right *after* the opening word group:

    Shaving in front of the steamy mirror, *Ed* nicked his chin.

Activity

1

Look at the opening words in each sentence and ask *who*. The subject that answers the question should be nearby in the sentence. If it is not, provide the logical subject by using either method of correction described above.

EXAMPLE

While pitching his tent, a snake bit Tony on the ankle.

While Tony was pitching his tent, a snake bit him on the ankle.

Or

While pitching his tent, Tony was bitten on the ankle by a snake.

1. Dancing on their hind legs, the audience cheered wildly as the elephants paraded by.

   _____

   _____

2. Last seen wearing dark glasses and a blond wig, the police spokesperson said the suspect was still being sought.

   _____

   _____

3. Applying a salve to the burn on my leg, the pain soon subsided.

   _____

   _____

4. Escorted by dozens of police motorcycles, I knew the limousine carried someone important.

   _____

   _____

5. Marching across the field, a river could be seen in the distance.

   _____

   _____

6. Packed tightly in a tiny can, Fran had difficulty removing the anchovies.

   _____

   _____

7. Practicing relaxation techniques daily, stress can be relieved.

   _____

   _____

8. Avoiding foods high in fat and calories, one's health can be drastically improved.

   _____

   _____

9. Sitting at a sidewalk café, all sorts of interesting people passed by.

_____

_____

10. Though somewhat warped, Uncle Zeke played his records from the forties.

_____

_____

Review Test 1

Write DM for *dangling modifier* or C for *correct* in the space provided for each sentence.

_____ 1. Having considered several models, the Ford mustang was finally agreed upon.

_____ 2. Having considered several models, we finally agreed upon the Ford Mustang.

_____ 3. After eating shellfish for the first time, Jim had a frightening allergic reaction.

_____ 4. After eating shellfish for the first time, Jim's allergic reaction was frightening.

_____ 5. Boring and silly, I turned the TV show off.

_____ 6. I turned off the boring and silly TV show.

_____ 7. Munching leaves from a tall tree, the giraffe fascinated the children.

_____ 8. Munching leaves from a tall tree, the children were fascinated by the giraffe.

_____ 9. At the age of twelve, several colleges had already accepted the boy genius.

_____ 10. At the age of twelve, the boy genius had already been accepted by several colleges.

Review Test 2

Make the changes needed to correct the dangling modifier in each sentence.

1. After dieting for several months, a loss of twenty pounds was Susan's reward.

   _____

   _____

2. Joined at the hip, a team of surgeons successfully separated the Siamese twins.

   _____

   _____

3. Flossing one's teeth daily, dental checkups should be less worrisome.

   _____

   _____

4. While being restrained by federal marshals, the judge sentenced the kidnapper.

   _____

   _____

5. In a sentimental frame of mind, the music brought tears to Beth's eyes.

   _____

   _____

Review Test 3

Complete the following so that a logical subject follows the opening words.

EXAMPLE

   Looking through the door's peephole, _I couldn't see who rang the doorbell._

   _____

1. Noticing the light turn yellow, _____

2. Being fragile, _____

3. While washing the car, _____

4. Graduating at the top of her class, _____

5. Driving past the cemetery, _____

PREVIEW

CHAPTER 34
Manuscript Form

CHAPTER 35
Capital Letters

CHAPTER 36
Numbers and
Abbreviations

People often forget to apply sentence skills to their writing when composing e-mails. What can be done to correct the sentence-skills mistakes in the e-mail pictured here? Do you think such mistakes should be excusable in e-mails?

re: texas alignment files — Inbox

Delete   Junk   Reply   Reply All   Forward   Print

From: Shirley Michels
Subject: **re: texas alignment files**
Date: April 4, 2007 11:26:06 AM CDT
To: Amanda Crawford

Good morning, Amanda,

I have found the reports you were asking about for the texas project. our finance Department will get back to you as soon as they finalize the budget spreadsheets.

thanks,
shirley

34

Manuscript Form

This chapter will describe manuscript from: the required format for any paper you hand in.

KEY TERMS

format: the formal characteristics of a manuscript, comprising such things as paper size, margins, spacing, and font.

manuscript: literally, a paper written by hand; in this text, any paper handed in for a grade.

When you hand in a paper for any course, it will probably be judged first by its format. It is important, then, to make the paper look attractive, neat, and easy to read. Here is a checklist you should use when preparing a paper for an instructor:

www.mhhe.com/langan

_____ • Is the paper full-size, 8½ by 11 inches?

_____ • Are there wide margins (1 to 1½ inches) all around the paper? In particular, have you been careful not to crowd the right-hand or bottom margin?

_____ • If the paper is handwritten, have you

    Used a blue or black pen?

    Been careful not to overlap letters or to make decorative loops on letters?

    Made all your letters distinct, with special attention to *a, e, i, o,* and *u*—five letters that people sometimes write illegibly?

    Kept all your capital letters clearly distinct from small letters?

_____ • Have you centered the title of your paper on the first line of page 1? Have you been careful *not* to put quotation marks around the title and *not* to underline it? Have you capitalized all the words in the title except short connecting words like *of, for, the, and, in,* and *to*?

‾‾‾‾‾‾‾ • Have you skipped a line between the title and the first line of your paper?

‾‾‾‾‾‾‾ • Have you indented the first line of each paragraph about five spaces (half an inch) from the left-hand margin?

‾‾‾‾‾‾‾ • Have you made commas, periods, and other punctuation marks firm and clear? If you are typing, have you left a double space after a period?

‾‾‾‾‾‾‾ • If you have broken any words at the end of a line, have you been careful to break only between syllables?

‾‾‾‾‾‾‾ • Have you put your name, the date, and other information at the end of the paper (or wherever your instructor has specified)?

Also ask yourself these important questions about the title and the first sentence of your paper:

‾‾‾‾‾‾‾ • Is your title made up of several words that tell what the paper is about? (The title should be just several words, not a complete sentence.)

‾‾‾‾‾‾‾ • Does the first sentence of your paper stand independent of the title? (The reader should *not* have to use the words in the title to make sense of the opening sentence.)

Activity 1

Use the checklist to locate the seven mistakes in format in the following lines from a student paper. Explain the mistakes in the spaces provided. One mistake is described for you as an example.

	"Being alone"
	This is something that I simply cannot tolerate, and I will predi-
	ctably go to great lengths to prevent it. For example, if I know that

1. <u>Hyphenate only between syllables (predict-ably, not predi-ctably).</u>

2. ‾‾

3. ‾‾

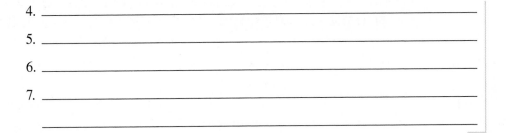

4. _____

5. _____

6. _____

7. _____

   _____

35

Capital Letters

This chapter will describe

- the main uses of capital letters
- secondary uses of capital letters
- unnecessary use of capital letters

INCORRECT:

The Bank is located on the corner.

"The" is capitalized correctly because it appears at the beginning of the sentence, but "bank" is not the building's official, specific name.

CORRECT:

The bank is located on the corner.

"The" is capitalized to start the sentence, but "bank" is left lowercase.

www.mhhe.com/langan

Main Uses of Capital Letters

Capital letters are used with

1. First word in a sentence or direct quotation
2. Names of persons and the word *I*
3. Names of particular places
4. Names of days of the week, months, and holidays
5. Names of commercial products
6. Titles of books, magazines, newspapers, articles, stories, poems, films, television shows, songs, papers that you write, and the like
7. Names of companies, associations, unions, clubs, religious and political groups, and other organizations

Each use is illustrated in this chapter.

First Word in a Sentence or Direct Quotation

The corner grocery was robbed last night.

The alien said, "Take me to your leader."

"If you need help," said Teri, "call me. I'll be over in no time."

In the third example above, *If* and *I'll* are capitalized because they start new sentences. But *call* is not capitalized, because it is part of the first sentence.

Names of Persons and the Word *I*

Last night, I saw *Elf,* a hilarious movie starring Will Ferrell and James Caan.

Names of Particular Places and Institutions

Although Bill dropped out of Port Charles High School, he eventually earned his degree and got a job with Atlas Realty Company.

But Use small letters if the specific name is not given.

Although Bill dropped out of high school, he eventually earned his degree and got a job with a real estate company.

Names of Days of the Week, Months, and Holidays

On the last Friday afternoon in May, the day before Memorial Day, my boss is having a barbecue for all the employees.

But Use small letters for the seasons—summer, fall, winter, spring.

Most people feel more energetic in the spring and fall.

Names of Commercial Products

Keith installed a new Sony stereo and a Motorola cell phone into his old Ford Ranger pickup.

But Use small letters for the *type* of product (stereo, cell phone, pickup, and so on).

Titles of Books, Magazines, Newspapers, Articles, Stories, Poems, Films, Television Shows, Songs, Papers That You Write, and the Like

We read the book *Hiroshima,* by John Hersey, for our history class.

In the doctor's waiting room, I watched *All My Children,* read an article in *Reader's Digest,* and leafed through the *Miami Herald.*

Names of Companies, Associations, Unions, Clubs, Religious and Political Groups, and Other Organizations

Joe Naples is a Roman Catholic, but his wife is a Methodist.

The Hilldale Square Dancers' Club has won many competitions.

Brian, a member of Bricklayers Local 431 and the Knights of Columbus, works for Ace Construction.

Activity

1

Underline the words that need capitals in the following sentences. Then write the capitalized form of each word in the space provided. The number of spaces tells you how many corrections to make in each case.

EXAMPLE

In our biology class, each student must do a report on an article in the maga-

zine *scientific american.* ___*Scientific*___   ___*American*___

1. Leon's collection of beatles souvenirs includes a pair of tickets from their last concert in candlestick park in San Francisco.

   _____   _____   _____

2. Yumi read in *natural health* magazine that abraham lincoln suffered from severe depression.

   _____   _____   _____   _____

3. When i have a cold, I use vicks ointment and chew listerine lozenges.

   _____   _____   _____

4. Since no man volunteered for the job, the boy scouts in springfield, illinois, have a woman troop leader.

   _____   _____   _____   _____

5. A nature trail for the blind in cape cod, massachusetts, has signs written in Braille that encourage visitors to smell and touch the plants.

   _____   _____   _____

6. Some of the most popular items at a restaurant called big river are chilean sea bass and atlantic clam chowder.

   _____   _____   _____   _____

7. We visited several theme parks in orlando, florida, including disney world.

   _____   _____   _____   _____

8. Stan was a big eater. For lunch he had a mcdonald's quarter-pounder, a big mac and a large coke.

   _____   _____   _____   _____

9. Vince listened to a U2 album called *The Joshua Tree* while Donna read an article in *glamour* titled "What Do men Really want?"

   _____   _____   _____

10. After having her baby, joan received a card from one of her friends that read, "congratulations, we all knew you had it in you."

   _____   _____

Other Uses of Capital Letters

www.mhhe.com/langan

Capital letters are used with

1. Names that show family relationships
2. Titles of persons when used with their names
3. Specific school courses
4. Languages
5. Geographic locations
6. Historical periods and events

7. Races, nations, and nationalities

8. Opening and closing of a letter

Each use is illustrated on the following pages.

Names That Show Family Relationships

All his life, Father has been addicted to gadgets.

I browsed through Grandmother's collection of old photographs.

Aunt Florence and Uncle Bill bought a mobile home.

But Do not capitalize words like *mother, father, grandmother, grandfather, uncle, aunt,* and so on when they are preceded by a possessive word (such as *my, your, his, her, our, their*).

All his life, my father has been addicted to gadgets.

I browsed through my grandmother's collection of old photographs.

My aunt and uncle bought a mobile home.

Titles of Persons When Used with Their Names

I contributed to Senator McGrath's campaign fund.

Is Dr. Gomez on vacation?

Professor Adams announced that there would be no tests in the course.

But Use lowercase letters when titles appear by themselves, without specific names.

I contributed to my senator's campaign fund.

Is the doctor on vacation?

The professor announced that there would be no tests in the course.

Specific School Courses

The college offers evening sections of Introductory Psychology I, Abnormal Psychology, Psychology and Statistics, and Educational Psychology.

But Use lowercase letters for general subject areas.

The college offers evening sections of many psychology courses.

Languages

My grandfather's Polish accent makes his English difficult to understand.

Geographic Locations

He grew up in the Midwest but moved to the South to look for a better job.

But Use lowercase letters in directions.

Head west for five blocks and then turn south on State Street.

Historical Periods and Events

During the Middle Ages, the Black Death killed over one-quarter of Europe's population.

Races, Nations, and Nationalities

The questionnaire asked whether the head of our household was Caucasian, African American, Asian, Latino, or Native American.

Tanya has lived on army bases in Germany, Italy, and Spain.

Denise's beautiful features reflect her Chinese and Mexican parentage.

Opening and Closing of a Letter

Dear Sir:	Sincerely yours,
Dear Ms. Henderson:	Truly yours,

Capitalize only the first word in a closing.

Underline the words that need capitals in the following sentences. Then write the capitalized forms of each words in the spaces provided. The number of spaces tells you how many corrections to make in each case.

Activity 2

1. The boston tea party was an act of defiance against the british government's policy of taxation in the american colonies.

   _____ _____ _____ _____ _____

2. On their job site in korea, the french, swiss, and chinese coworkers used English to communicate.

   _____ _____ _____ _____

3. When uncle harvey got the bill from his doctor, he called the American Medical Association to complain.

   _____ _____

4. Dr. Freeling of the business department is offering a new course called intro-duction to web design.

   _____   _____   _____

5. A new restaurant featuring vietnamese cuisine has just opened on the south side of the city.

   _____

Unnecessary Use of Capitals

Activity

3

Many errors occur when capitalization is used when it is not needed. Work-ing with a fellow classmate, underline the incorrectly capitalized words in the following sentences, and write the correct forms in the spaces provided. The number of spaces tells you how many corrections to make in each sentence.

1. George Washington's Forces starved at Valley Forge because Pennsylvania Farmers preferred to sell food to the British for cash.

   _____   _____

2. Minnesota is bordered by the Canadian Provinces of Manitoba and Ontario to the North, by Wisconsin to the East, and by North and South Dakota to the West.

   _____   _____   _____   _____

3. North America is the World's third largest Continent. It includes Canada, the United States, Mexico, the Countries of Central America, and the island Nations of the Caribbean.

   _____   _____   _____   _____

4. In his Book titled *Offbeat Museums,* Saul Rubin tells about various Unusual Museums, such as the Kansas Barbed Wire museum.

   _____   _____   _____   _____

5. Einstein's theory of relativity, which he developed when he was only twenty-six, led to the invention of the Electron Microscope, Television, and the Atomic bomb.

   _____   _____   _____

Review Test   1

Add capitals where needed in the following sentences.

EXAMPLE

> In an injured tone, Mary demanded, "ᵂwhy wasn't ᵁuncle Lou invited to the party?"

1. The white house is located at 1600 pennsylvania avenue in washington, d.c.

2. My favorite movie is *the godfather*, starring al pacino and marlon brando.

3. Insects living in mammoth cave in kentucky include blind crickets, spiders, and flies.

4. For practical purposes, the american civil war ended when general robert e. lee surrendered to general ulysses s. grant at appamatox on April 9, 1865.

5. In an old movie, an attractive young lady invites groucho marx to join her.

6. "why?" asks groucho. "are you coming apart?"

7. I was halfway to the wash & dry Laundromat on elm street when i realized that my box of tide was still home on the kitchen counter.

8. Although I know that mother loves holidays, even I was surprised when she announced a party in february to celebrate groundhog day.

9. *Rolling stone* magazine features an article about plans to remake the Alfred Hitchcock classic *the birds* and a review of a new biography about elvis presley.

10. Celebrities have earned big money by endorsing products, including nike shoes, trident gum, and jell-O pudding.

Review Test   2

On separate paper, write

1. Seven sentences demonstrating the seven main uses of capital letters.

2. Eight sentences demonstrating the eight other uses of capital letters.

36

Numbers and Abbreviations

This chapter will describe the proper use of numbers and abbreviations.

INCORRECT:

It took us 5 weeks to find an apt. we both liked.

"5" can be written as one word ("five") so it should be spelled out. "Apartment" can be abbreviated on an envelope, but should be written out in a sentence.

CORRECT:

It took us five weeks to find an apartment we both liked.

Spelling out "five" and "apartment" is correct in this format.

INCORRECT:

We'll have the report for you in 72 hours.

"72" can be written out as "seventy-two," which is fewer than three words.

CORRECT:

We'll have the report for you in seventy-two hours.

Because the number can be expressed in fewer than three words, it is spelled out.

KEY TERM

abbreviations: shortened forms of words, often used for convenience in writing. Certain abbreviations (such as *Mr.*, A.M., and *e.g.*) are acceptable in formal writing; in general, however, the complete form of words is preferred.

Numbers

Here are three helpful rules for using numbers.

Rule 1

Spell out numbers that take no more than two words. Otherwise, use the numbers themselves.

> In Jody's kitchen is her collection of seventy-two cookbooks.
>
> Jody has a file of 350 recipes.
>
> It will take about two weeks to fix the computer database.
>
> Since a number of people use the database, the company will lose over 150 workdays.
>
> Only twelve students have signed up for the field trip.
>
> Nearly 250 students came to the lecture.

Rule 2

Be consistent when you use a series of numbers. If some numbers in a sentence or paragraph require more than two words, then use numbers for the others, too.

> After the storm, maintenance workers unclogged 46 drains, removed 123 broken tree limbs, and rescued 3 kittens who were stuck in a drainpipe.

Rule 3

Use numbers to show dates, times, addresses, percentages, and chapters of a book.

> The burglary was committed on October 30, 2006, but was not discovered until January 2, 2007.
>
> Before I went to bed, I set my alarm for 6:45 A.M. (But spell out numbers before *o'clock*. For example: I didn't get out of bed until seven o'clock.)
>
> The library is located at 45 West 52nd Street.
>
> When you take the skin off a piece of chicken, you remove about 40 percent of the fat.
>
> The name of the murderer is revealed in Chapter 8 on page 236.

<table>
<tr><td>**Activity**</td></tr>
<tr><td>**1**</td></tr>
</table>

Activity 1

Cross out the mistakes in numbers and write the corrections in the spaces provided.

1. The Puerto Rican Pride Parade will begin at three-thirty in front of the newspaper office at one-oh-six South Forty-Second Street.

   _____   _____   _____

2. The governor is scheduled to arrive at four o'clock, but she is going to be twenty minutes late.

   _____   _____

3. We expect to have fifty percent of the work completed by March tenth.

   _____   _____

Abbreviations

www.mhhe.com/langan

Using abbreviations can save you time when you take notes. In formal writing, however, you should avoid most abbreviations. Listed below are some of the few abbreviations that are considered acceptable in compositions. Note that a period is used after most abbreviations.

1. Mr., Mrs., Ms., Jr., Sr., Dr. when used with names:
   Mrs. Johnson   Dr. Garcia   Howard Kelley Jr.

2. Time references:
   A.M.   P.M.   BC, AD

3. Initials in a person's name:
   J. Edgar Hoover   John F. Kennedy   Michael J. Fox

4. Organizations, technical words, and company names known primarily by their initials:
   IBM   UNICEF   ABC   IRS   NBA   AIDS

Activity 2

Cross out the words that should not be abbreviated, and correct them in the spaces provided.

1. Between mid-Nov. and the beginning of Jan., I typically gain about five lbs.

   _____   _____   _____

2. I have an appointment this A.M., but I can meet you for lunch in the caf. at noon.

_____   _____

3. I stopped at the p.o. at about twenty min. past ten and bought five dol. worth of stamps.

_____   _____   _____   _____

Review Test   1

Cross out the mistakes in numbers and abbreviations, and correct them in the spaces provided.

1. Sanjay was shocked when he transferred from a small h.s. to one with over 5,000 students.

_____   _____   _____   _____

2. Grandpa lived to be ninety-nine despite smoking 3 packs of cigs. every day.

_____   _____

3. Although the 2 girls are twins, they have different birthdays: one was born just before midnight on Feb. twenty-fifth and the other a few minutes later, after midnight.

_____   _____   _____

4. In their first week of Span. class, students learned to count from 1 to twenty-one and studied Chapter One in their textbook.

_____   _____   _____

5. United States banks belong to the Federal Reserve System, which consists of 12 regional member banks. Members of the Board of Governors serve for 14 year terms.

_____   _____

PREVIEW

CHAPTER 37
Apostrophe

CHAPTER 38
Quotation Marks

CHAPTER 39
Comma

CHAPTER 40
Other Punctuation
Marks

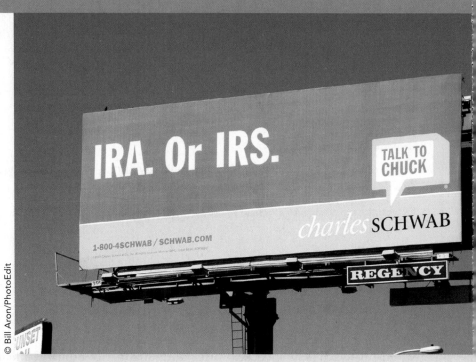

© Bill Aron/PhotoEdit

*Is there a punctuation error in the sign pictured here?
If so, how would you correct it?*

Apostrophe

This chapter will describe the two main uses of the apostrophe. The sentences below will introduce you to one of these uses—to show ownership or possession. See if you can guess the other main use of the apostrophe before turning the page.

INCORRECT:

Because of the dogs constant barking, I could not sleep all night.

An apostrophe is needed before the *s* in dogs to show possession of the constant barking.

CORRECT:

Because of the dog's constant barking, I could not sleep all night.

With the apostrophe included it is clear that the dog is the possessor of the constant barking.

KEY TERMS

apostrophe: a punctuation mark generally used in order to (1) show the omission of one or more letters in a contraction, and to (2) show ownership or possession.

contraction: the combination of two words through omission of one or more letters and use of an apostrophe. Example: *hasn't* (for *has not*)

The two main uses of the apostrophe are

1. To show the omission of one or more letters in a contraction
2. To show ownership or possession

www.mhhe.com/langan

Apostrophe in Contractions

A contraction is formed when two words are combined. An apostrophe shows where letters are omitted.

> have + not = haven't (the *o* in *not* has been omitted)
>
> I + will = I'll (the *wi* in *will* has been omitted)

Following are some other common contractions:

I + am = I'm	it + is = it's
I + have = I've	it + has = it's
I + had = I'd	is + not = isn't
who + is = who's	could + not = couldn't
do + not = don't	I + would = I'd
did + not = didn't	they + are = they're
	we + are = we're

Will + not has an unusual contraction: won't.

Activity

1

Write the contractions for the words in parentheses. One is done for you.

1. (Are not) _____ the reserve books in the library kept at the circulation desk?

2. If (they are) _____ going to Israel, they (do not) _____ want to miss visiting Jerusalem.

3. (I am) _____ the kind of student (who is) _____ extremely nervous before tests.

4. (Who is) _____ the clerk who discovered that (it is) _____

    cheaper to buy supplies online? (We are) _____ always interested in recognizing employees with good ideas.

5. I (cannot) _____ remember if (there is) _____ gas in the car or not.

> **TIP:** Even though contractions are common in everyday speech and in written dialogue, it is often best to avoid them in formal writing.

Apostrophe to Show Ownership or Possession

To show possession, we can use such words as *belongs to,* or *possessed by.*

the umbrella that belongs to Mark

the toys possessed by children

the tape recorder owned by the school

the gentleness of my father

But the apostrophe and *s* (if the word does't end in *s*) is often the easiest way to do this.

Mark's umbrella

the children's toys

the school's tape recorder

my father's gentleness

Points to Remember

1. The 's goes with the owner or possessor (in the examples given, *Mark, children, the school, my father*). What follows is the person or thing possessed (in the examples given, *the umbrella, the toys, the tape recorder, gentleness*).

2. There should always be a break between the word and *'s.*

   Mark's   not   Mark's
   Yes   No

3. An apostrophe and *s* are used to show possession with a singular word even if the word already ends in *s:* for example, Doris's purse (the purse belonging to Doris).

Activity

2

Working in groups of two or three, rewrite the *italicized* part of each of the sentences below, using *'s* to show possession. Remember that the *'s* goes with the owner or possessor.

EXAMPLE

> *The wing of the bluejay* was broken.
>
> The bluejay's wing was broken. _____

1. *The capital of Great Britain* is London.

   _____

2. *One of the major attractions of New York City* is the Emprire State Building.

   _____

3. *The three official languages of Switzerland* are German, French, and Italian.

   _____

4. *In the window of the jewelry store* is a sign reading "Ears Pierced While You Wait."

   _____

5. A fly flew into *the mouth of the TV weatherperson.*

   _____

6. *The new denim shirt belonging to Lamont* was as scratchy as sandpaper.

   _____

7. *The hair belonging to Rachel* is usually not green—she colored it for Halloween.

   _____

8. *The piano belonging to the Previn family* was once used in a symphony orchestra.

   _____

9. *The Honda owned by Donna* was crammed with boxes and furniture.

   _____

10. *The previous tenant of the apartment* had painted all the walls bright green.

    _____

Add *'s* to each of the following words to make it the possessor or owner of something. Then write sentences using the words. The first one is done for you.

1. rock star *rock star's* _____

   The rock star's limousine pulled up to the curb. _____

2. Felipe _____

   _____

3. The railroad conductor _____

   _____

   _____

4. neighbor _____

   _____

5. school _____

   _____

6. The government _____

   _____

   _____

Apostrophe versus Possessive Pronouns

Do not use an apostrophe with possessive pronouns. They already show ownership. Possessive pronouns include *his, hers, its, yours, ours,* and *theirs.*

Incorrect	Correct
The sun warped his' albums.	The sun warped his albums.
The restored Model T is theirs'.	The restored Model T is theirs.
The decision is yours'.	The decision is yours.
The lion charged its' prey.	The lion charged its prey.

Apostrophe versus Simple Plurals

To make a word plural, add only *s,* not an apostrophe. For example, the plural of the word *movie* is *movies,* not *movies'.*

Look at this sentence:

Tim coveted his roommate's collection of cassette tapes and compact discs.

The words *tapes* and *discs* are simple plurals, meaning more than one tape, more than one disc. The plural is shown by adding *s* only. On the other hand, the *'s* after *roommate* shows possession—that the roommate owns the tapes and discs.

Insert an apostrophe where needed to show possession in the following sentences. Write *plural* above words where the *s* ending simply means more than one. Then, compare your answers with that of a classmate.

EXAMPLE

Arlene's tinted contact *plural* lenses protect her eyes *plural* from glare.

1. Harry grasped his wifes arm as she stood on in-line skates for the first time.

2. Vonettes decision to study computer science is based on predictions of good opportunities for women in that field.

3. Pablo Picassos paintings are displayed in museums all over the world.

4. At the doctors request, Lyndon pulled up his shirt and revealed the zipperlike scars from his operation.

5. Of all the peoples names in all the worlds countries, the most common is Muhammad.

6. Sevilles many attractions include the beautiful Alcazar district built by the Moors, who ruled this Spanish city for five centuries.

7. The childrens shouts of delight grew louder as the clown added eggs, lightbulbs, and a bowling ball to the items he was juggling.

8. Tinas camping handbook suggests that we bring water purification tablets and nylon ropes.

9. *Black Beauty,* a childrens novel has entertained young readers for more than a hundred years.

10. The rattlesnakes head has a sensitive pit below the eyes, capable of detecting the body heat of warm-blooded prey.

Apostrophe with Plurals Ending in *s*

Plurals that end in *s* show possession simply by adding the apostrophe, rather than an apostrophe and *s*.

the Thompsons' porch

the players' victory

her parents' motor home

the Rolling Stones' last CD

the soldiers' hats

Add an apostrophe where needed.

1. Several campers tents collapsed during the storm.

2. Both of the Johnsons daughters have become attorneys.

3. Many cities subway and bus systems provide inexpensive and efficient transportation.

4. The twins habit of dressing alike was started by their mother when they were children.

5. At the crowded intersection, several young men rushed out to wash the cars windshields.

Activity

5

Review Test   1

In each sentence, underline the two words that need apostrophes. Then write the words correctly in the spaces provided.

_____ 1. Nigerias chief export is oil, the earnings from which make the

_____ countrys economy one of the richest in Africa.

_____ 2. A shaky rope ladder led from the barns wooden floor to the

_____ haylofts dusty shadows.

_____ 3. The paperback books glaring purple and orange cover was

_____ designed to attract a hurrying customers eye.

_____ 4. One of South Africas greatest writers is Alan Paton, the author

_____ of the novel *Cry, the Beloved Country*. Patons fiction deals with the conflicts between the races in his country.

_____ 5. While he waited in his bosss office, Charlies nervous fingers

_____ shredded a Styrofoam coffee cup into a pile of jagged white flakes.

_____ 6. Gregory couldnt remember whether he had left his wallet in

_____ his mothers car or at home.

_____ 7. Members of the parents association constructed a maze made

_____ of old tires for the childrens playground.

_____ 8. The cats great green eyes grew even wider as the curious dogs

_____ sniffing nose came too close to her.

_____ 9. The suns rays beat down until the streets blacktopped surface

_____ softened with the heat.

_____ 10. The Czars government was overthrown by the Bolshevik

_____ Revolution of 1917. Russias new government was based on communist principles.

38

Quotation Marks

Quotation marks are punctuation marks that indicate exact words or the titles of short works. This chapter will describe the two main uses of quotation marks. The sentences below will introduce you to one of these uses—to set off the exact words of a speaker or writer. See if you can guess the other main use of quotation marks before turning the page.

INCORRECT:

I'm giving up smoking tomorrow said Jason.

Because it is a direct quote, what Jason said should be in quotation marks.

CORRECT:

"I'm giving up smoking tomorrow," said Jason.

Jason's words are directly attributed by the quotation marks.

The two main uses of quotation marks are

1. To set off the exact words of a speaker or writer
2. To set off the titles of short works

Quotation Marks to Set Off the Words of a Speaker or Writer

Use quotation marks to show the exact words of a speaker or writer.

Ben Franklin once wrote, "To lengthen thy life, lessen thy meals." (Quotation marks set off the exact words that Ben Franklin wrote.)

"Did you know," said the nutrition expert, "that it's healthier to be ten pounds overweight?"

(Two pairs of quotation marks are used to enclose the nutrition expert's exact words.)

www.mhhe.com/langan

The biology professor said, "Ants are a lot like human beings. They farm their own food and raise smaller insects as livestock. And like humans, ants send armies to war."

(Note that the end quotation marks do not come until the end of the biology professor's speech. Place quotation marks before the first quoted word and after the last quoted word. As long as no interruption occurs in the speech, do not use quotation marks for each new sentence.)

> **TIP:** In the three examples above, notice that a comma sets the quoted part off from the rest of the sentence. Also, observe that commas and periods at the end of a quotation always go *inside* quotation marks.

Complete the following statements, which explain how capital letters, commas, and periods are used in quotations. Refer to the four examples above as guides.

1. Every quotation begins with a _____ letter.

2. When a quotation is split (as in the sentence about the nutrition expert), the second part does not begin with a capital letter unless it is a

   _____ sentence.

3. _____ are used to separate the quoted part of a sentence from the rest of the sentence.

4. Commas and periods that come at the end of a quotation go _____ the quotation marks.

The answers are *capital, new, Commas,* and *inside.*

Activity

1

Place quotation marks around the exact words of a speaker or writer in the sentences that follow.

1. Several people have been credited with saying, The more I see of people, the more I like dogs.

2. Let nature be your teacher, advised the poet William Wordsworth.

3. According to the Bible, the laborer is worthy of his hire.

4. The bumper sticker on the rear of the battered old car read, Don't laugh—it's paid for.

5. I know why Robin Hood robbed only the rich, said the comedian. The poor don't have any money.

6. The ballot, said Abraham Lincoln, is stronger than the bullet.

7. When chefs go to great lengths, the woman at the diet center said, I go to great widths.

8. If I go with you to the dinner party, my friend said, you must promise not to discuss politics.

9. On a tombstone in a Maryland cemetery are the words Here lies an atheist, all dressed up and no place to go.

10. The columnist advised, Be nice to people on your way up because you'll meet them on your way down.

1. Write a sentence in which you quote a favorite expression of someone you know. In the same sentence, identify the person's relationship to you.

Activity 2

EXAMPLE

My grandfather loves to say, "It can't be as bad as all that."

_____

_____

_____

2. Write a quotation that contains the words *Pablo asked Teresa*. Write a second quotation that includes the words *Teresa replied*.

_____

_____

_____

_____

3. Quote an interesting sentence or two from a book or magazine. In the same sentence, identify the title and author of the work.

EXAMPLE *In The Dilbert Desk Calendar, by Scott Adams, the cartoon character Dilbert says, "I can please only one person per day. Today isn't your day, and tomorrow isn't looking good either."*

_____

_____

_____

_____

_____

_____

4. Write a sentence in which the speaker of a quotation is identified in the middle of the quotation.

EXAMPLE *"Ralph ate a pound of pasta, six meatballs, and a slice of chocolate cake," said his wife, Alice, "but he was still hungry!"*

_____

_____

_____

_____

_____

Indirect Quotations

An indirect quotation is a rewording of someone else's comments rather than a word-for-word direct quotation. The word *that* often signals an indirect quotation.

Direct Quotation	Indirect Quotation
The nurse said, "Some babies cannot tolerate cows' milk." (The nurse's exact spoken words are given, so quotation marks are used.)	The nurse said that some babies cannot tolerate cows' milk. (We learn the nurse's words indirectly, so no quotation marks are used.)
Vicky's note to Dan read, "I'll be home by 7:30." (The exact words that Vicky wrote in the note are given, so quotation marks are used.)	Vicky left a note for Dan saying that she would be home by 7:30. (We learn Vicky's words indirectly, so no quotation marks are used.)

Rewrite the following sentences, changing words as necessary to convert the sentences into direct quotations. The first one has been done for you as an example.

1. Teddy asked Margie whether she wanted to see his spider collection.

   Teddy asked Margie, "Do you want to see my spider collection?"

   _____

2. According to Monica, her grandmother has been the role model for several women in her family.

   _____

   _____

3. Angelo said that he wanted a box of the extra-crispy chicken.

   _____

   _____

4. My history professor told us that tomatoes were first grown in Peru.

   _____

   _____

5. The instructor announced that Thursday's test had been canceled.

   _____

   _____

Quotation Marks to Set Off Titles of Short Works

www.mhhe.com/langan

Titles of short works are usually set off by quotation marks, while titles of long works are underlined (if writing longhand) or italicized (if writing on a computer). Use quotation marks to set off titles of such short works as articles in books, newspapers, or magazines; chapters in a book; short stories; poems; and songs. But you should underline or italicize titles of books, newspapers, magazines, plays, movies, CDs, and television shows. Following are some examples.

Quotation Marks	Underlines
the essay "On Self-Respect"	in the book <u>Slouching Towards Bethlehem</u>
the article "The Problem of Acid Rain"	in the newspaper the <u>New York Times</u>

the article "Living with Inflation"	in the magazine <u>Newsweek</u>
the chapter "Chinese Religion"	in the book <u>Paths of Faith</u>
the story "Hands"	in the book <u>Winesburg, Ohio</u>
the poem "When I Have Fears"	in the book <u>Complete Poems of John Keats</u>
the song "Ziggy Stardust"	in the CD <u>Changes</u>
	the television show <u>60 Minutes</u>
	the movie <u>High Noon</u>

Activity

4

Use quotation marks or underlines as needed. Review your answers with a partner.

1. In her short story A Sea Worry, Maxine Hong Kingston describes a group of teenage surfers and a mother who tries to understand them.

2. The January issue of Discover magazine included an article entitled Lost Cities of the Amazon.

3. We read the chapter Pulling Up Roots in Gail Sheehy's book Passages.

4. Raymond gave me a copy of last month   National Geographic magazine, which featured a story called Saving Energy: It Starts at Home.

5. The movie Casablanca, which starred Humphrey Bogart, was originally cast with Ronald Reagan in the leading role.

6. One of my grandfather's favorite old TV shows was Thriller, a horror series hosted by Boris Karloff, the man who starred in the 1931 movie Frankenstein.

7. When the Beatles' movie A Hard Day's Night was first shown, fans screamed so much that no one could hear the songs or the dialogue.

8. Pinned on Jeffery's wall is the cover of a recent issue of Rolling Stone. The cover has a photo of the British rock group The Rolling Stones.

9. The sociology test will cover the first two chapters: Culture and Diversity and Social Stratification.

10. An article in Consumer Reports called Which Cereal for Breakfast? claims that children can learn to like low-sugar cereals like Cheerios and Wheaties.

Other Uses of Quotation Marks

Quotation marks are also used as follows:

1. To set off special words or phrases from the rest of a sentence:

> In grade school, we were taught a little jingle about the spelling rule "*i* before *e*."

What is the difference between "it's" and "its"?

(In this and other books, *italics* are often used instead of quotation marks to set off words.)

2. To mark off a quotation within a quotation:

> The physics professor said, "For class on Friday, do the problems at the end of the chapter titled 'Work and Energy.'"

> Brendan remarked, "Did you know that Humphrey Bogart never actually said, 'Play it again, Sam,' in the movie *Casablanca*?"

TIP: A quotation within a quotation is indicated by *single* quotation marks, as shown above.

Review Test 1

Insert quotation marks where needed in the sentences that follow.

1. The psychology class read a short story called Silent Snow, Secret Snow, about a young boy who creates his own fantasy world.

2. While filming the movie *Vertigo,* the actress Kim Novak was agonizing over how to play a particular scene until the director, Alfred Hitchcock, reminded her, Kim, it's only a movie!

3. He that would thrive, said the writer John Clarke, must rise at five.

4. The composer George Gershwin wrote many hundreds of hit songs, including classics like Summertime and Somebody Loves Me.

5. When we finally found a motel that had rooms available, my wife shouted, Halleluiah! We won't have to stay with your relatives again!

6. I looked twice at the newspaper headline that read, Man in River Had Drinking Problem.

7. To learn more about the stock market for his business class, Jared began reading the column by Pablo Galarza in *Money* magazine called MarketRap.

8. When a guest at the wedding was asked what he was giving the couple, he replied, About six months.

9. Theodore Roosevelt, a pioneer in conservation, once said, When I hear of the destruction of a species, I feel as if all the works of some great writer had perished.

10. The assignment read as follows: Write an essay in which you explain the theme of Walt Whitman's poem When Lilacs Last in the Dooryard Bloom'd.

Review Test 2

In a newspaper's comic section find an amusing comic strip. Choose one where two or more characters speak to each other. Write a description that enables people who have not read the comic strip to appreciate its humor. Describe the setting and action in each panel, and enclose the speakers' words in quotation marks.

Comma

This chapter will describe the six main uses of the comma. The sentences below will introduce you to one of these uses—to set a direct quotation off from the rest of the sentence. The other five main uses of the comma are included below.

INCORRECT:

The journalist pleaded "Just one more question."

A comma is needed to set the direct quotation off from the rest of the sentence.

CORRECT:

The journalist pleaded, "Just one more question."

With the comma included, the direct quotation is properly set off from the rest of the sentence.

Six Main Uses of the Comma

Commas are used mainly as follows:

1. To separate items in a series
2. To set off introductory material
3. On both sides of words that interrupt the flow of thought in a sentence
4. Between two complete thoughts connected by *and, but, for, or, nor, so, yet*
5. To set off a direct quotation from the rest of a sentence
6. For certain everyday material

You may find it helpful to remember that the comma often marks a slight pause or break in a sentence. Read aloud the sentence examples given for each rule, and listen for the minor pauses or breaks that are signaled by commas.

1 Comma between Items in a Series

Use commas to separate items in a series.

> The street vendor sold watches, necklaces, and earrings.
>
> The pitcher adjusted his cap, pawed the ground, and peered over his shoulder.
>
> The exercise instructor told us to inhale, exhale, and relax.
>
> Joe peered into the hot, still-smoking engine.

A. The final comma in a series is optional, but it is often used. If you use a final comma in one series in an essay, use one in all the other series in the same essay.

B. A comma is used between two descriptive words in a series only if *and* inserted between the words sounds natural. You could say:

> Joe peered into the hot *and* still-smoking engine.

But notice in the following sentence that the descriptive words do not sound natural when *and* is inserted between them. In such cases, no comma is used.

> Tony wore a pale green tuxedo. (A pale *and* green tuxedo does not sound right, so no comma is used.)

Activity

1

Place commas between items in a series.

1. The American alligator lives in southern swamps, streams, lakes, and other bodies of water.

2. Rudy stretched out on the swaying, hammock popped open a frosty can of soda, and balanced, it carefully on his stomach.

3. The children splashed through the warm, deep, swirling, rainwater that flooded the street.

4. The police officer's warm brown eyes, relaxed, manner, and pleasant smile made her easy to talk to.

5. The soft warm woolen blankets comforted us, as we heard the cold north wind blow through the pines.

2 Comma after Introductory Material

Use a comma to set off introductory material.

> Just in time, Sherry applied the brakes and avoided a car accident.
>
> Muttering under his breath, Hassan reviewed the terms he had memorized.
>
> In a wolf pack, the dominant male holds his tail higher than the other pack members.

Although he had been first in the checkout line, Deion let an elderly woman go ahead of him.

After the fire, we slogged through the ashes of the burned-out house.

> **TIP:** If the introductory material is brief, the comma is sometimes omitted. In the activities here, you should include the comma.

Place commas after introductory material. Once you have completed the activity, review your answers with a partner.

1. Although it cannot kill certain bacteria penicillin is still a useful antibiotic.
2. His heart pounding wildly Jesse opened the letter that would tell him whether he had been accepted at college.
3. Passing through 14 states the Appalachian trail is over 2,000 miles long.
4. When the band hadn't taken the stage forty-five minutes after the concert was supposed to begin the audience members started shouting and stamping their feet.
5. Along the side of the brook we noticed a newborn fawn speckled brown and red.

3 Comma around Words That Interrupt the Flow of Thought

Use a comma on both sides of words or phrases that interrupt the flow of thought in a sentence.

The vinyl car seat, sticky from the heat, clung to my skin.

Marty's computer, which his wife got him as a birthday gift, occupies all his spare time.

The hallway, dingy and dark, was illuminated by a bare bulb hanging from a wire.

Usually, by reading a sentence aloud, you can hear the words that interrupt the flow of thought. In cases where you are not sure if certain words are interrupters, remove them from the sentence. If it still makes sense without the words, you know that the words are interrupters and that the information they give is nonessential. *Such nonessential or extra information is set off with commas.*

In the sentence

Sue Dodd, who goes to aerobics class with me, was in a serious car accident.

the words *who goes to aerobics class with me* are extra information not needed to identify the subject of the sentence, *Sue Dodd*. Commas go around such non-essential information. On the other hand, in the sentence

The woman who goes to aerobics class with me was in a serious accident.

the words *who goes to aerobics class with me* supply essential information—information needed for us to identify the woman being spoken of. If the words were removed from the sentence, we would no longer know exactly who was in the accident: "The woman was in a serious accident." Here is another example:

Watership Down, a novel by Richard Adams, is the most thrilling adventure story I've ever read.

Here the words *a novel by Richard Adams* could be left out, and we would still know the basic meaning of the sentence. Commas are placed around such non-essential material. But in the sentence

Richard Adams's novel *Watership Down* is the most thrilling adventure story I've ever read.

the title of the novel is essential. Without it the sentence would read, "Richard Adams's novel is the most thrilling adventure story I've ever read." We would not know which of Richard Adams's novels was so thrilling. Commas are not used around the title, because it provides essential information.

Most of the time you will be able to hear which words interrupt the flow of thought in a sentence and will not have to think about whether the words are essential or nonessential.

Activity 3

Use commas to set off interrupting words.

1. A slight breeze, hot and damp, ruffled the bedroom curtains.
2. Two large pines, swaying in the wind, signaled that cooler weather was coming.
3. Hawaii, which became the fiftieth state in 1959, is made up of eight major islands.
4. Mr. Delgado, who is an avid Yankees fan, remembers the grand days of Mickey Mantle and Yogi Berra.
5. The fleet of tall ships, a majestic sight, made its way into the harbor.

4 Comma between Complete Thoughts

Use a comma between two complete thoughts connected by *and, but, for, or, nor, so, yet.*

> Sam closed all the windows, but the predicted thunderstorm never arrived.
>
> I like wearing comfortable clothing, so I buy oversize shirts and sweaters.
>
> Peggy doesn't envy the skinny models in magazines, for she is happy with her own well-rounded body.

A. The comma is optional when the complete thoughts are short.

> The Ferris wheel started and Wilson closed his eyes.
>
> Many people left but the band played on.
>
> I made a wrong turn so I doubled back.

B. Be careful not to use a comma to separate two verbs that belong to one subject. The comma is used only in sentences made up of two complete thoughts (two subjects and two verbs). In the sentence

> The doctor stared over his bifocals and lectured me about smoking.

there is only one subject (*doctor*) and a double verb (*stared* and *lectured*). No comma is needed. Likewise, the sentence

> Dean switched the lamp on and off and then tapped it with his fingers.

has only one subject (*Dean*) and a double verb (*switched* and *tapped*); therefore, no comma is needed.

Place a comma before a joining word that connects two complete thoughts (two subjects and two verbs). Remember, do *not* place a comma within a sentence that has only one subject and a double verb. (Some items may be correct as given.)

Activity 4

1. The television sitcom was interrupted for a special news bulletin, and I poked my head out of the kitchen to listen to the announcement.
2. Before he led Confederate troops in the Civil War, General Robert E. Lee had fought in the Mexican War and had been superintendent at West Point.
3. The eccentric woman brought all her own clips and rollers to the beauty parlor, for she was afraid to use the ones there.
4. Orangutans are ideally suited for living in trees, and they rarely climb down to the ground.
5. Plastic surgery was developed to repair damaged tissue, but today it is often used to improve one's appearance.

6. Ruth was tired of summer reruns, so she visited the town library to pick up some interesting books.

7. You can spend hours driving all over town to look for a particular type of camera, or you can telephone a few stores to find it quickly.

8. Many people strolled among the exhibits at the comic book collectors' convention, and stopped to look at a rare first edition of *Superman*.

9. Our neighborhood crime patrol escorts elderly people to the local bank and installs free dead-bolt locks on their apartment doors.

10. Brendan tapped the small geraniums out of their pots, and carefully planted them on his grandfather's grave.

5 Comma with Direct Quotations

www.mhhe.com/langan

Use a comma to set off a direct quotation from the rest of a sentence.

The carnival barker cried, "Step right up and win a prize!"

"Now is the time to yield to temptation," my horoscope read.

"I'm sorry," said the restaurant hostess. "You'll have to wait."

"For my first writing assignment," said Scott, "I have to turn in a five-hundred-word description of a stone."

> **TIP:** Commas and periods at the end of a quotation go inside quotation marks. See also page 566.

Activity 5

Use commas to set off direct quotations from the rest of the sentence.

1. The coach announced, "In order to measure your lung capacity, you're going to attempt to blow up a plastic bag with one breath."

2. "A grapefruit," said the comedian, "is a lemon that had a chance and took advantage of it."

3. The child heard her mother whisper, "Ladybird, ladybird, fly away home."

4. "My heart is bursting," said Stella. "How can I ever repay you for all you've done?"

5. The zookeeper explained to the visitors, "We can't tell the sex of a giant tortoise for almost ten years after its birth."

6 Other Uses for Commas

Use a comma when addressing someone directly.

> If you're the last to leave, Paul, please switch off the lights.
>
> Fred, I think we're on the wrong road.
>
> Did you see the playoff game, Lisa?

Use a comma after the salutation of a friendly letter and after the salutation and closing of a friendly and a formal letter.

> Dear allie   Sincerely yours,
>
> Dear Roberto,   Yours truly,

TIP: In formal letters, a colon is used after the opening:
Dear Sir: *or* Dear Madam: *or* Dear Allan: *or* Dear Ms. Mohr:

Use commas in numbers of four digits or more, except for years and street numbers.

> In 2008, the insurance agent sold me a $50,000 term life insurance policy.

TIP: No comma is used before a zip code.

Place commas where needed.

1. The City of Dublin Maggie is the capital of the Republic of Ireland.
2. On July 15 2009, Philip Vassallo opened a legal office at 2600 Woodbridge Avenue Fort Myers Florida.
3. An estimated 875000 African American men participated in the Million Man March on Washington on October 16 1995.
4. The mileage chart shows Elaine that we'll have to drive 1231 miles to get to Sarasota Florida.
5. The coupon refund address is 2120 Industrial Highway Great Plains, Minnesota 55455.

Persons Spoken To

Openings and Closings of Letters

Numbers

www.mhhe.com/langan

Activity 6

Review Test   1

Insert commas where needed. In the space provided below each sentence, summarize briefly the rule that explains the comma or commas used.

1. "Kleenex tissues" said the history professor "were first used as gas mask filters in World War I."

   _____

2. The large juicy Barlett pear that I bit into was sweet cold and refreshing.

   _____

3. While waiting to enter the movie theater we studied the faces of the people just leaving to see if they had liked the show.

   _____

4. I had left my wallet on the store counter but the clerk called me at home to say that it was safe.

   _____

5. The demonstrators protesting nuclear arms carried signs reading "Humans have never invented a weapon that they haven't used."

   _____

6. Large cactus plants which now sell for very high prices are being stolen from national parks and protected desert areas.

   _____

7. At the age of twenty-one Tiger Woods won the 1997 Masters Tournament with the highest margin of victory in the golfing tournament's history.

   _____

8. Tucson a large city in Arizona is quite near the border with Mexico.

   _____

9. The North African nation of Algeria is bordered by five other countries: Tunisia Libya Niger Mali and Mauritania.

   _____

10. Cats and dogs like most animals love the taste of salt and will lick humans' hands to get it.

    _____

Review Test 2

Insert commas where needed. Mark the one sentence that is correct with a C.

1. Before leaving for the gym Nikki added extra socks and a tube of shampoo to the gear in her duffel bag.
2. My father said "Golf isn't for me. I can't afford to buy lots of expensive sticks so that I can lose lots of expensive white balls."
3. Reviewed by a committee of college faculty Jason's application for scholarship aid was approved unanimously.
4. Oscar took a time-exposure photo of the busy highway so the cars' taillights appeared in the developed print as winding red ribbons.
5. A line of dancing numerals on *Sesame Street* kicked across the screen like a chorus line.
6. During the summer graduation ceremony students fanned themselves with commencement programs and parents hid in the shade of trees.
7. Leaving seven astronauts dead the space shuttle *Columbia* broke apart as it returned to Earth on February 1 2003.
8. "When I was little" said Ernie "my brother told me it was illegal to kill praying mantises. I still don't know if that's true or not."
9. The Cloisters, a museum of medieval art which is part of the New York Metropolitan Museum of Art includes buildings brought to the United States from Europe.
10. On June 24 1948 the Soviet Union closed the German city of Berlin to traffic from the West. However this ill-fated venture lasted only until May 11 1949 when the Soviets were forced to reopen the city.

Review Test 3

In the following passage, there are ten missing commas. Add the commas where needed. The types of mistakes to look for are shown in the box below.

> 2 commas missing between items in a series
> 1 comma missing after introductory material
> 4 commas missing around interrupting words
> 2 commas missing between complete thoughts
> 1 comma missing with a direct quotation

When I was about ten years old, I developed several schemes to avoid eating liver, a food I despise. My first scheme involved my little brother. Timmy, too young to realize what a horrible food liver is, always ate every bit of his portion. On liver nights, I used to sit next to Tim and slide my slab of meat onto his plate when my parents weren't paying attention. This strategy worked until, older and wiser, Tim decided to reject his liver along with the rest of us. Another liver-disposal method I used was hiding the meat right on the plate. I'd cut the liver into tiny squares half the size of postage stamps, and then I would carefully hide the pieces. I'd put them inside the skin of my baked potato, beneath some mashed peas, or under a crumpled paper napkin. This strategy worked perfectly only if my mother didn't look too closely as she scraped the dishes. Once she said to me, "Do you know you left a lot of liver on your plate?" My best liver trick was to hide the disgusting stuff on a three-inch-wide wooden ledge that ran under our dining-room table. I'd put little pieces of liver on the ledge when Mom wasn't looking; I would sneak the driedup scraps into the garbage early the next day. Our dog would sometimes smell the liver, try to get at it, and bang his head noisily against the bottom of the table. These strategies seemed like a lot of work, but I never hesitated to take whatever steps I could. Anything was better than eating a piece of meat that tasted like old socks soaked in mud.

Review Test 4

On separate paper, write six sentences, one illustrating each of the six main comma rules.

1. I love to play basketball, soccer, and cricket.

2. If you got something in wrong, you will caught trouble or pushinent.

3. my friend Jamil, ~~who his is NYC~~, is very nect person.

4.

5. his birthday is on May 16, 2011.

6. Someone hit kid on the floor while man yell, "get out or else I will kill you;"

Other Punctuation Marks

This chapter will describe other punctuation marks including the colon, the dash, the hyphen, parentheses, and the semicolon.

KEY TERMS

colon: punctuation mark used at the end of a complete statement to introduce a list, a long quotation, or an explanation.

dash: punctuation mark used to signal a pause longer than that of a comma but not as long as that of a period.

hyphen: punctuation mark used with two or more words that act as a single unit or to divide a word at the end of a line.

parentheses: punctuation marks used to set off extra or incidental information from the rest of a sentence.

semicolon: punctuation mark used to mark a break between two complete thoughts or to mark off items in a series when the items themselves contain internal punctuation (such as commas).

Colon (:)

Use the colon at the end of a complete statement to introduce a list, a long quotation, or an explanation.

www.mhhe.com/langan

1. List:

> The store will close at noon on the following dates: November 26, December 24, and December 31.

2. Quotation:

> In his book *Life Lines,* Forrest Church maintains that people should cry more: "Life is difficult. Some people pretend that it is not, that we should be able to breeze through. Yet hardly a week passes in which most of us don't have something worth crying about."

3. Explanation:

> Here's a temporary solution to a dripping faucet: Tie a string to it, and let the drops slide down the string to the sink.

Activity

1

Place colons where needed in the sentences below:

1. There are eight parts of speech noun, pronoun, verb, adjective, adverb, preposition, conjunction, and article.

2. The Italian lira and the German mark are no longer used in 1999, the official currency of many European countries became the euro.

3. Willa Cather, the American author, had an insightful comment about plots "There are only two or three human stories, and they go on repeating themselves as fiercely as if they had never happened before."

Semicolon (;)

www.mhhe.com/langan

The main use of the semicolon is to mark a break between two complete thoughts, as explained on page 583. Another use is to mark off items in a series when the items themselves contain commas. Here are some examples:

> Maya's children are named Melantha, which means "black flower"; Yonina, which means "dove"; and Cynthia, which means "moon goddess."

> My parents' favorite albums are *Rubber Soul,* by the Beatles; *Songs in the Key of Life,* by Stevie Wonder; and *Bridge over Troubled Water,* by Simon and Garfunkel.

Activity

2

Working with a partner, place semicolons where needed in the sentences below.

1. Strange things happen at very low temperatures a rose will shatter like glass.

2. My sister had a profitable summer: by mowing lawns, she earned $125 by washing cars, $85 and by walking the neighbors' dogs, $110.

3. There are three major Hindu gods: Brahma, the power that creates Shiva, the power that destroys and Vishnu, the power that restores.

Dash (—)

A dash signals a pause longer than a comma but not as complete as a period. Use a dash to set off words for dramatic effect:

> I was so exhausted that I fell asleep within seconds—standing up.

> He had many good qualities—sincerity, honesty, and thoughtfulness—yet he had few friends.

> The pardon from the governor finally arrived—too late.

> **TIPS:** a. A dash can be formed using a keyboard by striking the hyphen twice (--). Computer software also has a symbol for the dash. In handwriting, a dash is as long as two letters would be.
>
> b. Be careful not to overuse dashes.

Place dashes where needed in the following sentences.

Activity

3

1. The victim's leg broken in three places lay twisted at an odd angle on the pavement.
2. On September 17, 2008, a phone call from the Lottery Commission changed the Richardsons' lives they were informed they had won $10 million.
3. After nine days of hiking in the wilderness, sleeping under the stars, and communing with nature, I could think of only one thing a hot shower.

Parentheses ( )

Parentheses are used to set off extra or incidental information from the rest of a sentence:

> In 1913, the tax on an annual income of four thousand dollars (a comfortable wage at that time) was one penny.

> Arthur C. Clarke, author of science fiction books (including *2001: A Space Odyssey*), was inspired as a young man by the magazine *Astounding Stories*.

www.mhhe.com/langan

> **TIP:** Do not use parentheses too often in your writing.

Add parentheses where needed.

Activity

4

1. Though the first *Star Trek* series originally ran for only three seasons 1965–1968, it gave rise to a number of spinoff shows that remain popular to this day.
2. Ukraine became independent the country had been part of the Soviet Union since 1922 in 1990, after the fall of communism in Eastern Europe.
3. When I opened the textbook, I discovered that many pages mostly in the first chapter were completely blank.

Hyphen (-)

1. Use a hyphen with two or more words that act as a single unit describing a noun.

> The light-footed burglar silently slipped open the sliding glass door.
>
> While being interviewed on the late-night talk show, the quarterback announced his intention to retire.
>
> With a needle, Rich punctured the fluid-filled blister on his toe.

2. Use a hyphen to divide a word at the end of a line of writing or typing. When you need to divide a word at the end of a line, divide it between syllables. Use your dictionary to be sure of correct syllable divisions.

> Selena's first year at college was a time filled with numer-
> ous new pressures and responsibilities.

TIPS: a. Do not divide words of one syllable.
  b. Do not divide a word if you can avoid dividing it.

Activity 5

Working with a partner, place hyphens where needed.

1. The blood red moon hanging low on the horizon made a picture-perfect atmosphere for Halloween night.

2. We walked by a beautiful lily covered pond, then through a sweet smelling pine forest, and finally up to the mountain's sun-bathed summit.

3. The well written article in *Newsweek* described the nerve racking experiences of a journalist who infiltrated the mob.

Review Test 1

At the appropriate spot, place the punctuation mark shown in the margin.

—   1. An A on my English paper, a raise in pay at the Dairy Delight, and the birth of my first nephew it's been a great week!

( )   2. My grandfather who will be ninety in May says that hard work and a glass of wine every day are the secrets of a long life.

3. Mark Twain offered this advice to writers "The difference between the right   :
word and the nearly right word is the difference between lightning and the
lightning bug."

4. The passengers in the glass bottomed boat stared at the colorful fish in the   -
water below.

5. Fermium named after Italian physicist Enrico Fermi, who helped develop the   ( )
atomic bomb is a radioactive element discovered in 1952.

6. The dog-show winners included Freckles, a springer spaniel King Leo, a   ;
German shepherd and Big Guy, a miniature schnauzer.

7. There are only two ways to get an A in Prof. Callahan's class read the material   —
carefully and write good papers.

8. Cold hearted stepmothers are a fixture in many famous fairy tales.   -

9. Some people need absolute quiet to study they can't concentrate with the soft   ;
sounds of a radio, air conditioner, or television in the background.

10. A critic reviewing a bad play wrote, "I saw the play under the worst possible   :
circumstances the curtain was up."

SECTION 4

WORD USE

PREVIEW

CHAPTER 41
Spelling
Improvement

CHAPTER 42
Commonly Confused
Words

CHAPTER 43
Effective Word
Choice

CHAPTER 44
Editing Tests

CHAPTER 45
ESL Pointers

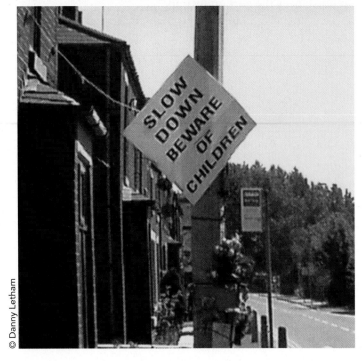

What is it about these signs that makes them funny? How could each one be fixed so that its message is clearer?

41

Spelling Improvement

This chapter will list six steps toward improving your spelling:

Step 1: Use a Dictionary

Step 2: Keep a Personal Spelling List

Step 3: Master Commonly Confused Words

Step 4: Learn Key Words in Major Subjects

Step 5: Study a Basic Word List

Step 6: Use Electronic Aids

KEY TERM

personal spelling list: a list of words you misspell written on the back page of a frequently used notebook or on a separate sheet of paper.

Poor spelling can be corrected. If you can write your name without misspelling it, learn to spell you can any word in the English language. You can use the next six steps to improve your spelling.

www.mhhe.com/langan

Step 1: Use a Dictionary

When writing a paper, leave time to look up the spelling of all words you are unsure about. Don't overlook the value of this step. Using a dictionary will help you improve your spelling significantly!

Step 2: Keep a Personal Spelling List

Keep a list of words you misspell, and study them regularly. Write the list on the back page of a frequently used notebook or on a separate sheet of paper entitled "Personal Spelling List."

1. Write down hints to help you remember a word's spelling. For example, note that *occasion* is spelled with two *c*'s or that *all right* is two words, not one.

2. Study a word by saying and spelling it. Write the word one or more times.

3. Break a long word into syllables. *Inadvertent* can be divided into four syllables: *in ad ver tent*. *Consternation* can be spelled easily if you hear its four syllables in turn: *con ster na tion*.

4. Review and repeatedly test yourself. When learning a series of words, go back after studying each new word and review all preceding ones.

Step 3: Master Commonly Confused Words

Master the meanings and spellings of the commonly confused words on pages 594–602. Your instructor may assign twenty words for you to study at a time and give you a series of quizzes until you have mastered the words.

Step 4: Learn Key Words in Major Subjects

www.mhhe.com/langan

Make up and master lists of words central to the vocabulary of your major subjects. For example, a list of key words in business might include *economics, management, resources, scarcity, capitalism, decentralization, productivity, enterprise,* and so on; in psychology, *behavior, investigation, experimentation, frustration, cognition, stimulus, response, organism,* and so on. Set aside a specific portion of your various course notebooks to be used only for such lists, and study them using the methods described above for learning words.

Step 5: Study a Basic Word List

Following is a list of 250 English words that are often misspelled. Study their spellings. Your instructor may assign 25 or 50 words for you to study at a time and give you a series of quizzes until you have mastered the entire list.

250 Basic Words

absence	appearance	believe
ache	appetite	beneficial
achieve	attempt	25 bottom
acknowledge	attendance	breathe
advice	autumn	brilliant
aisle	awful	bureau
all right	bachelor	business
already	balance	cafeteria
amateur	bargain	calendar
answer	basically	candidate
anxious	beautiful	category

ceiling

cemetery

chief

choose

cigarette

citizen

college

column

comfortable

committed

completely

conceit

conscience

conscious

conversation

cruelty

50 daughter

deceit

definite

deposit

dictionary

disastrous

disease

distance

doctor

doubt

efficient

eighth

either

emphasize

entrance

environment

exaggerate

examine

existence

familiar

fascinate

February

financial

foreign

forty

75 friend

furniture

government

grammar

grieve

guidance

hammer

handkerchief

harass

height

hospital

hundred

husband

imitation

incredible

independent

instant

instead

intelligence

interest

interfere

interrupt

irresistible

January

kindergarten

100 leisure

library

lightning

likely

livelihood

loneliness

loose

magazine

making

maintain

marriage

material

mathematics

medicine

minute

mortgage

muscle

naturally

necessary

neither

nickel

niece

ninety

noise

obedience

125 obstacle

occasion

occur

occurrence

omission

opinion

opportunity

optimist

ounce

outrageous

pageant

pamphlet	resistance	thousand
people	restaurant	through
perform	rhythm	tomorrow
persistent	ridiculous	tongue
physically	right	tonight
picnic	175 safety	tournament
plausible	said	toward
pleasant	salary	transferred
policeman	scarcely	trousers
possible	scholastic	truly
precede	science	twelfth
prefer	scissors	unanimous
preference	secretary	until
prejudice	seize	unusual
150 prescription	separate	usage
probably	sergeant	used
psychology	several	usual
pursue	severely	usually
quantity	shriek	vacuum
quarter	siege	valuable
quiet	similar	variety
quiz	sincerely	225 vegetable
raise	sophomore	vengeance
really	straight	view
recede	succeed	villain
receive	suppress	vision
recognize	telephone	visitor
recommend	temperature	voice
reference	tenant	Washington
region	tendency	wear
region	200 tenth	weather
relieve	than	Wednesday
religion	theater	weight
representative	though	weird

welcome	won't	yolk
whether	writing	your
which	written	**250** you're
woman	wrong	
women	yesterday	

Step 6: Use Electronic Aids

An electronic spell-checker looks like a pocket calculator, which has a tiny keyboard. You type the word the way you think it is spelled. Then the checker provides the correct spelling of related words. As part of a word processer, a spell-checker identifies incorrect words and suggests correct spellings.

42

Commonly Confused Words

This chapter will list homonyms and other commonly confused words and provide activities to help you learn to distinguish them.

KEY TERM

homonym: words such as *brake* and *break* that have the same sounds but different meanings.

www.mhhe.com/langan

Homonyms

Some words are commonly confused because they have the same sounds but different meanings and spellings; such words are known as *homonyms*. Following are a number of homonyms. Complete the activity for each set of words, and check off and study the words that give you trouble.

all ready completely prepared

already previously; before

> It was *already* four o'clock by the time I thought about lunch.
>
> My report was *all ready,* but the class was canceled.

Fill in the blanks: Tyrone was ___all ready___ to sign up for the course when he discovered that it had ___neared___ closed.

brake stop

break come apart

> The mechanic advised me to add *brake* fluid to my car.
>
> During a commercial *break,* Marie lay on the floor and did fifty sit-ups.

Fill in the blanks: Tim, a poor driver, would always ___brake___ at the last minute and would usually ___break___ the speed limit as well.

course part of a meal; a school subject; direction

coarse rough

At the movies, I tried to decide on a *course* of action that would put an end to the *coarse* language of the man behind me.

Fill in the blanks: Over the ___course___ of time, jagged, ___coarse___ rocks will be polished to smoothness by the pounding waves.

hear	perceive with the ear
here	in this place

I can *hear* the performers so well from *here* that I don't want to change my seat.

Fill in the blanks: The chairperson explained that the meeting was being held ___here___ in the auditorium to enable everyone to ___hear___ the debate.

hole	an empty spot
whole	entire

A *hole* in the crumbling brick mortar made a convenient home for a small bird and its *whole* family.

Fill in the blanks: The ___whole___ in Dave's argument wouldn't exist if he put his ___hole___ concentration into his thinking.

its	belonging to it
it's	shortened form of "it is" or "it has"

The tall giraffe lowered *its* head (the head belonging to the giraffe) to the level of the car window and peered in at us.

It's (it is) too late to sign up for the theater trip to New York.

Fill in the blanks: I decided not to take the course because ___its___ too easy; ___it's___ content offers no challenge whatsoever.

knew	past form of *know*
new	not old

No one *knew* our *new* phone number, but the obscene calls continued.

Fill in the blanks: Even people who ___knew___ Charlie well didn't recognize him with his ___new___ beard.

know   to understand

no   a negative

By the time students complete that course, they *know* two computer languages and have *no* trouble writing their own programs.

Fill in the blanks: Dogs and cats usually ___know___ by the tone of the speaker's voice when they are being told ___no___.

passed   went by; succeeded in; handed to

past   a time before the present; by, as in "I drove past the house"

As Yvonne *passed* exit six on the interstate, she knew she had gone *past* the correct turnoff.

Fill in the blanks: Lewis asked for a meeting with his boss to learn why he had been ___passed___ over for promotion twice in the ___past___ year.

peace   calm

piece   a part

The best *piece* of advice she ever received was to maintain her own inner *peace*.

Fill in the blanks: Upon hearing that ___peace___ of music, my angry mood was gradually replaced by one of ___piece___.

plain   simple

plane   aircraft

The *plain* box contained a very expensive model *plane* kit.

Fill in the blanks: After unsuccessfully trying to overcome her fear, Selena finally admitted the ___plain___ truth: she was terrified of flying in a ___plane___.

principal   main; a person in charge of a school

principle   a law or standard

If the *principal* ingredient in this stew is octopus, I'll abandon my *principle* of trying everything at least once.

Fill in the blanks: Our ___principle___ insists that all students adhere to every school ___principal___ regarding dress, tardiness, and smoking.

right   correct; opposite of "left"

write   to put words on paper

Without the *right* amount of advance planning, it is difficult to *write* a good research paper.

Fill in the blanks: Connie wanted to send for the CDs offered on TV, but she could not ___*right*___ fast enough to get all the ___*write*___ information down before the commercial ended.

than   (thăn) used in comparisons

then   (thĕn) at that time

I made more money *then,* but I've never been happier *than* I am now.

Fill in the blanks: When I was in high school, I wanted a racy two-seater convertible more ___*than*___ anything else; but ___*then*___ my friends pointed out that only one person would be able to ride with me.

their   belonging to them

there   at that place; a neutral word used with verbs like *is, are, was, were, have,* and *had*

they're   contraction of "they are"

The tenants *there* are complaining because *they're* being cheated by *their* landlord.

Fill in the blanks: The tomatoes I planted ___*their*___ in the back of the garden are finally ripening, but ___*their*___ bright red color will attract hungry raccoons, and I fear ___*they're*___ going to be eaten.

threw   past form of *throw*

through from one side to the other; finished

As the inexperienced pizza-maker *threw* the pie into the air, he punched a hole *through* its thin crust.

Fill in the blanks: As the president moved slowly ___*threw*___ the cheering crowd, the Secret Service agent suddenly ___*through*___ himself at a man waving a small metal object.

to	verb part, as in *to smile;* toward, as in "I'm going *to* heaven."
too	overly, as in "The pizza was *too* hot"; also, as in "The coffee was hot, *too.*"
two	the number 2

I ran *to* the car *to* roll up the windows. (The first *to* means "toward"; the second *to* is a verb part that goes with *roll.*)

That amusement park is *too* far away; I hear that it's expensive, *too* (The first *too* means "overly"; the second *too* means "also.")

The *two* players (2 players) jumped up to tap the basketball away.

Fill in the blanks: The ___two___ of them have been dating for a year, but lately they seem ___to___ be arguing ___too___ often to pretend nothing is wrong.

wear	to have on
where	in what place

Where I will *wear* a purple feather boa is not the point; I just want to buy it.

Fill in the blanks: ___where___ were we going the night I refused to ___wear___ a tie?

weather	atmospheric conditions
whether	if it happens that; in case; if

Although meteorologists are *weather* specialists, even they can't predict *whether* a hurricane will change course.

Fill in the blanks: The gloomy ___weather___ report in the paper this morning ended all discussion of ___whether___ to pack a picnic lunch for later.

whose	belonging to whom
who's	contraction of "who is" and "who has"

"*Who's* the patient *whose* filling fell out?" the dentist's assistant asked.

Fill in the blanks: ___who's___ the salesperson ___whose___ customers are always complaining about his high-pressure tactics?

your	belonging to you
you're	contraction of "you are"

You're making a fool of yourself; *your* Elvis imitation isn't funny.

Fill in the blanks: If _____you're_____ having trouble filling out _____your_____ tax return, why don't you call the IRS's toll-free hot line?

Other Words Frequently Confused

Not all frequently confused words are homonyms. Here is a list of other words that people often confuse. Complete the activities for each set of words, and check off and study the words that give you trouble.

a, an   Both *a* and *an* are used before other words to mean, approximately, "one."

Generally you should use *an* before words starting with a vowel (*a, e, i, o, u*):

> an orange   an umbrella   an indication   an ape   an effort

Generally you should use *a* before words starting with a consonant (all other letters):

> a genius   a movie   a speech   a study   a typewriter

Fill in the blanks: The morning after the party, I had _____a_____ pounding headache and _____an_____ upset stomach.

accept	(ăk sĕpt′)	to receive; agree to
except	(ĭk sĕpt′)	excluding; but

> It was easy to *accept* the book's plot, *except* for one unlikely coincidence at the very end.

Fill in the blanks: Ved would _____accept_____ the position, _____except_____ that it would add twenty minutes to his daily commute.

advice	(ăd vīs′)	noun meaning "an opinion"
advise	(ăd vīz′)	verb meaning "to counsel, to give advice"

> I have learned not to take my sister's *advice* on straightening out my life.
> A counselor can *advise* you about the courses you'll need next year.

Fill in the blanks: Karen is so troubled about losing her job that I will _____advise_____ her to seek the _____advice_____ of a professional counselor.

affect	(uh fĕkt′)	verb meaning "to influence"
effect	(ĭ fĕkt′)	verb meaning "to cause something"; noun meaning "result"

The bad weather will definitely *affect* the outcome of the election.

If we can *effect* a change in George's attitude, he may do better in his courses.

One *effect* of the strike will be dwindling supplies in the supermarkets.

Fill in the blanks: Scientists have studied the ___affect___ of large quantities of saccharine on lab animals but have yet to learn how similar amounts ___effect___ human beings.

among	implies three or more
between	implies only two

After the team of surgeons consulted *among* themselves, they decided that the bullet was lodged *between* two of the patient's ribs.

Fill in the blanks: ___among___ halves, one enthusiastic fan stood up ___between___ his equally fanatic friends and took off his coat and shirt.

beside	along the side of
besides	in addition to

Besides doing daily inventories, I have to stand *beside* the cashier whenever the store gets crowded.

Fill in the blanks: ___Beside___ those books on the table, I plan to use these magazines stacked ___besides___ me while doing my research paper.

fewer	used with things that can be counted
less	refers to amount, value, or degree

I've taken *fewer* classes this semester, so I hope to have *less* trouble finding time to study.

Fill in the blanks: This beer advertises that it has ___less___ calories and is ___fewer___ filling.

former	refers to the first of two items named
latter	refers to the second of two items named

Sue yelled at her sons, Greg and John, when she got home; the *former* (Greg) had left the refrigerator open and the *latter* (John) had left wet towels all over the bathroom.

Fill in the blanks: Eddy collects coupons and parking tickets: the ___Former___ save him money and the ___latter___ are going to cost him a great deal of money someday.

learn	to gain knowledge
teach	to give knowledge

I can't *learn* a new skill unless someone with lots of patience *teaches* me.

Fill in the blanks: Because she is quick to ___learn___ new things, Mandy has offered to ___teach___ me how to play the latest video games.

loose	(lōos)	not fastened; not tight-fitting
lose	(lōoz)	to misplace; fail to win

In this strong wind, the house may *lose* some of its *loose* roof shingles.

Fill in the blanks: A ___loose___ wire in the television set was causing us to ___lose___ the picture.

quiet	(kwī′ ĭt)	peaceful
quite	(kwīt)	entirely; really; rather

Jennifer seems *quiet* and demure, but she has *quite* a temper at times.

Fill in the blanks: Most people think the library is ___quite___ a good place to study, but I find the extreme ___quiet___ distracting.

These sentences check your understanding of *its, it's; there, their, they're; to, too, two;* and *your, you're.* Underline the two incorrect spellings in each sentence. Then spell the words correctly in the spaces provided.

_____ 1. "Its not a very good idea," yelled Alexandra's boss, "to tell
_____ you're customer that the striped dress she plans to buy makes
her look like a pregnant tiger."

_____ 2. You're long skirt got stuck in the car door, and now its
_____   sweeping the highway.

_____ 3. When your young, their is a tendency to confuse a crush with
_____   true love.

_____ 4. After too hours of typing, Lin was to tired to type any
_____   longer.

_____ 5. In its' long history, the island of Sicily has been a colony of
_____   Greece, a Norman kingdom, and an Arab emirate. Today, its
        part of the Republic of Italy.

_____ 6. The vampires bought a knife sharpener in order too sharpen
_____   there teeth.

_____ 7. Your never alone if your loved ones are in you're
_____   heart.

_____ 8. When the children get to quiet, Clare knows their getting
_____   into trouble.

_____ 9. There friendship developed into love as the years passed, and
_____   now, in midlife, their newlyweds.

_____ 10. It is to far to swim too Nantucket Island. The Massachusetts
_____   mainland is 25 miles away.

Review Test 1

Underline the correct word in the parentheses. Rather than guessing, look back at the explanations of the words when necessary.

1. I (know, no) that I need to manage my time better now that I am enrolled in classes on (to, too, two) campuses and that I have to take public transportation.

2. (Whose, Who's) the author of that book about the (affects, effects) of eating (to, too, two) much protein?

3. In our supermarket is a counter (where, wear) (your, you're) welcome to sit down and have free coffee and doughnuts.

4. (Its, It's) possible to (loose, lose) friends by constantly giving out unwanted (advice, advise).

5. Some scientists don't accept, except) the theory that human behavior is contributing to global warming more (than, then) ever before.

6. The (hole, whole) platoon of marines was recognized for valor after (braking, breaking) (through, thru) enemy lines and saving the (lives, lifes) of five hostages.

7. The newly appointed (principal, principle) is (quite, quiet) familiar with the problems (hear, here) at our school.

8. I found that our cat had (all ready, already) had her kittens (among, between) the weeds (beside, besides) the porch.

9. I (advice, advise) you not to take children to that movie; the special (affects, effects) are (to, too, two) frightening.

10. There were (fewer, less) than one hundred trout let (lose, loose) in our state's rivers and streams; now there are thousands.

Review Test 2

On separate paper, write short sentences using the ten words shown below.

www.mhhe.com/langan

1. accept
2. its
3. you're
4. too
5. then
6. course
7. their
8. passed
9. fewer
10. all ready

43

Effective Word Choice

This chapter will give you practice in avoiding slang, clichés, and pretentious words.

KEY TERMS

cliché: an expression that has been worn out through constant use. Example: *short but sweet*

pretentious language: artificial or stilted expressions that more often obscure meaning than communicate it clearly. Example: *It was a splendid opportunity to obtain some slumber* could be more simply expressed as *It was a good chance to get some sleep.*

slang: nonstandard language particular to a time and often to a specific locale; acceptable in everyday speech, slang should be avoided in formal contexts and, with few exceptions, in writing. Example: *I'm going to have to sweat it out for the next couple of days until the test results are posted* would be more appropriately expressed as *I'm going to have to wait anxiously for the next couple of days until the test results are posted.*

Choose your words carefully when you write. Always take the time to think about your word choices rather than simply use the first word that comes to mind. You want to develop the habit of selecting words that are precise and appropriate for your purpose. One way you can show sensitivity to language is by avoiding slang, clichés, and pretentious words.

Slang

We often use slang expressions when we talk because they are so vivid and colorful. However, slang is usually out of place in formal writing. Here are some examples of slang:

www.mhhe.com/langan

Someone *ripped off* Ken's new Adidas running shoes from his locker.

After the game, we *stuffed our faces* at the diner.

I finally told my parents to *get off my case*.

The movie really *grossed me out*.

Slang expressions have a number of drawbacks. They go out of date quickly, they become tiresome if used excessively in writing, and they may communicate clearly to some readers but not to others. Also, the use of slang can be an evasion of the specific details that are often needed to make one's meaning clear in writing. For example, in "The movie really grossed me out," the writer has not provided the specific details about the movie necessary for us to clearly understand the statement. Was it acting, special effects, or violent scenes that the writer found so disgusting? In general, then, you should avoid slang in your writing. If you are in doubt about whether an expression is slang, it may help to check a recently published hardbound dictionary.

Rewrite the following sentences, replacing the italicized slang words with more formal ones.

Activity

1

EXAMPLE

When we told the neighbors to *can the noise,* they *freaked out.*

When we told the neighbors to be quiet, they got upset.

1. When our car *died,* the *cops* were very *cool;* they called a tow truck, which got there *in a flash.*

_____

_____

_____

2. I was *like really freaked out* when I saw *Grams* and *Gramps* dancing to rock music at my cousin's anniversary *bash.*

_____

_____

_____

3. Theo was so *wiped out* after his workout at the gym that he couldn't *get it together* to defrost a frozen dinner.

_____

_____

_____

4. When Rick tried to *put the moves on* Lola at the school party, she told him to *shove off.*

_____

_____

_____

5. The entire town was *psyched* that the corrupt mayor *got busted.*

_____

_____

_____

Clichés

A *cliché* is an expression that has been worn out through constant use. Here are some typical clichés:

short but sweet	at a loss for words
drop in the bucket	taking a big chance
had a hard time of it	took a turn for the worse
word to the wise	singing the blues
it dawned on me	in the nick of time
sigh of relief	too close for comfort
too little, too late	saw the light
last but not least	easier said than done
work like a dog	on top of the world
all work and no play	time and time again
it goes without saying	make ends meet

Clichés are common in speech but make your writing seem tired and stale. Also, they are often an evasion of the specific details that you must work to provide in your writing. You should, then, avoid clichés and try to express your meaning in fresh, original ways.

Underline the cliché in each of the following sentences. Then substitute specific, fresh words for the trite expression. Partner with a classmate and go over your answers together.

EXAMPLE

My boyfriend has stuck with me <u>through thick and thin.</u>

through good times and bad. _____

1. As the only girl in an otherwise all-boy family, I got away with murder.

   _____

2. I was on top of the world when the doctor told me I was as healthy as a horse.

   _____

3. My suggestion is just a shot in the dark, but it's better than nothing.

   _____

4. Janice got more than she bargained for when she offered to help Larry with his math homework.

   _____

5. A stone's throw from the Colosseum in Rome are some restaurants, where the food is as good as it gets.

   _____

6. On a hot, sticky midsummer day, iced tea or any frosty drink really hits the spot.

   _____

7. Nadia thanks her lucky stars that she was born with brains, beauty, and humility.

   _____

8. Anything that involves mathematical ability has always been right up my alley.

   _____

9. The Montessori system of education is old hat now but, when it came upon the scene, it raised a few eyebrows.

   _____

10. Even when we are up to our eyeballs in work, our boss wonders if we have enough to do.

_____

Activity

3

Write a short paragraph describing the kind of day you had. Try to put as many clichés as possible into it. For example, "I got up at the crack of dawn, ready to take on the world. I grabbed a bite to eat. . . ." By making yourself aware of clichés in this way, you should lessen the chance that they will appear in your writing.

Pretentious Words

Some people feel that they can improve their writing by using fancy, elevated words rather than simple, natural words. They use artificial, stilted language that more often obscures their meaning than communicates it clearly. Here are some unnatural-sounding sentences:

It was a splendid opportunity to get some slumber.

We relished the delicious repast.

The officer apprehended the intoxicated operator of the vehicle.

This establishment sells women's apparel and children's garments.

The same thoughts can be expressed more clearly and effectively by using plain, natural language, as below:

It was a good chance to get some sleep.

We enjoyed the delicious meal.

The officer arrested the drunken driver.

This store sells women's and children's clothes.

Here are some other inflated words and simpler words that could replace them:

Inflated Words	Simpler Words
subsequent to	after
finalize	finish
transmit	send
facilitate	help
component	part
initiate	begin
delineate	describe
manifested	shown
to endeavor	to try

Cross out the inflated words in each sentence. Then substitute clear, simple language for the inflated words.

EXAMPLE

The ~~conflagration~~ was ~~initiated~~ by an arsonist.

  . . . fire was started by an arsonist.

1. Rico and his brother do not interrelate in a harmonious manner.

   _____

2. The meaning of the movie's conclusion eluded my comprehension.

   _____

3. The departmental conference will commence promptly at two o'clock.

   _____

4. Utilization of the left lane is proscribed except for buses.

   _____

5. When my writing implement malfunctioned, I asked the professor for another.

   _____

Review Test   1

Certain words are italicized in the following sentences. In the space provided at the left, identify the words as slang (S), a cliché (C), or pretentious words (PW). Then replace the words with more effective diction.

_____   1. Losing weight is *easier said than done* for someone who loves sweets.

          _____

_____   2. After dinner, we washed the *culinary utensils* and wrapped the *excess* food.

          _____

_____   3. After we set up camp, we watched a beautiful sunset, *then hit the sack*.

          _____

_____   4. Michelle spent the summer *watching the tube* and *catching rays.*

_____

_____   5. The fans, *all fired up* after the game, *peeled out* of the parking lot
and honked their horns.

_____

_____   6. The stew I made contained *everything but the kitchen sink.*

_____

_____   7. My parents never *laid guilt trips* on me when I was a *kid.*

_____

_____   8. A company cannot *implement changes and attain growth* without
input from its personnel.

_____

_____   9. Since I decided to study harder, math no longer seems *clear as mud.*

_____

_____   10. I *perused* several *periodicals* while I waited for the doctor.

_____

44

Editing Tests

This chapter will give you practice in editing, or revising, to correct sentence-skills mistakes.

> **KEY TERMS**
>
> **editing:** revising to correct sentence-skills mistakes.
>
> **proofreading:** carefully examining written text to correct typographical mistakes and other related errors.
>
> **proofreading symbols:** shorthand notations intended to call attention to typographical mistakes and other related errors.

www.mhhe.com/langan

The twelve editing tests in this chapter will give you practice in revising to correct sentence-skills mistakes. Remember that if you don't edit carefully, you run the risk of sabotaging much of the work you have put into a paper. If readers see too many surface flaws, they may assume that you don't place much value on what you have to say, and they may not give your ideas a fair hearing. Revising to eliminate sentence-skills errors is a basic part of clear, effective writing.

In five of the tests, the spots where errors occur have been underlined; your job is to identify and correct each error. In the rest of the tests, you must locate as well as identify and correct the errors.

EDITING HINTS

1. Have at hand two essential tools: a good dictionary and a sentence-skills handbook (you can use Chapter 5 and Part Four of this book).

2. Use a sheet of paper to cover your essay so that you will expose only one sentence at a time. Look for errors in grammar, spelling, and typing. It may help to read each sentence out loud. If a sentence does not read clearly and smoothly, chances are something is wrong.

3. Pay special attention to the kinds of errors you tend to make. For example, if you tend to write run-ons or fragments, be especially on the lookout for those errors.

4. Proofreading symbols that may be of particular help are the following:

ℓ	omit	draw two ~~two~~ conclusions	ℓ
^	insert missing letter or word	achi̯eve	
cap, lc	add a capital (or a lowercase) letter	(cap) My english class	(lc)

Editing Test   1

In the spaces at the bottom, write the numbers of the ten word groups that contain fragments or run-ons. Then, in the spaces between the lines and in the margin, edit by making the necessary corrections.

¹I remember my childhood as being generally happy and can recall experiencing some of the most carefree times of my life. ²But I can also remember, even more vividly, other moments. ³When I was deeply frightened. ⁴As a child, I was truly terrified of the dark and of getting lost. ⁵These fears were very real, they caused me some extremely uncomfortable moments.

⁶Maybe it was the strange way things looked and sounded in my familiar room at night. ⁷That scared me so much. ⁸The streetlight outside or passing

(continued)

car lights would create shadows in my room. ⁹As a result, clothes hung over a chair taking on the shape of an unknown beast.

¹⁰Out of the corner of my eye, I saw curtains move when there was no breeze. ¹¹A tiny creak in the floor would sound a hundred times louder than in daylight, my imagination would take over. ¹²Creating burglars and monsters on the prowl. ¹³Because darkness always made me feel so helpless. ¹⁴I would lie there motionless so that the "enemy" would not discover me.

¹⁵Another of my childhood fears was that I would get lost. ¹⁶Especially on the way home from school. ¹⁷After school, all the buses lined up along the curb, I was terrified that I'd get on the wrong one. ¹⁸Scanning the bus windows for the faces of my friends. ¹⁹I'd also look to make sure that the bus driver was the same one I had in the morning.

1. _____   3. _____   5. _____   7. _____   9. _____

2. _____   4. _____   6. _____   8. _____   10. _____

Editing Test 2

Identify the five mistakes in essay format in the student paper that follows. From the box below, choose the letters that describe the five mistakes and write those letters in the spaces provided. Then correct each mistake.

a. Title should not be underlined.
b. Title should not be set off in quotation marks.
c. There should not be a period at the end of a title.
d. All major words in a title should be capitalized.
e. Title should be a phrase, not a complete sentence.
f. First line of a paper should stand independent of the title.
g. One line should be skipped between title and first line of the paper.
h. First line of a paragraph should be indented.
i. Right-hand margin should not be crowded.
j. Hyphenation should occur only between syllables.

> *"eating in fast-food restaurants"*
> Doing so doesn't have to be terrible for your health. Although I often
> stop at Wendy's or Burger King, I find ways to make healthful
> choices there. For one thing, I order sandwiches that are as plain as
> possible. A broiled hamburger or fish sandwich isn't so bad for you,
> as long as it isn't covered with melted cheese, fatty sauces, bacon,
> or other "extras" that pile on the fat and calories. Another health-
> conscious choice is to skip deep-fat-fried potatoes loaded with salt
> and heavy with cholesterol; instead, I'll order a plain baked potato
> from Wendy's and add just a bit of butter and salt for taste. In
> addition, I take advantage of healthy items on menus. For example,
> most fast-food places now offer green salads and low-fat chicken
> choices. And finally, I order a sensible beverage—ice water or a diet
> soda—instead of soda or a milk shake.

1. _____   2. _____   3. _____   4. _____   5. _____

Editing Test   3

Identify the ten sentence-skills mistakes at the underlined spots in the student paper that follows. From the box below, choose the letter that describes each mistake and write that letter in the space provided. (The same kind of mistake may appear more than once.) Then, in the spaces between the lines, edit and correct each mistake.

a. fragment	d. dangling modifier
b. run-on	e. missing comma
c. inconsistent verb tense	f. spelling mistake

George Washington was a land <u>surveyor during</u> the French and Indian
<u>1</u>
Wars, he led the Virginia militia. Twenty years later, when the American

Revolution <u>broke out. Washington</u> commanded the Continental armies. In
<u>2</u>
1776, <u>after blockading Boston</u>, the city was taken from the British. Later,
<u>3</u>
however, Washington yielded New York City to the <u>enemy, he</u> retreated to
<u>4</u>
Pennsylvania. In December, he boosted the sagging morale of

his men <u>crossing</u> the Delaware River on Christmas night he <u>attacks</u> Trenton,
<u>5</u>   <u>6</u>
where Hessians (British allies) were <u>stationed. Then</u> went on to <u>defeet</u> a
<u>7</u>   <u>8</u>
British army at Princeton. In 1777–1788, the army spent a miserable winter at

<u>Valley Forge Pennsylvania</u>. Later, however, it defeated the British at
<u>9</u>
Monmouth, New Jersey. This battle marked a turning point. In 1781, by

winning the battle of <u>Yorktown, Washington</u> brought the war to an end.
<u>10</u>

1. _____	3. _____	5. _____	7. _____	9. _____
2. _____	4. _____	6. _____	8. _____	10. _____

Editing Test   4

Identify the ten sentence-skills mistakes at the underlined spots in the student
paper that follows. From the box below, choose the letter that describes each mistake and write that letter in the space provided. (The same kind of mistake may
appear more than once.) Then, in the spaces between the lines, edit and correct
each mistake.

a.	run-on	e.	wordiness
b.	mistake in subject-verb agreement	f.	slang
c.	faulty parallelism	g.	missing comma
d.	missing quotation marks		

It is this writer's opinion that smokers should quit smoking for the sake of
$\underline{}$
1
those who are around them. Perhaps the most helpless creatures that suffer

from being near a smoker is unborn babies, one study suggests that the risk of
      2   3
having an undersized baby is doubled if pregnant women are exposed to

cigarette smoke for about two hours a day. Pregnant women should refrain

from smoking and to avoid smoke-filled rooms. Spouses of smokers are also
              4
in big trouble. They are more likely than spouses of nonsmokers to die of
   5
heart disease and the development of fatal cancers. Office workers are a final
                    6
group that can be harmed by a smoke-filled environment. The U.S. Surgeon

General has said "Workers who smoke are a health risk to their coworkers.
              7   8
While it is undoubtedly true that one can argue that smokers have the right
                 9
to hurt themselves they do not have the right to hurt others. Smokers should
          10
abandon their deadly habit for the health of others at home and at work.

1. _____	3. _____	5. _____	7. _____	9. _____
2. _____	4. _____	6. _____	8. _____	10. _____

Editing Test 5

Identify the ten sentence-skills mistakes at the underlined spots in the student paper that follows. From the box below, choose the letter that describes each mistake and write that letter in the space provided. (The same kind of mistake may appear more than once.) Then, in the spaces between the lines, edit and correct each mistake.

a. fragment	e. dangling modifier
b. run-on	f. missing comma
c. mistake in subject-verb agreement	g. wordiness
d. misplaced modifier	h. slang

The United States will never be a drug-free society but we could eliminate
<u>   1   </u>
many of our drug-related problems by legalizing drugs. Drugs would be sold

by companies and not criminals <u>if they were legal.</u> The drug trade would then
                                            2
take place like any <u>business freeing</u> the police and courts to devote their time
                          3
to other problems. Lawful drugs would be sold at a fair <u>price, no one would</u>
                                                              4
need to steal in order to buy them. <u>By legalizing drugs,</u> organized crime
                                          5
would lose one of its major sources of revenue. <u>It goes without saying that</u>
                                                        6
<u>we would, instead,</u> create important tax revenues for the government Finally,

if drugs <u>was</u> sold through legal outlets, we could reduce drug problems
          7
among our young people. It would be illegal to sell drugs to people under

a certain age. <u>Just as is the case now with alcohol.</u> And because the profits
                          8
on drugs would no longer <u>be out of sight,</u> there would be little incentive
                                9
for drug pushers to sell to young people. Decriminalizing drugs, in short, could

be a solution. <u>To many of the problems that result from the illegal drug trade.</u>
                                      10

1. _____   3. _____   5. _____   7. _____   9. _____

2. _____   4. _____   6. _____   8. _____   10. _____

Editing Test   6

Identify the sentence-skills mistakes at the underlined spots in the paper that follows. From the box below, choose the letter that describes each mistake and write that letter in the space provided. (The same kind of mistake may appear more than once.) Then, in the spaces between the lines, edit and correct each mistake.

a. fragment	e. mistake with quotation marks
b. run-on	f. mistake in pronoun point of view
c. mistake in subject-verb agreement	g. spelling error
d. mistake in verb tense	h. missing comma

> One reason that I enjoy the commute to school is that the drive gives me uninterupted time to myself. The classes and socializing at college is great,
> 1   2
> and so is the time I spend with my family, but sometimes all this togetherness keeps you from being able to think. In fact, I look forward to the time I have
> 3
> alone, it gives me a chance to plan what I'll accomplish in the day ahead.
> 4
> For example, one Tuesday afternoon my history professor announces that a
> 5
> rough outline for our semester report was due that Friday. Fortunatly, I had
> 6
> already done some reading and I had checked my proposed topic with her the
> 7
> week before. Therefore, on the way home in the car that evening. I planned
> 8
> the entire history report in my mind. Then all I had to do when I got home was quickly jot it down before I forgot it. When I handed the professor the outline
> 9
> at 8:30 Wednesday morning. She asked me "if I had stayed up all night working
> 10
> on it." She was amazed when I told her that I owed it all to commuting.

1. _____   3. _____   5. _____   7. _____   9. _____

2. _____   4. _____   6. _____   8. _____   10. _____

Editing Test 7

Identify the ten sentence-skills mistakes at the underlined spots in the student paper that follows. From the box below, choose the letter that describes each mistake and write that letter in the space provided. (The same kind of mistake may appear more than once.) Then, in the spaces between the lines, edit and correct each mistake.

a. fragment	e. missing capital letter
b. run-on	f. dangling modifier
c. mistake in subject-verb agreement	g. homonym mistake
	h. missing apostrophe
d. missing comma	i. cliché

At one time doctors believed that diseases generated spontaneously—
          1
on their own. Louis Pasteur (1822–95), a french scientist, disproved that.
                                          2
Demonstrating that germs cause many diseases. Pasteur worked like a dog
                                         3   4
to convince doctors to sterilize their instruments and wash their hands
before delivering a baby. Pasteur new this would reduce the chances of
                                 5
infection as a result, it would save the lives of many women who otherwise
             6
would have died giving birth. Another of Pasteurs discoveries was a vaccine
                                          7
for rabies. Retarding the progress of the disease, a boy bitten by a rabid dog
was saved. Finally, Pasteur is responsible for a process that stop the growth
          8   9
of bacteria in wine and milk, it now bears his name: pasteurization.
                        10

1. _____   3. _____   5. _____   7. _____   9. _____

2. _____   4. _____   6. _____   8. _____   10. _____

Editing Test 8

Locate the ten sentence-skills mistakes in the following passage. The mistakes are listed in the box below. As you locate each mistake, write the number of the word group in the space provided. Then, in the space between the lines, edit and correct each mistake.

1 fragment _____	1 missing comma after
1 run-on _____	introductory material _____
1 mistake in verb tense _____	2 missing quotation
1 nonparallel structure _____	marks _____ _____
1 dangling modifier _____	1 missing apostrophe _____
1 mistake in pronoun point of	
view _____	

¹The greatest of my everyday fears is technology. ²Beginning when I couldn't master bike riding and extending to the present day. ³Fear kept me from learning to operate a jigsaw, start an outboard motor, or even using a simple tape recorder. ⁴I almost didn't learn to drive a car. ⁵At age sixteen, Dad lifted the hood of our Chevy and said, "All right, you're going to start learning to drive. ⁶Now, this is the distributor . . ." ⁷When my eyes glazed over, he shouted, "Well, I'm not going to bother if youre not interested!" ⁸Fortunately, the friend who later taught me to drive skipped what goes on under the hood. ⁹My most recent frustration is the digital camera, I would love to take professional-quality pictures, but all the buttons and tiny electronic menus confuse me. ¹⁰As a result, my unused camera is hidden away on a shelf in my closet. ¹¹Just last week, my sister gives me a beautiful digital watch for my birthday. ¹²I may have to put it on the shelf with the camera—the alarm keeps going off, and you can't figure out how to stop it.

Editing Test   11

Locate the ten sentence-skills mistakes in the following passage. The mistakes are listed in the box below. As you locate each mistake, write the number of the word group in the space provided. Then, in the space between the lines, edit and correct each mistake.

1 fragment _____	2 missing apostrophes
1 run-on _____	_____ _____
1 mistake in subject-verb agreement _____	1 nonparallel structure _____
2 missing commas after introductory material	1 dangling modifier _____
_____ _____	1 mistake in pronoun point of view _____

¹Being a waitress is an often underrated job. ²A waitress needs the tact of a diplomat, she must be as organized as a business executive, and the ability of an acrobat. ³Serving as the link between customers and kitchen, the most demanding diners must be satisfied, and the often temperamental kitchen help must be kept tamed. ⁴Both groups tend to blame the waitress whenever anything goes wrong. ⁵Somehow, she is held responsible by the customer for any delay (even if it's the kitchens fault), for an overcooked steak, or for an unavailable dessert. ⁶While the kitchen automatically blames her for the diners who change their orders or return those burned steaks. ⁷In addition she must simultaneously keep straight who ordered what at each table, who is yelling for the check, and whether the new arrivals want cocktails or not. ⁸She must be sure empty tables are cleared, everyone has refills of coffee, and no one is scowling because a request for more rolls are going unheard. ⁹Finally, the waitress must travel a hazardous route between the busy kitchen and the crowded dining room, she has to dodge a diners leg in the aisle or a swinging kitchen door. ¹⁰And you must do this while balancing a tray heaped with steaming platters. ¹¹The hardest task of the waitress, though, is trying to maintain a decent imitation of a smile on her face—most of the time.

Editing Test   12

Locate the ten sentence-skills mistakes in the following passage. The mistakes are listed in the box below. As you find each mistake, write the number of the word in the space provided. Then, in the space between the lines, correct each mistake.

2 fragments _____ _____	1 mistake in pronoun point of view _____
1 run-on _____	
1 mistake verb tense _____	1 mistake in pronoun agreement _____
1 misplaced modifier _____	
2 missing capital letters _____ _____	1 mistake in subject-verb agreement _____

¹The earliest type of paper appeared about five thousand years ago in Egypt it took its name from the papyrus plant. ²The fibers of which were used in its manufacture. ³The kind of paper that you use today probably originated in china in the second century. ⁴ However, some historians argue that paper have been invented in that country hundreds of years earlier. ⁵Made of hemp fiber and tree bark, the Arabs brought this new paper to Europe in the fifteenth century via spain. ⁶A country they controlled at the time. ⁷When printing was invented, the manufacture of paper increased greatly. ⁸Today, most paper consist of wood fiber, but they may also contain cotton and other textiles.

45

ESL Pointers

This chapter will cover rules useful for speakers of English as a second language (ESL).

INCORRECT:

The ball was thrown by the boy.

The verb is expressed in the passive voice.

CORRECT:

The boy threw the ball.

The action is attributed directly to the boy.

KEY TERMS

active voice: mode of expression in which the subject performs the action expressed by the verb.

count nouns: words that name people, places, things, or ideas that can be counted and made into plurals, such as *teacher, restroom,* and *joke.*

idiomatic: particular to a certain language.

noncount nouns: words that refer to things or ideas that cannot be counted, such as *water, bravery,* and *snow.*

qualifier: a word that expresses the quantity of a noncount noun. Example: *some* water

This section covers rules that most native speakers of English take for granted but that are useful for speakers of English as a second language (ESL).

Articles with Count and Noncount Nouns

Articles are noun markers—they signal that a noun will follow. (A noun is a word used to name something: a person, place, thing, or idea.) The indefinite articles are *a* and *an*. (Use *a* before a word that begins with a consonant sound: **a c**ar, **a p**iano, **a u**niform—the *u* in *uniform* sounds like the consonant *y* plus *u*. Use *an* before a word beginning with a vowel sound: **an e**gg, **an o**ffice, **an h**onor—the *h* in *honor* is silent.) The definite article is *the*. An article may immediately precede a noun: **a** smile, **the** reason. Or it may be separated from the noun by modifiers: **a** slight smile, **the** very best reason.

To know whether to use an article with a noun and which article to use, you must recognize count and noncount nouns.

Count nouns name people, places, things, or ideas that can be counted and made into plurals, such as *teacher, restroom,* and *joke (one teacher, two restrooms, three jokes).*

Noncount nouns refer to things or ideas that cannot be counted, such as *flour, history,* and *truth.* The following box lists and illustrates common types of noncount nouns.

TIP: There are various other noun markers besides articles, including quantity words *(some, several, a lot of),* numerals *(one, ten, 120),* demonstrative adjectives *(this, these),* possessive adjectives *(my, your, our),* and possessive nouns *(Jaime's, the school's).*

Common Noncount Nouns

Abstractions and emotions: anger, bravery, health, pride, truth

Activities: baseball, jogging, reading, teaching, travel

Foods: bread, broccoli, chocolate, cheese, flour

Gases and vapors: air, helium, oxygen, smoke, steam

Languages and areas of study: Korean, Spanish, algebra, history, physics

Liquids: blood, gasoline, lemonade, tea, water

Materials that come in bulk form: aluminum, cloth, dust, sand, soap

Natural occurrences: magnetism, moonlight, rain, snow, thunder

Other things that cannot be counted: clothing, furniture, homework, machinery, money, news, transportation, vocabulary, work

The quantity of a noncount noun can be expressed with a word or words called a **qualifier,** such as *some, a lot of, a unit of,* and so on. (In the following two examples, the qualifiers are shown in *italic* type, and the noncount nouns are shown in **boldface** type.)

Please have *some* **patience.**

We need to buy *two bags of* **flour** today.

Some words can be either count or noncount nouns, depending on whether they refer to one or more individual items or to something in general.

Certain **cheeses** give some people a headache.
(This sentence refers to individual cheeses; *cheese* in this case is a count noun.)

Cheese is made in almost every country where milk is produced.
(This sentence refers to cheese in general; in this case, *cheese* is a noncount noun.)

Using *a* or *an* with Nonspecific Singular Count Nouns

Use *a* or *an* with singular nouns that are nonspecific. A noun is nonspecific when the reader doesn't know its specific identity.

A left-hander faces special challenges with right-handed tools.
(The sentence refers to any left-hander, not a specific one.)

Today, our cat proudly brought **a** baby bird into the house.
(The reader isn't familiar with the bird. This is the first time it is mentioned.)

Using *the* with Specific Nouns

In general, use *the* with all specific nouns—specific singular, plural, and noncount nouns. Certain conditions make a noun specific and therefore require the article *the.*

A noun is specific in the following cases:

- When it has already been mentioned once

   Today, our cat proudly brought a baby bird into the house.
   Luckily, **the** bird was still alive.
   (*The* is used with the second mention of *bird*.)

- When it is identified by a word or phrase in the sentence

   The pockets in the boy's pants are often filled with sand and dirt.
   (*Pockets* is identified by the words *in the boy's pants*.)

- When its identity is suggested by the general context

  At Willy's Diner last night, **the** service was terrible and **the** food was worse.
  (The reader can conclude that the service and food being discussed were at Willy's Diner.)

- When it is unique

  There will be an eclipse of **the** moon tonight.
  (Earth has only one moon.)

- When it is preceded by a superlative adjective *(best, biggest, wisest)*

  The best way to store broccoli is to refrigerate it in an open plastic bag.

Omitting Articles

Omit articles with nonspecific plurals and noncount nouns. Plurals and noncount nouns are nonspecific when they refer to something in general.

Pockets didn't exist until the end of the 1700s.

Service is as important as **food** to a restaurant's success.

Iris serves her children homemade **lemonade.**

Using *the* with Proper Nouns

Proper nouns name particular people, places, things, or ideas and are always capitalized. Most proper nouns do not require articles; those that do, however, require *the*. Following are general guidelines about when and when not to use *the*.

1. Do not use *the* for most singular proper nouns, including names of the following:

   - *People and animals* (Benjamin Franklin, Fido)

   - *Continents, states, cities, streets, and parks* (North America, Illinois, Chicago, First Avenue, Washington Square)

   - *Most countries* (France, Mexico, Russia)

   - *Individual bodies of water, islands, and mountains* (Lake Erie, Long Island, Mount Everest)

2. Use *the* for the following types of proper nouns:

   - *Plural proper nouns* (the Turners, the United States, the Great Lakes, the Rocky Mountains)

- *Names of large geographic areas, deserts, oceans, seas, and rivers* (the South, the Gobi Desert, the Atlantic Ocean, the Black Sea, the Mississippi River)

- *Names with the format* the _____ of _____ (the Fourth of July, the People's Republic of China, the University of California)

Activity

1

Underline the correct form of the noun in parentheses.

1. (A library, Library) is a valuable addition to a town.
2. This morning, the mail carrier brought me (a letter, the letter) from my cousin.
3. As I read (a letter, the letter), I began to laugh at what my cousin wrote.
4. The Boy Scouts had to carry a great deal of equipment, equipments) when they marched out of camp.
5. Every day, Melissa reminds me that (jogging, joggings) can help me keep trim.
6. (Acrobatics, The acrobatics) requires a great deal of motor coordination.
7. The soldiers in battle showed a great deal of (courage, courages).
8. A famous sight in Arizona is (Grand Canyon, the Grand Canyon).
9. My son would like to eat (the spaghetti, spaghetti) at every meal.
10. It is dangerous to stare directly at (the sun, sun).

Activity

2

Underline the correct form of the noun in parentheses.

1. Last night, I went to (a restaurant, the restaurant) with my best friend.
2. (The restaurant, A restaurant) was a more expensive place than we had expected.
3. Jeremy was told he had been accepted to (the University, University) of Pennsylvania.
4. A newspaper reporter is supposed to write a story with (the honesty, honesty).
5. Armando was honored by (Republic of Italy, the Republic of Italy.)
6. Long-distance runners need lots of (determination, determinations) to succeed.
7. A hurricane crossed (Atlantic Ocean, the Atlantic Ocean) before it hit the United States.
8. (The Chilean, Chilean) sea bass at Emilio's Restaurant is the best I have ever tasted.
9. (Jupiter, The Jupiter) is the largest planet in our solar system.
10. Computers have been programmed to play (the chess, chess) and can now beat most human players.

Subjects and Verbs
Avoiding Repeated Subjects

In English, a particular subject can be used only once in a clause. Don't repeat a subject in the same clause by following a noun with a pronoun.

> Incorrect: The *manager he* asked Dmitri to lock up tonight.
> Correct: The **manager** asked Dmitri to lock up tonight.
> Correct: **He** asked Dmitri to lock up tonight.

Even when the subject and verb are separated by a long word group, the subject cannot be repeated in the same clause.

> Incorrect: The *girl* who danced with you *she is* my cousin.
> Correct: The **girl** who danced with you **is** my cousin.

Including Pronoun Subjects and Linking Verbs

Some languages may omit a pronoun as a subject, but in English, every clause other than a command must have a subject. In a command, the subject *you* is understood: (**You**) Hand in your papers now.

> Incorrect: The Grand Canyon is in Arizona. *Is* 217 miles long.
> Correct: The Grand Canyon is in Arizona. **It is** 217 miles long.

Every English clause must also have a verb, even when the meaning of the clause is clear without the verb.

> Incorrect: Angelita's piano teacher very patient.
> Correct: Angelita's piano teacher **is** very patient.

Including *There* and *Here* at the Beginning of Clauses

Some English sentences begin with *there* or *here* plus a linking verb (usually a form of *to be: is, are,* and so on). In such sentences, the verb comes before the subject.

> **There are** masks in every culture on Earth.
> The subject is the plural noun *masks*, so the plural verb *are* is used.
> **Here is** your driver's license.
> The subject is the singular noun *license*, so the singular verb *is* is used.

In sentences like those above, remember not to omit *there* or *here.*

> Incorrect: *Are* several chickens in the Bensons' yard.
>
> Correct: **There are** several chickens in the Bensons' yard.

Not Using the Progressive Tense of Certain Verbs

The progressive tenses are made up of forms of *be* plus the *-ing* form of the main verb. They express actions or conditions still in progress at a particular time.

> George **will be taking** classes this summer.

However, verbs for mental states, the senses, possession, and inclusion are normally not used in the progressive tense.

> Incorrect: All during the movie they *were hearing* whispers behind them.
>
> Correct: All during the movie they **heard** whispers behind them.
>
> Incorrect: That box *is containing* a surprise for Pedro.
>
> Correct: That box **contains** a surprise for Pedro.

Common verbs not generally used in the progressive tense are listed in the following box.

Common Verbs not Generally Used in the Progressive

Thoughts, attitudes, and desires: agree, believe, imagine, know, like, love, prefer, think, understand, want, wish

Sense perceptions: hear, see, smell, taste

Appearances: appear, seem

Possession: belong, have, own, possess

Inclusion: contain, include

Using Only Transitive Verbs for the Passive Voice

Only transitive verbs—verbs that need direct objects to complete their meaning—can have a passive form (one in which the subject receives the action instead of performing it). Intransitive verbs cannot be used in the passive voice.

> Incorrect: If you don't fix those brakes, an accident *may be happened.*
> (*Happen* is an intransitive verb—no object is needed to complete its meaning.)
>
> Correct: If you don't fix those brakes, an accident **may happen.**

If you aren't sure whether a verb is transitive or intransitive, check your dictionary. Transitive verbs are indicated with an abbreviation such as *tr. v.* or *v. t.* Intransitive verbs are indicated with an abbreviation such as *intr. v.* or *v. i.*

Using Gerunds and Infinitives after Verbs

A gerund is the *-ing* form of a verb that is used as a noun: For Walter, **eating** is a daylong activity. An infinitive is *to* and the basic form of the verb (the form in which the verb is listed in the dictionary): **to eat.** The infinitive can function as an adverb, an adjective, or a noun. Some verbs can be followed by only a gerund or only an infinitive; other verbs can be followed by either. Examples are given in the following lists. There are many others; watch for them in your reading.

Verb + gerund (admit + stealing)
Verb + preposition + gerund (apologize + for + yelling)

Some verbs can be followed by a gerund but not by an infinitive. In many cases, there is a preposition (such as *for, in,* or *of*) between the verb and the gerund. Following are some verbs and verb-preposition combinations that can be followed by gerunds but not by infinitives:

admit	deny	look forward to
apologize for	discuss	postpone
appreciate	dislike	practice
approve of	enjoy	suspect of
avoid	feel like	talk about
be used to	finish	thank for
believe in	insist on	think about

Incorrect: He must *avoid to jog* until his knee heals.

Correct: He must **avoid jogging** until his knee heals.

Incorrect: The instructor *apologized for to be* late to class.

Correct: The instructor **apologized for being** late to class.

Verb + infinitive (agree + to leave)

Following are common verbs that can be followed by an infinitive but not by a gerund:

agree	decide	plan
arrange	have	refuse
claim	manage	wait

Incorrect: The children *want going* to the beach.

Correct: The children **want to go** to the beach.

Verb + noun or pronoun + infinitive (cause + them + to flee)

Below are common verbs that are followed first by a noun or pronoun and then by an infinitive (not a gerund):

cause	force	remind
command	persuade	warn

Incorrect: The coach *persuaded Yasmin studying* harder.

Correct: The coach **persuaded Yasmin to study** harder.

Following are common verbs that can be followed either by an infinitive alone or by a noun or pronoun and an infinitive:

ask	need	want
expect	promise	would like

Dena asked to have a day off next week.

Her boss asked her to work on Saturday.

Verb + gerund or infinitive (begin + packing or begin + to pack)

Following are verbs that can be followed by either a gerund or an infinitive:

begin	hate	prefer
continue	love	start

The meaning of each of the above verbs remains the same or almost the same whether a gerund or an infinitive is used.

Faith hates **being** late.

Faith hates **to be** late.

With the verbs below, the gerunds and the infinitives have very different meanings.

forget	remember	stop

Esta **stopped to call** home.
(She interrupted something to call home.)

Esta **stopped calling** home.
(She discontinued calling home.)

Activity

3

Underline the correct form in parentheses.

1. The doctor (asked me, she asked me) if I smoked.
2. The day was sunny but a little cool. (It was, Was) the perfect day to run a marathon.
3. (Are several art galleries, There are several art galleries) in Florence, Italy.
4. The box (is containing, contains) a beautiful necklace.
5. Unless you take your foot off the brake, the car will not (be gone, go).
6. Most basketball players (very tall, are very tall).
7. Many people (enjoy to spend, enjoy spending) a day in the city.
8. The township committee (plans voting, plans to vote) on the new proposal Tuesday.
9. Some old men in my neighborhood (play cards, they play cards) every afternoon.
10. When I am happy, I feel like (to sing, singing).

Activity

4

Underline the correct form in parentheses.

1. My grandparents (are, they are) in their nineties.
2. The pizza is two days old. (Is, It is) dry and stale.
3. (Is, There is) no excuse for not seeking tutoring at our college; the learning center is open 18 hours a day.
4. The manager (owns, is owning) two SUVs: a Honda and a Ford.
5. The package will not (be arrived, arrive) until Friday morning.
6. During World War II, (there were, were) many countries that declared their neutrality.
7. Most adults need (to sleep, sleeping) at least seven hours each night.
8. Our new puppy (wants to be chewing, wants to chew) all the furniture in our apartment.

9. On their wedding day, the bride and groom (they seemed, seemed) very happy.

10. Whenever she hears music, Sara feels like (to dance, dancing).

Adjectives

Following the Order of Adjectives in English

Adjectives modify nouns and pronouns. In English, an adjective usually comes directly before the word it describes or after a linking verb (a form of *be* or a "sense" verb such as *look*, *seem*, and *taste*), in which case it modifies the subject. In each of the following two sentences, the adjective is **boldfaced** and the noun it describes is *italicized*.

That is a **false** *story*.

The *story* is **false.**

When more than one adjective modifies the same noun, the adjectives are usually stated in a certain order, though there are often exceptions. Following is the typical order of English adjectives:

Typical Order of Adjectives in a Series

1. **Article or other noun marker:** a, an, the, Lee's, this, three, your
2. **Opinion adjective:** dull, handsome, unfair, useful
3. **Size:** big, huge, little, tiny
4. **Shape:** long, short, round, square
5. **Age:** ancient, medieval, old, new, young
6. **Color:** blue, green, scarlet, white
7. **Nationality:** Italian, Korean, Mexican, Vietnamese
8. **Religion:** Buddhist, Catholic, Jewish, Muslim
9. **Material:** cardboard, gold, marble, silk
10. **Noun used as an adjective:** house (as in *house call*), tea (as in *tea bag*), wall (as in *wall hanging*)

Here are some examples of the above order:

a long cotton scarf

the beautiful little silver cup

your new lavender evening gown

Ana's sweet Mexican grandmother

In general, use no more than two or three adjectives after the article or another noun marker. Numerous adjectives in a series can be awkward: **the beautiful big new blue cotton** sweater.

Using the Present and Past Participles as Adjectives

The present participle ends in -*ing*. Past participles of regular verbs end in -*ed* or -*d;* a list of the past participles of many common irregular verbs appears on pages 495–497. Both types of participles may be used as adjectives. A participle used as an adjective may precede the word it describes: That was an **exciting** *ball game.* It may also follow a linking verb and describe the subject of the sentence: The *ball game* was **exciting.**

While both present and past participles of a particular verb may be used as adjectives, their meanings differ. Use the present participle to describe whoever or whatever causes a feeling: an **embarrassing** *incident* (the incident is what causes the embarrassment). Use the past participle to describe whoever or whatever experiences the feeling: the **embarrassed** *parents* (the parents are the ones who are embarrassed).

The long day of holiday shopping was **tiring.**

The shoppers were **tired.**

Following are pairs of present and past participles with similar distinctions:

annoying/annoyed	exhausting/exhausted
boring/bored	fascinating/fascinated
confusing/confused	frightening/frightened
depressing/depressed	surprising/surprised
exciting/excited	

<table>
<tr><td>**Activity**</td></tr>
<tr><td>**5**</td></tr>
</table>

Underline the correct form in parentheses.

1. The Renaissance was an era in which Europeans made (intellectual significant, significant intellectual) advances.

2. Mr. Kim runs a (popular Korean, Korean popular) restaurant.

3. For her party, the little girl asked if her mother would buy her a (beautiful long velvet, beautiful velvet long) dress.

4. The audience became (exciting, excited) when the president was announced.

5. In the center of the city is a church with (three enormous colorful stained-glass, three stained-glass colorful enormous) windows.

Underline the correct form in parentheses.

1. My mother is an (excellent public, public excellent) speaker.

2. The creek is spanned by (an old wooden, a wooden old) bridge.

3. The ancient Maya of Central America built (large stone, stone large) temples that can still be seen today.

4. Many people find public speaking a (terrifying, terrified) experience.

5. The museum acquired (an ancient marble, a marble ancient) statue from Greece.

Prepositions Used for Time and Place

The use of prepositions in English is often idiomatic—a word that means "peculiar to a certain language"—and there are many exceptions to general rules. Therefore, correct preposition use must be learned gradually through experience. Following is a chart showing how three of the most common prepositions are used in some customary references to time and place:

Use of *on*, *in*, and *at* to Refer to Time and Place

Time

On a specific day: on Monday, on January 1, on your anniversary

In a part of a day: in the morning, in the daytime (but at night)

In a month or a year: in December, in 1776

In a period of time: in an hour, in a few days, in a while

At a specific time: at 10:00 A.M., at midnight, at sunset, at dinnertime

Place

On a surface: on the desk, on the counter, on a ceiling

In a place that is enclosed: in my room, in the office, in the box

At a specific location: at the mall, at his house, at the ballpark

Underline the correct preposition in parentheses.

1. Can you babysit for my children (on, at) Thursday?

2. Please come to my office (on, at) 3:00.

3. You will find some computer disks (in, on) the desk drawer.

4. Miguel will begin his new job (in, at) two weeks.

5. A fight broke out between two groups of friends (on, at) the park.

Activity

8

Underline the correct preposition in parentheses.

1. Tina's husband always sends her flowers (on, at) her birthday.
2. The patients (at, in) the waiting room at the dentist's office all looked uneasy.
3. Let's meet (on, at) the coffee shop after work.
4. The bank is open (in, on) Thursday evenings, but only until six.
5. The Great Depression began when the stock market crashed (in, at) 1929.

Review Test   1

Underline the correct form in parentheses.

1. During the storm, I was startled by the loud (thunder, thunders).
2. The people (on, in) my community (are often working, often work) together to keep our streams, rivers, and lakes clean.
3. The ending of the movie was very (surprised, surprising).
4. Many animals that sleep all day are active (at, in) night.
5. (The people, People) in the photograph are my mother's relatives.
6. The city streets were full of (big yellow, yellow big) taxis.
7. Between the end of World War II and the fall of communism, (there were, were) two Germanys.
8. In the West, New Year's Day is celebrated (in, on) January 1.
9. If I were in London right now, I would certainly (consider, consider to) visiting the British Museum.
10. Most (cheese, cheeses) are made from cow's milk, but others are made from the milk of sheep or goats.

Review Test   2

Underline the correct form in parentheses.

1. (The computers, Computers) have revolutionized our society.
2. (There was, Was) hardly anything left to do after the children cleaned up the kichen and swept the floor.
3. The instructions for the new computer were very (confused, confusing).
4. The snow began to fall (in, at) dawn and continued all day.

5. I stopped at a newsstand to buy (the magazine, a magazine) to read on the train.

6. A (large hairy, hairy large) spider crawled across the basement floor.

7. Susan agreed (marrying, to marry) her boyfriend but then changed her mind.

8. In the United States, Halloween is celebrated (on, in) October 31.

9. After we finished dinner, we (decided to go, decided to be going) to the movies.

10. I was so (insulting, insulted) by the comedian's joke that I (was complaining, complained) to the club owner.

Correction Symbols

Here is a list of symbols the instructor may use when marking papers. The numbers in parentheses refer to the pages that explain the skill involved.

Agr	Correct the mistake in agreement of subject and verb (502–507) or pronoun and the word the pronoun refers to (514–517)
Apos	Correct the apostrophe mistake (557–564)
Bal	Balance the parts of the sentence so they have the same (parallel) form (111–112)
Cap	Correct the mistake in capital letters (544–551)
Coh	Revise to improve coherence (84–94, 154–157)
Comma	Add a comma (573–582)
CS	Correct the comma splice (479–491)
DM	Correct the dangling modifier (535–539)
Det	Support or develop the topic more fully by adding details (62–66)
Frag	Attach the fragment to a sentence or make it a sentence (465–478)
lc	Use a lowercase (small) letter rather than a capital (544–551)
MM	Correct the misplaced modifier (531–534)
¶	Indent for a new paragraph
No¶	Do not indent for a new paragraph
Pro	Correct the pronoun mistake (514–517)
Quot	Correct the mistake in quotation marks (565–572)
R-O	Correct the run-on (479–491)
Sp	Correct the spelling error (588–593)

Trans	Supply or improve a transition (87–91)
Und	Underline (569–570)
Verb	Correct the verb or verb form (492–501, 508–511)
Wordy	Omit needless words (121–122)
WW	Replace the word marked with a more accurate one
?	Write the illegible word clearly
/	Eliminate the word, letter, or punctuation mark so slashed
^	Add the omitted word or words
;/:/-/—	Add semicolon (584), colon (583), hyphen (586), or dash (584)
✓	You have something fine or good here: an expression, a detail, an idea

Credits

Text Credits

p. 1: "Have Yourself a Merry Little Christmas." Words and Music by Hugh Martin and Ralph Blane. © 1943 (Renewed) Metro-Goldwyn-Mayer, Inc. © 1944 (Renewed) EMI FEIST Catalog Inc. All rights controlled by EMI FEIST Catalog, Inc. (Publishing) and Alfred Publishing Co., Inc. (Print). All rights reserved. Used by permission.

p. 194: Beth Johnson, "Lou's Place." Reprinted by permission. Beth Johnson lives in Lederach, Pennsylvania.

p. 220: Pete Hamill essay, "The Yellow Ribbon." Reprinted by permission of International Creative Management, Inc. Copyright © 2010 Pete Hamill.

p. 226: "You Turn Me On, I'm a Radio," words and music by Joni Mitchell. Copyright © 1972 (Renewed) Crazy Crow Music. All rights administered by SONY/ATV Music Publishing, 8 Music Square West, Nashville, TN 37203. All rights reserved. Used by permission of Alfred Publishing Co., Inc.

p. 241: Andrew Malcolm, "Dad." Reprinted by permission.

p. 263: Glenda Davis, "How to Do Well on a Job Interview."

p. 286: "Taming the Anger Monster," by Anne Davidson.

p. 311: Camille Lewis, "Born to Be Different?"

p. 333: Marie Winn, "Cookies or Heroin?" from *The Plug-In Drug,* Revised and Updated-25th Anniversary Edition. Copyright © 1977, 1985, 2002 by Marie Winn Miller. Used by permission of Viking Penguin, a division of Penguin Group (USA) Inc.

p. 343: Screenshot: © Amazon.com, Inc. or its affiliates. All Rights Reserved.

p. 352: Tom Bodett, 1987, "Wait Divisions," from *Small Comforts.* Cambridge, MA: Perseus Books. Copyright © 1988 Tom Bodett. Reprinted by permission of Da Capo Press, a member of the Perseus Books Group.

p. 376: Molly Ivins, "Ban the Things. Ban Them All," *The Washington Post,* March 16, 1993. Copyright © Molly Ivins. Used by permission of the Estate of Molly Ivins.

p. 435: Screenshot: from www.bn.com © 2009. Used with permission from barnesandnoble .com, llc.

p. 440: "Cookies or Heroin?" from *The Plug-In Drug,* Revised and Updated-25th Anniversary Edition by Marie Winn. Copyright © 1977, 1985, 2002 by Marie Winn Miller. Used by permission of Viking Penguin, a division of Penguin Group (USA) Inc.

p. 441: Jane Brody, "New Respect for the Nap," *The New York Times,* January 4, 2000. Copyright © 2000 by The New York Times. All rights reserved. Used by permission and protected by the Copyright Laws of the U.S. The printing, copying, redistribution, or retransmission of the Material without express written permission is prohibited. www.nytimes.com

p. 442: James Henslin excerpt, from *Essentials of Sociology,* Fourth Edition, 2002, Allyn & Bacon.

Photo Credits

Chapter Opener 1: © Stock Image/SuperStock; p 14: © Jamie Grill/Corbis; Chapter Opener 2: © Blend Images/Imagestate; Chapter Opener 3: © Jiang Jin/SuperStock; p 82: © Comstock Select/ Corbis; Chapter Opener 4: © Tim Pannell/Corbis; p 102: © Getty; Chapter Opener 5: © Image Source/Corbis; p 119: © Paul Barton/Corbis; Chapter Opener 6: © Michael Ainsworth/Dallas Morning News/Corbis; Part 2 Opener top: © Lawrence Manning/Corbis; PO2 middle: © Eddie Gerald/Alamy; Chapter Opener 7: © Joel Gordon; Chapter Opener 8: © Photographers Choice RF/SuperStock; p 200: © James Leynse/Corbis; Chapter Opener 9: © James Leynse/Corbis; p 223: © Rachel Epstein/PhotoEdit; p 224 top: © Simon Marcus/Corbis; p 224 bottom: © Banana-Stock/Alamy; Chapter Opener 10: © AP Photo/James Nachtwey/VII; p 246: © Journal-Courier/ Steve Warmowski/The Image Works; p 247: © Anton Vengo/SuperStock; Chapter Opener 11: © Mike Watson Images/Corbis; p 267: © WoodyStock/Alamy; p 274: © Bloomimage/Corbis; Chapter Opener 12: Craig Sjodin/© ABC/Courtesy Everett Collection; p 292: © Micheal Newman/ PhotoEdit Inc.; p 293: © Greg Hinsdale/Corbis; p 294: © Bubbles Photolibrary/Alamy; Chapter Opener 13 top: © vario images GmbH & Co.KG/Alamy; Chapter Opener 13 bottom: © Photodisc/ SuperStock; p 320 top: © Bob Daemmrich/PhotoEdit; p 320 bottom: © Peter M. Fisher/Corbis; Chapter Opener 14: © Digital Vision/Getty; p 339 top: © BananaStock/SuperStock; p 339 bottom: © Joel Gordon; p 334: © BananaStock/SuperStock; p 353: © John Gress/Reuters/Corbis; p 356: © Myrleen Pearson/PhotoEdit; Chapter Opener 16: © Bill Aron/PhotoEdit; p 366: © Mary Kate Denny/PhotoEdit; p 380: © Tony Freeman/PhotoEdit; p 384: © BananaStock/Imagestate; PO 3: © Steve Boyle/NewSport/Corbis; Chapter Opener 17: © Comstock/Imagestate; Chapter Opener 18: © Bill Aron/PhotoEdit; © Kayte M. Deioma/PhotoEdit; © Alan D. Monyelle/U.S.Navy/Handout/ Reuters/Corbis; © Zave Smith/Corbis; © Natalie Hummel; © Bill Aron/PhotoEdit; © Photri MicroStock™/A.Kaplan; © Danny Letham; © Joe Tabacca/AP Photo; © Bettmann/Corbis; © Reuters NewMedia Inc./Corbis; © Cynthia Johnson/Time Life Pictures/Getty; © Mike Watson Images/Corbis; © Popperfoto/Getty; © North Wind Picture Archives/Alamy; Courtesy of Beth Johnson; Courtesy of John Langan; Courtesy of John Langan; Courtesy of John Langan; Courtesy of John Langan; © Chicago Tribune/Landov LLC; Courtesy of John Langan; © Bill Aron/ PhotoEdit; Courtesy of Joan Dunayer; © Kayte M. Deioma/PhotoEdit; © Susanne Oehlschlaeger/ VISUM/The Image Works; Courtesy of Sora Song; Courtesy of David Daniels; Courtesy of Daniel A. Sugarman; © Allstar Picture Library/Alamy; Courtesy of Mary Sherry; © Judy Griesedieck/ Time Life Pictures/Getty

Index

A

A/an, 599
Abbreviations, 552, 554–555
Abstract, 395
Accept/except, 599
Active voice, 120–121, 625
Added-detail fragments, 471–473
Addition signals, 87
Adequate details, 65–66
Adjectives
  defined, 525
  present and past participle as,
    636–637
  using to compare, 526–527
  using in a series, 129–130,
    635–636
  well and *good,* 528–528
Adverbs
  common mistake, 528
  conjunctive adverbs, 88
  defined, 525, 527–528
  well and *good,* 528–528
Advice/advise, 599
Affect/effect, 599
All ready/already, 594
Among/between, 600
Anecdotes, 237
Apostrophes
  in contractions, 558–559
  defined, 557
  to show ownership or possession,
    559–561
  vs. similar plurals, 561–563
Argument, 182
Argument essays
  argument strategies, 364–367
  "Ban the Things. Ban Them All."
    (Ivins), 376–377
  considering purpose and audi-
    ence, 371–372
  defined, 182
  introduced, 363–364
  prewriting, 372–375
  revising, 375
  student essays, 367–370

Articles (pieces of writing)
  citation of, 445–446
  finding in libraries, 424–426
  finding online, 428
  summarizing, 396–405
Audience, knowing and writing for,
    178, 189
Auxiliary verbs, 459, 462

B

Balanced sentences, 111–112
"Ban the Things. Ban Them All."
    (Ivins), 376–377
Beside/besides, 600
Between/among, 600
Bodett, Tom, 352–354
Books
  citation of, 445
  finding on the Internet, 427
  finding in libraries, 420–424
  summarizing, 405–406
  writing a report on, 408–411
"Born to be Different?" (Lewis),
    311–314
Brainstorming, 26–28
Brake/break, 594

C

Call number, 421
Capital letters
  main uses, 544–547
  other uses, 547–550
  unnecessary use of, 550
Catch phrase, 388, 391
Cause-and-effect essays
  considering purpose and
    audience, 280–282
  prewriting, 282–284
  revising, 284–285
  overview of, 276–277
  student essays, 277–279
  "Taming the Anger Monster"
    (Davidson), 286–290
Change-of-direction signals, 87

Chronological order, 84–85
Chronological résumés, 413–414
Citations, in research papers,
    443–447
Clause, 479
Cliché, 604, 606–608
Clustering, 28–29
Coherence, 154–157
Colon, 583–584
Comma splices, 479–480
Commas, 482–483, 573–579
Comparison or contrast essays
  "Born to be Different?" (Lewis),
    311–314
  considering purpose and
    audience, 307–308
  defined, 301
  one side at a time development,
    301–302
  point by point development,
    302–303
  prewriting, 308–310
  revising, 310–311
  student essays, 303–305
Comparisons, using adjectives,
    526–527
Complex sentences, 125–130
Compound sentences, 124–125
Compound subjects, 502,
    504–505
Computers, in the writing process,
    15–17
Conclusion signals, 87
Conclusions and concluding
    paragraphs
  in traditional essay, 9–10
  methods of, 98–100
  using to summarize, 396, 406
Conjunctive adverbs, 88
Connecting words, 91–94
Contractions, 557–559
Contrast, 301. *See also* Comparison
    or contrast essays
Coordination, 124–125
Correction symbols, 639–640

Count nouns
   defined, 625
   using articles with, 626–629
Course/coarse, 594–595
Cover letters, 416–418

D

"Dad" (Malcolm), 241–243
Dangling modifiers, 535–536
Dash, 584–585
Davidson, Anne, 286–290
Davis, Glenda, 263–265
Definition essays
   considering purpose and audi-
     ence, 329
   introduction to, 325
   prewriting, 329–331
   revising, 331–333
   student essays, 325–327
   "Television Addiction" (Winn),
     333–335
Demonstrative pronouns, 518, 523
Dependent clause, 125n, 479
Dependent thought, using in sen-
   tences, 125–130
Dependent words, 465–466
Dependent-word fragments,
   465–468
Description, 182
Descriptive essays
   considering purpose and audi-
     ence, 189–191
   introduction to, 185
   "Lou's Place," 194–198
   prewriting, 191–192
   revising, 193–194
   student essays, 185–189
Details, 62–66. *See also* Evidence
Dewey decimal cataloging system,
   423–424
Diagramming, 28–29
Dialogue, 214–216
Direct quotations
   in note taking, 437
   using quotation marks with, 565–568
Direction words, 389
Division-classification essays
   considering purpose and
     audience, 348

   introduction to, 344
   prewriting, 348–351
   revising, 351
   student essays, 344–346
   "Wait Divisions" (Bodett),
     352–354

E

-ed words, 127
Editing
   on computer, 17
   importance of, 611
   strategies, 612
   in the writing process, 35–37
Editorials, citation of, 445
Effect/affect, 600
Electronic mail, citation of, 446
Ellipsis points, 437–438
Emphatic order, 85–86
ESL pointers
   adjectives, 635–637
   articles with count and noncount
     nouns, 626–629
   correction symbols, 639–640
   prepositions, 637–639
   subjects and verbs, 630–635
Essay development
   description, 189–194
   important considerations in,
     177–181
   patterns of, 182–183
Essay exams
   before writing, 389–390
   anticipate probable questions,
     387
   introduced, 386
   organization, 392–394
   outlines and, 388–389, 391–392
Essays
   benefits of writing, 11
   conclusion, 98–100
   connecting words, 91–94
   defined, 5
   development of, 177–183,
     189–194
   diagram of, 10
   editing, 35–37
   first draft, 31–33
   introductions, 94–98

   one-three-one form, 10
   organization of, 84–87
   parts of, 7–10
   prewriting (*see* Prewriting)
   proofreading, 132–133
   point and support, 3–6
   revising (*see* Revising)
   sentence skills and (*see*
     Sentences; Sentence skills)
   thesis statement (*see* Thesis and
     thesis statements)
   title, 100–101
   traditional structure of, 6–11
   transitions, 87–91
   see also specific essay types
Evidence
   connecting words, 91–94
   organization of, 84–87
   supporting a thesis with, 60–66
   transitions, 87–91
Examinations. *See* Essay exams
Except/accept, 599
Exemplification essays
   considering purpose and
     audience, 236–237
   "Dad" (Malcolm), 241–243
   defined, 182, 231
   prewriting, 237–239
   revising, 240–241
   student essays, 231–234
Exposition, 182

F

Fewer/less, 600
Films, citation of, 446
Final outline, 442
First draft
   on computer, 16
   in writing process, 31–33
First-person approach, 178–179
Format, 542
Former/latter, 600–601
Fragments
   added-detail fragments,
     471–473
   checking for, 475
   defined, 465
   dependent-word fragments,
     465–468

-*ing* and *to* fragments, 469–471
missing-subject fragments, 473–474
Freewriting, 23–25
Functional résumés, 414–415
Fused sentences, 479–480

G

Gerund, 508, 511, 632–634
Good, 528–529
Grammar
    adjectives and adverbs, 525–529
    dangling modifiers, 535–536
    misplaced modifiers, 531–533
    pronoun agreement and reference, 512–516
    pronoun types, 518–523
    regular and irregular verbs, 492–500
    run-on sentences, 479–488
    sentence fragments, 465–475
    subjects and verbs, 459–464
    subject-verb agreement, 502–505

H

Hamill, Pete, 220–221
Hear/here, 595
Helping verbs, 459, 462, 509–510
Hole/whole, 595
Homonyms
    common examples, 594–599
    defined, 594
"How to Do Well on a Job Interview" (Davis), 263–265
Hyphens, 583, 586

I

Idiomatic, 625
Illustration signals, 87
Indefinite pronouns
    agreement, 505, 514–515
    defined, 502, 512
Independent clause, 125n, 479
Indirect quotations, 568–569
Infinitive
    after verbs, 632–634
    defined, 508, 510

-*ing* fragments, 469–471
-*ing* words, 127
Internet
    evaluating sources, 428–430
    finding articles on a topic, 428
    finding books on a topic, 427
    online periodical databases, 425–426
    and plagiarism, 440
    and research paper topic selection, 434–435
    search engines, 428
Introductions and introductory paragraphs
    function of, 94
    methods of, 94–97
    in research papers, 442
    in traditional essays, 7–8
    using to summarize, 396, 406
Irregular verbs, 492, 495–500
Its/it's, 595
Ivins, Molly, 376–377

J

Job application letters, 416–418
Johnson, Beth, 194–198
Journaling, 14–15
Journals, locating articles in, 424–426, 428

K

Key words, 388, 391
Knew/new, 595
Know/no, 596

L

Latter/former, 600–601
Learn/teach, 601
Less/fewer, 600
Lewis, Camille, 311–314
Libraries
    book stacks, 423–424
    catalog of holdings, 420–422
    main desk, 420
    periodicals, 424–426
    and research paper topic selection, 433–434

Library of Congress
    cataloging system, 423
    online, 427
Linking sentences, 91
Linking verbs, 459
List making, 26–28
List of works cited, 444–447
Loose/lose, 601
"Lou's Place" (Johnson), 194–198
-*ly* words, 127

M

Magazines, locating articles in, 424–426, 428
Making a list, 26–28
Malcolm, Andrew H., 241–243
Manuscript, 541
Manuscript form, 541–542
Mapping, 28–29
Mechanics
    capital letters, 544–550
    manuscript form, 541–542
    numbers and abbreviations, 553–555
Misplaced modifiers, 531–533
Misused words
    common examples, 599–602
    homonyms, 594–599
Missing-subject fragments, 473–474
Modifiers
    dangling, 535–536
    misplaced, 531–533

N

Narration, 182, 209–210
Narrative essays
    considering purpose and audience, 214
    dialogue in, 214–216
    prewriting, 216–218
    revising, 218–219
    as storytelling, 209–210
    student essays, 210–212
    "The Yellow Ribbon" (Hamill), 220–221
New/knew, 595
Newspaper articles, finding on a topic, 424–426, 428

No/know, 596
Noncount nouns
  defined, 625
  using articles with, 626–629
Note taking, for research papers,
    437–439
Nouns
  capitalization of, 544–546
  defined, 512–513
  article use with, 626–629
Numbers, 552–554

O

Object pronouns, 518, 520–521
One-three-one essay, 10
Online periodical databases,
    425–426
Opening words/phrases, 127–129
Organization
  checking for in content
      revision, 34
  common methods of, 84–87
  of essay exams, 392–394
  in report writing, 409
Outlines
  for essay exams, 388–389,
      391–392
  in prewriting, 29–31
  for research papers, 436–437

P

Pamphlets, citation of, 446
Paragraphs
  concluding, 9–10, 98–100
  introductory, 7–8, 94–97
  point and support in, 4–5
  see also Support and supporting
      paragraphs
Parallelism, 111–112
Paraphrasing, 437–438
Parentheses, 583, 585
Participle, 508, 511
Passed/past, 596
Passive voice, 120–121, 631–632
Past participle, 492–493, 636
Past tense, 492–494
Peace/piece, 596
Peer review, 180–181

Periodicals
  in libraries, 424–426
  online, 428
Personal interviews, citation of, 446
Personal review, 181–182
Plagiarism, 439–442
Plain/plane, 596
Plan of development, 7
Plan of organization, 409
Plural subject, 502
Plural words, 561–563
Point of view, 178–180
Points, supporting in writing, 3–6
Possessives, forming with
      apostrophes, 561–563
Possessive pronouns, 518, 522, 561
Précis, 395
Predictions, 99
Prefaces, 406
Prepositional phrase, 128, 461
Prepositions, 459, 461, 637–639
Present participle, 492–493, 636
Present tense, 492–494
Pretentious words, 604, 608–609
Prewriting
  clustering, 28–29
  computer in, 15–16
  freewriting, 23–25
  making a list, 26–28
  questioning, 25–26
  scratch outline, 29–31
Principal/principle, 596
Principal parts of verbs, 492
Process essays
  considering purpose and
      audience, 258–259
  defined, 254
  "How to Do Well on a Job
      Interview" (Davis), 263–265
  prewriting, 260–262
  revising, 262
  structure, content, and style,
      259–260
  student essays, 255–257
Pronoun agreement, 512, 513–515
Pronoun reference, 512, 515–516
Pronouns
  agreement of, 513–515
  as connecting words, 92

  consistency in use of, 114–116
  defined, 512
  demonstrative pronouns, 523
  possessive pronouns, 522, 561
  reference, 515–516
  subject and object types, 518–521
Proofreading
  on computer, 17
  defined, 611
  overview of, 132–133
Proofreading symbols, 611
Punctuation
  apostrophes, 557–564
  commas, 573–579
  other punctuation marks,
      583–586
  quotation marks, 565–571

Q

Qualifier, 625
Questioning, 25–26
Questions
  in conclusions, 98–99
  in introductions, 96
  essay exams and, 387
Quiet/quite, 601
Quotation marks
  direct quotations, 565–568
  indirect quotations, 568–569
  other uses, 570–571
  to set off titles, 569–570
Quotations, 96

R

*Reader's Guide to Periodical
    Literature,* 424–425
Recommendations, 99
Regular verbs, 492–495
Repeated words, 92
Report writing, 407–411
Research. *See* Internet, Libraries
Research papers
  documentation of sources,
      443–447
  limiting topic, 435–436
  model paper, 447–456
  note-taking, 437–439
  plagiarism, 439–442

preparing outline, 436–437, 442
topic selection, 433–435
writing, 442
Résumés, 412–416
Revising sentences
active verbs, 120–121
concise words, 121–123
consistent point of view, 113–116
parallelism, 111–112
specific words, 116–119
Revising
coherence, 154–157
with computer, 16–17
sentence skills, 157–161
support, 150–154
in writing process, 33–34
unity, 147–150
Right/write, 597
Run-on sentences
checking for, 488
correcting, 480–488
defined, 479–480

S

Scratch outline
in peer review, 180–181
in prewriting, 29–31
Search engines, using in research, 428
Second-person approach, 179
Semicolon, 583, 584
Semicolon
correcting run-on sentences with, 485–487
defined, 583
uses, 585
Sentence outline, 442
Sentence skills
consistent point of view, 113–116
editing and, 35
editing practice, 612–624
revising essays and, 157–161
using active verbs, 120–121
using concise words, 121–123
using specific words, 116–119
varying sentences, 124–130
see also Grammar, Mechanics, Punctuation, Word Use

Sentences
editing, 130–131
parallel (balanced), 111–112
revising (*see* Revising sentences)
transitional, 91
Singular subject, 502
Slang, 604–606
Sound recordings, citation of, 446
Sources, documenting in research paper, 443–447
Space signals, 87
Specific details, 62–65
Specific evidence. *See* Details, Evidence
Spelling, 589–593
Subject headings, in library research, 421
Subject pronouns, 518–520
Subjects
agreement with verbs, 502–505
avoiding repeating, 630
in sentences, 459–464
Subjects of essays. *See* Topics
Subordinate clause, 479, 488
Subordination, 125–127, 488
Subtitles, using to summarize, 405
Summaries and summarizing
of an article, 396–405
of a book, 405–406
in concluding paragraphs, 98
defined, 395
in report writing, 407
in research papers, 437–438
Support and supporting paragraphs
checking for in content revision, 34
in effective writing, 3–6
revising essays for, 150–154
thesis statements and, 60–66
in traditional essay, 8–9
Synonyms, 92–93

T

Table of contents, 405
"Taming the Anger Monster" (Davidson), 286–290
Teach/learn, 601
"Television Addiction" (Winn), 333–335

Television programs, citation of, 446
Tense. *See* Verb tense
Than/then, 597
Their/there/they're, 597
Thesis and thesis statements
avoiding common mistakes, 57–60
in introductory paragraph, 5–6, 7
narrowing topic, 52–57
supporting with specific evidence, 60–66
understanding, 51–52
Third-person approach, 179–180
Threw/through, 597
Time order, 84–84
Time signals, 87
Titles
capitalization of, 546
choosing for an essay, 100–101
of research papers, 447
using quotation marks to set off, 569–570
using to summarize, 396, 405
To/too/two, 598
to fragments, 128, 469–471
Topic outline, 442
Topic sentence, 8
Topics
limiting for research papers, 435–436
selecting, 177, 189, 433–435
thesis statement and, 51, 52–57
Transitional phrases, 88
Transitional sentences, 91
Transitions
connecting words, 91–94
transitional words, 87–91
Transitive verb, 631–632

U

Unity
checking for in content revision, 34
revising essays and, 147–150

V

Verb tense
consistency in, 113–114

Verb tense (*continued*)
    defined, 492, 508–509
    progressive tense, 631
    subject-verb agreement, 502–505
Verbals, 508, 510–511
Verbs
    active vs. passive voice, 120–121
    agreement with subjects,
        502–505
    gerunds and infinitives, 632–634
    helping verbs, 459, 462, 509–510
    irregular, 495–500
    regular, 492–495
    in sentences, 459–464
    transitive verbs, 631–632
    using in a series, 129–130
    verbals, 510–511
Viewpoints, considering in argument
    essays, 365–367

W

"Wait Divisions" (Bodett), 352–354
Wear/where, 598

Weather/whether, 598
Well, 528–529
Whole/hole, 595
Whose/who's, 598
Winn, Marie, 333–335
Word choice
    clichés, 606–608
    pretentious words, 608–609
    slang, 604–606
Word list, for spelling, 590–593
Word use
    commonly confused words,
        599–602
    effective word choice, 604–609
    homonyms, 594–599
    spelling improvement, 589–593
Wordiness, 121–123
Works-cited list, 444–447
Write/right, 597
Writing process
    computers in, 15–17
    editing, 35–37
    first draft, 31–33

prewriting (*see* Prewriting)
    revising, 33–34
Writing
    compared to talking, 3–4
    keeping a journal, 14–15
    as a means of communication, 13
    point and support, 3–6
    as a process of discovery, 12–13
    as a skill, 11–12
    using a computer, 15–17

Y

Your/you're, 598–599
"The Yellow Ribbon" (Hamill),
    220–221

Z

Zip codes, 579